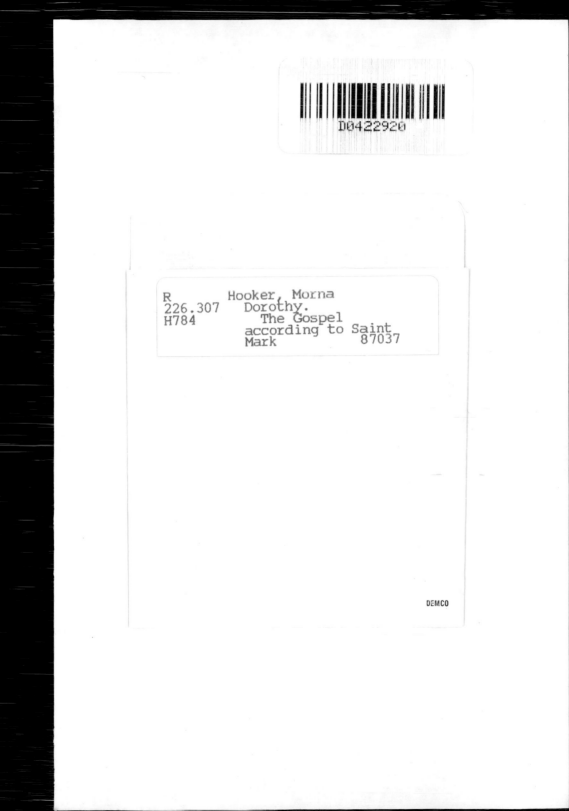

BLACK'S NEW TESTAMENT COMMENTARIES

General Editor: Henry Chadwick, DD, FBA

# THE GOSPEL ACCORDING TO ST MARK

BLACK'S NEW TESTAMENT COMMENTARY

# THE GOSPEL ACCORDING TO SAINT MARK

## MORNA D. HOOKER

 HENDRICKSON
PUBLISHERS
PEABODY, MASSACHUSETTS 01961-3473

First published 1991

A & C Black (Publishers) Limited, London

Copyright © 1991 Morna D. Hooker

Hendrickson Publishers, Inc. Edition

ISBN 1-56563-010-6

Reprinted by arrangement with A & C Black (Publishers) Limited.

The mosaic fretwork on the cover comes from the Galla Placidia
Mausoleum in Ravenna and is used courtesy of ITALCARDS, Bologna, Italy.

# CONTENTS

# PREFACE

The translation which is used in this commentary is, as is customary in this series, my own, and is intended to help the reader understand the meaning of the text, not to provide an elegant piece of English prose. Because I was originally invited to write the commentary for another series, the initial work for it was based on the text of the *New English Bible*, and (because of a change of format) a first draft was subsequently completed on the text of the *Revised Standard Version*. The requirement to produce my own translation for this series demonstrated how much easier it is to point out the errors in the work of others than to produce an adequate translation of one's own!

In the many years since I began work on this commentary, there has been an explosion of Markan studies which has caused me to revise again and again. I have attempted, in the tradition of this series, not to overburden the reader with names and theories. References to Greek are given for those who may be helped by them, but knowledge of Greek is not essential.

I acknowledge with thanks those who have helped with work on this commentary. I am grateful to the Revd Professor Henry Chadwick for his invitation to complete the commentary for this series, and for his judicious comments on the typescript. Various institutions have assisted in its preparation: Clare Hall, Cambridge, who invited me as Visiting Fellow in 1974; Duke University Divinity School, North Carolina, who gave me the freedom of their Library when I was there as Visiting Professor in 1983, 1987 and 1989; and the Rockefeller Foundation who invited me in 1988 as a Visiting Scholar to the Villa Serbelloni, where I was able to revise the typescript of the 'final' draft. One of my graduate students, Mary Ann Beavis, offered helpful comments on some of the early chapters. Above all I am grateful to my husband, David Stacey, who not only read the whole commentary and made many helpful criticisms, but who goaded me into completing it.

Cambridge, January 1990                                    Morna D. Hooker

# ABBREVIATIONS

| | |
|---|---|
| *A.V.* | *Authorized Version* |
| *B.J.R.L.* | *Bulletin of the John Rylands Library* |
| *C.B.Q.* | *Catholic Biblical Quarterly* |
| *E.tr.* | English translation |
| *Eph. Th. L.* | *Ephemerides Theologicae Lovanienses* |
| *Exp. Tim.* | *Expository Times* |
| *H.T.R.* | *Harvard Theological Review* |
| *J.B.L.* | *Journal of Biblical Literature* |
| *J.R.* | *Journal of Religion* |
| *J.S.N.T.* | *Journal for the Study of the New Testament* |
| *J.T.S.* | *Journal of Theological Studies* |
| LXX | Septuagint |
| MS, MSS | manuscript, manuscripts |
| n.s. | new series |
| *N.E.B.* | *New English Bible* |
| *N.T.* | *Novum Testamentum* |
| *N.T.S.* | *New Testament Studies* |
| *R.S.V.* | *Revised Standard Bible* |
| S.B.L. | Society of Biblical Literature |
| Sib.Or. | Sibylline Oracles |
| *T.D.N.T.* | *Theological Dictionary of the New Testament* |
| *Z.N.W.* | *Zeitschrift für die Neutestamentliche Wissenschaft* |
| *Z.Th.K.* | *Zeitschrift für Theologie und Kirche* |

References to the tractates of the Mishnah are preceded by the letter M; those to the Babylonian Talmud by the letter B, and those to the Jerusalem Talmud by the letter J. References to the Tosefta are indicated by the abbreviation Tos.

References to Josephus are given according to the system used in the edition of W. Whiston, rather than that in the Loeb edition, since Whiston's translation is more likely to be available to readers of this commentary than the Loeb. These references can in any case be easily followed in the Loeb edition.

The sigla used in referring to New Testament manuscripts and versions are explained in Nestle-Aland's *Novum Testamentum Graece*, on which text our English translation is based.

In the translation, words that do not occur in the Greek are enclosed in square brackets.

References to the psalms follow the English enumeration; where necessary the Septuagint numbers are given in brackets.

# INTRODUCTION

## The task of a commentator

Commentators have long posed the question 'What is a gospel?' The time has perhaps come to raise the question 'What is a commentary?' For though the 'genre' of a commentary may remain more or less constant, the presuppositions or questions which commentators bring to bear on the text vary enormously. Anyone who examines commentaries on Mark written over the centuries will soon become aware of the very different ways in which the gospel has been expounded at different periods of time. Some of the most dramatic changes, however, have come about quite recently, as we can see by considering a few of the many commentaries which have been published in the last forty years.

The year 1952 saw the publication of a commentary which quickly established itself as a classic – Vincent Taylor's *The Gospel According to St Mark*. Taylor was typical of the British scholars of his period: approaching the gospels from the stand-point of the source critics, he took it as axiomatic that Mark was the earliest of the gospels, and that it was composed by a companion of Peter, an eye-witness of the events which are recorded. Thus though Taylor was familiar with the work of the form critics, and used their literary classification in analysing Mark's material, he did not allow the recognition that the early Church might have shaped the stories to raise questions about their historical value. The chief questions Taylor addressed to the text were very largely at the historical level: what had Jesus done and said, or what had been the order of events in the course of his ministry? He assumed that Mark was able to provide the answers to such questions.

A very different approach was taken by Dennis Nineham, whose Pelican Commentary on *Saint Mark* appeared eleven years later. Versed in the methods of form criticism, he saw the gospel as reflecting primarily the beliefs and concerns of the early Christian community. Though he did not deny that the tradition might embody historical recollection, he recognized the difficulty of separating history from interpretation. The questions posed by Nineham were thus chiefly questions about how Jesus was seen and interpreted by the early communities and by the evangelist who wrote the gospel, rather than questions about what Jesus himself had done and said. The form critics tended to see the evangelists as collectors of material, rather than as theologians with minds of their own. Thus though Nineham discusses Mark's arrangement and presentation of the tradition, he regards him as representing the view-point of the church c. AD 75, rather than as a creative writer. It was left to the redaction critics to focus on the concerns of the evangelist and his method in handling the story overall, rather than concentrating on the smaller units of tradition within the gospel. Redaction criticism is concerned with the way in which tradition has been handled and modified; with what has been selected and what has been omitted. It thus attempts to separate the redaction from the tradition by concentrating on particular features of an evangelist's vocabulary or style or method. If we assume Markan priority, discussion of Matthaean and Lukan redaction of the material taken from Mark by the later evangelists is comparatively easy – though complications arise where 'Q' material overlaps with Mark, and where the text of one gospel has been assimilated to that of another. In the case of Mark, the separation of redaction from tradition is much more complicated – though the summaries, 'seams' and parentheses provide an obvious starting point for discovering Markan redaction (see E. Best, *The Temptation and The Passion*, for an example of this approach). The work of the redaction critics opened up a third '*Sitz im Leben*': questions were now being asked, not about the setting of the tradition in the life of Jesus, nor about its use by the early Christian communities, but about its significance for the evangelist. Eduard Schweizer's commentary, *The Good News according to Mark*, originally published in German in 1967, only a few years after Nineham's, marked a new approach, since it concentrated on how Mark himself interpreted 'the good news'.

Just as form criticism involved far more than an analysis of the material into forms, so redaction criticism has led to far more than a study of the redaction of the tradition. The way had now been opened up to study each gospel as a whole – as a presentation of the Christian gospel. But no book is written in a vacuum; nor is it read in one. Questions were now raised about the community for which Mark was writing – about its situations and concerns: these must surely have influenced the way in which Mark wrote, and are thus reflected in his book. Similarly, the way in which the gospel is read depends very largely on the situation and concerns of the reader, with the result that it is interpreted in different ways at different times and in different places. New methods of literary criticism now being used are based on the belief that the text can properly be considered in its own right, without any consideration of the original author's intention. (An interesting example of interpreting the text primarily from the reader's view-point is found in Fernando Belo's *A Materialist Reading of the Gospel of Mark* (originally published in 1974)).

These few examples serve to show the many different ways in which, in the course of a few years, a commentary can be written: the focus of concern has shifted from the historical Jesus, through the early history of the traditions, through Mark the evangelist, through the community for which he wrote, to what modern readers can make of the text. Cynics might well say that the questions addressed to the text have been changed as each set of questions has proved impossible to answer! The source critics supposed that Mark could be used as an historical source providing them with information about Jesus, but the historical Jesus proved elusive, and investigations came to an impasse. Form critics concentrated on the belief of the early communities – but were in fact unable to provide clear evidence about either the communities or their beliefs, since the traditions had already been taken over by the evangelist and incorporated into his gospel. With some relief the redaction critics turned to the gospels themselves: here, surely, one is in touch with what was actually written by a particular person in a particular time and place. But who *was* this person – and what *were* the time and place? If we knew the answers to these questions we might better understand what the evangelist has written. And how much of the gospel is due to the author and how much to the tradition? Is it any easier to separate redaction from tradition than it is to separate interpretation from history? Is it possible to distinguish deliberate alteration from chance? And can we be certain that the particular theory of literary relationships between the Synoptics on which our redaction-critical analysis is based is correct? Certainly a different theory will lead to different results, and if we have chosen the wrong one our conclusions will be false. Deducing the situation and concerns of Mark's community is equally complex, for it can be done only through an analysis of the gospel, which we are attempting to interpret in the light of the community's needs! We cannot be certain how the gospel would have been read (or rather heard) in that community. Moreover, the community was not itself static, and so almost immediately the gospel would have been read in new ways, a process of reinterpretation which has been at work ever since. It is hardly surprising if the new form of literary-critical analysis has now become popular, for here the text alone is important. When interpretation is a matter of the text's speaking to the interpreter, then it is no longer necessary to strive for 'objective' exegesis. The presuppositions which influenced earlier commentators, and which are so clearly reflected in their work, are no longer hindrances, but

3

part of the interpretative process, once we recognize that every reading of a text involves some kind of interpretation.

This present commentary has been in the process of preparation for over twenty years, and I am therefore very much aware of these changes in approach. Some of the questions which were raised at the beginning of my research no longer seem relevant, but they have been replaced by many more. It seems proper, however, to ask questions at every level. The work of the new literary critics reminds us that it is important to recognize that our own reading of the text plays a very large part in the interpretation that we give to it, but the author, his community, the men and women who handed on and moulded the tradition, and, beyond them all, Jesus himself, all play a significant part in its meaning. The primary concern in this commentary is with the interpretation of the evangelist himself – always recognizing, however, that we may be imposing our own understanding of the text on to him, or be attributing to him ideas that are embedded in the tradition. It is not strictly a 'redaction-critical' approach, in that it is not primarily concerned with the changes Mark has made in the tradition. Rather, it attempts to look at the finished product, not simply analysing individual units but examining the structure of the book as a whole, in order to discover, if possible, what lessons the evangelist is trying to convey to his readers. Since we think of Mark as writing for a particular community, we regard him (like Paul) as being a pastor, as well as a theologian. By asking questions about the original audience (who would have heard the gospel read, as a congregation, rather than reading it themselves, as individuals), we hope to keep in contact with the author and his intentions, and to learn something of his understanding of the nature of 'the good news about Jesus Christ'.

One crucial question which has played an important role in the interpretation of Mark's gospel is that of the relationship between history and *kerygma*. If we recognize that the authors of the gospels were 'evangelists' – preachers of the gospel – we still have to deal with the question of the importance for them (if any!) of history. Those who interpret Mark as 'kerygmatic history' include both those who see him primarily as a careful recorder of the tradition, and those who believe that his only concern was to present the significance of Jesus for his own community, with little or no interest in the original Jesus. Did Mark simply preserve the tradition or freely create it? The approach adopted here falls between these extremes. While we believe that Mark was an evangelist, and that he selected and arranged the material to proclaim the significance of Jesus for the community of his day, we do not think that the fact that Mark addressed his gospel to the needs of his readers means that he had no interest in history.[1] it seems unlikely that he created material *ex nihilo*. His creative activity is seen, rather, in the way in which he used the tradition which was available to him – in its selection, arrangement, presentation, wording, adaptation and in the added explanations. We do not believe that every word and phrase in Mark need necessarily be traced to the hand of the evangelist or receive the explanation for its position in his gospel from his grand theological design; some material may have been included because it was already attached to incidents he deliberately chose to include. Those who find significance in every word and phrase Mark used are as likely to distort our understanding of the gospel as much as those who insist that his presentation is an accurate historical record of what Jesus did and said.

In the course of the commentary there are frequent references to the words and actions of Jesus. These references are not intended to beg the question of historicity, but it would clearly be tedious to raise historical questions on every occasion. Usually we mean 'Jesus as Mark presents him'; occasionally our intention is to distinguish Jesus' own words from those of Mark's interpretation, but in these cases the distinction is clear.

## Authorship, place and date

The earliest statement about Mark's gospel to have come down to us was made by Papias, Bishop of Hierapolis, in about AD 130, and is preserved by Eusebius in his *Ecclesiastical History* (iii.39.15). In a book since lost, Papias recalled the tradition which had been told to him by 'the Elder' (i.e. John) about Mark, who, 'having been the interpreter (ἑρμηνευτής)) of Peter, wrote down accurately (ἀκριβῶς)), but not in order (οὐ μέντοι τάξει), all that he remembered of the Lord's sayings and doings'. Papias adds what is probably his own comment: Mark 'had not heard the Lord, nor been a follower of his, but later (as I said) of Peter; who used to adapt his reading to the needs [of the situation], but not so as to make an orderly account of the Lord's sayings. So Mark did no wrong in writing down some things just as he recalled them. For he had one purpose only – to omit nothing of what he had heard, and to state nothing falsely.'

This early testimony is frequently appealed to by those who wish to affirm the historical reliability of Mark's account. If Mark records

---

1 It is worth remembering that historical information can be conveyed even when this is not an author's primary concern. A great deal of the material used by historians (whether documents or inscriptions) is not in fact intended to inform us about historical questions, but historical information can nevertheless be gleaned from it.

tradition which he had received from Peter, does this not put us in touch with 'eye-witness' tradition? This view has often been passionately maintained, in contrast to the form-critical position that the material has all been passed on through the community and adapted to its needs. But how reliable is Papias' evidence? Is it simply, as has been argued, based on conjecture? Is it merely an attempt to provide credentials for the gospel by linking it with the name of an apostle?

Assuming that Papias is right in attributing the gospel to someone called Mark, what more do we know about him? We may reasonably accept his statement that Mark knew Peter, for this tradition is supported by 1 Peter 5.13 (whoever may have been the author of that epistle). At the same time, we need to note that this tradition is often questioned, since Papias might well have identified Mark with Peter's companion *on the basis of* 1 Peter 5.13. Papias' description of Mark as Peter's 'interpreter' seems strange, but the word can also mean 'translator', and this seems a natural explanation: Peter would probably have needed a translator if he addressed congregations whose language was Greek. Mark is often identified with the 'John whose other name was Mark' referred to in Acts (12.12,25; 15.37–9), who is presumably the 'Mark' referred to in Col. 4.10, Philemon 24 and 2 Tim. 4.11. Apart from the somewhat tenuous link in Acts 12.12, however, there is nothing to connect this figure with Peter. Moreover, we have to remember that 'Mark' was a very common name at the time. It would be no surprise if there were two men with this name in the early Christian community. Nothing else is known about the Mark who wrote the gospel. It has often been suggested that the young man who fled naked from Gethsemane (14.51f.) was in fact the evangelist, but this speculation has no evidence to support it; indeed, if we accept Papias' evidence, it is contradicted in his statement that Mark had neither heard the Lord nor been his follower.

Papias may well be right, therefore, in claiming that the gospel was written by someone who had known Peter. Does this tell us anything about the nature of the tradition the evangelist includes? Now one of the interesting things about Papias' statement is the way in which he in effect apologizes for Mark's presentation of his material. To be sure, he tells us that Mark wrote accurately, and took care to omit nothing and to get nothing wrong. But twice he says that the material was not arranged in order, and he also remarks that 'he (presumably Peter) used to adapt his teaching to the needs' (perhaps of the moment or of his hearers) – statements which all tally with the insight of the form critics. The whole passage reads like a defence of Mark – perhaps because his gospel was already being unfavourably compared with those of the other evangelists. Papias does not claim that Mark presented the material in the correct chronological order –

the very opposite; and he speaks of its having been adapted: this does not amount to very strong support for the idea that Mark was presenting an 'eye-witness account' of Jesus' ministry.

The tradition linking Mark with Peter is repeated by various writers in the next couple of centuries, though they may, of course, be dependent on Papias: Justin Martyr (c. 150) refers to the 'memoirs of Peter'; the Anti-Marcionite Prologue (c. 160–80) tells us that Mark (known as 'stump-fingered') was the interpreter of Peter, and that he wrote his gospel after Peter's death in the regions of Italy; Irenaeus (c. 180–200) similarly describes Mark as the disciple and interpreter of Peter and says that he wrote after the deaths of Peter and Paul; this tradition conflicts with that recorded by Clement of Alexandria (c. 180) who refers several times to Mark's writing down the words of Peter during the latter's lifetime; Origen (c. 200) also speaks of Mark's doing as Peter instructed him.

It was undoubtedly this association with Peter that preserved the gospel for posterity, for it appears to have been less used than the other gospels and was somewhat neglected by commentators. Yet Mark's gospel was included in the canon from the beginning (though it was sometimes placed last of the four) and was sufficiently established to be used by Tatian (c. 170) in his *Diatessaron*, or compilation of four gospels. Since almost all of Mark's material is found also in either Matthew or Luke, it is remarkable that the gospel survived.

According to Clement of Alexandria, Mark wrote the gospel in Rome, a tradition which is backed up by the reference to 'the regions of Italy' in the Anti-Marcionite Prologue; Irenaeus, too, implies that the gospel was composed in Rome, since he speaks of Peter's work there. But the belief that Mark wrote in Rome could well be based on the link between Peter and Mark. The suggestion that the tradition of a Roman origin is backed up by Mark's use of 'Latin' words has no substance, since these words would have been used throughout the Roman Empire. Similarly, arguments that the constant warnings in Mark about suffering would be especially appropriate for a Roman congregation enduring the Neronian persecution ignore the fact that Christians elsewhere also suffered for their faith. Chrysostom (writing at the end of the fourth century) said that Mark wrote in Egypt, but he was perhaps misinterpreting Eusebius' comment that Mark went to Egypt and preached there the gospel which he had composed; certainly there is nothing to support this suggestion. Some have suggested Antioch as the place of origin, but this is simply a guess with little to support it. Another suggestion, that the gospel was written in Galilee, is based on the belief that it was intended to summon Christians to flee to Galilee in expectation of the parousia. This theory, put forward by Marxsen, has received little support, and the location in Galilee is at odds with Mark's lack of geographical knowledge and his explanation of Aramaic terms. All we can say with certainty, therefore, is that the gospel was composed somewhere in the Roman Empire – a conclusion that scarcely narrows the field at all!

The gospel is usually dated between AD 65 and 75. An earlier date has sometimes been advocated (notably by J.A.T. Robinson, in his *Redating the New Testament*), but a date after 65 seems likely, partly because this agrees with the evidence of the Anti-Marcionite Prologue and of Irenaeus (though not with that of Clement and Origen) that Mark wrote after the death of Peter (who died in AD 64), and partly because evidence in the gospel itself suggests a date of this period. Arguments that the tradition indicates a certain period of development, or that it reflects concern for the Gentile mission (7.19; 13.10; 14.9) or persecution (8.34–8; 10.35–40; 13.9–13) are too imprecise to allow us to pinpoint the date; but the sayings in Mark 13 appear to reflect events associated with the Jewish revolt which began in AD 64, and which led to the destruction of the temple in AD 70. The belief that the gospel was written before AD 75 depends on the view that Mark was the first of the four gospels to be written, and that it was used by Matthew and Luke as a source for their own gospels. Since the latter are usually dated between AD 80–90, Mark (or at least an early form of Mark) must have been written previously. Those who argue that Mark is dependent on Matthew and Luke must necessarily date Mark later.

Among those who accept a dating between AD 65 and 75, however, there is considerable disagreement as to whether the gospel was written before or after the destruction of the temple in the year 70. Although many commentators believe that Mark was written before AD 70, our own view is that it was written subsequently, and that Mark 13 reflects the trauma of those who had assumed that the temple's destruction was the sign which heralded the end of this era.[1] Whatever one decides on this particular point, the evidence points to a date just before or just after the events of AD 70.

## Interpretation of the gospel

Mark is the shortest of our four gospels, and almost the whole of it is closely paralleled in either Matthew or Luke, often in both. The relationship between the three gospels is so close as to suggest that two of the evangelists must have copied this parallel material. The first to consider this problem was Augustine, who examined the

1 See introductory note on Mark 13, pp. 297–303.

relationship between the gospels in his *De Consensu Evangelistarum* (*c.* 400). He regarded Mark's gospel as an abbreviation of Matthew's and apparently saw no conflict between this explanation of their relationship and the patristic tradition that Mark had been the interpreter of Peter.

It was no doubt the close relationship between Mark and Matthew which caused the comparative neglect of Mark by scholars and commentators for many centuries. Their preference for the longer gospel is understandable: it contained almost the whole of Mark and more besides; it was believed to be by an apostle, while Mark was not; its arrangement made it easy to comprehend. Mark was generally ignored, except for those short sections which have no parallel in Matthew. One of the few exceptions was the commentary by the Venerable Bede (676–735).

The modern era of Synoptic studies began with the publication by J. J. Griesbach of a synopsis of the gospels (replacing earlier harmonies) in 1774. Griesbach himself argued that Mark wrote after Matthew and Luke, and that he used both gospels, his purpose being to produce a shorter book. Griesbach also suggested that verses 9–20 of chapter 16 were spurious, and that the original ending of the gospel had been lost. His theory of synoptic relationships was accepted by many scholars in the early part of the nineteenth century, though by no means all. One theory (suggested by G.E. Lessing, and developed by J.G. Eichorn) was that all three synoptic evangelists had used a written Aramaic gospel, another (argued by J.G. Herder) that this source was oral. The idea that Mark's was the earliest gospel, and that it had been used by Matthew and Luke, was first seriously argued (independently) by C.J. Wilke and C.H. Weisse in 1838.

The importance of this debate lay in its relevance for the question of the nature of the gospels, and their value as historical documents. In contrast to D.F. Strauss, who had interpreted the gospel tradition as primarily mythical, scholars were now able to maintain that they were on firm historical ground with Mark, whose account of the ministry of Jesus was basically reliable. To Mark was now added 'Q', the sayings source believed to lie behind Matthew and Luke, and the two-document hypothesis of synoptic relations was born. For the next hundred years, the priority of Mark was almost universally accepted by Protestant scholars. After centuries of neglect, Mark's gospel was suddenly the focus of scholarly attention.

But the assumption that, because Mark was the earliest, it was therefore historically reliable did not go unchallenged. In 1892, Martin Kähler argued that the gospels could not be used as sources for the life of Jesus, since the figure they portray is the Christ believed in by the Christian community. In a famous phrase he described Mark as a 'passion narrative with an extended introduction'. William

Wrede, similarly, writing in 1901, argued that the Christ of faith had been superimposed on the historical Jesus, and that Mark's gospel was a theological work comparable to John's, not an account of the life of Jesus. Wrede's discussion of the part played by the messianic secret in Mark foreshadows the work of the redaction critics half a century later.[1] Wrede's book was not translated into English until 1971, but its influence, especially in Germany, was enormous. The belief that Mark could be used as the basis of a life of Jesus came under further attack from the form critics. The work of K.L. Schmidt, M. Dibelius and R. Bultmann in particular focused scholarly attention on the individual pericopae that made up the gospel, and attempted to ascertain the function of each pericope within the Christian community. The evangelists were now seen as mere collectors of material, and the historical value of the Markan outline was obviously suspect, since it was regarded as editorial. The recognition that the gospel stories reflected the beliefs and practices of the early Christian communities seemed to some of these scholars to point to the conclusion that they had been created by those communities and were therefore of no historical value. Although the extreme scepticism of certain form critics led many scholars (especially outside Germany) to reject their views, their contribution to Markan studies has ultimately proved enormous. It is now generally accepted that in the oral period the material was shaped (not necessarily created) by the believing communities, and that it cannot therefore be used directly as evidence for a 'life of Jesus' (though it is well to remember that the fact that the communities transmitted the tradition indicates that they valued it). Equally important has been the recognition that the Markan framework does not provide a chronological outline of the ministry. Few would now wish to argue, as C.H. Dodd did in 1932, that the framework itself represents 'a genuine succession of events'.[2] for as D. E. Nineham pointed out 25 years later, even if Mark's framework were traditional rather than editorial, it amounts to little more than a summary statement that Jesus taught and healed.[3]

But if the framework is editorial rather than historical, then perhaps it reflects the interests and concerns of Mark himself. The form critics had compared Mark's gospel to a haphazard collection of beads on a string – but might those beads perhaps have been arranged in a deliberate order? If so, then the evangelist must be seen as an author who chose and arranged his material with particular purposes in mind, rather than as a mere collector. Mark returned to the centre of scholarly interest – not, this time, because he was being

1 See additional note on the messianic secret, pp. 66–9.
2 *Exp. Tim.* 43, 1932, p.400.
3 *Studies in the Gospels*, pp. 223–39.

thought of as the closest of the evangelists to the historical Jesus, but because he was regarded as a theologian. We have already noted that the work of the redaction critics was foreshadowed by that of Wrede. Another precursor of the method was R.H. Lightfoot whose primary concern was with the purpose of the evangelists, in particular Mark. Other scholars, too, began to stress the creative role of the evangelist in presenting his material, and to see theological emphases in his gospel.

It was W. Marxsen, however, who coined the term 'redaction criticism', and applied this new method to Mark, in a study originally published in German in 1956. A flood of redaction-critical studies followed. This method still treats the gospels as essentially collections of traditional material, but assumes that the way in which the material is handled indicates the evangelist's own theological approach. In order to distinguish redaction from tradition it is necessary to consider literary factors, such as vocabulary and style: there are words (not just εὐθύς, straight away) which are particularly common in Mark; similarly, certain features of style (e.g.) parataxis and pleonasm) are especially frequent.[1] Compositional techniques, too, such as Mark's love for sandwiching incidents together (as, for example, in 5.21–43), betray his hand at work. Attempts to isolate pre-Markan blocks of tradition have been less successful. What seems to one generation of scholars to be a collection of similar pericopae from the oral period (e.g. 2.1–3.6) appears to the next to be a carefully designed section of the gospel! Unlike redactional-critical studies of Matthew and Luke, it was impossible to compare the evangelist's finished work with a document which was assumed to be his source. An alternative approach was to examine particular Markan concerns. Some studies concentrated on particular passages (e.g. Mark 13), others on prominent themes (e.g. the messianic secret), but all were based on the assumption that one could learn something of the theology of the evangelist himself from his gospel, and all took Markan priority for granted. Questions were now raised concerning the *Gattung* or 'genre' of the gospel. What kind of a document had Mark supposed himself to be writing? If the form critics were right in asserting that his gospel could no longer be seen as a biography, or as the memoirs of the apostle Peter, then what was it? Some critics saw it as an aretalogy, portraying Jesus as a hero figure, others as an apocalyptic message to the Christian community. Other suggestions were that it was modelled on Greek drama, or that it was intended to be used as a lectionary. One obvious reply to all these suggestions is that Mark wrote a gospel, and that this was a new literary genre,

---

1 For discussion of these features, see E.J. Pryke, *Redactional Style in the Marcan Gospel*, and F. Neirynck, *Duality in Mark*.

designed to proclaim the good news. But since nothing is ever entirely new, attempts to discover partial antecedents in various literary models have continued. It has, for example, been argued that the gospels are, after all, similar to some of the biographies written in the ancient world, and that Mark's gospel is written in the style of Xenophon's *Memorabilia* which defends the central character against misunderstanding and provides a true image of the hero for others to follow.[1] Yet there are important differences: while it is true that the *Memorabilia* is a collection of anecdotes about Socrates (frequently introduced, as in Mark, with a vague phrase such as 'one day' or 'on one occasion' or 'he used to'), these anecdotes are all much longer than the Markan pericopae and consist entirely of conversations. Moreover, they are woven into an argument defending Socrates against the charges brought against him, whereas Mark claims to be writing 'good news' about Jesus, not defending him.

Linked with this interest in the genre of the gospel went concern to discover the situation which it addressed. What was it that led Mark to tell his story in the precise way that he did? Since the passion narrative dominates the gospel, this suggests that Mark was particularly concerned to show why Jesus came to die. Did he perhaps feel that the gospel of a crucified Messiah needed careful explanation? But if Mark is a 'passion narrative with a long introduction', we need to look at the introduction also: clearly one of Mark's central concerns is with the identity of Jesus, although this is deliberately concealed throughout his ministry. Was Mark anxious to present a particular aspect of Jesus' messiahship – as Son of God, or as Son of man? And if so, why?

One popular answer to these questions was that Mark wrote in an attempt to correct a false understanding of the gospel with a correct one. This approach was advocated in a remarkable exposition of the gospel by T. Weeden who argued that Mark's purpose was to combat a false christology with a true understanding of Jesus as the suffering Son of man: the first eight chapters of Mark's gospel present the false christology, which represent Jesus as a θεῖος ἀνήρ, or 'divine man', exercising miraculous powers, and this is then corrected, in the last eight chapters, with teaching about the suffering Son of man. The disciples represent the church leaders of Mark's day who hold the false belief in Jesus as a wonder-worker and ignore the message of the Cross.[2] Weeden's interpretation of Mark had moved on, beyond redaction criticism proper to a literary analysis of the gospel which

1 Cf. C. Talbert, *What is a Gospel?*
2 T. Weeden, *Mark – Traditions in Conflict*

attempted to understand the setting in which it was written, as well as the purpose of the evangelist. It is a good example of the dangers which beset such attempts. Much of Weeden's interpretation is based on the belief that Mark was totally opposed to the Twelve and conducted a vendetta against them, and on the understanding of the scene at Caesarea Philippi as a rejection by Jesus of Peter's acknowledgement of him as Messiah. These assumptions go far beyond the evidence and can, indeed, be refuted from the gospel itself. Moreover, the notion that the gospel had its origins in a situation of conflict is itself an assumption. In asking questions about the purpose and situations of the author and his community, we need to be careful not to read them in the light of our own presuppositions.

In spite of its popularity, there is no reason to suppose that the antagonistic model of the gospel is necessarily correct. In fact, the notion that Mark was correcting a 'heresy' is clearly anachronistic. And though he might be correcting a view that he believed to be mistaken, he could equally well simply be stating what he believed to be the truth. Emphasis on Jesus' suffering can certainly be explained as due to Mark's desire to combat a false christology which interpreted Jesus' messiahship in terms of glory without reference to the Cross; but it can equally well be seen as due to Mark's need to explain to his community the necessity for Christ's death, and to help them come to terms with the scandal of the Cross. Similarly, Mark's insistence that the disciples must share Jesus' suffering could well be due, not to the fact that the leaders of the church had played down the need for Christians to suffer, but because (as tradition has maintained) Mark's contemporaries were suffering persecution at the time. Mark certainly presents the disciples as hard of heart, but they may well represent Christian believers rather than heretical Church leaders, for their obtuseness is tied up with the 'messianic secret', and represents the inability of men and women to grasp the truth about Jesus until this is revealed through his death and resurrection.

The problem of separating tradition from redaction had thus proved as complex, in its way, as that of separating history from interpretation; in each case, the results depend very largely on a prior decision about the creativity of the evangelist or the community. Concern to discover the purpose of the evangelist and his *Sitz im Leben* meant that the gospel was now being analysed as a whole. But there was an inbuilt circularity in the method, for the answers one gave to questions about Mark's purpose and theology depended to a large extent on how much of the material one attributed to Mark, and how much to his sources. Since we do not have his sources, to act as a 'control', we cannot say how much of the material is directly attributable to Mark himself.[1] This circularity became even more apparent when scholars such as Howard Kee attempted to answer questions about the community for whom Mark was writing: it might be possible to guess the social structure of a society from a sermon if there were no constraints on the author (such as history, sources and traditions), but in the case of Mark (which is far more than a simple sermon), such guesses have too little basis.

But the story as Mark tells it is a fascinating one, and there are various ways of approaching it. Since answering historical questions about the evangelist and his community has proved as difficult as answering questions about Jesus, it is hardly surprising if there has recently been a shift from concern with historical matters to interest in literary criticism. Here we find, at one extreme, those who are still concerned primarily with the author's intention: redaction criticism may help to pinpoint his special emphases, rhetorical criticism may reveal something of the methods he uses to say it. At the other extreme, there are those who have abandoned historical questions altogether, and who focus on the gospel as a document in its own right: they are not interested in the concerns of the evangelist, but in the literary-critical analysis of his gospel, and the way in which it is read by the reader.

Redaction-critical studies, building on the work of source critics, have assumed the priority of Mark. For the past hundred years or so, the 'Markan hypothesis' has tended to be regarded as one of the 'assured results' of New Testament criticism. It is true that the official Catholic view for much of that time was that Mark was the abbreviation of Matthew,[2] but the general view was that the Synoptic problem had been solved. Recently, however, the priority of Mark has been challenged by a revival of the Griesbach hypothesis, which holds that Mark was written last of the Synoptics and used the other two.[3]

---

1 The problems of applying redaction criticism to Mark have been analysed in a recent study by C.C. Black entitled *The Disciples according to Mark*.
2 This view was ably defended by B.C. Butler, in his book *The Originality of St Matthew*.
3 See W.R. Farmer, *The Synoptic Problem*, and H.-H. Stoldt, *History and Criticism of the Marcan Hypothesis*. For a critical assessment of the Griesbach hypothesis, leading to the conclusion that it is 'considerably less viable as a solution to the Synoptic Problem than the two-document hypothesis' (p. 186), see C. Tuckett, *The Revival of the Griesbach Hypothesis*.

Whatever solution we adopt, Mark occupies the crucial position, because of its close relationship with the other two, in both wording and ordering of the material. The possibilities are:

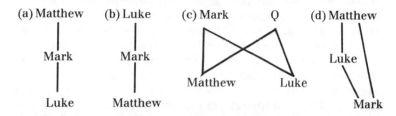

(a) Matthew    (b) Luke    (c) Mark    Q    (d) Matthew

Mark      Mark          Matthew   Luke      Luke

Luke      Matthew                               Mark

The vast majority of scholars still believe that (c) is the most likely explanation, on the grounds that Matthew and Luke frequently appear to 'correct' Mark, expressing things more carefully, more elegantly, more grammatically and more succinctly: but the arguments used in the heyday of source criticism can no longer be used without qualification, for the recognition that the evangelists are authors means that Mark could have written last and have chosen, quite deliberately, to concentrate on the miracles and the passion narrative and to have left on one side traditions about Jesus' teaching included by Matthew and Luke. Moreover, the relationships between the gospels are not as simple as the 'Two Document Hypothesis' (Mark + Q) suggests; supporters of the Griesbach hypothesis are right to this extent, that sometimes the evidence suggests that the Matthaean (or Lukan) version of a saying or incident is earlier than the Markan. This has led to the suggestion that Matthew and Luke made use of an earlier version of Mark's gospel ('*Ur-Markus*'), and that all three synoptic evangelists made use of this document. There may, indeed, have been other gospels or sources (written or oral) of which we know nothing. Certainly the fact that no theory fits all the facts suggests that there may be hidden factors contributing to the situation.

All we can say with certainty is that, on the evidence available, the hypothesis of Markan priority solves more problems than any other. But no hypothesis should ever be given the status of an 'assured result', and we may be grateful to those who have challenged this particular theory for reminding us of this fact.

## The shape of the gospel

The gospel was almost certainly intended to be read aloud in a congregation, not privately. Although it has been argued that it was designed to be used as a lectionary,[1] it seems far more likely that it

1 See P. Carrington, *The Primitive Christian Calendar*, and M.D. Goulder, *The Evangelists' Calendar*.

was originally read *in toto*, or at least in fairly large sections. The fact that the gospel was composed for the ear, rather than for the eye, is reflected in the constant repetitions, and in the summaries, recapitulations and variations on a theme. The word πάλιν, 'again', is used no less than 26 times and serves to remind us of the previous occasion on which something occurred. Words, stories and geographical locations are repeated or echoed later in the gospel, so welding the whole narrative into a unity. Since hearers had to rely on what they heard and could not thumb back through the pages of the gospel, the editorial links between sections and the juxtaposition of material underlined the relationship of the various stories to one another. Reading the gospel today, we tend to analyse it, dividing it into sections and sub-sections which deal with different themes, but those who first heard it would have been far more aware of the links between different parts of the story rather than of the divisions.

This means that we must recognize that any attempt to analyse the gospel is bound to be arbitrary, since we are imposing our own pattern on the material. It is true that the gospel does have a clear shape: after the opening few verses, we have an account of Jesus' ministry in Galilee, in which the inability of Jesus' contemporaries (first the religious authorities, then the crowd, finally even the disciples) to comprehend the truth about him is more and more stressed. After the incident at Caesarea Philippi (8.27–30), Jesus teaches his disciples about his own future suffering and the meaning of true discipleship. At 11.1 he arrives at the gates of Jerusalem, and in 14.1 Mark begins the story of the passion; the gospel ends with the account of the empty tomb in 16.1–8. But one interesting feature of this scheme is the fact that commentators have found it difficult to agree as to where the divisions should be made. There is frequent discussion as to whether 1.14–15 belong to the 'Prologue' (vv. 1–13) or introduce the first main section; 3.7–12 and 6.7–13 are sometimes regarded as the opening paragraphs in new sections, sometimes as the closing paragraphs in the previous ones. So, too, at the major division at the end of chapter 8: does the new section begin in 8.22, 8.27 or 8.31? The very fact that the answer is not clear encourages us to believe that we are right in seeing these paragraphs as turning points – but wrong if we place them firmly 'before' or 'after' the division. We suggest, rather, that those paragraphs which tend to 'wander' in scholarly analyses do so precisely because they look both backwards and forwards; such passages have the nature of overlapping hinges. It is possible, of course, that breaks were made in the reading of the gospel, and that the summaries in 3.7–12 and 6.7–13 were designed to remind the congregation of 'the story so far'; one interesting fact is that the six major divisions usually descried in the gospel are of very similar length, suggesting that this plan may not be so arbitrary after all.[1] Nevertheless, we do well to remember that these divisions are artificial in the sense that they result from *our* reading of the gospel and do not necessarily agree with Mark's own intentions. But since we today read the gospel as written word, we have felt obliged to assist readers of this commentary to find their way around the gospel by adopting the conventional approach and dividing the gospel into sections.

For those who listened, rather than read the gospel, then, repeated words and ideas would have been significant. The setting of incidents in particular places may have rung bells, frequently reminding the gospel's hearers of other events set in the same spot, and sometimes linking with important Old Testament passages. Significant events take place at the very beginning in the 'wilderness' (ἔρημος: 1.3,4,12,13); the same word is used to describe a 'lonely place' where Jesus takes refuge (1.35, 45; 6.31, 32, 35). Many incidents take place beside the sea (1.16; 2.13; 3.7; 4.1; 5.21; 7.31), and three significant self-revelations of Jesus to his disciples are located *on* the sea, the first two reminiscent of theophanies in the Old Testament (4.35–41; 6.45–52; 8.13–21). Other incidents are set in 'a house' (1.29; 2.1,15; 3.20; 5.38; 7.17, 24; 9.28, 33; 10.10; 14.3). Again, there are constant references to the 'way' (ὁδός), and we soon learn that this way frequently refers, not simply to a road, but to a very particular way: it is the way of the Lord (1.2f.; 12.14), the way Jesus and his disciples take to Jerusalem (9.33f.; 10.32, 46, 52; 11.8).

The importance of ideas is underlined by repetition: the three-fold prophecy of the Son of man's suffering and resurrection (8.31; 9.31; 10.33) is an obvious example. The significance of events is also stressed by the frequent references to the amazement, fear or awe of those who witnessed them (e.g.1.22, 27; 2.12; 4.41; 5.15, 20, 42; 6.2, 51; 7.37; 9.6,15; 10.32; 12.17; 16.8). The use of paradox (often in the sayings of Jesus) keeps Mark's readers alert: the statement that one must lose one's life in order to save it, for example (8.35), and the declaration that whoever wishes to be first must be the slave of all (10.44) shock those who have not been lulled into complacency by familiarity. Nor would the use of irony be lost on Mark's readers (see, e.g., 3.1–6; 14.65; 15.31).

The juxtaposition of material on similar themes would help to impress an idea on Mark's readers. Of particular importance here is his fondness for sandwiching together two stories which have something in common, as in 3.21–35; 5.22–43; 11.12–26; 14.54–72. Sometimes two stories simply stand side by side (e.g. 7.1–23, 24–30;

---

1 B. Standaert, *L'Évangile selon Marc*, divides the gospel somewhat differently: he finds three major divisions instead of six (1.14–6.13; 6.14–10.52; 11.1–15.47), but he also traces concentric patterns in each division.

8.22–6, 27–38). Occasionally a series of stories builds up an idea, as with the 'conflict' stories in 2.1–3.6; most notable of all here is the block of material which falls between the two stories about blind men who were given their sight, since every incident between these two stories demonstrates the 'blindness' of the disciples and their inability to understand Jesus and his teaching (cf. 8.31ff.; 9.2–13, 14ff., 30–2, 33–7, 38–50; 10.10f., 13–16, 23–31, 32–45).

All four of our gospels end with the passion narrative, followed by an account of the empty tomb and the news of Jesus' resurrection; Mark alone lacks a resurrection appearance, since 16.8 is certainly the last verse in the gospel from his hand.[1] The four introductions, on the other hand, are strikingly different: yet they have this in common – they all begin with a section which is markedly different from the rest of the gospel. John 1.1–18 and Mark 1.1–13 are commonly referred to as the 'Johannine prologue' and the 'Markan prologue' respectively, but Matthew 1–2 and Luke 1–2 perform the same function, spelling out the significance of Jesus without any suggestion of secrecy.[2] This means that all four gospels have a 'second introduction' (Matt. 3.1f.; Mark 1.14f.; Luke 3.1f.; John 1.19), where the story proper begins; it is interesting to note that John the Baptist features in all four, even though in Mark he receives only a bare mention, since his work has been adequately described already.

Mark's prologue has frequently been compared with the prologue of a Greek play, in which the chorus introduces the story to the audience and explains the significance of the scenes they are about to see. The device is familiar to many modern readers who have not necessarily watched Greek drama, because it is used by Shakespeare in *Henry V*, though Shakespeare uses it to tell parts of the story which take place offstage, rather than to reveal the hidden meaning of the events taking place on the stage. Whether or not Mark himself attended the theatre we do not know.[3] He is certainly not the only biblical writer to use this dramatic device, for, in addition to the parallels in the other gospels, there is an interesting precedent in the book of Job: after the scene has been set in 1.1–5, the explanation of the story is given in the first scene, vv. 6–12, which is set in heaven. The story then returns to earth and thereafter, apart from 2.1–7 which provides us with the second part of the explanation, it is told from the point of view of Job and his contemporaries, who are totally unaware of the real issues which are being decided by their reactions to events. Only because we, the readers of the story, have been allowed to witness the scenes set in the heavenly court, do we

---

1 See below, additional note on Mark's ending, pp. 391–4.
2 M.D. Hooker, in *N.T.S.*, 21, 1974, pp.51f.
3 M.A. Beavis, *Mark's Audience*, argues strongly that he did.

appreciate the significance of the story. In a similar way, Mark 1.1–13 provides us with the key information about Jesus which enables us to understand the drama which is about to be unfolded before us. Occasional comments 'from beyond' (the heavenly voice at 9.7, and the unclean spirits at 1.24; 3.11; 5.7) punctuate the narrative and remind us of the real meaning of the story.

## The theology of Mark

Because of the difficulty of separating Markan interpretation from the material which he inherited, and because of the impossibility of isolating Mark's own understanding of the story from that which we ourselves read into the text, we cannot claim to be able to present Mark's theological position with any certainty. We can, however, point out what appear to us to be the important issues in his presentation of the gospel. Several of these issues are dealt with in more detail in the additional notes in the commentary.

Mark introduces his gospel with the declaration that it is 'good news'. The good news which he unfolds, however, is strangely disturbing. It brings salvation, but it also brings the threat of destruction – symbolized by torn garments (2.21; 14.63) and burst wineskins (2.22) – not simply for the temple (13; 14.58; 15.29, 38), but for the nation as well (11.12–14, 20–5; 12.9). The climax of the story is the gruesome death of its hero who has summoned men and women to abandon everything they value (10.17–31) and follow him to the scaffold (8.34–8). The 'good news' must be good indeed to justify Mark's title! His claim is that those who abandon everything to follow Jesus will 'be repaid a hundred times' (10.30), and that those who lose their lives for Jesus' sake will save them (8.35). The radical challenge presented to men and women is to abandon their old way of life in order to do the will of God; those who do this belong to the new community (3.35). The new existence is symbolized by miracles of healing, restoration and forgiveness, as well as by parables which describe abundant harvests (4.1–32). But no one in the story seems capable of responding to the call: the disciples, who follow Jesus as far as Jerusalem, run away at the critical point; even the women, who are present when he dies, flee from the empty tomb (16.8).

The gospel is 'good news about Jesus Christ', and the whole book is focused on the figure of Jesus. Earlier commentators who discussed Mark's christology began from an investigation of the christological titles in the gospel. But titles are simply a form of shorthand – a useful way of summarizing beliefs – which became important at a later stage as confessions of Christian faith. Moreover, it appears that many of these titles were originally far more 'fluid' than we once supposed. The term 'messiah', for example, could be used for a variety of figures and was not nearly as specific as Christians later supposed it to be. Though Mark himself sometimes uses one or other of these titles as the climax of particular stories, they sum up truths which have already been demonstrated in the course of the narrative. The confession of Peter at Caesarea Philippi (8.29) and that of the centurion at the moment of Jesus' death (15.39) point Mark's readers to the true interpretation of the story which he has been telling.

Recent investigation of Mark has stressed the importance of the fact that he presents his gospel in narrative form. A great deal of Mark's christology is implicit, conveyed by the way in which he presents the material. The identity of Jesus is deliberately concealed from the characters in the story.[1] A glance at John's gospel reveals a very different approach: there, Jesus frequently makes specific claims for himself, e.g. in the 'I am' sayings; he refers to himself as the Son, and to God as his Father. In Mark, Jesus nowhere preaches himself: his own 'good news' is summed up in 1.15 – it is good news about the Kingdom of God. Jesus calls men and women to follow him (to a scaffold!), but it is left to others to make statements about who he is; the only 'claims' he makes are those in which he refers to himself obliquely as 'the Son of man'.[2] Nevertheless every part of Mark's story makes implicit claims on his behalf. His every action is characterized by authority; though he does not teach about himself, his teaching challenges men and women with a choice between believing in him and rejecting him. In Jesus, Mark's readers are confronted by the Kingdom of God in action, and they must decide for or against him.

Not surprisingly, the theme of discipleship runs throughout the gospel: the disciples are called (1.16–18,19f.; 2.14), chosen (3.13–19) and sent out (6.7–13). Much of the teaching in the second part of the gospel concerns the meaning of discipleship (8.34–8; 9.42–50; 10.23–31, 35–45), and the story, when it is not the story of Jesus, is the story of the disciples' failure – of their misunderstanding and lack of faith (4.13, 40; 6.37, 52; 7.18; 8.4, 14–21, 32f.; 9.5f., 10, 14–29, 32–41; 10.10, 24–6, 32, 35–41), and of their final collapse (14.33–42, 50), Judas' betrayal (14.10f., 43–6) and Peter's denial (14.54, 66–72). Their failure is so great that it is sometimes suggested that Mark is launching a deliberate attack on the Twelve, who perhaps represent a group in his own community.[3] It is more likely, however, that Mark's emphasis on the inability of the Twelve to comprehend the truth about Jesus is due to his insistence that this truth is revealed through the Cross and resurrection. The disciples thus act as a foil to

1 See additional note on the messianic secret, pp. 66–9.
2 See additional note on the Son of man, pp. 88–93.
3 So, e.g., T. Weeden, *op. cit.*

Mark's own readers who are able to recognize the good news for what it is. There are three ways in which the Twelve fail to comprehend. First, they do not understand Jesus' teaching (4.13; 7.17f.; 10.10; 10.23–6); second, they cannot grasp the significance of his divine authority (4.35–41; 6.45–52; 8.14–21); and third, they are bewildered by his teaching about his approaching death and resurrection (8.31–3; 9.9f.; 9.30–7; 10.32–45). To those who read the gospel all these things should be plain.

The disciples are not the only characters in the story to fail to comprehend its significance, however: indeed they do better than most, since they have *some* inkling of the truth (4.11f.; 8.27–30; 9.2–8). If Mark's story is a story about the meaning of discipleship (barely understood), it is also a story about misunderstanding and opposition, incomprehension and rejection. It begins with the authorities, in the series of 'conflict stories' found in 2.1–3.6 and continues in the confrontation between Jesus and the scribes from Jerusalem in 3.20–30. Linked into this last story is that of Jesus' rejection by his own family (3.20f., 31–5). At the same time, in contrast to these 'outsiders' (v.31), we find a group emerging who have chosen to be with Jesus (3.13–19, 32–5). In the next chapter, the contrast between those who are with Jesus and those 'outside' continues, but now it is the crowd who, though they listen to Jesus, are without understanding (4.10–12). In 5.17, the inhabitants of 'the district of the Gerasenes' beg him to leave their country, and in 6.1–6, echoing the rejection by his own family, we find the inhabitants of his own home village refusing to believe in him. From this point on, Mark emphasizes the hostility of the religious authorities who have rejected Jesus' authority (7.1–23; 8.11–13; 10.1–12; 11.15–33; 12; 14–15), and the incomprehension of the disciples who have accepted it. The divisions are not always clear, however. True, some groups (scribes and Pharisees, Herodians, elders and chief priests) are always opposed to Jesus; even so, individuals are sometimes sympathetic (12.28–34; 15.42–7). The crowds are ambivalent; though they follow Jesus, they are without understanding (4.11f.). Others besides the Twelve are called to follow Jesus (2.13f.; 8.34–8; 10.21): and outsiders often show greater faith in Jesus than do the disciples (7.24–30, cf. 7.17f.; 9.24, cf. 9.28f.; 10.46–52; 15.39), sometimes persisting in spite of discouragement (2.4f.; 5.35f.; 7.27–9; 10.47f.). Only the women are consistently shown in a positive light (5.25–34; 7.24–30; 12.41–4; 14.3–9; 15.40f., 47), and even here there is one suprising exception – his own mother (3.31).

We have already referred to the fact that Mark's story is dominated by the death of Jesus. Why is this so? Is it perhaps merely a reflection of early Christian preaching? Or is there some other reason why Mark devotes so much space to this theme? One obvious explanation is that Mark felt it necessary to explain the scandal of the Cross: Paul had described the message of a crucified Messiah as 'an offence to Jews, and folly to Gentiles' (1 Cor. 1.23), and such it certainly was. By emphasizing that the death of Jesus was 'necessary', that it took place in accordance with God's will and was foretold in scripture, Mark would be able to deal with this particular problem. Another explanation links up with the traditional belief that Mark was written in a time of persecution. The stress on Jesus' willing acceptance of suffering, and on his call to his followers to share his suffering, may well have encouraged Christians facing persecution for their faith.

A very different explanation suggests that the Markan community, like the Corinthian church, was ignoring the message of the Cross altogether, and interpreting the Christian life (as do James and John in Mark 10.35–45) in terms of glory and honour; they emphasized the nearness of the End and forgot that distress and persecution must come first (cf. Mark 13). In such circumstances, Mark felt it necessary to tell the story of Jesus' sufferings at some length, and to emphasize that those who wished to be his disciples must be prepared to follow him along the same way of rejection and shame.

The appropriateness of Mark's message to these very different situations illustrates the difficulty of recovering the original situation which Mark was addressing. It also demonstrates very well the part which readers themselves play in the interpretation of the gospel, since clearly this can mean very different things in different circumstances.

Whatever the reason, Mark's story deals with the question 'Why did Jesus die?' and answers it at various levels. At one level, his answer is that Jesus died because it was the will of God; at another, that he died because he was obedient; at a third (paradoxically!), that he died because of the wickedness of his enemies and the treachery of Judas. All three explanations tell us how it came about that Jesus died: they do not tell us what his death achieved. None of the evangelists has a great deal to say about what we would call 'the atonement'. Nevertheless, there are in Mark two passages where Jesus describes his death as being 'for many' (10.45; 14.24); his death is a 'ransom' and effects a 'covenant'. These two terms remind us of God's choice of Israel to be his people, of the Exodus from Egypt and the covenant made with them on Sinai: Jesus' death creates a new people of God, who will inherit the Kingdom of God (14.25).

But Jesus' death cannot be separated from his resurrection (as we see in all the so-called passion predictions), and Jesus himself is not separated from the redeemed community: he too will drink wine in the Kingdom of God (14.25); he himself leads the disciples into Galilee (14.28; 16.7); he is raised up by God to be the chief stone in the new building (12.10) – a theme which is echoed in the accusations about his threat to replace the temple with a new one (14.58; 15.29). The life of the new community depends upon his death *and resurrection*. Nevertheless, it is only because of Jesus' obedient acceptance of suffering and death that he is vindicated, and Mark's narrative concentrates on the story of the passion. One of the remarkable features of this section of the gospel is the way in which, in contrast to the earlier chapters, implicitly rather than explicitly, but nevertheless clearly to those with eyes to see, Jesus is now revealed as Christ and Son of God. It begins with Bartimaeus' acknowledgement of Jesus as 'Son of David' as he approaches Jerusalem; Jesus then enters the city on a donkey, while his followers greet the one who comes in the name of the Lord, together with 'the coming kingdom of our father David'. He comes to the temple in judgement (as Mal. 3.1 foretold of 'the Lord'), and looks for fruit on the barren tree of Israel which fails to respond to its Messiah; Jesus' question about John the Baptist in 11.30 makes the significance of this section clear. He then tells a parable and, unlike the parables in 4, the meaning of this one is plain (12.12): there is no doubt that Mark understood it as a claim by Jesus to be God's final messenger, his 'beloved son' (12.6). Jesus then demonstrates, in a series of debates, an authority to teach which is superior to that of the Pharisees, Sadducees and scribes, and finally claims to be greater than the son of David (12.35–40). After chapter 13, which spells out the judgement on the temple and the nation, we come to the passion narrative itself. This begins with the anointing of Jesus (by a woman!), an incident which is interpreted as pointing forward to his burial: the story is a symbol of the fact that Jesus is to be proclaimed King through his death. But only with the 'trial' and crucifixion of Jesus is this theme brought out into the open. Remarkably, the three men who pass sentence of death on him and carry it out all proclaim the truth about him, though the first two merely ask (incredulous) questions: the high priest asks 'Are you the Christ, the Son of the Blessed?' (14.61), Pilate asks 'Are you the King of the Jews?' (15.2) and the centurion declares 'Truly this man was [the] son of God' (15.39). Throughout chapter 15, Mark hammers home the truth that Jesus was crucified as King of the Jews: Pilate refers to him as such (vv. 9,12), the Roman soldiers mock him as a king and salute him as 'King of the Jews', and the inscription on the cross reads 'the King of the Jews'; finally, the chief priests and scribes mock him as 'the Christ, the King of Israel'. The one who saved others cannot save himself, and the Christ the King of Israel cannot come down from the cross, because that would be a denial of his kingship (vv. 31f.). In his dying, as in his living, Jesus embodies his own teaching: by losing his life he saves it (8.35), by being last he is first (9.35), and by serving and giving his life as a ransom for many, he is acknowledged to be great (10.42–5). Through his death he is proclaimed Messiah and Son of God. This is why the full truth about Jesus cannot be grasped by men and women until after his death and resurrection. They cannot comprehend who he is because they refuse to accept the necessity for shame and death – something Mark emphasizes by linking every reference to the fate which lies in store for the Son of man with the disciples' failure to understand (8.31ff.; 9.9–13, 30–7; 10.32–45; 14.17–21, 41f.).

It is not surprising if the event which reveals Jesus as Messiah also brings about the redemption of the people of God. Nor, since this new community replaces the old, is it surprising to find another theme interwoven into it – namely, that of Israel's condemnation. The link is clearly set out in the parable of the vineyard tenants in 12.1–12: because the tenants kill the beloved son, they will themselves be destroyed. The chief priests and scribes and elders refuse to recognize Jesus' authority in the temple (11.27–33) and plot his death (11.18; 14.1f.); they accuse him of speaking against the temple and condemn him to death (14.53–64). By doing so, they bring judgement on themselves and seal their own fate and that of the temple (11.12–22; 13; 15.38). In seeking to destroy their Messiah, Israel's rulers destroy their nation: it is they, not he, who have broken the Law and who are therefore condemned. Mark's bitter portrait of the Jerusalem authorities may have been influenced by the events of AD 70.

The new community is established by Jesus' death, but it has already been called into being earlier in the gospel. The people who have already experienced the benefits of God's Kingdom have *not* been the 'religious'. Jesus has included 'sinners and tax-gatherers' (2.16)', men and women who were excluded from society because of some infirmity or impurity (1.40–5; 5.25–34), those with 'unclean' spirits, those who were not over scrupulous in their interpretation of the requirements of the Law (2.23–8; 7.1–23). The community he calls is Jewish; but a Gentile woman creeps in because of her faith (7.24–30) and at the end of the story Mark depicts a Gentile centurion as the one who acknowledges Jesus as son of God.

The gospel reflects the tensions of a time when Jewish Christians were coming to terms with the failure of their fellow Jews to respond to the gospel. The rejection of Jesus' own message by his contemporaries had been followed by the rejection of the message about him by the great majority of Jews. But the Jewish background is still vitally important: Jesus was a Jew, his whole ministry was spent among Jews, and finally he is proclaimed King of the Jews on the cross. Although he is attacked by his opponents for laxity towards the Law, Mark affirms that Jesus is in fact *loyal* to the Law (1.44; 3.4; 10.19; 12.29–31); it is his enemies who ignore the Law and are castigated by Jesus for doing so (3.4; 7.8–13). The debates in the gospel are concerned with the interpretation of the Mosaic tradition, and the question at issue is whether it is Jesus and his followers or their Jewish opponents who are faithful to it. Yet Mark's picture is not entirely consistent, for he attributes to Jesus teaching which in effect challenges the Law and frees the community from the obligation to keep the Jewish food laws, teaching which was of vital importance for Gentile Christians of Mark's own day (7.19).

Jesus' loyalty to Judaism is demonstrated also in his use of scripture. Apart from the Pharisees in 10.4 (who are referred to Moses by Jesus himself), the scribe in 12.28–34 (who simply echoes Jesus' own words) and the Sadducees in 12.19, the quotations from scripture in Mark's gospel are all found in the mouth of Jesus, often in arguing against his attackers (7.6f., 10; 10.6–8; cf. also 2.25f.; 4.12; 10.19; 11.17; 12.10; 12.26; 12.36; 14.27, as well as many echoes of scripture which are not specifically introduced as quotations). Jesus appeals to Moses and is supported by Moses (see 9.2–8), for, at the end of the day, Jesus is greater than Moses (1.41; 2.7; 6.50–2; 9.7; 10.2–12; 10.21; 12.1–12).

Because of the misunderstanding which surrounds the word 'Law', the Jewish word Torah ('teaching') has frequently been used in this commentary in referring to the Mosaic tradition; its use helps to remind us that the idea that the religion of the Old Testament is a legalistic one is a caricature. Judaism (like Christianity after it) was open to a legalistic interpretation, but the disputes in Mark about the interpretation of Torah imply acceptance of the Torah itself, and we should avoid reading back into the gospel the later antithesis between Law and Gospel.

We have suggested already that the opening verses of Mark's gospel are equivalent to a prologue in a classical play. The analogy of a drama is a helpful one in understanding the gospel as a whole, for it consists of a series of short, crisp scenes; the action moves speedily from one incident to another, but what unites them all is the fact that every scene in the drama is focused on the figure of Jesus. Moreover, the arrangement of these scenes means that they demand a response from those who watch, as well as from those who play a part in them. 'What is this?' the characters ask, then '*Who* is this?' The answer seems clear to us, but not to the participants in the play: we are surprised at their incomprehension, forgetting that they have not been present for the prologue and have not understood the comments of the vanquished demons. We are relieved when Peter finally acknowledges that Jesus is greater than anyone who has gone before (8.27–9). But we are still involved as the story proceeds, because Jesus addresses the crowd as well as the Twelve: this drama involves audience participation, and we, too, are summoned to take up a cross and follow him. And at the end of the story, we are invited to leave the theatre and to go, not to our own homes, but 'to Galilee', where we shall see the Risen Lord, for the promise of Easter morning is made to anyone who is prepared to follow Jesus on the path of discipleship. Mark's gospel is above all a powerful challenge to faith and to commitment.

Mark's story is written from a standpoint of faith. No one who reads it can be neutral towards it: inevitably we read it in the light of our own presuppositions, and this goes for the commentator also! It is not the commentator's task to make judgements about Mark's interpretation of the story, and we have tried to avoid doing so: it is for each individual reader of the gospel to decide the extent to which Mark's interpretation rings true.

# ANALYSIS OF THE GOSPEL

A  *The Prologue: the basis of Jesus' authority*  1.1–13

  1  The beginning  1.1 – 8
    Additional note: the baptism of John
  2  The baptism of Jesus  1.9–11
  3  The battle with Satan  1.12–13

B  *Authority at work: success and opposition in Galilee*
                                         1.14–3.6

  1  Jesus proclaims the Good News  1.14–15
    Additional note: the Kingdom of God
  2  The call to discipleship  1.16–20
  3  Authority in teaching and exorcism  1.21–8
    Additional note: the messianic secret
  4  Jesus heals a friend  1.29–31
  5  Healings and exorcisms  1.32–4
    Additional note: miracles
  6  Jesus extends his ministry  1.35–9
  7  Jesus makes a leper clean  1.40–5
  8  Authority to forgive sins  2.1–12
    Additional note: the Son of man
  9  Jesus and the outcasts  2.13–17
 10  Old and new  2.18–22
 11  Lord of the Sabbath  2.23–8
 12  The opposition hardens  3.1–6

C  *Truth hidden and revealed: parables and miracles*  3.7–6.6

  1  The crowds follow Jesus  3.7–12
  2  Appointment of the Twelve  3.13–19
  3  Misunderstanding  3.20–35
  4  The parable of the sower  4.1–9
    Additional note: parables
  5  The purpose of the parables  4.10–12
  6  The parable explained  4.13–20
  7  More sayings on the same theme  4.21–5

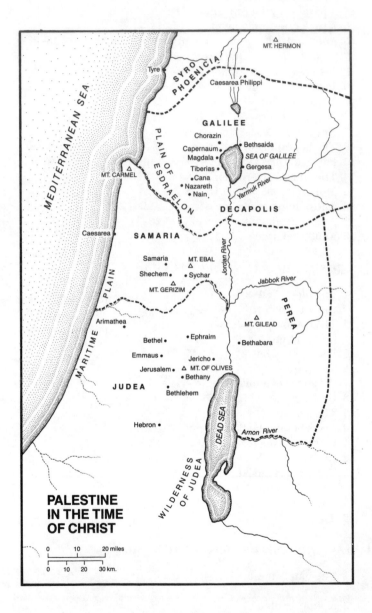

MEDITERRANEAN SEA

△ MT. HERMON

Tyre •

SYRO-
PHOENICIA

• Caesarea Philippi

GALILEE

Chorazin •
Capernaum •   • Bethsaida
Magdala •   *SEA OF GALILEE*
Tiberias •
• Cana   • Gergesa
• Nazareth
• Nain

PLAIN OF ESDRAELON

△ MT. CARMEL

Yarmuk River

DECAPOLIS

Caesarea •

SAMARIA

Samaria •   MT. EBAL △
Shechem •   • Sychar
MT. GERIZIM △

Jordan River

Jabbok River

PEREA

△ MT. GILEAD

Arimathea •

MARITIME PLAIN

Bethel •   • Ephraim

Emmaus •   • Bethabara
Jericho •
Jerusalem •   △ MT. OF OLIVES
• Bethany

JUDEA   • Bethlehem

DEAD SEA

Hebron •

Arnon River

WILDERNESS OF JUDEA

**PALESTINE
IN THE TIME
OF CHRIST**

0    10    20 miles
0   10   20   30 km.

# THE GOSPEL ACCORDING TO ST MARK

## A   The Prologue: the basis of Jesus' authority                    1.1–13

These first thirteen verses stand apart from the rest of the gospel and provide the key to what follows. They give us certain information about Jesus which enables us to understand the significance of the events that follow. In this respect they may be compared with the prologue of John's gospel (John 1.1–18). The two passages perhaps appear very different in character, the one consisting of narrative, the other of philosophical exposition. Nevertheless, both set out to give us information about Jesus which will provide the key to our understanding of the rest of the gospel – and what they tell us is in some ways remarkably similar. John speaks of the Logos, and Mark of Jesus Christ, the Son of God, but both explain who Jesus is by comparing him with the Baptist, and by stressing Jesus' superiority. John speaks of his activity in creation, and Mark of the fact that the creative spirit of God rests on him. In both, Jesus is Son of God, and his relationship to the Father is described in similar terms – 'beloved' (ἀγαπητός, used especially of an only child) in Mark, 'only' (μονογενής) in John.

It is, of course, possible to read the stories as straightforward accounts of a series of events: the work of John the Baptist, the baptism of Jesus and the temptation in the wilderness; but this is to miss their true significance. For the information these stories convey is primarily christological: the story of John tells us that Jesus is the one whose coming is expected in scripture, the baptism reveals Jesus as God's beloved Son and the bearer of the Holy Spirit, and the story of the temptation shows us Jesus confronting Satan in the power of the Holy Spirit.

It is important to realize that the events described in these opening verses of Mark are different in character from those that take place in most of the remaining pages of the gospel. Elsewhere, though unusual things happen, we do not find visions or voices from heaven (except once, in chapter 9); nor do we read about the activity of the Holy Spirit and Satan (apart from a discussion about them in chapter 3); we do not even have the meaning of what is going on spelt out for

31

us by Mark with the help of Old Testament texts, as it is here. In other words, we have here a concentration of christological material – information about the identity of Jesus and the meaning of his ministry. Remarkably, it is concentrated into these few verses, before the ministry of Jesus begins. It is as though Mark were allowing us to view the drama from a heavenly vantage-point (whence we see things as they really are) before he brings us down to earth, where we find characters in the story totally bewildered by what is going on. In these opening pages there is no secret about who Jesus is: on the contrary, the truth about him is spelt out several times; but it is only we who read the gospel who overhear what is said. We need to take careful note of the information about Jesus with which Mark here provides us, for he expects us to hold it in our hands as a guide as we thread our way through the rest of the story, but we need to remember that Mark is letting us into secrets which remain hidden, throughout most of the drama, from the great majority of the characters in the story. These verses are important, therefore, in providing us with a summary of Mark's own beliefs about Jesus – beliefs which he wants to share with his readers.

Some commentators argue that vv.14–15 should be included in this section (see, e.g., the article by L.E. Keck in *N.T.S.*, 12, 1966, pp. 352–70). But vv.14–15 lead us into the story of the ministry of Jesus with a summary of his proclamation of the Kingdom, whereas vv.1–13 provide us with the key to understanding that story, and the basis for his declaration that the Kingdom is at hand. Vv.1–13 stand apart from the rest of the gospel precisely because they provide this basic insight into the identity and significance of Jesus.

# 1   THE BEGINNING                                    1.1–8

*(Matt. 3.1–12; Luke 3.1–18)*

**(1) The beginning of the good news of Jesus Christ, [the] Son of God:**[1]

**(2) As it is written in Isaiah the prophet:**[2]
> **'Look, I am sending my messenger ahead of you**
> **to prepare your way:**
> **(3) a voice crying in the wilderness –**
> **"Prepare the way of the Lord;**
> **make his paths straight."'**

1 The words *Son of God* are missing from a few MSS, including the original hand of ℵ and Θ.
2 Some MSS read *in the prophets*.

(4) So it was that John the Baptizer appeared in the wilderness,[1] proclaiming a baptism of repentance for the forgiveness of sins. (5) And the whole district of Judaea flocked to him, together with everyone from Jerusalem; and they were baptized by him in the river Jordan, confessing their sins. (6) Now John was dressed in camel's hair, with a leather belt round his waist, and he ate locusts and wild honey.

(7) And this was the message he proclaimed: 'After me comes one who is mightier than I; I am not worthy to stoop down and unfasten the straps of his sandals. (8) I baptized you in water, but he will baptize you in the Holy Spirit.'

Since Mark heads his work **the beginning of the good news of Jesus** 1 **Christ**, it might be possible to take this as a title for the whole work, and to understand him to mean that his whole account of the life and ministry of Jesus is the beginning or basis (ἀρχή) of the good news. But since Jesus himself proclaims the good news in v.14, it seems clear that it is the activity of John the Baptist that is to be regarded as its beginning. A similar understanding of the work of John as the beginning of the good news is found in Acts (1.22; 10.37; 13.24f.). Some commentators have brought out this meaning by treating the scripture quotation in vv.2–3 as a parenthesis, and translating 'The beginning of the good news . . . was John the Baptist'. It seems unlikely, however, that Mark intended the passage to be read in this way; rather, we should take the first verse on its own. With this somewhat abrupt introduction we may compare the LXX version of Hosea 1.2, which reads, 'The beginning of the word of the Lord through Hosea': instead of introducing the word of God, spoken through a prophet, however, we have the good news of Jesus Christ.

In fact, Mark's purpose is clearly to set out not just the beginning of the good news, but the good news itself. The Greek word εὐαγγέλιον is normally translated 'gospel', but we have chosen to translate it 'good news' because in Mark's time the term was not yet a technical term meaning a document. It was no false instinct that later led to Mark's book being termed 'a gospel', but as far as we know, nobody before Mark had written a 'gospel', and his first readers would have understood him to be referring to a message – the good news which was proclaimed by the early Christian preachers – not to a particular literary form. The book is not in itself 'a gospel'; rather, it contains the gospel, which is something to be believed (1.15). The background of the term εὐαγγέλιον is to be found in the LXX, where the cognate verb (εὐαγγελίζω) means 'to proclaim good news'. In particular, we find it

1 Following B 33 and a few other MSS. The article is omitted before βαπτίζων in many MSS.

used several times in Isa. 40–66, where the good news that is proclaimed is the imminent salvation which God is going to work for his people (cf. Isa. 40.9; 52.7; 60.6; 61.1). By using this term, Mark claims that this salvation has come in Jesus.

The good news is about **Jesus Christ**. It is possible to understand the genitive here ('Iησοῦ Χριστοῦ) as either objective (about Jesus Christ) or subjective (from Jesus Christ); it is not necessary to choose between these two senses, and Mark may well have had both meanings in mind, since for him the gospel preached by the Church is identical with the gospel proclaimed by Jesus. But the emphasis is probably on the former meaning here, since Jesus is certainly the content of Mark's gospel. Throughout the rest of the book, Jesus is known simply by that name, but here Mark is setting out the basis for affirming that his news is indeed 'good'. The term 'Christ', meaning 'anointed', the Greek equivalent of the Hebrew 'Messiah', is used here almost as a proper name; its significance, however, would not have been missed by Mark's first readers, and we shall find it used later in the gospel in two crucial passages where Jesus' identity is at issue (8.29; 14.61). The description of Jesus as **Son of God** is missing from a few MSS. It is possible that it was added to the text subsequently, by a copyist, in order to make plain the truth about Jesus in the opening line; on the other hand, the phrase could have dropped out accidentally, owing to the similarity in the endings of the Greek words. Whichever is the true explanation, the phrase is certainly in keeping with Mark's own beliefs, and forms an appropriate heading to his book.

After this introduction, we may well be surprised to find Mark writing about John, not Jesus. But though these next verses are concerned with the Baptist, his significance for Mark lies entirely in his relationship with Jesus: he is important only because he points forward, by his words and actions, to the one who follows him. John's appearance at the beginning of the gospel is due to the fact that he marks out his successor as the Coming One. As we shall see, he has this function wherever he is mentioned (cf. 1.14; 6.14–29; 9.11–13; 11.27–33). But John is not the only witness to Jesus. Scripture also points forward to Jesus and, though it is in a sense John who 'fulfils' it, the written word and crying voice combine to point unmistakably to Jesus. The prominent position given to the Old Testament quotation at the very beginning of the book is even more striking when it is remembered that this is the only occasion on which Mark himself refers in this way to the fulfilment of Old Testament prophecy; other references are found only in the mouth of Jesus.

2–3     The beginning of the good news took place **as it is written in Isaiah the prophet.** Although introduced as a prophecy from Isaiah, the quotation is in fact a composite one: the first two lines appear to be a combination of Exod. 23.20 and Mal. 3.1, while v.3 comes from Isa. 40.3. The variant reading 'in the prophets' is a later emendation by someone who wished to correct the error. There are various explanations for this mistake. Mark may have taken over the combination of texts from Christian tradition – possibly already gathered together in a testimony-book (i.e. a collection of Old Testament passages used by the early Church) – and perhaps wrongly assumed that the whole of what he was quoting came from Isaiah. Or perhaps he chose to mention Isaiah because it was of special importance to him. Another possibility is that Mark quoted only the passage from Isaiah, and that v.2 was added later. There is no manuscript evidence for this last suggestion, but it receives some slight support from the fact that, though Matthew and Luke follow Mark here in quoting Isa. 40.3, both of them lack the words from Exodus and Malachi at this point and use them in another context (Matt. 11.10; Luke 7.27). The fact that the confusion is found in Mark, but not in Matthew and Luke, provides a good example of a passage where the evidence can be explained more easily on the basis of the theory that Mark was written *after* the other two gospels rather than before them. The text of the quotations also suggests that the combination has been made in stages: the first line – **Look, I am sending my messenger ahead of you** – agrees with the LXX version of Exodus 23, the second – **to prepare your way** – with the Hebrew of Malachi 3 (except that 'my' has become 'your'), and the quotation of Isaiah 40,

> **a voice crying in the wilderness –**
> **"Prepare the way of the Lord;**
> **make his paths straight",**

with the LXX (with the substitution of αὐτοῦ for τοῦ Θεοῦ ἡμῶν). In their original context, the words from Exodus are addressed to Israel in the wilderness; both Mal. 3.1 and Isa. 40.3 refer to one who announces the coming of God himself in salvation and judgement. In later rabbinic interpretation the messenger of Malachi 3 who prepares **the way** is identified with the returning Elijah of Mal. 4.5, who comes before the day of the Lord; he is seen as the herald of the Messiah who will act as God's agent. It is possible that this idea that the returning Elijah would act specifically as the forerunner of the Messiah was already known in first-century Judaism, and that it has influenced Mark's account. It has to be remembered, however, that none of these Old Testament passages was in itself 'messianic'. For Mark, **the Lord** would already be familiar as a title used of the risen Jesus, making it easier for Old Testament passages referring to the Lord to be applied to him. Nevertheless, since the title is used in the LXX to translate the tetragrammaton (i.e. the four letters of the divine name, Yahweh), its use here is a significant christological development. God's advent in salvation and judgement has taken place in Jesus. The minor changes to two of the passages noted above have been introduced in order to make them appropriate, and whereas the Hebrew of Isaiah 40 understands the wilderness as the place where the way is to be prepared ('in the wilderness prepare the way of the Lord'), Mark follows the LXX in attaching the phrase 'in the wilderness' to the voice, so introducing the figure of John the Baptist as a **voice crying in the wilderness**. The messenger who is sent to **prepare** the **way** (v.2) is thus more closely defined as the voice crying '**prepare the way of the Lord**' (v.3).

4    In keeping with this introduction, **John** makes his appearance in **the wilderness**. One would not normally describe the banks of the Jordan, where John baptized, as part of the wilderness, but both the location and the somewhat strange reference to **baptism** as something that he was **proclaiming** show at once that John is the one who cries in the wilderness. Both John himself and the baptism that he proclaims point forward to the one who follows him. Mark's emphasis on John's presence in the wilderness is by no means surprising. Because of Israel's original sojourn there, the wilderness came to be associated (as in Isaiah 40) with the idea of a new Exodus. Some of the prophets, protesting about the nation's sin, looked back to the years spent in the wilderness as an ideal period, and regarded the nomadic life as divinely approved, in contrast to agrarian settlement (Jer. 2.2; 31.2; Hos. 2.14; 9.10; Amos 5.25). The eschatological hope came to be centred on the wilderness, and leaders of revolts led their men into the wilderness (cf. Acts 21.38; Josephus, *Wars* II.13. 4f.; VII.11.1), which suggests that the Messiah may have been expected to appear there (perhaps Matt. 24.26), and to repeat the miracles performed by Moses. Others besides John associated the wilderness with preparation and repentance. We find Isa. 40.3 being used by the Qumran society in support of their withdrawal into the desert: those who join the community 'shall separate from the habitation of ungodly men and shall go into the wilderness to prepare the way of Him; as it is written...' (1QS 8.12–16). In this case, the 'way' is interpreted as the study of the Mosaic Law. (On the significance of the wilderness for Mark, see U. Mauser, *Christ in the Wilderness*, pp. 77–102.)

The distinctive and striking feature of John's teaching was that which gave him the title 'the Baptist' (ὁ βαπτιστής), a title which is used in 6.25 and 8.28, as well as by Matthew and Luke. Here, however, Mark uses the participle of the verb 'to baptize'. In some MSS (which have been followed in our translation), this is preceded by a definite article, and so is to be understood as an unusual title – **the Baptizer** (ὁ βαπτίζων). Other MSS omit the definite article and so understand the participle not as a title but as a statement of his activity (he was baptizing and proclaiming). However, Mark refers to John as ὁ βαπτίζων in 6.14, and this supports the belief that we should interpret the participle as a title here. If the reading we have followed is right, then the first thing that John does in Mark's account is to *proclaim* baptism, and Mark's stress on John as the voice crying in the wilderness is even clearer than if he introduces John as 'baptizing and proclaiming'. The textual evidence is divided, however, and it is difficult to decide whether the article was added because scribes were used to John's being referred to as 'the Baptist' or deleted because they were puzzled by the unusual title. (For a defence of the text we have chosen, see C.H. Turner, *J.T.S.*, 28, 1926, p. 150. For a discussion of John's baptism, see the additional note on pp. 39–43.)

Mark describes this baptism as being one of **repentance for the forgiveness of sins**. The Greek word for repentance (μετάνοια) means literally 'a change of mind'. Although in popular usage it often has a sense of regret for what is past, it is generally used in a more positive way in the New Testament, implying a deliberate turning, or conversion, to God.

The statement that **the whole district of Judaea flocked to him, together with everyone from Jerusalem**, is clearly an exaggeration but should not be dismissed as mere hyperbole. The words indicate the accomplishment of John's task; sufficient representatives of the nation heard the message of John for it to be said that he had completed his work and prepared the people for the coming of God in judgement and salvation.

We might perhaps have expected Mark to introduce John with the description he now provides. But it is John's proclamation of baptism which is all important, and with which he therefore begins. The details of John's dress and diet mark him out as a man of the wilderness, for they are part of the nomad's life. The rough garment of **camel's hair** is probably to be taken as an indication that he was a prophet (cf. Zech. 13.4). More particularly, the reference to the **leather belt** is an almost exact echo of the description of Elijah in 2 Kgs. 1.8: the details of John's clothing, therefore, suggest again that he is seen as 'Elijah the prophet' who is sent to call the nation to repent 'before the great and terrible day of the Lord' (Mal. 4.5f.; cf. Mark 9.12f.). The **locusts** and **honey** of wild bees are typical food for the wayfarer in the wilderness, and there is no need to follow the suggestion that the reference to locusts results from a confusion between two similar Hebrew words meaning 'locusts' and 'carob-pods'. Locusts and honey would not be John's entire diet but might well be his greatest delicacies. Although the diet was frugal, it was permitted in the Torah (Lev. 11.21f.): John stands in the Mosaic tradition.

Mark does not record John's ethical teaching, which is found in Luke, but the omission of such material does not necessarily mean that it was not known to him; he may simply have wished to concen-

5

6

7–8

trate here on his central theme. The brief summary Mark provides of John's preaching serves only one purpose – to point forward to Jesus. This is done by means of a three-fold contrast between John and the one who follows him, in terms of strength, worth, and mode of baptism. (1) The term **mightier** (ἰσχυρότερος) may seem a strange one in John's mouth, since John himself was hardly mighty in the ordinary sense of that word. Yet, as the prophet who inaugurated the setting of things to rights, he proclaimed the will of God and acted with his authority. In the Old Testament the idea of God as powerful – to save and to judge – is a familiar one, and if John himself used such a term, he would have been thinking of the supernatural power which he expected to see manifested at the eschatological judgement: the one who will bring this judgement will be God himself. For Mark, of course, the mighty one is Jesus whose power will be demonstrated in the following pages. (2) The action of unfastening **sandals** was regarded by the Jews as the most menial of all the tasks performed by a slave. It is said in the Talmud that a disciple must do for his teacher everything that a slave will do for his master, except this one act (B. Kethuboth 96a). John's statement that he is **not worthy** to perform this service for his successor thus emphasizes the vast superiority of the latter in a striking way. (3) The third contrast sets the whole mission of John over against that of his successor: the baptism **in water**, symbolizing repentance, purification and preparation for the eschatological drama, is but the prelude to baptism **in the Holy Spirit** (ἐν πνεύματι ἁγίῳ), an odd phrase which must owe its origin to this contrast. This time the superiority of the coming one is emphasized by the use of personal pronouns (ἐγὼ. . .αὐτὸς). The use of the Aorist tense, **I baptized** (ἐβάπτισα), may simply represent a Semitic perfect which would make it the equivalent of a present tense; it seems more likely, however, that the aorist marks the fact that in Mark's mind the mission of John is at this point complete: as soon as Jesus appears on the scene, John's work is over. The pouring out of the Holy Spirit is another eschatolgical theme; in the Old Testament we find the hope that God himself will pour out his Spirit on both men and women (Isa. 44.3; Ezek. 39.29: Joel 3.1f. [Eng. 2.28f.]). If Johns call to baptism marks the eleventh hour, baptism with Holy Spirit is a sign of the arrival of the eschatological era.

The prophecy that Jesus will baptize men and women in the Holy Spirit is not fulfilled in the course of Mark's gospel; presumably he is thinking of an experience such as that described by Luke in Acts 2. Mark is writing for those who acknowledge Jesus as Lord, and who have themselves experienced the 'baptism' to which John here refers. What Mark *does* describe is Jesus' own baptism with the Holy Spirit; he then goes on to show Jesus himself working in the power of the Spirit; he leaves his readers to draw the link with their own baptism in the Spirit. The saying is clearly appropriate to Mark's story but, since it does not fit perfectly, it looks very much as though he is using the traditional material available to him. This is confirmed by the Johannine parallel to the saying (John 1.33).

In Mark's account of John's preaching we find ideas which, like the quotations from Malachi and Isaiah, were used in the Old Testament with reference to God himself. It is God who is the Mighty One, in whose presence John might well feel unworthy; it is God who comes in judgement; it is God who pours out the Spirit. Some of these ideas were, of course, transferred in time to a Messiah who was expected to act as God's vicegerent. The reference here to sandals certainly suggests a human figure, but anthropomorphic metaphors concerning God are common in the Old Testament, and it seems at least possible that John was expecting, not a Messiah, but the advent of God himself. Surprisingly, there is no suggestion in Mark's narrative (in contrast to Matt. 3.14 and John 1.29ff.) that John recognized Jesus as the one whose coming he had proclaimed. Mark leaves his readers to make the connection between John's words and Jesus' arrival for themselves.

## Additional note: the baptism of John

No real parallel to John's baptism has been discovered in contemporary Jewish practice. The Torah prescribed various lustrations, but these were intended for ritual purification, not for what we understand by 'the forgiveness of sins'. The Qumran community also made frequent use of water for ritual purification, and it is possible that the number of these lustrations (in a community which did not acknowledge the temple regime) had been multiplied to make up for the absence of sacrifices and were thus believed to have some atoning power. Some of these lustrations at least, in contrast to those prescribed in the Torah, involved immersion rather than sprinkling. None of these rites was a once only event, however; all of them could be repeated as often as necessary. John's baptism, on the contrary, was an act performed once and for all and stood as a decisive turning-point in a person's life. Some writers have suggested that a similar initiatory act took place at Qumran (e.g. C.H.H. Scobie, *John the Baptist*, pp.102–10), but there is no clear evidence for this, and the most that can be said with confidence is that the first occasion on which a member of the community shared in the special rite held there would (like first communion) be of particular significance (Cf. H.H. Rowley in *New Testament Essays*, ed. A.J.B. Higgins, pp. 218–29).

The closest analogy to John's baptism appears to be the rite of proselyte baptism. Although it is often objected that the evidence for proselyte baptism is later than the time of John, this does not rule out the possibility that it was already being practised then (see the discussion in G.R. Beasley-Murray, *Baptism in the New Testament*, pp. 18–31). Indeed, since Gentiles were by definition 'unclean', it is difficult to think that they were ever admitted into the Jewish community without some such rite. Baptism was not only a means of purification by which the Gentile was freed from his uncleanness, however; it was also the ceremony which (together with circumcision and sacrifice) marked his entry into Judaism, and in the case of women, for whom there was no circumcision, it was especially significant. The immersion beneath the waters and re-emergence were an appropriate symbol of the end of one life and the beginning of a new one. One possible influence in the development of the rite of proselyte baptism may have been the story of Naaman in 2 Kgs. 5, a Gentile who is cured of his leprosy by dipping himself (the LXX uses the verb $\beta\alpha\pi\tau\acute{\iota}\zeta\omega$) in the Jordan in response to Elisha's command to 'Wash and be clean'. His cure leads him to affirm that 'there is no God in all the earth but in Israel' and to carry home 'two mules' burden of earth' in order to worship Yahweh in a foreign land. His immersion in the Jordan thus leads to his conversion.

It seems probable that it is the rite of proselyte baptism which provides the clue to the origin of John's baptism. It has been objected that it would have been inappropriate to adapt a rite intended for Gentiles who wished to become members of the chosen nation and apply it to Jews. But figures such as John have an uncomfortable habit of doing and demanding what seems inappropriate, and according to Matt. 3.9//Luke 3.8, this denial of special privilege to the Jews was part of his message. If Jewish descent was no security against the wrath of God, then it was necessary to take some action in face of the imminent judgement. John's message appears to have been based on the conviction that the time was short, and that the Day of the Lord was at hand; in this situation he called on men and women to repent and join themselves to the remnant of Israel. Baptism thus served not only as a symbol of their moral purification, but also as the sign that they were members of the true Israel; passages in the Old Testament which speak of the washing of the faithful in preparation for judgement and vindication (Isa. 4.4; Ezek. 36.25) would add weight to the significance of the rite. The link with moral purification is spelt out specifically in Mark's account in the reference to the forgiveness of sins. Although the lustrations provided in the Torah were intended for ceremonial uncleanness, the idea of washing was an obvious metaphor for moral cleansing, and we find it used in various Old Testament passages (e.g. Ps. 51.7; Isa. 1.16). It would be wrong, therefore, to draw a hard and fast line between ritual and moral purification (cf. W.F. Flemington, *Baptism*, p.3).

One difference between proselyte baptism and that of John is that the former was self administered, while the latter was probably administered by John himself. Some commentators, indeed, believe that John only supervised the rite, and that the penitents immersed themselves in his presence (so Wellhausen, Branscomb, Johnson); it is argued that the middle voice (ἐβαπτίζοντο), translated 'they were baptized', in Mark 1.5 properly has this reflexive meaning, and that ὑπ'αὐτοῦ means 'under his direction' rather than 'by him' – an interpretation which is supported by the 'Western' reading (D it) of Luke 3.7, which has ἐνώπιον αὐτοῦ ('in his presence') for ὑπ' αὐτοῦ. However, John's title of 'the Baptizer' and the emphatic 'I baptised' (ἐβάπτισα) in v.8, when taken with the phrase 'by him' (ὑπ' αὐτοῦ), suggest that John himself performed the rite (cf. Flemington, *Baptism*, p.16). The stress which he laid on baptism indicates that he regarded it as the essential sign of the new life to which he was summoning the nation; through repentance and baptism, men and women were forgiven and made members of the real people of God, prepared for the coming of God which John expected.

In addition to the gospels, we have one other source of information regarding the significance of John's baptism, and that is a reference to it by the Jewish historian Josephus (*Antiquities*, XVIII.5.2). He mentions John's execution by Herod, describing him as a good man who exhorted men to practise virtue; the baptism to which John summoned them served, he says, not for the remission of sins, but for the purifying of the body if the soul had already been purified by virtue. This distinction certainly reflects Josephus' interpretation of the rite, rather than John's. Josephus goes on to tell us that Herod put John to death because of his fear of a rebellion, but while this indicates the strength of popular response to John, there is no hint as to why Herod should have considered his religious teaching subversive; nor is there any explanation for John's insistence on a baptism which is described simply as another rite of lustration, a seemingly unnecessary addition to those that existed already. One phrase used by Jospehus, however, perhaps betrays John's purpose: he writes that John urged the people βαπτισμῷ συνιέναι, which should probably be translated 'to unite by baptism' rather than simply 'to come together for baptism'. It is possible that we have here an echo of the idea that John's baptism was an initiation into the true Israel and so an act which not only affected men and women as individuals, but bound them together. (For a discussion of the significance of Josephus' reference, see C.K. Barrett, *The Holy Spirit*, pp. 26–8,32.)

Attempts have been made in recent years to link John with the Qumran community (see, e.g., C.H.H. Scobie, *John the Baptist*, and his essay in *The Scrolls and Christianity*). Certainly there are interesting parallels between his teaching and theirs; the fact that John was a man of the wilderness may also be suggestive (see especially Luke

1.80). It may be that John's movement should he seen as parallel to that at Qumran, however, rather than as dependent on it. As usual, it is best to treat the material from Qumran as illustrative of contemporary ideas, rather than as providing the origin of particular developments within the New Testament.

John's contrast between his own baptism and that of Jesus raises further problems: John has baptized with water, but his successor will baptize with Holy Spirit. The Johannine version of this saying in John 1.33 is very similar, but in both Matthew and Luke water is contrasted with 'Holy Spirit and fire' – an odd combination which has led to the suggestion that the original saying referred to *wind* and fire (with the word πνεῦμα being understood to mean 'wind', not 'spirit'). In other words, John baptized with water, urging men and women to repent, lest the one who followed him baptized them calamitously with wind and fire (see, e.g., C.K. Barrett, *The Holy Spirit*, pp. 125f.). This would make excellent sense in John's mouth, for he preached, so Mark tells us, a baptism of repentance. In support of this interpretation, we may point to the words that follow immediately after the saying in both Matthew and Luke, which speak of the coming one winnowing the wheat and burning the chaff: in this operation, wind and fire are the instruments of judgement and punishment – though it should be remembered that the chief purpose is the positive one of storing the corn. An even more drastic suggestion is that the original contrast was between water and fire – between the water of cleansing and the fire of judgement; this 'fire' was then interpreted in terms of the early Christian experience of the Holy Spirit (see T.W. Manson, *The Sayings of Jesus*, pp. 40f.). The fact that the Holy Spirit was associated with Christian baptism (1 Cor. 12.13) might encourage this development, and there is evidence elsewhere that the relationship between John's baptism and Christian baptism was a matter of concern (Acts 19.1–7).

We might well expect John to refer to the eschatological fire of judgement, such as is referrred to in Mal. 3.2. But neither Mark nor the fourth gospel contains the reference to fire, while all four evangelists refer to the Holy Spirit; is it then possible that John himself drew the contrast in terms of water and Holy Spirit? If he thought of himself as the prophet of the eschatological age, then he may well have pointed to a future pouring out of the Spirit, for this was already part of Old Testament expectation (e.g. Isa. 44.3; Joel 3.1f. [Eng. 2.28f.]). So, too, was the recognition of the need for washing and judgement (e.g. Isa. 4.4). But the two ideas had already come together in Ezek. 36.25–7, where cleansing is the preliminary step to the gift of God's Spirit:

'I shall pour clean water over you and you shall be cleansed;
I shall cleanse you of all your defilement and all your idols.

I shall give you a new heart, and put a new spirit in you;
I shall remove the heart of stone from your bodies and give you a
heart of flesh instead.
I shall put my spirit within you, and make you keep my laws and
sincerely respect my ordinances.'

Another interesting parallel is found in the Qumran literature (in 1QS 4.20f.), where we are told that God will cleanse mankind and root out the spirit of falsehood. 'He will cleanse him of all wicked deeds with the spirit of holiness; like purifying waters He will shed on him the spirit of truth, to cleanse him of all abomination and falsehood. And he shall be plunged into the spirit of purification that he may instruct the upright in the knowledge of the Most High. . . .' We have here, also, in the reference to being plunged into the spirit of purification, an idea similar to that of being baptized with the Holy Spirit. There is thus evidence in Judaism, not simply for the eschatological hope of the Spirit, but for linking the Spirit with the themes of purification and judgement, as well as of renewal. It is easy to see how the twin themes of water and spirit could be used either as parallels (as in 1QS 4), or to express the ideas of preparation followed by renewal (as in Ezek. 36). John may well have seen his own role as a cleansing which prepared men and women for the coming renewal by the Spirit. In common with the other evangelists, Mark sees the significance of John the Baptist solely in terms of his witness to Jesus. But he appears to have been an important figure in his own right. Like Jesus, he had a group of disciples (2.18; 6.29; Matt. 11.2ff.//Luke 7.18ff.; John 3.25). It has even been argued that Jesus himself began his ministry as one of them. There is evidence of a continuing Baptist sect in Acts 19.1–5. The Gnostic sect of Mandaeans (still in existence) claims to go back to John but in fact is probably post-Christian in origin.

For further discussion, see: G.R. Beasley-Murray, *Baptism in the New Testament*, pp. 1–44; W.F. Flemington, *The New Testament Doctrine of Baptism*, pp. 3–24; A. Oepke in *T.D.N.T.*, I, pp. 529–46; H.H. Rowley, in *New Testament Essays*, ed. A.J.B. Higgins, pp. 218–29; C.H.H. Scobie, *John the Baptist*.

# 2　THE BAPTISM OF JESUS　　　　　1.9–11

*(Matt. 3.13–17; Luke 3.21–2)*

**(9) It was at this time that Jesus came from Nazareth in Galilee and was baptized in the Jordan by John. (10) And straight away, as he came up out of the water, he saw the heavens breaking open, and the Spirit coming down on him like a dove. (11) And a voice came from heaven: 'You are my beloved Son; with you I am well pleased.'**

It is natural for modern readers of the gospel to interpret this event as a great spiritual experience in the life of Jesus, and to seek in it information regarding his 'messianic consciousness'. Although his baptism must certainly have been a significant experience, however, it is idle to look to Mark for answers to speculations as to whether the incident was in the nature of a call, or a confirmation of a vocation already accepted, or for information regarding the precise way in which Jesus understood the role laid upon him. Mark's purpose is not to write a spiritual biography, but to present a christological statement. Even though the story may well go back to Jesus himself, it is told now from the viewpoint of one who sees Jesus through the eyes of faith and knows him to be the Son of God, in whom God's Spirit is at work; if the story was once told in an earlier form, it has been overlaid by interpretation. This is not to deny the historicity of the event, nor the reality of the experience, but merely to recognize that the story of the baptism is related here only in order to demonstrate the truth about Jesus as Mark understands it. The story provides a setting for the revelation of Jesus' identity, spelt out in terms of the descent of the Spirit and the words addressed to Jesus from heaven.

Mark is apparently unembarrassed by the problems raised by this story which troubled later writers. Matthew's description of John's hesitation regarding the propriety of baptizing Jesus (Matt. 3.14f.) and even more the account in *The Gospel according to the Hebrews*, which stresses the sinlessness of Jesus, both demonstrate the difficulties which were felt regarding Jesus' submission to baptism at the hands of an inferior, a baptism described by Mark as intended for the forgiveness of sins. The same difficulties may explain why Luke does not emphasize the baptism of Jesus, and why the fourth gospel does not mention it at all. Mark does not seem to feel these difficulties, though a comparision with v.5 indicates a difference between the baptism of Jesus and that of those who came confessing their sins. The problems perhaps arise from a misunderstanding of Mark's narrative, together with an emphasis on the negative aspect of repentance. It is unnecessary, and indeed unwarranted, to explain the baptism of Jesus, as some modern commentators have done, as a vicarious act of repentance, or an identification with sinners. If John's baptism was intended to be the preparation for the New Age, the rite which gathered together a holy people of God who affirmed in this act of committal that they were ready for his coming, then it was natural for Jesus to associate himself with this movement, and to join those who by baptism showed that they looked for the coming Kingdom of God.

The words addressed to Jesus are spoken from heaven, and Mark therefore unquestionably intends them to be accepted as true. Although we may have doubts about how Mark regards some of the other declarations of Jesus' identity later in the gospel (since they are found in the mouths of those who cannot fully comprehend what is happening, 3.11; 5.7), there can be no such hesitation here. If the term 'Son' occurs rarely in the rest of the gospel, this is because men and women cannot comprehend the truth, not because it is unimportant for Mark himself. The words are repeated in 9.7, in the story of the transfiguration, and in the ensuing conversation that scene is specifically linked with Jesus' death and resurrection; they are echoed in 15.39, when the centurion declares him to be God's son at the moment of his death. Jesus' identity as Son is also hinted at in 12.1–11, where the 'only son' is put to death. Jesus' sonship is thus linked in Mark's understanding with the crucifixion, and paradoxically revealed through it. Moreover, there is good reason to link the scene of Jesus' baptism with his death – not, as has often been done, via an imagined link with Isaiah 53 (see below, on v.11), but because the imagery of baptism is linked with death. This imagery is specifically used in 10.38, where Jesus speaks of suffering and death in terms of a baptism. The rite of baptism was an obvious symbol for death and resurrection, and one wonders whether the Markan community knew the kind of teaching about Christian baptism as a baptism into Christ's death which Paul expounds in Romans 6. Certainly it seems likely that when Mark related the story of the divine proclamation of Jesus' identity as Son within the setting of the baptism, he would have seen the link with the moment at the end of his life when that truth was proclaimed by his executioner (15.39).

Since Mark has already reminded his readers of their own 'baptism with Holy Spirit' in v.8, they might well remember their own experience as they read this account of Jesus' baptism.

The introductory phrase, translated **it was at this time** (καὶ **9** ἐγένετο ἐν ἐκείναις ταῖς ἡμέραις), uses Old Testament phraseology (e.g. Judg. 19.1; 1 Sam. 28.1). It serves to link the narrative that follows to the preceding description of John's baptism, and so to underline the fact that Jesus is the fulfilment of the expectation aroused by John. We are told nothing at all about Jesus' background (at the human level), except that he **came** to John **from Nazareth**. Jesus **was baptized in the Jordan by John**: as we have already noted, there is no hint in Mark's narrative that John recognized Jesus as the one whose coming he had proclaimed.

For the first time we meet one of Mark's favourite words (εὐθύς), **10** which we have normally translated **straight away**. The frequent use of this term gives a sense of urgency to the narrative, though, because it is used so often, it has a weakened sense and often means little more than 'so next'. According to Mark, it was Jesus who **saw** the events described in v.10, and presumably it was he alone who heard the words spoken in v.11, since they are addressed to him; the wording in Matthew and Luke suggests a wider audience, and according to the fourth gospel, John the Baptist saw and announced the descent of the Spirit – evidence that the idea was gaining ground that Jesus' status had been clear from the beginning of the ministry. But seeing and hearing are in Mark's gospel ways of comprehending the truth, and what he sets out here is the truth about Jesus, which cannot yet be grasped by anyone except Jesus himself.

The breaking open of **the heavens** was an obvious image for revelation at a time when God was believed to dwell in the top storey of a three-decker universe. Perhaps more significant, however, is its use in Isa. 64.1 in an appeal to God to come down and save his people. Certainly the idea of a new activity of God on earth is conveyed here by the descent of the Spirit, for in Jewish thought the Spirit of God represents his creative activity (cf. Gen. 1.2). In the Old Testament, the Spirit is described as resting on a variety of men – especially leaders, prophets and kings – giving them the power which they need for their different tasks. It was an obvious step to assume that the Spirit would also be given to any future 'Messiah'; so, for example, Ps. Sol. 17.37, describing the future king: 'For God made him mighty by means of his Holy Spirit, and wise by means of the counsel of understanding, with strength and righteousness.'

It is not clear what Mark means by the statement that Jesus saw **the Spirit coming down. . .like a dove**. Luke's understanding of the scene was that the Spirit came down 'in bodily form, as a dove' (Luke 3.22), but it is possible that Mark is thinking of the manner in which the Spirit descended, rather than the shape (so L.E. Keck, *N.T.S.*, 17, 1970, pp. 41–67). Whether or not the dove is a significant symbol is also uncertain: in rabbinic literature the dove is sometimes used to symbolize Israel, but this fact does not seem to be relevant here. In a few passages, however, it is mentioned in connection with the Spirit: e.g. the Targum to the Song of Solomon 2.12 equates the voice of the turtle-dove with the voice of the Holy Spirit, and a comment in the Babylonian Talmud refers to Gen. 1.2 in this way: 'And the Spirit of God was brooding on the face of the waters like a dove which broods over her young but does not touch them' (B. Hagiga 15a). These passages are late, but they lend support to the suggestion that in first-century Judaism the dove was already associated with the Spirit of God.

11    The **voice. . .from heaven** is usually explained in terms of the *baṭ qôl*. This Hebrew term, which means literally 'daughter of a voice', was used by the rabbis to denote the echo of a voice uttered in heaven. When the Spirit had withdrawn from Israel, and there were no more prophets, then, so it was said, the *baṭ qôl* was occasionally heard. The *baṭ qôl* was thus a means of revelation to men, a substitute for the direct word of God which had formerly been given by the Spirit. It

might be significant that its sound was at times compared to the cry of a bird (see Midrash Rab. Eccles. 12.7), and once to the moaning of a dove (B. Berakoth 3a). Even if this idea of the *bat qôl* were known to Mark, however, it seems unlikely that it could have been of any significance for his understanding of this event. For the *bat qôl* was essentially inferior – a substitute for the direct gift of God's Spirit – and Mark certainly had no intention of suggesting that Jesus was the recipient of anything inferior. There is, indeed, no need for a substitute, since Jesus has already been given the Spirit; the voice from heaven is no mere echo, but the direct word of God himself.

The words spoken from heaven are commonly traced to a combination of phrases from Ps. 2.7 and Isa. 42.1. The statement that '**You are my. . .son**' is certainly reminiscent of Ps. 2.7 and was evidently considered to be a quotation from that passage by some early Christians, since the 'western' text of the parallel account in Luke 3.22 continues by quoting the rest of the verse. The link with Isa. 42.1 is far more dubious, since none of the words used by Mark appears in the LXX version of that verse. It is misleading to try to press the words into either quotation, however, since they are reminiscent of other Old Testament passages also. The idea of an individual as God's son is not a common one in Jewish thought. Occasionally – as in Pss. 2.7 and 89.27 – the idea that the king is 'adopted' as God's son appears; in the book of Wisdom we find the idea that the righteous man is the 'child' of God (2.13–18; 5.5). The king is the representative of his nation, while the righteous man fulfils God's calling for the nation, and these passages reflect the more fundamental understanding of the whole nation as God's son which was one way in which the relationship between Yahweh and his chosen people was seen (see Exod. 4.22f.; Deut.1.31; Hos. 11.1). It is certainly significant that Jesus is addressed in terms used in the Old Testament of the relationship which should exist between Israel and God – in other words, precisely the relationship to which John the Baptist is calling the people through repentance and baptism: Jesus is here revealed as the one man in whom that role of Israel's sonship is realized.

The term **beloved** (ἀγαπητός) is traced by most commentators to Isa. 42.1, although none of the Greek versions of the Old Testament which have come down to us uses it here (or elsewhere) to translate the Hebrew *bāḥîr*, which means 'chosen'; it is, however, used in the very different translation of part of Isa. 42 given in Matt. 12.18–21. More significant, however, is the fact that on the majority of occasions when it occurs in the Greek Old Testament, it is used (with or without a noun) to refer to an only child; it is, for example, used several times of Abraham's only son Isaac. Its position after υἱός in both Mark 1.11 and 9.7 suggests that we should perhaps take the two words together, and translate them as 'my only son' (so C.H. Turner,

*J.T.S.*, 27, 1926, pp. 113–129). The phrase thus denotes Jesus' unique status. The final words, **with you I am well pleased**, echo a phrase used in the Old Testament of God's delight in his people Israel (e.g. Ps. 44.3 [LXX 43.4]; 149.4; Isa. 62.4; the Greek of Isa. 42.1 is once again a less exact parallel) and suggests the obedient response of Jesus to the divine will which causes God to delight in him.

There is an interesting parallel to this story in *The Testaments of the Twelve Patriarchs*. Although it has sometimes been argued that this is a Christian work, it now seems to be agreed that the basis of the book is Jewish, and that this has been reworked by Christian redactors. Since the passage in Test. Levi 18 may be a Christian addition, we cannot regard it as providing Jewish 'background' material to Mark's story; whether it is indeed Jewish, or a Christian exposition of the story of Jesus' baptism, however, it is worth noting that the voice from heaven in that passage is described as 'the Father's voice as from Abraham to Isaac'.

The words spoken to Jesus from heaven have sometimes been interpreted as an 'adoption formula' – that is, as an indication that at this point he was 'made' Son of God, as is the king in Psalm 2. Even if Mark had Ps. 2.7 in mind, however, there is no reason to suppose that he thought of the words in this way; it is far more likely that he interpreted them simply as a declaration of Jesus' identity. Certainly Matthew and Luke do not seem to have understood the words as an adoption formula, for they see no difficulty in using them after their own birth narratives – something especially striking if we accept the 'western' text of Luke 3.22 ('today I have begotten you'). Moreover, the repetition of the words in Mark 9.7 shows clearly that he regards them as a declaration and not as an adoption. Nor is there any basis for the common assumption that Jesus is here shown as accepting the mission of the Suffering Servant of Isaiah. 53. Even if we accept the tenuous link with Isa. 42.1, there is no hint whatever in Mark 1.11 of the later passage from that book, and no reason to suppose that Mark saw any connection between them.

# 3   THE BATTLE WITH SATAN                    1.12–13

*(Matt. 4.1–11; Luke 4.1–13)*

**(12) And straight away the Spirit drove him out into the wilderness. (13) And he was in the wilderness for forty days, being tempted by Satan. He was among the wild beasts, and angels looked after him.**

The account Mark gives of the temptation is so brief as to be enigmatic. Unlike Matthew and Luke, he does not record the content of the temptations encountered by Jesus but concentrates on the confrontation between Jesus and Satan. There is nothing here to suggest that Mark thought of this as the period when Jesus deliberated about what kind of a Messiah he was to be. Neither is there any sign – whatever later interpreters and preachers may have done with his account – that Mark's purpose is to portray Jesus' spiritual pilgrimage, passing through a psychological trough after the peak of his experience at the baptism. Nor is it primarily his intention to depict Jesus as one whose example of steadfastness in temptation must be imitated by his followers and by the readers of the gospel. For this is no ordinary temptation, but the temptation – or testing – of the Son of God. Just as the account of the baptism is a theological statement about Jesus, so too is the story of the temptation; it provides us with vital information about Jesus which will enable us to understand the narratives which follow.

The narrative is linked with that of the baptism of Jesus with **12** another use of Mark's characteristic phrase **straight away** (καὶ εὐθύς). In the encounter between Jesus and Satan, the initiative is taken by **the Spirit** who drives Jesus **into the wilderness**. The verb translated **drove out** (ἐκβάλλω) is a forceful one and, even though it is said to have lost something of its force in Hellenistic Greek, it retains to some extent its sense of compulsion: it is, for example, used repeatedly by Mark of the expulsion of demons; neither Matthew nor Luke uses it here. The fact that Jesus now enters the wilderness indicates (as we would expect) that the Jordan is not located in the wilderness, in spite of vv.4f.

Jesus is said to have remained **in the wilderness for forty days. 13** There are many possible interpretations of the period of forty days. Some have understood them as representing the forty years which Israel – God's son – spent in the wilderness while being tested by God. The allusion is however somewhat obscure, since forty days and forty years are by no means the same thing – though see Num. 14.34 and Ezek. 4.5f.; moreover, the testing in Jesus' case is hostile, even though he is in the wilderness at the instigation of the Spirit. There is much more to be said for this interpretation in Matthew and Luke, where Jesus' words are taken from the story of Israel's wilderness wanderings in Deuteronomy (see B. Gerhardsson, *The Testing of God's Son*, pp. 42f.). Another explanation links the forty days in the wilderness with the forty days spent by Moses on Sinai (Exod. 34.28) and the similar period spent by Elijah in travelling to Horeb (I Kgs. 19. 8); but both men went to meet with God, not Satan, and the only connection between their stories and that of Jesus' temptation is that Moses and Elijah fasted during the forty days – and, of course, Mark makes no reference to Jesus fasting. If we wish to discover Mark's own interpretation of the story, we must not read details from Matthew and Luke into his account. Mark may not have thought of Jesus as being without food in the wilderness; certainly he suggests that John found enough food to sustain him there. It is perhaps best, then, to understand the forty days as the conventional biblical round number, indicating a long period.

**Satan** (the Greek Σατανας is a transliteration of the Aramaic *sātānā'*) first appears in Jewish thought in Job 1–2, where he is simply *haśśāṭān*, the accuser, one of the servants of God, but in later literature he develops into an evil power, the opponent of God, seeking to destroy the relationship between God and man. Although the verb πειράζω means basically 'to test' or 'to attempt', there is no doubt that in the present context it means 'to tempt' in an evil sense. The information that Jesus was **among the wild beasts** is another feature that is open to various interpretations. It has been seen as an indication of the loneliness of the wilderness, but this seems unlikely in view of the presence of the angels. Certainly the presence of wild beasts can be seen as a sign of desolation and of danger (cf. Isa. 13.21f.; Ps. 22.12–21); they came to be used as symbols of Israel's enemies (Ezek. 34.5,8; Dan. 7.1–8). Demons were thought to live in the wilderness (e.g. Deut. 32.17; Isa. 34.14), and it was a short step to the identification of the demons with wild beasts. Thus we find the hope of a future defeat of demons linked with the idea of the subjection of wild beasts in Test. Issach. 7.7:

> 'Every spirit of Beliar shall flee from you,
> And no deed of wicked men shall rule over you;
> And every wild beast shall ye subdue.'

Similarly, in Test. Benj. 5.2 we read: 'If ye do well, even the unclean spirits will flee from you, and the beasts will dread you.' The subjugation of wild beasts and demons became part of the hope for 'Paradise restored' – the renewal of creation which included the dominion of man over the animals that had been enjoyed by Adam before he succumbed to temptation (cf. Isa. 11.6–9). It is possible, therefore, that Mark understands the scene as the reversal of Genesis 3: unlike Adam, Jesus resists temptation, and nature's harmony is restored (cf. Paul's use of this idea in Rom. 8). If so, however, it is remarkable that Mark says nothing about Jesus' victory; he simply tells us that Jesus was **among** the animals, and we should therefore be wary of reading too much into this verse.

The function of the **angels** is equally enigmatic. In Matthew they appear after Satan has departed, and presumably he understood them to be bringing Jesus food at the end of his forty-day fast. It is possible that Mark interpreted their presence in a similar way; if so, however, he perhaps assumed that they **looked after** Jesus throughout the period of forty days, much as Elijah was supplied with food in 1 Kings 19 (the verb διαχονέω means 'to serve' or 'to wait on'). It may be that Mark has not worked out the nature of their service, however: the angels are there to support Jesus in his conflict with Satan, just as the wild beasts oppose him. Ps. 91.11–13 couples service by the angels with a promise that lions and serpents will be trampled underfoot, and there is an interesting parallel in Test. Naph. 8.4:

> 'The devil shall flee from you,
> and the wild beasts shall fear you,
> and the Lord shall love you,
> and the angels shall cleave to you.'

One remarkable feature of Mark's account of the temptation is that it ends without any indication as to the outcome. It is possible that he regarded this as so obvious that it was unnecessary to spell it out, but his failure to do so has left commentators arguing about how he understood the relationship between this scene and the rest of Jesus' ministry. Some (e.g. James Robinson, Kallas, Mauser) have understood the temptation as initiating Jesus' struggle with evil, and have seen the later exorcisms, Jesus' struggle with obtuse and antagonistic men and the passion itself, as part of a continuous conflict between Jesus and Satan. Others (e.g. Best, Barrett) have seen the temptation conflict as decisive and have likened the later exorcisms to 'mopping-up' operations. But perhaps this distinction is unreal. If we are right in understanding these events as part of Mark's dramatic statement of the truth about Jesus, then the conquest of Satan by Jesus which takes place throughout his healing ministry is at this point proclaimed in another mode; the idea that the truth about how things are can be brought into focus and expressed in a dramatic act lies at the heart of a great deal of Old Testament ritual, and Mark's readers may not have been so puzzled by the representation of truth on two levels as we sometimes are today. The picture of the Son of God doing battle with Satan in the wilderness is the key which will enable us to understand Jesus' authority over unclean spirits: the stronger one has confronted the prince of demons, and is plundering his house (Mark 3.22–7).

Before leaving Mark's prologue, we should note that the three short paragraphs in vv.2–13 are linked together by the occurrence of a reference to the Spirit in all three of them – in vv.8, 10 and 12. In view of the paucity of references to the Spirit in Mark, this is a noteworthy feature. They are also linked by the setting of all three narratives in the wilderness. Both these themes point to the fact that Mark is writing of a time of fulfilment.

We are now in possession of the information which Mark considers we need to know in order to understand the rest of his narrative. The ministry of John has shown that we can expect the coming of the Lord; the voice from heaven has identified Jesus as the beloved Son of God; the temptation has meant the defeat of Satan. These themes will be worked out in the following chapters: but from now on they will not often be stated so clearly. It is part of Mark's understanding of the 'messianic secret' that the titles and powers which are here attributed to Jesus will be hidden during his ministry; they can be grasped only by those who have faith in him as God's Son, but this is something which men and women experience fully only through his death and resurrection.

## B   Authority at work: success and opposition in Galilee                                       1.14–3.6

Mark begins his account of the ministry of Jesus with a series of incidents which demonstrate the authority of Jesus and the response of men and women to his words and actions. Whether deliberately or not, he has included in the next few pages material that is typical of the whole ministry. Jesus proclaims the gospel, teaches and heals with authority, calls men to follow him as disciples, and offers health and salvation to outcasts of all kinds including a leper, a paralytic whose sins he pronounces forgiven, and a crowd of tax-collectors and 'sinners'. The reaction to Jesus is immediate: on the one hand, the crowds marvel at his authority and flock to hear and see him; on the other, the religious authorities are offended by his actions – which are in their eyes at the very least inconsistent with true piety, and at worst contrary to the Torah – and are already plotting to destroy him (3.6). The disciples, at this stage, hardly emerge as a distinct group; they are simply those who accompany Jesus, having responded to his call.

In presenting his material in this way, Mark impresses us with the authority of Jesus: here is a man who astonishes his hearers with his teaching (1.22), who possesses the power to subdue evil spirits (1.24) and to forgive sins (2.10). Yet he is not one of the scribes, the official religious teachers in Israel, and what he proclaims is something essentially new (1.15, 27; 2.21f.), which challenges the scribes' understanding of the Torah (2.6–10, 23–8; 3.1–6). Moreover, Jesus does not belong to the 'religious' party of Judaism, the Pharisees: his attitudes are in many ways totally contrary to theirs, for he does not teach his disciples to fast (2.18), or observe the traditions which had grown up to ensure that the Torah is kept (2.23–8; 3.1–6); he mixes with those whom the Pharisees regard as sinners (2.15–17), and even invites a tax-collector (an outcast from Jewish society) to join his band of disciples (2.13f.). Here is a religious teacher, healer and leader who comes from outside the system, apparently without credentials, and yet preaches with tremendous effect. It is hardly surprising if ordinary people ask one another 'What is this?' (1.27), or if the religious authorities are resentful and indignant.

# 1 JESUS PROCLAIMS THE GOOD NEWS          1.14–15

### (Matt. 4.12–17; Luke 4.14–15)

**(14) After John had been handed over, Jesus came into Galilee, proclaiming the good news from God (15) and saying: 'The time has come, and the Kingdom of God is at hand; repent and believe the good news.'**

The story begins with a summary of Jesus' preaching. Jesus himself must have spelt out his message at much greater length than this, which means that this succinct account may be either Mark's own summary of what Jesus had taught, or one that had been handed down to him. **The good news** proclaimed by Jesus centred on **the Kingdom of God**, and this theme reappears in his teaching later in the gospel. But the call to **repent and believe** reminds us of the preaching of the Church (cf. Acts 2.38; 3.19; 15.7), and is addressed to all who hear or read it. The message is the good news proclaimed by Mark to his readers (cf. 1.1), as well as the good news proclaimed by Jesus in Galilee, and the words may well reflect the language of Mark, rather than the language of Jesus. This means that when we ask questions about the precise meaning of particular words, such as the verb here translated **is at hand** (ἤγγικεν), we are asking questions about Mark's use of language, and his understanding as to whether Jesus announced the Kingdom as present or imminent, rather than about Jesus' own words.

According to Mark, the ministry of Jesus begins **after John had 14 been handed over**. These introductory words are far more than an indication of date. There is, indeed, some doubt as to whether John was in fact imprisoned so soon, since according to John 3.22–30 the ministries of John and Jesus overlapped. The significance of Mark's words lies rather in his belief that the work of the forerunner is now complete, and the work of Jesus can therefore begin. The word translated 'handed over' can be used as a technical term for delivering up a prisoner, but its choice here suggests that Mark is thinking of John being handed over by God into the power of men. The verb (παραδίδωμι) is used several times by Mark in the predictions of the passion to refer to the handing over of Jesus, and often seems to imply that God himself is responsible for this handing over: its use here, at the very beginning of the gospel, is an early pointer to the fact that John is the forerunner of Jesus in death as well as in life, a theme that will be taken up later in the gospel (see 6.17–29 and 9.13).

Jesus' ministry is set in **Galilee** – a region which was perhaps as strange a setting for messianic activity as the wilderness was appropriate. Unlike John the Baptist, Jesus does not withdraw from society for a ministry in the wilderness; nor, according to Mark, does he as yet proclaim his message in Jerusalem, the centre of Judaism, or even in Judaea; instead, he travels around semi-pagan Galilee, and preaches there.

In contrast to John, who proclaimed a baptism of repentance, Jesus comes **proclaiming** (κηρύσσων) **the good news from God**. Once again we have the word εὐαγγέλιον, echoing the introduction in 1.1: Jesus himself proclaims the 'good news' or 'gospel', but this time the genitive (τοῦ θεοῦ) has been understood in our translation as a subjective genitive meaning 'from God' rather than as objective ('about 15 God'). This good news is that **the time has come**. The word translated 'time' (καιρός) denotes a particular, significant point in time. It is the time of salvation (and of judgement) appointed by God which has at long last arrived (Dan. 12.4,9). Throughout the Old Testament and in intertestamental literature there are many references to a coming time: there is no unified expectation, and the hope varies according to circumstances, but in different ways writers look forward to a future period of salvation. Yet the reality never arrived; however near the promised time might come, it was never grasped. But now Jesus announces that it is fulfilled, here at last. Here, in this proclamation of the good news, we already have the fulfilment of John's expectations, but in contrast to what we might have expected from John's declaration about his successor, Jesus says nothing at all about himself or his own position. He speaks instead of **the Kingdom of God** (see additional note on pp. 55–8). The message of Jesus, as Mark understands it, is that this Kingdom **is at hand**. The verb ἐγγίζω means 'to draw near', and is therefore generally understood here as referring to the close approach of the Kingdom. C.H. Dodd, however, maintained that the verb can mean 'to arrive' and understood it in that sense here (see Dodd, *The Parables of the Kingdom*, pp. 4f.). This interpretation, which was based on an examination of the use of the verb in the LXX, seems less likely than the translation suggested here (see the arguments of J.Y. Campbell, in *Exp.Tim.*, 48, 1936–7, pp. 91–4; W.G. Kümmel, *Promise and Fulfilment*, pp. 19–25; R.H. Fuller, *The Mission* *and Achievement of Jesus*, pp. 21–5).

The response demanded from men and women is once again – as with John – that they should **repent**: but this time the 'conversion' to a new way of living involves, not a baptism signifying forgiveness, but that they should **believe the good news**. Already we notice the authority with which Jesus presents his message and challenges his hearers to respond – the authority that belongs to him because he is all that has already been spelt out to us. But the challenge is not confined to the inhabitants of Galilee; in this summary of Jesus' message Mark at the same time challenges his own readers in language familiar to them: this is the good news from God; repent and believe.

## Additional note: the Kingdom of God

According to Mark's summary in 1.15, the Kingdom of God was the central theme of Jesus' teaching, and this is borne out by the rest of the gospel, as well as by Matthew and Luke. Its arrival is good news, but it brings judgement as well as salvation, and so demands repentance as well as faith.

The Aramaic phrase underlying the Greek ἡ βασιλεία τοῦ θεοῦ would perhaps be better translated as 'the kingship of God': the emphasis is on the rule of God, rather than on the territory where this rule is exercised. The idea of God's kingship is basic in the Old Testament, even though the phrase 'the Kingdom of God' itself is not found there; many of the psalms speak of him as king, or as ruling over the earth (e.g. Pss. 47.7; 97.1; 99.1; 103.19). But side by side with this declaration went the realization that men and nations did not acknowledge Israel's God as king; though this did not diminish God's omnipotence, their disobedience meant that God was not seen to reign. There arose, therefore, the hope of a time when God would assert his authority in such a way that rebellion against him would be defeated, and all men would henceforth be obedient to his will (e.g. Isa. 24.23). This hope is expressed in different terms and different forms by prophets, apocalyptists and rabbis, but basically it remains the same – the expectation that God would finally establish his Kingdom.

When Jesus declares that the Kingdom of God has drawn near, therefore, he is speaking within the context of this expectation. As we have already seen, Mark 1.15 raises the much debated question as to whether Jesus himself meant that the Kingdom had in some sense arrived, or whether he was referring to an event which was still to come. Whereas some passages in Mark imply that it can be entered now (10.14f.; 12.34), others speak of entering it in the future (9.47; 10.23–5), and 9.1 describes it as coming in a dramatic way in the near future. The question ought not, perhaps, to be posed in the form of a stark either/or; we have already noted that the Old Testament speaks of the rule of God as something which is both present and future. Nevertheless, the preaching of Jesus does bring a new factor into the situation which is expressed in his words 'the time is fulfilled'. In 4.11 we read that the secret of the Kingdom of God is given to his disciples, but that it is hidden from outsiders; two parables (4.26–9 and 30–2) suggest that it is hidden now but will be revealed later; the saying in 14.25 could perhaps mean that Jesus' death may serve to bring the Kingdom into being. In some sense, the coming of Jesus is linked with that of the Kingdom, either because he brings it, or because he announces it: certainly signs of its coming are demonstrated in the ministry of Jesus. This tension between present and future is found throughout all the gospels.

It is important to remember that kingship can be seen from two points of view. On the one hand, it can be understood in terms of loyalty to a monarch. In ancient Israel, David was acclaimed king, first by the house of Judah, then by all the tribes (2 Sam. 2.1–4; 5.1–5): in theory, at least, every Israelite accepted him and acknowledged him as king. On the other, it can be understood in terms of the absolute authority exercised by a monarch over a circumscribed area: in this case, there may well be those within the kingdom who refuse to recognize the monarch's claims. The ambiguity in the idea contributes to our difficulty in understanding the image of the Kingdom in the New Testament.

Interpretation of the meaning of the Kingdom of God in modern biblical criticism has tended to divide into two very different approaches. On the one hand, there have been those who have emphasized that the Kingdom of God implies obedience to God's will. An early advocate of this view was Albrecht Ritschl who thought of Jesus as primarily a moral teacher setting out the ethical demands of God as the goal towards which men and women had to strive. The Kingdom of God was thus seen as something which Christians could build on earth. Within this Kingdom, everyone would acclaim God as King: those who do not accept his rule will not enter it.

In reaction to Ritschl, Johannes Weiss argued that the Kingdom was not something which would arrive gradually, as men and women accepted its claims, but that it would burst into history, bringing cataclysmic judgement and renewal. Only God could bring the Kingdom; all men and women could do was to repent and prepare for its coming. The background to this belief is to be found in Jewish apocalyptic literature which expected God to intervene to establish his rule on earth. Here, the model is that of a rule which is imposed from above: any malcontents will be thrown out of the Kingdom.

Weiss' interpretation was developed by Albert Schweitzer and Rudolf Bultmann, who understood Jesus to be announcing the imminent arrival of the Kingdom of God. Schweitzer shocked the scholarly world of his day by concluding that Jesus was mistaken in this expectation, for no such intervention took place. Nevertheless, this understanding of the Kingdom as a future, eschatological event has been very widely held by biblical scholars. There have always been others, however, such as T.W. Manson, who have understood the Kingdom to have been manifested in Jesus' own obedience to God's rule and in the obedience of those who respond to his challenge to repent and believe. T.F. Glasson has pointed out that there is very little evidence for the widespread assumption that there was in the first century of this era a widespread Jewish expectation that the Kingdom would be established in a cosmic catastrophe bringing this world to an end.

The great strength of the 'futuristic' interpretation, however, was that it took seriously the proclamation by Jesus that something new was about to take place. This interpretation was challenged from a new quarter when C.H. Dodd argued, on the basis of the references in the gospels to the Kingdom as present, that Jesus announced that the Kingdom had already arrived in his person – an interpretation which was given the name of 'realized eschatology'. Dodd subsequently conceded that the Kingdom was not wholly here and therefore accepted the modified expression 'eschatology in the process of realization'. Much recent scholarship has acknowledged the truth in both positions and conceded that, while Jesus proclaimed a future coming of the Kingdom, there is a sense in which it is already here – proleptically – in the person of Jesus himself. (For a summary of the debate about whether the Kingdom is present or future, see N. Perrin, *The Kingdom of God.*)

As for Mark, it seems that he, too, believes that, though the final coming of the Kingdom lies in the future (9.1), it has nevertheless drawn near in the person of Jesus himself (1.15). According to the prologue, Jesus is the one with whom God is well pleased, the Son who is obedient to God's will, who has been given the Spirit of God and who has done battle with Satan: in a sense, then, Jesus is the very embodiment of the Kingdom. Thus, although Jesus speaks of the Kingdom, and not of himself, his words are nevertheless an indirect testimony to himself; it is because he himself lives in obedience to God's rule that he can announce the dawning of God's Kingdom and demonstrate its presence in his miracles. The key to Mark's understanding is found in the parables in chapter 4: the secret of the Kingdom is given to those who respond to Jesus' teaching (v.11); it is present already like seed (v.26) or a grain of mustard seed (v.31); but what will happen in the future (presumably when the Kingdom 'comes in power') will by comparison be overwhelming.

But if, in fact, the Kingdom is in some sense already here, then can it still be understood as a future cataclysmic event? It is perhaps significant that Jesus' teaching about the Kingdom makes no reference to apocalyptic speculation about the End. Is not our problem very largely due to the fact that we interpret symbols literally? We assume that apocalyptic writers intended their symbols to be interpreted literally, of the break-up of the universe, even though, when they were first used, these symbols were used metaphorically. As for the phrase 'the Kingdom of God', that is clearly a metaphor, and like all metaphors it has its limitations. One of these limitations is that it may convey false ideas, as when James and John interpret Jesus' role in the Kingdom in the wrong way (10.35–45). Another is that there is a clear problem in speaking about the Kingdom of God's 'coming': rule can be imposed from on high or acknowledged from below, but it can hardly 'come'. Perhaps a more important question than the one concerning present/future which so concerns scholars is whether Jesus (and the evangelists) were thinking primarily of a rule which is accepted or of a rule which is imposed. Perhaps the answer – for both Jesus and the evangelists – is 'both'. But, in so far as there is a growing emphasis in the tradition on the judgement which will befall those who are excluded from the Kingdom, we suggest that Jesus will have been closer to the 'rule acclaimed' end of the spectrum, and Matthew to the 'rule imposed' end, with Mark somewhere in between. Inevitably the emphasis shifts from that found in the teaching of Jesus himself, because his proclamation of the Kingdom has been rejected and judgement has come. As for the question about present/future, if God's rule involves obedience to his will, as it surely does, is there not a sense in which one can enter it here and now, even though it will not be established universally until some future date? And since Jesus' challenge to Israel demands that individuals repent and believe, does this not necessarily involve opting to obey the will of God here and now – i.e., accepting his rule over one's life? Perhaps we can learn from the Old Testament's juxtaposition of the assertion that God already rules with the conviction that he *will* rule. How that rule will finally be established we do not know; but the evangelists are confident that we see something of it embodied already in the person of Jesus, who is obedient to God and who confronts men and women with the challenge to share his obedience.

For further discussion, see: T.W. Manson, *The Teaching of Jesus*; T.F. Glasson, *The Second Advent*; N. Perrin, *The Kingdom of God in the Teaching of Jesus*; *Jesus and the Language of the Kingdom*; R. Schnackenburg, *God's Rule and Kingdom*; B. Chilton, ed., *The Kingdom of God*; M.D. Hooker, 'The Kingdom of God'.

# 2   THE CALL TO DISCIPLESHIP                    1.16–20

*(Matt. 4.18–22; Luke 5.1–11)*

(16) And as Jesus was walking by the Sea of Galilee, he saw Simon and his brother Andrew casting a net into the sea – for they were fishermen. (17) And Jesus said to them, 'Come after me, and I will make you fishers of men.' (18) And straight away they left their nets and followed him. (19) And going a little further, he saw James son of Zebedee and John his brother; they were in their boat mending the nets. (20) And straight away he called them, and they left their father Zebedee in the boat with the hired men, and went after him.

The theme of discipleship is prominent in Mark's gospel; those who first heard his story, who had recently responded to the call to be Jesus' disciples, would no doubt have identified themselves with the men and women in this book who struggle to learn what it means to follow him. The theme appears already in the call of the fishermen. The description of their immediate response to the summons of Jesus conveys vividly the authority and power which he exercises. Mark does not tell us whether these men had already met or heard Jesus, and it is possible that they had; according to John (1.40), Andrew was a disciple of John the Baptist, and Luke (5.1–11) provides an explanation for their willingness to follow Jesus. The impression given by Mark, however, is that the personality and authority of Jesus were such that the four men responded to his call at their first meeting. By telling the story in this way, Mark not only impresses his readers with the authority of Jesus, but reminds them that they, too, are called by Jesus to obey the same command.

**Jesus was walking by the Sea of Galilee.** Mark always refers to   16 the lake of Galilee as θάλασσα, a word which normally has the meaning 'sea' (though Aristotle once uses it of a lake, *Meteorologica* 351ᵃ9); Luke is perhaps more correct in using the word λίμνη (lake). The Greek (παράγων παρὰ τὴν θάλασσαν) is odd (lit. 'and passing by along the sea'), and it seems likely that Mark has added the reference to the Sea of Galilee to a story which began simply 'And passing by. . .' But why? Did he think that the explanation was necessary? Anyone familiar with the geography of Palestine would know that fishermen worked on the Sea of Galilee. Perhaps this detail has been added for the benefit of readers living outside Palestine. An alternative suggestion is that the addition is an indication that Mark's readers *come* from Galilee (W. Marxsen, *Mark the Evangelist*, pp. 58–66). Perhaps, however, it is due rather to Mark's emphasis on Galilee as the place of discipleship (see below, on 16.7). Although Mark always refers to the

*Sea* of Galilee, it is really only a large inland lake. In the time of Jesus, it was of great importance because of its excellent supply of fish. The thriving fishing industry, which was known far beyond Palestine through the sale of cured fish, supported many towns and villages on the lake's shores. **Simon and his brother Andrew** are said to have been **casting a net into the sea.** The casting net was a circular net with stones attached to its edge to weight it, and a draw rope which was pulled, to enclose the fish in the net.

17    Jesus calls Simon and Andrew to **come after** him; the use of the word 'after' (ὀπίσω) indicates that he calls them as disciples, not equals. Jesus' call to discipleship has sometimes been likened to that of a rabbi summoning pupils, but far more is involved in following Jesus than learning a particular form of teaching. According to Mark, it involves already the call to become **fishers of men.** The summons picks up the word ἁλιεῖς from Mark's explanatory comment at the end of v.17. Although this metaphor seems apt to us now, it was certainly not an obvious one at the time. The only examples which we have of its previous use apply the metaphor of catching men in an unpleasant sense, e.g. for judgement (so Jer.16.16). It has indeed been argued (see C.W.F. Smith, in *H.T.R.*, 52,1959, pp.187–203) that the brothers' task was to summon the people for judgement. In the present context, however, the metaphor seems to mean that the brothers are commissioned to win men for the Kingdom. The saying is a striking one, and there is no reason to deny it to Jesus himself, though it may perhaps have been spoken on a later occasion. Mark, however, brings out the fact that the brothers are called from the beginning to share in Jesus' own task: for them, at least, the call to discipleship means also a call to ministry (cf. 3.14). Mark's readers may well have understood their own call to discipleship to involve a similar task.

18    The reaction of Simon and Andrew is immediate; they down tools **straight away** and follow. Mark vividly conveys the effect of Jesus' command, for the abruptness of the narrative suggests that there is no delay for them to settle their affairs. Response to Jesus is decisive, and the brothers therefore abandon **their nets** and their old life and livelihood. There are indications in Mark's narrative that the break may not have been quite as sudden as this incident suggests, since throughout the next eight chapters of the gospel Jesus remains in the vicinity of the brothers' homes, and a boat (presumably belonging to one of the fishermen) is always available (see Mark 3.9; 4.1, 35; 5. 21; 6.32, 45; 8.13).

19    **James son of Zebedee and John his brother,** together with Peter, form the group of disciples mentioned most often by Mark, and
20    apparently closest to Jesus. Their response to Jesus' call is as immediate as that of the first two disciples: they sever their family ties, leaving **their father Zebedee in the boat with the hired men.** For

this renunciation, compare the words of Jesus in 10.29f. The reference to hired men indicates that the brothers were by no means poor men. As **fishermen** they would all have been reasonably prosperous, and Peter's boast in 10.28 is not an idle one.

# 3 AUTHORITY IN TEACHING AND EXORCISM                                  1.21–8

*(Matt. 4.13; 7.28–9; Luke 4.31–7)*

**(21) And he entered Capernaum, and straight away on the sabbath he went into the synagogue and taught. (22) And the people were astonished at his teaching, for unlike the scribes, he taught them as one who had authority. (23) Now there was in their synagogue a man with an unclean spirit, and straight away he shrieked out, (24) 'What do you want with us, Jesus of Nazareth? Have you come to destroy us? I know who you are – the Holy One of God.' (25) But Jesus reproved him; 'Be silent,' he said, 'and come out of him.' (26) Then the unclean spirit convulsed the man, cried with a loud voice and came out of him. (27) And they were all amazed and began to ask one another: 'What is this? A new kind of teaching, spoken with authority; he gives commands even to unclean spirits, and they obey him.' (28) And the news about him spread straight away in all directions, throughout the whole region of Galilee.**

Mark refers repeatedly to the fact that Jesus taught and devotes a considerable amount of space to what he taught, even though he records far less of the content of Jesus' teaching than do the other evangelists. Here he is concerned not with what Jesus taught, but only with the manner in which he taught, and the extraordinary effect which his teaching had on his hearers. For Mark's readers, as well as for those who heard Jesus in the synagogue, Jesus is one with an authority far greater than that of the scribes.

   Linked with the description of Jesus' authoritative teaching is the first account in the gospel of an exorcism. Belief in demons was widespread in Judaism at this time, having developed over the previous few centuries during which Jewish beliefs had been subjected to many foreign influences. Their existence offered an explanation of evil, and they were increasingly regarded as representatives of the forces opposed to God. Their allegiance was to Satan, the prince of demons (cf. Mark 3.22), who by this time was no longer regarded as God's servant (as in Job) but as his opponent. Satan was in no sense regarded as God's equal, but as one who had rebelled against his authority, who for the moment was allowed his own way, but who ultimately would be crushed. Demon-possession was the explanation commonly given for certain types of illness. By no means all sickness was attributed to demons, and it was probably mainly mental illnesses, with their disturbing symptoms, which were thought to be caused by possession. Exorcisms were not unknown; there are examples given in rabbinic literature and, although this evidence comes from a time later than that of Jesus, the reference to exorcisms in Matt. 12.27 and Luke 11.19 suggests that the rabbinic material reflects earlier beliefs and practices (see also G. Vermes, *Jesus the Jew*, pp. 61–9). There are also stories of exorcisms from outside Judaism, though once again most of the evidence dates from a later period (cf. J.M. Hull, *Hellenistic Magic and the Synoptic Tradition*, pp. 61–72). There is no reason to doubt that Jesus performed exorcisms. We scarcely need the Jewish charge that he practised magic which is recorded in B. Sanhedrin 107b, to confirm the evidence of the gospels that he had this power.

Mark links this exorcism firmly with the teaching of Jesus: it is while teaching that Jesus performs the exorcism. Since Mark frequently weaves two stories together, he may well have done the same here. Certainly the comment in v.27 (however it is punctuated) underlines the connection between Jesus' authoritative teaching and his control of the unclean spirits. Later passages also link preaching or teaching and exorcism together – see 1.39; 3.14f.; 6.12f. Mark is perhaps concerned lest Jesus should appear to be simply a wonder-worker (as in the Talmud reference above): the overthrow of the demons must be seen as part of his proclamation of the Kingdom of God.

The account of the exorcism shows many of the characteristic features of such stories. In Mark's setting, however, these take on a deeper significance: the demon's submission to Jesus is understood as an acknowledgement of his status, and Jesus' reaction is seen as part of the mystery surrounding his identity. Teaching and exorcism together confront Mark's readers with the question posed in v.27.

21 **Capernaum** is generally identified with *Tell Ḥûm* and lay on the north-west shore of the lake, in the best fishing area. The synagogue whose remains still exist there was built after the time of Jesus, though the foundations of an earlier building may lie beneath it. Mark uses once again his characteristic phrase **and straight away** (καὶ εὐθύς), but as so often it has little meaning; the events described in vv.16–20 cannot have happened **on the sabbath**, since the brothers were all working when Jesus called them. Mark presumably means 'on the next sabbath'.

Worship in **the synagogue** consisted of prayers, benedictions,

readings from the Law and the Prophets together with renderings
into Aramaic, and expositions of the readings. Its conduct was not in
the hands of the priests, who were concerned only with worship in
the temple at Jerusalem, but was regulated by local elders. Any man
who wished to do so and who was competent could contribute an exposition at the invitation of the synagogue ruler, as Jesus does here.
The effect of his teaching was to make his hearers **astonished**. The 22
verb ἐξεπλήσσομαι is used several times by Mark to express the
crowd's amazement at Jesus' activity (cf. 6.2; 7.37; 11.18). Here, it is
the **authority** with which he teaches that causes their astonishment –
an authority which contrasted markedly with the kind of teaching
they were accustomed to hearing.

**The scribes** (οἱ γραμματεῖς) were learned men who did not necessarily belong to any party, though they were probably mostly
Pharisees. They studied the Torah and the oral tradition which had
been built up round it and passed their teaching on to their disciples,
who learned it by heart through constant repetition: the teaching
thus consisted largely of a recital of precedents. The rabbinic teaching which has been recorded in the Talmud is of a period later than
that of Jesus, and is not intended for public worship; nevertheless, it
gives some indication of the way in which the scribes would have
taught. Certainly they would have laid great emphasis on tradition,
quoting at length what previous teachers had said, but hesitating to
make any authoritative judgement; by contrast, Jesus taught directly,
decisively, and on his own authority. Not all teachers of the Torah,
however, were content simply to quote the opinions of others: some
of them must have formulated the teaching which others quoted.
D. Daube (*J.T.S.*, 39, 1938, pp. 45–59) has suggested that there were
two categories of scribes – those rabbis who had been authorized to
lay down doctrines, and inferior teachers who were not entitled to introduce fresh rules. The people of Capernaum, accustomed to hearing only the second kind, were naturally astonished at the kind of
teaching given them by someone who taught like a fully authorized
rabbi. Although this might be a possible explanation of the story's
origin, it is certainly not the kind of distinction that Mark has in mind;
for him, the authority of Jesus is unique, and totally unlike that of
anyone else. It has not been given to him by any human agency; in
teaching – as in all else – Jesus' authority comes from God.

Another use of the phrase **straight away** links the exorcism with 23
what has already happened **in their synagogue**. The use of 'their'
here perhaps hints at a division between Mark's own community and
the Jews. Mark describes the sick man as having **an unclean spirit**;
this is one of his normal expressions for a demon (he uses the phrase
seven times, and the word 'demon' the same number of times). In the
present context, the term may have been chosen deliberately to con-

trast with the word 'holy' in the next verse, where Jesus is addressed as 'the Holy One of God'. In Hebrew thought everything and everyone was either clean or unclean, and whatever came into the latter category needed to be put right before it could come into God's presence. Mark's understanding of the spirit world is an extension of this belief: the description 'unclean' indicates that the spirit is at odds with the divine ordering, though not necessarily irrevocably evil. The man's presence in the synagogue is strange, since someone who was already believed to be possessed by an unclean spirit would normally have been excluded from worship. The man **shrieked out**: the Greek word (ἀνέκραξε) denotes deep emotion; such cries are usual in stories of exorcisms. Although the words are spoken by the unfortunate man, they are understood to be those of the unclean spirit, uttered through its victim's mouth. It is notable that this healing is depicted wholly in terms of an encounter between the spirit and Jesus; the attitude of the man himself to Jesus is not mentioned. His first

24 question, **'What do you want with us?'** (τί ἡμῖν καὶ σοί;), can mean in Classical Greek 'What have we in common?' – an appropriate question from an unclean spirit to one whom it addresses as 'the Holy One of God'. The Greek phrase is, however, an exact rendering of a Hebrew expression used in Judges 11.12 and 1 Kings 17.18 with the meaning 'Why are you interfering with us?', and this is probably its meaning here. The question is immediately answered in the words of the second – **'Have you come to destroy us?'** – which can and perhaps should be read as a statement rather than another question. The twice-used plural, **us**, suggests that the demon speaks in the name of all demons: Jesus is attacking and destroying the whole race. This destruction is said to be the purpose of Jesus' coming, and this is the significance of the story for Mark: we see the one who has already overcome Satan waging war against God's enemies.

The unclean spirit addresses Jesus by two names. The first, **Jesus of Nazareth**, is presumably a name by which Jesus would readily be recognized. The word Ναζαρηνός probably means 'from Nazareth' (cf. 1.9), although alternative explanations have linked the word with two Hebrew terms meaning 'branch' and 'consecrated'. The second name, **the Holy One of God**, expresses a deeper truth about Jesus, unknown to the bystanders but recognized by the demon, which was no doubt assumed to have supernatural knowledge. As far as is known, this phrase was not a messianic title in Judaism. It is occasionally used in the Old Testament, for example of Aaron in Ps. 106.16 and Elisha in 2 Kgs. 4.9; the term 'the Holy One' is used of God himself in Isa. 40.25 and 57.15. The plural, in the form 'the saints of the Most High', is used in Dan. 7.18–27, where 'the holy ones' are represented by the one like a son of man. It is possible that 'the Holy One of God' was among the titles given to Jesus by the early Church (cf. Acts 3.14;

Acts 2.27 and 13.35, quoting Ps. 16.10, use a different word – ὅσιος instead of ἅγιος). The fact that the unclean spirit is said to have addressed Jesus by name probably reflects the belief that the knowledge of a man's name gave one power over him, and so suggests an attempt to gain the upper hand; the use of names in this way played an important part in exorcisms. For Mark, however, the words have a deeper significance; he sees them as an acknowledgement by the unclean spirit of the superior power of Jesus who has already conquered Satan and can therefore destroy his minions.

**Jesus reproved him**: his word of rebuke, **Be silent** (φιμώθητι), was  25 used in the ancient world in magic spells for binding people and demons. It is possible to read Mark's story as a straightforward account of an exorcism but, in view of references later in the gospel to the secrecy concerning Jesus' identity, it seems likely that Mark sees another significance in this command for silence and expects it to be taken in connection with the demon's words in the preceding verse (cf. v.34). This introduces an element of incongruity into the story: the man announces Jesus' identity, whereupon Jesus tells him to be silent. Though the words have already been uttered, nevertheless none of those present (including the disciples) takes any notice of what the demon has said. We meet here for the first time the so-called 'messianic secret' which runs through the whole gospel; the demand for silence and the total failure of everyone to hear what has been said will become familiar to us as we read Mark's story. The reader, having been let into this secret at the very beginning, is perhaps not unduly surprised by the occasional references to Jesus' messianic status, but the participants in the story apparently do not comprehend the truth, even when it is spelt out for them.

The command of Jesus to **come out of him** is enough: the spirit  26 leaves, demonstrating its departure by a final convulsion and loud cry. The effect on the bystanders, as so often in Mark, is to cause them  27 **all** to be **amazed**. This is a natural enough reaction to such an event, for although exorcisms were performed by others before and after Jesus, they would hardly be everyday occurrences in Capernaum. It is more likely, however, that Mark is attributing the crowd's amazement to the manner in which Jesus healed – that is, once again, to his authority. The exact wording and punctuation of this verse are uncertain. The translation given here follows the text and punctuation favoured by most modern editors of the Greek New Testament: **'What is this? A new kind of teaching, spoken with authority; he gives commands even to unclean spirits, and they obey him.'** Other translations link the authority of Jesus with his power over unclean spirits, and the onlookers' response then forms a parallel with the statement made in v.22 that his teaching was with authority: 'What is this? A new teaching! With authority he commands even the unclean spirits and they obey him' (*R.S.V.*). A similar link is made in the text read by the Textus Receptus (followed by the *A.V.*) which takes the second clause as another question: 'What is this? What new teaching is this?' (This reading, usually regarded as inferior, has been supported as the original by G.D. Kilpatrick in *Neotestamentica et Semitica*, pp. 198–201). Whichever of these three interpretations we follow, it seems clear that Mark is trying to emphasize that there is a close link between Jesus' activities of teaching and exorcism: the two must be seen as belonging together. Moreover, what he does is essentially new because it is part of a new era. No reaction is recorded to the acknowledgement of Jesus as 'the Holy One of God': it is as though these words had not been spoken.

28    The result of this incident is that Jesus' fame **spread. . .in all directions, throughout the whole region of Galilee.** The Greek (ὅλην τὴν περίχωρον τῆς Γαλιλαίας) is ambiguous: it could mean 'that part of Galilee which surrounds Capernaum' or possibly 'the region surrounding Galilee'. But the translation we have given seems the most likely: Galilee is the place where Jesus' message is proclaimed, and the statement that the news spread throughout the whole area underlines the great effect of Jesus' authoritative actions.

## Additional note: the messianic secret

The notion of secrecy occurs from time to time in various forms in the first half of Mark's gospel. Jesus silences the demons, who claim to know who he is (1.24f., 34; 3.11f.), and orders the disciples to remain silent when they learn that he is Messiah and Son of God (8.30; 9.9). But it is not only the identity of Jesus which is to be kept secret, for we also find him commanding those who are healed to say nothing about their cure (1.44; 5.43; 7.36; 8.26).

It was William Wrede who first attempted to explain the theme of secrecy (which he termed 'the messianic secret') in Mark's gospel by suggesting that it reflects a tension between the belief of the early Church in Jesus as Messiah and the unmessianic character of Jesus' ministry. Jesus' commands to secrecy, he argued, cannot be taken as historical but are a dogmatic device to explain why he was not acknowledged as Messiah during his ministry. The interpretation of Jesus' words and deeds as messianic belongs to the post-Easter faith of the community and has been imposed upon the tradition (W. Wrede, *Das Messiasgeheimnis in den Evangelien*, 1901; E.tr. *The Messianic Secret*, 1971).

In stark contrast to this interpretation, various commentators continued for many years to maintain that the messianic secret was basically historical (so, e.g., Taylor and Cranfield). The commands to secrecy were explained as the result of Jesus' wish to conceal his messiahship from men and women during his ministry for fear that it would have been misunderstood as a claim to political kingship; instead, it was argued, he chose to use the ambiguous term 'the Son of man', which could be given the content he desired.

Both these views raise problems. The view which takes the secret to be historical fails to explain why Jesus should have chosen to confuse his disciples by using an enigmatic title, leaving them bewildered about his own understanding of his messiahship. It also assumes that there are in fact 'unclean spirits' who possess supernatural knowledge, and leaves unsolved the problems of how the bystanders could ignore the confessions of Jesus' identity made by the men and women who were possessed by these spirits, and why Jesus should give such unrealistic commands – e.g. the command to keep silent about the fact that he has raised a child from the dead (5.43)! Wrede's solution is equally problematic: since Jesus was put to death as a messianic pretender, it seems that during his ministry questions about his messiahship were already being asked, even if no clear answer was yet being given. To describe the whole ministry of Jesus as 'unmessianic' is to ignore totally the plain evidence of the gospels in favour of a complex theory as to how that evidence came to be arranged. If there is any agreement among New Testament scholars today, it is in believing that Jesus acted with authority and believed himself to have been commissioned by God: it is difficult not to use the term 'messianic' to describe such authority. And were the Church – or the evangelist – to have imposed a messianic interpretation on to totally non-messianic material, one would hardly have expected the messianic secret to have emerged: rather, one would have expected much clearer statements of Jesus' messiahship.

But Wrede was surely right in pointing to Easter as the crucial turning-point. It is not until the resurrection that men and women are able to understand who Jesus is and what he signifies. It is not that the Church imposes a messianic interpretation on to a non-messianic life and death: rather, in the light of Easter faith the disciples see events from a new perspective. If we ask how Mark makes use of the secret, then it is important to notice that *it functions in precisely the opposite way to what one expects*: it serves as a means of revelation to the hearers/readers of the gospel. When Jesus commands the unclean spirits to be silent about his identity it is too late, since they have already spoken (1.24f.; 3.11f.). Yet no one in the story hears them, and the truth they utter remains hidden – as it must, to all whose eyes and ears have not been opened: their words are intelligible only to those who already believe that Jesus is what they declare him to be – the Son of God. Jesus' instructions that nothing should be said about the restoration of a child to life (5.43) or about the opening of a deaf man's ears (7.36) and a blind man's eyes (8.26) are equally implausible as historical commands: such things cannot be hidden and are spoken of all over Galilee. But Jesus' instructions that nothing should be said about what he has done suggest that the real significance of these miracles is hidden from the crowd and revealed only to those who are committed to him. It is perhaps no accident that the secret is associated here with miracles of resurrection and the restoration of hearing and sight, for Mark himself makes use of these themes as symbols of understanding and belief (See additional note on miracles, pp. 71–5.) It is only after the resurrection that the truth about Jesus will be made known (9.9); and, while many have ears to hear, they do not all listen or understand (4.1–12); as for the miracle of the restoration of sight in 8.22–6, this itself is used by Mark as a symbol for the dawning of the disciples' faith (8.27–33).

It is significant, too, that the secret is not universally imposed. It occurs in two contexts. First, there are the commands for secrecy which are given immediately after some declaration about who Jesus is has been made: 1.24f., 34; 3.11; 8.30 and 9.9; a remarkable example occurs in 10.48, where the *crowd* tries to silence Bartimaeus and refuses to hear what he proclaims. Second, there are the three miracles we have just noted, where restoration to life, and the restoration of hearing and sight, seem to be used in a symbolic way. The one example which does not fit into either category is 1.44, where the command to say nothing is subsidiary to the order to the healed leper to show himself to the priest. In contrast to these commands for secrecy we have frequent references to the fact that men and women talked freely about what Jesus was doing (1.28, 45; 2.12), that Jesus made no secret of his healing (5.19, 30), and that crowds flocked to him as a result (3.10; 6.54ff.). The exorcisms themselves are common knowledge (3.20–30). The secret is thus only one side of the story; just as important is Mark's insistence that everyone in Palestine knew about Jesus' teaching and healing and was marvelling at it.

It seems clear that the commands to secrecy are largely (though not necessarily entirely) artificial, and that they are a narrative device which has been used by Mark to draw his readers' attention to the real significance of his story. Secrecy and disclosure are part of a theme which pervades the whole of Mark's gospel. Throughout the narrative, Jesus acts with supreme authority yet makes no open claims for himself. Even when he challenges his disciples by asking them about his identity, he orders them to say nothing (8.27–30); when he makes a dramatic entrance into Jerusalem and into the temple (11.1–18), the significance of his actions is not understood and he refuses to explain the basis of his authority directly (11.27–33). Yet for those with eyes and ears to see and hear, the meaning is plain: they know why the Son of man must suffer (8.31), they understand why he rides into Jerusalem on the back of a colt (11.1–10), and they comprehend why he appeals to John the Baptist as the witness to his own authority (11.27–33). The truth about Jesus is displayed in his miracles – yet men's normal reaction is fear and uncomprehending amazement (2.12; 5.15, 33, 42; 7.37). Even the disciples are bewildered (4.41; 8.14–21). He teaches the word to those who have ears to hear (4.1–9); yet the disciples are mystified and have to ask for an explanation (4.10–12). From time to time the truth about Jesus is openly proclaimed – at the baptism (1.10f.); by unclean spirits (1.24; 3.11; 5.7); at the transfiguration (9.2–8). But no one hears the voice or sees the Spirit descend at the baptism; the unclean spirits are silenced whenever they cry out; and the discples are told to say nothing about the transfiguration until after the resurrection. The truth about Jesus is at once hidden from view and yet spelt out on every page of the gospel.

Mark has perhaps used this technique to explain not merely the failure of Jesus' disciples to grasp the whole truth about him before his death and resurrection, but also the failure of the religious authorities to recognize him at all. The rejection of Jesus by his own people raised real problems for the early Christian community: how was it that Israel rejected her Messiah? The answer was sought in the plan and purpose of God. If Jesus' death was foreordained, so too was his rejection by the nation's leaders, and the only explanation must be that the truth was deliberately concealed from them – and that meant that it was concealed by Jesus himself.

It remains an open question whether Mark has created the messianic secret *ex nihilo*, or made use of a theme which he found in the tradition. Our answer to this question depends on the degree of creativity which we attribute to Mark himself. On the assumption that he is in fact making use of earlier traditions, we may ask whether any of this has its origins in Jesus' own ministry. If we believe that Jesus' actions were characterized by an authority which may fairly be termed 'messianic', then it is possible that the so-called secret reflects not simply the tension between Jesus as he was perceived in his lifetime and as he was confessed after the resurrection, but the reluctance of Jesus to make claims about himself: for his message was centred on God and on his Kingdom, not on himself, and, if he believed himself to be in any sense the Messiah, the last thing he would do was to claim the title for himself. Artificial though the secret may be, there is a sense in which it corresponds to the truth about the way in which Jesus came to be acknowledged as Messiah only through suffering and death.

For further discussion, see: W. Wrede, *The Messianic Secret*; G.H. Boobyer, *N.T.S.*, 6, pp. 225–35; C.M. Tuckett, ed., *The Messianic Secret*.

# 4 JESUS HEALS A FRIEND 1.29–31

## *(Matt. 8.14–15; Luke 4.38–9)*

**(29) They left[1] the synagogue and went straight away to the house of Simon and Andrew, together with James and John. (30) Now Simon's mother-in-law lay sick with a fever, and they told him about her straight away. (31) And he came to her, grasped her by the hand and lifted her up; and the fever left her, and she waited on them.**

29    The fact that this story is linked with the name of **Simon** has been regarded by many commentators as evidence supporting the tradition that this gospel consists of Peter's 'memoirs'; it has been suggested, moreover, that the verb **they left** (more likely to be original than the variant reading 'he left') represents an oral tradition in
30    the form 'we left the synagogue and went straight home'. More significant, perhaps, is the fact that this first account in Mark of the healing of an illness is personal in the sense that the patient is identified as **Simon's mother-in-law**. Though we cannot generalize from this story to the rest of the gospel, it may well be that the tradition of this particular incident was handed down because it was of special importance to Peter. As in the story of the exorcism, the healing power of Jesus is used in response to a particular, urgent situation, and once again we note how the response of Jesus demonstrates his authority, this time in his power over diseases. **Andrew ... James and John** are not mentioned in the Matthean and Lukan parallels, and some commentators (e.g. Nineham, following Bultmann) think that the names may be a later gloss. But there is no textual evidence for their omission in Mark, and it is more likely that the later evangelists omitted them because they play no part in the story.
31    In the case of the exorcism in the synagogue, Jesus drove out the unclean spirit with a word. Here, as so often in healings of this kind in Mark, he heals through physical contact with the patient: **he. . . grasped her by the hand and lifted her up**. Similar cases of healing by raising the patient are reported of some of the rabbis (e.g. B. Berakoth 5b). The fact that **she waited on them** is proof of her recovery; not only had **the fever left her**, but she had regained her strength. It seems clear that Mark means that she did so 'straight away', but for once he omits to say so. He has already used the word εὐθύς twice in the preceding two verses.

---

1 Some MSS (including B, D, W, Θ, fams. 1,13, it) read *he left*.

# 5 HEALINGS AND EXORCISMS 1.32–4

## (Matt. 8.16–17; Luke 4.40–1)

(32) When evening came and the sun had set, they brought to him all those who were ill or possessed by demons: (33) the whole town was gathered round the door. (34) And he healed many who were suffering from various diseases and drove out many demons; and he would not allow the demons to speak, because they knew who he was.

This short section summarizes Jesus' activity in healing. A similar passage occurs later, at 3.11f. Mark regards these scenes as typical, not unique. Once again, he emphasizes the authority of Jesus, this time by stressing the large number of those who are healed.

The sabbath ended at sunset, so that when **evening came and the** 32 **sun had set**, it was permissible to carry the sick through the streets. The imperfect **brought** (ἔφεϱον) implies a constant stream of sufferers. Mark specifies two classes of sickness, distinguishing between **those who were ill** and **those possessed by demons**: Jesus has already healed one case of each kind, and now he is called on to cure many more in both categories. Mark uses hyperbole once more when 33 he says that **the whole town was gathered round the door**, but this serves to indicate the response of Capernaum to Jesus. In this context, the door must be understood to be that belonging to Peter's house. In saying that Jesus healed **many who were suffering from various** 34 **diseases and drove out many demons**, Mark is not making a distinction between the **all** referred to in v.32 and the many whom Jesus **healed**; 'many' is often used in Hebrew and Aramaic in an inclusive, rather than an exclusive, sense. The exorcism and healing described in vv.28 and 29–31 are thus seen as typical, not unique. Once again, Jesus **would not allow the demons to speak**, and this time we are told plainly that this was **because they knew who he was**: it is Jesus' identity which must not be publicly proclaimed. The echo of the earlier scene reminds us that his activity now fulfils the words spoken by the unclean spirit in v.24: that first exorcism in the synagogue was not an isolated event, but demonstrated the overthrow of all demonic powers.

## Additional note: miracles

It is clear from the amount of space which Mark devotes to miracles that he considers them to be important. They fall into two broad groups: healing miracles (which can be further subdivided into exorcisms and other healings) and those which are often termed 'nature' miracles, though this is hardly a good description, since it suggests a belief that in these particular cases Jesus was controlling nature, but that he was not doing so in the miracles of healing. Already in the first couple of pages of his account of Jesus' ministry, Mark has told us of miracles bringing healing to two individuals – one involving an exorcism, the other a general restoration. It is significant that each story implies that the power of Jesus to heal is universal: the unclean spirit's response to Jesus suggests that his coming destroys all unclean spirits; the healing of Peter's mother-in-law leads to a scene in which everyone who is ill comes to Jesus, and he heals them all.

Significant, too, is the link between Jesus' authoritative teaching and his power to heal, seen in the way these two themes are woven together in 1.21–8. Mark has already told us in 1.14f. the theme of Jesus' teaching – it is the proclamation of the Kingdom of God. Now we know that this proclamation involves healing: in Jesus the power of God's Kingdom is at work, destroying the unclean spirits. Elsewhere, we discover that the inbreaking of the Kingdom in Jesus' healing miracles means more than mere physical healing: those who were excluded from the community because of their infirmity are restored to membership of God's people (1.44; 5.15, 34).

But for Mark, miracles not only demonstrate the power of God's Kingdom but reveal the identity of Jesus himself. The authority invested in him is unique – it is the authority of the Son of God (as we know from 1.11). So the unclean spirit acknowledges Jesus to be 'the Holy One of God', v.24; in v.34 the demons are silenced because they know him. Healing takes place when his authority is acknowledged, either by the spirits, who know who he is (see also 3.11f.; 5.7), or by the sick, who come to him in the faith that he has the power to heal them; this faith is implicit in the fact that they come at all, but is underlined by comments such as we find in 1.40; 2.5; 5.28, 34, 36; 9.24; 10.47f., 51f. Where there is no faith – no acknowledgement of his authority – there are no healings. So Jesus *cannot* heal in his home town, 6.1–6; he refuses to perform miracles to order, 8.11–13. Particularly interesting is the conversation between Jesus and the Syro-Phoenician woman in 7.24–30. Jesus' initial response to the woman indicates that miracles belong in the context of faith and are part of the good news offered to the children, i.e. to God's people Israel: a healing outside the context of the proclamation of the Kingdom is inappropriate because it does not belong within the context of faith in the power of God. The woman gains healing for her child because of her persistence: her answer demonstrates that she understands Jesus' ability to heal to be due, not to magic, but to the power of God, working for the salvation of his people. By her insight into what is taking place she shows that she too has faith; must we not conclude then that she too belongs to the Kingdom?

In Mark's presentation, miracles are thus essentially christologi-cal: they present us with the authority of Jesus and demand a re-sponse from us. For this reason they are able to serve as symbols for belief in Jesus as the Son of God. The clearest example is found in the story of the blind man whose eyes are gradually opened just before Caesarea Philippi; his semi-restored sight symbolizes the imperfect faith of the disciples (8.22–6). Another blind man, Bartimaeus, who gains his sight as Jesus sets out from Jericho, and who follows him 'on the road' to Jerusalem, is also a symbol of those who understand something of the truth about Jesus (10.46–52). Similarly, the deaf man who gains his hearing (7.32–7) and is able to tell the story em-bodies the command of Jesus in 4.3–9 to hear the 'word'. These stories remind us that true faith in Jesus is not simply faith in his power as a mighty man of God (like John the Baptist or Elijah or one of the prophets) but faith in him as the Christ who is proclaimed as Son of God through suffering. That faith is born only at the very end of the story, but already some in the story see and hear part of the truth about him. This is why the blind man in ch. 8 and the deaf man in ch. 7 are bound to secrecy; similarly, those who witness the raising of Jairus' daughter are told to keep silent, because that points forward to Jesus' own resurrection. (See additional note on the messianic secret, pp. 66–9.) Bartimaeus, on the other hand, has already acknow-ledged Jesus as Son of David and, when he receives his sight, he fol-lows Jesus on the way to Jerusalem; secrecy is no longer appropriate, because Jesus is about to enter Jerusalem, where his identity will be openly proclaimed, even though no one believes the proclamation (11.1–10; 12.1–9; 35–7; 14.61f.; 15.2, 9, 12, 16–19, 26, 32), until the moment of his death, when one man finally sees the truth (15.39).

There is thus a sense in which Mark's miracles function as 'signs', very much like the Johannine signs, even though he avoids the term σημεῖα itself in speaking of the miracles of Jesus (though he uses it in 13.22 to describe the works of the false Christs and false prophets), and records that Jesus refused the demand to perform them. The Pharisees' request in 8.11–13 underlines the irony of the situation, for Jesus has just performed a 'sign' by feeding the crowd – how absurd, then, for them to demand one! (Cf. the equally absurd question of the crowd in John 6.30.) By failing to see the significance of the miracle, they demonstrate their own blindness and hardheartedness. The miracles are 'signs' of Jesus' authority, but only to those who are pre pared to see their true meaning. In other words, they are not signs which *lead* to faith, but signs to those who *have* faith.

The fact that Jesus heals and exorcises demons is not denied by his opponents, but they give these miracles the wrong explanation: they cannot deny the authority of Jesus, but they attribute that authority to the wrong source. Herod thinks Jesus is John the Baptist come back to haunt him; the scribes from Jerusalem ascribe his authority to Beelzebul. Jesus' response to them (3.22–30) gives us the true explanation: his power over unclean spirits is given to him by the Holy Spirit. But more than this, he himself is the 'strong one' who has bound Satan, and the unclean spirits acknowledge him as the Holy One and Son of God (1.24, 34; 3.11; 5.7).

We have said that Jesus' authority is unique and points to his identity. Nevertheless, it is an authority he is able to delegate to others. The Twelve are appointed to be with him, to preach and to have authority to cast out demons. Preaching (the good news of the Kingdom) and the exorcism of demons go hand in hand: so when they are sent out in 6.7–12, they preach repentance and cast out demons and heal many. On a subsequent occasion, however, we read of the dismal failure of the disciples to heal a child (9.14–29): the story assumes that both the crowd and the disciples expected that they would have the power to cure him. This last story reminds us of the importance of faith for healing. Jesus alone has the faith which enables him to do all things, in contrast to the faithless generation which he has to bear. The disciples lack the faith to cast out the unclean spirit, and the child's father doubts Jesus' ability to heal him. Because Jesus' life is rooted in the Kingdom, he has the faith to grapple with Satan and defeat him; the disciples are not yet wholly committed. The cry of the child's father would be an appropriate one for them: 'I believe, help my unbelief.' Mark may well have felt that it was apposite, also, for Christians of his own generation, if they, too, found themselves unable to perform miracles in Jesus' name.

The five so-called 'nature miracles' are also essentially christological. After the calming of the storm, in 4.35–41, the disciples are left asking, 'Who is this, that wind and sea obey him?' As usual, we are left to supply the answer: Ps. 107.25–9 is an obvious place to look. When Jesus walks on the water, in 6.47–52, he announces 'It is I': superficially, the words might seem reassuring, but in this context they remind us of the divine name in the Old Testament, for it is God alone who 'trampled the waves of the sea' (Job 9.8). The two feeding miracles, also, remind us of the way in which God fed the Israelites in the wilderness with manna and quails. These two stories clearly had great importance for Mark: not only does he tell virtually the same story twice over, but in 6.52 he refers back to the first occasion, and in 8.14–21 he refers to them both. Both these reminders occur in the course of stories about Jesus and his disciples crossing the lake by boat, and underline the disciples' failure to understand what is taking place. In 6.52, Mark makes a link between the feeding of the crowd and Jesus' ability to walk on the water; the disciples are terrified by Jesus' power, and the reason for their fear is that 'they had not understood about the loaves'. In 8.14–21, the disciples discuss the fact that they have brought only one loaf with them, and Jesus reminds them of the two occasions when he has fed huge crowds. On both occasions, the disciples are said to have hardened hearts – it is this which prevents them from seeing the true significance of the miracles: they are unprepared for the power of God at work in him.

These four miracles demonstrate the power of God to save. The fifth miracle in this category depicts the obverse side of this power, seen in God's judgement. The destruction of the barren fig tree (11.12–14, 20–5) seems oddly out of place in Mark's narrative – the very antithesis of the miracles by which Jesus restores men and women to health. But the story symbolizes the judgement which is going to fall on those who reject the message of the Kingdom, and whose hard hearts prevent them from seeing the power of God at work in Jesus.

For further discussion, see: A. Richardson, *The Miracle-Stories of the Gospels*; R.H. Fuller, *Interpreting the Miracles*; M.E. Glasswell, 'The use of miracles in the Markan gospel'; J.M. Hull, *Hellenistic Magic and the Synoptic Tradition*; D. Wenham and C. Blomberg, eds., *The Miracles of Jesus*.

# 6   JESUS EXTENDS HIS MINISTRY               1.35–9

### (Matt. 4.23; Luke 4.42–4)

**(35) And early in the morning, while it was still quite dark, he got up, left the house and went away to a lonely place where he prayed. (36) But Simon and his companions pursued him; (37) and when they found him they said, 'Everyone is looking for you.' (38) But he answered, 'Let us go elsewhere, into the neighbouring villages, so that I may preach there: that is what I came out to do.' (39) So he travelled through the whole of Galilee, preaching in their synagogues and driving out demons.**

This apparently simple narrative is more difficult to understand than at first appears. It has often been suggested that Jesus left Capernaum **early in the morning** in order to escape from the pressure of those who had seen his healing miracles and now regarded him as a wonder-worker. Such a departure, however, would not change the impression which Jesus had made upon the people; neither does he repudiate the role of healer, for when he leaves Capernaum he continues to cast out demons. Moreover, it would be strange if Jesus, having called four men to follow him, should almost immediately set off elsewhere, leaving them behind. Such problems show that discussion at this level is unhelpful; we cannot answer such detailed historical questions from this narrative. Those who have read and reread the gospel may well think forward to the final scene in the story, which is also set very early in the morning (λίαν πρωΐ: cf. πρωῒ ἔννυχα λίαν here), when Jesus 'got up' and left the tomb, and when the disciples were told to follow him into Galilee. Links such as this did not necessarily occur to Mark himself but contribute to the significance of the story once they have been seen. Mark's own explanation is that Jesus left Capernaum early in the morning in order to pray. This suggests that Mark sees this as an important point in the ministry, at which Jesus seeks guidance. This is confirmed in Jesus' words to the disciples, where he provides a second reason for his departure: his intention is to preach in **the neighbouring villages**. The real contrast is not between preaching and healing, but between a ministry confined to one spot and a mission to the whole area. There is no suggestion here that Mark thinks of Jesus' leaving Capernaum because he feels that his reception there has been mistaken; he leaves because he must do in the rest of Galilee what he has already done in Capernaum. The refusal to limit his ministry to one city points forward to the wider proclamation of the good news by his followers to which Mark's readers have already responded.

35     Jesus **went away to a lonely place**. The word ἔρημος(translated
36 'lonely place') can mean 'wilderness' (see 1.3f., 12), but is perhaps used here primarily in contrast to **the house**. The phrase **Simon and his companions** is an odd one. Those who trace Mark's material back to Peter find more support here for their belief that this group of narratives in chapter 1 is told from his point of view. Alternatively, it has been suggested that the term 'disciples' is deliberately avoided because the four men do not behave here like disciples (Nineham): the four act here as representatives of the crowd and share its attitudes (cf. 8.33). But the word 'disciples' is not used by Mark at all until 2.18, and the fact that it is not used here may be accidental. Moreover, it is characteristic of the disciples throughout Mark's narrative that they fail to behave as disciples and again and again prove to have no better understanding of Jesus than the crowds. On this occasion they **pursued him** – the verb καταδιώκω has the sense of 'to track down', and its use here suggests an unwelcome intrusion. Though Jesus has called them to 'follow' him, this is certainly not what was meant; what following does involve will be spelt out later
37 (8.34; 10.52). The disciples were not alone, however, in **looking for** Jesus; **everyone, they said**, was doing so; here, too, the verb (ζητέω) seems to imply an unwelcome following, since those who seek Jesus in Mark always do it in the wrong way (cf. 3.32 and 16.6).
38     Jesus' explanation of his action – **that is what I came out to do –** could mean simply 'that is why I left Capernaum', but this hardly fits

the context, since we have been told that he came out to pray. It may well be an independent saying which Mark has placed at this point. One possible explanation is to understand it as a reference to Jesus' coming from God; this interpretation may well lie behind Luke's version of the words, 'I was sent for this purpose' (Luke 4.43). In Mark, however, the most natural explanation of the words is that they mean 'This is why I left home and came into the rest of Galilee – in order that I might preach in the whole region.' This task is accomplished in the next verse, which summarizes Jesus' activity. The statement that 39 **he travelled through the whole of Galilee** emphasizes the completion of Jesus' purpose: now it is not simply a rumour which travels through the whole district (v.28) but Jesus himself, **preaching in their synagogues and driving out demons**, so that the whole area is evangelized.

Mark's summary of Jesus' ministry is worthy of note: he went throughout Galilee, **preaching in their synagogues and driving out demons**. These words continue the theme of the overthrow of Satan found in the prologue: the proclamation of the gospel includes the defeat of the demonic powers. They also demonstrate that Jesus' ministry in Galilee was the extension of what he had done in Capernaum. Just as he had taught in the synagogue at Capernaum and proclaimed the good news there, so now he does the same in all the synagogues of Galilee; just as he had rescued one man from the power of a demon in the synagogue at Capernaum, so now he casts out demons from many people throughout the whole area. In this sense what Mark describes as having happened in Capernaum is typical of what happens elsewhere. It matters little, therefore, whether the closely knit series of events from v.21 to v.39 are understood in the way that they have often been understood, as the recollection of the first sabbath that the disciples spent with Jesus, or whether we interpret the links as artificial, and see the narrative as an account of a typical sabbath; whether or not this particular series of events took place in Capernaum during one particular period of 24 hours, Mark uses them to present to us the impact which Jesus made, not only there, but in **the whole of Galilee**.

It is interesting to note that Mark refers again to 'their' synagogues (cf. 1.23), suggesting that those for whom he is writing feel themselves distinct from the Jewish community; we begin to see here the separation between church and synagogue which leads the fourth evangelist to speak of Jesus' contemporaries as 'the Jews'.

# 7  JESUS MAKES A LEPER CLEAN  1.40–5

*(Matt. 8.2–4; Luke 5.12–16)*

(40) There came to him a leper who knelt before him and begged his help. 'If you are willing,' he said, 'you can make me clean.' (41) And Jesus, moved with anger,[1] stretched out his hand and touched him, saying, 'I am willing: be clean!' (42) And the leprosy left him straight away, and he was clean. (43) And giving him a stern warning, Jesus immediately sent him away: (44) 'See that you say nothing to anyone', he said, 'but go and show yourself to the priest, and make the offering for your cleansing which Moses commanded, as evidence to them.' (45) But he went out and began to announce it freely and to spread the news far and wide, so that [Jesus] could no longer enter a city openly. Instead he stayed outside in lonely places, and people flocked to him from all directions.

This story is not part of the close complex of stories which has just ended and is introduced abruptly into the narrative. Mark probably included it at this point because it continues the theme of healing and introduces an example of Jesus' healing powers going beyond anything that has been related so far. There is no certainty as to the exact nature of the man's complaint: on the one hand, the word translated as **leprosy** (λέπρα, cf. the Hebrew *ṣāra'aṯ*) seems to have been used at the time to cover various skin-diseases, some of which were curable; the legislation given in Leviticus 13 and 14 for the 'cleansing' of a leper illustrates that some at least of the complaints covered by the term were self-limiting. On the other hand, leprosy as we understand it was until very recently incurable, and the rabbinic saying that the healing of a leper was as difficult as the raising of the dead demonstrates that the Hebrew term included this disease, while the story of Naaman in 2 Kings 5 shows the near impossibility of curing leprosy proper. The special treatment which Mark gives to this story, together with the amazement aroused by the cure, indicate that he understands the man to have been suffering from a form of the disease regarded as incurable.

The significance of the story lies in Jesus' amazing power to heal even this condition. To us, leprosy seems the most loathsome of diseases; to the Jew, it was also the most strident example of uncleanness. Whether or not the so-called leper was suffering from what we should recognize as a contagious disease, he was certainly *regarded*

---

1 Reading ὀργισθείς with D and some MSS of the Old Latin version. The majority of MSS read σπλαγχνισθείς, *moved with compassion.*

as contagious: he was not allowed to come into contact with other human beings or with their property and was thus totally cut off from society. In touching this man, Jesus did not simply run the risk of catching the leprosy, but also made himself unclean according to the regulations of the Mosaic Law. Yet the outcome of the story is not that Jesus is made unclean, but that the leper is made clean! Jesus' power to cleanse is thus demonstrably greater than the power of the leprosy to contaminate.

The story also has important implications for the status of the Torah in Christian teaching. Jesus commands the man to go to the priest in fulfilment of the requirements of Leviticus 14. Only the priest could carry out the official examination of those who had lost the symptoms of leprosy and pronounce them clean: hence the man is told to go straight to the priest, and to say nothing about his cure until the proper procedures have been carried out. It seems likely that this represents Jesus' own attitude to the Torah but, by the time Mark writes, there is an element of tension in the story. Jesus himself acts in accordance with the Torah, but the healed man declares what Jesus has done without bothering to go to the priest for cleansing. In other words, Jesus' action in healing the leper is seen as sufficient in itself, and the Torah's pronouncements are no longer needed. Jesus has thus in a sense replaced the Torah; indeed, he has done 'what the Law could not do' (Rom. 8.3), since he has routed the power of leprosy itself, not simply pronounced as clean someone who had already lost his symptoms.

**There came to him a leper.** The man was breaking the regulations  40 in approaching Jesus, since a leper was forbidden to come near other people. The statement that he **knelt before him** is omitted in a few MSS, but an equivalent expression is found in both Matthew and Luke, so that the omission was probably accidental. The gesture emphasizes the man's entreaty as he **begged his help.** He shows remarkable confidence in Jesus' ability to **make** him **clean**; it is hardly strange that he should doubt whether he would be **willing** to do so, since this involved the leper's coming near him.

One of the great difficulties in this narrative is to understand the  41 emotion attributed to Jesus. The translation given here, **moved with anger,** represents the Greek word ὀργισθείς which is found in a minority of manuscripts. This is almost certainly the correct reading, though it is relegated to the margin by almost all editors of the text, and ignored by many translators, who prefer the reading found in the majority of manuscripts; according to most translations, therefore, Jesus was moved with *pity* (σπλαγχνισθείς), not anger. It is easy to see why translators prefer the majority text – but, for precisely that reason, it seems that the minority text is more likely to be correct; scribes might well have changed a statement that Jesus felt anger to one that he felt compassion, but it is difficult to see why they should have made the opposite change. If the original text referred to Jesus' anger, this would also explain why Matthew and Luke omit the reference to Jesus' emotion altogether. But if 'moved with anger' represents the original reading, why did Mark consider it appropriate to attribute anger to Jesus? Did he understand the anger to be directed against the leper, and if so, why? One suggestion is that Mark supposes Jesus to be angry because the man approached him, whereas according to the Mosaic law he should have avoided all human contact; but he goes on to say that Jesus voluntarily touched him, so making himself ritually unclean, and this scarcely indicates displeasure with the man's action. Another suggestion is that Jesus might have been thought to be angry with the leper's doubts concerning his willingness to heal. A third explanation attributes the anger to the fact that Jesus has been interrupted in his preaching tour, but this is totally in conflict with Mark's presentation of Jesus' mission as one where preaching and healing go hand in hand. It seems best to conclude that Mark does not intend us to understand Jesus' anger as directed against the leper at all, but against the evil forces which have claimed the man as their victim. The responsibility of Satan for illness is referred to in Luke 13.16, and is probably assumed here, even though Satan is not specifically mentioned. Anger is an appropriate emotion when one is confronted with the devastating effects of disease.

**Jesus ... stretched out his hand and touched him.** The action is a normal one in healing stories, but amazing in the circumstances. 2 Kgs. 5.11 records that Naaman expected Elisha to 'wave his hand over' his sores. Mark says nothing of the fact that Jesus might have been expected to be made ceremonially unclean by such contact: his power is greater than that of the leprosy, so that he cannot himself be affected by it. Only a priest could declare a man to be clean, but Jesus, in issuing the command 'Be clean!' deals with the root of the

42 problem, the illness itself. **The leprosy left him straight away, and he was clean.** Although Mark once again uses his favourite phrase (καὶ εὐθύς), a cure from leprosy could scarcely be so immediate. A somewhat more plausible picture is given in Luke's account of the cure of ten lepers, who were healed as they travelled to Jerusalem (Luke 17.14). Perhaps Mark means that the power of the leprosy left the man at that moment (cf. 5.29).

43 The next stage in the story also takes place **immediately**. The **stern warning** in our translation is an attempt to represent a rare Greek verb (ἐμβριμᾶσθαι) whose normal meaning is 'to snort' or 'to be indignant'; it is used in John 11.33,38 to indicate Jesus' deep emotion at the tomb of Lazarus; in Mark 14.5 it is used of the disciples' indignation with the woman who anointed Jesus' head. In the present

passage, and in Matt. 9.30, the word indicates the emotion of Jesus towards those whom he has healed, and whom he is about to command to secrecy. The verb translated **sent. . .away** (ἐκβάλλω) was used in v.12 of the Spirit driving Jesus into the wilderness, and in vv.34 and 39 of the expulsion of demons; it perhaps conveys something of the same compulsion here. Why should Jesus drive the man away? This has been interpreted as yet another indication that Mark thinks of Jesus as angry with the man himself; it is possible that Jesus drives him away because he is still unclean. However, it is perhaps used simply to indicate the urgency with which Jesus sends him to fulfil the regulations of the Law: he is not to stop on the way to tell people what has happened, but is to go straight to the priest (v.44); a similar use of this verb can be found in James 2.25.

We have now met three Greek words in this story (ὀγισθείς . . . ἐμβριμησάμενος . . . ἐξέβαλεν) which suggest agitation or strong emotion on Jesus' part. One explanation of these various strange words is that they belong to an earlier version of the story which told how Jesus drove a 'leprous spirit' out of the man: in this context, all three of these strong verbs could have been used in the description of the cure itself (see, e.g., Nineham). The problem is that in this case, two of them occur at the wrong point in the story, after the man has been healed; if this is the explanation, Mark's editing has been very clumsy. Whatever the origin of these features, whether they have been taken over by Mark or originate with him, it is probable that Mark himself understood Jesus' anger and emotion as caused by the forces of evil and disease with which he is here in conflict. The whole verse is omitted by Matthew and Luke in their accounts, who thus avoid all reference to emotion on Jesus' part.

**'See that you say nothing to anyone.'** The command to keep silent **44** is introduced by a strong negative (μηδενὶ μηδὲν), and this time it is not Jesus' identity (as in v.34) but the cure which is not to be spoken of. The instruction has a very specific purpose here, since it is linked with the instruction to go straight to the priest, but it will be echoed later in the gospel, when Jesus imposes silence on those whom he has healed. Since similar commands after other miracles symbolize the inability of men and women at the time to understand their significance, Mark may well have understood this command in the same way. The significance of what Jesus has done cannot be grasped at this stage – the crowds can only marvel at what they hear without understanding. If Mark intends the story to be read in this way, then we have another example of a command to silence which originally had one purpose being reinterpreted by the evangelist.

The leper is however commanded to tell of his cure to the priest, and only when he has done so will he be legally able to mix in society again: **go and show yourself to the priest, and make the offering**

**for your cleansing which Moses commanded, as evidence to them**. The last phrase is ambiguous: to whom is the evidence to be given? The word 'them' can be understood as a reference to 'the people' – presumably those who mob Jesus in v.45 (so the *R.S.V.*); the evidence would then be of Jesus' ability to heal. But there seems no reason why Jesus should need to give evidence of a power which everyone seems to acknowledge. Another possible explanation is that Mark is thinking of the opponents of Jesus, who will shortly be accusing him of laxity in keeping the Torah; in this case, the 'evidence' he offers is of his adherence to the Torah. But this group has not yet appeared in the gospel and, though it is possible that everyone in the community for whom Mark was writing would immediately recognize 'them' as a reference to the Pharisees and scribes, it seems unlikely that this is what he means here. The one person who has been mentioned in the story so far is the priest to whom the leper is sent, and the most natural interpretation in the context is that showing himself to him will be evidence of his cure; if Mark writes 'them' rather than 'him', that is perhaps because the one priest is representative of them all. When the healed leper has fulfilled the legal requirements and has been declared as no longer suffering from the disease, then he can be restored to his place within Israel. Mark has perhaps deliberately placed this indication of Jesus' adherence to the Torah immediately before the account in 2.1–3.6 of the opposition which he encountered from those who claimed to uphold the Torah: his words show that he is in fact no transgressor of the Torah.

45 **But he went out.** The change of subject at this point – from Jesus to the leper – is harsh, and it has been suggested (e.g. by Klostermann) that the 'he' refers to Jesus himself. This is attractive, in view of Mark's use here of two words which elsewhere are used of the proclamation of the gospel: **to announce it** represents the verb κηρύσσειν, which is elsewhere used of preaching, and **the news** translates the Greek ὁ λόγος, 'the word', which can be used of the word of the gospel. But the abrupt change of subject is possible for Mark, and it is more likely that it is the healed leper who, in contrast to Jesus' command, blazons news of his cure **far and wide**; and, of course, what he proclaims is indeed the good news, even though Jesus had tried to prevent him spreading it abroad. The result of the miracle is thus once again an overwhelming response from all who hear what has happened, even though, unlike the readers of the gospel, they do not understand the significance of what they hear. From this time onward, Jesus **could no longer enter a city openly. Instead he stayed outside in lonely places, and people flocked to him from all directions.**

# 8 AUTHORITY TO FORGIVE SINS 2.1–12

*(Matt. 9.1–8; Luke 5.17–26)*

(1) Some days later he returned to Capernaum, and the news went round that he was in the house. (2) So many people collected that there was no room left, even in front of the door; and he preached the word to them. (3) Then some people arrived, bringing a paralysed man to him. There were four men carrying him, (4) and when they could not get near because of the crowd, they broke through the roof above the place where Jesus was; and when they had made a hole, they lowered the mat on which the paralysed man was lying. (5) And when Jesus saw their faith, he said to the paralysed man, 'My son, your sins are forgiven.' (6) Now there were some scribes sitting there who thought to themselves: (7) 'Why is this fellow talking like this? It is blasphemy! Who can forgive sins but God alone?' (8) Jesus realized straight away what they were thinking and said to them: 'Why are you thinking like this? (9) Which is easier – to say to this paralysed man, "Your sins are forgiven", or to say "Get up! Pick up your mat, and walk"? (10) But so that you may know that the Son of man has authority on earth to forgive sins' – he said to the paralysed man, (11) 'I say to you, "Get up! Pick up your mat and go home."' (12) And he got up, straight away picked up his mat and went out in front of everyone; then they were all astounded and praised God saying, 'We have never seen anything like this before!'

This next story about Jesus' authority introduces a new theme – that of conflict between Jesus and the Jewish leaders. It is the first of a group of five stories involving conflict (2.1–3.6). Most commentators believe that the grouping is pre-Markan, but it is not obvious what use such a collection of stories would have been, and it seems more likely that Mark himself has gathered them together in order to show how the authority of Jesus was rejected by the Jewish authorities. Certainly it is for this purpose that he includes the stories here, and it is this refusal to accept Jesus' authority which leads to his rejection and ultimately to his death, a fate foreshadowed in 2.20 and 3.6. This chapter, therefore, is not simply a collection of 'conflict stories', but a demonstration of Jesus' authority and the refusal of the Jewish religious leaders to recognize it.

As well as introducing the theme of conflict, the story is also linked by its topic to the preceding healing narrative. The leper was excluded from society because of his disease; this paralytic is shut off from life in another way. In both cases Jesus deals with the root of the complaint, and thus shows an authority superior to that of the priests who could pronounce a man clean or forgiven only when the cure had been effected and the proper sacrifices had been made. Joanna Dewey (*Markan Public Debate*, pp. 117f.) points out that the two stories are linked also by 'hook words' in 1.45 and 2.1f. (τὸν λόγον, ὥστε μηκέτι. . .εἰσελθεῖν, repeated in reverse order).

The form of this first conflict story is unusual. It has the framework of a 'miracle story' – the description of the man's complaint, his cure by Jesus, and finally the demonstration of his recovery as he marches off carrying his bed; but in the middle of this we have a discussion about Jesus' authority to forgive sins. It is possible that this middle section has been added to an original straightforward account of a healing in vv. 1–5a and 11–12 (which could stand on their own): the break in construction in v.10 gives some support to this interpretation. The expansion is often explained as an attempt by the early Church to justify its claim to forgive sins in the name of Jesus (cf. Matt. 16.19; John 20.23). Since it is typical of Mark's style to place one story within another, it is possible that he is responsible for this juxtaposition – though in this particular case the 'insertion' (if such it is) is not an independent story. But stories did not necessarily fall into the neat categories identified by the form critics, and this one may have been more complicated from the beginning. In its present form, the story provides a neat parallel to the last in the series of conflict stories, in 3.1–6, which also includes questions addressed by Jesus to his opponents before the actual healing. Just as exorcism was linked with Jesus' teaching in 1.21–8, so now healing is linked with forgiveness. Jesus is not to be seen as a mere wonder-worker, but as one who proclaims the good news of God's salvation.

For the readers of the gospel, the story brings assurance of the power of Jesus to forgive sins. They, too, may be gathered in a house listening to someone preach **the word**. Just as teaching and exorcism belong together (1.21–82), so do 'speaking the word' and forgiveness. Whether or not the congregation of Mark's day experienced healings, they would certainly know about the new life which comes to those who are forgiven.

1    The statement that Jesus **returned to Capernaum** suggests that he had already carried out his intention to preach throughout the neighbourhood (1.38); the information scarcely tallies with what we were told in 1.45 – namely, that he was unable to enter a town, but perhaps Mark supposes that **some days later** the commotion has died down. The inconsistencies could be the result of editing, since it is possible that 2.1–3.6 is an insertion into an earlier account, in which case 3.7 at one time followed 1.45. **The news went round that he was in the house.** The phrase ἐν οἴκῳ means literally 'in a house', but could also be used idiomatically to mean 'at home'. Since Jesus

himself came from Nazareth (1.9), Mark perhaps means that he is staying in Peter's house, but the phrase could refer to any house in Capernaum; those who first heard Mark's gospel might well envisage a setting very similar to the house in which they were meeting to hear the story read. **So many people collected that there was no room** 2 **left, even in front of the door**: the crowd overflowed into the street, thronging the doorway. Jesus **preached** (lit. 'spoke to them') **the word** – ὁ λόγος, as in 1.45 – a term used in the early Christian community to denote the gospel or good news (cf. Acts 8.4; 17.11). As in 1.21–8, Mark gives us an account of healing set within the context of preaching. The **four men** carrying the **paralysed man**, finding that 3–4 they were unable to get near the doorway, climbed the outside staircase to the flat roof. There they **broke through the roof**. It would have been a fairly simple matter to break up the mixture of twigs, matting and earth which filled the space between the beams of the roof, although a considerable amount of debris would have fallen on the crowd below in the process. **They lowered the mat**: the Greek word (ὁ κράββατος) indicates a cheap bed or mattress which could easily be carried.

**And when Jesus saw their faith. . . .**For the first time, Mark refers 5 to the faith of those who came for healing; it is not, however, the faith of the paralytic alone (though he is presumably included), but that of his four friends as well. Jesus' response is surprising; instead of the expected word of healing, he says **'My son, your sins are forgiven.'** Mark does not tell us whether this man was supposed to have led a particularly sinful life, but we do know that popular opinion regarded physical misfortune as the result of sin (cf. John 9.1–3); Paul took a similar view (1 Cor. 11.30). The belief is common in pagan literature, and Jewish teaching is well illustrated by the Talmudic saying: 'No one gets up from his sick-bed until all his sins are forgiven' (B. Ned. 41a). If the victim shared the prevailing attitude, this might well be sufficient to maintain his state of paralysis and prevent him from responding to a bodily cure. A psychiatrist friend tells the story of a woman who was totally paralysed for two years. When questioned, it was discovered that she had succumbed to the paralysis immediately after witnessing on television a violent killing, which had by chance been broadcast as it took place. Reassurance that she was in no way responsible for the crime resulted in a cure as instantaneous and dramatic as the paralysis. While such cases are undoubtedly rarer than popular imagination supposes, the fact that they happen at all confirms the likelihood that a sense of guilt could cause paralysis, and that the assurance of forgiveness could bring about a cure. Jesus' response is therefore by no means unnatural or digressionary, and is not in itself sufficient reason for supposing that two stories have been joined together. Certainly for Mark, healing and forgiveness belong together.

Jesus' words are striking. The idea of the free forgiveness of sins which they imply was something entirely outside the scope of the Law, where forgiveness was associated with ritual cleansing. Even at Qumran, where we find passages which express confidence that God will forgive sins through his mercy and grace, these are spoken by men who have become members of the community and have atoned for sins by their prayers and by their obedience to the rigorous rules of the community (1QS 9–11). The belief that suffering was a punishment for sins pervades the book of Deuteronomy and is echoed by the prophets (e.g. Isa. 40.2), and perhaps that is the implication of Jesus' words here: the man's illness is sufficient punishment for his sins. The closest parallel in the Old Testament is the declaration of forgiveness in 2 Sam. 12.13, where Nathan tells David 'The Lord has put away your sin' – but where a penalty is exacted in the death of David's child. But do Jesus' words go beyond those of Nathan? Is he assuring the paralytic of God's forgiveness, or is he claiming that he himself has the authority to forgive? There can be no doubt how Mark understands the story, for he spells this out for us in v.10, as well as in the reaction of the Jewish leaders. Jesus is once again doing something which the Law could not do, dealing with the root of the problem, and in that sense the act of forgiveness is parallel to the act of cleansing in the previous story. On that occasion, however, the leper was instructed to carry out the legal requirements; here, no conditions are made, no penalty demanded, and forgiveness is a matter of sheer grace. Such an attitude might well lead to objections from the scribes, who would consider this to be treating sin in an appallingly light way.

6    **Now there were some scribes sitting there.** The sudden introduction of these men into the story appears artificial: why should they be present? The fact that their criticism is unspoken suggests that it was made on a later occasion. Such criticism could certainly have been made during the lifetime of Jesus and so be included in the story from the earliest days, but it would also undoubtedly be familiar both to Mark and to his readers from their own experience, since arguments about Jesus' power to forgive would certainly have taken place between Christians and the Jewish religious leaders in their own day.

7    Jesus' critics refer to him contemptuously as **this fellow.** His words are **blasphemy**, since forgiveness was the prerogative of **God alone.** The Greek idiom emphasizes the internal character of their thoughts:

8    **Jesus realized** (lit. 'in his spirit') ... **what they were thinking** (lit, 'in themselves'), **and said to them: 'Why are you thinking like this?**

9    (lit. 'in your hearts'). **Which is easier – to say. . ."Your sins are forgiven", or to say "Get up! Pick up your mat, and walk?"'** Every conceivable answer has been given to this question. Since forgive-

86

ness is possible for God alone, it is no doubt easier to heal than to forgive. But Jesus asks here whether it is easier *to say* the word of forgiveness or of healing. The form of wording may well be deliberate: since the scribes clearly regard Jesus as having used empty words, he will now demonstrate that for him, as for God, to speak is to act. The scribes can hardly reply that it is easier to say 'Get up and walk', since that will be to acknowledge that Jesus has already done the more difficult thing. But neither can they reply that it is easier to say 'Your sins are forgiven', since Jesus' next action is to speak the word of healing, so demonstrating not only that he is able to do the more difficult thing, but that his words are neither empty nor blasphemous. For a similar question posed by Jesus to his critics cf. 11.29f. The verb translated **get up** (ἔγειρε), which is repeated in vv.11 and 12, is used in 16.6 of Jesus' resurrection: Mark's readers may well have been aware of this implication of the word, which suggests that the man is being offered new life.

'**But so that you may know. . . .**' The sentence is awkward and   10 lacks a main verb. It is possible that we should understand something like 'This has happened. . . .' (For a similar elliptical construction, cf. the Greek of 14.49 with Matt. 26.56.) An alternative suggestion is that the sentence should be understood as a command (the ἵνα being imperative; cf. ἵνα ἐλθὼν ἐπιθῇς in 5.23, and perhaps ἵνα πληρωθῶσιν in 14.49): 'Know that the Son of man has authority. . . .' It is much more likely, however, that Mark's sentence is simply clumsy. We now learn that it is as **the Son of man** that Jesus has authority to forgive sins. It is sometimes suggested that the use of the phrase here results from a misunderstanding, and that the original Aramaic phrase *bar nāšā'* meant simply 'man'; this would mean that the saying originally referred to an authority given to man in general. This interpretation is unsatisfactory: for Jesus to claim that man has the power to forgive sin would certainly justify the charge of blasphemy. Nor would such a general authority have any relationship with Jesus' power to heal, with which forgiveness is so closely linked in this story. Mark clearly believes that the phrase has a more specific meaning than this. For the possible interpretations of Jesus' own use of the phrase, see the additional note on the Son of man (pp. 88–93). Although Mark's use of the phrase 'the Son of man' at this point in his narrative has frequently puzzled commentators, it may well be significant. In Dan. 7.14, the authority exercised by the one like a son of man is authority delivered to him by the Ancient of Days. The scribes protest that only God can forgive sins – and they are right – but Jesus acts here as God's representative and with divine authority. It is not in his own name or in his own strength that he acts, since he exercises a power which has been given to him, and yet he it is who exercises it. For Mark and his readers, the authority of Jesus to forgive sins was an important part of their Christian experience, and it was an authority he exercised now, **on earth**, not simply at the parousia. Whether Jesus himself claimed this wider authority cannot be established with any certainty, since the Church's experience of forgiveness meant that his actions inevitably came to be interpreted in that way. Mark's account of the story reflects a time when the story was being seen as an example of forgiveness, rather than one particular incident: the authority delegated to Jesus is permanent and of universal scope.

This is the first occasion in Mark on which Jesus is said to have offered an explanation of his authoritative action, and it is noteworthy that the reason is that he is accused of claiming to do what only God can do; his previous activity, however remarkable and authoritative it may have been, did not go beyond the boundaries of what was possible for a prophetic or charismatic person. But there is nothing in Jewish literature to suggest that any man – not even a messiah – would have the authority to forgive sins. It is also true that nothing is said in Jewish literature about such authority being given to the Son of man, but it would certainly be appropriate for a figure who acts as God's representative on earth and shares in his judgement to be given this power.

Jesus backs his claim by healing the man. Although this is said to be done so that his opponents **may know that the Son of man has authority**, this demonstration of authority is very different from the demands for a sign which are made by the Pharisees later in the gospel: forgiveness and healing are not here two distinct acts, but belong together as different aspects of one thing, the total restoration of the paralysed man; this act of healing is a sign which is received only by those with faith to recognize its significance.

**He said to the paralysed man**: the break in construction may be the result of an insertion. As the story now runs, it cannot be avoided. 12 The man **got up, straight away picked up his mat and went out**. His action not only demonstrates the reality of the cure, but also indicates his own faith in the healing power of Jesus: a paralysed man cannot stand up – yet he obeys the command instantly! As before, the crowd **were all astounded**, declaring '**We have never seen anything like this before!**' Since Mark has recorded previous healings in Capernaum, he perhaps intends us to understand that this cure – linked as it is with forgiveness – was particularly impressive.

## Additional note: the Son of man

'The Son of man' represents a clumsy Greek phrase – ὁ υἱὸς τοῦ ἀνθρώπου – which is a literal translation of the Aramaic *bar nāšā*'; the anarthrous form, 'a son of man' (*bar nāš*), is used with the meaning 'a man' or 'a human being'. The Greek phrase is used in all four gospels as a self-designation by Jesus, and on only one occasion (John 12.34, where the crowd ask 'Who is this Son of man?') is it attributed to anyone other than Jesus. Although Mark apparently understands it to have been a title used by Jesus of himself, he does not treat it as a christological title comparable to 'Christ' or 'Son of God', since it is not included in the messianic secret but is used openly by Jesus: it is in keeping with this that there is no record of Jesus ever having been 'confessed' as 'Son of man' by the early Church (Acts 7.56 and Rev. 1.13 are no exception to this). The evidence is thus overwhelmingly in favour of the phrase having been used by Jesus himself. But did he use it to refer to himself? And if so, was this some kind of 'messianic' claim?

The phrase is used fourteen times in Mark, and in the great majority of cases it is used in connection with suffering and future vindication. The stress on the necessity of suffering for the Son of man is particularly noticeable in Mark, who has fewer sayings overall than Matthew and Luke, but all three Synoptists emphasize this aspect of the Son of man's destiny, as well as his future vindication; John neatly compresses the two ideas into a single statement by talking about the 'exaltation' or 'glorification' of the Son of man on the cross. The Synoptic sayings are generally divided into three categories: those about the present activity of the Son of man (in Mark, 2.10 and 28); those which refer to his sufferings (in Mark, 8.31; 9.9, 12, 31; 10.33, 45; 14.21 (bis), 41); and those which predict his future vindication (in Mark, 8.38; 13.26; 14.62). But it is well to remember that these categories are not as clear cut as is often assumed, and that there is a certain overlap of ideas: Mark 10.45 describes Jesus' present activity, as well as his future suffering; Mark 8.31, 9.31 and 10.33 all speak of future vindication as well as suffering, and Mark 9.9 refers to the resurrection which follows the suffering of 9.12; significantly, all three sayings about eschatological vindication are found in contexts which describe present persecution and suffering.

In the Old Testament, the equivalent Hebrew phrase, *ben 'āḏām*, is used occasionally, chiefly in poetic passages, as a synonym for man (e.g. Ps. 8.4). Its most striking use is in the book of Ezekiel, where the prophet is frequently addressed by God as 'Son of man' (so too, Dan. 8.17). The Aramaic phrase is used in Dan. 7.13, at the climax of a vision in which the prophet sees four beasts destroying and devouring, until the Ancient of Days sits in judgement and the beasts are slain: one like a son of man then appears on the clouds and is given dominion and glory and kingdom. The ensuing explanation tells us that the beasts represent four kingdoms which make war on the Ancient of Days and the saints of the Most High, and that the kingdom and dominion will finally be given to the saints of the Most High.

Daniel's imagery seems to be derived from ancient creation myths, in which God destroys the powers of chaos and puts man in control of the world. His vision is expounded by the author of the Similitudes of Enoch (1 Enoch 37–71), who refers to the manlike figure as 'the Son of man', and identifies him with the Messiah: he is interpreted as the head of the redeemed and righteous community. Many commentators on the gospels have based their interpretation of the Son of man sayings on the figure in 1 Enoch, but the dating of this book is problematic. It now seems likely that it was composed towards the end of the first century AD – too late to be of relevance to the gospel sayings, except as an interesting contemporary development. The description in 4 Ezra 13 of a man who emerges from the sea and annihilates his enemies dates from the same period.

Beginning from the evangelists' clear belief that Jesus was referring to himself when he spoke of 'the Son of man', the phrase has often been understood as a messianic claim on his part. Some have argued that an eschatological Son of man was expected at the time of Jesus, and that he identified himself with this figure (so Jeremias, *Theology*, pp. 257–76); as we have seen, however, evidence for this expectation is scanty. Others have taken the opposite view, suggesting that the term had little significance in itself and that Jesus saw his vocation primarily in terms of the Suffering Servant of Isaiah (so Dodd, *The Founder of Christianity*, pp. 110–13); but why, in this case, did he refer to himself as 'the Son of man', rather than as 'Servant of the Lord'? Suggestions that the term is derived from Ezekiel have met with little support for, while it might seem appropriate that Jesus should apply to himself a phrase which had been used in addressing a prophet, this in itself cannot explain why the Son of man must suffer or should be expected to come in glory. An interesting variation of this view was, however, put forward by E. Schweizer (e.g. in *Good News*, pp. 166–71) who argued that Jesus used the phrase to express his prophetic calling, which he linked with the innocent sufferings of the righteous described in Isaiah 53 and Wisdom 2–5; the eschatological sayings are therefore a later addition to the tradition.

Since there are frequent echoes of Daniel 7 in the Synoptic sayings, there is perhaps more to be said for the view that Jesus was deliberately referring to Daniel's vision, and that he believed himself to be fulfilling the role of the one like a Son of man – or rather, the role of those who are symbolized by this figure. In other words, he accepted the calling of the saints of the Most High, who suffer at the hands of God's enemies, but who are promised final vindication (so Hooker, *The Son of Man in Mark*, pp. 174–98; C.F.D. Moule, *The Origin of Christology*, pp. 11–22). The phrase was used, not as a title, but as an allusion to this role. Moreover, it may well have been used by Jesus with a corporate significance (as in Daniel 7); Jesus is the nucleus of the righteous and elect community in Israel (see T.W. Manson, *The Teaching of Jesus*, pp. 211–36). This interpretation assumes that the echoes of Daniel 7 are (a) significant and (b) traceable to Jesus himself; both of these assumptions have been challenged (M. Casey, *The Son of Man*); but its greatest difficulty is that it fails to explain how Jesus could refer to himself as 'the Son of man' in this strange, circumlocutionary way.

A very different line of approach has argued that the evangelists were mistaken in assuming that Jesus was referring to himself in speaking about the Son of man. Since Jesus always refers to 'the Son of man' as though he were speaking of someone else, and since he sometimes appears to make a distinction between himself and the Son of man (most notably in 8.38), it has become almost axiomatic for many scholars, especially in Germany, that Jesus spoke about the coming, eschatological Son of man, and that the early Church identified him with this figure after the resurrection (among many others, Bultmann, *Theology of the New Testament*, I, pp. 28–32; F. Hahn, *The Titles of Jesus in Christology*, pp. 15–53). The community then went on to create other 'Son of man' sayings which referred to Jesus' suffering and ministry. This explanation founders on the lack of evidence for first-century expectation of an eschatological Son of man. It also assumes that an extraordinary leap was made by the community, which is credited with creating Son of man sayings of an apparently entirely inappropriate kind. Although this view has long dominated discussion of the question, it is badly flawed.

An even more radical solution to the problem is that which argues that Jesus never used the phrase at all, whether with reference to himself or someone else, and that all the sayings are therefore creations of the early community (e.g. P.Vielhauer, *Z.Th.K.*, 60, 1963, pp.133–77; H. Conzelmann, *An Outline of Theology*, pp.131–7). This solution fails to explain the remarkable fact that, according to the gospels, every occurrence of the phrase is found in the mouth of Jesus.

A fresh approach has been opened up by scholars working on the Aramaic background of the phrase who have found new evidence to support an old suggestion that the phrase is little more than an Aramaic idiom meaning 'I'. In an appendix to Matthew Black's *Aramaic Approach to the Gospels and Acts*, Geza Vermes argued that the Aramaic phrase *bar nāš(ā')* was used in the first century AD, not only with the meaning 'man', but as a circumlocution for 'I'. A parallel Aramaic idiom, *hāhû' gabrā'*, 'this person', is used in a similar way. But Vermes' suggestion that the sayings clearly refer to the speaker is too specific; in none of the examples which he supplies is the phrase clearly equivalent to 'I'; rather, the speaker happens to be in the circumstances described in the saying. (See also *Jesus the Jew*, pp. 160–

91). Maurice Casey has defined the idiom more precisely when he says that a speaker could use it in a general statement in order to say something about himself. If this interpretation is correct, we have an explanation for some of the more general Son of man sayings: men in general have authority to forgive sins – hence Jesus claims that authority; men in general must die – hence Jesus must die. But the sayings about the future glory of the Son of man – the sayings which according to some scholars form the core of authentic utterances – must be creations of the early Church, the result of interpreting Jesus' chosen way of referring to himself in the light of Daniel 7. But why should Jesus choose this somewhat odd self-designation? And why should a literal translation of the phrase into Greek be so carefully preserved by the evangelists? And why should there be such an emphasis in the sayings on the necessity for suffering and the certainty of future vindication? This explanation leaves all these questions unanswered.

Building on the work of Vermes and Casey, Barnabas Lindars has suggested that the phrase refers, not to men in general, nor to 'I' in particular, but to someone in the particular circumstances in which the speaker finds himself (*Jesus Son of Man*, pp. 17–28). In Jesus' case, it is used to refer to his mission: Lindars identifies nine sayings which are 'authentic', all of which refer to the present authority of the Son of man or to his destiny of suffering. The phrase is thus used by Jesus as a way of referring to his vocation, rather than as a claim to personal authority.

These investigations have shown that it was possible for Jesus to use the phrase 'the Son of man' as a way of referring to himself. But why should he have done so? And why should the sayings in which the phrase is used refer specifically to his mission? We suggest that the answer to these questions may perhaps be found in Daniel 7 and Ezekiel: in other words, the discovery that the phrase could be used as an acceptable way of referring to oneself provides the answer to the problem as to how Jesus could have applied the imagery of Daniel 7 to himself. Indeed, if the vision of Daniel 7 was widely known at the time of Jesus (as it appears to have been, judging from its use in both Jewish and Christian documents), and if the repeated use of the term in Ezekiel made any impact on the book's readers (as it surely must have done), it seems unlikely that Jesus could have used the phrase to refer to his own mission *without* reminding his readers of its use in Daniel and Ezekiel. If the researches of Aramaic scholars have provided the answer to the question as to how Jesus could have used the term as a self-designation, study of those Old Testament passages where it is used has suggested an answer to the question as to why he should have done so. The phrase was by no means a colourless way of referring to oneself: it conjured up all kinds of associations: the prophetic calling; the mission of God's obedient people; the possibility of suffering for those who were faithful to his will; the promise of final vindication. Jesus used the phrase, we suggest, not as a title, not because he was claiming to 'be' the messianic Son of man, but because he accepted for himself the role of obedient faith which the term evokes, and because he called others to share that calling with him. (See further, M.D. Hooker, 'Is the Son of Man problem really insoluble?')

All these ideas are used in Mark's gospel, but they are by no means confined to Mark. We cannot assume that any of the Son of man sayings represents Jesus' own words accurately, since they are all likely to have been adapted and elaborated with the passing of time. But taken together, the sayings provide overwhelming evidence that Jesus did use the phrase, and that he used it of himself; though they are so varied, it seems possible that in their different ways they reflect various aspects of the significance which he himself saw in the term.

For further discussion, see: M.D. Hooker, *The Son of Man in Mark*; Maurice Casey, *Son of Man*; B. Lindars, *Jesus Son of Man*.

# 9   JESUS AND THE OUTCASTS                    2.13–17

## *(Matt. 9.9–13; Luke 5.27–32)*

**(13) He went out again beside the shore of the lake; and the whole crowd came to him, and he taught them. (14) And as he went along, he saw Levi,[1] son of Alphaeus, at his seat in the customhouse, and he said to him, 'Follow me'; and he got up and followed him. (15) And when [Jesus] was having a meal in his house, there were many tax-gatherers and sinners who reclined with Jesus and his disciples, for there were many who followed him. (16) And some scribes who were Pharisees saw him eating with sinners and tax-gatherers, and said to his disciples: 'Why does he eat[2] with tax-gatherers and sinners?' (17) Jesus heard them and answered: 'Those who are well do not need a doctor, only those who are sick. I have not come to summon the righteous, but sinners.'**

Two brief stories – the call of another disciple (vv.13–14) and the account of a meal (vv.15–17) – are linked by the fact that, in both, Jesus

---

1 D, Θ, fam. 13 and a few other mss read *James*.
2 Following B D W. Many mss add *and drink*.

is dealing with outcasts from society, so demonstrating again his authority to forgive sinners: there is thus an obvious link with the previous narrative. For Mark's first readers, Jesus' call of an outsider like Levi to be his disciple and his willingness to consort with men and women who were regarded as irreligious by pious Jews would both be amazing; since many of them would themselves have been outsiders, it was also truly good news. No one is excluded from the forgiving grace of God.

13 Returning to **the shore of the lake**, where he had already called four men to follow him, Jesus **taught** the assembled **crowd**; as so
14 often happens, Mark does not tell us what he taught. **Levi, son of Alphaeus**, is not included in the list of the Twelve in 3.16–19, although there is reference there to a 'James, son of Alphaeus'. This apparent discrepancy has been solved in some MSS by the substitution of James' name for Levi's in the present passage. Matthew also identifies the tax-gatherer with one of the Twelve, but in his account it is the name of Matthew himself which replaces Levi's. It has sometimes been suggested that this conflicting evidence results from one man having two names, but to explain all the variations he would have needed three! It is possible that James and Levi were brothers; the substitution of other names for Levi's is probably due to the difficulty which was felt in finding someone outside the circle of the Twelve apparently called to discipleship in a manner exactly parallel to the call of the four fishermen in Mark 1.16–20. But Mark himself does not appear to be aware of the difficulty, nor to believe that the call to follow Jesus is limited to the Twelve; the call comes to others in his story (see 8.34; 10.21 and 52), and it comes to all who hear his gospel: indeed, he may well have deliberately included this story of someone who was called to be a disciple but was *not* one of the Twelve.

Jesus finds Levi **at his seat in the custom-house**. As the Sea of Galilee divided the tetrarchy of Herod Antipas from that of Philip, to the east of the lake, Levi would have been an officer in the employ of Herod. Like the tax-gatherers employed directly by the Romans, he would have been regarded askance by his fellow countrymen, and especially by those who aspired to religious purity, not only because all these officials were notoriously dishonest, but because they were continuously in contact with Gentiles. For Jesus to call ordinary fishermen to be his disciples was extraordinary; but to call a tax-gatherer to follow him was nothing short of scandalous. This perhaps explains why Mark has told the story at this point, for the call of a notorious sinner to be a disciple must have seemed to Mark an act of forgiveness parallel to that in the preceding story. It is a story about saving grace, for there are no penalties, and no demands, except to follow Jesus.

15 It is by no means clear where the story in vv.15–17 is set. Mark says

simply that 'he' **was having a meal in his house**. Many commentators suppose that the house is Levi's , and that he had invited Jesus and his other disciples to a meal; this is how Luke understood the verse (Luke 5.29). But the last word of v.14 referred to Jesus (αὐτῷ), and it is probable that Mark means that Jesus himself is the host. The explanation of this ambiguity may well be that vv.15–17 circulated as a separate story in which the 'he' would obviously refer to Jesus. The guests **reclined** at table – the verb (κατακεῖσθαι) suggests that this was a feast rather than an ordinary meal; the saying in v.19 will explain why. The phrase **tax-gatherers and sinners**, used three times in this short story, combines two nouns in a somewhat odd way, as though sinning were an occupation. Mark probably means 'other sinners'. It is often supposed that the term was used by the Pharisees to refer to 'the people of the land', i.e. all those who did not keep the Pharisaic ideal of purity (which would mean the great majority of Jews). Even if the Pharisees referred to the rest of their countrymen as 'sinners', however – and it is by no means certain that this was the case – it is unlikely that Mark would do so; the term is more likely to refer to notorious sinners who deliberately violated the Law, and who were thus treated as religious and social outcasts. (See E.P. Sanders, *Jesus and Judaism*, pp. 174–211.) They ate with **Jesus and his disciples**. This is the first time Mark has referred to a group of disciples, and he probably has in mind a somewhat larger number than the five men whose names he has already given, since he tells us immediately that **there were many who followed him** (lit. 'there were many and they followed him'), a phrase which might, however, refer to the 'many tax-gatherers and sinners'. It was customary for Jewish rabbis to have a group of pupils (μαθηταί); the use of this word here for Jesus' disciples emphasizes again the importance of his teaching role. For Mark, however, a disciple is primarily one who follows Jesus (1.17f., 20; 2.14; 8.34; 10.21, 52 ) and shares his ministry (3.14f.; 6.12f.).

**Pharisees** were pious men who adhered very strictly to the written  16
Law, and who regarded the oral tradition (which had grown up as an explanation of the written code and was designed to defend it against possible breaches) as equally binding. They were undoubtedly sincere and devout men, but their desire to be faithful to the minutiae of the Torah inevitably separated them from other people. The derivation of the term 'Pharisees' is uncertain, but the word probably means 'separated ones' (from the Hebrew root *pāraš*). In doctrine, they were more progressive than the priestly party of the Sadducees, believing both in the resurrection of the dead and in angels, and in this respect they were closer to the position of Jesus. But their very piety and devotion to the Torah, and their resulting condemnation of all who fell short of their own standards, inevitably led to a clash with Jesus. The

opposition of the Pharisees to Jesus has probably been exaggerated, however, because of the later antagonism between the Pharisees and the Christian community. This antagonism inevitably coloured the evangelist's understanding of the Pharisees and can be seen most clearly in the 'Woes' of Matthew 23. The **scribes** would tend to belong to this group. (On the Pharisees, see Josephus, *Wars*, II.8.14; *Antiquities*, XIII.10.6; XVIII.1.3; Schürer, *History*, II, pp. 385–403.) Mark tells us that they **saw him eating**, but their scruples would certainly have prevented them from joining such company, so that if a conversation with Jesus took place it could only have been at a later time. They are said to have spoken to Jesus' **disciples** – a detail which seems to reflect later disputes between the early Christian community and the synagogue. It is likely that this story was used to justify the practice of Jewish and Gentile Christians eating together, but this does not necessarily exclude the possibility that such an incident took place in the ministry of Jesus himself.

**'Why does he eat with tax-gatherers and sinners?'** It is possible to understand these words as a statement expressing the scribes' astonishment at Jesus' conduct, but it seems best to take them as a question (the introductory ὅτι being used interrogatively). We then have in chapter 2 a series of questions posed by Jesus' opponents regarding his own behaviour and that of his disciples, all introduced by the query 'Why?' (vv.7, 16, 18, 24). Since they themselves adhered to the kind of regulation set out in Mark 7.1–8, their disapproval of Jesus eating in such company would be due in part to the possibility that the food provided would not have been tithed in accordance with the Law (e.g. Deut. 14.22; cf. Matt. 23.23) or prepared in the proper way (see the discussion of 7.1–8), and to the possibility that he might come into contact with unclean garments or dishes. This particular accusation does not feature in this story, however. Instead, the Pharisees protest that Jesus mixes with sinners – with men and women who have deliberately excluded themselves from the people of God. They would naturally be indignant if Jesus, who claimed to teach and heal with God-given authority, mixed with such people, apparently indifferent to their violation of the commandments of God. Mark's first readers must certainly have seen the relevance of this story for their own situation, for many of them had been outsiders – perhaps 'sinners', perhaps Gentiles. If the early Christian community came to set aside the regulations regarding table-fellowship with outsiders, then it was because they became aware that the coming of Jesus had created a new situation in which there was no division between the so-called 'righteous' and 'sinners'. A new division has, however, been created – between those who respond to Jesus and those who reject him. (The words 'and drink', which occur in many MSS, are a natural addition, and possibly due to assimilation to Luke 5.30.)

Jesus replies by using a familar proverb, the point of which is 17
drawn out in the final words, **'I have not come to summon the righteous, but sinners.'** The reference to 'coming' perhaps reflects a later
understanding of Jesus' ministry, but the contrast between 'not this . . .
but that' (οὐ . . . ἀλλά) is typical of many of Jesus' sayings in Mark. It is
intriguing to note that the saying implies that there were some who
*were* **righteous!** Are we meant to understand this as irony? It is
difficult to think that Mark supposed that those who considered
themselves to be righteous were anything of the sort. But might Jesus
himself perhaps have believed that there were some who were in fact
obeying God's will and who did not need his help? At any rate, his concern was with **sinners.** If Mark means that Jesus himself was the host
at the meal, then the verb 'to summon' (καλέσθαι) could have the
sense 'to invite', though Luke (5.32) has understood it of a summons
to repentance. The attitude expressed in the saying seems as characteristic of Jesus as righteous indignation was of the scribes. As in the
story of the leper, it seems that Jesus' own power to bring forgiveness
is understood as greater than the power of uncleanness to contaminate: like a doctor dealing with the sick, he is able to venture among
sinners and help them. Once again, the story demonstrates the extraordinary authority of Jesus.

# 10   OLD AND NEW                                        2.18–22

### *(Matt. 9.14–17; Luke 5.33–9; Thomas 47;104)*

**(18) Now John's disciples and the Pharisees were fasting; and
some people came and asked him, 'Why do the disciples of John
and the disciples of the Pharisees fast, but your disciples do not
fast?' (19) And Jesus said to them, 'Can the friends of the bridegroom fast while he is with them? As long as the bridegroom is
with them, they cannot fast. (20) But the time will come when the
bridegroom is taken away from them, and when that day comes,
they will fast. (21) No one sews a patch of unwashed cloth on to an
old garment; if he does, the patch tears away from it, the new from
the old, and makes a bigger hole. (22) And no one pours new wine
into old skins; if he does, the wine will burst the skins and both the
wine and the skins will be lost. New wine goes into fresh skins.'[1]**

Once again we have two short sections, each complete in itself,
joined together because of their common theme, the new situation

---

1 The omission of the last clause of v.22 in some (Western) MSS was probably
accidental.

brought about by the ministry of Jesus. The element of conflict is hinted at in both. The first, vv.18–20, is a short pronouncement story about fasting: the verb 'to fast' is used no fewer than six times in these few lines. Although those who question Jesus criticize the behaviour of the disciples, he supports them: so far in Mark we have not met the criticism which will later be brought against the disciples by Jesus himself, on the grounds that they are blind and deaf when confronted with his words and deeds; indeed, in this chapter and the next they stand in clear contrast to those who, because of their blindness and hardness of heart, are opposed to Jesus.

The wording of Jesus' reply reflects the situation of the Church: **the bridegroom** has been **taken away**. The community's joy in the gospel is tempered with sorrow at the absence of its Lord, and this sorrow provides a very different cause for fasting. The two sayings which follow reflect the tensions between old and new, between Judaism and Christianity, which meant that Christians found it impossible to continue within the mother faith.

The reference to John the Baptist's disciples may reflect the problems of the early Christian community in understanding John's relation to the age of salvation. If his followers fasted, were they in fact not trying to patch the old garment (albeit with a suitably preshrunken patch of material)? Certainly they are found here in company with the Pharisees, representatives of the old order.

18    Although Mark regards the Baptist as Jesus' forerunner, **John's disciples** are here coupled with **the Pharisees** as belonging to the old order. It is possible that this reference to the Pharisees, together with the strange phrase **the disciples of the Pharisees** (Pharisees did not have disciples), are editorial additions intended to integrate this story into the series of conflict stories. If so, the original narrative would have pointed simply to the contrast between Jesus and John, as in Matt. 11.18f.//Luke 7.33f. Those who belonged to the old era **were fasting**. The main fast of the Jews was that of the Day of Atonement (Lev. 16.29; cf. Acts 27.9), but the Pharisees fasted on the second and fourth days of the week (cf. Luke 18.12). As for the followers of John the Baptist, one would expect them to share his asceticism. If the story originally referred to his disciples alone, and not to the Pharisees, then it is possible that they were mourning his imprisonment or even (if the incident belongs to a later period in Jesus' ministry) his death. In this case there would be no particular reason to expect the disciples of Jesus to fast also, unless – as is possible – Jesus was regarded as a follower of the Baptist. But since fasting was a normal practice for the pious, it would be natural to expect a religious leader to follow suit, and there is no need to link this incident with John's fate. **But your disciples**: the question concerns the behaviour of Jesus' disciples, but it is put to Jesus, since their failure to fast is as-

sumed, correctly, to reflect his teaching. The disciples' behaviour reflects more than his teaching, however, since it reflects his presence: Jesus brings in a new order, and his followers can only rejoice. But the fact that the criticism is brought against the disciples, rather than against Jesus himself, could be a sign that the story in its present form reflects a later dispute between Christians and their Jewish opponents. It was natural for Christians under pressure to look back to the ministry of Jesus and seek guidance there.

Jesus responds with a short parable – the first that Mark has given       19–20
us: **Can the friends of the bridegroom fast while he is with them?**
The main point is clear enough: the disciples do not fast, because this is the time of joy and fulfilment. The problem is in knowing how much of vv.19f. belongs to the original parable. It seems clear that the statement in v.20 that **the time will come when the bridegroom is taken away from them** is a later addition, for it is not usual for a bridegroom to be 'taken away'. This verse is an allegorical expansion, which contrasts the time of joy with the subsequent period when Jesus is no longer present. The parallel saying in Thomas 104 (used in a context where Jesus is justifying his own refusal to fast) avoids the awkward reference to the bridegroom's removal: 'But when the bridegroom comes out of the bride-chamber, then let them fast and pray.' This sounds like an echo of Joel 2.16, which is a call to the people to 'sanctify a fast'. The information that **when that day comes, they will fast** suggests that by Mark's time the practice of fasting had grown up in the Christian community, and that the expansion is meant to justify this: it is far more relevant to this later situation than to the discussion as Mark depicts it, where indeed it somewhat blunts the point that Jesus is making. V.19b is not found in either Matthew or Luke and this sentence too, with its implication that **the bridegroom is with them** for a limited time, may well be an addition to the original saying. This would leave us with v.19a – **Can the friends of the bridegroom fast while he is with them?** Yet even this in its present form seems to suggest by its wording that the presence of the bridegroom is only temporary (**while** = ἐν ᾧ = ἐν τῷ χρονῷ ᾧ). It is clear that Mark understands the bridegroom to be Jesus himself, and when vv.19b–20 are included, this is the only possible interpretation. But was this the original meaning? Many recent commentators have argued against the existence of any allegorical details in the parables, and for this reason alone would eliminate vv.19b–20, suggesting that Jesus spoke originally simply of guests rejoicing at a wedding. In this case, the point of Jesus' saying must be that because the Kingdom of God is near, this is a time of rejoicing, comparable to a wedding-feast.

But the assumption that parables never contain allegory is too dogmatic, and in this particular case the saying in v.19a focuses on the bridegroom, implying a comparison between Jesus and the bridegroom: it is because he is present that his disciples rejoice, and their joy is entirely dependent on him. There is no precedent in the Old Testament for referring to any 'messianic' figure as a bridegroom, but the image is used of God (Isa. 54.4–8; 62.5; Ezek. 16.7ff.). Whether or not Jesus intended to identify himself with the bridegroom, the identification quickly became inevitable. For Mark, the saying points once again to the significance of Jesus: his presence is the occasion for such rejoicing that – as at a wedding – ordinary duties are put aside as of lesser importance. The events which are taking place in Jesus overrule even religious practices like fasting.

21    The radical nature of what is taking place is summed up in the two parabolic sayings which follow. The old forms of Judaism – symbolized by the practice of fasting – cannot contain the new factors introduced into the situation by the coming of Jesus and his proclamation of the Kingdom of God. In the first saying, we have a new **patch** which makes the **hole** in **an old garment** worse. The meaning was apparently incomprehensible to Luke, who refers to cutting a patch out of a new garment to mend an old one! Thomas (who has both of these sayings) speaks of sewing an old patch on a new garment, which seems equally confused, but would make sense in the *Markan* context as a rejection of the Jewish custom of fasting. Mark perhaps envisages the garment tearing when it is washed and the **unwashed cloth** shrinks. Or perhaps the meaning is simply that the patch of new material is so strong that it pulls away from the hole, in which case the saying is a close parallel to the one that follows in v.22,

22    where the **new wine** is clearly too strong for the **old skins**, which are brittle with age. Yet the conclusions of the two parables are certainly different: **new wine goes into fresh skins**, but an old garment presumably needs to be patched with a piece of old material. In the first saying, it is the old garment which is the centre of interest and which is ruined, and even in the second, where the emphasis is on the new wine, the loss of the skins seems to be as much a disaster as the loss of the new wine (this is even clearer in Matthew). Both sayings show concern lest the old be lost; yet both point to the truth that something new and fresh cannot be contained within the limits of the old and indeed must inevitably destroy the old. So, for Mark, the new religion could not be contained within Judaism. The different versions of these two parables in the Synoptic Gospels probably reflect the debate which went on in the early Christian communities regarding the relationship between Judaism and Christianity. Cf. also the story of the water intended for the rites of purification which becomes wine in John 2.1–10. In the mouth of Jesus, the sayings would have been a challenge to his hearers to recognize the change in attitude which the coming of the Kingdom required. His message was not merely (like John's), 'Repent!' but 'Believe in the good news': the time

for restoration was past, and the time to accept the new age had arrived. It is perhaps no accident that the symbolism of tearing a garment reappears in the scene in chapter 14 where Caiaphas tears his clothes, for at that moment the old forms of religion are, in Mark's view, doomed. Similarly, the tearing of the temple veil in 15.38 signifies the end of the old and the birth of the new.

# 11  LORD OF THE SABBATH                              2.23–8

### (Matt. 12.1–8; Luke 6.1–5)

**(23) One sabbath he was walking through the cornfields, and his disciples began to make their way, plucking the ears of corn. (24) Then the Pharisees said to him: 'Look! Why are they doing what is forbidden on the sabbath?' (25) And he answered, 'Have you never read what David did when he was in need, and when he and his companions were hungry? (26) He went into the house of God, in the time of Abiathar the high priest, and ate the sacred bread which it is forbidden to eat – except for the priests – and he even gave it to his companions.' (27) And he said to them, 'The sabbath was made for man, and not man for the sabbath. (28) Therefore the Son of man is Lord even of the sabbath.'**

In this incident Jesus is again challenged about the actions of his disciples, but this time they are accused not of neglecting extra religious observance, but of doing something which is forbidden. Both this narrative and the next, in 3.1–6, are concerned with what may and may not be done on the sabbath. The question of sabbath observance was of importance for the early Christian community and a point of dispute between Jews and Jewish Christians, who came under attack for their lax interpretation of the regulations. These stories would clearly have been relevant to this situation, but this does not necessarily mean that they originated there, as some (e.g. Bultmann) have suggested; there is no reason to deny the possibility that such disputes took place between the Jewish authorities and Jesus himself. Nevertheless, stories which appear to us to be primarily of historical interest probably had a much more existential significance for Mark's first readers, who might well have been worried about whether or not it was necessary for them to keep the sabbath. Most Gentile Christians apparently did not keep the sabbath (or other Jewish regulations), but celebrated the 'Lord's day' instead. Jewish Christians would continue to observe the sabbath, but while some of them felt that *all* Christians should do so, others took a more liberal attitude. Jewish readers would find here assurance that their Lord was greater than the sabbath. But if (as is likely) Mark's first readers were Gentiles, then they would probably have seen in these stories a somewhat different significance, and understood them to mean that they were not in any way bound by the command to keep the Jewish sabbath. Certainly that is the way in which they have been interpreted in the Christian community ever since.

23    As usual, there is little indication of time and place, except that the incident took place **one sabbath**, as Jesus and his disciples were **walking through the cornfields**: in Palestine, grain is ripe and ready for reaping in early summer (our April or May). **His disciples began to make their way, plucking the ears of corn**: the strangeness of Mark's statement is normally disguised in English by the fact that the verbs are usually turned around and translated 'as the disciples made their way, they began to pluck the ears of corn', which is the picture we expect. The verb translated **make their way** (ὁδὸν ποιεῖν) means literally 'to make or build a road'. It is usually explained as a latinism (= *iter facere*), meaning 'to make a journey', but is sometimes understood as meaning that the disciples made a path by tearing up the corn. Had they indeed behaved in this way, one would expect the field's owner to protest even more vigorously than the Pharisees! What could have led the disciples to destroy the corn in such an apparently wanton manner? Duncan Derrett has suggested that the answer lies in the right of the king (set out in later Jewish law) to break through private property and build himself a road (e.g. M. Sanhedrin 2.4); we are to understand the disciples as 'making a way' by tramping down the standing corn (*Studies in the New Testament*, I, pp. 85ff.). At the historical level, such an action seems extremely unlikely, but in view of the comparison with David later in the pericope, it is certainly possible that Mark deliberately chose language which suggested that the disciples made a path for Jesus through the fields. Cf. also 1.2f., where John's mission is to 'prepare the way' for Jesus; later in the gospel, the same word (ὁδός) is used of the road to Jerusalem and the path of discipleship (see, especially, 10.32, 52). Mark describes the disciples also as **plucking the ears of corn**. Derrett argues that the action described by Mark (τίλλοντες τοὺς στάχυας) was in fact that of picking the grain out of the ears, rather than plucking it from the stalk – the idle rubbing of wheat in the hands, rather than pulling it from the ground: it was thus 'threshing' rather than 'reaping'. Whatever the exact meaning of the Greek, it seems that Mark thinks of the disciples as both picking and rubbing the grain.

24    The action of gathering ears of grain while passing through the fields is permitted in Deut. 23.25. The protest of **the Pharisees** is due to the fact that it was **the sabbath**. Both reaping and threshing were included in the thirty-nine primary activities which were defined as

'work' (M. Shabbath 7.2). In fact, Deut. 23.25 distinguishes between plucking a few ears by hand and cutting the corn with a sickle, and it would therefore have been reasonable to suppose that using a sickle was truly work, but plucking by hand was not. The scribal interpretation, however, appears to have been more rigorous. Yet it is only according to the scribal view that the disciples' action in plucking a few ears can be understood as work and so be said to contravene the Torah. The sudden appearance of the Pharisees on the scene again seems artificial, and one may well wonder what they were doing in a field on the sabbath. Their presence there is not impossible, since there is no suggestion that the disciples have walked more than the distance permitted on the sabbath, and the fields could have been close to the town, within the sabbath's day's journey of approximately 1,000 yards. Nevertheless, an attack by Pharisees on the activity of disciples suggests that the story may well owe something to a later dispute.

Jesus replies with a counter-question and a reference to scripture. **25–6** He refers the Pharisees to the example of David, generally regarded in Jewish tradition – in spite of some Old Testament stories – as a model of piety, whose actions had in fact contravened the Torah: **'Have you never read what David did when he was in need, and when he and his companions were hungry? He went into the house of God ... and ate the sacred bread which it is forbidden to eat – except for the priests – and he even gave it to his companions.'** The statement that this took place **in the time of Abiathar the high priest** is incorrect; the high priest at the time was Ahimelech, father of Abiathar (1 Sam. 21.1–6) but, since the latter was much better known, the mistake is a natural one. David, like the disciples, did something which is **forbidden** (the phrase οὐκ ἔξεστιν, used in v.24, is repeated here) by eating the sacred bread or 'shewbread', the twelve loaves which were set out each week in the sanctuary in the presence of God. In fact the command in Lev. 24.5–9 that the bread should be eaten only by priests belonged to a tradition later than the time of David, though we may assume that the Levitical passage incorporates an ancient prohibition. This apparent breach of the regulations was explained by rabbinic exegetes as due to necessity: the saving of life took precedence over the regulations. It is doubtful whether David's need and that of **his companions** was as desperate as this, even though they are described as **hungry**; certainly there is no reason to suppose that the disciples were so hungry that it was necessary for them to pluck the corn. In fact, the circumstances of the two stories are quite different: the disciples are criticized, not for eating the grain, but for plucking it on the sabbath. The events in 1 Sam. 21 may well have taken place on the sabbath, since the bread was set out before the Lord each sabbath (Lev. 24.8) and according to the

Midrash (Midrash Rabbah Lev. 32.3), the bread was removed and eaten by the priests on the following sabbath. But even if this is so, it is only incidental to the story in 1 Samuel. Why, then, is the parallel drawn? To Christians reading this story, the obvious explanation is that the parallel is between David and Jesus: if the regulations regarding what is holy (the shewbread) were set aside for **David** and **his companions**, how much more can the regulations regarding what is holy (the sabbath) be set aside for Jesus and *his* companions? Such an argument was entirely appropriate in the early Christian community, where it was allegiance to Jesus which divided men and women from Judaism. But if this reply goes back to Jesus himself, then perhaps the comparison was originally between the special situations rather than between David and Jesus; in other words, Jesus is claiming that a new situation has arisen in which rules are set aside – a claim very similar to that made in v.19a.

The real reason why the disciples are **doing what is forbidden** is not, however, the fact that they are disciples of Jesus, or that a new situation has arisen, but simply that they have never bothered with the niceties of the oral tradition on which the Pharisees placed such importance. Jesus sides with them over against the Pharisees, who hedge the Torah around with innumerable regulations for fear that they might accidentally or unknowingly transgress the will of God.

27 A second answer to their accusation, given in vv.27f., fits this situation better, since it suggests that the Pharisees were so eager not to transgress that they lost sight of the real purpose of the commandments. In spite of all their endeavours, the will of God – that men and women should rest and enjoy the sabbath – was not performed; they had failed to understand that **the sabbath was made for man, and not man for the sabbath**. The fresh introduction to this saying – **and he said to them** – indicates that this is an independent reply. Since it fits the incident better, this response has the better claim to being the original; vv. 25f., which reflect a rabbinic style of argument, may be a later addition to the story.

It must not be supposed that Jesus' position here is entirely revolutionary: a parallel saying in the Midrash (Mekilta 109b on Ex. 31.14) – 'the sabbath is delivered unto you, and you are not delivered to the sabbath' – suggests that some Jewish rabbis would have agreed with his attitude for, although the rabbi to whom this saying is attributed lived later than Jesus, he was probably repeating earlier tradition. Jewish interpretation is also of interest in that it consistently understands the sabbath to be God's gift to Israel, instituted for the sake of the chosen people, not mankind in general.

28 The climax of the narrative comes with the concluding statement, **Therefore the Son of man is Lord even of the sabbath**. It has often been suggested that 'the Son of man' here is a mistake for 'man', and

that Mark misunderstood the Aramaic parallelism of the original, in which *bar nāšā'* was simply a variant for 'man' in v.27. It seems unlikely, however, that Jesus would have spoken of mankind in general as Lord of the sabbath. Certainly Mark understands the saying as referring to Jesus himself. An alternative explanation holds v.28 to be an addition to the original saying in v.27, reflecting the early Christian community's desire to stress the personal lordship of Jesus over the sabbath (so many commentators, including Klostermann, Rawlinson, Taylor, Nineham, Anderson). It is significant, however, that v.28 follows logically from the previous verse, and that the use of the term 'the Son of man' here appears to be by no means accidental. If the sabbath was made for man (i.e. for Israel), then it is to be expected that the Son of man (representing obedient Israel, restored to dominion in the world) should be Lord even of the sabbath (see the additional note on the Son of man, pp. 88–93): the original purpose of God, set out in v.27, is fulfilled through him. If Jesus allows his disciples to continue to be 'irreligious', that demonstrates not carelessness in respect of the Torah, but the freedom of one who is confident that he is doing God's will; and the justification for their action, offered in v.27, is not merely the opinion of one Jewish rabbi over against that of others but is the authoritative statement of the Son of man. In Mark's presentation, this second response, like the first, centres on the status of Jesus and underlines his authority.

# 12   THE OPPOSITION HARDENS                      3.1–6

*(Matt. 12.9–14; Luke 6.6–11)*

**(1) He entered the synagogue once more, and a man was there with a withered hand. (2) And they watched him, to see whether he would heal him on the sabbath, so that they might bring a charge against him. (3) Then he said to the man with the withered hand, 'Come and stand out here.' (4) And he asked them, 'Is it permitted to do good on the sabbath, or to do evil? To save life, or to kill?' But they said nothing. (5) And he looked round at them with anger, grieved at their hardness of heart. Then he said to the man, 'Stretch out your hand.' And he stretched it out, and his hand was restored to normal. (6) And the Pharisees went out straight away, and began to plot against him with the Herodians, looking for a way to destroy him.**

The series of conflict stories reaches its climax in this narrative. Like the story of the paralytic in 2.1–10, this is a miracle story with a difference: in form-critical categories, each is as much a pronouncement story as a miracle story. In both cases, the account of the cure contains a question put by Jesus to his critics, so that the focus of the story is not the cure in itself but its significance. In this instance, the question at issue is again that of sabbath observance. As in 2.1–10, Jesus makes his point by curing the sick man and restoring life to withered limbs. The saying in v.4 reminds us of the significance of Jesus for the Christian community, since it is he who 'does good' and who 'saves life'. The story would have been relevant to the problem which concerned many in the early Church – namely, the place of the Torah. Jesus' action is in no way contrary to the Torah: rather, he points to its real intention. It is important to note that Mark's account suggests that the real issue is not whether or not the sabbath should be kept, but *how* it should be kept. Throughout his gospel, Mark depicts Jesus as a faithful upholder of the Torah (1.44; 3.4; 7.8–13; 10.3–9; 12.29–31; cf. M.D. Hooker, in *It is Written*), who attacks not the Torah itself, but the interpretation given to its demands by the religious authorities of his day. It is not, then, the Torah which is at fault but those who misunderstand it; the purpose of the Torah is to bring life, but when it is wrongly interpreted, it becomes an instrument of evil and the bearer of death. With this, compare Paul's teaching in Romans 7.

This incident forms a climax to the story so far: in dramatic terms, it points forward to the 'trial' scene before Caiaphas at the end of the gospel. Jesus' opponents watch him because they wish to bring an accusation against him; his claims in chapter 2 to have authority as the Son of man, together with the charge of blasphemy brought against him in 2.7, will be echoed in 14.62–4. Those who plot his death are a remarkable combination of religious and political leaders – Pharisees and Herodians: those who bring it about will also be religious and political leaders, though it will be the priests and the Roman authorities who succeed. And here as there, we notice the irony in the story: the religious authorities plan to accuse Jesus, but in reality it is they who are on trial and they who are judged, because in spite of their concern for the Torah, they are failing to do God's will. Finally, we note that here, in the synagogue, Jesus **looked round. . .with anger**; when he arrives in the temple, he looks round (Mark 11.11) and shows his anger at what he sees in actions which lead directly to his death. Whether Mark himself was aware of this dramatic foreshadowing or not we do not know.

Early readers of the gospel who were familiar with the Old Testament may have seen a link with the story of the healing of Jeroboam's withered hand by 'a man of God' in 1 Kings 13.4–6; the two stories are in fact very different, however.

1     **He entered the synagogue.** No particular synagogue is mentioned; the phrase is the equivalent of 'he went to church'. Mark once again

depicts Jesus as one who – in spite of the charges brought against him – faithfully adhered to Jewish religious practices. **And they watched** 2 **him . . . so that they might bring a charge against him.** In Mark's context, 'they' must clearly be understood as the Pharisees who are mentioned in v.6. It is notable how their opposition has grown throughout 2.1–3.6; hitherto they have responded indignantly to those actions of Jesus which they have witnessed, but now they are said to be watching him with the deliberate purpose of bringing a charge against him. According to Ex. 31.14 the penalty for sabbath breaking was death, and although it was unlikely that this could be enforced in the time of Jesus, a charge of sabbath breaking would be sufficient to discredit Jesus as a prophet. His power to heal is apparently here taken for granted – the only question is **whether he would heal. . .on the sabbath.**

'Come **and stand out here'** – literally, 'Get up into the middle!' 3 Mark once again uses the verb ἔγειρε (see 2.9). As in 2.8f., Jesus 4 comprehends the unspoken thoughts of his critics and answers them with a question. The issue, as in the previous story, concerns what is **permitted. . .on the sabbath.** It was not normally permissible to heal on the sabbath, since healing was classified as work but, if life was in danger, then emergency treatment was allowed (see M. Yoma 8.6). It is to this principle that Jesus appeals and which he extends, since in this case the man's life is not in danger. In drawing a sharp antithesis between doing **good** and doing **evil**, and between attitudes which either **save life** or **kill**, Jesus refuses to draw a distinction between saving life in the narrowest sense and the offer of full life which characterizes his whole ministry. To delay healing for a day is to deny the Torah's true intention, which is the glory of God and the benefit of man. By their attitude the Pharisees destroy life rather than save it; by neglecting opportunities to do good they do harm. It is therefore they who are the sabbath breakers, and Jesus himself who fulfils the Torah which commands men to do good and offers life to those who obey it. The irony of the situation is that at this very moment the Pharisees are planning to do harm and to kill Jesus, whose only purpose is to do good and to save life.

The Pharisees **said nothing**, being incapable of response because of **their hardness of heart.** In Jewish thought the heart was the seat 5 of understanding rather than of emotion, and the phrase therefore refers to intellectual blindness or obtuseness. Throughout Mark's gospel, failure to understand Jesus and refusal to respond to him are described by this phrase, which sums up human opposition to the power of God at work in him. Unlike the later evangelists, Mark speaks of the **anger** and grief of Jesus at this deliberate blindness which refuses to acknowledge the truth. By contrast to these silent critics, the man with the withered hand makes an immediate response to Jesus' command, **'Stretch out your hand.'** His complaint seems to have been some form of paralysis, and it is possible that the whole arm was affected, since the word χείρ, here translated 'hand', can also mean 'arm'. If so, then the man's use of an immobile limb is itself (as in the case of the paralytic) an act of faith that he is already cured. On this occasion Jesus cures the man by command alone, and there is no physical contact between them; this may be significant, since Jewish scholars argue that to heal by word alone was not contrary to the Torah, and that Jesus was therefore blameless (so, e.g., Vermes, *Jesus the Jew*, p. 25).

6       **The Pharisees went out straight away.** If we take Mark's 'straight away' seriously, then it was still the sabbath, and the irony is complete: while Jesus saves life on the sabbath, they plot to kill. **The Herodians** were not a party, but Mark presumably refers to those who supported Herod Antipas, tetrarch of Galilee. An alliance between such men and **the Pharisees**, who were completely opposed to them in attitude and interest, is extraordinary; if such an alliance was in fact made, bringing together two such groups to fight a common danger, this indicates the strength of the hostility to Jesus. (The two groups are found together again, trying to trip Jesus up, in 12.13.) Mark presents a picture of Jesus opposed both by religious authorities and by supporters of the secular power.

The two groups **began to plot against him...looking for a way to destroy him**. It has sometimes been argued that Mark has placed this comment too 'early' in the ministry of Jesus; but Mark has given us few indications of chronology, and it is impossible to make any judgement on this question. It may be that a more accurate historical presentation of the material would have spread the conflict stories out through the ministry of Jesus but, by placing them together in the early stages of his gospel, Mark emphasizes the implacable opposition of official Judaism to Jesus and explains – at a human level – his final rejection. Already, Jesus has been judged and found guilty, and the shadow of the Cross has fallen over the story.

It is perhaps significant that the phrase translated **began to plot** (συμβούλιον ἐδίδουν) is echoed in 15.1, where συμβούλιον occurs again, either in the sense of 'decision', or with the meaning 'consultation'. The verb **destroy** (ἀπόλλυμι) is picked up in 11.18, where it is the chief priests and scribes who plot Jesus' destruction.

## C Truth hidden and revealed: parables and miracles          3.7–6.6

## 1 THE CROWDS FOLLOW JESUS          3.7–12

*(Matt. 12.15–21; 4.25; Luke 6.17–19; 4.41)*

**(7) Jesus withdrew to the lakeside with his disciples, and a huge number of people followed him – from Galilee and from Judaea, (8) from Jerusalem and from Idumaea and beyond the Jordan and the neighbourhood of Tyre and Sidon – a huge number, having heard what he was doing, came to him. (9) And because of the crowd he asked his disciples to have a boat ready for him, lest they should crush him; (10) for he had healed many people, so that all those who had diseases crowded in on him in order to touch him. (11) And whenever the unclean spirits saw him, they fell at his feet, and cried aloud, 'You are the Son of God'; (12) and he gave them strict instructions not to make him known.**

Most commentators make a major break at this point, but such divisions are largely arbitrary. There are plenty of links with previous sections: the theme of conflict which came to a climax in 3.6 will be taken up again in 3.20ff., and in the same story we are given the explanation of the exorcism narratives in chapter 1. But the scene shifts at this point to the lakeside (3.7), and Mark gives us a compressed account of Jesus' healing activity before moving on to a new theme – the commissioning of the Twelve disciples. An important theme throughout the next three chapters is the response which men and women make to Jesus: the truth about him is spelt out in a series of parables and miracles, but this truth is hidden from the majority of those in the story, who hear and see but fail to comprehend.

Vv.7–12 seem to be an editorial summary of Jesus' activity (cf. 1.14–15; 32–4). The statement that **Jesus withdrew to the lakeside** 7 can be understood to mean that he left the town because of the plots against his life mentioned in v.6; this was how Matthew interpreted it. Or we can understand it to mean that Jesus deliberately abandoned the official representatives of Judaism in order to concentrate on the ordinary people. Certainly there is no suggestion that the move was in any sense a retreat in the scope of the ministry. Rather it was an extension, for **a huge number of people followed him**, not only **from Galilee**, but also **from Judaea, from Jerusalem and from Idumaea** 8 **and beyond the Jordan and the neighbourhood of Tyre and Sidon.** This comprehensive description covers the whole of Palestine apart from Samaria and the mainly Gentile region of the Decapolis; the land beyond the Jordan was known as Peraea; the area of Tyre and Sidon, though not Jewish, had a large Jewish population and was closely linked with Galilee. Just as all Judaea and all Jerusalem responded to John the Baptist in 1.5, so now an even larger crowd representing every Jewish territory flocks to Jesus. The contrast between his popularity with the ordinary people and his rejection by the authorities in 3.6 is clear, but Mark does not draw this contrast simply for dramatic effect: the significant point is that, though official Judaism has already rejected Jesus, all Israel gathers to him.

9–10   **A boat** is made **ready for him**, in case the people **should crush him**: Mark here introduces the boat which will be used in 4.2. Many of those in the vast **crowd** have apparently come in the hope of healing. Such is Jesus' reputation that they now try **to touch him**, rather than waiting for him to touch them: his power is treated as magical (cf. 5.28). **Those who had diseases**: the Greek word used here, μάστιξ, means 'scourge', a reminder that disease was originally seen as a divine chastisement for sin, but Mark attributes much of the illness

11   to the work of unclean spirits. Like the unclean spirit in 1.24, these spirits recognize Jesus and acknowledge him as **the Son of God**. The statement that **they fell at his feet** must in fact refer to those who were possessed by unclean spirits; in this context, the action should

12   probably be interpreted as homage. The command **not to make him known** emphasizes once again the secrecy regarding Jesus' identity: bystanders are unaware of the meaning of the demoniacs' strange cries, but readers of the gospel understand that in submitting to Jesus the spirits recognize the source of his authority.

# 2   APPOINTMENT OF THE TWELVE    3.13–19

*(Matt.10.1–4; Luke 6.12–16)*

(13) Then Jesus went up the mountain and summoned those he wanted, and they came to him. (14) And he appointed twelve[1] so that they might be with him, and so that he might send them out to preach, (15) and to have authority to drive out demons. (16) He appointed twelve:[2] Simon, to whom he gave the name 'Peter', (17) and James son of Zebedee and John the brother of James, to whom he gave the name 'Boanerges', which means 'Sons of Thunder'; (18) Andrew and Philip and Bartholomew and Matthew and Thomas and James son of Alphaeus and Thaddaeus[3] and Simon the zealot (19) and Judas Iscariot, the man who betrayed him.

Following A C[2] D fam. 1 and other MSS. Many MSS add *whom he called apostles.*
2 Following ℵ B and other MSS. Many MSS omit *He appointed twelve*
3 D and the old Latin read *Lebbaeus.*

There has been considerable discussion as to whether or not this narrative is a reading-back of a later idea into the ministry of Jesus. On the one hand, it has been urged that the notion of the Twelve is an artificial construction, and that the evangelists themselves indicate that the circle of Jesus' followers was a much wider one. On the other hand, the Twelve (as such) seem to have played little part in the life of the early Church, and the inclusion of Judas in the list suggests that the choice of the group goes back to Jesus himself. The uncertainty in the tradition concerning one of the names can be explained either way: perhaps the closed group of twelve disciples did not exist during Jesus' ministry, or perhaps some of the group played no significant role in the life of the Christian community.

The number twelve is clearly symbolic (cf. Matt. 19.28 and Luke 22.30), and Mark shows his awareness of this by placing the account after his statement in vv.7f. about the nation's response to Jesus. The Twelve represent the whole nation, since Israel consisted of twelve tribes. The tradition is united in affirming that Jesus appointed twelve men in addition to himself: in other words, Jesus is seen as in some sense standing over against the nation. Had he chosen eleven men to join him, then he would still have been gathering together a nucleus of the true Israel (as did John the Baptist); but if the tradition is correct, then his choice of twelve men represents an implicit claim regarding his own status. For Mark, certainly, Jesus is the leader of this community, and it is as such that Jesus now delegates authority to those whom he has called to be his disciples.

**Then Jesus went up the mountain.** Mark does not identify the 13 mountain, and it does not matter which it might have been, since its significance is primarily theological. The mountain is a normal setting in biblical narratives for divine activity and revelation (cf. Exod. 3, 1 Kgs. 19, March 9), but in this case it reminds us in particular of the creation of the nation of Israel in Exodus 19–20. The initiative of Jesus is emphasized in the statement that he **summoned those he wanted**. This group is probably meant to be identical with the twelve who are chosen, though Mark's somewhat awkward expression could mean that Jesus selected twelve men from a larger number. **And he appointed twelve**: the addition *whom he named apostles* 14 found in some manuscripts has probably crept in from Luke 6.13. Luke's belief that Jesus used the term 'apostles' (ἀπόστολοι) of the Twelve is probably anachronistic, but it is a development from the picture given by Mark of Jesus' commissioning them and sending them out (ἀποστέλλω). The purpose of their appointment, according to Mark, is two-fold: first, they are to **be with him** (i.e. to learn from him), and second, Jesus will **send them out to preach, and to have** 15 **authority to drive out demons**. This second function is not fulfilled until 6.7; until then, the Twelve simply accompany Jesus. (Cf. Acts

1.21f., for the importance placed on being with Jesus as a qualification for being one of the Twelve.) In calling these men to preach, and in giving them authority to drive out demons, Jesus is calling them to share his own mission (cf. 1.39).

16     The words **He appointed twelve** are missing from some MSS. They were probably dropped because they simply repeat what we have already been told in v.14, but they could have been added at some stage by mistake. Mark does not explain why **Simon** was given **the name 'Peter'**, which is used throughout the rest of the gospel (apart from 14.37), but the Greek word πέτρος means 'stone'. Matthew offers one explanation as to why Jesus gave him the name in Matt. 16.18, where there is a play on the words πέτρος (referring to Peter) and πέτρα (rock); the two terms are in fact alternative Greek renderings of the Aramaic word *Kêpā'* (meaning 'rock' or 'stone'), and Peter's name is sometimes given as Kephas (Κηφᾶς). It seems unlikely that the name – which is given to him as a nickname rather than a surname – corresponded to Peter's character, since Peter is portrayed as anything but rocklike in the gospel! In spite of his later denial, Peter heads the list of disciples. Although **'Boanerges'** is explained as

17     meaning **'Sons of Thunder'**, the derivation is obscure. If Mark's explanation is correct, then perhaps this time the term did refer to the character of **James. . .and John** (cf. 9.38 and Luke 9.54); alternative suggestions are that it referred to their style of preaching or was a term given to twins. These three disciples are mentioned more than any of the others in Mark's story.

18     **Bartholomew** is really a 'surname', since *bar* is the Aramaic word meaning 'son of'. Mark does not identify **Matthew** with Levi (2.13f.), and Levi is therefore not included among the Twelve; there is no real difficulty in this, since Mark clearly envisages a circle of disciples wider than the Twelve. In Luke's lists of the Twelve (Luke 6.14–16 and Acts 1.13) the name of **Thaddaeus** is replaced by that of Judas son of James. Some texts of Matthew (10.2–4) agree with Mark, but a considerable number of MSS there (and a few here) read 'Lebbaeus'. There is thus considerable disagreement over this disciple's identity, and this is by no means surprising if he did not play any important part in the early Christian community; the absence of material about some of the Twelve in the tradition suggests that they did not all occupy important roles in the Church.

A second **Simon** is described as **the zealot**; many translations refer to him as 'the Cananaean', but the Greek word Καναναῖος used here comes from an Aramaic word meaning 'zealot' or 'enthusiast' (cf. Luke 6.15, where he is called ζηλωτής). It is sometimes argued that Simon was a member of the Zealot party, an extreme nationalistic movement which attempted to drive the Romans from Palestine by force; there is, however, no evidence that the term was used in this

technical sense until after the time of Jesus. If the word refers to
Simon's political activities, then he may have belonged to a group
with similar aims. Attempts have been made to link Jesus himself
with these anti-Roman extremists (notably by S.G.F. Brandon, *Jesus
and the Zealots*), but the fact that Simon's allegiance (if this is the
meaning) is mentioned indicates that his views were exceptional in
the circle surrounding Jesus. It is possible, however, that the word
describes Simon's character, and does not have these political implications at all.

The meaning of the word **Iscariot** is uncertain, the most likely   19
explanation being that it means 'man of Kerioth' (there were villages
of that name in both Judaea and Moab). It is possible that Mark himself did not understand the term, since he fails to explain it, though he
normally translates Semitic terms. The reference to the fact that it
was Judas **who betrayed him** points forward again to Jesus' coming
death.


# 3   MISUNDERSTANDING                         3.20–35

*(Matt. 12.22–32, 46–50; Luke 11.14–23; 8.19–21; Thomas 35; 44; 99)*

**(20) Then he went indoors. And once again a crowd gathered, so
that they had no chance even to eat. (21) And when his family
heard it they set out to take charge of him, for they said, 'He is out
of his mind'. (22) And scribes who had come down from
Jerusalem, said, 'He is possessed by Beelzebul',[1] and 'He drives out
demons by the prince of demons'. (23) Then he summoned them
and spoke to them in parables: 'How can Satan drive out Satan?
(24) For if a kingdom is divided against itself, that kingdom cannot stand; (25) and if a household is divided against itself, that
household will not be able to stand. (26) And if Satan has rebelled
against himself and is divided, he cannot stand; that is the end of
him. (27) But no one can break into a strong man's house and
plunder his goods unless he first binds the strong man; then he
can plunder his house. (28) Truly I tell you: the sons of men will be
forgiven all their sins, and blasphemies of every kind; (29) but
whoever blasphemes against the Holy Spirit will never be forgiven; he is guilty of an eternal sin.' (30) [He said this] because
they had said, 'He has an unclean spirit'.
(31) Then his mother and his brothers arrived. They stood outside and sent a message to him to come out. (32) There was a**

1 Syriac MSS and the Vulgate read *Beelzebub*.

crowd sitting round him when the message was brought to him, 'Your mother and your brothers[2] are outside, asking for you.' (33) And he answered, 'Who are my mother and brothers?' (34) And looking round at those who were sitting in the circle about him he said, 'Here are my mother and my brothers. (35) Whoever does the will of God is my brother, sister and mother'.

In this section we move back into the atmosphere of conflict which characterized the narratives in 2.1–3.6 but move another step forward in the development of this theme, since now Jesus' opponents do not merely watch him and criticize, but offer their own – utterly false – interpretation of the source of his authority and power. A number of stories have been woven together, probably by Mark himself, since we have here an example of the intercalation of incidents of which he is so fond. Material about the scribes, whom we now expect to be hostile to Jesus (vv.22–30), is sandwiched between material about his relatives and friends, whom we might expect to be sympathetic (vv.21,31–5). This device serves to bring out the parallel between the religious authorities and Jesus' own family circle: both offer false explanations of his activity, and are therefore blind to the truth. Attempts have been made to tone down this indictment of Jesus' family: Matthew and Luke both omitted vv.20f.; some translators take v.21 to refer to Jesus' friends rather than his relatives; commentators have attributed sympathetic motives to his family. But the sequel in vv.31–5, together with the parallel between the two groups in v.21 and v.22, indicate that Mark believed that Jesus was as misunderstood by his own family as by the scribes.

By his arrangement of the material, Mark confronts us with the all-important question of the nature of Jesus' authority. To attribute his activity to Satan is not only demonstrably absurd; it is a blasphemy against the Holy Spirit. Jesus himself has already been silently accused of blasphemy by the scribes (2.7): now the accusation is thrown back, and the real blasphemers are revealed. Religious leaders are blind to the truth, and so are Jesus' own relatives; their places of privilege are taken by those who follow Jesus and whose concern, like his, is to do God's will. They recognize that the power by which Jesus wages war on unclean spirits is that of the Holy Spirit, not of Satan; among these men and women are numbered not only Jesus' contemporaries, but the members of Mark's community, together with all who read the gospel and respond to its challenge.

The first incident is very brief and lacks a conclusion: we are not told whether an attempt was made to seize Jesus. The verses may be a scrap of independent tradition; more probable is the suggestion

---

1 Some MSS (including A and D) add *and your sisters*.

that they originally belonged to vv.31–5, and that Mark is responsible for dividing the material in order to insert vv.22–30. In both Matthew and Luke, the accusation about Beelzebul follows the cure of a demoniac, a logical setting which would not, however, have suited Mark's purpose in placing the accusations of vv.21 and 22 side by side. A comparison with Matthew and Luke also shows how sayings become attached to a basic narrative: it is possible that v.27 and vv.28–30 were separate sayings which have been added at some stage to the original nucleus of vv.22–6.

**Then he went indoors.** As in 2.1, the Greek phrase (εἰς οἶκον) is 20 ambiguous, and can be understood to mean either 'he went home' or 'he entered a house'. Jesus and those who respond to his teaching are now gathered in a house, and those who first listened to the gospel being read, also gathered in a house, would identify with the crowd. **Once again a crowd gathered**, and Mark emphasizes the popular response to Jesus in the comment that he and his companions **had no chance even to eat.** The crowd's enthusiasm stands in contrast to the attitudes which Mark is about to describe. **His family** represents the 21 Greek phrase οἱ παρ' αὐτοῦ – literally 'those from beside him'. In both the LXX and contemporary colloquial Greek it meant 'relatives' or 'friends'. Since the narrative begun here is taken up again in v.31 with the arrival of Jesus' mother and brothers, the phrase must refer in this context to Jesus' relatives. **They intended to take charge of him**; the verb (κρατέω) is a violent one, and is used in 6.17 and 12.12 of arrest; their purpose was therefore similar to that of the authorities. **They** is most naturally interpreted of the relatives; they believed Jesus to be **out of his mind.** Since madness was often regarded as due to possession by a demon, it is arguable that their judgement on the situation was close to that of the scribes in the next verse. Mark gives no explanation for their belief.

The **scribes** referred to in this incident are of greater authority than 22 those previously mentioned, since they are **from Jerusalem.** Mark probably means that they came down to Galilee in order to investigate the situation by watching and listening to Jesus; he intends us to understand how great an impact the ministry of Jesus was making. The derivation of the name **Beelzebul** is obscure, but the word may be derived from the Hebrew *ba'al z<sup>e</sup>bul*, meaning 'Lord of the dwelling'; this would be appropriate here in view of v.27, and receives further support from the saying in Matt.10.25. The well-known variant, 'Beelzebub', is found here in Syriac MSS and the Vulgate, and probably derives from 'Baalzebub', meaning 'Lord of flies', the God of Ekron (2 Kings 1.2.). Mark apparently identifies Beelzebul with **the prince of demons**, i.e. Satan, in whose power Jesus is accused of working; this, at least, is how Matthew and Luke interpret the two charges, since they run them together. From the view-point of the authorities, the accusation that Jesus is in league with the devil is a natural one. They are unable to deny his ability to work miracles, and this indicates that he is possessed by some supernatural power; his teaching, however, is in their opinion contrary to the Torah, which represents the revealed will of God: if his teaching is false, then clearly his miraculous power cannot derive from heaven and must be demonic.

23 Jesus replies to their charges **in parables**. This is the first time that Mark has used this term, though he has already recorded some in 2.19–22. It is noteworthy that there, as here, the parables are used in debates with Jesus' critics: far from being stories expressing general religious truths, as has sometimes been supposed, the parables of Jesus seem always to have been supplied to very particular situations. The Greek word for parable, παραβολή, means literally a 'setting beside', i.e. a comparison or analogy. In the LXX it is used to translate the Hebrew *māšāl*, which covers a variety of forms: riddles, fables, short pithy sayings, proverbs, etc.; the parables in the gospels also vary considerably in form and length.

**How can Satan drive out Satan?** Jesus' initial answer is as logical as the charge brought by his opponents. It is absurd to suggest that he is using satanic power to cast out demons – Satan has more sense

24–6 than to destroy his own kingdom. The argument in vv.24–6 appears to assume that Satan's kingdom still stands firm and is not breaking up: if his kingdom were crumbling, then we might conclude that civil war had broken out but, since it is not, the scribes' accusations must be false (C.K. Barrett, *The Holy Spirit and the Gospel Tradition*, p. 61). But internal revolution is not the only way to topple a regime; an alternative method is invasion, and this, the true explanation, is set

27 out in v.27, introduced by the strong adversative **but** (ἀλλά). The assumption behind this second saying is that Satan's kingdom is, after all, breaking up. Mark appears to have put together two separate sayings, and their juxtaposition shows that he believed that Satan's rule was indeed crumbling, not because Satan was divided against himself, but because he had been overcome by someone stronger. This second saying is found also in the Gospel of Thomas (35).

The language of v.27 is reminiscent of Isa. 49.24f., where the mighty one is overcome by Yahweh himself. Here, however, the one who **binds the strong man** (ὁ ἰσχυρός) must be Jesus, and the implication that he is stronger than Satan reminds us not only of the Baptist's statement that the one who follows him is mightier (ἰσχυρότερος) than he, but also of the temptation narrative and its implied result: it is because Jesus has already overcome Satan that he is able to **plunder his goods** by releasing men and women from his power. (For Satan's defeat, cf. Luke 10.18.) As in Isa. 49.24f., where the 'prey' are the captive Israelites, this short parable demands allegorical interpretation.

V.28 introduces a new saying, which brings out the serious implica- **28** tions – for themselves – of the scribes' charge. Its solemn nature is seen in the introductory word **Truly**, literally 'Amen' ('Aμὴν), the transliteration of a Hebrew word meaning 'true'. The gospels are unique in placing the word at the beginning of statements instead of at the end (as was normal in Jewish liturgy), and this seems to have been characteristic of the sayings of Jesus, and an indication of the authority with which he spoke. A different form of the saying in vv.28f. is found in another context in Luke 12.10, which contrasts blasphemy against the Son of man with the sin against the Holy Spirit; Matthew (12.31f.) records both forms. The version in Thomas 44, contrasting blasphemy against the Father and against the Son with blasphemy against the Holy Spirit, is clearly late. It seems probable that the Markan version is the more original, though some commentators have postulated an earlier form from which our two existing versions are derived, in which blasphemy against the sons of men was contrasted with that against the Holy Spirit. The relevance of the saying to the argument is underlined in the Matthaean parallel, where already in 12.28 we have been told that it is by the Spirit of God that Jesus casts out demons. **The sons of men** is simply a Semitic way of saying 'men' (cf. Pss. 21.10 and 115.16). The word **blasphemies** is probably used here, not in the technical sense as defined by the rabbis (see on 14.64) but, as often, of the denial of the power and greatness of God. Jesus again speaks of forgiveness, this time for all sinners. The one exception to this is the person who **blasphemes** **29** against the Holy Spirit. It is clear from the context, as well as from the editorial note in v.30, that Mark has interpreted this as the deliberate refusal to acknowledge the activity of God's Spirit in Jesus' ministry: it is the attitude which makes a man attribute the work of God to Satan and confuse goodness and evil, truth and falsehood. Such behaviour indicates that an individual **is guilty of an eternal sin**; his attitude of mind is so fixed and obstinate that it forms a permanent obstacle betwen God and man. The singling out of one unforgivable sin has its parallels in rabbinic writings, where those who have committed certain sins are said to have no share in the world to come. Once again we see the irony of a situation in which the Jerusalem scribes, guardians of orthodoxy and upholders of the Torah, are themselves found guilty of the one truly heinous sin, and by their attitude to and condemnation of Jesus are themselves condemned. Mark's final comment ensures that we understand Jesus' meaning; **30** those who are in the grip of this sin are those who have accused Jesus of having an unclean spirit – i.e., of being in the power of Satan. They have confused the work of the *Holy* Spirit with that of an *unclean* spirit.

31    Jesus' **mother and his brothers**, who had set out on their journey in v.21, now arrive and stand **outside** (ἔξω); presumably this means outside the house referred to in v.20, but by using this word here, and by repeating it in v.32, Mark stresses their dissociation from Jesus and his circle of adherents. The term ἀδελφός (translated 'brother') can be used of any male relative, and since the plural, ἀδελφοί, can include females, it is possible to understand it here as a reference to brothers and sisters or, more generally, to relatives. By the second century, Mary was felt to be the embodiment of the ascetic ideal, and belief in the perpetuity of her virginity led some of the Fathers to interpret the word ἀδελφοί as a reference to the sons of Joseph by a former wife (so Clement of Alexandria and Origen) or cousins of Jesus (so Jerome). Joseph does not appear outside the infancy narratives of Matthew and Luke and is generally assumed to be already dead.

There is an obvious parallel between Jesus' own estrangement from his family and what he demands of his followers in 10.29. The point here, however, is not Jesus' attitude to his mother and brothers (his departure from home and his apparent indifference to them) but their attitude to him, already made plain in v.21. Regarding Jesus as

32    demented, they stood outside, in contrast to the **crowd sitting round him**. There is no direct contact between Jesus and his family: a **message was brought to him, 'Your mother and your brothers are outside, asking for you.'** The phrase *and your sisters* is added here (but not in vv.31 or 33) by a few MSS – probably by analogy with the

34    saying in v.35. Jesus looks round **the circle** of those whom he now acknowledges as members of his family, and says: **here are my mother and my brothers**. Those **about him** (περὶ αὐτὸν, cf.4.10), who have responded to him and are listening to his teaching, have replaced those who were once beside him (οἱ παρ' αὐτοῦ, v.21). His commendation apparently includes the whole group (i.e. the **crowd**

35    of v.32), not the disciples alone (contrast 4.10). The contrast is underlined in Jesus' comment: his true kinsmen are not those who are related to him by blood, but those who do **the will of God**. (A similar contrast is found in the story used by Luke at this point, Luke 11.27f.). The idea that man's true life consists in doing the will of God is a thoroughly Jewish one, and if those who do God's will are close to Jesus, then it is because he himself is closely associated with obedience to that will. Rejected and misunderstood by his own family and by the nation's religious leaders, Jesus is nevertheless accepted by a nucleus of those who are obedient to God and prepared for the coming of the Kingdom. The parallel saying in Thomas 99 actually makes the link: 'Those here who do the will of my Father are my brothers

and my mother; these are they who will enter the kingdom of my Father.' The fact that Jesus' final saying refers, not simply to **mother and. . .brothers**, but to **brother, sister and mother**, may perhaps reflect the inclusion of women in the early Christian community. Certainly the members of Mark's community would have felt that these words were addressed to them.

# 4  THE PARABLE OF THE SOWER                          4.1 0

*(Matt. 13.1–9; Luke 8.4–8; Thomas 9)*

**(1) He began to teach again by the lakeside, and a large crowd gathered round him, so he got into a boat on the lake and sat there; and the whole crowd was on the shore, at the edge of the water. (2) And he taught them many things in parables, and in his teaching he said to them: (3) 'Listen! A sower went out to sow. (4) And it happened that as he sowed, some of the seed fell beside the path; and the birds came and ate it. (5) And some fell on stony ground, where it had little soil, and it sprouted straight away, because it had no depth of soil; (6) and when the sun came up it was scorched and, because it had no root, it withered away. (7) And some fell among thistles, and the thistles sprang up and choked it, and it produced nothing. (8) And some seeds fell on good soil where they sprang up and grew and produced a crop: some bore thirty grains, some sixty and some a hundred.' (9) And he said, 'Whoever has ears to hear, let him hear!'**

Although Mark has several times referred to the fact that Jesus taught, he has so far told us nothing about the content of that teaching, apart from the brief summary in 1.15 and the sayings in the various conflict stories. It has often been noted that Mark gives us far less of the teaching of Jesus than the other evangelists and, though it is easy to exaggerate this (for it is, after all, the shortest of the gospels), it is true that it contains no equivalent of the Sermon on the Mount or on the Plain, and that Mark has included relatively few of the parables: by comparison with the other evangelists, he devotes less space to the teaching of Jesus and more to his miracles. This does not mean, however, that Mark considered Jesus' teaching in any sense unimportant: he has already emphasized its authority and effect, and it is clear from his vocabulary – the word διδαχή (teaching) is used five times, διδάσκω (to teach) seventeen – that he regards teaching as one of Jesus' main activities. Nor need we assume that the material used by the other evangelists was unknown to him, for he did not necessarily wish to provide a complete or even a typical picture of Jesus' teaching: sayings and parables which have been treasured by later generations of Christians may quite simply not have suited his particular purpose.

It is significant that the teaching which Mark first records is teaching about teaching, a parable about parables. The explanation of the parable of the sower is introduced in v.13 with the words: **Don't you understand this parable? Then how will you understand any of the parables?** Clearly Mark regards this introductory parable as the key to understanding the rest. The clue to his own interpretation of the parable is found in vv.11–12, intercalated between the two versions of the parable, though because of their difficulty their importance for Mark himself is often overlooked. In his teaching Jesus confronts men with an all-important decision which is a matter of life and death. Those who do not respond are those whose hearts are hardened, whom Satan has in his power; those who respond, who hear and follow Jesus, are those to whom the secret of the Kingdom is given. Although Jesus does not preach himself, or announce himself as the Christ, the effect of his teaching, as presented to us by Mark, is to do precisely that. Jesus confronts the reader as the one who brings salvation: to accept or reject his teaching about the Kingdom is to accept or reject both the Kingdom itself and the one who brings it.

## Additional note: parables

For Mark, the parables of Jesus both reveal and conceal: for those who have ears to hear they convey the good news of the Kingdom, to those who refuse to listen their message is obscure. The parables are thus in some ways similar to crossword clues, making sense to those who are prepared to accept their challenge. The Hebrew word *māšāl*, which is translated into Greek as παραβολή, means 'proverb' or 'riddle' as well as 'parable', and Mark may not be wrong in believing that Jesus' parables contained a certain enigmatic quality. Nevertheless, by the time that Mark was writing, the enigma seemed much greater. For one thing, it is clear that he saw in the parables some explanation for Israel's rejection of Jesus: they had failed to respond to him because they had not understood his teaching, and they had not understood his teaching because they had not been able to decipher the parables. A second reason why Mark would be conscious of the parables' obscurity was the shift in situation from Jesus' time to his own. Parables spoken by a wandering teacher in Galilee sounded very differently when recited as words of the Master whom the community acknowledged as risen Lord. Inevitably parables took on a new meaning in a new situation, and inevitably, in the process, their relevance sometimes seemed obscure.

It was natural, once the parables seemed unduly puzzling, to add explanatory comments: application to a new situation often involved allegorization. We can see this happening especially clearly in many of the parables used by Matthew and Luke; here, in Mark 4.14–20, we find an allegorical interpretation of the sower which sounds very much like an early preacher's exposition of the parable, warning Christians of the dangers that might overcome their faith. Later expositors used allegory constantly as a method of exegesis and extracted innumerable meanings – and sermons – from one parable in this way: the parables were assumed to be allegories which required a special understanding to unravel their hidden meaning. It was this approach that Adolf Jülicher challenged at the end of the nineteenth century, maintaining that the parables of Jesus were not allegories at all and should not be interpreted as such: each parable had one point and one point only – and this was a universal truth which anyone could grasp.

Later scholars (e.g. C.H. Dodd and J. Jeremias) built on Jülicher's work. But Jülicher's basic assumption that the parables of Jesus are not intended to be allegories and that each one contains only one point has proved to be too rigid. While it is easy to see the difference between extremes – between a simple parable and an artificial allegory (e.g. a fable in which animals or plants are substituted for people) – the line between parable and allegory is not always so simple to draw. The issue has been further complicated by the fact that some commentators have read allegorical details into the parables where none was intended – as, for example, in the case of Augustine's famous interpretation of the Good Samaritan – but this does not mean that all allegorical interpretation is eisegesis. A parable involves a comparison and, once the comparison is made, then something or somebody in the parable is in a sense 'identified' with a thing or person in the real world. If the parable is relevant to its hearers, they are likely to find themselves addressed, as David was by the words 'You are the man' (2 Sam. 12.7). In Mark 12, for example, Jesus tells a story about a vineyard; everyone who heard him must have been familiar with the description of Israel as a vineyard in Isaiah 5. The song of the vineyard in Isaiah 5 is an allegory, and if Jesus makes use of well-known imagery, then we may expect his story to be an allegory also. This does not mean that every detail in the story will have an allegorical interpretation (e.g. the winepress, the tower) but it does mean that we should beware of assuming that there cannot be any allegorical details at all or that a parable can have only one point. It is probable that other images would have been equally evocative of Old Testament and intertestamental ideas.

Most of the parables found in Mark are very brief, often amounting to little more than pithy sayings. Only two are of any length – those about the Sower and the Vineyard. Mark's use of the former suggests that he sees it, not simply as a key to the teaching of Jesus (4.13), but as a key to his whole ministry. This is brought out in the explanation of the parable in vv.13–20: the seed represents the word proclaimed by Jesus, the crop the response of men and women to him. The end of the story is told in the parable of the Vineyard, where the failure to respond to the messengers leads ultimately to the death (and resurrection!) of the son of the owner of the vineyard. The fact that each parable is placed immediately after a challenge by the Jerusalem religious authorities concerning the nature of Jesus' authority (3.20–35; 11.27–33), as well as at the head of a block of teaching linked with the theme of the parable, suggests that Mark regarded both of them as allegories of Israel's response to and rejection of Jesus. Taken together, they encapsulate the whole story of the ministry.

For further discussion, see: C.H. Dodd, *The Parables of the Kingdom*; J. Jeremias, *The Parables of Jesus*; M. Boucher, *The Mysterious Parable*; J. Drury, *The Parables in the Gospels*.

1–2 The setting is again **by the lakeside**, and the popular response to Jesus is underlined once more in the reference to **a large crowd** which has **gathered** to hear him. These first two verses are a good example of Mark's repetitious style: **the...crowd** is mentioned twice, **the lake** three times, and the **teaching** of Jesus is emphasized by being referred to three times. **He got into a boat on the lake and sat there**: the boat has been ready for use since 3.9; in sitting, Jesus adopts the posture typical of a teacher (cf. 13.3). **And he taught them many things in parables**: there is no hint in this statement that there was any failure in communication, or that Jesus' words were found obscure. Mark's version of the parable reflects the Semitic phraseology
3 of the underlying Aramaic. The opening command – **Listen!** – emphasizes the importance of the teaching which is to follow. Moreover, it echoes the opening word of Deut. 6.4, known as the *Shema*, which was recited daily by the pious Jew as a reminder of the core of his faith. The word is derived from a Hebrew verb which means not only 'to listen' and 'to hear' (v.9), but also 'to obey', and thus implies an active response to what is heard. It has indeed been suggested that the parable and its interpretation was originally based on the command of the *Shema* to love God with heart and mind and might (B. Gerhardsson, *N.T.S.*, 14, 1968, pp. 165–93). If that was Jesus' own intention, then the parable confronted men and women with the central demand of the Jewish faith.

   **A sower went out to sow.** Since for Mark the parable presents the choice which confronts men and women in the person of Jesus, it is clear that for him the sower represents Christ himself. Although he does not make the identification, he has perhaps dropped hints. J. Marcus (*The Mystery of the Kingdom of God*, pp. 37–9) points out that the verb 'went out', ἐξῆλθεν, echoes the verb used by Jesus of his own mission in 1.38, and that the sowing of the seed on the good soil (v.8 – εἰς τήν γῆν τὴν καλὴν) echoes the statement that Jesus addressed the crowd gathered on the shore (v.1 – ἐπι τῆς γῆς – lit. 'on the land'). A very similar parable is told, much more briefly, in 4 Ezra 8.41, which dates from the end of the first century AD.

The sowing of seed in the autumn was followed by ploughing, 4 which would bury the seed under the soil. Most commentators accept the interpretation given by Jeremias (*Parables*, pp. 11f.), who assumes that the field was therefore unploughed when the seed was sown, and that the path was a temporary one which would be ploughed together with the field; the fact that some of the seed fell beside the path would therefore be remedied when the path was ploughed – unless, in the interval, the birds spotted the seed in this vulnerable position and came and ate it. But Jeremias' interpretation is based on a few ambiguous rabbinic references, and the picture he draws is a difficult one; it would be strange if the field were unprepared for the crop: clods of earth and last year's stubble would need to be broken up before the seed was sown. This seems better agricultural practice and more likely to be what is in mind. The field was bounded by a path, which was thus a permanent, not a temporary one (cf. K.D. White in *J.T.S.*, n.s., 15, 1962, pp. 300ff.; J. Drury in *J.T.S.*, n.s., 24, 1973, pp. 367ff.). If this is the correct picture, then seed scattered near the edge of the field or next to the path might not be covered over when the field was ploughed once more, and so would be vulnerable; some might even fall on the path itself. This was not bad farming, but part of the risk involved if the whole field was to be utilized.

Jeremias' explanation of the parable lent support to the interpretation of the phrase παρὰ τὴν ὁδόν (here translated literally) which takes it to mean 'on the path'. C.C. Torrey (followed by M. Black, *An Aramaic Approach*, p. 162) suggested that behind Mark's Greek there lay an ambiguous Aramaic phrase which could be understood to mean either 'on the path' or 'beside it', but this hardly seems necessary to explain the parable, and certainly Mark chose to write a word which means 'beside', not 'on'. In view of the significance given to the word ὁδός later in the gospel (see, especially, on 8.27; 9.33f.; 10.32 and 52), one is tempted to suggest that Mark's readers might well have seen special significance in the fact that those who immediately rejected the word (4.15) were *beside* the way: but this path is an unproductive one, not the way of discipleship, and if sowing practices were as we have described, then παρά was the natural word for Mark himself to use in this context, and may not have had any deeper meaning for him.

5     The presence of **stony ground** in the field is not surprising, since the soil in Galilee is sometimes thin, barely covering the underlying limestone rock. The fact that the seed **had no depth of soil** did not, of course, make it sprout any faster, as Mark suggests, but in shallow ground it would be nearer the surface, and its shoots might well

6   appear above the ground more quickly. In the hot **sun**, however, the

7   plants would soon be **scorched**. Jeremias' picture (*loc. cit.*) of a farmer deliberately sowing among thistles because he is going to plough them up is contradicted by the parable itself, since we are told that **the thistles sprang up** and choked the seed. Because the farmer sowed broadcast, some seed inevitably fell among the weeds outside the area of prepared land. **It produced nothing**: J. Marcus (*op. cit.*, p. 22) points out that each of the 'failures' is lost at a different stage of growth. The first batch of seed does not even germinate; the second withers away as soon as it springs up; the third apparently grew, but produced nothing (lit. 'did not give fruit').

8     **And some seeds fell on good soil**: finally, in contrast to those which failed, we have seeds which thrived. **They sprang up and grew and produced a crop: some bore. . . .**All the verbs in the story so far have been in the Aorist tense, expressing punctiliar action. Now Mark uses two present participles (lit. 'springing up and growing'), together with two imperfect verbs (lit. 'were producing'. . .'were bearing'). Whether intentionally or accidentally, he has succeeded in conveying the contrast between the transitory and the enduring. The figures **thirty. . .sixty and. . .a hundred** refer not to the total yield of the crop (the average would be less), but to the produce from individual seeds; the original Aramaic probably ran 'yielding one thirtyfold, one sixtyfold, one hundredfold'. It was by no means impossible to produce thirty, sixty or even a hundred grains from one plant, though the last would certainly be an exceptional yield.

    It is far from easy to determine the original meaning of the parable. It is usually interpreted as a parable about the Kingdom of God, a theme central to Jesus' teaching, in which case the harvest is understood to symbolize the coming of that Kingdom; the debate then centres on whether the harvest is taking place in the ministry of Jesus (so C.H. Dodd, *Parables*, pp. 180ff.), or whether it lies in the future, the ministry of Jesus being the time of sowing. It should be noted, however, that the parable is not specifically said to be about the Kingdom, though Mark's comment in vv.10–12 clearly interprets it as such. One traditional interpretation of the parable has been that it was intended to encourage the disciples in the work of evangelism as they proclaimed the 'word' of the gospel; this is in fact an extension of the interpretation of the parable given by Mark himself, who understands it of the ministry of Jesus and the response made to him, but the application of the parable to the work of the disciples is clearly an interpretation deriving from a later situation. Within the setting of the ministry of Jesus himself, however, it is the word that he speaks which challenges his hearers. If Gerhardsson is right in his suggestion that the parable is based on the *Shema*, this serves to remind us that Jesus' teaching stands in continuity with the words of God to Israel in the past. To this extent, at least, Dodd is right in supposing that the word has been delivered in the past, and that the present is the time for harvesting. The symbolism of bearing fruit is common in both the Old Testament and the teaching of Jesus, and it is possible that the parable was originally intended to present the distinction between those who were responsive to God's commands, and so true members of his people, and those who had failed to obey his will. The Lord looks for the harvest in his field, as he looks for grapes in his vineyard (12.1–9). In so far as Jesus' teaching represents a final challenge to Israel to respond to God's demands, however, Mark has correctly interpreted the parable in terms of the response made to Jesus himself. The challenge is driven home in the words of v.9,  9 which take up the opening command to listen in v.3: the verb (ἀκούω) is the same, but it is impossible to translate this verb by one English word throughout this chapter, and we have therefore retained here the familiar translation, 'Whoever has ears to hear, let him hear!'


# 5   THE PURPOSE OF THE PARABLES   4.10–12

*(Matt. 13.10–15; Luke 8.9–10)*

(10) And when he was alone, those round him, together with the Twelve, asked him about the parables. (11) And he said to them, 'To you has been given the secret of God's Kingdom. But to those who are outside, everything is in parables, (12) in order that

"They may look and look, yet perceive nothing;
they may listen and listen, yet understand nothing.
Otherwise they might turn and be forgiven."'

These are perhaps the most difficult and the most discussed verses in the whole of Mark's gospel. Their meaning for the evangelist is, however, clear enough. Mark shares the fundamental Jewish conviction that God is at work both in historical events and in people, whose actions are ultimately the result of his decree: for the Christian community, looking back on the ministry of Jesus, the rejection by Israel of her Messiah and the continued obduracy of the Jewish nation when confronted by the Christian gospel could be explained only as part of God's mysterious purpose. If men and women had refused to accept Jesus, then it must be part of the will of God that this should happen. In spite of attempts to soften the harshness of Mark's words, there can be no doubt that this was his meaning.

It must be noted, however, that there is for Mark another aspect to this picture. Those outside, to whom everything comes in parables, stand in contrast to those who were about him with the Twelve. It will be remembered that the previous incident in 3.31–5 also underlined the contrast between those who remained outside (ἔξω) and those who were about Jesus (οἱ περὶ αὐτὸν). On that occasion, however, the crowd was included in the circle surrounding him. Although the choice between being a disciple or an outsider is such a vital one, there is no rigid line between the two groups. Mark will later show the Twelve behaving with no greater understanding than the crowds; and in 4.3,9, the invitation of Jesus to listen is addressed to everyone. For those who refuse to accept the challenge of the teaching of Jesus, his parables inevitably remain nothing more than parables, and those who see and hear him are totally without comprehension – and without the salvation he brings. But to those who respond, the meaning of the parables is explained; to them, the secret of God's Kingdom is given. For a similar saying about revelation cf. Matt. 11.25–7 = Luke 10.21f.

Yet the saying appears to stand in marked contrast to Mark's story; for from this point onwards, the Twelve behave with a singular lack of understanding, while some outsiders show remarkable faith. The disciples fail to understand the parables (4.13) and the power of Jesus (4.40f.; 6.37, 49–52; 8.4,14–21); they are mystified by his teaching (7.18) – especially on the need for suffering (8.32–4; 9.32–4; 10.32, 35–41) – and they fail him at the crucial hour (14.32–42, 47, 50, 66–72). But to those outside, faith is given: to the woman with a haemorrhage (5.34), the Syro-Phoenician woman (7.29), the father of the epileptic boy (9.24), the children who are brought for blessing (10, 13–16), the woman who anoints Jesus (14.3–9) and – most remarkable of all – the centurion at the Cross (15.39). How is it that those to whom the secret of the Kingdom is revealed fail to comprehend, while those from whom it is hidden grasp it? This is the enigma of Mark's gospel: the statement in 4.12 proves to be true, but the identity of those to whom the secret is in fact given provides some surprises. Mark has perhaps prepared us for this by including a reference to others besides the Twelve in v.10.

In their present form and context, these verses seem to reflect a time when the parables had become somewhat puzzling to the early Church, because their original context had been lost. Although it is customary to contrast the self-evident character of Jesus' original parables with the attempts of the early community to extract meaning from what had become obscure, it is possible to exaggerate the

difference. It seems likely that Jesus' intention in teaching in parables was to challenge his listeners and make them think for themselves. Whether or not it was necessary for Jesus to spell out their
meaning to his disciples as Mark suggests we do not know: but Mark
is certainly right in picturing the disciples as representing those for
whom – through their response to Jesus – the parables had become
meaningful, while for those outside the Christian community, their
significance was lost because their challenge was rejected.

The quotation in v.12 comes from Isa. 6.9f. Although the words
occur in the acount of Isaiah's call, it seems probable that they represent his understanding of his ministry to Israel at the end of his life
rather than at the beginning, as he looks back on what seems to him a
complete failure to convert his people: even this he sees as part of
God's purpose. His words would seem appropriate to early Christians
wrestling with the problem of Jesus' rejection. The fact that the
version of Isa. 6.9f. given here is closer to the Targum than to the LXX
suggests that it may go back to an Aramaic source, and it is possible
that Jesus himself commented on his failure to convert Israel (with so
few exceptions) in words reminiscent of Isaiah. Certainly Mark understood Isaiah's words to have been fulfilled in Jesus' ministry. (On
the importance of this saying for Mark, see M.A. Beavis, *Mark's
Audience.*)

The scene has changed from the crowded lakeside to a place where **10**
Jesus and his closest followers are by themselves. The Greek is
awkward, for we are told first that Jesus **was alone**, and then given
two groups of people who were with him. One possibility is that the
tradition inherited by Mark read 'And when he was alone with the
Twelve...' (E. Best, 'Mark's use of the Twelve'). If so, then perhaps he
has deliberately introduced the reference to **those round him** (οἱ
περὶ αὐτον) in order to link back to the group referred to in 3.34f., who
are prepared to do the will of God. It is not **the Twelve** alone who
have come to Jesus to ask **about the parables.** Clearly Mark believes
that there were others in the crowd who responded to his warning to
hear. The cumbersome Greek expression also gives Mark's readers
the opportunity to see themselves among the group surrounding
Jesus, and to identify themselves with those to whom the secret of the
Kingdom is given. **Secret** (μυστήριον) is a word used in Greek of the **11**
mystery known to those initiated into the mystery religions. But the
equivalent Hebrew and Aramaic terms are also used in Jewish
apocalyptic literature and at Qumran of a secret purpose of God
which he reveals to his people, and the word is often used by Paul in
this sense (cf. Rom. 11.25; 16.25; 1 Cor 2.7; 15.51; Col. 1.26f.; 2.2). This
is probably the meaning of the word here, though Gentile readers
would of course tend to interpret it in the light of their own
background. This secret is **of God's Kingdom** (lit.'the Kingdom of

God'), and presumably allows those who possess it to enter that Kingdom. It **has been given** to them – i.e. by God: this use of the passive in speaking of the activity of God reflects the Jewish reluctance to speak directly of God and is characteristic of the teaching of Jesus. How is the secret of God's Kingdom given? Paradoxically it is given in the parable itself, but it is not understood until Jesus gives the explanation as well: Jesus' word, human response to his word and explanation are all essential.

In contrast, we have **those who are outside** (ἔξω, cf. 3.31f.). This term clearly does not refer to the whole crowd, since some of them are included in the circle gathered round Jesus, but presumably it includes those whose attitudes are represented by the first three kinds of soil. For them, **everything is in parables**. It has been suggested by Jeremias (*Parables* pp. 14–18) that the original Aramaic of this phrase meant 'everything is obscure', and that Mark misunderstood the Greek ἐν παραβολαῖς, meaning 'in riddles', as a reference to parables; if Jeremias is correct, then it was this misunderstanding which led to these two verses, originally a separate saying, being linked to the theme of parables. Whether it was originally a general saying about the effect of Jesus' ministry as a whole, however, or referred, as Mark believed, to his teaching in particular, these two verses sum up Mark's understanding of the events he describes: in Jesus, the power of God's Kingdom is breaking into the world, and the signs of its coming are present for all to see; but only his followers grasp the true significance of what is happening.

12     This happens **in order that** (ἵνα. . . .We come here to the crux of the problem. Commentators have made innumerable attempts to tone these words down, suggesting, for example, that they are a mistranslation of the Aramaic. (See, e.g., T.W. Manson, *The Teaching of Jesus*, pp. 76–80.) For Mark, however, there is no doubt that the paradoxical result – and therefore the purpose – of the ministry was that many failed to comprehend the truth even when they saw and heard it. Jewish thought tended to blur the distinction between purpose and result; if God was sovereign, then of course what happened must be his will, however strange this appeared. The quotation therefore fits Mark's theology admirably. It is less easy to see what place the words could have had in the ministry of Jesus, for we may confidently assume that the purpose of his teaching was to stimulate response, not prevent it. If he used the quotation, the most likely explanation is that he felt Isaiah's words were being fulfilled in his own ministry: the people were as unresponsive to his mission as they had been to Isaiah.

The people **look and look. . .listen and listen**. The construction in both lines is a Semitic one; in each case Mark uses one verb twice, so intensifying the action. The parable began and ended with exhortations to listen, and the word 'listen' picks up the same verb (ἀκούω), used in vv. 3 and 9; here it is used in parallel with the verb 'look' (βλέπω). It is perhaps significant that the other long section of teaching, in chapter 13, is punctuated by the command: Watch! (βλέπετε). These two images of seeing/watching and hearing/listening for spiritual perceptiveness will be used again. **Otherwise**, lit. 'lest' (μήποτε) is as harsh as **in order that**: if they perceived and understood, **they might turn and be forgiven**. There is no mercy for those who refuse to see and hear; we need to remember, however, that this harsh statement implies that there *is* forgiveness for those who *do* respond. Those who listened to Mark's gospel would themselves have experienced this forgiveness.

# 6   THE PARABLE EXPLAINED                    4.13–20

## *(Matt. 13.18–23; Luke 8.11–15)*

**(13) And he said to them: 'Don't you understand this parable? Then how will you understand any of the parables? (14) The sower sows the word. (15) The ones who are beside the path, where the word is sown, are these: when they hear it, then straight away Satan comes and takes away the word which has been sown in them. (16) Similarly,[1] the ones who are sown on stony ground are these: when they hear the word, they receive it straight away with joy; (17) but they have no root in them, and are short-lived, and when there is trouble or persecution on account of the word, they fall away at once. (18) And there are others who are sown among the thistles; these hear the word, (19) but worldly cares and the seduction of wealth and desires of other kinds crowd in and choke the word, and it yields nothing. (20) And there are those who are sown on good soil, who hear the word and accept it and bear fruit, some thirty, some sixty and some a hundredfold.'**

Most commentators believe that this explanation of the parable of the sower originated in the early Christian community and represents an early 'exegesis' of it. This is supported by the fact that many of the words used in this section do not occur elsewhere in the teaching of Jesus, but are found in the epistles – e.g. **the word** (ὁ λόγος) in the sense of 'gospel' (Gal. 6.6; 1 Thess. 1.6), **short-lived** (πρόσκαιρος, 2 Cor. 4.18), **cares** (μέριμναι, I Pet. 5.7) and **seduction** (ἡ ἀπάτη, Col.

---

1 Some MSS omit *Similarly*.

2.8). The interpretation also seems to presuppose a fairly long period during which the faith of Christians is tested in various ways, and to reflect the harsh experience of Christian preachers and communities. The setbacks encountered by the seed are allegorized, and though there is no reason to deny (as some have done) that Jesus ever used allegory, the allegorization of details is often a sign of later attempts to expound the parables; this seems especially likely here, since the explanations suit the period of Christian mission better than the lifetime of Jesus. However, though the interpretation may come from the Church, rather than from Jesus, it has perhaps not distorted the original parable as much as is sometimes suggested: rather, as with the account of Nathan's parable in 2 Sam. 12, we detect at each point the warning of an early preacher – 'this could mean you'.

Jesus' rebuke of the disciples for their failure to understand reads somewhat strangely after the previous section. Yet this juxtaposition of comprehension and incomprehension is typical of Mark's gospel. A notable parallel occurs in 8.27ff., where Jesus' identity is revealed to the Twelve, but is hidden from others; immediately following this we find Peter rebuked for his total failure to understand Jesus' teaching, which was spoken 'plainly' (vv.31–3). The theme of the disciples' failure to understand Jesus, which recurs frequently in the rest of the gospel, reflects the contrast between the time of Jesus' ministry and the period of the Church (see additional note on the messianic secret, pp. 66–9). Perhaps it also suggests that similar problems still beset the Christian community, even after the resurrection (see J. Marcus, *Mystery of the Kingdom*, pp. 100f.).

13    **Don't you understand this parable?** Jesus now takes up the request of the disciples in v.10. This is the first indication in Mark of the disciples' failure to understand Jesus. Their question was about parables, and though this present section is about one parable in particular, it is linked to other parables by Jesus' next words: **Then how will you understand any of the parables?** Mark clearly regards this introductory parable about the sower as the key to the rest; for him, the words of Jesus mean not simply that if the disciples cannot understand one parable they will not be able to understand others, but that this particular parable will enable them to see the meaning of others. It is for this reason that Mark has inserted the explanatory paragraphs vv.10–12 and 13–20 at this point. This confuses some modern commentators, who apparently think that Mark has been careless in his editing, since although vv.10–20 are spoken in private, the editorial notes in 4.33f., 35f., show that the parables in 4.21–32 were addressed, like vv.1–9, to the crowd from the boat. Mark, however, has used his favourite device of intercalating the material: it is neces-

sary for him to insert the saying about the effect of Jesus' parables and the explanation of the sower at this point, because to Mark this is a parable about parables, and the rest of Jesus' teaching can be understood only by those who have grasped the meaning of these words. The fact that this allegorical explanation of the sower is the key to all the parables is significant also, because it suggests that Mark sees *all* the parables as allegories.

**The sower sows the word** – i.e. the gospel; cf. Acts 6.4; 10.36f.; **14** 1 Thess. 1.6. Jesus himself has already preached the word to the crowd in 2.2. Mark does not identify the sower, perhaps because, even though the parable is about the word spoken by Jesus, it is clear from the explanation that for Mark's community the word will be spoken by Christian preachers. **The ones who are beside the path, where** **15** **the word is sown are these:** the Greek is awkward, but the sense is plain; the first group of hearers is identified as being 'beside the path', i.e. as the unproductive strip of soil bordering the path. The analogy is already strained; the idea is presumably that their hearts are like the ground, totally unreceptive. It makes no sense, in the context of this explanation, to suggest that these hearers should have been *on* the path; ὁδός here certainly has a neutral meaning (see above, on v.4). Since **Satan comes and takes away the word which has been sown in them,** he is here still active, and not bound (contrast 3.27).

**Similarly** is scarcely accurate, since the comparison has shifted, **16** and the seed which is **sown on stony ground** is now – somewhat oddly – identified with those who **hear the word** and **receive it.** This may explain the omission of the word 'similarly' in some MSS. The explanation has become somewhat muddled in the telling, since the point which is being made is not that there are differences in the character of the seed, but that the nature of the response to it differs greatly. These people **have no root in them, and are short-lived,** **17** **and. . .they fall away:** the Greek verb σκανδαλίζομαι means to stumble, and the noun from which it is derived, τό σκάνδαλον, is used frequently in the New Testament, especially by Paul, of the offence of the Cross; similarly, here, the cause of offence is the arrival of **trouble or persecution on account of the word.** Ephemeral discipleship is of no value. Persecution for the sake of the gospel was part of the experience of the early Christian communities, and it is natural that the parable has been interpreted in this way for them. With the third group, in vv.18f., who are overcome by **worldly cares** **18–19** **and the seduction of wealth and desires of other kinds,** compare the saying in Matt. 6.24f.

The elaboration of the misfortunes of the unfruitful seed in vv.15–19 has shifted the balance of the parable, so that there is now far more emphasis on the failures than there was in the original story in vv.1–

9. The triple failure in production, though recounted there in some detail, was balanced by the triple success; but in the explanation, the various difficulties seem overwhelming.

Why does Mark ascribe such importance to this parable, and see it as the key to understanding them all? The answer lies in v.14: the parable is about the proclamation of the gospel and how it is received – i.e. the response which is made to Jesus himself. The existence of four groups of hearers should not conceal the fact that basically there are only two: those whose hearing of the word bears fruit, and those whose hearing proves to be fruitless. The parable conveys the same message as the saying in v.11: the proclamation of Jesus divides mankind into two camps, and the number of those 'outside' is large by comparison with the circle who accept him. The authorities whose hearts are hardened and who reject Jesus' teaching, the crowds who hear Jesus gladly but are not prepared to accept the way of discipleship, those men and women whose concerns are centred on themselves to the exclusion of thought of God's Kingdom – all these groups
20   stand in opposition to the small band of disciples who **hear the word and accept it**. The challenge to the members of Mark's community, who have gathered together to listen to the parable and to its explanation, is clear: they must ensure that they are found in the last group. Those who **bear fruit** are those to whom the Kingdom is given: it is because the parable expresses the same truth as v.11 that it is primary for Mark, and if the disciples cannot understand this parable about their own response, they are numbering themselves with the outsiders. For another parable about the two possible responses to Jesus, compare the story of the builders used by Matthew at the close of the Sermon on the Mount (7.24–7) to express the same theme of the two ways that are open to those who hear his words.

# 7   MORE SAYINGS ON THE SAME THEME   4.21–5

*(Matt. 13.12; Luke 8.16–18; Thomas 5; 6; 8; 33; 41)*

**(21) And he said to them, 'Do you fetch a lamp in order to place it under the measure or under the bed? Isn't it in order to place it on the lampstand? (22) For nothing is hidden except to be revealed, and nothing is concealed except to be brought into the open. (23) If anyone has ears to hear, let him hear!' (24) And he said to them, 'Pay attention to what you hear! The measure with which you measure is the measure by which you will receive – and more besides; (25) for whoever has, will be given more, and whoever has nothing, will have what he has taken away.'**

This paragraph brings together four sayings which seem originally to have been separate, since in addition to the three sayings included by Luke in the Markan context (Luke 8.16–18), they are found scattered throughout Matthew and Luke (Matt. 5.15; 10.26; 7.2; 13.12, repeated at 25.29; Luke 11.33; 12.2; 6.38; 19.26). Thomas has the parable about the lamp, as well as sayings similar to those in vv.22, 23 and 25. Mark – or someone before him – has arranged the sayings in two pairs (vv.21f., 24f.), and in each pair the second saying is linked to the first by the word for (γάϱ); the importance of the sayings is underlined in both cases by an injunction to listen carefully (vv.23, 24a). A comparison of the contexts shows that the evangelists have understood these sayings in very different ways, and this suggests that it is impossible for us now to recover their original application. All we can do is attempt to discover how Mark understood them, and even this is extraordinarily difficult.

**And he said to them**: Mark does not tell us whom Jesus is now 21 addressing; it could be the disciples (as in vv.13 – 20) or the crowd (as in vv.33f.). The theme of this section – the contrast between what is hidden and what is revealed – suggests that the audience consists still of the disciples, though the injunctions to listen in vv.23f. remind us of earlier commands addressed to the crowd, and indicate that even the disciples are in danger of failure. **Do you fetch a lamp?** The Greek reads literally 'Does a lamp come?' (ἔϱχεται); the active tense suggests that Jesus himself is to be seen as the lamp that comes. The form of the Greek question (introduced by μήτι) indicates that the answer expected is 'No, of course it is not meant to be concealed, but to be put **on the lampstand**.' It would be absurd to hide it **under the measure**. The Greek word ὁ μόδιος refers to a measure for grain which could contain approximately two gallons; clearly an empty measure is meant, not one containing meal. The absurdity of hiding the light here **or under the bed** underlines the fundamental fact that a lamp is meant to give light and cannot do so if it is hidden. It has, however, been argued by Duncan Derrett that the picture is not as absurd as it seems, since the light was sometimes hidden in precisely this way because it was not permitted to extinguish it deliberately on sabbaths and holy days (*Law in the New Testament*, pp. 189ff.). Even if this was done in Jesus' time, however, it is still true that a lamp was not lit for the purpose of being concealed.

By linking the saying with the next verse, however, Mark shows 22 that he believes that the light was in fact hidden during the ministry of Jesus. Nevertheless, this was an anomaly, and of a temporary nature: the true purpose of the light will finally be achieved. The Greek word ἵνα – here translated **in order to** (v.21) and **to be** (v.22) – is used four times in these two verses: the notion that things are deliberately **hidden** in order that they may be **revealed** and **concealed**...

**to be brought into the open** is on the face of it absurd, but it is in keeping with Mark's understanding of the messianic secret. The concealment of Jesus' true identity is a necessary part of God's purpose, which embraces his crucifixion and resurrection.

23–4    The two pairs of sayings are linked together with two more injunctions to listen (again using the verb ἀκούω). The first repeats the command in v.9 almost verbatim: **If anyone has ears to hear, let him hear!** The second echoes the comment in v.12 about looking and listening: **Pay attention to what you hear!** (lit. 'Look what you hear'). Apart from this, there appears to be little connection between the rest of v.24 and vv.21f. **The measure with which you measure is the measure by which you will receive**: this saying seems much more at home in the context given it by Matthew (7.1f.) and Luke (6.37f.), where the theme is that of judging others. In the Markan setting, the words apparently mean that those who listen to Jesus will receive according to their response: i.e., in this case the warning about hearing is explained by the sayings which follow, rather than, as in the previous two cases, by underlining the words which preceded it.

25    The principle of v.24b is underlined by the next saying, **whoever has, will be given more, and whoever has nothing, will have what he has taken away**. It is possible that this was originally a proverbial saying. There is an interesting parallel in B. Berakoth 40a, though it is ascribed to teachers of about AD 300: God 'puts more into a full vessel, but not into an empty one; for it says "If hearkening you will hearken" (Exod. 15.26), implying, if you hearken you will go on hearkening, and if not you will not hearken.' Interestingly enough, the saying is here used with a meaning very close to that which it has in Mark, of 'hearkening' to the words of God. So, too, in another similar passage in B.Sukkah 46a–b: 'According to the standards of mortal man, an empty vessel is able to contain [what is put into it], and a full vessel cannot contain it, but according to the standards of the Holy One, blessed be He, a full vessel is able to contain it while an empty one cannot'; the passage then quotes Deut. 28.1. Within the setting of the ministry of Jesus, the saying might refer to those on the one hand who possess the Kingdom and those on the other who imagine that they are within the community of Israel, but who will find that they have lost that privilege. In its present context, it is perhaps understood by Mark to sum up the ideas in vv.1–20: those who accept the word – who have the secret of the Kingdom – will receive all the joys of the Kingdom, but those who do not have this secret will lose even what they had – the word which was offered and rejected.

However diverse these sayings once were, therefore, they have been related to the previous passage by the position which Mark has given them. The images remind us of the theme of vv.11–12, and the contrast there between the secret which was given to some and the truth which was hidden from many. These verses emphasize the positive message of vv.12–20: the word is meant to be heard, the seed to grow, the lamp to give light; ultimately God's purpose will be victorious. But the responsibility of men and women to respond remains: anyone with ears to hear may hear; therefore everyone must take care how he hears.

# 8　TWO PARABLES ABOUT THE KINGDOM　4.26–32

*(Matt. 13.31f.; Luke 13.18f.; Thomas 20)*

**(26) And he said, 'The Kingdom of God is like this: a man scatters seed on the earth; (27) he sleeps at night, gets up in the daytime, and the seed sprouts and grows – how he does not know. (28) The earth produces a crop by itself; first the blade, then the ear, then the full grain in the ear. (29) But when the crop is ripe, he sets to work straight away with the sickle, because harvest time has come.'**

**(30) And he said, 'How can we picture the Kingdom of God? What parable shall we use for it? (31) It is like a mustard seed; when it is sown in the ground it is smaller than any other seed; (32) and when it is sown, it springs up and grows bigger than any other plant, and puts out such large branches that the birds of the air can build nests in its shade.'**

Mark now gives us two parables which – unlike that of the sower – are specifically about **the Kingdom of God**. The first, in vv.26–9, has no parallel in the other gospels (though Matthew's parable of the tares, in 13.24–30, may be an elaboration of it). Why the other two synoptic evangelists should both omit this parable we do not know, but it is possible that they regarded it as an abbreviated version of the parable of the sower. Mark makes no mention at all of Jesus' audience, but it seems clear from vv.33f. that he thought of these parables as addressed to the crowd.

The Jew reckoned time from sunset (as is demonstrated in Gen. 26–7 1.5), so that it was natural to mention **night** before **day**. After the initial act of scattering the **seed on the earth**, the man's activities have no effect on the seed, which **sprouts and grows – how he does not know**. The **earth produces a crop by itself**, since God alone 28

controls the mysterious process of growth, which produces **first the**
29 **blade, then the ear, then the full grain in the ear.** The concluding
words, **he sets to work straight away with the sickle, because
harvest time has come,** echo Joel 3.13, which refers to the final
judgement.

30 The second parable, in vv.30–2, forms a pair with the first, but the
new introduction, **And he said,** shows that it circulated independently
in the tradition. **'How can we picture the Kingdom of God? What
parable shall we use for it?'** The opening formula, with its parallel
phrases, may be compared with similar introductions to parables in
31 Jewish sources. **Mustard seed** was apparently proverbial for its
32 smallness, cf. Matt. 17.20 and Luke 17.6, but **when it is sown, it
springs up and grows bigger than any other plant** (though
Matthew and Luke exaggerate in describing it as a tree). It grows so
large **that the birds of the air can build nests** there, or perhaps
'roost': the verb κατασκηνοῦν means literally 'to live'. Like the conclusion of the previous parable, these words echo Old Testament
imagery: the symbol of a tree in whose shade birds take shelter is
found in Ezek. 17.23 and 31.6; in Dan. 4.12, 14 and 21 the birds nest in
the branches (cf. Matt. 13.32 and Luke 13.19), and the reference is to a
great kingdom which gives protection to subject nations. If the
Markan parable also is interpreted allegorically, the birds may represent the Gentiles, who will one day have a place in the Kingdom – and
indeed, in Mark's day, are perhaps already flocking in; but the important point is the contrast between the almost invisible seed and the
enormous bush.

Many different interpretations have been given to these two
parables. One suggestion is that they teach that there is to be a long
period between sowing and maturity. However, this point is not
stressed in the first parable, and in the second is quite inappropriate,
since the mustard is a fast-growing plant which **springs up**
(ἀναβαίνει, v.32) at a great pace. Others emphasize the harvest as a
symbol of the Eschaton, either as a still future event, or as dawning in
the ministry of Jesus: the parables are assurances of the coming of
God's Kingdom. The early Christian communities may well have
taken comfort from the belief that, though response to the gospel was
often indiscernible, God was in fact in control: though they did not
understand what was taking place, they could be confident that the
harvest would eventually appear. Since the first parable stresses that
the growth of the seed is due to God, not man, it could have been used
by Jesus to teach that the Kingdom will come when God's purpose is
complete and cannot be hastened by violence (cf. Matt.11.12//Luke
16.16). In the second parable, the contrast between the tiny seed and
the large plant which grows from it fits well in the Markan context,
for it illustrates the theme of v.22. Since Mark has placed the two

parables together as a pair, it is probable that he understands them both to be conveying the same message, especially since both end in language reminiscent of Old Testament references to the final unfolding of God's purpose. It is significant that the parables are about the Kingdom of God. One would naturally expect the Kingdom to be spoken of in terms of judgement, of setting things right, and of obedience to God's will; instead, we have parables which imply that the Kingdom is present and yet not present, and which continue the theme of the previous paragraph of the contrast between what is now hidden and what will assuredly be revealed. For Mark, the Kingdom of God is displayed in the life of Jesus, but it is displayed like seed thrown on to the earth: you do not know that it is there unless you are let into the secret. But what the Kingdom will finally be is a very different matter: its greatness comes by the power of God, as silent and mysterious and inevitable as the power of growth. Just as the harvest comes from the grain sown in the earth, and the mustard bush springs from the almost invisible seed, so the Kingdom will follow from the ministry of Jesus. Unlike the parable of the sower, there is no hint here of even partial failure. By his presentation of these parables, Mark delivers a message of hope to his community, which lives in the period between the initiation of the Kingdom and its final consummation.

# 9   JESUS' USE OF PARABLES                     4.33–4

## (Matt. 13.34f.)

**(33) With many parables like these he used to teach them the word, as far as they could grasp it. (34) He never spoke to them without a parable; but when they were on their own, he explained everything to his disciples.**

Mark now sums up the theme of vv.1–32: Jesus regularly taught in parables, the full significance of which he then explained to his disciples. Mark's readers would presumably identify themselves with this smaller group, since they were among those who had responded to Jesus' challenge and were thus able to comprehend **everything**.

Jesus taught **with many parables like these**: Mark implies that 33 there were many more; presumably he has selected those parables which are most appropriate for his purpose. **He used to teach them the word** – the imperfect, ἐλάλει, suggests that teaching in parables was Jesus' normal practice – **as far as they could grasp it** (ἀκούω once again). These words have seemed to some to be inconsistent with vv.10–12, but they show us clearly Mark's understanding of that section. The parables are a challenge, but response to them lies within the power of those who hear, as vv.9, 23 and 24 have underlined. The contrast between vv.33–4a and 34b suggests that Mark is now thinking of the parables as addressed to the crowds, though they 34 have not been mentioned since v.1. **His disciples** are those who have responded to the challenge of the parables, and to them **he explained everything**: 'For whoever has, will be given more, and whoever has nothing, will have what he has taken away.'

## 10 POWER OVER WIND AND WAVES 4.35–41

*(Matt. 8.18, 23–7; Luke 8.22–5)*

**(35) That day, in the evening, he said to them, 'Let us go across to the other side.' (36) So they left the crowd and took him, as he was, in the boat; and there were other boats accompanying him. (37) A heavy squall blew up, and the waves broke over the boat, so that it quickly filled with water. (38) And he was in the stern asleep on a cushion; and they roused him and said, 'Teacher, don't you care that we are sinking?' (39) He woke up, reproved the wind and said to the sea, 'Quiet! Be silent!' And the wind dropped and there was a great calm. (40) And he said to them, 'Why are you so cowardly? Don't you have faith yet?' (41) And they were terrified, and said to one another, 'Who can this be? Even the wind and the sea obey him.'**

Having brought the section on parables to a conclusion, Mark turns his attention to a group of four miracles, which form two pairs. The first story, that of the stilling of the storm, is also the first of the so-called 'nature miracles', but the difference between these and healing miracles is probably more obvious to us than to Mark, for whom they are all indications of the authority of Jesus.

Some commentators have interpreted the story as symbolizing the storms of persecution experienced by the Church, and her appeal to an apparently indifferent Lord to come to her aid (so Nineham); although this kind of allegorical interpretation was made as early as Tertullian, there is no indication in the narrative that Mark himself intended it to be understood in this way. For him, the main point seems to be that which is implied by the final question of the disciples, 'Who then is this?' Like all Mark's material, this narrative is christological and points the reader to the significance of Jesus' action. The background of the story is to be found in Old Testament passages such as Ps. 107.23–32 and Jonah 1.1–16, which describe

God's control of the sea, and Exod. 14.21–31, the account of Israel's deliverance from the sea through Moses. The story may be based on some incident in the life of Jesus, but, if so, it is impossible now to say anything about the nature of that incident. The account is indeed intrinsically improbable, since we find experienced fishermen, not merely taken by surprise by the weather, but apparently scared out of their wits by a sudden storm, while Jesus, the landlubber, sleeps calmly in the stern; the unlikelihood of these events suggests that we are meant to see a deeper significance in the narrative. Whatever the origin of the story, its point for Mark is the divine power at work in Jesus, a power which was experienced by the disciples during his ministry and affirmed by subsequent generations of men and women who had faith in him.

The story is linked to the preceding narrative, either by Mark or 35 by a previous narrator, with the words **That day, in the evening.** Another link is found in the phrase **as he was**, which presumably 36 means 'without disembarking': **the boat** is the one Jesus entered in 4.1. The **other boats accompanying him** play no further part in the story, and it is not clear why they are mentioned. The **heavy squall** 37 obviously blew up suddenly, filling the boat **with water**. Because of its position, the Lake of Galilee is subject to storms caused by sudden inrushes of wind which begin and end abruptly. For Jesus to sleep 38 in these conditions suggests confidence in his disciples' seamanship, but to sleep when surrounded by danger is also a sign of trust in God (e.g. Ps. 4.8), and no doubt Mark interpreted Jesus' sleep in that way. The **cushion** on which he slept seems to refer to the helmsman's seat which, being **in the stern**, would be comparatively dry. **And they roused him and said. . .** : the urgency of the situation is graphically conveyed in the Greek by Mark's use of historic presents. **'Teacher, don't you care that we are sinking?'** The disciples' words to Jesus are rough and indignant, and they are toned down by Matthew and Luke; apart from 1.37, they are the first words addressed to Jesus by his disciples in the gospel, and it is to be noted that they address him as **Teacher**; the word Διδάσκαλε presumably represents the Aramaic 'rabbi'.

Jesus **reproved** (ἐπετίμησεν) **the wind**. The form of the verb is 39 exactly that used in 1.25, where Jesus reproved an unclean spirit; since the sea, in ancient mythology, symbolized the powers of chaos and evil, it is not surprising that storms were thought to be caused by rebellious powers, or that the narrative is so closely parallel to accounts of exorcisms. The command **Be silent** also echoes the narrative of 1.25, using another form of the verb (φιμόω) used there in silencing the unclean spirit. As in the exorcism narratives, the result of Jesus' command is dramatic: **the wind dropped and there was a great calm** – a calm as great as the great storm in v.37 (the word translated 'great' here and 'heavy' there is the same, i.e. μεγάλη).

Jesus now rebukes the disciples for their timidity and lack of faith: **'Why are you so cowardly? Don't you have faith yet?'** The contrast between their behaviour and his demonstrates their different attitudes to God: Jesus trusts, while the disciples panic. For Mark, however, the point of the narrative is the disciples' failure to understand and believe what is happening in the ministry of Jesus: why do they not believe, when they have seen what they have seen, and heard what they have heard? The narrative ends with the effect of the incident on the disciples: **they were terrified.** The verb φοβέω, to fear, is used repeatedly in later sections of the gospel to describe reaction to Jesus and usually seems to indicate an attitude which, though responding to the power of God seen in Jesus, nevertheless stands in contrast to faith (e.g. 5.36; 6.50;10.32;16.8). The form of wording here echoes the LXX of Jonah 1.10, and there are other parallels between the two stories: e.g. Jonah, too, is asleep and has to be roused, 1.5f.; the fear of the sailors in Jonah is evoked by his statement that he serves Yahweh who made the sea and the dry land, while the disciples' fear is occasioned by Jesus' power to control the sea.

**Who can this be? Even the wind and the sea obey him.** As in 1.27, those who witness the activity of Jesus are left wondering about the source and character of his authority, though to the reader of the gospel the answer to their question is obvious. It is God who made the sea, and God alone who controls it, e.g. Ps. 89.8f. The authority with which Jesus acts, as in 2.1–10, is that of God himself.

# 11 POWER OVER DEMONS 5.1–20

## *(Matt. 8.28–34; Luke 8.26–39)*

**(1) And they came to the other side of the lake, to the district of the Gerasenes.[1] (2) And as soon as he got out of the boat, a man with an unclean spirit came to meet him out of the tombs. (3) He had made his home among the tombs, and nobody was able any longer to bind him with a chain; (4) for though he had been bound many times with fetters and chains, he had torn the chains apart and smashed the fetters: no one was strong enough to subdue him. (5) Night and day, among the tombs and on the hillsides, he cried aloud and cut himself with stones. (6) And when he saw Jesus from afar, he ran and threw himself down before him,**

1 Some MSS read *Gergesenes*, other *Gadarenes*.

(7) and cried in a loud voice, 'What do you want with me, Jesus, Son of the Most High God? In God's name, do not torment me.' (8) (For Jesus was saying to him, 'Unclean spirit, come out of the man.') (9) And he asked him, 'What is your name?' And he said, 'My name is Legion, for we are many.' (10) And he begged hard that he would not send them out of that district. (11) Now there was a large herd of pigs nearby, feeding on the hillside. (12) And they begged him, 'Send us into the pigs; let us go into them.' (13) And he gave them leave; and the unclean spirits came out and entered the pigs, and the herd of about two thousand rushed down the steep bank into the lake, and were drowned in the lake.

(14) And the men who were in charge of them took to their heels and brought the news to the town and countryside; and people came to see what had happened. (15) And when they came to Jesus and saw the demoniac who had been possessed by the legion of demons sitting there, clothed and in his right mind, they were afraid. (16) And the eyewitnesses described to them what had happened to the demoniac, and about the pigs. (17) Then they began to beg him to leave their district. (18) As he was getting into the boat, the man who had been possessed begged to go with him. (19) But Jesus would not allow him; 'Go home to your own people,' he said, 'and tell them how much the Lord has done for you, and how he had mercy on you.' (20) And he went off and began to proclaim throughout the Decapolis how much Jesus had done for him; and everyone marvelled.

Mark has already given us one brief account of an exorcism, in 1.23–7. Now, in a much more detailed narrative, he gives an even more remarkable example of Jesus' authority over unclean spirits. The expulsion of a whole army of spirits is a dramatic fulfilment of the cry in 1.24: 'Have you come to destroy us?' The source of Jesus' authority and its significance have already been made clear in 3.22–30. The story forms a pair with the account in 4.35–41 of the stilling of the storm: Jesus is able to control both the raging of wind and waves and the raging of a possessed demoniac, since in both cases the forces responsible for the outbursts recognize his superior authority. Once again, those who witness what happens react with tremendous fear.

The detail in the story serves to emphasize its point: the extraordinary strength of the demoniac (vv.3–5) demonstrates the even greater power of Jesus to whom these forces must yield. The destruction of the pigs perhaps indicates the destruction of the unclean spirits and certainly underlines the cure of the demoniac. There is, indeed, an embarrassing amount of detail, and the narrative does not run smoothly: vv.3–5 are somewhat intrusive and v.6 seems strange after v.2b.; v.8 is clumsy, and we have two 'proofs' of the demoniac's cure, in vv.11–13 and 15. Luke has made an attempt – not wholly satisfactory – to tidy up the narrative by moving the description of the demoniac. One possibility is that Mark has combined two accounts of the miracle, one of which included vv.1–2, 7–8, and perhaps 15, where the demoniac's cure is demonstrated by his behaviour, and the other vv.3–6 and 9ff., where the account centres on the man's strength, his belief that he was possessed by a legion of spirits, and the removal of these spirits to the pigs. The parallel account in Matthew, although, as is usual with stories of healing miracles, much shorter than Mark's version, speaks of two demoniacs instead of one, but Matthew may have been combining Mark's narrative here with that of Mark 1.23–7, which he omits; a similar phenomenon occurs at Matt. 20.29–34 (//Mark 10.46–52, and cf. 8.22–6).

It has often been suggested that this narrative is a combination of a miracle-story and a popular tale about an unknown exorcist who tricked some demons into self-destruction. Apart from the difficulties just noted, which do suggest the bringing together of two separate tales of exorcism, the real reason for this particular suggestion seems to be a dislike for the idea that Jesus permitted the destruction of the herd of pigs (see below, on v.13).

Those who heard this story in Mark's community would conclude that if Jesus was able to deal with a whole legion of unclean spirits, then the power of Satan was finally destroyed.

For details paralleled in 1.23 – 7, see the notes on that passage.

The scene now changes from Galilee to the neighbouring Decapolis.

1 The place on **the other side of the lake** where Jesus and his disciples landed is identified by Mark as **the district of the Gerasenes**. The difficulty of this reading is reflected in the variants 'Gergesenes' and 'Gadarenes' (as in Matthew), which seem to be attempts at emendation by those aware of the fact that Gerasa was situated 30 miles from the lake; it seems unlikely that the coastal region was known by this name, and probable that Mark's knowledge of the geography of the area was vague. Gadara is on a hill six miles from the lake, and Gergesa (apparently suggested by Origen) cannot

2–3 now be positively identified. **The tombs** in which the man **had made his home** were thought to be the haunt of demons, as well as being regarded as unclean: they were a suitable spot for one who was cut

4–5 off from ordinary life and as good as dead. The statement that **night and day...he cried aloud and cut himself with stones** suggests that he was attempting to destroy himself. The description of the man's enormous strength in vv.3f. concludes with the statement that **no one was strong enough** (ἴσχυε) **to subdue him**. Now, however, he is confronted by the mightier one (ὁ ἰσχυρότερος, 1.7) who has already bound the strong man Satan (ὁ ἰσχυρός, 3.27); Jesus is therefore able to subdue him without needing **to bind him with a chain**.

6 **And when he saw Jesus from afar, he ran. . . .**This continues

naturally after the description in vv.3–5 but reads strangely after v.2.
Either Mark has pieced two stories together, or he has forgotten what
he wrote there. The statement that **he threw himself down before**
Jesus suggests a recognition of the latter's authority; the verb (προσ-
κυνέω) can mean 'to worship', but its basic meaning is to kneel or
prostrate oneself, in supplication or respect. **What do you want with**    7
**me?** The demoniac's words (τί ἐμοὶ καὶ σοί) repeat those used in 1.24,
except for the rather strange fact that here we have the singular 'me'
instead of the plural 'us', a form which would have seemed more appropriate here; this is another indication that these words probably
belonged originally to one story, and the conversation about Legion
which follows to another. The demoniac addresses Jesus as **Jesus,**
**Son of the Most High God**; once again, we see how unclean spirits
are depicted as aware of Jesus' true identity (cf. 1.24 and 3.11). The
term 'the Most High God' is one found in the Old Testament, mostly
used by non-Israelites in speaking of Israel's God: it is therefore appropriate in the mouth of one who was living in Gentile territory and
was presumably himself a Gentile. **In God's name**: the equivalent
phrase was used in Jewish exorcisms but seems somewhat ludicrous
in the mouth of a demoniac; presumably it represents a last attempt
to resist the powers of Jesus. Matthew understands the request **do**
**not torment me** as a reference to the eschatological punishment,
already breaking in because of the coming of Jesus, but in Mark it
probably means a simple entreaty to be spared the agony of exorcism: the victim is so possessed by the unclean spirit that he desires
his own destruction (v.5), not release.

If the suggestion that Mark has pieced together two exorcism    8
narratives is correct, v.8 may once have followed naturally after the
preceding words with a simple 'and'. Now, however, it reads as a
somewhat awkward parenthesis. The fact that Jesus asks the name    9
of the man (or spirit) reflects the contemporary belief that knowledge
of a name gave one a certain power over that person. Some commentators have seen the reply **My name is Legion** as an attempt to dodge
the issue, but it seems more likely that it is understood by Mark as
another example of the power of Jesus: the unclean spirits have to
submit to him, even to the extent of giving him the information which
will lead to their expulsion. The significance of the name is seen in
the comment **for we are many**: a Roman legion consisted of over
6,000 men. **And he begged hard that he would not send them.** . . .    10
Mark's grammar reflects not only the difficulty of speaking consistently of one man with many demons, but the divided condition of the
man himself. Their request not to be sent **out of that district** is a concession of defeat and reflects a belief that demons are associated with
a particular locality (cf. Luke 11.24–7).

The presence of **a large herd of pigs** is another indication of the    11
Gentile locality. It was entirely appropriate that the unclean spirits

should choose to live in a herd of unclean animals. Their request to enter them is hardly an intelligent one, however, since the pigs promptly **rushed down the steep bank into the lake, and were drowned**: the impulse towards self-destruction, seen already in the demoniac, now comes to fruition. At best, this would make the demons homeless again, but we are perhaps meant to understand the incident as involving their destruction: Jesus has not only rescued the man from their power but has destroyed the demons as well. The death of such a vast herd of animals is a dramatic sign that Satan's kingdom is crumbling, and his house being plundered.

12–13

Modern readers are often disturbed by this story, because of the 'unethical' behaviour attributed to Jesus in permitting the destruction of 'innocent' animals who were the property of someone else. For Mark, of course, such problems would not arise: pigs were unclean animals (their meat forbidden to Jews), and their destruction was as appropriate as that of the unclean spirits. Some have tried to explain the incident by suggesting that a paroxysm accompanying the exorcism terrified the nearby herd and sent them rushing headlong over a precipice (κρημνός, translated **steep bank**, can also mean a cliff or precipice), but it is useless for us to try to reconstruct what might have happened. The interpretation given to the incident by Mark was the natural deduction from the available facts, granted the basic belief of those concerned that the man had been possessed by a large number of unclean spirits, and that these had been driven out.

14    As usual, news of what Jesus has done spread throughout the land, this time taken by the only witnesses, **the men who** had been **in**

15  **charge of** the pigs. The recovery of **the demoniac** is demonstrated by the fact that he is found **sitting...clothed and in his right mind**. The reaction of those who **came to see what had happened** and found this transformation in the man is typical: **they were afraid**.

16  **And the eyewitnesses described to them what had happened to the demoniac, and about the pigs.** The repetitive style again

17  suggests the piecing together of two narratives. **Then they began to beg him to leave their district**: this demand has been interpreted by some as an expression of indignation at the loss of the pigs. It is much more likely, however, that Mark understood it as an indication of the inhabitants' fear of Jesus' uncanny power, as Luke makes

18  clear (Luke 8.37; cf. also 5.8). By contrast, the healed demoniac **begged to go with him** – lit. 'that he might be with him' (ἵνα ᾖ μετ' αὐτοῦ), a somewhat odd way of expressing his desire to accompany Jesus which echoes the phrase used in 3.14, when Jesus appointed

19  twelve to be with him (ἵνα ὦσιν μετ' αὐτοῦ). **But Jesus would not allow him**, though it is not clear why. The number of disciples is not complete, since others, later, are called to follow Jesus (8.34) or do follow him (10.52). Such a request may, however, have been made

and refused: there is no reason to assume that Jesus accepted all would-be disciples as intimates, and indeed Mark indicates that he made a choice (3.13–19). Moreover, if the man was a Gentile, and Jesus confined his ministry to Jews (cf. 7.24–30), we would not expect him to include the man among his followers. Jesus' command that the man should **go home** and tell his **own people** what had happened has sometimes been seen as a remarkable exception to Mark's theme of secrecy, and attempts have even been made to understand the words as meaning 'keep it in the family', with v.20 indicating the man's disobedience. However, the verse is not as exceptional as has been suggested. The only instances of secrecy so far have been occasions when Jesus silenced unclean spirits, forbidding them to announce his identity publicly (1.25, 34; 3.12), and his command to the leper to say nothing to anyone (1.44). Healings and exorcisms, far from being secret, have taken place in public and have been the cause of much amazement (1.32–4; 2.1–12; 3.1–6, 7–12). It is misleading to impose a theory of secrecy on all the Markan material. If there is a difference between the command to the leper in 1.44 and that given here, it may be because the circumstances in the two cases are different. In the former narrative, the command to silence stands in contrast to the instruction to the man to show himself to the priest to make the appropriate offering: the man's first duty is to go to the priest for authentication of his cleansing, and to fulfil the requirement of the Law, so that he may take his place again as a member of the Jewish nation. In the present story, however, there is no need for authentication, and the man is sent immediately to his own home and family. In different ways, the command of Jesus, **Go. . .** symbolizes in each case the restoration of a former outcast to his own people. Here, the man is told to report **how much the Lord has done for you.** 'The Lord' (ὁ Κύριος) may refer to Jesus himself, as it does in 1.3 and 12.36f., but in words attributed to Jesus it is perhaps more likely that it is used, as in the LXX, of God; Luke understands it that way and replaces the title with the word 'God'. Since the healing miracles of Jesus are linked with his proclamation of God's Kingdom, they are a part of God's salvific activity, and it is especially appropriate that this should be made clear to everyone who hears about this particular miracle, which has taken place in an area where Jesus has not taught: the miracles of Jesus are not to be detached from the good news and spoken of simply as marvels. If this man, unlike anyone else in Mark's gospel, is told to spread the news of what has happened, it may be precisely because it was an area where Jesus himself did not preach.

The former demoniac **began to proclaim.** . . .The verb 'to pro-  20
claim' (κηρύσσω) is used regularly of preaching the gospel (cf. Mark 1.4, 7, 14, 38, 39; 3.14; 6.12; 13.10; 14.9). What he announced was **how**

**much Jesus had done for him**; the parallelism between this and Jesus' words in the previous verse suggests that Mark is deliberately underlining the fact that in the activity of Jesus is to be seen the activity of God himself (cf. 1.3). **The Decapolis** (lit. 'ten cities') was a confederation of ten Greek cities, mostly east of the Jordan, under the protection of the Roman governor of Syria, but enjoying a certain degree of independence. The population was mixed and very much influenced by Greek culture. Since the area was predominantly Gentile, it is possible that Mark understood the man's commission as a precursor of the mission to the Gentiles: though Jesus himself did not preach in Gentile territory and stayed there only briefly, he nevertheless commanded that God's activity and mercy should be announced there. Here, as in Galilee, the news of what Jesus has done results in amazement: **everyone marvelled**.

# 12   POWER TO RESTORE LIFE                      5.21–43

*(Matth. 9.18–26; Luke 8.40–56)*

**(21) And when Jesus had again crossed by boat to the other shore, a large crowd gathered round him; and he was by the lakeside. (22) And one of the synagogue leaders, named Jairus,[1] came up; and seeing Jesus, he fell at his feet (23) and pleaded with him, saying, 'My little daughter is dying. Come and lay your hands on her, so that she may be saved, and live.' (24) And he went with him; and a great crowd followed him, pressing round him.**

**(25) And a woman who had suffered from a haemorrhage for twelve years (26) and had endured much at the hands of many doctors and had spent all she had, yet was no better, but instead had grown worse, (27) hearing the reports about Jesus, came up in the crowd from behind and touched his garment; (28) for she said, 'If I can only touch his clothes, I shall be saved.' (29) And immediately the flow of blood dried up, and she felt in her body that she was cured of her affliction. (30) Jesus knew straight away that power had gone out of him, and turning round in the crowd, he asked, 'Who touched my clothes?' (31) And his disciples said to him, 'You see the crowd pressing round you; yet you say, "Who touched me?"' (32) But he was looking round to see who had done it. (33) And the woman, fearful and trembling, knowing what had happened to her, came and fell before him and told him the whole truth. (34) He said to her, 'Daughter, your faith has saved you. Go in peace, and be free of your affliction.'**

1 The words *named Jairus* are missing from D and the old Latin MSS.

(35) While he was still speaking, a message arrived from the house of the synagogue leader, saying, 'Your daughter is dead. Why trouble the teacher any more?' (36) Jesus, overhearing the message, said to the leader of the synagogue, 'Don't be afraid; just believe.' (37) And he allowed no one to accompany him, except for Peter and James and John, James' brother. (38) And they came to the house of the synagogue leader, and he saw the commotion – weeping and loud wailing; (39) and he went in and said to them, 'Why are you making this commotion? Why are you weeping? The child is not dead – she is asleep.' (40) And they laughed at him. Then he turned everyone out, took the child's father and mother and his companions and entered [the room] where the child was. (41) And grasping the child's hand, he said to her, '*Talitha cum*', which means, 'Little girl, I tell you, get up,' (42) And straight away the girl got up and walked about; she was twelve years old. And they were utterly astounded. (43) Then he gave them strict orders to let no one know what had happened, and he told them to give her something to eat.

Mark narrates a second pair of miracles, this time using one as an interlude within the other. The stories may have been told in this way from the beginning, but it seems highly likely that they have been put together by Mark, since he is certainly fond of this kind of sandwich arrangement. As in 3.21–35 and 11.12–25, the second story not only fills up a space in the narrative, allowing time for other events to occur, but is related thematically to the first: the life which Jesus restores to the twelve-year-old child is paralleled by the life which he gives to the woman, from whom strength has been draining away for twelve years. The two stories are also linked by the theme of faith (vv.34 and 36).

The story raises obvious problems: was the child really dead? Matthew and Luke interpreted the narrative in this way, and it seems unlikely that Mark intended anything else. Whether or not the story developed from a narrative about a child in a coma, as many have suggested, it is now impossible to make any judgement about the origin of the story on the basis of Mark's account, and speculations about this cannot help us to understand his interpretation of the story.

One notable feature of the story about the child is that her father is said to be a leader of the synagogue; unusually in Mark, a member of the Jewish 'establishment' not only accepts Jesus' authority but appeals to him for help and apparently continues to believe in him, even when all human hope has gone. Another very interesting feature of this story is the vocabulary, much of which would be appropriate to the resurrection hope of the Christian community: the verbs 'save' and 'live' in v.23, the contrast between death and sleep in v.39, the command to **get up** in v.41 (once again we have ἔγειρε – see 2.9 and 3.3), the mockery of the bystanders in v.42, all suggest that those who heard the story would see another significance in it: the child's restoration would be understood as a symbol of their own future resurrection. The story of the woman would have been of special interest to Gentiles, since they, too, had once been 'outsiders', excluded from the community of God's people. Both stories would have brought reassurance of the new life and salvation which came to believers through the power of Jesus.

21    Jesus crosses the lake **again...to the other shore**, and is presumably back in Galilee: the suggestion of some commentators that he is in Capernaum is only a guess. The scene is similar to that in 3.7 and 4.1: Jesus remains **by the lakeside** and is surrounded by **a large crowd**.

22    The information that **the synagogue leader** was **named Jairus** is missing in some MSS and may have crept into Mark's account from Luke 8.41. His undignifed behaviour in throwing himself at Jesus'

23    feet underlines the surprising fact that this prominent religious official is prepared to come to him for help. His **daughter** is at death's door – not, as in Matthew, already dead; the distracted father approaches Jesus because all else has failed. His request that Jesus should **come and lay** his **hands on her** assumes that Jesus follows the normal practice in healing: the child can thereby **be saved and live**; the verb 'to save' (σῴζω) means to restore to health, but in the context of the gospel it has a wider significance.

24    The fact that **a great crowd followed him, pressing round him**, provides the setting for the next story, which is dove-tailed into that

25    of the official's daughter. The details of the woman's illness emphasize

26    its severity: it has lasted **for twelve years**, she has **endured much at the hands of many doctors**, and she has **spent all she had** to no effect. Mark's description of her ailment is far more dramatic than Matthew's brief account. Like the child, the woman is beyond human aid. Her affliction is not simply physical, however; her complaint was presumably vaginal bleeding (a vital fact that male commentators assume, but which most coyly omit to state!), and she is therefore

27–8    unclean (Lev. 15.25–30) and thus an outcast from society. It is for this reason, and not simply because of natural shyness or modesty, that she approaches Jesus secretly, saying to herself, **'If I can only touch his clothes, I shall be saved.'** Her confidence that a mere touch of his garment could restore her seems to us to border on a belief in magic, but was based on **the reports about Jesus** that had reached her. It was common at the time to think of clothing as an extension of personality, and the woman's desire to **touch his clothes** was natural.

29    Having done so, the woman knew **that she was cured of her affliction**. The word translated 'affliction', here and in v.34, is μάστιξ

30    (see on 3.10). **Jesus knew...that power had gone out of him.** It is

impossible to translate the Greek neatly into English, for the phrase
**out of him** belongs to **power**, and not to the verb: Jesus is the source
of the power and does not simply act like the conductor of an electric
current. The word **power** (δύναμις) is used in the LXX primarily of
the power of God himself, or of the result of that power – i.e. a 'mighty
work': it is this power which resides in Jesus. As with the leper in
1.40–5, this power is greater than the contaminating force of the
woman's impurity. The question **'Who touched my clothes?'** seems 31
absurd to **the disciples**, with **the crowd pressing round** him; Luke
tones down their abrupt reply and Matthew omits it. Luke appears to 33
attribute the fact that the woman is **fearful and trembling** to the fact
that she has been found out; she might well have expected Jesus to be
angry, since in a state of impurity she should neither have been mix-
ing in a crowd nor touching Jesus. But Mark links the woman's
emotion with the fact that she knew **what had happened to her**,
which suggests that he understands her reaction as one of awe in
response to the amazing power (δύναμις) of Jesus. Cf. the similar
reaction of the disciples in 4.41, of the spectators in 5.15, and of the
women in 16.8.

**He said to her, 'Daughter'**: Jesus' words to the woman acknowledge 34
her **faith**, and the incident is removed from the realm of magic into
that of a personal relationship with Jesus. Matthew achieves the
same end by omitting part of the story, so that the woman is not
healed until Jesus speaks to her. For both evangelists, it is the
woman's faith which has **saved** her: the verb σῴζω is used here for
the third time in this section. Again it implies more than physical
healing: she has been restored not only to health but to society. The
final command, **be free of your affliction**, sounds tautologous, but in
fact it looks forward, rather than repeating the cure, since the Greek
(ἴσθι ὑγιής, translated **be free**) means 'be healthy'. Just as the father's
request for his child in v.23 was for salvation and life, so the woman
has gained salvation and health.

Mark links the two miracles closely together with the phrase **while** 35
**he was still speaking**. The **message. . .from the house of the syna-**
**gogue leader** dashes his last hope: there is no point in troubling
Jesus to come further. The Greek word translated **overhearing** 36
(παρακούσας) can equally well be translated 'ignoring', which explains why this translation is sometimes given. Although the verb is
used in the sense of 'ignore' elsewhere in the Greek Bible (seven
times in the LXX and in Matt. 18.17), the meaning 'overhear' suits the
context here better, since Jesus does not ignore **the message** – on the
contrary, he is led by what he has heard to urge Jairus not to **be**
**afraid**, but to go on believing (**just believe** translates a present imperative) in spite of the news which he has received: it is Jairus who is
to ignore the message!

37    The three disciples chosen to **accompany** Jesus – **Peter . . . James and John** – seem to form an inner circle in Mark: they are with Jesus again at the transfiguration and in Gethsemane and are mentioned
38    together with Andrew in Mark 13. **The commotion** at **the house of the synagogue leader** is caused either by professional mourners, who would arrive at such times, or by members of the official's own
39    household. Jesus' words to those who were lamenting the child's death with **weeping and loud wailing** has caused endless discussion. It has sometimes been argued that his words are to be understood literally: **the child is not dead,** and those who have reported otherwise to Jairus are mistaken – in other words, Mark is attributing super-
40    natural knowledge to Jesus, who has not yet seen the child. Certainly the characters in the story who **laughed at him** assume him to be making this kind of claim. But readers of the gospel understand that Jesus' diagnosis is of quite a different kind: his declaration that the child **is asleep** makes perfectly good sense in the context of the miracle. The child is to be restored and so is not irrevocably dead; since she is to be given life, her death has the nature of sleep. There is an interesting rabbinic parallel in Genesis Rabbah 96.60f., where Jacob is told, 'Thou shalt sleep, but thou shalt not die.' The contrast there is clearly between physical death and final resurrection, and it is this contrast which is symbolized in this story. See also the discussion in John 11.4, 11–14.

       **Then he turned everyone out, took the child's father and mother and his companions and entered [the room] where the child was.** This miracle is performed privately, because it is to be
41    kept secret (cf. 7.33; 8.23). The words *Talitha cum* are a transliteration of an Aramaic phrase, whose literal meaning is 'Lamb, get up'. Contemporary miracle stories sometimes contain foreign formulae, and this might explain why the Aramaic words were preserved in a Greek account: the story apparently conforms to the normal pattern of miracle stories. But *this* formula is in fact not mumbo-jumbo. The words would have been perfectly comprehensible in their original setting, whether this was an incident in Jesus' ministry or a story emanating from Aramaic-speaking Christians, and Mark takes care to translate them for his readers, so that they, too, will understand them. Thus they do not *function* as a foreign formula in Mark's account. Mark translates the words for us: **'Little girl, I tell you, get up'** – lit. 'Rise!' (once again, he uses the injunction ἔγειρε).
42    The response is dramatic: **straight away the girl got up and walked about.** Mark's comment that the child **was twelve years old** is perhaps an afterthought to explain that she was old enough to walk, but he may well have seen significance in the fact that the woman whom Jesus had just cured had been ill, and thus debarred (probably by her medical and certainly by her social condition) from the possi-

bility of bearing a child, for twelve years. **They were utterly astounded**: the amazement of the onlookers, expressed in a vivid Greek phrase (ἐξέστησαν ἐκστάσει μεγάλῃ) is understandable, but Jesus' **strict orders to let no one know what had happened** are 43 extraordinary: it would obviously be impossible to keep secret the resurrection of a child whom everyone knew to have been dead. Jesus might well have urged those who were present not to rush around talking about what had happened, but Mark's emphatic language is certainly more than an extravagant way of saying this. We have here once again the theme of secrecy in connection with one of Jesus' miracles: the child's cure must not be announced to those who are unable to comprehend it – which include, of course, all Jesus' contemporaries. The miracle of resurrection can only be understood by those who believe in the one who has himself been raised from the dead.

One aspect of this question which is often overlooked is the interesting contrast between Jesus' treatment of the woman and the child. The woman attempted to be healed in complete secrecy but was not allowed to keep her restoration to herself; the cure of her complaint could not be openly demonstrated or cause wonder, but it was nevertheless brought out into the open by Jesus himself. In the case of the child, however, whose restoration would inevitably be a nine days' wonder, the witnesses of the cure are told to keep quiet. Although the reaction of Jesus in the two stories is so different, it is possible that Mark assumes a common underlying motive; the danger in both cases is of detaching the miracle from the wider context of what is happening in Jesus. The woman could easily treat Jesus as a magician-healer, and the friends of the family babble about his ability to raise the dead; but these things must only be spoken of in the context of faith in Jesus and must not be detached from his proclamation of God's Kingdom. Another link between the two stories is that both victims are ceremonially unclean. In both cases, Jesus comes into contact with defiling forces, but his own power is demonstrably greater.

The final command, **to give her something to eat**, underlines the reality of the child's restoration to life.


# 13   DISBELIEF IN HIS OWN TOWN          6.1–6a

*(Matt. 13.53–8; Luke 4.16–30; Thomas 31)*

**(1) And he left that place and came to his home town, and his disciples followed him. (2) And on the sabbath, he began to teach**

in the synagogue, and many who heard him were astonished, saying, 'Where did he come by all this? What wisdom is this that has been given him? What are these mighty works that are performed at his hands? (3) Isn't this the carpenter, the son of Mary[1] and the brother of James and Joses and Judas and Simon? And aren't his sisters here with us?' And they were offended by him. (4) And Jesus said to them, 'A prophet is not without honour except in his home town, among his own family and in his own home.' (5) And he was unable to do any mighty work there, except that he put his hands on a few sick people and healed them. (6) And he marvelled at their lack of faith.

In contrast to the faith (however inadequate and wavering) of those who come to Jesus for help, Mark gives us this account of the refusal of those who had once been Jesus' neighbours to accept his teaching or respond to him. Jesus' rejection by 'his own' (cf. John 1.11) is emphasized throughout Mark's gospel. His own family have already shown their lack of faith in him (3.21, 31–5) and been disowned as a result. The failure of his own nation to respond to him, and their consequent rejection by God, will form the climax of the story. For the citizens of his own town also there is rejection: those who are offended by Jesus and do not believe in him are unable to experience any mighty work.

For the early Christian community, the story of Jesus' rejection in his own town was symbolic of the failure of Israel to respond to the gospel; however, Jesus was not 'without honour' among those who had once been outsiders but who now had faith in him.

1  By **his home town** (πατρίς) Mark probably means Nazareth, which
2  he mentioned by name in 1.9. The scene returns to **the synagogue**, where Jesus is presumably invited to speak. **Many** in English suggests less than everyone, but in the LXX, following Semitic idiom, πολλοί usually means 'all'; Mark does not intend to imply that some were unmoved. The congregation is **astonished** at his **wisdom** and at the **mighty works** (in Greek 'powers', δυνάμεις) **that are performed at his hands**: they recognize him as the agent of a supernatural power. But their astonishment quickly turns to disbelief: he cannot be what he seems, since they know who he is and where he comes
3  from. **Isn't this the carpenter, the son of Mary?** The variant reading, *Isn't this the son of the carpenter and Mary?* is read by a significant minority of MSS, including the important early 𝔓45. It is difficult to choose between these two readings. If the text in our translation is correct, the easiest explanation of the variant is that there has been an assimilation to Matt. 13.55. An alternative explanation is that the

1 Following the great majority of MSS. A few, including 𝔓45 and fam. 13, read *Isn't this the son of the carpenter and Mary?*

change (like Matthew's change of Mark) is due to an early dislike of the idea that Jesus could have been a manual worker. This attitude is found in Origen who denies that any gospel describes Jesus as working with his hands (*Contra Celsum*, vi.36); presumably he knew only the variant text of Mark. If the less well-attested reading is correct, then we have an explanation for Matthew's version (Luke seems to follow an independent tradition), but it is difficult to understand how the reading we have accepted arose. The suggestion that the alternative was thought to contradict belief in the Virgin Birth can be dismissed, since both Matthew and Luke (who alone record the Nativity) refer to Jesus as the son of Joseph the carpenter. On balance, the reading given above therefore seems the more likely.

It was an insult in Jewish society to describe anyone as the son of his mother alone, and it is possible that the phrase reflects rumours that Jesus' birth was illegitimate, in which case the objection to Jesus is not merely that he was a local boy. Mark, however, may not have realized that the description might have these implications. The reference to four brothers of Jesus, **James and Joses and Judas and Simon**, was interpreted later as meaning half-brothers or cousins, because of the doctrine of Mary's perpertual virginity, but Mark knows nothing of this belief. The fact that everyone knew Jesus' brothers, not to mention **his sisters** (Mark does not, in fact, name them, and they tend to be omitted from any discussion of the identity of Jesus' relatives!), indicates that Jesus must be quite ordinary and cannot possibly be remarkable in any way.

**And they were offended by him.** The Greek verb used here (σκανδαλίζειν) means 'to cause to fall', and so can have the meaning in the passive of 'to stumble', or 'to be offended' (cf. 4.17); the cognate noun (τό σκάνδαλον) has the sense of 'temptation' or 'cause of offence' and is used of Jesus himself in Rom. 9.33 and I Pet. 2.8 in a quotation from Isa. 8.14 ('a rock that will make them fall'), and of the Cross in I Cor. 1.23 ('a stumbling-block'). In using the verb here, Mark perhaps has in mind the idea that Jesus is the one who is appointed by God but whom the Jews find it impossible to accept, who will therefore paradoxically cause their rejection: it is not simply that they took offence at him.

**And Jesus said to them, 'A prophet is not without honour except** 4 **in his home town, among his own family and in his own home.'** A partial parallel to Jesus' words is found in the Gospel of Thomas 31, and both versions may derive from a proverbial saying. It has been suggested that the words were attributed to Jesus, and the incident then built up round them. This seems improbable, since it is far more likely that Jesus applied the term 'prophet' to himself than that it was considered an appropriate title for him by the early Church. Nor is the

5 scene in Nazareth an unlikely one. **And he was unable to do any mighty work there.** Mark apparently did not share Matthew's feeling that it was inappropriate to speak of Jesus' inability to heal (cf. Matt. 13.58). It is not simply that Jesus refuses to perform miracles; mighty works cannot be done except in a context of faith – and this faith (with a few exceptions) was lacking, for the people have rejected his teaching (v.2f.). Once again, therefore, Mark links the healing miracles closely with the preaching of Jesus and with the
6 response made to him. **And he marvelled at their lack of faith:** this time it is Jesus' turn to be amazed – at the failure of his own people to respond to the good news.

# D   Hard hearts and lack of faith                6.6b–8.26

Mark 6.1–6 can fairly be seen as the climax to the previous section of the gospel, and as parallel to 3.1–6. Just as 1.14–3.6 ended with the rejection of Jesus by the Pharisees, so 3.7–6.6 ends with the rejection of Jesus by his neighbours. In spite of his authoritative teaching and the four remarkable miracles that he has performed, they do not believe in him. This new section of the gospel begins, like the two previous ones, with a summary of Jesus' activity (this time very brief – 6.6b only!), followed by a section dealing with the disciples: this time, instead of being called (1.16–20) or appointed (3.13–19), they are sent out. Once again, however, we must remember that the divisions we are making are artificial and are not necessarily part of Mark's own understanding. It is possible to arrange the material differently – e.g., to take either the summaries or the references to the disciples as marking the beginning and end of a section (so forming what is known as an 'inclusio'). Perhaps each of our major divisions overlaps with the next, so that it is impossible to separate them at any one point in the narrative. Certainly themes reappear: so, here, we have the commissioning of the Twelve (picking up the account of their call in 3.13–19), followed by the death of John the Baptist (picking up 1.14), leading into the continuation of the story of the commissioning of the Twelve. And in the following chapters, we have a complicated structure of parallel stories about the feeding of the crowd (6.32–45; 8.1–10), disputes with the Pharisees (7.1–23; 8.11–13), and private healing narratives (7.31–7; 8.22–6).

# 1   JESUS SENDS OUT THE TWELVE          6.6b–13

*(Matt. 9.35; 10.1–15; Luke 9.1–6)*

(6) Then Jesus went through the villages round about, teaching. (7) And he summoned the Twelve, and began to send them out, two by two; and he gave them authority over the unclean spirits. (8) And he instructed them to take nothing for the journey except a stick: no bread, no bag, no money in their belts; (9) they might wear sandals, but not a second tunic. (10) And he told them, 'Whenever you enter a house, stay there until you leave that place. (11) And if any place will not receive you, and they will not listen to you, shake the dust from your feet as you leave, as testimony to them.' (12) And they set out and proclaimed that people should repent; (13) and they drove out many demons, and anointed many sick people with oil and healed them.

Material about the mission of the Twelve is to be found not only in Mark's account, but in the tradition shared by Matthew and Luke, and perhaps also in independent traditions used by each of them (see Matthew 10 and Luke 10). Some commentators have questioned whether Jesus did send out the disciples during his lifetime, as their commissioning reflects the circumstances of the early Church. The tradition is certainly pre-Markan, since this picture of a mission by the disciples to some extent contradicts Mark's own portrayal of them as far from comprehending the truth about Jesus – and therefore about the gospel – at this stage of the ministry. The gospel proclaimed in Mark's own day was not identical with that of Jesus himself, but if Jesus called men to be his followers, he may well have called them to share in his own task of announcing the Kingdom and calling for repentance. For Mark himself, the task entrusted to the Twelve is now carried on by members of his own community, and it is hardly surprising if the details of the instructions given here to the Twelve reflect the conditions of his day.

**Then Jesus went through the villages round about, teaching.** 6 Mark perhaps intends us to see, in this brief summary, a contrast with Jesus' home town, which was unwilling to listen to his teaching.

Jesus **summoned the Twelve, and began to send them out:** Mark 7 picks up here the statement in 3.14 that Jesus appointed the Twelve 'so that he might send them out'. Sending them **two by two** would provide the disciples with mutual support, but this detail probably reflects the Jewish belief that the testimony of one unsupported witness was not sufficient. The Old Testament references (e.g. Deut. 17.6; 19.15) refer to judicial proceedings, but the idea that any kind of testimony needs corroboration seems a natural corollary. Moreover, in v.11 the disciples are required to testify to those who refuse to hear them that they are under judgement. According to Acts, the apostles (not just the Twelve) regularly travelled in twos (see Acts 8.14; 13.1f.; 15.22, 39f.). Jesus now passes on to **the Twelve** his own **authority** (ἐξουσία) **over the unclean spirits**; the power which he has and which has already been the subject of comment in 1.27 is no freak occurrence, but something of which he has full command. The control of demons is central to the ministry of Jesus, as it is presented by Mark, and it is not surprising to find Jesus entrusting this task to the Twelve as an essential part of their mission. The fact that he is able to pass on this power emphasizes his own authority – a theme which is of vital importance for Mark. The fundamental question of the basis of this authority will be raised finally in 11.27–33.

8    The disciples are **instructed. . .to take nothing for the journey** (εἰς ὁδὸν): the Greek word ὁδός, normally translated 'way', is used frequently in Mark and would remind his readers that the journey which the Twelve are making is the one undertaken by disciples. They are commanded to travel light – an indication, possibly, of the urgency of their task. In Mark they are permitted **a stick** (forbidden in Matt. 10.10 and Luke 9.3), but they are not to take provisions – **no bread, no bag, no money in their belts**. The bag is perhaps a beggar's collecting bag rather than a knapsack, since the Greek word (ἡ πήρα) can be used of such a bag, carried for example by itinerant

9    Cynic preachers; small coins were often carried in a belt. According to Mark, **they might wear sandals** (σανδάλια), but in Matthew and Luke (10.4), shoes (ὑποδήματα) are forbidden. Some commentators think that Mark is permitting sandals, while excluding shoes, but it is doubtful whether he intends a distinction between two forms of footwear: the word he uses is probably the equivalent of that used by Matthew and Luke. Mark's less stringent rules perhaps reflect the conditions of a later missionary journey: it was possible to travel around Palestine without stick or shoes, but these became necessary when more arduous journeys were undertaken. But they are not allowed **a second tunic**: the Greek changes abruptly into the second person plural here (lit. 'and you shall not wear two tunics'), perhaps indicating a different source (though we have a new beginning in the following verse). The tunic or shirt is the inner garment, and it is not clear why anyone would wish to wear two. The second is perhaps a spare: Matthew and Luke forbid the disciples to 'take' or 'have' two tunics. There is an interesting echo of these instructions in a passage in the Mishnah (M. Berakoth 9.5) which forbids entry into the temple mount with staff or sandal or wallet, or with dust on one's feet, and it was suggested by T.W. Manson (*Sayings*, p. 181), that this is due to the fact that Jesus was sending his disciples out on a sacred errand. Since Matt. 10.9f. is closer to the Mishnah than Mark, it may be that

Matthew's account has been adapted to some such tradition about the temple, and that this explains the differences in detail between the two gospels.

If hospitality is offered, the disciples are to accept it, and not to 10 move if better accommodation is offered subsequently. If they are not 11 received in any area, however, they are to **shake the dust from** their **feet ... as testimony to them.** At the very least, this suggests that those who have proclaimed the gospel in places which **will not receive** or **listen to** them take no further responsibility for them. But shaking the dust from the feet was a symbolic action normally performed by a Jew who had been abroad on his re-entry into Palestine: foreign dust must not contaminate Jewish soil. (For the idea that the earth from Gentile countries is unclean, see M. Oholoth 2.3; M. Tohoroth 4.5; B. Shab. 15b.) Such an action on the part of the disciples was clearly meant to indicate that the village or town which had rejected them was no longer to be regarded as part of the Jewish nation. It is not clear whether Mark means that the action is to be understood as a warning to the inhabitants of that place before it is too late and they find themselves cut off, or whether it is to serve as a witness against them at the final Judgement (as Luke apparently interprets it, 9.5; 10.10–12). Perhaps Mark intends both meanings. Certainly these words indicate the urgency of the situation. Jesus' words read ominously, coming so soon after the story of his own rejection in his home town.

Mark tells us nothing of the content of the disciples' message, except 12 that they **proclaimed that people should repent.** While this echoes the brief summary of Jesus' own preaching in 1.15, it is closer to the message of John the Baptist in 1.4: it is possible that Mark thinks of the Twelve, as he thinks of John, as preparing the way for Jesus himself. However, he seems to regard them as sharing his ministry, 13 for the account of their activity also echoes the summaries of Jesus' activities in 1.34 and 3.10f., except for the addition of the detail about the use of **oil** which was widely used as a medicament at the time: the disciples, given authority by Jesus, extend his work.

## 2   THE DEATH OF JOHN THE BAPTIST          6.14–29

*(Matt. 14.1–12; Luke 9.7–9)*

**(14) And King Herod heard [about Jesus], for his fame had spread, and people were saying,**[1] **'John the Baptizer has been raised from**

1 Many MSS read the singular, ἔλεγεν, *he said*, instead of the plural, ἔλεγον, which is read by B W and some Latin MSS.

the dead, and that is why these powers are at work in him';
(15) but others said, 'It is Elijah,' and others said, 'He is a prophet,
like one of the prophets [of old].' (16) But when Herod heard
[these reports] he said, 'John, whom I beheaded, has been raised.'

(17) For Herod had sent and seized John and had bound him in
prison, on account of Herodias (his brother Philip's wife), because
he had married her. (18) For John had told Herod, 'It is not right
for you to have your brother's wife.' (19) And Herodias had a
grudge against him and wanted to kill him, but could not,
(20) because Herod feared John, knowing him to be a righteous
and holy man; and he kept him in safety and liked to listen to him,
though he was greatly disturbed by what he heard.[1]

(21) An opportunity came on Herod's birthday, when he gave a
banquet to his chief officials and military commanders, and to the
leading men of Galilee; (22) Herodias' daughter[2] came in and
danced, and she pleased Herod and his guests. The king said to
the girl, 'Ask me whatever you like, and I will give it to you';
(23) and he swore an oath to her: 'Whatever you ask me I will give
you, up to half my kingdom.' (24) And she went out and said to her
mother, 'What shall I ask for?' She replied, 'The head of John the
Baptist.' (25) And she hurried back in straight away to the king
and demanded, 'I want you to give me, at once, on a dish, the head
of John the Baptist.' (26) And though he was deeply grieved, the
king did not wish to refuse her, because of his vows and his guests.
(27) And straight away the king sent one of the guards with orders
to bring his head; and he went off and beheaded him in prison,
(28) and brought his head on a dish and gave it to the girl, and the
girl gave it to her mother. (29) And when his disciples heard, they
came and took his body away and laid it in a tomb.

Between the account of the sending-out of the Twelve and that of
their return, Mark inserts an account of Herod's reaction to the
rumours about Jesus, together with the story of his beheading of John
the Baptist. There seems no logical connection between the two
themes, but the somewhat artificial insertion provides an interlude
for the disciples to complete their mission.

The story of John the Baptist is the only section in the gospel which
is not specifically about Jesus. Even this, however, is narrated
because what happens to John points to the one who follows him – as
did the earlier section about John at the beginning of the gospel.
John's death foreshadows that of Jesus: there are even similarities in

1 Some MSS (including A C D fam. 1 and the Latin and Syriac versions) read
ἐποίει, *he did,* instead of ἠπόρει, *he was disturbed.*
2 The text is confused. Some important MSS, including אB D, read τῆς θυγατρὸς
αὐτοῦ Ἡρωδιάδος, *his daughter Herodias.*

the stories, since both John and Jesus are put to death by political rulers who recognize their goodness, but who are described as weakly giving in to pressure. The idea that John's death points forward to Jesus' own will be underlined in 9.12f., where John is identified with Elijah. Mark presumably intends his readers to see also the contrast between John, who is buried and about whom only rumours of resurrection circulate, and Jesus, who is buried and raised from the dead.

**King Herod**: Herod Antipas (son of Herod the Great) was not in fact  14 king, but tetrarch (as Matthew and Luke both correctly record) of Galilee and Peraea from 4 BC to AD 39. A tetrarch exercised limited authority, being himself subject to and dependent on Rome. It was Herod's request to Rome for the title of king which led to his deposition and banishment. Mark's mistake may reflect popular usage, which was unconcerned with the niceties of Roman officialdom. Mark writes simply that he **heard** without specifying what was heard. The context suggests that he heard about the journey of the Twelve, but sense demands that he heard about Jesus, who in fact is not mentioned by name throughout this story. Mark appears to have fitted the stories together somewhat clumsily at this point.

These introductory verses raise again the all-important question: who is Jesus? **People were saying . . . others said . . . and others said. . . .** Mark now introduces the various rumours about Jesus – rumours which perhaps reached the ears of Herod. The variant reading in v.14 is well attested, but Herod's own comment is given in v.16, and the singular form of the verb has probably been wrongly transferred to v.14 from there. It is not clear what is meant by the suggestion that **John the Baptizer has been raised from the dead**; if such a rumour ever circulated, then the idea of an individual being raised was presumably not incredible in popular imagination; it is a vain hope which stands in contrast to the resurrection of Jesus. In the mouth of Herod, in v.16, the same suggestion can only mean 'This is John the Baptist all over again.' It seems strange that Jesus should be thought to be John *redivivus* because of the **powers** (δυνάμεις) **. . . at work in him**, since nothing of the kind is attributed to John: presumably the idea is that he now has greater powers than before. **Elijah**  15 was popularly expected to return before the End – a belief based on Mal. 4.5f. In his case, there was no need to think of a resurrection, since he was said to have been taken up into heaven without dying (2 Kgs. 2). The third suggestion, that Jesus **is a prophet, like one of the prophets [of old]**, seems less dramatic, but is nevertheless a significant one, since prophets belonged very much to the past (an idea we have tried to convey by adding the words 'of old', which are not in the Greek), and the emergence of a new prophet therefore indicates an important new event in God's dealings with his people. All three opinions thus attribute high status to Jesus: nevertheless, none of them is adequate.

16  **But when Herod heard [these reports] he said, 'John, whom I beheaded, has been raised.'** The reference to the beheading of John by Herod Antipas leads into the narrative of the events which led to

17  John's death. **For Herod had sent and seized John and had bound him in prison, on account of Herodias (his brother Philip's wife), because he had married her.** According to Josephus (*Antiquities,* XVIII.5.2), John was held prisoner in the fortress of Machaerus, to the east of the Dead Sea. Mark gives no indication of place, but since the guests at the banquet are described in v.21 as from Galilee, it is natural to think of this being held at Herod's palace in Tiberias, on the shore of the lake, and the story implies that John was imprisoned in the same place. There are also some differences between Josephus and Mark concerning the details of Herod's marriage. According to the former, **Herodias,** who was a daughter of Aristobulus (half-brother of Herod Antipas), and so herself a grand-daughter of Herod the Great and half-niece of Herod Antipas) was first married to another Herod, yet another half-brother of Herod Antipas. **Philip,** who like the two Herods, was a son of Herod the Great, was married to Salome, and not to her mother. The family tree of the Herods is extraordinarily complex, and full of incestuous relationships. If Mark was confused about the members of the Herod family and wrongly thought that Herodias, not her daughter, was married to Philip, the confusion is understandable. According to Josephus, again, Herod's motive for killing the Baptist was fear of a rebellion by the people; interestingly, he also links John's death with Herod's marriage, but in a very different way, since he states that Aretas, the King of Arabia, the father of Herod Antipas' first wife (whom he had divorced to marry Herodias), waged war on his son-in-law because of his conduct, and the people regarded the defeat of Herod's army as a punishment from God for the murder of the Baptist.

18  **For John had told Herod, 'It is not right for you to have your brother's wife.'** John's objection to the liaison between Herod and Herodias is based on the prohibitions expressed in Lev. 18.16 and 20.21. Presumably Herodias' first husband had not divorced her, and according to Jewish law a woman was unable to divorce her husband; even if Herodias had divorced her first husband under Roman law, this would not be acceptable in Jewish eyes. Throughout this narrative there are interesting parallels with the story of Elijah, Ahab and Jezebel in 1 Kgs. Like Herod, Ahab's great sin is said to be his marriage (1 Kgs. 16.31) – in his case because it led him into idolatry. In both stories the king is a weak man, afraid of the prophet and prepared to listen to him (1 Kgs. 21.20–9) but led astray by his wife (1 Kgs. 21.5–16). Elijah's attack on the worship of Baal, introduced by

Jezebel, leads her to plot his destruction (1 Kgs. 19.1f.), but whereas
Jezebel failed, **Herodias**, after nursing **a grudge against him**, finally 19
succeeds in getting rid of the Baptist.

Herod's ambivalent attitude to John is reflected in his behaviour: 20
although he had imprisoned the prophet, he knew him **to be a
righteous and holy man**. There is an interesting parallel in 15.14,
where Pilate recognizes Jesus' innocence, yet eventually hands him
over to be crucified. **And he kept him in safety**: this last phrase is
sometimes understood as meaning 'he kept him in custody', but the
verb (συντηϱέω) means 'to protect', and the meaning seems to be that
Herod protected John from Herodias' designs. Herod **liked to listen
to** his prisoner, but **was greatly disturbed by what** John said to him.
The alternative reading perhaps means that Herod, having once
heard John, did so often (taking πολλά as = 'often') and heard him
gladly, but this is perhaps an attempt to smooth out the difficulties of
Mark's picture.

The **opportunity** Herodias seized was an occasion to wreak her 21
revenge on John, and it was provided by **a banquet** in celebration of
**Herod's birthday**. One puzzling feature of the ensuing narrative is
the picture of a Herodian princess dancing in public. In a society
where it was considered improper for women to mix freely in male
company, it may seem surprising that Salome should have performed
in this manner. It needs to be remembered, however, that the dance
was not necessarily performed with the eroticism with which later
tradition has imbued it. Moreover, it can be argued that members of
the Herodian family clearly did not consider themselves bound to
adopt conventional behaviour. However scurrilous the story, there
was sufficient likelihood of truth in the account for it to be recounted.
It is generally supposed that **Herodias' daughter** was Salome, daughter 22
of Herodias by her previous marriage. The Greek is somewhat
awkward, which could explain the variant reading, 'his daughter
Herodias', which has some claim to being the right one, however,
since it is supported by some important MSS. If so, then this could be a
child of the union condemned by John.

The banquet, the dance, the extravagant promise of Herod to give 23
**'whatever you ask me...up to half my kingdom,'** and the macabre
detail about the **dish** are all part of the story-teller's art: the account 24–5
may owe something to the story of Esther (Esther 5.1–8). The girl
appears to be an eager accomplice of **her mother**. Herod, on the 26–8
other hand, is **deeply grieved** and reluctant to fulfil his promise, but
feels bound to do so: he is trapped by his own weakness and sin into a
position where he is blind to the real issues, and John is treated as a
political puppet instead of as a prophet of God. John's death could
scarcely have been more wickedly contrived or more useless: yet for
Mark it points forward to the passion of Jesus. So does his burial:

John's **disciples came and took his body away and laid it in a tomb**. The same word for body (τό πτῶμα) is used of Jesus in 15.45, and the same (or a similar) word for tomb (τό μνημεῖον) in 15.46 and 16.2 (some MSS read τό μνῆμα in chapters 15 and 16). But in John's case, this is the end of the story, apart from the rumours which again point to Jesus.

# 3 THE TWELVE RETURN 6.30–1

## *(Luke 9.10)*

**(30) And the apostles returned to Jesus and reported to him all the things they had done, and everything they had taught. (31) And he said to them, 'Come away to a lonely place by yourselves and rest for a while'; for there were so many people coming and going that they had no opportunity even to eat.**

Mark does not describe what Jesus did while his disciples were absent: the gap until their return has been filled by the story of the Baptist's

30  death. The disciples are here referred to as **the apostles**. The word ἀπόστολος, which is used only here in Mark (see note on 3.14), denotes in classical Greek a military or naval expedition. It is used in the LXX to translate the Hebrew *šālîaḥ*, a word which is used also in Rabbinic Hebrew to mean an authorized agent or representative. The term denotes a function rather than status, and the *šālîaḥ* was appointed for a particular mission, not to a permanent post. While he was engaged in his task, he was empowered to act with the full authority of the one to whom he was responsible (cf. Matt. 10.40). The term is therefore entirely appropriate in the present context where it is used of those to whom Jesus has given authority to extend his own activities of preaching and healing. Both Mark and his readers, however, would have been conscious of the fact that it had become a technical term in the Christian community, although in the earliest period (and perhaps still in Mark's) it was certainly not one which

31  was confined to the Twelve. The comment that the pressure from the crowd was such that they had **no opportunity even to eat** echoes that made in 3.20, after the appointment of the Twelve. Jesus suggests withdrawal to **a lonely place** (see below, vv.32, 35).

# 4   JESUS FEEDS FIVE THOUSAND        6.32–45

*(Matt. 14.13–22; Luke 9.10–17; John 6.1–17)*

(32) And they left in the boat for a lonely place on their own. (33) And many people saw them leave and recognized them; and they hurried to the spot on foot from all the cities and arrived there before them. (34) And when he landed, he saw a great crowd. And he was full of pity for them, because they were like sheep without a shepherd, and he began to teach them many things. (35) And when it grew late, his disciples came to him and said, 'This is a lonely place, and it is now late. (36) Send them away, so that they may go to the nearby farms and villages, and buy themselves something to eat.' (37) But he answered them, 'Give them something to eat yourselves.' And they said to him, 'Are we to go and spend two hundred denarii on bread, and give them that to eat?' (38) But he said to them, 'How many loaves do you have? Go and see.' And when they had found out, they told him, 'Five – and two fish.' (39) And he commanded them all to sit down in groups on the green grass; (40) and they sat in companies of fifty and a hundred. (41) And taking the five loaves and two fish, he looked up to heaven, blessed [God], broke the loaves and gave them to the disciples to set before them; and he divided the two fish among them all. (42) And they all ate, and were satisfied. (43) And they picked up twelve basketfuls of pieces, and of the fish. (44) And there were about five thousand men who ate. (45) And straight away he made his disciples get into the boat and go ahead to the other side of the lake, to Bethsaida, while he himself dismissed the crowd.

Mark's account of the return of the disciples leads straight into another miracle story – the only miracle, apart from the one which immediately follows it, which is described by John as well as by all three Synoptic writers. It is, indeed, more often recorded than any other miracle, since the feeding of the four thousand in Mark 8.1–10 (parallel to Matt. 15.32–9) appears to be a doublet of this story. It is possible that Mark has incorporated two parallel independent cycles of tradition into his gospel, each of which begins with a miraculous feeding (6.32–44; 8.1–10) followed by a journey across the lake (6.45–52; 8.11–21), includes a dispute with Pharisees (7.1–13; 8.11–13) and a discussion about bread (7.27–9; 8.14–21) and concludes with the restoration of sight or hearing to those who lack these faculties (7.31–7; 8.22–6). (Alternatively, P.J. Achtemeier in *J.B.L.*, 89, 1970, pp. 265–91, suggests that Mark has incorporated a pre-Markan cycle of miracles consisting of two catenae.) But Mark himself is certainly aware of some of these parallels (cf. 8.17–21) and may have used independent pericopae to build up the scheme. John's order is similar: the feeding of the crowd (6.1–15) is followed by an account of the walking on the water (6.16–21) similar to Mark 6.45–52; after the long discourse on the meaning of the feeding miracle and the dispute with the Jews (6.22–65) we have the acclamation of Jesus by Simon Peter (6.66–71), which is the Johannine equivalent of the narrative of Caesarea Philippi which concludes Mark's second cycle (Mark 8.27–33). Although it is often argued that John is dependent on Mark, there is very little indication of this, and it seems highly probable that John is using another cycle of tradition parallel to that used by Mark in 6.32–52. This widespread use suggests that the feeding miracle, whatever its difficulties for the modern reader, was of considerable importance in early Christian circles. It also indicates that the story of the feeding was closely linked with that of the walking on the water at an early stage. See below, on 8.1–10, for further discussion of the relationship between the two stories of feedings.

A great deal of attention has been concentrated by commentators on attempts to answer the question 'What happened?' Unfortunately this question has proved unanswerable. Suggestions that the numbers involved were exaggerated (Wellhausen) or that the feeding was a symbolic one involving only tiny fragments of food (A. Schweitzer, *The Mystery of the Kingdom of God*, pp. 103–6), or that the people were persuaded to share the food which they had brought with them (Branscomb), cannot explain the belief of all the evangelists that this was a miraculous feeding. Whatever the historical basis for the story, it is now impossible to separate this out from the interpretation given to the event in which various ideas have been employed to bring out the significance of Jesus' person. It is thus a much more rewarding question to ask what truths about Jesus the evangelist is trying to convey to his readers in retelling this story.

It is important, first of all, to recognize the important role of Old Testament narrative and symbolism in this story. There is an interesting parallel to the account of the feeding in the miracle attributed to Elisha in 2 Kings 4.42–4, but the most important background to the Markan narrative is the story of God's provision of manna for Israel in the wilderness (cf. Exodus 16; Numbers 11). This story was of great importance to the Jews, not only as an account of God's salvation in the past, but as a pointer to the future. The rabbis' messianic expectation included the hope of a Messiah like Moses who would again give the people manna, an idea which certainly lies behind the discourse of John 6. Another hope linked with this was the image of the messianic banquet, of which the feeding narrative was perhaps regarded as a symbol – even though bread and fish may seem to us scarcely to constitute a feast. The narrative of the feeding has verbal links with the account of the Last Supper in 14.22–5, and Mark himself may therefore have understood it as pointing forward to the eucharist; certainly bread and fish became eucharistic symbols at an early stage, and the story would have been interpreted in that way by many of his early readers (see Q. Quesnell, *The Mind of Mark*). The fourth evangelist clearly interpreted the story in terms of the eucharist (cf. John 6.52–9).

In Jewish thought, the manna given to the people through Moses became a symbol of the Torah – another idea which is taken up and developed in the Johannine discourse on the bread, though for John the true bread is not the Torah, but Jesus himself. In Mark, too, there is perhaps a hint of this symbolism: Jesus has compassion on the crowd and cares for the leaderless people of Israel (v.34) by giving them first an abundance of teaching, then an abundance of food.

As with the healing miracles, this miracle too is linked with Jesus' ministry of teaching: he is like Moses, not only in providing the people with food in the wilderness, but in acting as their shepherd and teaching them. Both activities testify as to who Jesus is. Moreover, those whom he feeds belong to God's people – among whom are numbered the members of Mark's community who would recall, as they heard these words read, the occasions when bread was taken, a blessing said, the bread broken and given to all who called themselves disciples. The fact that so much food was left over at the end suggests that there is enough to feed those who were not present at the time, but who now gather together to listen to the words of their Lord and to share in the broken bread.

Jesus and his disciples set off **for a lonely place**. This phrase, 32 repeated from v.31, is perhaps intended to convey more than the idea of isolation, since the adjective translated 'lonely' (ἔρημος) can be used as a noun to mean 'desert' or 'wilderness' (see 1.4,12): the spot thus provides a suitable setting for a miracle recalling the provision of manna in the wilderness. Mark is vague about the precise location: probably he thinks of it as close to the departure point (also unidentified), since it was possible for those **on foot** to arrive first. Apparently 33 he locates the scene across the lake from Bethsaida (v.45), and so on the western shore – a detail which is contradicted by Luke, who places the feeding in Bethsaida itself (9.10).

Jesus regards the **crowd** as being **like sheep without a shepherd**. 34 The description implies criticism of the nation's leaders who are failing to guide the people. This same image is used in the Old Testament of leaderless Israel (cf. Num. 27.17; 1 Kings 22.17; Ezek. 34.5). Moses, as well as David, was a shepherd before becoming leader of the nation, so the metaphor was an obvious one; various passages speak of the future Davidic leader as the shepherd of this people: Jer. 23.1–6; Ezek. 34.22f.; cf. Ps. Sol. 17.40f. The crowd's need was apparently for instruction; Jesus **began to teach them many things** (or perhaps, taking πολλά adverbially, 'at length').

35 **This is a lonely place.** This statement by the disciples emphasizes
37 once again the character of the place (cf. vv.31f.). Jesus' reply indicates that the disciples should take responsibility for the crowd – **Give them something to eat yourselves.** It is a natural enough command in view of the fact that they have just returned from the mission on which they exercised the authority he gave them. To be sure, when engaged on that mission, they were commanded to take 'no bread . . .no money in their belts' – so how can they be expected to feed the crowd now? Perhaps Mark has forgotten that earlier command – or perhaps he has placed the two narratives in close proximity in order to hint that the miracle that follows is about something more significant than ordinary bread (cf. the comment about the season of figs in 11.13). At any rate, the disciples are not yet ready to respond to Jesus' challenge. Their rough reaction here is toned down in Matthew and Luke but is understandable: they would clearly have to scour the countryside for miles around in order to find the vast quantity of bread required. Their response fits Mark's picture of the disciples as continually failing to understand what Jesus is doing. Changes in standards of living, as well as inflation, make it impossible to translate **two hundred denarii** into any modern currency: in Matt. 20.2, however, a denarius is apparently an acceptable daily wage for a
38 labourer. The source of the **loaves** is not specified by Mark: it appears to be food which the disciples have with them. Each loaf would have been round and flat, about an inch thick and eight inches across (2½ cm × 20 cm). The number **five** has sometimes been explained as symbolic; it might perhaps represent the five books of the Law, in which case the **two fish** could symbolize the two tablets. But why should Jesus distribute the Law? It is unlikely that Mark saw any such significance in the numbers.
39 Jesus commands the people to **sit down in groups** (συμπόσια συμπόσια – group by group); the word συμπόσιον means 'drinking-party', and so a group of people eating together. The reference to **the green grass** has often been used in attempts to calculate the length of Jesus' ministry, since grass is green in Palestine only in the spring: since Mark's arrangement of material is not necessarily chronological, however, this cannot be done. Possibly the phrase is meant to remind us that in the messianic age, the desert will be fertile (Isa. 35.1); it is appropriate that Jesus should feed the people in a fertile
40 spot. **They sat in companies** (πρασιαὶ πρασιαί); this time, the Greek word means 'garden plot', and the idea is apparently of orderly groups. They sat in groups of **fifty and a hundred** – lit. 'by a hundred and by fifty'; this may mean simply that the groups numbered approximately 50–100 people, but if Mark intended the numbers to be un-

derstood strictly – i.e. if he meant that the groups consisted of either 100 or 50 men – he perhaps had in mind the organizing of Israel by Moses in Exod. 18.21. It is appropriate that the new shepherd of Israel should organize the people in this way. Another possibility is that by 'groups' Mark meant 'rows', and that what he had in mind was a rectangle consisting of 100 rows of 50 men. Duncan Derrett (*Studies in the New Testament*, II, pp. 1–3) points out that the word is derived from the word for 'leek', and so means properly a bed of leeks: the image suggests plants arranged in straight rows for the purpose of irrigation. It seems unlikely that the unorganized throng listening to Jesus could have been persuaded to sit down in this fashion (though it would have helped the distribution of food!) but it is conceivable that there is in this description a hint that the crowd could easily become an army prepared to march behind Jesus (cf. John 6.15).

Jesus' actions in **taking** the bread, which he then **broke. . .and 41 gave. . .to the disciples**, after having **blessed** God, is described in language closely paralleled in 14.22. This might be accidental, since they were the natural actions for the head of the household or host, but inevitably they suggest a eucharistic interpretation of the miracle – a theme which is developed in the final verses of the discourse in John 6. Mark's words remind his readers of their own eucharistic celebrations.

Whatever symbolic meaning Mark may have attached to the feeding, 42 he certainly regarded the occasion as a real meal: the people **all ate, and were satisfied** – the verb χορτάζω, to satisfy (sometimes used of fattening animals), implies an abundance of food. The amazing 43 character of the miracle is emphasized by the quantity of surplus food collected up afterwards: **they picked up twelve basketfuls of pieces**. A similar story is told about Elisha in 2 Kgs. 4.42–4, where a hundred men are fed on a mere twenty loaves, and there is food left over, but in Mark's account, there is far more food at the end of the day than there was at the beginning! Moreover, the broken pieces of bread are carefully gathered up: why? Such fragments would soon have become stale and inedible, so there was little point in collecting them. Nor would it have occurred to anyone that they constituted 'litter' that needed to be taken home! This suggests that the surplus is to be interpreted symbolically. Perhaps Mark is hinting at a contrast with the manna provided in the wilderness which could not be preserved, except on the eve of the sabbath (Exod. 16.13–30; c f. John 6.30–5). If food is left over, it will perhaps be available for others, who were not present with God's people in the wilderness. This inference is apparently drawn in 7.28.

The statement that **there were about five thousand men who ate 44 also underlines the greatness of the miracle; the phrase is ambiguous, since Mark may well mean 'men, not counting women and children', which is how Matthew interprets it (Matt. 14.21); this would be appropriate if they were drawn up in formation like an army. On the other hand, he may well be using the term ἄνδρες in the sense of 'people'.

One feature which is missing from this narrative is any expression of astonishment on the part of the crowd; nor does Jesus command secrecy. Mark perhaps supposes that the crowd were unaware of what had happened, and that the disciples alone realized that five thousand people had been fed on five loaves. Certainly he emphasizes later that, even though the disciples had witnessed the miracle, they did not understand its significance and were therefore in the same
45 condition as the crowd (6.52; 8.17–21). Jesus' somewhat abrupt dispatch of **his disciples. . .to the other side of the lake, to Bethsaida, while he himself dismissed the crowd,** perhaps replaces the command for secrecy and the sending away found in some of the healing miracles. For this reason v.45, though it serves as a link with what follows, is here treated as the conclusion of the story of the feeding, rather than the beginning of the next narrative.


# 5   JESUS WALKS ON WATER                    6.46–52

*(Matt. 14.23–33; John 6.15–21)*

**(46) And when he had taken leave of them, he went up the mountain to pray. (47) And when evening came, the boat was in the middle of the lake, and he was alone on land. (48) And seeing them labouring at the oars – for the wind was blowing against them – he came to them, about the fourth watch of the night, walking on the lake; and he was going to pass by them. (49) When they saw him walking on the lake, they thought it was a ghost and cried out, (50) for they all saw him, and were terrified; but he straight away spoke to them: 'Courage!' he said, 'It is I; do not be afraid.' (51) Then he climbed into the boat and the wind dropped; and they were utterly astounded, (52) for they had not understood about the loaves: their hearts were hardened.**

This short narrative bristles with difficulties for the modern reader. The most obvious is the apparent contravention of scientific principles: men do not walk on water – a basic fact which points us immediately to a second area of difficulty, which is doctrinal. Other miracles depict Jesus as possessing a more than human power which enables him to heal the sick and perform other extraordinary feats; this one – although it, too, demonstrates his superhuman gifts – is in danger of presenting him in docetic terms, that is as less than fully human, because more than merely human. In contrast, also, with the great majority of miracles (the exception is the withered fig tree in 11.12–14, 20f.), is the 'uselessness' of this particular miracle: the disciples do not seem to be in danger, and the miracle is really an epiphany (similar to the transfiguration) rather than a rescue operation. There are, it is true, some parallels here to the stilling of the storm in chapter 4, and these present us with a further difficulty, since there are inconsistencies in the story as it exists at present which have led to the suggestion that two narratives (or parts thereof) have been pieced together (see v.51).

Yet another problem is to discover the meaning which the story has for Mark. He appears to consider its significance plain, but the modern reader often feels as perplexed as the disciples. Mark does, however, provide one important clue: the meaning should be obvious to those who understand the story of the multiplication of the loaves, with which this narrative is so closely linked. The disciples have watched Jesus feed the people and should therefore not be surprised to see him walking across the water. If we search the Old Testament for a background to this idea, we find that only God is able to control the sea and to walk on the waves (cf. Job 9.8); in particular, however, he is said to have made his path through the sea at the Exodus, when he brought his people across the water (cf. Ps. 77.19f.; Isa. 43.16; 51.10). Jesus has already revealed himself to the disciples as Moses' successor by feeding the people – indeed, as greater than Moses, since he himself provided the people with bread: if he now reveals himself as one who is able to cross the sea, this too would seem to point him out not merely as Moses' successor, but as one who is far greater. The crossing of the sea and the gift of manna are the central miracles in the Exodus story, and it is therefore not surprising to find Mark tying these two miracles of Jesus closely together (cf. Ps. 78.13–25). If Mark means us to understand the narrative in this way, we have an explanation for its strange anomalies: Jesus does not come to rescue the disciples from a storm; they are there to witness his epiphany.

As with the stilling of the storm, this miracle has been interpreted from patristic times as an allegory of the Church, subjected to hardship and persecution, and wondering if the Lord would ever return: the story is then understood as a message of hope in a dark hour – a promise that Christ will indeed come. This interpretation was natural enough for those in that situation, but Mark himself gives no indication that he understands the story in that way; rather his concern here, as elsewhere, seems to be with the question 'Who is Jesus?' The answer is clear to those who grasp the significance of the story.

**He went up the mountain to pray**: Mark gives an explanation of 46 the separation of Jesus from his disciples. Although he may mean

simply that Jesus wished to get away from the crowd, he may have recognized the parallel with Moses, going up the mountain to speak
47 with God, and terrifying the people on his descent (Ex. 34.29f.). **And when evening came**: it was already late in v.35, so that evening should have come long ago – the detail may belong to a stage when the stories were told separately. **The boat** was apparently making extraordinarily slow progress, since it is still out **in the middle of**
48 **the lake** at **about the fourth watch of the night** – a Roman reckoning, equivalent to 3 a.m. Mark's explanation is that **the wind was blowing against them** – presumably a north-east wind, blowing from Bethsaida. In Ex. 14.21, we read that 'the Lord drove the sea back by a strong east wind all night'. The disciples are not said to be in danger – rather they are present as witnesses to the miracle, and to the accompanying weather conditions.

Attempts have often been made to rationalize the story by suggesting that Jesus was wading in shallow water when he was seen by the disciples – an explanation which totally fails to explain the reaction attributed to a group of men which included experienced Galilaean fishermen. The origin of the story is not likely to lie in a misunderstanding of this kind. Moreover, Mark has said that the boat was **in the middle of the lake**, and he describes Jesus twice as **walking on**
49 **the lake**. The statement that he intended **to pass by them** is incomprehensible if the narrative is a description of Jesus coming to the aid of the storm-tossed disciples, but makes good sense if it is understood as a symbolic repetition of the crossing of the sea by Moses and the Israelites; there was no reason for him to stop – until they **cried out** in terror. The contrary wind does not prove the same hindrance to him
50 as to the disciples, for he is able to walk faster than they can row. **It is I**: since the words can mean also 'I am', they could be a reference to the divine name and so have a deeper significance than a simple self-identification: this would certainly be appropriate in the context. It is not clear that Mark interpreted the words in this way, but others may well have soon done so (cf. John 18.5f.).
51 **Then he climbed into the boat and the wind dropped**: in Ex. 14.24–7 the sea returns (the wind presumably having dropped) 'in the morning watch'. In Mark's account, this detail suggests a rescue rather than an epiphany, and may be an addition to the story. The disciples are **utterly astounded** by Jesus' power, and the reason,
52 according to Mark, is their inability to understand **about the loaves**; for the evangelist, astonishment on the part of those who see Jesus at work is the result of incomprehension and lack of faith. The disciples were apparently as far from understanding Jesus as were the crowds (4.10–12); indeed, since **their hearts were hardened**, their condition was even dangerously close to that of the Pharisees (3.5).

# 6   MANY ARE HEALED         6.53–6

*(Matt. 14.34–6)*

(53) And when they had crossed over, they came to land at Gennesaret, where they tied up. (54) And when they left the boat, people straight away recognized him; (55) and they ran about the whole region, and began to bring sick people on their mats, wherever they heard he was. (56) And wherever he went, to villages, towns or farms, they laid those who were ill in the market places, and begged him to let them touch just the edge of his garment; and all who touched him were made well.

These few verses give us another summary of Jesus' activity (cf. 1.32–4 and 3.7–12). This summary was probably written largely by Mark himself, since the vocabulary echoes previous incidents: his meaning seems to be that the healings he has described in detail are typical of what happened again and again.

**And when they had crossed over**: this phrase does not follow the  53 last narrative easily. It can hardly be meant as a summary of such a strange voyage. Even stranger is the statement that **they came to land at Gennesaret,** since the destination in v.45 was said to be Bethsaida. Gennesaret was a plain on the north-west shore of the lake and lay south of Capernaum. One explanation is that the boat had been blown off course by the wind! Yet the wind is said to have dropped in v.51. Another possibility is that Mark's geography is vague, and he does not know where the places he names are: Gennesaret was also the name given to the lake itself (cf. Luke 5.1), but Mark does not describe it by this title. The most likely explanation is that Mark has combined different traditions at this point, which means that these few verses are not simply editorial but embody earlier tradition. It is interesting to note that John's account is close to Mark here, since he says that the boat came to Capernaum (John 6.24). Even more interesting, however, is Mark's statement in 8.22, after the second pair of narratives about a feeding and a crossing, that Jesus and the disciples arrived at Bethsaida. One solution is that Mark has split up an earlier collection of narratives and has inserted 6.53–8.21. This would mean that the original cycle of tradition consisted of a feeding and a crossing (6.32–52), followed by a healing and Peter's confession (8.22–30). The double cycle would then be largely Mark's own creation, formed by the addition of further traditional material which he ordered deliberately in order to emphasize the significance of the stories.

**Those who were ill** sought to touch. . .**the edge of his garment:** this probably refers, not to a decorative border, but to one of the four blue tassels worn by a Jew in accordance with the Law (cf. Num. 15.38f.; Deut. 22.12). As in 5.27f., Jesus' garment is seen as an extension of his personality.

# 7   A DISPUTE ABOUT PURITY                    7.1–23

*(Matt. 15.1–20; Thomas 14)*

(1) Then the Pharisees and certain scribes who had come from Jerusalem gathered round him, (2) and seeing some of his disciples eating bread with 'unclean' – that is unwashed – hands (3) (for the Pharisees and all the Jews do not eat unless they wash their hands 'with the fist',[1] firmly maintaining the tradition of the elders; (4) and [on coming] from the market place they never eat without purifying themselves;[2] and there are many other customs which they maintain – the washing of cups and jugs and copper bowls[3]), (5) the Pharisees and scribes asked him, 'Why don't your disciples observe the tradition of the elders, but eat food with unclean hands?' (6) And he said to them, 'Isaiah prophesied truly about you hypocrites; for it is written:

> "This people honours me with their lips,
> but their heart is far away from me.
> (7) In vain they worship me,
> teaching as doctrines the precepts of men."

(8) You abandon the commandment of God and maintain the tradition of men.' (9) And he said to them, 'How good you are at setting aside the commandment of God, in order to establish your own tradition! (10) For Moses said, "Honour your father and your mother", and "Whoever curses his father or mother shall be put to death". (11) But you say, "If a man says to his father or mother, 'What you might have received from me is *corban* (that is, a gift [to God])'" (12) – you no longer allow him to do anything for his father or mother, (13) revoking the word of God through your tradition which you hand on; and many such things you do.'

(14) And calling the crowd to him again, he said to them, 'Hear me, all of you, and understand. (15) There is nothing outside a

1 The word πυγμῇ (*with the fist*) is omitted by Δ, the Syriac and the Sahidic, while ℵ W, and some other versions read πυκνά, meaning *often*, instead.
2 A D and many other MSS read βαπτίσωνται, *washing themselves thoroughly*, instead of ῥαντίσωνται, *purifying themselves*.
3 Many MSS (including A D W Θ fams. 1 and 13) add *and beds*.

man which can make him unclean by entering him; but the things which come out of him are what make him unclean. [(16) If anyone has ears to hear, let him hear.]'[1] (17) And when they had gone indoors, away from the crowd, his disciples asked him about the parable. (18) And he said to them, 'Are you so dull? Don't you understand that nothing that enters a man from outside can make him unclean, (19) because it does not enter his heart but his stomach, and goes out into the sewer?' (Thus he declared all foods clean.) (20) And he said, 'It is what comes out of a man that defiles him; (21) for from inside, out of the hearts of men, come evil intentions: acts of fornication, thefts, murders, (22) adulteries, deeds of avarice, malicious acts, deceit, indecency, envy, slander, arrogance, folly. (23) These evil things all come from inside, and it is they that make a man unclean.'

Mark returns to the theme of official Judaism's disapproval of Jesus, and at the same time gives us another collection of his teaching. The repeated introductory phrases, in vv.6, 9, 14, 18 and 20, suggest that either Mark or a predecessor has gathered together sayings which originally circulated separately. The origin of the material has been much debated: some exegetes attribute a great deal of it to Mark himself, while others trace much of it back to Jesus. A detailed examination of the pericope is made by J. Lambrecht (*Eph. Th. L.*, 53, 1977, pp. 24–79) who points out the careful structure which Mark has built up out of the diverse elements: the introduction (vv.1–5) raises two questions – why do the disciples not behave according to the tradition of the elders, and why do they eat with unclean hands? It is these two questions which are dealt with in vv.6–13 and 14–23. Yet this careful structure conceals tensions in the material. The first two sayings answer the criticism of the authorities by means of a counter-attack: the complaint about the disciples is based on the Pharisees' own traditions, not on the Torah, and by concentrating on the former they are in danger of ignoring the latter. But in the parable and its explanation (vv.14ff.) a different and much more radical answer is given which questions the Torah itself by challenging its demands for Levitical purity. If we are surprised to find Jesus condemning the scrupulous Pharisees in vv.6–13 for failing to keep the Torah, it is even more surprising to find him, immediately afterwards, apparently abrogating the teaching of the Torah. We have here a tension found repeatedly in the New Testament: the strict adherents of the Torah are accused of failing to keep it, and their Christian accusers claim on the one hand to be fulfilling it, on the other to be free from its restrictions. These attitudes are not incompatible however: their

1 This verse is omitted by some important MSS, including ℵ B L Δ*.

consistency depends on the fact that it is the purpose of the Torah, rather than its detailed requirements, which is seen as important. The answers attributed to Jesus here approach the problem in two different ways, and it seems unlikely that they were given at the same time, even if they both go back to him.

Much of this material is likely to have been used in arguments between Jews and Christians in the period between Jesus and Mark: vv.1–13 suggest a debate in which **the tradition of the elders** is under attack as contrary to the Torah's true commands. The tradition of the elders was the oral law, handed on from rabbi to pupil; the tradition was meant to protect the Torah, but grew so complex that in time it tended to conceal the Law's real intent. This is the basis of the criticism here. By adding the more radical challenge of v.15, however, Mark seems to wish to go further. The meaning of this saying is then expounded to the disciples inside the house: this typical Markan device leads once again to criticism of the disciples for being without understanding, but provides the scene for what Mark presumably wishes his readers to grasp as the true explanation of Jesus' words. This is set out in vv.19–23 and may well reflect early preaching on the theme provided by v.15. It is not surprising that this challenge to the Law focuses on the matter of clean and unclean food. This section perhaps provided Mark's community with a necessary justification for what was taking place among them.

1    As in 3.22, the opposition to Jesus is said to stem **from Jerusalem**, which is for Mark the home of official opposition. The complaint, as
2    often, is about the behaviour of **some of his disciples**. Why is the behaviour of Jesus himself not queried? Are we to suppose that Jesus kept the Pharisaic rules, while his disciples did not? It seems that in its present form at least, the story reflects a dispute between the early Christian community and the Jewish authorities. Even if the form of the narrative is influenced by a later situation, however, the nucleus of the debate may go back to the ministry of Jesus, since the criticism that he kept company with lawbreakers seems authentic enough.

The complaint is that the disciples eat with **'unclean' – that is unwashed – hands**. The Greek word κοινός means 'common', and so acquires the meaning 'unclean', being used of anything which is not
3    'holy' or devoted to God. In a parenthesis, Mark explains the point of the dispute for the benefit of his Gentile readers. Unfortunately, however, his explanation only adds to our difficulties, since his statement that **all the Jews do not eat unless they wash their hands** is untrue. The origin of this custom seems to have been the necessity for priests to wash before eating 'holy' food which had been offered as a sacrifice (as in Num. 18.8–13), a principle which was then extended to their 'ordinary' food. This rule that hands must be ceremonially washed before meals was later applied to laymen, on the basis that all food

should be treated as though offered in the temple (see B. Hullin 105a; 106a–b; B. Shab.13b–14b). The first to apply this rule seem to have been the *ḥaberim* – a group whose relationship to the Pharisees is by no means clear; it is probable that the *ḥaberim* were Pharisees, though not all Pharisees were *ḥaberim*. Mark may thus be mistaken even in thinking that all **Pharisees** insisted on this rule in the time of Jesus, and it was not until about AD 100 that it came to be seen as a general religious obligation. One of our problems here is that our Jewish sources date from a later period and so cannot be regarded as an infallible guide to what was believed in the first century – and certainly should not be treated as a complete one. Mark's own account is evidence for first-century Judaism and cannot be ignored. Clearly the rule was being advocated in some Pharisaic circles, even though it was by no means universally accepted.

**They wash their hands 'with the fist'**; this last phrase is a literal translation of the Greek πυγμῇ. Various explanations of this term have been given: one is that it means 'with a fistful of water', another that it means 'up to the wrist', a third that it means 'cupping the hand' (to make it small). Whatever the exact meaning, it would seem that the purpose was to cleanse the hands with as little water as possible (water being scarce). This is reflected in a passage in the Mishnah which rules that 'a quarterlog or more must be poured over the hands (i.e. the equivalent of 1½ eggs!) to clean them, and that 'the hands . . .are rendered clean [by pouring water over them] up to the wrist' (M. Yadaim 1.1; 2.3; cf. B. Hullin 106a–b, where washing up to the second or third joint of the fingers is required). The early variant for πυγμῇ – πυκνά, meaning *often* – is clearly an attempt to make the Markan text intelligible.

It is **the tradition of the elders**, not the Torah itself, that is under attack. **From the market place** (ἀπὸ ἀγοϱᾶς) seems a somewhat 4 irrelevant phrase and creates further difficulties, since there is no reference anywhere in Jewish literature to such a custom. It is possible that we ought to translate it 'anything from the market', and understand it as the object of **purifying**, but this is equally difficult, since there are no regulations in the Jewish Law about washing the food itself. Perhaps Mark is simply trying to explain why Pharisees might consider the hand-washing necessary – namely, that in the market place they might have inadvertently come into contact with those who were ritually unclean. **Without purifying themselves**: the verb used here, ῥαντίζω, means 'to sprinkle', and once again refers to a ceremonial cleansing. The verb βαπτίζω, which occurs in the variant reading, really means 'to wash thoroughly' and does not necessarily carry the technical sense 'to baptize'; but its use here would be in contrast with the token wash of the previous verse and so hardly offers the necessary explanation. The cognate noun, **washing** (βαπτισμός), occurs later in the verse, so it is possible that the reading arose from confusion with this. **The washing of cups and jugs and copper bowls** derives from the commands in Leviticus 11–15, which deal with the cleansing of articles that have been in contact with those thought to be unclean. These rules were elaborated in great detail at a later period, and the last twelve tractates of the Mishnah deal with questions of Tohoroth – 'cleannesses'. It seems likely that these rules had already developed by the first century AD: certainly this verse suggests that they were already of considerable importance for many Jews in Mark's day. The reference to *beds* in some MSS is probably an addition, made under the influence of Leviticus 15. If, on the other hand, it was original, it could have been omitted by someone puzzled by the notion of washing a bed.

5    **Why do...your disciples...eat food with unclean hands?** A recent examination of this section (Roger Booth, *Jesus and the Laws of Purity*) isolates this question (without reference to **the tradition of the elders**) as the original cause of the dispute, and takes v.15 to be Jesus' original reply. (A similar view was held by Rawlinson.) The question would have been put by a group of *ḥaberim* (not **Pharisees and scribes**), who expected Jesus and his disciples to adopt their own high standards of piety.

6–7    According to Mark, Jesus' first reply is a counter-attack on his critics and deals with the basis of their criticism rather than the particular objection which they have made. **You hypocrites**: the word 'hypocrite' means originally an actor, and so comes to have the meaning of 'dissembler'
**It is written:**

> **'This people honours me with their lips,**
> **but their heart is far away from me.**
> **In vain they worship me,**
> **teaching as doctrines the precepts of men.'**

This passage comes from Isa. 29.13, and is closer to the LXX than to the Hebrew text, which is concerned with the unaccceptability of the people's lip-worship, rather than with the relative position of true doctrines and human precepts. We would expect Jesus to quote from the Hebrew, not the LXX, and this means either that its use derives from a later period, or that its form has been assimilated to the Greek version. In its present setting, however, linked as it is with v.8, the quotation would be inappropriate in the Hebrew version; if Jesus himself used this passage, it could only have been in another context.

8    The concluding saying opposes **the commandment of God** to **the tradition of men**. By giving the latter equal authority with the former, the Pharisees are in effect subordinating the Torah to their own interpretation.

9    **How good you are at setting aside the commandment of God, in**

176

**order to establish your own tradition!** This saying, which repeats
the accusation made in v.8, introduces a specific example. **'Honour** 10
**your father and your mother', and 'Whoever curses his father or
mother shall be put to death'.** The quotations are from Exod. 20.12
(//Deut. 5.16) and 21.17; the death penalty was no longer applied in
the time of Jesus. Here what **Moses said** (passing on the commandment
of God) is contrasted with what **you say** (maintaining the tradition of 11
men). Surprisingly, in the next paragraph, Jesus' own teaching will
apparently be set in opposition to that of Moses.

But you say **'If a man says to his father or mother, "What you
might have received from me is** *corban* **(that is, a gift [to God]"' –
you no longer allow him to do anything for his father or mother.** 12
Mark's syntax is clumsy, but the general sense is clear. He explains
the meaning of the Hebrew word **corban** for his Gentile readers. Anything that has been offered to God is holy, and cannot be used for
ordinary purposes. If the case is meant literally, then the son apparently denies support to his parents by dedicating to the temple the
money he might have spent on them. An alternative explanation is
that the son has not in fact parted with any property, but simply
makes a rash oath, saying 'the money is *corban* as far as you are
concerned', meaning that his parents may not benefit from it, an oath
which he is then not allowed to annul. There are plenty of parallels to
this kind of oath (using the word *corban* or a substitute) in one of the
tractates of the Mishnah called Nedarim (Oaths). An interesting use
of the word has recently been discovered on an ossuary lid in a tomb
dating from the beginning of the Christian era. The lid bears the inscription: 'All that a man may find to his profit in this ossuary is an
offering (*corban*) to God from him who is within it' (translation by J.A.
Fitzmyer; see *Essays*, pp. 93–100). Anything that is *corban* is thus set
aside for God. Whether the debate in Mark is about a real gift to the
temple, or simply an oath which denies the use of the money to a'
man's parents, the question at issue is whether an oath should be
allowed to take priority over a commandment from the Decalogue.
The example hardly fits the argument, however, since the inviolabil-
ity of an oath is affirmed in the Torah itself (Num. 30.2; Deut. 23.21–
3), and the question is therefore not one of Law versus tradition at all,
but rather of the relative weight to be given to different parts of the
Law; the saying may well have belonged originally to a different context. It is not clear whether the attitude attributed to the Pharisees
accords with the contemporary rabbinic attitude to the question. The
Jewish scholar C.G. Montefiore maintained that the rabbis were not
strict in the matter of oaths, as this passage in Mark suggests, but
looked for escape-routes from them. Moreover, in the Mishnah (Ned.
viii.7) a case similar to this one is considered, and the judgement
given agrees with Jesus' attitude here. However, a contrary opinion is

cited, and the fact that the matter was discussed shows that there was room for debate. It looks as if Jesus may have sided with one party of the Pharisees over against another, a possibility which the evangelists have obscured by suggesting that Jesus was opposed to the teaching of all Pharisees.

The scribal judgement that the oath takes precedence over the duty to father and mother is certainly a strange one, and possibly

13   more unusual than the concluding **many such things you do** suggests; it could perhaps be made only by those who failed to realize that such actions did in fact dishonour father and mother. Since the honouring of oaths is scriptural, the **tradition** which is described as **revoking the word of God** must be understood as the decision that the oath must be kept at whatever cost.

14   The summoning of **the crowd** in v.14 suggests that what follows is a separate saying which Mark considers appropriate to the theme. The opening authoritative command, **Hear me**, is reminiscent of Moses' address to Israel (cf. Deut. 6.4), and echoes the introduction to the parable of the sower, which provides the first account of Jesus' teaching to the crowd, in 4.3 (the verb is again ἀκούω). Although the crowd is also ordered to **understand**, Jesus' words to them are described in v.17 as a 'parable' which the disciples – and presumably

16   the crowd – cannot understand (cf. 4.10). The concluding **If anyone has ears to hear, let him hear** completes the parallel to the parable of the sower, since that concludes in the same way, though since v.16 is textually suspect, it may well have been added from 4.9.

15   These opening words (and the conclusion, if it is original) suggest that Mark regards Jesus' saying in v.15 as especially significant: **There is nothing outside a man which can make him unclean by entering him; but the things which come out of him are what make him unclean.** This saying (found in a different context entirely in the Gospel of Thomas) returns to the subject of food and therefore seems relevant to the question posed in v.5, but is really less appropriate than at first appears, since the hand-washing required there was not intended as a safeguard against eating defiled food. Knowledge of modern hygiene suggests to us that dirty hands can contaminate food, and that this then harms the eater, but the two problems here are quite separate: the question in v.5 concerned the condition of the eater, while the saying here concerns the character of the food itself. To be relevant to the dispute in vv.1–5, we must assume that the Pharisees believed that cultic impurity could be passed from unwashed hands to food to eater (as has been argued recently by R.P. Booth, *op. cit.* chs. 4 and 5). If the saying goes back to Jesus – and comparatively few scholars have questioned its authenticity – then the problem is to understand its meaning. The difficulty with the saying is that it appears to contravene the Mosaic Law as set out in Leviticus

11: did Jesus himself intend to deny the Law's validity, and challenge the prohibition of 'unclean foods'? This is the obvious meaning of the saying, though Matthew has attempted to avoid it by relating it back to the issue of washing hands (15.11, 20). Yet this raises a problem: if Jesus spoke so clearly against the food laws, why was there such debate on the issue in the early Church, and why did no one ever appeal to this saying? For this reason Heikki Räisänen (*J.S.N.T.*, 16, 1982, pp.79–100) suggests that the saying has its origins in the Gentile mission.

If the saying is in fact original, then one possible solution may be found in the structure of the sentence, with its antithesis – not this but that – which can be understood as an emphatic way of saying that one thing is more important than another: the use of antithesis was in fact a common form of argument in Hebrew tradition. In this case, the saying means that what really defiles men is not this but that (cf. Hos. 6.6). For Jesus to pronounce on the relative importance of two commands would not be unusual, since the scribes also discussed which of two commands had precedence (as in vv.9–13); in the present case, the two commands are not incompatible, so that the meaning could only be 'you are so busy with ritual cleanliness that you are ignoring moral cleanliness'. Once again, however, the two commands are both part of the Mosaic code, so that the contrast is again between two sections of the Law itself, and not between the commandment of God and the tradition of men: indeed, what is dismissed now as being of lesser importance is more clearly set out in the Law than what is here regarded as essential! Even if we understand Jesus' words as a comparison, therefore, rather than a stark choice, they still raise questions about the importance of rules which form part of God's Law. The saying is a radical one, since it challenges the attitude which treats all the commandments on an equal level, and in doing so stands in the prophetic tradition (cf. Jer. 7.22f.; Hos. 6.6).

Mark, however, has not understood the saying in this way, as can 19 be seen from his comment in v.19: **Thus he declared all foods clean.** For him, Jesus has not simply declared that morality is more important than ceremonial cleansing, but has swept the Mosaic regulations about what is clean and unclean aside. The belief that the prohibitions to eat certain foods had been abolished was of vital importance for the Gentile Christian community at the time that Mark was writing, and Jesus' words must have found new relevance when Jewish food regulations became a burning issue in the Church, but the saying would hardly have been understood in this way in its original context. Nevertheless, the Markan interpretation is a valid development from the principle set out by Jesus.

Not surprisingly, Jesus has been accused of inconsistency (e.g. by C.G. Montefiore), because he attacks the scribes for rejecting God's commandments and then himself challenges the validity of one of those commandments. If Jesus is regarded simply as an interpreter of the Torah, then we must agree that his teaching, as it is presented and interpreted here, is inconsistent. Yet Mark was able to set v.19 within the context of vv.8 and 9. By the time he was writing, it seems that even the Torah itself was being interpreted to some extent as embodying the traditions of men. If we understand Jesus to be claiming the kind of authority attributed to him in Mark 1.22, the logic behind Mark's presentation of his teaching becomes clearer. Since Jesus is depicted here as challenging not only scribal interpretation of the Torah but the Torah itself (an unthinkable thing to do!), it must be because he is teaching with an authority given to him by God: he is not a scribe who debates the meaning of the Torah, but one who – like Moses – is entrusted by God to declare his commandments directly. This is Mark's understanding of Jesus' role, and if v.15 is authentic, it is evidence that Jesus himself claimed to teach with this kind of authority.

17–18   The explanatory saying in v.19 falls in the context of Jesus' private explanation of **the parable**. We have noted the similarity of the form of vv.14–16 to 4.3–9; parallel too are the request here by **his disciples** for an explanation when they are alone, **away from the crowd** (cf. 4.10), and Jesus' surprise that they do not understand: **Are you so dull?** (cf. 4.13). The conversation takes place **when they had gone indoors** – lit. 'into a house' (εἰς οἶκον): once again, Jesus and his followers are gathered in a house (see above, on 2.1 and 3.20). To Mark, the saying in v.15 is a **parable**, since it is a cryptic saying which needs explanation; its meaning is spelt out in a way which was highly relevant to the debates which were taking place as to whether Jewish food laws must be kept by Gentile Christians: **Don't you understand that nothing that enters a man from outside can make him**

19   **unclean, because it does not enter his heart but his stomach, and goes out into the sewer?** Mark's own comment, **Thus he declared all foods clean**, is abrupt. The Greek means literally 'cleansing all foods', and it has been suggested that it is a misunderstanding of an Aramaic phrase referring to food being purged from the body; it is, however, best understood as Mark's own editorial comment.

20   Another introductory **and he said** suggests a separate saying, but if vv.18f. expound the first part of the parable, vv.20–3 expound the second part. The general category of **evil intentions** introduces a list

21–2   of twelve possible varieties. The first six nouns – translated **acts of fornication, thefts, murders, adulteries, deeds of avarice, malicious acts** – are all in the plural, suggesting repeated actions, while the remainder – **deceit, indecency, envy, slander, arrogance, folly** – are in the singular, denoting different vices. Similar lists are found elsewhere in the New Testament (e.g. Rom. 1.29–31) and in Greek literature generally. **These evil things all come from inside, and it is they that make a man unclean.** It is typical of Jesus' teaching that 23 he should emphasize God's radical demands for righteousness; if these are met, the other requirements of the Torah fall into place. Cf. 3.4; 10.2–9; 12.33, 43.

# 8 A GENTILE GIRL IS HEALED                7.24–30

*(Matt. 15.21–8)*

**(24) Then he left that place and went away to the district of Tyre;[1] and he went into a house and did not want anyone to know it, but he could not escape notice. (25) Straight away a woman whose little daughter had an unclean spirit heard about him and came and fell at his feet; (26) now the woman was a Gentile, a Syro-Phoenician by birth, and she besought him to drive the demon out of her daughter. (27) And he said to her, 'Let the children be fed first, for it is not right to take the children's bread and throw it to the dogs.' (28) But she answered him, 'Sir, even the dogs under the table eat the children's scraps.' (29) And he said to her, 'For this reply – go: the demon has come out of your daughter.' (30) And returning home, she found the child lying on the bed, and the demon gone.**

Some commentators regard this as the beginning of a new section, which they term a 'Gentile mission'. In fact, however, Mark tells us nothing of such a mission: this is the only occasion when he specifically refers to a Gentile being cured, and there is no account of Jesus teaching on Gentile soil. Tyre (and Sidon) lay outside the borders of Galilee, and came under the jurisdiction of Philip, but the population was as mixed as in Galilee. The incident itself is presented as a departure from Jesus' plans: the extension of his ministry to a Gentile is treated as an exception and anomaly, forming no part of his intention.

The occurrence of the story at this particular point in the narrative, however, is certainly significant. It seems clear that Mark wishes us to see a link between this incident and the teaching which he has placed immediately before, in vv.1–23, where Jesus challenged the basis of the levitical distinction between what is 'clean' and what is 'unclean'. If 'cleanness' depends only on men's attitudes, then the distinction between Jew and Gentile will also fall: Jews may produce

---

1 Following the text of D L W Δ Θ 28, and the Old Latin and Syriac versions. Some MSS add *and Sidon.*

evil thoughts and Gentiles good ones (cf. Rom. 2.13f.). The real problem of the narrative, however, is its presentation of Jesus as almost churlish in his reluctance to help the Gentile woman, and erratic in the way in which he then changed his mind. Most readers of the gospel feel that this is out of character with what they otherwise know of Jesus. Yet it seems unlikely that such a story would have been invented. If it was developed in the course of the church's discussions about the admission of Gentiles to the Christian community, then it seems too vacillating to have lent much support to either side in the argument.

Part of our difficulty is perhaps that we tend to assume that Jesus himself must have included Gentiles in his ministry. Yet the evidence is firmly in favour of the theory that he confined his attention to the Jews (cf. J. Jeremias, *Jesus' Promise to the Nations*). This is not really surprising when we remember the constant emphasis in Jewish thought on God's election of Israel, and on the nation's consequent responsibility. Although there is some reference also in the Old Testament to Israel's missionary role, the prophets saw their own task as directed to the nation. If Jesus understood his own role as in any sense messianic, we would expect him to do the same; it would be for the renewed and obedient Israel to undertake the mission to the nations.

Jesus' mission, then, is to Israel. Moreover, as Mark has constantly emphasized, his healing miracles are closely linked with his preaching: they are part of the breaking-in of God's Kingdom. Jesus calls Israel to repent and believe the gospel, and Israel's response is a mixture of enthusiasm and incomprehension, belief and rejection; the healing miracles are closely tied up with his proclamation and take place only where there is faith. The Gentile woman requests a cure outside the context of Jesus' call to Israel; she seems to be asking for a cure which is detached from the inbreaking of God's Kingdom, merely taking advantage of the opportunity provided by the presence of a miracle worker. This is perhaps the reason for Jesus' stern answer; his healings are part of something greater and cannot be torn out of that context. Mark does not interpret the woman's reply as simply a witty retort; by accepting Jesus' terms, she recognizes that salvation belongs to Israel and shows her faith in something more far reaching than a miraculous power to heal the sick.

Many of Mark's readers will themselves have been Gentiles. For them, the story will have provided reassurance that Jesus himself responded to the faith of a Gentile and gave her a share in the blessings of the Kingdom.

24     **Then he left that place.** No explanation is given for Jesus' journey. If Mark's account is historically correct, then one possible explanation is that Jesus wished to leave Galilee, because that was under Herod's jurisdiction. He **went away to the district of Tyre;** the words

*and Sidon* may be original but have probably been added by assimilation with Matt. 15.21. Mark perhaps sees this journey as another
attempt to get away from the crowd, since in Tyre **he went into a
house**, seeking privacy; the attempt was unsuccessful, however,
since though he **did not want anyone to know it. . .he could not
escape notice.**

The **woman** is described as 'Greek' (Ἑλληνίς), a word which is   25–6
regularly used in the New Testament as the equivalent of **Gentile**;
she was **Syro-Phoenician by birth** – i.e. a Phoenician from Syria. Her
**little daughter had an unclean spirit**, and she therefore came to
Jesus and **besought him to drive the demon out of her daughter.**
Jesus rebuffed her, but since his reply refers to **the children's** being   27
**fed first**, it contains at least a hint that there may be something later
for **the dogs**. This may, of course, reflect later knowledge of the
Gentile mission (cf. the Pauline declaration that the gospel brings
salvation 'to the Jews first, and also to the Gentile', Rom. 1.16).
Moreover, readers of Mark know that the children have already been
fed (6.32–44), and that there were plenty of carefully gathered fragments left over; the verb translated **be fed** (χορτάζω) was in fact used
in 6.42 of the satisfaction of the children's hunger.

The unflattering appellation **dogs** was regularly used by Jews for
all Gentiles. Many attempts have been made to rid Jesus' reply of the
offence which belongs to the term. It has, for example, been
suggested that the word is a diminutive and therefore an affectionate
one, or that Jesus' words were 'spoken. . .half whimsically, and with a
smile' (Rawlinson). There is no reason to suppose that a Gentile
would consider it any less offensive to be called a 'little dog' rather
than a 'dog', and descriptions of Jesus' manner and tone of speech
are, of course, sheer imagination. In its present context, the term is a
challenge to the woman to justify her request.

The woman addresses Jesus as **Sir** (Κύριε). Since the word is a   28
normal form of polite Gentile address, we should probably understand it in that way here, though it is not used in that sense elsewhere
in this gospel. The word could, however, be translated 'Lord', and it is
possible that Mark sees a deeper significance in it: certainly those
who called Jesus Lord would soon come to feel that this woman, like
the Gentile centurion in 15.39, showed true insight into the identity of
Jesus. **Even the dogs under the table eat the children's scraps.** The
word for 'scraps' (ψιχία) denotes very small bits, and the suggestion
that these were pieces of bread used for cleaning the hands seems
unlikely. By her reply the woman acknowledges that the children are
already being fed, and that, in spite of their recognized priority, there
is therefore hope for her now. Her words are an indication of her faith
that the power of God is at work in Jesus, and the healing is therefore
linked with the same kind of faith-response that characterizes the
other miracles. She has no claims to assistance but depends wholly

29   on grace. **And for this reply...the demon** leaves her **daughter.**
30     **And...she found the child lying on the bed, and the demon gone.**
The fact that the cure is said to have been performed at a distance is
perhaps to be understood as symbolic of the salvation which comes to
the Gentiles, hitherto far away; the similar case of a Gentile cure in
Matt. 8.5–13//Luke 7.1–10 is also performed at a distance. Unusually,
there is no final expression of astonishment, perhaps because Mark
pictures the woman **returning home** alone.

# 9   A DEAF MAN HEARS         7.31–7

*(Matt. 15.29–31)*

**(31) Returning again from the district of Tyre, he came through
Sidon to the Sea of Galilee, right through the district of the
Decapolis. (32) And they brought to him a deaf and dumb man,
and begged him to lay his hand on him. (33) And taking him on his
own, apart from the crowd, he put his fingers into his ears; and he
spat and touched his tongue. (34) And looking up to heaven he
sighed and said to him, 'Ephphatha' – which means 'Be opened'.
(35) And straight away his ears were opened, and the bond on his
tongue was loosened, and he spoke clearly. (36) Then he gave
them strict instructions to tell no one; but the more he instructed
them, the more they proclaimed it. (37) And they were astonished
beyond all measure. 'He has done everything well,' they said; 'he
makes the deaf hear and the dumb speak.'**

Hitherto in Mark, Jesus has been described as healing a great variety
of diseases, but this is the first case of deafness to be recorded. This
miracle and the parallel story of the blind man in 8.22–6 are apparently both understood symbolically by Mark: the physical restoration of the two men represents the ability to hear and see spiritually
which is given to those who believe in Jesus. Jesus has taught the
crowds many things (6.34), and urged the people to listen to his
teaching (7.14–16); but even the disciples have failed to understand
what they have heard (7.17f., cf. 6.52). Now a man without hearing is
enabled to hear – and so to speak of what he has heard. The miracle
ends with Jesus' command to tell no one. This motif of secrecy is not
found as commonly in connection with the miracles as is sometimes
supposed: the unclean spirits are, of course, forbidden to make Jesus
known (1.25, 34; 3.11f.); the leper is told to say nothing to anyone, but
he is nevertheless to show himself to the priest as a proof of his cure
(1.44); only the raising of the dead child (the most impossible of all

miracles to conceal!) is to be kept secret (5.43). Again, the parallel story of the blind man will contain what is apparently meant to be a command for secrecy (8.26). See additional note on the messianic secret, pp. 66–9.

It is the exception rather than the rule, then, for Jesus to command secrecy – and his command here, as in 1.45, is disregarded. Strangely, it is the onlookers, as in 5.43, not the man himself, who are told to keep silent. Mark's use of the idea of secrecy in connection with the miracles may be no more than a foil to the much more frequent emphasis on Jesus' fame and the people's astonishment: the commands for secrecy stress the sheer impossibility of keeping his activity quiet. Alternatively, it may have a theological significance: it may be part of the 'messianic secret', in which case Mark presumably thinks that the particular miracles where secrecy is enjoined are especially clear demonstrations of the identity of Jesus. Another possibility is that these miracles are linked with secrecy because they symbolize Christian faith – sight, hearing, resurrection – which become full realities only after the death and resurrection of Jesus; these physical cures cannot really be spoken of with understanding at this stage, because they point forward to events and spiritual changes which still lie in the future. The secrecy motif underlines the fact that it is only those who believe in the risen Lord who can understand the full significance of what was taking place in Jesus' ministry. Mark presumably expected those for whom he was writing to be among those who were able to comprehend.

**Returning again from the district of Tyre, he came through** 31 **Sidon to the Sea of Galilee, right through the district of the Decapolis.** The route given by Mark is an extremely circuitous one, since it takes Jesus twenty miles to the north before he begins to go south. It is often argued that Mark's knowledge of the geography must be vague. This is possible, but there is no reason why we should suppose, either that Jesus necessarily went from one place to another by the quickest route, or that Mark believed that he always did so. If this journey to Sidon is apparently without motive, so are most of the other movements attributed to Jesus in the gospel. Mark may perhaps be giving us a compressed summary of a journey which he believes Jesus to have made in the north, the details of which he perhaps does not know and certainly does not record. Whatever the explanation, he describes the next incident in his narrative as taking place on the eastern shore of the Sea of Galilee, in a region whose inhabitants were predominately Gentile. On Jesus' previous visit to this area, the inhabitants had asked him to leave them (5.1–20); this time, they appeal for his help. For **the Decapolis**, or 'Ten Towns', see the note on 5.20. It is not clear whether Mark understands the deaf man 32 to be a Gentile; if he does, this fact plays no part in the story. The **man**

is described as not only **deaf**, but as **dumb**. The word used here (μογιλάλος) means literally 'speaking with difficulty', and since in v.35 we are told that **he spoke clearly**, Mark may be thinking of a man with a speech impediment. On the other hand, in v.37, the people acclaim the fact that Jesus has made **the dumb speak**, and this was how the early versions understood v.32 also. Mark has probably chosen the rare word deliberately, because it echoes the LXX version of Isa. 35.5f.

33 Jesus takes the man **on his own, apart from the crowd.** Once again we meet the idea of withdrawal. Until now, it is the disciples who have been taken aside privately (cf. 4.33f.; 6.31f.), but it is interesting to note that both the deaf mute and the blind man (8.23) are taken away from the crowd (cf. also the dead child, 5.37, 40). This detail perhaps reflects Mark's symbolic understanding of the stories: just as Jesus restores hearing and sight to these two men, so he gives the spiritual faculty to understand what is obscure to the disciples, who think that they can hear and see but show by their behaviour how little they in fact understand.

Jesus **put his fingers into his ears; and he spat and touched his tongue.** The method of the cure, involving physical contact and the
34 use of spittle, is typical of the period. **And looking up to heaven he sighed** – or perhaps 'groaned'. This has been interpreted as an expression of power, of anger, of grief, of compassion, as a prayer, a magical action, or an indication of the difficulty of the cure! Like the other details in the story, however, it is typical of contemporary accounts of cures. As in 5.41, the word used by Jesus – **Ephphatha** – is
35 recorded but also translated: **Be opened.** The cure is immediate: **straight away his ears were opened, and the bond on his tongue was loosened:** Mark may be thinking of the man as having been
36 bound by Satan (cf. Luke 13.16). Jesus **gave them** (presumably those who witnessed the change in the man) **strict instructions to tell**
37 **no one; but,** inevitably, **they proclaimed it.** Their reaction is described in superlatives: **they were astonished beyond all measure.** Mark apparently regards this miracle as highly remarkable: Jesus is able even to restore the faculties of hearing and speech to one who was deaf and dumb, and is therefore seen to have **done everything well.**

# 10   JESUS FEEDS FOUR THOUSAND          8.1–10

*(Matt. 15.32–9)*

(1) In those days, when a great crowd had once again gathered and had nothing to eat, he called his disciples and said to them, (2) 'I am full of pity for these people, for they have stayed with me now for three days, and they have nothing to eat, (3) and if I send them home hungry, they will faint on the way; some of them have come a long distance.' (4) And his disciples answered him, 'Where could anyone get bread here in the wilderness to satisfy all these people?' (5) And he asked them, 'How many loaves do you have?' They said, 'Seven.' (6) And he instructed the crowd to sit down on the ground. And having taken the seven loaves and given thanks, he broke and gave them to the disciples to distribute, and they distributed them to the crowd. (7) And they had a few small fishes; and having blessed them, he ordered these to be distributed. (8) And they ate and were satisfied; and they picked up what was left over – seven large baskets of pieces. (9) There were about four thousand people. And he sent them away, (10) and straight away getting into the boat with his disciples, he went to the region of Dalmanutha.[1]

The similarities and differences between this narrative and the account of the feeding of the five thousand suggest that it represents a different tradition of the same event: the miracle is basically the same; it is the details which vary. The real problem, then, is to know why Mark included both accounts in his gospel. He, of course, will almost certainly have assumed that the narratives are about different events but, unless we suppose that he used every tradition about Jesus known to him, this is not sufficient explanation for his inclusion of two such similar stories. The suggestion that Mark took over two cycles of tradition, both of which included a feeding narrative, does not in itself explain why he gave space to both. It is clear, however, that Mark himself recognized the narratives as extremely significant (6.52; 8.17–21); but what was this significance?

From at least as early as the time of Augustine, the two narratives have been understood as symbolizing the giving of the bread of life to Jews and Gentiles; in support of this interpretation it is argued that the first feeding takes place on Jewish territory, the second on Gentile, and that the details in the stories, in particular the numbers, have an allegorical meaning. Although this interpretation has become very popular among commentators (see A. Richardson, *The Miracle Stories of the Gospels*, pp. 97f., for a classic exposition), it has

1 This is the reading of most MSS. Some read *Magadan* (D) or *Magdala* (Θ, fams. 1 and 13).

187

no real foundation in the text. It is not at all clear that Mark supposes the second feeding to have taken place on Gentile soil; the last reference to the geographical setting certainly stated that Jesus journeyed to the Sea of Galilee through the district of the Ten Towns (7.31), but the introductory phrase **in those days** links the present narrative only loosely with the preceding one, and the story itself contains no indication of place. In the absence of further information, we may perhaps assume that Jesus is still in the Decapolis, but Mark makes no reference to his being on Gentile territory. Nor does he indicate that the crowd consisted of Gentiles; we might perhaps expect this to be the case in the Decapolis (though the population was a mixed one) but it is apparently not sufficiently important to mention (contrast 7.26). We learn only that some of the people **have come a long distance**, which could well mean that we are to understand that they have come from Galilee.

In terms of symbolism, it has been suggested that the five loaves in the first story represent the five books of the Law, and the twelve baskets the twelve disciples. To some extent this tallies with the interpretation of Mark's story given above, though we may well wonder why Jesus should be distributing the Law in his teaching. Attempts to give similar interpretations to the numbers in the second story, however, become absurd: here the seven loaves are said to represent the seventy nations, and the seven baskets the seven deacons of Acts 6.1–6. But the loaves are fed to the people and cannot represent them, seven does not equal seventy, and we must not import deacons from Acts to explain what Mark is doing here. This kind of interpretation becomes artificial and is not justified by Mark's narrative. Moreover, it ignores the hint given by Mark himself in 7.28, that the Gentiles will be fed on the abundant leftovers. The final detail which is seen as significant is that, in the two narratives, two different words are used to describe the baskets. In 6.43 we find the noun κόφινος, a term which is normally used of a basket considered typical of the Jews, whereas in 8.8 we have σπυρίς, a word used in everyday Greek. But we ought not to be surprised if a typically Jewish basket is envisaged in 6.43, and this certainly does not make the basket in 8.8 a typically Gentile one! It seems more likely that this difference, like the differences in the figures, is accounted for by the details already present in the two traditions (see further on 8.19f.). We must therefore disagree radically with Vincent Taylor's opinion that Mark 'tells the story in such a way as to suggest that he has in mind the Gentile Church of his day' (p. 357).

It has recently been argued by Robert M. Fowler (*Loaves and Fishes*) that Mark took over this narrative from the tradition, but that the earlier account, in 6.30–44, was created by the evangelist himself. In an analysis of the material he argues that it is possible to separate

Markan redaction (8.1-2, 10) from tradition in this second story, but that the former account betrays its Markan composition. This means that any tensions and conflicts betwen the two stories are deliberate, and that we are certainly meant to read the second narrative in the light of the first; Mark's purpose in creating a second story is to underline the stupidity and incomprehension of the disciples. The separation of redaction from tradition is notoriously difficult, and the evidence is not sufficient to justify the suggestion that Mark created 6.30-44: it seems much more likely that he used traditional material creatively. Nevertheless, Fowler is right to stress the way in which Mark has handled the stories to underline the inability of the disciples to understand Jesus' power.

The various explanations offered regarding the story's origin and meaning are similar to those given for 6.32-44.

**A great crowd** has **once again gathered**, and Jesus is again said 1-2 to feel **pity for the people** – this time, however, because **they have nothing to eat**, rather than because they are without a shepherd; the two ideas, however, clearly belong closely together for Mark. **He called his disciples and said to them**: whereas in 6.35f. it was the disciples who pointed out the need for action, the initiative here is taken by Jesus: this may be an indication of a later development in the tradition. The time the crowd has spent with Jesus has lengthened from one day to **three days**; the long period serves to emphasize the great need of the people when Jesus at last feeds them – as does the 3 **long distance** they have come from home. Mark does not tell us what took place during that time, but it is natural to suppose that he thinks of Jesus teaching the crowd throughout that period. The suggestion that those who had listened eagerly to Jesus might **faint on the way** (ὁδός) could well have reminded Mark's readers that would-be disciples did not always persevere in the way of discipleship (see below, on 8.27; 9.33f.; 10.17, 32 and 52).

The disciples' question, which is entirely sensible if the story is 4 taken on its own, seems incredibly stupid within the Markan framework, since Jesus has already shown them **where** to find **bread**. This is certainly not carelessness on Mark's part, however, since in his view the disciples were extraordinarily insensitive to what was happpening. The setting of the miracle is stressed: it takes place **here in the wilderness**. The noun ἐρημία (wilderness) is cognate with the adjective ἔρημος, which we have translated 'lonely' (cf. 6.31,32,35). In the wilderness there is no food; nevertheless, God may be expected to provide for his people, as he did at the Exodus. This time the absurd notion of going on a foraging expedition is not mentioned. In asking where bread could be found, the disciples use words which might well have been spoken by the Israelites in the wilderness immediately before God provided the manna (Ex. 16.1-5).

5    Once again, Jesus asks 'How many loaves do you have?' and this time receives the answer 'Seven'.

6    As before, Jesus instructed the crowd to sit down on the ground, and his next actions are described in language almost identical with that used on the previous occasion: having taken the seven loaves and given thanks, he broke and gave them to the disciples. The only differences are that here bread and fish are separated: the loaves are distributed after Jesus has given thanks (εὐχαριστήσας),

7    and the participle having blessed (εὐλογήσας) is this time referred to the few small fishes. The language would very soon remind Mark's readers of their own eucharistic gatherings. The fishes appear in the story almost as an afterthought, probably because of the importance placed originally on the bread, with its obvious parallel to the Exodus

8    story. The people once again ate and were satisfied (χορτάζω, 6.42; 7.27; 8.4), and again there was more than sufficient food for their needs (cf. Exod. 16.18). They picked up what was left over, collecting it in seven large baskets: the Greek word σπυρίς refers to a large basket, and we have therefore used this translation here as a way of distinguishing the term from κόφινος, used in 6.43, and not because

9    there is any emphasis on the size. The number who ate is this time put at about four thousand people, and nothing is said to indicate whether this figure includes only men. On this occasion Jesus is said

10   to have sent...away the crowd but not the disciples. His own destination, Dalmanutha, is unknown, and the alternative readings (assimilations to Matt. 15.39) indicate that it was unknown also in antiquity. Either Mark's geography is faulty, or the place disappeared at an early date.

## 11    THE PHARISEES DEMAND A SIGN    8.11-12

*(Matt. 12.38f.; 16.1-4; Luke 11.16,29)*

**(11) Then the Pharisees came out and began to dispute with him, testing him by demanding from him a sign from heaven. (12) And with a deep sigh within himself he said, 'Why does this generation demand a sign? Truly I tell you, a sign shall not be given to this generation.'**

This short incident, coming immediately after the dramatic event in vv.1–10, serves to demonstrate what Mark regards as incredible blindness on the part of the Jewish religious leaders. Immediately after this obvious 'sign from heaven' they come to Jesus and demand that he give them one! Mark himself is very probably responsible for this arrangement, for though nothing is said to indicate that the

**Pharisees** were present at the feeding, the juxtaposition of the two stories suggests that they should have known about the feeding, and the irony is certainly in keeping with his theme. There is an interesting parallel in John, however, where the crowd which has been fed by Jesus ask him what sign he can show them so that they may believe in him – and then remind him how Moses had fed their fathers with manna in the wilderness (John 6.30f.). Both evangelists, therefore, stress this inability of the Jews to comprehend what was happening before their very eyes.

Jesus' outright refusal to give **a sign** (σημεῖον) is often contrasted with John's use of this term for the miracles. Although Mark may refer to the miracles as acts of power (δυνάμεις) and not as signs (σημεῖα), however, there is no real difference in understanding between the two evangelists. For John, the miracles are signs to those who believe that they are the work of God himself; those who do not recognize Jesus do not recognize the signs. For Mark, also, the miracles are clear demonstrations of the activity of God; only those who are completely blind can ask for a sign from heaven. The real signs are not miracles done to order but are part and parcel of the breaking-in of God's Kingdom.

Miracles and parables have a parallel function in Mark. To those who have eyes to see and ears to hear, both miracles and parables demonstrate the power of the Kingdom of God. But those without ears hear only parables and do not understand the secret of the Kingdom (4.11f.), while those without eyes see only amazing acts, so that to them no sign from heaven is given.

Readers of the gospel will naturally interpret the sign demanded by the Pharisees as a sign of Jesus' messianic status, but if any such demand was ever made, it is much more likely that it concerned his authority to teach doctrine that was contrary to their own. There are occasional examples, both in the Old Testament (1 Sam. 2.30–4; 2 Kgs. 20.1–11; Isa. 7.10–11) and in rabbinic literature (B. Sanhedrin 98a and B. Baba. Meziah 59b), of signs being offered as a guarantee of the truth of the utterances of a prophet or rabbi. Yet a 'sign or wonder' is in fact in itself no guarantee of the truth of a prophet's words (Deut. 13.1f.), and the only true test of prophecy is if it proves to be fulfilled (Deut. 18.21f.; cf. the argument used by Gamaliel, Acts 5.38f.). In demanding **a sign from heaven**, therefore, the Pharisees are refusing to allow the principle that truth validates itself. A similar demand is made in John 2.18, where Jesus is asked for a sign of his authority to act as he does (in prophetic action).

By the time Mark was writing, the Pharisees were regarded as the implacable opponents of Christianity. They thus typify the generation which, through its own stubbornness, refused to recognize the truth of the gospel.

Jesus' refusal of a sign is emphatic: he will not perform a miracle to order, simply to provide a 'proof' of his authority. In **demanding. . .a sign**, the Pharisees are said to be **testing him**: the verb πειράζω was used in 1.13 of Satan's activity in tempting Jesus, and the scene here accords with the interpretation given to that narrative by Matthew and Luke, who understand the temptations as demands to display divine power. Jesus' teaching and actions validate themselves, and the truth of both should be plain to those whose ears are not hardened by unbelief. By relating this incident after the second feeding miracle, Mark suggests that the truth which these men fail to grasp is the truth about Jesus himself. Out of context, Jesus' words might seem harsh – like those in 4.11f.: but the refusal is to be understood as the result of the Pharisees' own perversity. Jesus' **deep sigh** is due to anger – or grief – at the Pharisees' hardness of heart. **Why does this generation demand a sign?** These words are reminiscent of a constant Old Testament theme – the sin of Israel in doubting the Lord, in spite of the signs which he had performed. The term 'generation' (γενεά) is often used in connection with this condemnation (cf. Ps. 95.10 (LXX 94.10); Deut. 32.5): just as the generation of Israelites in the wilderness had shown themselves perverse and foolish (Deut. 32.5f.), trying to test God by demanding signs from Moses (Exod. 17.2), while ignoring those which had been shown them (Num. 14.10–12, 22f.), until the Lord was grieved with them (Ps. 95.8–11), so now the generation of Jesus' contemporaries show themselves equally senseless and wicked when confronted with God at work in Moses' successor.

# 12 THE BLINDNESS OF THE DISCIPLES 8.13–21

*(Matt. 16.5–12; Luke 12.1)*

**(13) And leaving them, he embarked once more and went across to the other shore. (14) Now they had forgotten to take any bread, and they had only one loaf with them in the boat. (15) And he warned them, 'Look out! Beware of the leaven of the Pharisees and the leaven of Herod.'[1] (16) And they began to discuss with one another why they had[2] no bread. (17) And knowing it, he said to them, 'Why do you argue about having no bread? Do you still not understand? Don't you comprehend? Are your hearts hardened?**

1 Some MSS, including 𝔓45 W Θ fams. 1 and 13 read *the Herodians*.
2 ἔχουσιν is read by 𝔓45 B W fam. 1 and the Coptic D and old Latin read εἶχαν. Many MSS, including ℵ A C L Θ fam. 13, the Vulgate, Syriac and Bohairic read ἔχομεν *we have*.

(18) "You have eyes – can you not see?
You have ears – can you not hear?"

Do you not remember (19) how many basketfuls of pieces you
picked up when I broke five loaves for five thousand people?'
They answered, 'Twelve.' (20) 'When [I broke] seven for four
thousand people, how many large baskets were filled with the
pieces you picked up?' And they answered, 'Seven.' (21) And he
said to them: 'Do you still not comprehend?'

In this incident, more clearly than anywhere else, Mark spells out his
belief that the miracles of Jesus were a means of revelation which the
disciples failed to comprehend at the time. By their demand for a sign,
the Pharisees have just demonstrated their inability to see the power
of God at work in Jesus. Now the disciples show their failure to comprehend the two miracles of the loaves by their own incredibly stupid
anxiety over the small amount of food they have brought with them in
the boat. These two accounts of spiritual blindness are followed in
the Markan account by two stories about men who receive their
sight; the first, vv.22–6, is the story of the cure of a blind man, and the
second, vv.27–30, is the story of the opening of the disciples' eyes.

By underlining the details of the two feeding miracles, Mark brings
home to his readers the significance of these stories: for those whose
hearts are *not* hardened, they provide clear pointers to the identity of
Jesus, the one who supplies the needs of his people. Moreover, Jesus
provides more than enough food for each occasion – enough to feed
not only the crowds who originally flocked to him, but all those who
subsequently respond to the gospel. This is the third story in which
Jesus and his disciples cross to the other side of the lake by boat. On
the first occasion (4.35–41), he rebuked them because of their lack of
faith, and they are described as terrified. On the second (6.45–52),
Jesus joined them half way, and the disciples are said to have been
terrified and astounded, 'for they had not understood about the
loaves: their hearts were hardened.' This time, they once again fail to
comprehend Jesus' power, and his rebuke underlines their lack of
faith and understanding.

The story is closely linked with the previous one, since the setting is 13–14
**the boat** in which he **embarked** on **leaving** the Pharisees, but the
stories belong to each other thematically, rather than chronologi-
cally. Mark's account is confused; although he tells us that the
disciples **had forgotten to take any bread**, and in the ensuing conversation they confirm that **they had no bread**, we are told also that
**they had. . .one loaf with them**; perhaps he means that they had
forgotten to renew their supplies but happened to have one loaf left
over. This introduction betrays no knowledge of the feeding mira-

cles, which might seem to make it unnecessary to take more than one loaf; if the food supply has run low, there are this time only thirteen people, not thousands, to be fed. The ensuing conversation will make it clear that Mark is fully aware of the irony of the situation: the disciples may have forgotten the miracles, as well as the bread, but Mark will not allow his readers to do so.

The conversation between Jesus and the disciples is remarkable: it is hard to believe that men who had witnessed two feeding miracles such as Mark has described could argue like this! Mark has perhaps used a tradition about a conversation on the theme of bread, adding the references to the two miracles in vv.19–20 to stress the disciples' lack of comprehension; certainly those verses show signs of Mark's redaction. There is an apparent lack of connection between what Jesus says to the disciples in v.15 and the rest of the conversation: the failure in communication reminds one of many Johannine passages in which Jesus and those with whom he converses appear to speak on different planes, so that the real sense of his words remains uncomprehended by his hearers. A possible explanation of this could be that v.15 is an independent saying which Mark has inserted into the story; this suggestion is supported by the fact that another form of the saying is found in isolation in Luke 12.1. If so, then Mark has placed the saying here – not, as has been sometimes suggested, because he did not know where else to put it – but because it seemed to him relevant to the situation.

15    The saying warns the disciples against **the leaven of the Pharisees and the leaven of Herod**. 'Leaven' is a familiar metaphor in the New Testament and rabbinic literature, and usually stands for something evil (cf. I Cor. 5.6–8; Gal. 5.9; contrast Matt. 13.33//Luke 13.20f.). Matthew understands this saying as referring to teaching (substituting Sadducees for Herod); Luke's parallel (which speaks of Pharisees alone) defines it as hypocrisy. The combination of Pharisees with Herod is strange – so strange, perhaps, as to have led to the alternative reading *the Herodians*, which is usually regarded as secondary; on the other hand, it is tempting to adopt this alternative reading, since the combination of Pharisees and Herodians is found in 3.6 and in 12.13, but the same reasoning could well have led a copyist to alter 'Herod' to 'Herodians'. Herod has been mentioned only in the story of the Baptist's death (though the parallel between the fate of John and Jesus makes Herod's attitude significant), but Pharisees have appeared repeatedly throughout Mark's narrative – always disbelieving and hostile. In 3.6, at the climax of a series of clashes with Jesus in which they demonstrated their hardness of heart, they plotted with the Herodians to get rid of him. The same remarkable combination occurs in 12.13, where again Pharisees and Herodians join forces in trying to entrap Jesus. The attitude of Pharisees and Herodians to

Jesus is therefore one of consistent hostility. The leaven of which the disciples are to **beware**, however, was perhaps understood by Mark as the *cause* of this hostility and of Herod's treatment of John – namely, the refusal to recognize and accept the truth. It is this hardness of heart which leads to their hostile attitude, and it is this which the disciples are in danger of sharing. Jesus' anxiety about the disciples is in Mark's view well founded: they are so infected by the same disease as Jesus' opponents that they cannot understand even his warning. By using this saying here, Mark demonstrates the incomprehension of the disciples – no doubt somewhat unfairly – and so stresses their danger. Like the crowds, they have eyes and ears, but neither see nor understand; worse still, since these men have been privileged to witness all Jesus' mighty works and have still failed to recognize the power of God in them, they seem to share the hardened hearts of Jesus' opponents, who cannot acknowledge the truth of what they see and hear.

**And they began to discuss with one another why they had no** 16 **bread.** This comment follows uneasily after v.15, and the text is uncertain; we have read the third person plural (ἔχουσιν) and taken the introductory ὅτι as an indirect interrogative (see C.H. Turner, *J.T.S.*, 27, 1925, p. 59). If we read the first person plural instead of the third, then we may translate: 'they began to say (διελογίζοντο, an imperfect) to one another "It is because we have no bread"' (taking ὅτι as *recitativum*). In either case, the disciples apparently ignore Jesus' words in the previous verse. This may be, as we have suggested, because v.15 is a separate tradition which Mark has inserted into the story and, if we omit v.15, we are left with a conversation about the disciples' lack of faith. After seeing two miraculous feedings, they are still concerned about whether they have enough food with them! The disciples have shown repeatedly that they lack faith (4.40) and 17 understanding (4.13; 6.52; 7.18), and the **still** in v.17 is therefore appropriate: their **hearts**, like those of the Pharisees (3.5), appear to be **hardened**. Most commentators regard the lack of correlation between vv.15 and 16 as clumsy editing. Yet this strange juxtaposition seems to underline the very point which Mark is making. With Jesus and the disciples talking at cross-purposes, the meaning of his first question in v.17 – **'Why do you argue about having no bread?'** – seems to be: why are you discussing the lack of bread, when I am talking about something quite different? The verb διαλογίζομαι, 'to discuss' or 'argue' is used of the deliberations of Jesus' enemies in 2.6 and 8 (where it is translated by 'to think') and in 11.31; cf. also 9.33, where it is used of the disciples when they are again clearly failing to understand Jesus. This suggests that Mark has used it here deliberately to indicate the kind of discussion which stems from unbelief.

The accusations in v.18 are reminiscent of the quotations from 18

Isa. 6.9f. in 4.12, though the actual form of words is closer to Jer. 5.21 and Ezek. 12.2; the disciples are apparently as uncomprehending as those who were there described as outsiders. True, they **have eyes**

19–20 and **ears** and, in answer to Jesus' questions, they recall the amount of surplus food left over when Jesus fed the two crowds. Yet even when

21 they are reminded of what they saw and heard, they cannot **comprehend**. The reason is that their **hearts** are **hardened**.

What they have failed to understand is the *meaning* of the feeding miracles. Commentators have often argued that, for Mark, this meaning is their eucharistic significance (the most thorough exposition of this theory is set out by Q. Quesnell in *The Mind of Mark*); but this theme is hardly prominent in Mark. Others have argued for the Jewish-Gentile interpretation of the feeding miracles which we have already discussed. It seems clear that Mark understands these miracles to reveal the truth which is hidden from those whose ears are deaf and whose eyes are blind – and that is the truth about Jesus himself. The miracles are recalled in precise detail: the number of persons fed and the amount of bread available and left over; even the two different Greek words for 'baskets' are retained. It is this careful rehearsal of the details which has led some commentators to look for some significance in the actual numbers. There is an alternative explanation, however – and this is that the details are recalled in order to remind the disciples (or rather, the readers) of the magnitude of the miracles. If **five loaves** fed **five thousand people**, with **twelve basketfuls** to spare, and if **seven** loaves fed **four thousand people**, and **seven large baskets were filled with the pieces**, then the power of Jesus is sufficient to deal with any situation. He is even greater than Moses who went before him. In 4.41 the disciples asked one another, 'Who then is this?' Several mighty signs later, they still have not grasped the answer, but readers of the gospel can hardly be so uncomprehending.

This passage raises great problems for the modern reader. Is Mark implying that the disciples are foolish to worry about bread because, whenever they are short of food, Jesus can always multiply it? The fact that Jesus talks here about **the leaven of the Pharisees and the leaven of Herod**, however, and that this leaven cannot be interpreted literally suggest that Mark is hinting that the real significance of the feeding miracles is to be found at a deeper level than the physical. He does not suppose that Jesus will always satisfy hunger or that his followers will never go short again. Rather, in multiplying the loaves, Jesus has demonstrated his divine power and revealed who he is. Because they have failed to see the point and do not realize who Jesus is, the disciples show that they are indeed in great danger from the leaven of the Pharisees and of Herod.

# 13   A BLIND MAN SEES                        8.22–6

(22) And they came to Bethsaida; and they brought to him a blind man and begged him to touch him. (23) And taking the blind man by the hand, he led him out of the village; and he spat on his eyes, laid his hands on him and asked, 'Can you see anything?' (24) And looking up he said, 'I see men – they look like trees, walking about.' (25) Then he laid his hands on his eyes again; and he opened them wide and was cured and saw everything clearly. (26) And he sent him home, saying 'Do not even enter the village.'[1]

Although Matthew and Luke have not included this miracle in their gospels, there is an interesting parallel in John 9, in the account of the healing of the man born blind: the two stories are different, but the use made of the miracle by the fourth evangelist, to show the gradual development of the healed man's faith in Jesus in contrast to the blindness of the Pharisees, is similar to the significance which is implicit in the Markan narrative; whereas John spells out the parallel between physical and spiritual sight, however, Mark presents it by his juxtaposition of various pericopae concerned with the two themes.

There is also a remarkable parallel between this story and that about the deaf mute in Mark 7.32–7. The two accounts are so close that it has even been suggested that they are doublets referring to the same incident, but this is improbable, since the complaints healed are different; it seems more likely that Mark has deliberately used the two stories as parallels, and the similarities between them may well be the result of his editing. The following phrases are identical: **And they brought to him. . .and begged him to. . .and he spat. . . .** There are also close similarities in the request to Jesus to touch the victim, his response to this request, the taking aside and the request for secrecy.

There is yet another parallel to this narrative in the story of the healing of another blind man, Bartimaeus, in 10.46–52. In this story, too, the themes of faith (Bartimaeus appeals to Jesus as 'Son of David') and discipleship (he follows Jesus 'in the way') are close to the surface. Some commentators therefore divide the gospel at 8.22, arguing that these two healings of blind men form an 'inclusio' and mark the beginning and end of the section about the way of the Cross and the meaning of discipleship.

These parallels with other narratives point to Mark's intention that his readers should understand them not only as cures, but also as

1 Following ℵ B L fam. 1, the Syriac and Coptic. There are many variant readings which add or substitute the command *Do not tell anyone in the village.*

'acted parables' of the miracle of faith. Just as the story of the deaf man follows closely after a section where Jesus calls on men to hear and understand his teaching (and both Pharisees and disciples show that they have failed to do so), the story of the blind man in chapter 8 follows a section where Jesus rebukes Pharisees and disciples for failing to see and understand his miracles. It is the deaf man and the blind man, when they are taken aside by Jesus, who receive hearing and sight and so stand symbolically for those to whom understanding is to be given. But the significance of what is taking place remains hidden from those who are still deaf and blind to the truth.

The most unusual feature of this particular miracle is the statement that it was completed in two stages: for once, Mark makes no use of his favourite term εὐθύς, 'straight away'. Is this meant to indicate that it was particularly difficult? If so, it can be understood, some believe, as a mark of authentic tradition; more significantly, it demonstrates the amazing power of Jesus who can heal even such difficult cases. Or is the gradual recovery of sight symbolic of the disciples' poor progress in grasping the significance of Jesus? If so, we can understand Mark to mean either that the story of Caesarea Philippi which follows is parallel to the full recovery of sight (the view put forward by R.H. Lightfoot, *History and Interpretation of the Gospels*, pp. 90f.), or that the disciples, even after Caesarea Philippi, are men who comprehend only half the truth. The constant inability of the disciples in the chapters that follow this scene to understand Jesus' teaching about suffering – a failure which is remarkably similar to their inability beforehand to understand the significance of his words and deeds – suggests that Mark regards the disciples as semi-blind until the resurrection; until then, they are in the position of the half-cured man who could barely distinguish between men and trees.

Mark's community lives on this side of the resurrection and should therefore understand the significance of these events. But this story may reflect a fear that there are some within that community who do not fully understand the gospel for, as 8.31–3 shows, it is possible to have one's eyes half open, i.e. to grasp part only of the truth. Certainly the story could easily be reapplied to those in the early Church who, like Peter, were offended by the message of the Cross.

22  Jesus and his disciples at last reach **Bethsaida** (whither they set out in 6.45), on the north-east shore of the lake. Bethsaida was a town rather than a **village** (vv.23, 26), but Mark does not seem to have

23  realized this. **He led him out of the village**: the healing is once again private – a feature of those miracles in Mark which seem to symbolize faith. The method of healing – the use of spittle and the laying on of hands – is the same as in 7.32–7; there is a well-known parallel in Tacitus (*Histories*, IV.81), where Vespasian is said to have cured a

blind man in Alexandria by wetting his eyes with spittle. The next part of the story is, however, unusual: Jesus **asked, 'Can you see anything?'** We do not expect Jesus to doubt his own ability to heal. But the question as to what the man can see will be echoed in v. 29 in Jesus' question to the disciples as to what they believe about him, and the parallel may be deliberate. **And looking up:** this verb (ἀναβλέπω) 24 was used in 7.34 of Jesus. It can also mean 'to recover sight' (as in 10.51f.) and could have that meaning here (though the partial nature of the recovery is against this). Similarly, the verb translated **he 25 opened them wide** (διαβλέπω) can mean 'to see clearly', and Mark may therefore be describing the result of the cure, rather than the man's actions; but this is unlikely since this is already conveyed by the final phrase, **and saw everything clearly.** At first, however, the healing was only partial; in answer to Jesus' question, the man **said 'I see men – they look like trees, walking about.'** We cannot deduce from this somewhat odd description that the man had previously been able to see and therefore recognized the shape of a tree; the image conveys a remarkable (and apposite) impression of semi-comprehension. The man is sent **home,** with instructions **not even to 26 enter the village.** If this is the correct text, we are presumably to understand that the man lives outside the village, and that he is to go straight home, and not to make a detour in order to tell people what has happened. The textual evidence is confused, and there are many variants, most of which forbid him to *tell anyone* in the village. It is difficult to decide which reading is the more original. The instruction to say nothing could certainly be Markan, for it is in keeping with other commands for secrecy in the gospel and, like them, it would be impossible to carry out.

# E   The way of the Cross: teaching on discipleship                        8.27–10.52

# 1   THE DISCIPLES' EYES ARE OPENED        8.27–30

*(Matt. 16.13–20; Luke 9.18–21)*

(27) Jesus and his disciples left for the villages of Caesarea Philippi, and on the way he questioned his disciples, saying to them, 'Who do people say I am?' (28) They answered him, 'John the Baptist, and others, Elijah; others, one of the prophets.' (29) And he asked them, 'But you – who do you say I am?' Peter replied: 'You are the Christ.' (30) And he gave them strict instructions to say nothing about him.

This paragraph has long been seen as the watershed of Mark's gospel. In many ways, the character of the story changes at this point. The framework of the next two chapters is a journey: the details of this journey are not obtrusive, and the route is somewhat vague, yet Jesus is brought from Caesarea Philippi in the far north, via the mount of transfiguration, back to Galilee (9.30); from Capernaum (9.33) he sets out through Judea and the Transjordan (10.1), and finally comes to Jericho (10.46) and so to the gates of Jerusalem. The journey is the journey of Jesus to the Cross, and the teaching which he tries to impart to his disciples as they take that road together concerns the meaning of his own mission and the manner of their discipleship. Not surprisingly, there is far more teaching in this section, and it is addressed primarily to the disciples. Only two miracles occur *en route*; one is the story of the epileptic boy, which becomes the occasion of a discussion about the meaning of faith; the other is the account of a blind man, Bartimaeus, who hails Jesus as 'Son of David' and follows him 'on the way' when his sight is restored. We note, then, that Mark has enclosed Jesus' teaching about his own role and the meaning of discipleship between two miracles of restored sight: the first blind man had difficulties in seeing even after his encounter with Jesus; the second followed Jesus on the way to Jerusalem. The two together stand as symbols of the disciples' blundering attempts to follow Jesus. Some commentators suggest that these two stories mark the beginning and end of a section (e.g. E. Best, *Following Jesus*, pp. 134–45, who regards both stories as 'transition sections').

The story of Caesarea Philippi is aptly called a 'watershed', for it is an important pivot in Mark's narrative, belonging as closely to the preceding paragraph as to the one that follows, and we might well have made it the climax to the last division, rather than the opening of a new one. These divisions are arbitrary, and they must not be allowed to impose a pattern on the gospel. We have already noted the links with the previous story: like the blind man, the disciples at last have their eyes opened to the truth – or, rather, half opened. But their new understanding of Jesus, though still inadequate, forms the foundation of the teaching which follows, not only in vv.31–3, but throughout the next two chapters.

Traditionally, this story has been regarded not only as the watershed of Mark's gospel, but as an equally important event in the ministry of Jesus. It used to be assumed that Peter's confession was an important turning-point in Jesus' life, and that Mark's arrangement of the tradition before and after Caesarea Philippi was historically accurate: according to this view, Jesus proclaimed the gospel in word and deed in the early days of his ministry; then after Caesarea Philippi he taught the disciples about the necessity for his death, and set his face toward Jerusalem. More recently, the tendency has been to treat the story as a legend which carries back into the life of Jesus the early Church's confession of him as the Messiah. Those who maintain that Jesus made no messianic claims and that the identification was first made after the resurrection are bound to conclude that the story has no historical basis. Yet it seems almost inevitable that the question of messiahship would have been raised during his lifetime, a probability which seems confirmed by the accusation brought against him at the crucifixion (15.26; cf. also 14.61; 15.2, 18), so that we cannot rule out the possiblility that the disciples believed him to be Messiah; they must at least have asked questions about the strange charismatic teacher to whom they had committed themselves. But Mark's account tells us nothing of the meaning of such an affirmation for Jesus himself, and from the rest of his story it is clear that for Jesus it was the proclamation of God's Kingdom, not his own messianic status, that was central.

Some scholars argue that the historical basis of the story was in fact the rejection by Jesus of Peter's 'confession', and that a vestige of this rejection is to be found in Jesus' rebuke of Peter as Satan (so, e.g., F. Hahn, *The Titles of Jesus in Christology*, pp. 223–8). It seems hard to believe, however, that an indignant rejection by Jesus could have been transformed by degrees into the enthusiastic acceptance that we have in Matthew's account of the scene. Another suggestion is that Mark himself intends us to understand the story as Jesus' rejection of Peter's affirmation: Peter's declaration sums up the view of Jesus as *theios aner* – a divine man, working miracles and demonstrating divine power – but Jesus rejects this and substitutes his own teaching about the suffering Son of man (T. Weeden, *Mark – Traditions in Conflict*, pp. 64ff.). Although Jesus certainly rejects Peter's understanding of what messiahship means, it is difficult to suppose that Mark intends to portray him as rejecting the title: certainly Matthew did not understand his story that way. Moreover, Mark himself has already used the term Χριστός of Jesus in 1.1.

So at this half-way point in the story, we have a reiteration of the truth about Jesus' identity. Peter's acclamation of Jesus as Messiah is then endorsed by a scene in which the divine voice again affirms that Jesus is the beloved Son. From now on, Jesus' teaching spells out both the meaning of his own role, and what it means to be his disciple. Not surprisingly, the material in this section shows signs of its application to the needs of the Christian community as it sought to understand the nature of discipleship. A number of the sayings, for example, are cast in the form of 'community rules': 'Whoever. . .' (see 8.35, 38; 9.37, 39, 40, 41, 42; 10.11, 15, 29f., 43, 44). The overall theme of Jesus' teaching spells out what it means to follow one who sees his own mission in terms of service and suffering; his own attitudes must be reflected in the community which claims to belong to him.

27    Jesus and his disciples are again on their own. **The villages of Caesarea Philippi** were presumably in the neigbourhood of the town of that name which was situated near Mt Hermon in the north of Palestine, at the source of the Jordan, and which had been rebuilt by the tetrarch Philip, son of Herod the Great. The geographical reference may well be an historical reminiscence, as many have argued, since there is no other obvious reason why the area should be mentioned. The statement that the incident took place **on the way**, however, could in this context be a deliberate reminder that these men are following Jesus in 'the Way' (cf. Acts 9.2; 19.23, etc.), which is the only way to know him. The path which Jesus himself is pursuing is in fact 'the way of the Lord' (cf. 1.2f., and see also 9.33f.; 10.17, 32 and 52). **He questioned his disciples:** Jesus takes the initiative, challenging the disciples by asking direct questions about his own identity. Bultmann (*Synoptic Tradition*, pp. 66, 257f.) suggested that this marks the narrative out as secondary, pointing out that in rabbinic dialogues it was the disciples, not the rabbi, who asked the questions; moreover, the question is artificial, since Jesus knew as well as his disciples what men were saying about him. Yet Jesus must clearly frequently have taken the initiative, and there is no reason why he should have conformed to the practices of a Jewish rabbi; indeed, Bultmann himself elsewhere attached great importance to those characteristics which differentiated Jesus from his contemporaries. Our decision regarding the historicity of this narrative will in fact depend ultimately on our judgement about Jesus' 'messianic self-consciousness'.

28    **'Who do people say I am?'** The various opinions about Jesus echo the earlier comments in 6.14f.; some believe him to be **John the Baptist**. . .others, **Elijah**, though this time Jesus is said to be **one of the prophets** rather than 'a prophet like one of the prophets'. Presumably the suggestion here is that he is one of the prophets raised from the dead. Cf. Matt. 16.14, which refers to Jeremiah. 2 Esdras 2.18 expects the return of Isaiah and Jeremiah at the End, and may embody Jewish ideas, even though this passage is a Christian addition to the original apocalypse.

29    **'But you – who do you say I am?'** The contrast between the beliefs of others and the disciples is brought out by the emphatic 'you' (Ὑμεῖς). Mark stresses the confession which in his day differentiates the disciple from the outsider, but in the lifetime of Jesus the distinction between the two was probably not so clear cut. **Peter** acts as spokesman for the group of disciples, but his dramatic answer – **'You are the Christ'** – receives no acknowledgment from Jesus. (For a comment on the term 'Christ', see above, on 1.1.) If Mark has not added (as Matthew has done) a commendation of Peter by Jesus, it could be because it did not occur to him that it was necessary to spell

out that Peter's 'confession' represents the truth. Could any of his readers reach this point in his story and still not understand who Jesus was? Moreover, in Mark's story, Peter scarcely deserves commendation, since it is only now that he at last grasps what to Mark's readers seems so obvious. **He gave them strict instructions**: the 30 verb (ἐπιτιμάω) was used in 1.25 and 3.12 of silencing unclean spirits. Mark regards both Peter's 'confession' and the cries of the spirits in 1.24 and 3.12 as declarations of the truth about Jesus: the spirits acknowledge Jesus as the Son of God – a fundamental title for Jesus in Mark – while the term 'Christ' is acknowledged by Jesus in 14.61f. There is certainly no hint in Mark's story that he considered the term 'Christ' inappropriate for Jesus, or that he has adapted a version of the story in which Jesus rejected the term. The command **to say nothing about him** is not understood by Mark as a denial of messiahship, but as part of the messianic secret, which explains the failure of men to recognize Jesus. If Jesus commands secrecy, this is because the truth about his identity can be grasped only by those who are his disciples.

Up to this point the disciples themselves have asked the question 'Who then is this?' (4.41) but have been unable to answer it; repeatedly they have been rebuked by Jesus for their lack of faith and understanding. Now by their answer they separate themselves from other people who view Jesus merely in the role of a prophet. The 'confession' at Caesarea Philippi marks an important division – but this is not simply between 'before' and 'after'; it is a division between those who recognize Jesus as the Christ and those to whom his identity remains obscure. Yet we shall find that even the disciples are still only half aware of the truth, and that they continue to grope in a state of semi-blindness, frequently failing to understand what Jesus now teaches them plainly. From this point onwards, however, the truth which they cannot grasp is the necessity for suffering: in other words, it is the *nature* of Jesus' messiahship and of their own discipleship.

Mark's readers number themselves among those who have made the confession that Jesus is the Christ. They, too, must be aware of the division between their own understanding of Jesus and that of most of their contemporaries. But for them, too, that confession is only the half-way point in understanding who Jesus is and what discipleship involves.

# 2 JESUS PREDICTS HIS DEATH 8.31–3

*(Matt. 16.21–23; Luke 9.22)*

(31) Then he began to teach them that the Son of man must endure great suffering and be rejected by the elders and chief priests and scribes, be put to death and rise up three days later. (32) And he spoke the word plainly. And Peter took him aside and began to reprove him. (33) But turning round and seeing his disciples, he reproved Peter and said, 'Get behind me, Satan! You are thinking in men's way, not God's.'

At this point the atmosphere of the gospel changes dramatically: from now on the dominant theme is that of the Cross. Once again, however, this paragraph is closely linked with the one immediately preceding. The two paragraphs belong together because it is necessary for the disciples to acknowledge who Jesus is before they can begin to understand his paradoxical destiny. Yet they show themselves as uncomprehending in this matter as they were in answering the question 'Who is he?'

The inevitability of the Cross is underlined five times in this section (8.31; 9.9, 12; 9.31; 10.33f.; 10.45). This theme is interwoven with another – that of the meaning of discipleship: throughout the next two chapters, Jesus attempts to teach his disciples that following him involves accepting the same path themselves. Each time Jesus speaks of his suffering and death, the disciples show their total incomprehension, sometimes of what it means for him (8.32; 9.10f.), sometimes of what it means for themselves (9.33–7; 10.33–45).

The authenticity of the passion predictions has been the subject of considerable debate, and it has been argued that they are later formulations which have been read back into the life of Jesus. Certainly it is difficult to believe that Jesus could have predicted his death and resurrection with the precision attributed to him, for though Mark tells us that Jesus spoke plainly, the subsequent behaviour of the disciples is incomprehensible if the predictions were as clear as Mark suggests. On the other hand, it seems incredible that Jesus should not have foreseen at least the likelihood (if not the inevitability) of his death. The conviction that suffering was likely may well have arisen from the hostility of the authorities and would have been confirmed from his reading of scripture, where obedience to God frequently involves suffering. The pattern of suffering for the righteous and prosperity for the wicked is especially prominent in the psalms. The fact that the early Christian communities combed the scriptures for passages which would explain the death of Jesus does not rule out the possibility that he, too, looked in the scriptures for guidance. It has indeed often been assumed that Isaiah 53 was especially influential on Jesus' own thought, but there is no verbal link with that chapter here, and no use of the idea of vicarious suffering which is distinctive of that passage (see M.D. Hooker, *Jesus and the Servant*, pp. 92–7). It seems probable, then, that he did predict rejection and death, both for himself and for his followers, but that the tradition of his words has been influenced by later knowledge of events. Although the details of the passion predictions may be *vaticinia ex eventu*, there seems no reason to deny that he spoke of his rejection in general terms.

If we allow Jesus to have spoken in advance of his rejection, then he must also have expressed confidence in his subsequent vindication. Again, this may have been done with less precision than Mark suggests: the specific reference to resurrection may reflect Christian experience of the way in which Jesus was in fact vindicated, but certainly he must have expressed his confidence that God would not put him to shame.

The suffering and death of Jesus raised theological problems for the early Christian community. If Jesus was indeed God's messiah or 'anointed one', why had he allowed him to be rejected and put to death? This story served to reassure Mark's readers that the answer was to be found in the divine plan, a plan which could be traced in the scriptures by those whose eyes had been fully opened to the truth.

The initial declaration that Jesus was God's beloved Son (1.11) was followed 'immediately' by his temptation by Satan in the wilderness. Now the drama is played out again at a human level. Peter's declaration that Jesus is the Messiah is followed by another attack attributed to Satan, this time working through Peter. The latter's ambivalent reaction is typical of the disciples' response to Jesus throughout the gospel.

**Then he began**: Mark uses the verb ἄρχομαι (to begin) too frequently 31 for us to lay much stress on these words; nevertheless, this is certainly the beginning of a new stage in Jesus' teaching. All the Markan passion sayings speak of the sufferings of **the Son of man**, a title which occurred twice in chapter 2 in passages which claim unusual authority for Jesus, but which has not been used since. (See the additional note on the Son of man, pp. 88–93.) Those who believe that the term refers to a glorious eschatological being (possibly someone other than Jesus) explain its occurrence here as due to the reinterpretation of the term by the early Christian community. If the phrase is understood as a first-century idiom for 'I', there is no problem in finding it used here, though this solution does nothing to explain why suffering is necessary. If, however, we understand the term in the light of Daniel 7, then it is possible that Jesus used the phrase to speak of his own destiny (and that of his followers) as one who would be finally vindicated by God, though present rebellion against God meant suffering meanwhile. For Mark, the phrase is clearly understood as a title, and as the one which Jesus chose to use of himself. The word **must** (δεῖ) is extremely emphatic: Jesus' teaching implies an inevitability about what is to happen, based on the will of God. The wording may reflect scripture: the verb ἀποδοκιμασθῆναι, **be rejected**, is perhaps an echo of Ps. 118.22, a verse that is frequently appealed to in the New Testament. **The elders and chief priests and scribes** together comprised the Jerusalem Sanhedrin, the supreme Jewish ruling body (see below, on 14.53). The elders were lay members, and the chief priests were probably members of those priestly families from whom the high priests might be drawn; this term is used in the singular (ἀρχιερεύς) of the high priest; for scribes, see 1.22. He will **be put to death**: none of the predictions refers to the specific form of death which Jesus suffered, as one might have expected in sayings which have to some extent been shaped by the course of events. The phrase **three days later** has the same meaning as 'on the third day', but the fact that Matthew and Luke both prefer the latter phrase suggests that this was regarded as a more precise reference to the interval between the crucifixion and the resurrection than Mark's expression, which can also mean 'a short time later'.

32    The fact that Jesus now **spoke...plainly** is in marked contrast to the teaching in parables given to the crowds, who have no understanding of who he is. Yet however plainly Mark believes him to have spoken, the disciples are totally incapable of comprehending him! There is Markan irony here: as in 4.10ff., the truth is spelt out to Jesus' disciples, yet they are unable to grasp it. What he speaks is **the word** (ὁ λόγος) – a term which is perhaps intended to hint at the fact that this message is (paradoxically) the gospel or good news.

**Peter** now takes it on himself to give instructions to Jesus. He **took him aside and began to reprove him** – and Jesus, in turn,

33.  **reproved** Peter: the verb ἐπιτιμάω which occurs twice here was used in v.30 of Jesus' strict injunction to the disciples to say nothing. Immediately following his recognition of Jesus as God's anointed one – a recognition which differentiated the disciples' understanding from that of other men – Peter demonstrates that he is in fact still **thinking in men's way, not God's**. He has grasped only part of the truth, and this partial understanding can be misused by Satan himself. Peter acted as the spokesman of all the disciples in v.29, and the description here of Jesus **turning round and seeing his disciples** suggests that he is understood to be so here also. The command **Get behind me** probably means 'Get out of my sight'; there is an interesting echo of the words in the next verse, however, where the same Greek phrase (ὀπίσω μου) is translated 'after me', and it is with this idea of following that the words are used elsewhere in Mark. It is

possible, therefore, to understand the words here in the sense 'Get back into line, Peter', but in this case the use of the term **Satan** is very strange. The reproof of Peter by Jesus is generally felt to be part of the bedrock tradition; the suggestion by Weeden (*op. cit.*) that it represents Mark's own attack on heretical opponents is not persuasive.

# 3  THE WAY OF DISCIPLESHIP          8.34–9.1

*(Matt. 16.24–8; Luke 9.23–7)*

**(34) And calling to him the crowd, together with his disciples, he said to them, 'If anyone wishes to follow[1] after me, he must renounce himself, take up his cross and follow me. (35) For whoever wants to save his life will lose it, but whoever loses his life for my sake and the gospel's[2] will save it. (36) For what profit is it, to gain the whole world and lose one's own life? (37) For what can one give in exchange for one's life? (38) For whoever is ashamed of me and my words[3] in this godless and wicked age, the Son of man will be ashamed of him, when he comes in the glory of his Father, with the holy angels.'**

**(9.1) And he told them, 'Truly I tell you, there are some standing here who will not taste death before they see the Kingdom of God come with power.'**

Jesus' original summons to the disciples had been a simple demand that they follow him, linked with a call to share his mission (1.17; 3.14f.). Now that the cost of that mission has been spelt out, the implications for those who follow him are quickly explained. There is clearly a close thematic link between Jesus' prediction of his own fate in vv.31–3, and his warning to would-be disciples. Since the opening words of v.34 suggest the beginning of a separate pericope, Mark may have been responsible for bringing the two sections together and so underlining the truth that those who follow the Son of man must expect to share his sufferings, but the link between the two themes is firmly rooted in the tradition. The Johannine parallel to v.35 is also linked with the theme of the passion – or in Johannine terms 'glorification' – of the Son of man (cf. John 12.23–6). Mark, however, makes the point again in 10.32–45 and 13.9–13.

The section was perhaps itself already a collection of isolated sayings, brought together because of their common theme. In addition to

---

1 Some MSS, including ℵ A B, read ἐλθελν, *come*, for ἀκολουθειν, *follow*, but this is probably due to assimilation to Matt, 16.24.
2 𝔓45 D and a few other MSS read simply *for the gospel's sake.*
3 A few MSS omit λόγους, reading simply *and mine.*

the parallel passages in Matt. 16.24–7 and Luke 9.23–6, we find the
following parallels:

v.34 Matt. 10.38 = Luke 14.27
v.35 Matt. 10.39 = Luke 17.33    John 12.25
v.38 Matt. 10.33 = Luke 12.9

The distribution of the sayings in Luke suggests that they came to
him separately in the tradition, whereas Matthew either received
them together or brought them together.

In Mark's context, the sayings point to the fact that the crucial
divide is not between those who acknowledge Jesus as the Messiah
and those who do not, but between those disciples who are prepared
to follow him on the way of suffering and those who are not. Those
who know the end of the story realize with a shock that in its final
scenes the Twelve will be found among those who are ashamed of
Jesus.

The challenge of Jesus is addressed not merely to **the crowd,
together with his disciples**, but to all who read or hear the gospel.
The only way in which one can be a disciple is to follow Jesus. The
cost is comprehensive, but so is the reward.

34    **And calling to him the crowd, together with his disciples**: This
reference to the crowd may have come to Mark in the tradition, but if
it is due to his own editing, then he perhaps wished to stress that the
call to follow Jesus is not limited to the Twelve. Neither are the demands of discipleship, but unless these are understood in the light of
the preceding sayings about Jesus' own suffering and death, such
sayings must inevitably seem as enigmatic as the parables addressed
to the crowd in chapter 4.

The disciple of Jesus **must renounce himself**. The verb ἀπαρνέομαι
means 'to disown' and is used in 14.30f., 72, in the story of Peter's
denial. The traditional translation, 'deny himself', has been warped
through being interpreted in terms of asceticism. The attitude called
for is one in which self-interest and personal desires are no longer
central. The disciple must also **take up his cross**. This vivid image, in
which the disciple of Jesus is likened to a condemned criminal carrying the transverse beam of his own cross to the place of execution (cf.
Plutarch, *De sera num. vind.* 9.554b: 'Every criminal who is executed
carries his own cross'), is an obvious one to use of Christian discipleship after the crucifixion of Jesus himself. It is not so clear whether it
would have been meaningful before that event. Certainly crucifixions were sufficiently common for the comparison to be used, but
some have questioned whether Jesus was likely – unless he foresaw
the manner of his own death – to have used this particular image,
since crucifixion was associated in men's minds with the activity of
criminals: the words might even have seemed to be a call to rebel

against Rome, and risk the consequences. If the image does go back to Jesus, then presumably he used it to convey – in a way which would certainly shock his hearers – the shame and disgrace which discipleship might mean. The third requirement of a disciple is that he should **follow** Jesus. To say that **anyone who wishes to follow after** Jesus must **follow** him seems tautologous – the verb ἀκολουθέω is used twice in some texts, and even if we read ἐλθεῖν in the first instance, 'to come after' and 'to follow' seem to be synonymous in Mark (cf. 1.17f., 20; 2.14f.). But the repetition emphasizes the fact that discipleship means following in the same path, and being ready to share in the same fate, as the one who leads: those who want to follow Jesus must follow him even when he is carrying a cross. The apparently clumsy wording thus points to the irony in Mark's story: when the climax comes, those who have opted to follow Jesus will *not*, in fact, be prepared to follow him to the scaffold but will take to their heels and run.

The sayings in the next few verses may once have been independent, 35 but they are now linked together with the introductory **for** at the beginning of each verse. **Whoever wants to save his life will lose it, but whoever loses his life...will save it.** The word ψυχή, translated 'life', is used with a double meaning: to cling to life (existence) is to lose one's real self. Although this paradoxical statement can be applied to life within the bounds of this world, the context indicates that it is to be understood of an eschatological recompense. Some MSS omit **for my sake**, but this must be accidental. The words **and the gospel's** are not found in Matthew and Luke, and are perhaps Mark's own addition to the saying. For Mark, Jesus and the gospel about him proclaimed by the Church belong firmly together and provide the motivation for this radical disregard of the disciple's own interests. If the words 'for my sake' are authentic words of Jesus, they indicate a claim to absolute authority, but perhaps these, too, have been added at an earlier stage in the tradition, since the saying – like those in the next two verses – will stand without it. **For what profit is it, to gain** 36–7 **the whole world and lose one's own life? For what can one give in exchange for one's life?** These sayings may (so it has been argued) have been taken over from Jewish proverbial comments on the significance of human life, but in their present context they refer to life in the world to come. Verse 36 echoes the language of Ps. 49.7–8.

**For whoever is ashamed of me and my words:** the omission of 38 'words' in some MSS is attractive, since the resulting 'me and mine' links the followers of Jesus closely with him as a group; but the evidence for the omission is slight, and it is probable that it is Jesus and his authoritative demands which were seen by Mark as the cause of offence. (The saying is missing from Matthew, and Luke 9.26 includes the word λόγους.) The contrast between present and future is underlined by the reference to **this godless and wicked age**.

**The Son of man will be ashamed of him**: the alternative so-called 'Q' version of this saying has 'I' instead of 'the Son of man' in its Matthaean form (10.33) and uses the passive instead of either in Luke (12.9). It has been argued that the 'I' version is more original, but the reference to the Son of man is certainly appropriate in this context. It is not clear in which direction the Son of man **comes**; in Daniel 7 he comes to the Ancient of Days and is there given glory and dominion, but the reference to **the holy angels** suggests that Mark understands him to be coming to earth (cf. 2 Thess. 1.7). The expression **in the glory of his Father** is unusual, combining the ideas of Son of man and Son of God; the phrase 'of his Father' is therefore best understood as a later addition to the picture – possibly made to link the saying with 9.7. The idea that the Son of man will be ashamed of those who have been ashamed of Jesus indicates a judgement scene, in which the Son of man exercises either the role of judge or that of advocate. In the Old Testament, to be put to shame is to be proved, by misfortune, to lack God's favour, and so to be a sinner; the psalmist who prays that he may not be put to shame prays for divine vindication (Pss. 25.3; 119.6; cf. Isa. 41.10f.; Jer. 17.18).

The saying in v.38 is a negative one, and it is remarkable that no clear statement of future reward for Jesus' disciples is included here. We are left to infer that the Son of man will not be ashamed of those who have not been ashamed of Jesus – and of the shame which following him involves. The alternative version of the saying found in Matthew 10 and Luke 12 is in fact joined to a positive affirmation: 'Everyone who acknowledges me before men, the Son of man also will acknowledge before the angels of God' (Luke 12.8f.; cf. Matt. 10.32f.).

Much debate has centred on the apparent distinction between Jesus and the figure of the Son of man in v.38, which has been seen as an indication that Jesus thought of the Son of man as someone other than himself (see the discussion in the additional note on the Son of man, pp. 88–93). But Mark himself clearly assumed that they were identical. This could be because the early Christian community had already identified Jesus with the Son of man and so solved the problem; it could also be because the identification was implicit in the saying from the beginning, and that there was therefore no problem to be solved. To the Christian reader, 'me' and 'the Son of man' appear to be synonymous, used together very much in the way that synonyms are used as parallels in the psalms. In the context, it is appropriate for Jesus to speak in the first person in the first part of the saying, since he is referring to those who are ashamed of him, and to speak of the Son of man in the second part, where he speaks of final vindication. The paradox is in fact brought out fully only when these two terms are used, for there would be no logic in speaking of being ashamed of the Son of man unless (as was clearly not the case) that term was already recognized as referring to a shameful figure. On the other hand, there is every reason to speak of the Son of man in a scene of final vindication (as in Dan. 7.13ff.).

Another introductory phrase, **And he told them,** suggests that 9.1 **9.1** was originally a separate saying, though whether the link with 8.38 was made by Mark or someone before him it is impossible to say. Whoever was responsible for joining the sayings together presumably regarded the coming of the Son of man in glory and the coming of the Kingdom of God in power as closely associated, if not identical: Matthew has tidied things up by changing 'the Kingdom of God' to 'the Son of man coming in his kingdom'. The opening **truly** (ἀμήν) emphasizes the saying's solemnity and importance, and the emphasis is continued in Greek with a double negative.

**There are some standing here who will not taste death before they see the Kingdom of God come with power.** This is one of the most discussed verses in the whole of Mark's gospel. Part of the difficulty is the fact that it contains an apparently unfulfilled prophecy, since, almost twenty centuries after the words were spoken, there is little sign of the Kingdom of God being established in the world, let alone of its coming 'with power', a phrase which indicates the finality and universality of its coming. Was Jesus then wrong? Many of the contorted explanations which exegetes have managed to twist out of these words have been based on the conviction that Jesus could not have been mistaken, and that some fulfilment of his words must therefore be found in history. The coming of the Kingdom has been identified with such varied events as the resurrection, the gift of the Holy Spirit, and the fall of Jerusalem. It is difficult to see how any of these can convincingly be described as the final manifestation of God's Kingdom; the fact that an event is linked with the power of God does not mean that it is therefore to be identified with his Kingdom.

One popular explanation of the saying was that put forward by C.H. Dodd, who interpreted it in the light of his theory of realized eschatology. Dodd laid stress on the fact that the word translated 'come' represents a Greek perfect participle (ἐληλυθυῖαν). He took the verb 'see' to refer to intellectual perception rather than physical sight and understood the saying to be a promise that some of the bystanders 'shall come to see that the Kingdom of God *has already come*, at some point before they became aware of it' (*Parables*, p. 53). This interpretation has found its way into some translations. (*The Common Bible* renders this clause as 'before they see that the kingdom of God has come with power', and the *N.E.B.* translates it 'before they have seen the kingdom of God already come in power'.) But though it might

211

tally with Mark's portrait of the disciples to suggest that only a few of them will grasp the truth about what is taking place in Jesus before it is too late, it is clear elsewhere that, though the Kingdom may be present in the ministry of Jesus, it is not yet fully here.

Yet another explanation of 9.1 links it with the narrative which follows – i.e. the transfiguration. This suggestion hardly solves the problem about the meaning of the saying in Jesus' mouth, but it has certain attractions as far as Mark's interpretation is concerned, since the two passages are closely linked together (in a way that is unusual in Mark) by the opening phrase of 9.2. But it is not obvious how the transfiguration can be understood to be the coming of the Kingdom in power. And if this is Mark's meaning, he has not noticed the absurdity of following a solemn announcement that some of Jesus' hearers will live to see the Kingdom with an account of how three of them saw it less than a week later. If Mark intends us to see a close link here, then we should probably understand the transfiguration to be a 'preview' of what is going to happen – and, though for Mark the two events belong together, it is a preview of the Son of man in glory, rather than of the Kingdom of God coming in power.

Since all attempts to find the fulfilment of Jesus' words in an historical event founder, the alternative is to suggest that he was mistaken in expecting the establishment of the Kingdom within the lifetime of some of his hearers. Christians have often been reluctant on doctrinal grounds to come to such a conclusion, though this reluctance could be seen as a failure to grasp the doctrine of incarnation and the limits of human knowledge which that implies. But this problem of the non-arrival of the Kingdom in power has tended to obscure the fact that the saying is not so much a prediction of a particular event as a confident declaration of the final establishment of God's purposes. Although the affirmation that the Kingdom will arrive within the lifetime of some of Jesus' hearers is repeated in Mark 13.30, both these promises lack any precise dating and contain none of the elusive references to future dating which are found in apocalyptic writings: the Kingdom is expected in the foreseeable future, but not on any particular day. Even if we conclude that Jesus was in some sense wrong, we may well wish to affirm also that he was in some sense right: the vindication he confidently expected took place – in the resurrection – but the final 'coming' of the Kingdom and of the Son of man still belong to the future.

It is, of course, possible that the saying does not go back to Jesus at all but was created in the early Christian community; if so, it was formulated early enough for it to cause no difficulties as an unfulfilled prophecy. Whatever its origins, it would have been used in the community to encourage Christians with the assurance that God's final intervention was at hand.

The phrase 'taste death' is a Semitic idiom: see 4 Ezra 6.26; Heb. 2.9. The whole section presents a challenge to Mark's readers, since for them, too, the way of discipleship involves taking up a cross and being prepared to lose one's life in following Jesus. If persecution threatened the members of Mark's community at the time he wrote, these words may well have seemed all too relevant. Those who were not prepared to accept the shame involved in following Jesus would themselves be put to shame when the Son of man was finally vindicated; but his followers could take comfort from his assurance that, whatever tribulations might lie in store, the Kingdom of God would eventually be established.

# 4  THE TRANSFIGURATION                      9.2–8

*(Matt. 17.1–8; Luke 9.28–36)*

**(2) And six days later, Jesus took Peter and James and John and led them up a high mountain by themselves; and in their presence he was transformed. (3) And his clothes became dazzling white, with a whiteness no bleacher on earth could achieve. (4) And Elijah appeared to them, with Moses, and they were talking with Jesus. (5) And Peter said to Jesus, 'Rabbi, it is good that we are here. Let us make three booths – one for you, and one for Moses and one for Elijah.' (6) For he did not know what to say; for they were terrified. (7) And a cloud came, overshadowing them, and a voice came out of the cloud: 'This is my beloved Son: listen to him.' (8) And suddenly, looking round, they saw no one any longer, except Jesus, alone with themselves.**

The story of the transfiguration is without parallel in the gospels, a fact which makes its interpretation all the more problematic. The question of its origin has also caused considerable difficulties. If the narrative has an historical basis, we must understand it as some kind of corporate vision (as does Rawlinson). Examples can be cited of men at prayer who have been so caught up in their experiences that their physical appearance has been changed. Such parallels offer some explanation of the change which Mark describes in Jesus, but the appearance and disappearance of Elijah and Moses are more difficult to explain.

An alternative explanation of the story is that it is an account of a resurrection narrative that has been put back into the earthly life of Jesus by Mark (so Bultmann). There are very marked differences, however, between this story and the resurrection narratives found in the other gospels: normally it is Jesus (not Elijah and Moses) who is unexpectedly seen by the disciples, and his appearance, though altered, is not a dazzling one; here Jesus says and does nothing, and it is the voice from heaven which announces his identity, whereas in resurrection narratives it is the risen Lord who announces himself. The narrative therefore cannot be convincingly interpreted as a misplaced resurrection story.

A third explanation regards the narrative as a piece of symbolic writing (so Lohmeyer). As we shall see, the story contains echoes of the account of Moses' ascent of Sinai, and could have been composed in order to express the community's conviction that Jesus was the Messiah. The Old Testament links are perhaps too allusive and too imprecise for this to be the whole truth, but they do indicate the possible significance of some of the puzzling details in the story. It seems likely that an historical 'happening' of some kind has been interpreted with the aid of Old Testament allusions to produce the narrative as we have it, but the two have been so fused together that it is impossible for us now to separate the two. H. Riesenfeld (*Jésus transfiguré*) has shown how the motifs of the story are illuminated by Old Testament eschatological hopes and by the ideas associated with the Feast of Tabernacles.

Although the story causes problems for the modern reader, it is unlikely that Mark was aware of them. In his God-filled universe, a heavenly confirmation of Jesus' identity would have seemed no more out of place than the acknowledgement of his identity by the unclean spirits. The true nature of Jesus is a hidden mystery which breaks out from time to time, and for Mark these revelations do not require explanations.

For Mark's readers, the story spells out the truth about Jesus and confirms their belief in him as God's beloved son. For a brief moment, the three disciples are said to have shared a vision of the understanding of Jesus which belongs to the post-resurrection situation.

2    **And six days later.** A precise reference to time is unusual for Mark and is found elsewhere only in 14.1. The phrase may well have come down to him in the tradition, and the apparently independent reference to time in the Lukan parallel, 'Now about eight days after' (Luke 9.28) supports this. It could, therefore, be explained as mere historical reminiscence, but its use in this context inevitably serves to link the story of the transfiguration thematically with what goes before. But it is not immediately clear which part of the story Mark is thinking of as taking place six days earlier. Is he linking this story with the declaration that Jesus is the Messiah in 8.29? Or with the prediction of the passion and resurrection in 8.31? Or with the affirmations about the coming of the Son of man and the Kingdom of God in 8.38 and 9.1? There is an obvious link with the first of these sections, since the

declaration in 9.7, **'This is my beloved Son'**, is a divine confirmation of Peter's confession in 8.29. The terms used are, of course, different, but they stand together (cf. 14.61), not over against each other. A link can be seen, too, with the prediction of the death and resurrection of the Son of man in 8.31, since immediately after the account of the transfiguration, Jesus warns his disciples **to tell no one what they had seen until the Son of man should have risen from the dead.** This new demand for secrecy suggests that the vision of Jesus which the disciples have shared is of the glory which belongs to him after the resurrection. The transfiguration, then, is to be understood as a confirmation not only of Jesus' messianic status, but of the necessity of the suffering, death and resurrection which lie before him. (See M.E. Thrall in *N.T.S.*, 16, 1970, pp. 305ff.) There are links, too, with the sayings in 8.38 and 9.1. We have already noted the suggestion that the transfiguration is understood by Mark as the fulfilment of 9.1. An alternative is to see it as a proleptic fulfilment, but this too has its difficulties, for why should the transfiguration of Jesus be a prefigurement of the coming Kingdom of God? It seems more likely that Mark might have understood it as a prefigurement of 8.38, and it has been forcefully argued that the story is intended as as an anticipation of the parousia: Jesus is revealed to the three disciples as he will be when he comes in the glory of his Father. (For the transfiguration as an anticipation of the parousia, see G.H. Boobyer, *St Mark and the Transfiguration Story*.)

Although there has been a spirited debate between the theories that the transfiguration points forward to the resurrection on the one hand or the parousia on the other, it is probable that Mark himself would not have understood the controversy. For though he certainly distinguished between the resurrection and the parousia, both were aspects of the vindication of Jesus, and the transfiguration is a symbol of that vindication. It is doubtful whether he would have wished to emphasize one aspect to the exclusion of the other. If Jesus' identity cannot be understood apart from his suffering, resurrection and final vindication, the scene on the mountain must be understood in relation to all these themes.

But Mark's introductory phrase also points outside his own narrative altogether, since it reminds us of Ex. 24.16, where Moses (accompanied by Joshua) spends six days on the mountain, before the Lord calls to him out of the cloud on the seventh. Though the details are not exactly parallel, there are sufficient echoes of this story in the rest of the narrative to suggest that Mark had it in mind. Choosing three companions rather than one, **Jesus took Peter and James and John and led them up a high mountain**: the traditional site of the transfiguration is Mount Tabor, which can hardly be described in these terms, but the exact location is unimportant, for the mountain is understood to be the new Sinai – the place of revelation – of the messianic era. They went **by themselves**: as usual, we find that this disclosure of truth takes place in private.

Mark does not explain in what way Jesus **was transformed**. Unlike Matthew, who refers to his face shining like the sun, Mark describes

3  only **his clothes**, which **became dazzling white**. The whiteness of garments often features in apocalyptic writings which attempt to describe heavenly scenes (cf. e.g. Dan. 7.9); the dazzling **whiteness** of Jesus' clothes is presumably a reflection of divine glory, but Mark is out of his depth in trying to describe it, since his experience is limited to what a **bleacher on earth could achieve**. His account suggests that Jesus' transformation took place for the benefit of the disciples, since it was **in their presence** (lit. 'before them'), and the

4  two Old Testament figures are said to have **appeared to them**. The presence of **Elijah. . .with Moses** is clearly symbolic, but the precise significance of these two figures is difficult to determine. The traditional explanation is that Moses represents the Law and Elijah the prophets: but this does not explain the puzzling order ('corrected' by Matthew and Luke) which places Elijah first, suggesting that Moses is playing a subsidiary role; moreover, in Jewish tradition Moses was regarded as the first and greatest of the prophets as well as the Lawgiver. Another explanation is that they are present as faithful servants of God who both suffered because of their obedience to his word – a theme taken up in vv.12f.; like those who are prepared to share Jesus' suffering, they share his glory (cf. 8.34–8). Relevant, too, is the belief that Elijah was carried up to heaven (2 Kgs. 2.1–12), and so did not 'taste death' (9.1); according to Jewish tradition, Moses shared this experience (Josephus, *Antiquities*, IV, 8.48), even though Deut. 34.5 records his death. Another link between the two figures, and one relevant to the transfiguration, is the belief that they both experienced theophanies on mountains. But, while all these suggestions point to ideas which may have contributed to the scene, none of them explains why Elijah is mentioned before Moses, the earlier and more significant figure.

The explanation of this perhaps lies in the use Mark makes of the figure of Elijah in the surrounding narrative. In the preceding chapter, the identification of Jesus with Elijah has been rejected (8.28); immediately following the transfiguration, Jesus affirms that Elijah has already come (so identifying him with John) and has suffered what was written of him. Elijah is clearly interpreted as the herald of Jesus' coming. But in the same passages, an appeal is made to 'what is written' about the Son of man. We normally turn to the prophets and psalms for these passages of scripture, but since the term 'Torah' could be loosely used of the the whole of scripture, not just the Pentateuch, Moses would be an obvious symbol for 'what is written' and so may appear here as another 'herald' of Jesus, pointing forward to his coming. It is entirely appropriate then, not only that these two figures should be present on the mountain, but that Elijah, who acts as Jesus' forerunner, should be mentioned first. (See M.D. Hooker, 'What doest thou here, Elijah?')

Mark tells us that **they were talking with Jesus** but, unlike Luke (9.31), does not tell us the subject of their conversation. Peter's use of **Rabbi** to address Jesus seems strange so soon after Caesarea Philippi, especially in a scene of this nature. It has often been explained as a 'primitive' trait in the story – an indication that it rests on early tradition. More probably its occurrence here is deliberate, a further sign that Peter is to be understood as still groping after the truth. He thinks of Jesus still as a rabbi who expounds the Law taught by Moses and he has not grasped the truth set out at Caesarea Philippi – that Jesus is not to be identified with the Baptist, or Elijah, or one of the prophets, and is thus greater than even Moses. It is not clear whether Peter's words mean that **it is good** for the disciples that they are present, or good for Moses, Elijah and Jesus! If it is the latter, it is so that they can **make three booths** or 'tabernacles' (σκηναί). These booths, made of plaited branches, were used at harvest time in the fields, but in the celebration of the Feast of Tabernacles, they came to be interpreted as a reminder of the tents which had been used in the wilderness (Lev. 23.42f.). Eventually, therefore, the notion arose that in the messianic era the people would again live in tents, and God would live with his people as he had done in the past. Mark clearly regards Peter's comment as foolish: **he did not know what to say.** It 6 is often suggested that Peter's mistake is that he is premature; he thinks that the messianic era has dawned and ignores the need for suffering and shame. But he speaks only of building **three booths – one for you, and one for Moses and one for Elijah**; he says nothing about booths for the disciples. The offer seems to be a way of honouring Jesus and the two great prophets. Peter's real mistake, therefore, is that he thinks of the three figures as being on a par: thinking to honour Jesus by ranking him with Moses and Elijah, he is still far from recognizing his master's true status. The disciples **were terrified**, experiencing once again the awe which has overcome them before in the presence of Jesus (cf. 4.41; 6.50).

The **cloud** symbolizes the Shekinah or presence of God. (The word 7 'Shekinah' – lit. 'that which dwells' – comes from the verb *šāḵan*, 'to dwell', and was used in later Jewish writings as a circumlocution for God. It expresses the traditional ideas of the manifestation of God's presence, e.g. in glory, Ezek. 1.28; 11.23, or in a cloud, Exod. 13.21f.; 33.7–11.) The cloud **came, overshadowing them** – or perhaps 'covering' them (the verb is ἐπισκιάζω – in which case 'them' presumably refers to Jesus, Elijah and Moses: since the voice comes *out* of the cloud, the disciples apparently remain outside. Cf. also Exod. 40.34f., where Moses cannot enter the tabernacle (in the LXX σκηνή – the word used here in v.5) because it is covered (the verb in the LXX is ἐπισκιάζω) by the cloud. On Sinai, God spoke to Moses out of the cloud (Exod. 24.16; cf. 34.5), a significant combination which is repeated here in the voice which **came out of the cloud.**

'**This is my beloved Son.**' The first words of the divine voice echo those addressed to Jesus in 1.11 (q.v.). The command to the disciples – **listen to him** – is reminiscent of Moses' promise regarding a prophet like himself in Deut. 18.15,18, but the authority exercised by Jesus is in fact far greater than that given to any prophet (even Moses!), for it is the authority of one who is uniquely Son of God, and the words remind us also of the repeated commands in the Old Testa-
8  ment to listen to – and to obey – God himself. Because of his unique authority, the other figures give way to Jesus and vanish from the scene, so that the disciples' attention may be focused on him alone: **And suddenly, looking round, they saw no one any longer, except Jesus, alone with themselves.**

## 5  ELIJAH AND THE SON OF MAN    9.9–13

*(Matt. 17.9–13)*

**(9) On their way down from the mountain he gave them strict orders to tell no one what they had seen until the Son of man should have risen from the dead. (10) And they seized on this saying, discussing among themselves what this rising from the dead might mean. (11) And they asked him, 'Why do the scribes say that Elijah must come first?' (12) He told them, 'Elijah does indeed come first and puts everything in order. (And how is it that the scriptures say of the Son of man that he is to endure great suffering and be treated with contempt?) (13) Yet I tell you that Elijah has come, and they have done to him whatever they wished, as the scriptures say of him.'**

9  Immediately following the transfiguration, we have another command for secrecy. **On their way down from the mountain he gave them strict orders to tell no one what they had seen until the Son of man should have risen from the dead.** Here a new note enters the secrecy theme: the truth about Jesus will be made plain by the paradoxical path of death and resurrection. For Jesus, as for his followers, life will be found through losing it, and vindication come because he is prepared to take up his cross. We see now why Mark links the transfiguration closely to the theme of vv.31–3 and 34–8, as well as to 27–30.

Those who argue that the transfiguration is a misplaced resurrection story find support for this theory in the final phrase; they suggest that Mark is here justifying his use of a story that was originally about a resurrection appearance as though it were an account of an earlier experience. But the secrecy motif is necessary to the story, even if its original setting was within the ministry of Jesus. For whether we take the story to have some kind of historical basis, treat it as a later creation of the Church, or conclude that both happening and interpretation have contributed to the narrative in its present form, ordinary men and women were certainly unaware of Jesus' heavenly glory during his lifetime, and the fact that the disciples said nothing about such an experience until later required some kind of explanation. The command for secrecy may be an attempt to explain the tension between the understanding of Jesus that his contemporaries had during his ministry, and the beliefs about him which they now hold. Mark thus uses this story to assure his community that what they believe about Jesus is indeed the truth, even though men and women were unable to comprehend it during his lifetime, and even though the few who glimpsed the truth after the resurrection were still bewildered by it.

**And they seized on this saying.** The meaning of the Greek (καὶ 10 τὸν λόγον ἐκράτησαν) is not clear, but this seems the most probable translation; less likely is the view which takes the phrase with the next two words (πρὸς ἑαυτούς) and interprets it as meaning 'they kept the matter to themselves'. Since the idea of resurrection was well known in first-century Judaism, the disciples' bemusement at **what this rising from the dead might mean** presumably concerned the meaning of resurrection for the Son of man, not resurrection in general: by **discussing among themselves** the meaning of Jesus' words, the disciples demonstrate yet again that they have failed to understand also his words about the inevitability of suffering.

**And they asked him, 'Why do the scribes say that Elijah must 11 come first?'** The logic behind the disciples' question is far from clear, since it seems to introduce an abrupt change of subject. It is possible that Mark has in fact added a separate tradition at this point, joining it to the story of the transfiguration because of the common reference to Elijah. Another attractive suggestion (made by Bultmann) is that in Mark's source v.11 came immediately after v.1: in this case, the questioners in the original story were concerned to know why Jesus is confidently predicting the arrival of the Kingdom of God, when Elijah has not yet arrived on the scene. In the Markan context, however, the disciples' question follows on from vv.9f. and presumably relates back to the transfiguration itself, which must not be spoken of until the Son of man has risen from the dead.

The teaching attributed to the scribes is based on Mal. 4.5, which speaks of the return of Elijah 'before the great and terrible day of the

219

Lord'. From this developed the idea that Elijah would return as the forerunner of the Messiah, and most commentators assume that this is what is in mind here. If so, then we may understand the disciples' question to mean: if the Messiah (Jesus himself) is already here, why do the scribes expect Elijah to come first? However, Mark's 'first' may mean 'before the day of the Lord' – i.e. before the day of judgement and vindication (and resurrection), as in Malachi. Perhaps, then, we should relate the question to the command for secrecy and understand it to mean: why must they keep silent about what they have seen until after the resurrection? Is not Elijah (whom they have seen on the mountain) to appear publicly *before* the final time, as the scribes say? Will not everyone see him soon?

12–13    The reply of Jesus is even more enigmatic, but holds together these two themes of Elijah's coming and the suffering and resurrection of the Son of man – themes which are linked together because the reception given to Elijah prefigures that which will be given to the Son of man. The logic of his reply seems to be as follows: **Elijah does indeed come first** – indeed, **Elijah has come** already, in the person of John the Baptist – and look what has happened to him! People **have done to him whatever they wished, as the scriptures say of him**; similarly, **the scriptures say of the Son of man that he is to endure great suffering and be treated with contempt**, and this, too, will just as surely take place. The death of John the Baptist thus seals the fate of the Son of man. One difficulty with this reply is the statement that Elijah **puts everything in order** (ἀποκαθιστάνει πάντα). How can John the Baptist be said to have put all things in order? The difficulty has led some to punctuate v.12a as a question, but since this is a clear reference to the Old Testament, it is better to understand it as an affirmation. In his presentation of John in 1.2–8, Mark clearly understands him to have accomplished his mission successfully, since everyone in Judaea and Jerusalem went to him, confessing their sins and being baptized; the task of the new Elijah was thus completed, and everything put in order.

There is more to be said for punctuating v.12b as a question and taking 12c to be the answer: 'How is it written of the Son of man? That he should endure great suffering.' Whatever punctuation we adopt, there is no direct prophecy of suffering for the Son of man in the Old Testament, any more than there is for Elijah, but it is perhaps implied in the description of the suffering of the remnant of Israel in Daniel 7. The Greek verb ἐξουδενηθῇ, translated 'be treated with contempt', echoes the LXX of Ps. 22.6 (LXX 21.7).

Another puzzling feature is the final phrase in v.13, since there is no prophecy of suffering for the returning Elijah. This has led to speculation about a prophecy in some lost apocryphal work, but the most likely explanation is that the reference is to the attempt on

Elijah's life spoken of in 1 Kings 19.1–3; Herodias has succeeded in doing to the second Elijah what Jezebel tried to do to the first.

In this section John the Baptist is clearly identified with the returning Elijah. Since an alternative tradition persisted that John was *not* Elijah (cf. John 1.21), it is unlikely that the identification was made by Jesus himself. The narrative may reflect attempts to deal with Jewish objections that Jesus could not be the Messiah because Elijah had not yet returned (cf. Justin, *Dialogue with Trypho*, 49).

# 6   A DUMB SPIRIT IS DRIVEN OUT              9.14–29

## (Matt. 17.14–21; Luke 9.37–43)

(14) When they came back to the disciples, they saw a large crowd round them, and scribes arguing with them. (15) And straight away, when they saw him, the whole crowd were astounded; and they ran to greet him. (16) And he asked them, 'What are you arguing about?' (17) And one of the crowd answered him: 'Teacher, I brought my son to you; he has a dumb spirit, (18) and whenever it takes hold of him it throws him to the ground, and he foams at the mouth and grinds his teeth and goes rigid. And I asked your disciples to drive it out, but they could not.' (19) [Jesus] answered: 'You faithless[1] generation! How long shall I be with you? How long must I put up with you? Bring him to me.' (20) And they brought him to him. And when the spirit saw him, it straight away threw [the boy] into convulsions; and he fell to the ground, rolling about and foaming at the mouth. (21) And he asked his father, 'How long has he been like this?' 'Since he was a young child,' he said, (22) 'and it has often thrown him both into the fire and into the water, in order to destroy him. But if you can do anything, have pity on us and help us.' (23) 'If you can!' replied Jesus. 'Everything is possible to one who believes!' (24) Straight away the child's father cried out:[2] 'I believe; help my unbelief!' (25) Seeing a crowd gathering, Jesus reproved the unclean spirit; 'Deaf and dumb spirit,' he said, 'I command you: come out of him and never return!' (26) And with a loud cry and many convulsions it came out. And [the boy] looked like a corpse, so that most of them said, 'He is dead.' (27) But Jesus grasped his hand and lifted him up; and he got up. (28) And when he went indoors, his disciples asked him privately, 'Why couldn't we drive it out?' (29) And

1 A few MSS add *and perverse.*
2 Some MSS (including D Θ fams. 1 and 13) add *with tears.*

**he told them, 'This sort cannot be cast out by anything except prayer'.**[1]

This unusually detailed account of an exorcism is not only longer than other Markan exorcism narratives, but somewhat repetitive: it contains, for example, two accounts of the child's illness (vv.18, 22), while a crowd mysteriously gathers in v.25, although one has been present from the beginning (vv.14ff.). It has been suggested that Mark may have combined two accounts of the story, one (vv.14–19, 28f.) emphasizing the failure of the disciples, the other (vv.20–7) concentrating on the question of the father's faith: if this is so, however, some parts of the two accounts have been omitted. Certainly these two themes both play their part in Mark's telling of the story. The contrast between the disciples' failure to cope and Jesus' own mastery over the demon perhaps explains why Mark has chosen to include this particular exorcism in this section: though (like all exorcism stories) it demonstrates the power of Jesus, it is not related primarily as an example of Jesus' power, but because it plays a part in the training of his followers in the meaning of discipleship. The emphasis on faith is equally relevant to this section, and the significant response to Jesus is the cry of belief uttered by the boy's father. Perhaps for this reason, the narrative does not conclude with the customary expression of the onlookers' astonishment.

This story has often been seen as a paradigm of Christian faith, expressed in the father's agonized cry, **'I believe; help my unbelief'.** Like the disciples, this man has faith in Jesus, but his faith is insecure. For the early community, his response would be an encouragement to those who were beginners in the Christian faith to deepen their commitment to the gospel. It may also have been relevant in another way: were they perhaps attempting to exorcise unclean spirits and failing to do so? If so, the story would suggest to them that their failure was due to their lack of faith and their neglect of prayer.

15 Strangely the story *begins*, not ends, with a statement about the crowd's astonishment: **when they saw him, the whole crowd were astounded; and they ran to greet him.** Since the crowd, like the father and his child, had presumably come in the expectation of seeing Jesus, their surprise is out of place, and the suggestion that Mark merely means that they were astounded by his sudden arrival on the scene is inadequate: unless Mark has devalued the Greek verb ἐκθαμβέομαι (used in the New Testament only by Mark – cf. 14.33 and 16.5, 6, where it refers to strong emotion), he must mean that there was something about Jesus' appearance which gave them good

---

1 Many MSS add *and fasting*. The shorter text is read by the first hand of ℵ and by B.

reason to be astonished. The only possible explanation seems to be that Mark means us to understand that Jesus' appearance is still in some way affected by the transfiguration. If Moses, coming down the mountain after speaking with God, reflected the glory of God from his face without knowing it, and so caused all the people to be afraid (Exod. 34.29f.), it is not surprising if Jesus also, coming down the mountain from a similar experience, caused astonishment among the crowd. Our problem is that Mark does not spell this out, but the implication would probably have been much more obvious to his first readers than it is to us: the opening phrase – **When they came back** 14 **to the disciples** – links the two stories together, and the **large crowd** is reminiscent of Exod. 34.30; perhaps these hints gave sufficient indication as to why the people were astonished.

The **scribes** play no part in the story, and their presence probably reflects later disputes between Jews and Christians. Mark offers no explanation as to why they should be **arguing with** the disciples, since Jesus' question – **'What are you arguing about?'** – is answered 16 by **one of the crowd** (the child's father) in terms of his own dealings with the disciples; perhaps we are to understand the scribes to be arguing (as happened in later disputes) about the authority and power of Jesus – an authority and power which on this occasion the disciples had been unable to demonstrate. The suggestion that the dispute is modelled on that in Ex. 32 seems hardly likely, since the two scenes are very different.

The father addresses Jesus, entirely appropriately, as **'Teacher'** 17–18 (διδάσκαλε). **I brought my son to you; he has a dumb spirit, and whenever it takes hold of him it throws him to the ground, and he foams at the mouth and grinds his teeth and goes rigid.** The symptoms of the child, both here and in v.22, suggest that he suffered from epilepsy, but these were naturally explained at the time in terms of possession by an evil spirit. **And I asked your disciples to drive it out, but they could not.** The disciples are assumed to exercise the same authority as their master – an authority which has indeed been specifically given to them (6.7). **'You faithless generation! How long** 19 **shall I be with you? How long must I put up with you? Bring him to me.'** Jesus' reaction to the disciples' failure is reminiscent of many Old Testament passages – the closest of which is perhaps Deut. 32.20, a passage which includes the description 'perverse' which is found in a few MSS here, as well as in the Matthaean and Lukan parallels (Matt.17.17 = Luke 9.41). The sweeping condemnation of Jesus' whole generation seems more appropriate to a general indictment of the nation's failure to respond to him, rather than to a rebuke of the disciples for their lack of faith in his power. But perhaps it is the crowd, as much as the disciples, who are to blame; when Jesus himself was unable to perform cures in 6.1–6, it was the inhabitants of

Nazareth (not Jesus!) who had insufficient faith.

20 Since this spirit is described as 'dumb', it cannot react like most, when confronted by Jesus, by crying out his identity: instead, **when the spirit saw him, it straight away threw [the boy] into convul-**

21 **sions, and he fell to the ground, rolling about and foaming at the mouth.** The gravity of the illness is emphasized by the fact that the

22 boy has **been like this...since he was a young child.** The father now explains the boy's symptoms again: **it has often thrown him both into the fire and into the water, in order to destroy him**; understandably, perhaps, after the disciples' failure, the man is hesitant about Jesus' ability to help. His appeal demonstrates his lack of faith; nevertheless, he has not quite given up hope: **if you can do anything,**

23 **have pity on us and help us.** Jesus' initial response – **'If you can!'** – is best understood as an astonished echo of the man's words: of course Jesus is able to help! **Everything is possible to** him because he believes, and he challenges the child's father to share his faith.

24 The point at issue shifts from Jesus' ability to heal (in v.22) to the father's ability to believe (in v.24), via Jesus' statement in v.23, where the **one who believes** could be either the one who works miracles or the one who benefits. The man responds **straight away**, and the anguish of his appeal has been emphasized at some stage by the addition of the phrase 'with tears'. His cry is the real climax of the story: **'I believe; help my unbelief!'** It is an apt summary of the response to Jesus that we meet elsewhere in Mark's gospel, for like the disciples who half see the truth, this man half believes in Jesus. He is the typical disciple: he has the faith to respond which is the essential first step – yet this faith is never complete and must continue to grow, and precisely because it is response to Jesus, it depends on him and is a gift from him. For Mark's readers, the story is a reminder of the importance of faith. Though they, too, may often find their faith faltering, they know that their failures are due to their own inability to believe, and not to any limitation in Christ's power.

25 The reference to **a crowd gathering** is odd after the earlier setting in vv.14–17, and a possible indication that two narratives have been joined together. Nor is the relevance of the remark to the story clear – unless the original account described a healing which was performed as privately as possible. The cure is effected by Jesus'

26 authoritative command, **'come out of him and never return!'** The spirit obeys, though not without **a loud cry and many convulsions.** There are interesting parallels between vv.26f. and the story of the raising of Jairus' daughter in 5.39ff. Because the boy **looked like a corpse...most of them said, 'He is dead'**, though perhaps with less

27 justification here than in her case. **Jesus grasped his hand and lifted him up; and he got up**: the same three Greek verbs (κρατήσας, ἤγειρεν, ἀνέστη) were used in 5.41f. Mark may simply be using the

most natural terms, but certainly this vocabulary will have reminded many of Mark's readers of the greater miracle of resurrection, and will have encouraged them with the belief that Jesus will one day raise those who appear to unbelievers to have died (cf. John 11).

**And when he went indoors** (lit. 'into a house', εἰς οἶκον), **his** 28 **disciples asked him privately.** . . . The scene is by now a familiar one in Mark's gospel: Jesus teaches the disciples in a house (see above 2.1; 3.20; 7.17), and away from the crowds. In this concluding scene, we return to the failure of the disciples: **'Why couldn't we drive it out?'** they ask. The answer, **'This sort cannot be cast out by any-** 29 **thing except prayer'**, is strangely at variance with the stress in the story on the need for faith – another indication perhaps that two accounts have been pieced together; Matthew in fact substitutes a saying about faith. The words *and fasting* are found in the great majority of manuscripts, but are not included in some of the earliest and most important. These words were often added subsequently to references to prayer in the New Testament, and this alone makes them suspect. Here, moreover, they are particularly inappropriate: in a context which has stressed faith and dependence on the power of God, the suggestion that it is necessary to fast in order to perform mighty works strikes the wrong note; prayer, on the other hand, though not the word we expect, indicates a dependence on God.

# 7   JESUS AGAIN PREDICTS HIS DEATH          9.30–2

## (Matt. 17.22f.; Luke 9.43–5)

**(30) Then they left that area and made their way through Galilee; and he did not want anyone to know, (31) for he was teaching his disciples, and telling them, 'The Son of man is to be delivered into the hands of men, and they will kill him; and three days after he has been put to death, he will rise up.' (32) But they did not understand what he said, and were afraid to ask him.**

The second prediction of the passion comes without prelude; Jesus 30 and his disciples have **left that area**, and are making **their way through Galilee**, presumably on the way to Jerusalem. **And he did not want anyone to know**: the time of his public ministry in Galilee is over, and his task now is to teach his disciples privately. Whether or not Mark's sequence corresponds with historical events, we cannot of course know. What is certain is that by his arrangement of the material he concentrates his readers' attention on the suffering, death and resurrection of Jesus.

Of the three so-called passion predictions (8.31, 9.31 and 10.33), this is the least detailed and possibly the most primitive. Some commentators assume them to be three Markan compositions – or, perhaps, one traditional saying and two Markan reproductions; their differences, however, suggest that perhaps they all came to him in the tradition. Whatever their origin, Mark has chosen to emphasize the theme by repetition: set at Caesarea Philippi, in Galilee and on the road leading to Jerusalem, the sayings have been likened to the solemn tolling of a bell; certainly they dominate this section of the Markan narrative and remind us of the inevitable destiny of the Son of man which Jesus obediently accepts.

31    The prediction once again concerns **the Son of man, who is to be delivered into the hands of men** – a paradoxical state of affairs since, if we are right in linking the phrase with Daniel 7, it is he who should exercise authority over them. The verb παραδίδωμι, translated 'delivered', is ambiguous: it can have the special meaning of 'betrayed' (as in 3.19 and 14.18–21), or the more general sense of 'handed over' (as in Rom. 8.32). Here, the second of these meanings seems the more appropriate, for if Mark is thinking of the betrayal by Judas, this is the only detail of the passion story which he has included in this prediction; moreover, we would in that case expect a reference to the chief priests and scribes (as in 10.33) rather than to 'men'. It seems likely, then, that the meaning is that God himself will deliver the Son of man into the hands of men, who **will kill him**. But **three days after he has been put to death, he will rise up**: as with all the predictions, this one concludes with an affirmation of final triumph.

32    Mark again emphasizes the inability of the disciples to **understand what he said**. It may seem odd that they are said to be **afraid to ask him** what he means, but their reaction to the teaching of Jesus about his death and resurrection – like their reactions to his mighty acts – is one of incomprehension and fear.

# 8   TRUE GREATNESS                              9.33–7

*(Matt. 18.1–5; Luke 9.46–8)*

**(33) And they came to Capernaum; and when he had gone indoors, he asked them: 'What were you arguing about on the way?' (34) But they were silent, for on the way they had been disputing with one another about which of them was the greatest. (35) He**

**sat down and called the Twelve and said to them, 'If anyone wishes to be first, let him be last of all and servant of all.' (36) And taking a little child, he set it in the centre; and putting his arms around [the child], he said to them, (37) 'Whoever receives one of these little children in my name receives me; and whoever receives me, receives not me but the one who sent me.'**

Once again, following immediately after a prediction of Jesus' passion, the disciples give a clear demonstration of their complete inability to understand his words about death and resurrection. This time it is not by questioning his teaching, as in 8.32 – for they are afraid to ask him about it – but by failing to see its implications for themselves, and so arguing among themselves about their own order of precedence. And once again this leads to teaching by Jesus on the paradoxical reversal of standards and the meaning of discipleship.

The relevance of this section for Mark's readers is obvious. Whether or not there were wranglings about precedence going on in his own church we do not know, but it was perhaps inevitable that disputes about who was the greatest would arise in any community. For the church leaders of his own day, as well as for the Twelve, the implications of Jesus' own path to Jerusalem were not easy to accept.

The scene moves back **to Capernaum**, and once again we have an 33 incident which is described as taking place **indoors** (lit. 'in the house'): those present are committed disciples. Mark's hearers might well look round the circle of those gathered in a house to listen while Jesus' words were read. Jesus' question – **'What were you arguing about on the way?'** – meets with silence; even the disciples recognize 34 the inappropriateness of their disputes **about which of them was the greatest.** Mark tells us once again that it was **on the way** that **they had been disputing with one another:** what looks like clumsy repetition may well be a deliberate reminder that they are on a journey which ultimately takes them to Jerusalem: for Jesus, the 'way' leads to the Cross; for the disciples, the way should be the path of discipleship (cf. 8.27; 10.17, 32, 52). V.35 has the appearance of a 35 separate saying that has been somewhat clumsily added at some stage to the story: Jesus **sat down** (as teachers customarily did) **and called the Twelve** – an unnecessary action in the present context, since he is already talking to the disciples. It may well be Mark himself who is responsible for bringing together the theme of the disciples' failure to grasp Jesus' point and the saying about greatness. **'If anyone wishes to be first, let him be last of all and servant of all.'** The saying has parallels elsewhere in the gospels – cf. Mark 10.43f. //Matt. 20.26f.; Matt. 23.11; Luke 22.26. This suggests that it was a well-known saying, perhaps circulating without any particular context.

36 An ingenious explanation by Matthew Black (*Aramaic Approach*, pp. 218–23), suggests that in **taking a little child**, Jesus was making a dramatized play on the Aramaic word *ṭalyā'*, which can mean both **child** and **servant**; his action in setting the child **in the centre and putting his arms around** it would therefore be an acted *māšāl* or parable. But vv.36f. may well record a separate incident. The difficulty is that the saying about receiving a child does not really suit the present context, which is concerned with the humility which ought to characterize a disciple, not with receiving those who are humble. It is interesting to note that in 10.15, in the context of another narrative about children, we find a saying which is much more appropriate to the story in 9.36f. – and the saying here fits much better there. Matthew seems to agree, since in his version of this story in 18.1–4 he uses a saying parallel to Mark 10.15 (though he seems to be using his own tradition rather than adapting Mark), and omits it in 19.13–15 (the parallel to Mark 10.13–16). This apparent mix-up is remarkable. It is perhaps most easily explained by suggesting that the sayings in the stories about children were accidentally reversed during the oral stage of the tradition; Matthew's accounts may reflect knowledge of independent traditions, rather than an editorial tidying of the material. But the 'mistake' could, of course, be the result of Mark's own deliberate editing; for even though the saying fits awkwardly into its immediate setting, it is nevertheless entirely appropriate to

37 Mark's overall theme. For the somewhat surprising conclusion to the pericope in v.37 draws out the implications of the teaching addressed to the disciples in this section. Jesus' followers have been quarrelling about which of them is greatest. Instead of worrying about their own positions, they should be concerned for the weakest and most humble member of the community – typified by **these little children** – and in receiving those who are weak and humble, they will be receiving Jesus himself. The idea that one **receives** Jesus by receiving one of his representatives is found in Matt. 10.40–2 and Luke 10.16 in the context of a missionary discourse. It is possible that Mark has again used an isolated saying out of context, and it has been suggested that the saying originally referred to 'little ones' meaning 'disciples' (cf. v.42) and that Mark misunderstood this and took it to refer to children. The saying reflects the Jewish belief that a man's agent or representative should be received as the man himself. **In my name** probably means simply 'for my sake'. Once again, the disciples – and Mark's readers also – are pointed firmly to Jesus' own example, who identifies himself with the lowly. Finally, we are reminded that Jesus himself is the envoy and representative of another: **'whoever receives me, receives not me but the one who sent me.'**

# 9   FOR AND AGAINST JESUS                    9.38–40

*(Luke 9.49f.)*

(38) John said to him, 'Teacher, we saw someone driving out demons in your name, and we tried to stop him, because he was not following us.' (39) But Jesus said, 'Do not stop him; for no one who does a miracle in my name will be able the next moment to speak evil of me. (40) For he who is not against us is on our side.'

The story of the exorcist seems to have been joined to the previous saying (probably when the tradition was being passed on orally) because of the linking phrase 'in my/your name', even though it is used here with a very different sense from that which it has in v 37. A similar story is narrated in Acts 19.13–17, and this kind of dispute is more likely to have arisen after rather than during the lifetime of Jesus. The present story has a very different application from the one in Acts, however: the disciples are rebuked for their exclusive attitude, and the strange exorcist is vindicated. It may well reflect disputes within the early community in which some leaders tried to exercise a monopoly in certain gifts. For Mark, however, the narrative is perhaps primarily of interest because it is on the theme of discipleship, and underlines the all important distinction between being for Jesus or against him.

**John** appears on his own only here in Mark, so the name must have 38 been part of the tradition which Mark received. He addresses Jesus as **Teacher**, a term normally used by 'outsiders' in Mark. This has sometimes been interpreted as a sign of early tradition, but Mark may well have used it here because John is not behaving as a disciple should (similarly, 4.38; 10.35). **We saw someone driving out demons in your name**: a name was believed to have power in itself, and the name of a known wonder-worker would clearly be thought to have power to effect cures. Many examples of names being used in a similar way have been found in contemporary papyri. **We tried to stop him, because he was not following us**: the reference to 'us' rather than 'you' betrays the influence of the early community.

**But Jesus said, 'Do not stop him.'** There is an interesting Old 39 Testament parallel to Jesus' attitude in Num. 11.26–30. His tolerance strikes us as remarkable, because he appears to condone the working of miracles unrelated to faith. But this impression has been given to us by Mark who has suggested that there is a deep divide between the disciples, who have faith (however inadequate), and outsiders. Jesus' reply suggests that the real issue is not whether the exorcist is using his name without believing in him, but whether the disciples are falling into the danger of cliquishness which sets more store on whether someone belongs to the right party than whether he acknowledges Jesus as lord – the kind of situation described in 1 Corinthians (cf. especially 1 Cor. 12.3).

40     The saying in v.40 was possibly proverbial. It is given in reverse form in Matt. 12.30 = Luke 11.23. Cf. also Cicero, *Oratio pro Ligario* XI: 'We have often heard you say that, while we considered all who were not with us as our enemies, you considered all who were not against you as your friends.'

# 10   SAYINGS ABOUT LIFE AND DEATH    9.41–50

*(Matt. 18.6–9; 5.13; Luke 17.1f.; 14.34)*

**(41) 'For truly I tell you, whoever gives you a cup of water on the grounds that you belong to Christ will certainly not go unrewarded.**

**(42) 'And whoever causes one of these little ones who believes in me to fall, it would be better for him if a large millstone were hung round his neck and he were thrown into the sea.**

**(43) 'And if your hand causes you to fall, cut it off! It is better for you to enter life maimed, than to have two hands and go into Gehenna, into the unquenchable fire.[1] (45) And if your foot causes you to fall, cut it off! It is better for you to enter life a cripple, than to have two hands and be thrown into Gehenna.[2] (47) And if your eye causes you to fall, pluck it out! It is better for you to enter the Kingdom of God with one eye, than to have two eyes and be thrown into Gehenna, (48) where "their worm never dies, and the fire never goes out".**

**(49) 'For everyone will be salted with fire.[3] (50) Salt is good, but if salt loses its taste, with what will you season it? Have salt in yourselves, and be at peace with one another.'**

This collection of sayings completes the section of teaching addressed to the disciples. The main theme of these verses is that of reward and punishment, and though the whole section from vv.33–50 seems to have been pieced together largely on the basis of common catch-

---

1 Some MSS including A D Θ fam. 13, add (44) *where "their worm never dies, and the fire never goes out".*

2 The same MSS add (46) *where "their worm never dies, and the fire never goes out"* (see v.44).

3 D and the old Latin read: *every sacrifice will be salted with salt;* others (including A) read: *everyone will be salted with fire, and every sacrifice will be salted with salt;* there are various other readings.

words, suggesting that it was built up during the oral stage of the tradition, it nevertheless possesses a unity and an emphasis which is remarkably close to that of 8.34–8. It is probable that in each case Mark has deliberately chosen to place paradoxical teaching about the meaning of discipleship and about true reward immediately after the misunderstanding about Jesus' prediction of his passion.

Taken together, these sayings remind Mark's readers of the vital importance of their response to Jesus and to the gospel. On the one hand lies the promise of reward, and entry into life; on the other hand we have the threat of punishment and destruction.

The first saying, in v.41, appears to be an independent saying which **41** might well have followed v.37 rather than vv.38–40; cf. Matt. 10.40–2. It was perhaps linked to v.40 (either by Mark or by a predecessor) because in Greek the phrase translated **on the grounds that you belong to Christ** picks up the **in my name** of v.39. The Greek (ἐν ὀνόματι ὅτι Χριστου ἐστε) is obscure, but ὄνομα appears to be used here in a more general sense than its usual meaning of 'name'. However we translate the phrase, 'Christ' is used here as a proper name, and this is the only place in Mark (apart from 1.1, where it is a quasi-title), where it is used in that way. The phrase obviously reflects the standpoint of the Christian community, but the saying itself, promising reward to those who do not seek it, has an authentic ring; a similar promise of reward for those who show compassion to those who belong to Christ is found in Matt. 25.31–46.

The theme of punishment in the independent saying in v.42 forms **42** a natural contrast to v.41. Matthew understands the **little ones** to be children and links the saying with that in v.37 (Matt. 18.5f.); it is difficult to know whether his version represents a more original order, or whether he has made a logical rearrangement to the tradition. Mark has understood Jesus to be talking about Christian disciples, and the saying therefore makes a pair with v.41, even though it refers to **one of these little ones** instead of to **you**. In 8.34,38, future reward and punishment depend on whether or not one is ashamed of the Son of man; here, they are dependent on one's attitude towards Christ's disciples.

**And whoever causes one. . .who believes in me to fall**: the verb σκανδαλίζω has the sense of 'to cause to stumble', which in the New Testament means to stumble as a Christian disciple; it was used (in the passive) in 4.17. The **millstone** is in Greek μύλος ὀνικός, a millstone turned by a donkey, and so **a large** one. The commonest millstones were small ones, used in the handmills turned by women; this is a very heavy one indeed. **It would be better for him if. . .he were thrown into the sea.** Drowning was apparently used by the Romans as a form of capital punishment and was presumably known as such in Palestine; certainly Josephus refers to an occasion when

Galilaeans turned on the members of Herod's party and drowned them 'in the lake' (*Antiquities*, XIV, 15.10). If such a death is **better**, the saying implies a worse fate in store for those who cause Christians to deny their faith.

**43–8** The verb σκανδαλίζω forms the link with vv.43–8, where it is used in each of the three warnings addressed to the disciples themselves concerning things which might lead to their own downfall. These three sayings echo the words of Job about the purity of his eyes, foot and hands (Job 31.1,5,7). The importance of the outcome is emphasized by the hyperbolic commands to sacrifice **hand** or **foot** or **eye** rather than lose **life** (cf. 8.35–7). It has been argued by Duncan Derrett (*Studies in the New Testament*, I, pp. 4–31) that the forfeiture of hand, foot or eye was commonly used as a punishment in the time of Jesus. Although there is no reference to such a custom in the Jewish Torah (with the sole exception of Deut. 25.11f.; *the lex talionis* of Ex. 21.24 is different), Derrett quotes evidence to show that other nations did practise amputation of foot or hand for such crimes as theft, and the loss of eyes for adultery. Moreover, Josephus refers to the amputation of hands for forgery (*Life*, 35) and for sedition (*Life*, 34; *War*, II. 21.10). Such mutilation was used, Derrett argues, as an alternative to the death penalty: clearly it was better to live with only one hand or foot than to keep both but lose one's life altogether. If such punishments were familiar to Jesus' hearers, then one can understand how relevant the imagery would be in speaking about the value of the reward he offers them. As for Mark's arrangement of the material, the theme of punishment provides an extra link between v.42 and vv.43ff., in addition to the use of the verb: opponents of the gospel are warned that the punishment that awaits them is worse than mere loss of life, while disciples are urged to accept discipline now, for the sake of entering into life. **Life** in vv.43 and 45 is paralleled by the **Kingdom of God** in v.47. The alternative to entering life is to **be thrown into Gehenna**. Gehenna was a valley near Jerusalem where human sacrifices were once offered to the god Moloch. After it had been defiled by the reforming Josiah (2 Kgs. 23.10), it was used as a city rubbish tip, where fires burned continually, and so came to be a symbol for the place of future destruction for the wicked. It should be noted that nothing is said here about eternal punishment: on the contrary, the image seems to be one of annihilation, in contrast to life; it is the **fire**, and not the torment, which is **unquenchable**.

V.v.44 and 46 are probably late additions, since the manuscript evidence is against their inclusion in the text. They are identical with v.48 (**where 'their worm never dies, and the fire never goes out'**), which is a quotation from Isa. 66.24, emphasizing the theme of destruction.

**49** The enigmatic saying in v.49, **For everyone will be salted with**

fire, seems to have been added at some stage because it contains the word 'fire'. Its meaning is obscure, and the variant readings, substituting or adding the words 'and every sacrifice will be salted with salt', suggest that an attempt was made to explain it by quoting Lev. 2.13; whoever was responsible for this gloss interpreted the fire as a sacrificial one and was probably thinking of suffering and persecution, which would purify the Christian community in the way that salt purified a sacrifice. On its own the saying could refer to the final judgement; Paul uses the image of testing by fire in 1 Cor. 3.10–15. But the use of the verb **salted** in this connection is strange, unless we understand it in the sense of 'purified': the sentence then means 'everyone is purified by fire'. It seems that the paradox of being 'saved through fire' (1 Cor. 3.15) is the key to Mark's use of the saying here. Like fire, salt is an agent of purification (Ezek. 16.4; 43.24); it can also bring desolation and destruction (Judg. 9.45; Zeph. 2.9). But unlike fire, salt is a source of life (2 Kgs. 2.19–22); it can be used to preserve food from putrefaction. However mixed the metaphor may be, therefore, the idea that men can be **salted with fire** sums up exactly the message of vv.43, 45 and 47: the purificatory process may destroy, but it can also preserve. The paradox of these sayings is thus in line with what we found in 8.34–8, offering the same promise of life to those who are prepared to suffer loss.

Two more sayings about **salt** complete the collection. Pedantic 50 commentators point out that the first of them is nonsensical, since **salt** cannot lose **its taste**: a substance without the salty taste is in fact not salt at all but something else. In Mark's day, however, the deposits of the Dead Sea must have appeared like salt, even after the actual salt had been washed out; to an observer, it would seem very much as though the salt had lost its taste. Once again, although the saying is linked to the previous one because of a catchword, it is relevant to Mark's theme. Salt is recognized by its taste: disciples who do not show the characteristics of disciples are as useless as 'salt' that proves not to be salt at all, and cannot be counted as disciples.

Finally, the disciples are told to **have salt in** themselves, and to **be at peace with one another**. The first part of this command may be taken with the previous saying and interpreted as a command to 'be salty' (cf. Matt. 5.13). If we take it with the final words, however (the most natural way of understanding it), the meaning may be 'have salt among yourselves'; in this case it is a reference to 'sharing salt', which symbolized eating together, and the whole verse will then be a command to live in fellowship and peace together. However we interpret these enigmatic words, the final command is also relevant to Mark's theme, pointing us back to the dispute in vv.33–7 and reminding us of its inappropriateness.

# 11   A QUESTION ABOUT DIVORCE   10.1–12

*(Matt. 19.1–12)*

(1) And leaving that area, he came into the districts of Judaea and the far side of Jordan,[1] and once again crowds collected round, him, and again as usual he taught them. (2) And some Pharisees approached him,[2] and in order to test him, they asked, 'Is it lawful for a man to divorce his wife?' (3) He answered them, 'What did Moses command you?' (4) They said, 'Moses permitted [a man] to write a certificate of annulment, and so to divorce [his wife].' (5) Jesus said to them, 'It was because of the hardness of your hearts that he wrote you this commandment. (6) But from the beginning of creation, "[God] made them male and female": (7) "This is why a man will leave his father and mother and be joined to his wife,[3] (8) and the two will become one flesh"; so they are no longer two, but one flesh. (9) So then, what God has joined together, man must not divide.'

(10) And when they were indoors again, the disciples asked him about this; (11) and he said to them, 'Whoever divorces his wife and marries someone else commits adultery against her. (12) And if she divorces[4] her husband and marries someone else, she commits adultery.'

In this section Jesus again addresses his teaching to the **crowds**, though the disciples have its significance spelt out for them in vv.10–12. It is perhaps the contrast between the concessions allowed by the Law and its basic rigorous demand that led Mark to place this incident in a context concerned with the demands of discipleship: those who follow Jesus are those whose aim is to do the will of God, not to look for concessions. The climax of the story for Mark, however, is found in the pronouncements of Jesus (vv.9,11f.), rather than in the Mosaic Law; as in Matthew's Sermon on the Mount, Jesus is here seen to be the one who reveals fully the divine will to which the Law bore witness.

This issue may well have been an important one for Mark's community: certainly for many Christian groups the question of the relationship between the Jewish Torah and the teaching of Jesus was a

---

1 Following ℵ B C* L Ψ and the Coptic. Many MSS read: *the district of Judaea on the far side of Jordan.*
2 The reference to the Pharisees is omitted by D and some MSS of the Old Latin version, which read: *some people asked him, in order to test him.*
3 The words *and be joined to his wife* are missing from ℵ B Ψ 892*.
4 D Θ fam. 13 and other MSS, and some versions read: *leaves.*

burning one. It is significant that Mark does not suggest here that Jesus contradicted the Torah, but rather that he pointed to its true fulfilment.

Jesus begins the journey towards the south which will eventually 1 bring him to Jerusalem, but his route is obscure. Many Jews crossed the Jordan into Peraea in order to avoid Samaria, but the statement that **he came into the districts of Judaea and the far side of Jordan** (i.e. Peraea) reverses the natural order, and early copyists were obviously puzzled. Perhaps Mark's geography was vague, or his expression clumsy; perhaps his wording reflects knowledge of a longer stay in Judaea than he describes (cf. the Fourth Gospel) or simply the fact that Judaea was the goal of the journey.

The identification of Jesus' interrogators as **Pharisees** may be due 2 to assimilation to Matthew. If so, then we have a typical Markan impersonal plural, 'they asked'. The real difficulty, however, is that it seems unlikely that any Jew would have asked Jesus whether it was **lawful for a man to divorce his wife,** since divorce was permitted in the Law and, as far as we know, the matter was not under dispute. Contemporary discussion was concerned rather with the grounds on which divorce was possible, and here entirely different positions were held by the schools of Hillel and Shammai, the former allowing the husband to divorce his wife on trivial grounds, while the latter insisted that only adultery was a sufficient cause: in the Matthaean version of the incident (Matt. 19.1–9), Jesus is asked to give his opinion on this dispute. Yet we cannot rule out completely the possibility that Mark's setting is original, since there are signs that a rigid attitude to divorce was already developing within Judaism; this seems to be implied not only in the obscure reference in Mal. 2.13–16, but also in a passage in the Damascus Rule (CD 4). If so, a teacher with radical views, like Jesus, might perhaps have been questioned on this point **in order to test him** (πειράζοντες αὐτόν), with the aim of trapping him. In this case, we should have to conclude that Matthew has adapted the story to bring it into line with the more usual contemporary Jewish debate.

Jesus answers by appealing to the Torah: **'What did Moses** 3 **command you?'** Whatever the original question, there seems no reason to doubt that the reply reflects Jesus' own attitude to the issue of divorce; he is more strict than the official rabbis in his approach. Nevertheless, because his concern is with what God wills, rather than with what the Law allows, he stands in opposition to legalism, which is concerned with definitions rather than with wholehearted obedience. Whereas the enquiry asked what is permitted, the answer points to what is commanded; the contrast reflects negative and positive attitudes to the Law.

The legislation in Deut. 24.1 **permitted [a man]...to divorce [his** 4

**wife]** if she found no favour in his eyes. The **certificate of annulment** was intended to protect the woman's positiòn. If the aim of the question is to trap Jesus into speaking against the Law, it is unsuc-
5 cessful. Jesus does not dispute the validity of the Deuteronomic rule, but sees it as concessionary: it was introduced because of man's weakness – **the hardness of your hearts** – and does not affect the
6–8 principle set out in Gen. 1.27 and 2.24, quoted in vv.6–8, which has been in force **from the beginning of creation**. There is no suggestion here that Moses commanded one thing and God another: all three passages quoted would have been understood as part of the teaching given by God through Moses. There is a similar use of Gen. 1.27 in CD 4. The words **and be joined to his wife**, missing from some MSS, were probably omitted accidentally at some stage; they are needed
9 for the sense of the passage. The climax of the pericope comes with the judgement of Jesus in v.9: **what God has joined together, man must not divide**. 'Man' here refers not to lawyers, but to the husband, who alone had the power to divorce his wife. The verb 'divide' (χωρίζω) is used in Greek papyri with the special meaning of 'divorce'. In affirming the principle set out at the creation, Jesus is perhaps proclaiming that the time for the eschatological ideal (or new creation) has arrived.
10 The editorial link in v.10 shifts the scene **indoors** (lit. 'into the house'), where **the disciples asked him about this** and were given
11 private teaching. This introduces what is either a separate saying or the community's interpretation of Jesus' teaching. The picture of private coaching is perhaps Mark's way of spelling out what he believes to be the implications of Jesus' words for the Christian community. The saying takes the form of a 'community rule' and may represent a maxim familiar to the Church (represented by the disciples). There is in fact a basic contradiction between v.9, where divorce itself is inconceivable, and vv.10–12, where it is remarriage *after* divorce which is forbidden because it leads to adultery (condemned in 10.19; cf. also 7.22). Nevertheless, Mark uses the saying to reinforce what has already been said by taking the argument one stage further. Since marriage has made a man and woman indissolubly one, a husband who **divorces his wife and marries someone else commits adultery against her**. The logic of this conclusion may seem clear, but it has to be remembered that in Jewish law adultery was committed only against a husband – i.e. by his wife and by her lover: the suggestion that a husband could commit adultery against his *wife* (implying that the woman had equal rights!) must have been
12 a startling one. The same rule is then applied to the woman: **if she divorces her husband and marries someone else, she commits adultery**. In Jewish law, however, a woman could not divorce her husband, and there seems little point in denouncing what could not

happen. This suggests that v.12 has been added in a society where Roman law gave the woman this right; there is no question here of a masculine privilege being extended to women, since the 'privilege' has been denounced. The variant reading *leaves* is probably a scribal 'correction' to make the saying agree with Jewish law, though it is just possible that it is original. F.C. Burkitt (*Gospel Transmission*, pp. 99–101), who accepted the saying as going back to Jesus, made the interesting suggestion that it is a reference to the well-known case of Herodias, who had left one husband and 'married' another. In this case Jesus would indeed be putting men and women on an equal footing and the force of his argument would be: 'You agree in condemning a woman who leaves her husband (without divorce) and lives with another man as an adulteress; the man who divorces his wife and marries again is equally guilty.' A few MSS in fact reverse the order of vv.11 and 12, perhaps because the logic of this argument was recognized.

The existence of a 'Q' version of the saying (Matt. 5.32 = Luke 16.18) supports the belief that it goes back to Jesus himself. This is much more Jewish in form, since it refers only to the man's action in divorcing and remarrying (though Matthew and Luke vary considerably in sense). Paul also refers to 'a word of the Lord' charging a wife not to leave her husband and a husband not to divorce his wife (1 Cor. 7.10f.).

If these words seem harsh, it must be remembered that the teaching in Mark is seen as directed to disciples, and in 1 Corinthians Paul is addressing the Christian community: there is no question at this stage of applying them to others who are not committed to Christian discipleship. The demand is an eschatological challenge which calls for perfection by pointing to the ideal for mankind set out at creation. As for Jesus himself, whatever form of the saying we attribute to him, it seems that his aim may have been to shock men out of the complacency which led them to congratulate themselves on keeping the Law, while they condemned those who ignored its niceties. Although discussion about the Law's requirements was for some rabbis an expression of their genuine concern to obey God, it could easily become a substitute for heartfelt obedience, and a delineation of what God demanded. Jesus points to the basic demands of God, which cannot be calculated in this way (cf. also Matt. 5).

Since hardness of heart (and human weakness) continues, even within the Christian community, it seems that the possibility of divorce must also continue, but always with the recognition that it is necessary because of human failure, and never (as in certain Jewish circles in the first century) as an automatic right, to be justified as a Mosaic 'command'.

# 12   JESUS BLESSES THE CHILDREN   10.13–16

*(Matt. 19.13–15; Luke 18.15–17)*

**(13) And people were bringing little children to him, so that he might touch them.** The disciples reproved them, **(14)** but when Jesus noticed he was indignant and said to them, 'Let the children come to me; do not prevent them, for it is to people like these that the Kingdom of God belongs. **(15)** Truly I tell you, whoever does not receive the Kingdom like a little child will never enter it.' **(16) And putting his arms round them, he laid his hands on them and blessed them.**

This section has been used from very early times to support the practice of infant baptism, and it has even been suggested that the story itself reflects a controversy as to whether children should be baptized. The story itself does not refer to baptism, but if such a debate were already taking place when Mark wrote, this might explain his description of the behaviour of the disciples and the indignation of Jesus; it seem unlikely, however, that this matter would have become an issue so early, and it is perhaps more probable that the passage was first interpreted in this way soon after Mark's time. Since the disciples are once again rebuked for their exclusive attitude (cf. 9.34–40) the story could, however, reflect an attack on the narrowness of some church leaders in their attitude towards children. Mark's inclusion of the story at this point has been seen as topical, a narrative about children following naturally after one on marriage and divorce. For him, however, its importance is more likely to lie in the sayings about the Kingdom in vv.14 and 15: once again, he has used a story which is linked to his basic theme of the meaning of discipleship.

This story is a reminder that the Kingdom is given to those who are content to receive it as a gift without laying claim to it, and a warning to those in the community who claim the right to exercise authority over others.

13   The story begins abruptly with the statement that 'they' **were bringing little children to him.** Mark does not explain who did so, nor why **the disciples reproved them,** though the context suggests that the disciples are again concerned with matters of status (cf. 9.33–7). The children are brought **so that he might touch them:** it was natural to suppose that blessing could be conveyed by touching

14   (cf. Gen. 48.14). **Jesus. . .was indignant,** perhaps because the disciples seemed to be claiming exclusive privileges, thus showing themselves no better than other religious leaders. Matthew and Luke omit the reference to Jesus' indignation, being less ready than Mark to criticize the disciples. The words **do not prevent them** have been interpreted

as a baptismal formula (cf. Acts 8.36), but it may well be that the formula was derived from this story. Jesus' declaration that it is to people like these that the Kingdom of God belongs is echoed in the opening beatitude: 'Blessed are those who know that they are poor; the Kingdom of heaven is theirs' (Matt. 5.3). The Kingdom belongs to them because they have nothing on which they base a claim, but are content to receive the Kingdom as a gift; their attitude is akin to what Paul describes as 'faith', which humbly receives God's grace. This is why children are said to show the appropriate attitude – not because they are presumed to be innocent or without sin.

The words Truly I tell you may introduce what was originally a 15 separate saying in v.15, which is omitted in the parallel Matthaean account but occurs at Matt. 18.3, in the parallel to Mark 9.36f. As we have already seen, the saying seems to fit that context better, and the saying in Mark 9.37 fits well here. But Mark has perhaps inserted v.15 into this section deliberately, in order to underline the attitude which is required of a disciple, and which the children possess. The tension between the present and future aspects of the Kingdom is seen here, in the juxtaposition of the idea that one can receive the Kingdom now with the hope that one will enter it in the future; but the Kingdom, whether present or future, is God's gift; there is no suggestion in the gospels that men can build the Kingdom for themselves.

By linking Jesus' words about entering the Kingdom with his action 16 in blessing the children, Mark reminds us that to come to Jesus is to be confronted by the claims and benefits of the Kingdom; his blessing is a symbol of the joy which the Kingdom brings.

# 13  A RICH MAN LOSES ETERNAL LIFE, BUT OTHERS FIND IT                          10.17–31

*(Matt. 19.16–30; Luke 18.18–30)*

(17) And as he was setting out on his journey, a man ran up, and kneeling before him asked him, 'Good Teacher, what must I do to inherit eternal life?' (18) Jesus said to him, 'Why do you call me good? No one is good except God alone. (19) You know the commandments: "Do not kill; do not commit adultery; do not steal; do not give false witness; do not defraud; honour your father and mother."' (20) But he replied, 'Teacher, I have kept all these [commandments] since my youth.' (21) Jesus looked at him steadily and loved him. 'One thing you lack,' he said. 'Go and sell everything you have and give [the money] to the poor, and you will have treasure in heaven. And come! Follow me.' (22) But at these

words his face fell and he went away sad at heart, for he was a man of great wealth.

(23) Then Jesus looked around and said to his disciples, 'How difficult it will be for those who have riches to enter the Kingdom of God!' (24) The disciples were amazed at his words. But Jesus said to them again, 'Children, how difficult it is[1] to enter the Kingdom of God.' (25) It is easier for a camel[2] to get through the eye of a needle than for a rich man to enter the Kingdom of heaven!' (26) They were more astonished than ever and said to one another,[3] 'Then who can be saved?' (27) Jesus looked steadily at them: 'For men it is impossible,' he said, 'but not for God; everything is possible for God.'

(28) At this, Peter asked him, 'What about us? We have left everything and followed you.' (29) Jesus said, 'Truly I tell you, there is no one who has given up home, or brothers, or sisters, or mother, or father, or children, or land, for my sake and for the sake of the gospel, (30) who will not be repaid a hundred times over in this present age: houses and brothers and sisters and mothers and children and land – with persecutions – and in the age to come, eternal life. (31) Many who are first will be last, and the last first.'

This section consists of what may originally have been four separate items: the story of the rich man, vv.17–22, Jesus' words about wealth, vv.23–7, the promise of reward to his disciples, vv.28–30, and the concluding sentence of v.31. Whatever their origin, by placing the sayings together Mark once again confronts his readers with the demands of discipleship. Following after the previous narrative, the story of the rich man who could not abandon his possessions for the sake of eternal life makes an interesting contrast with the saying about those who are able to enter the Kingdom because they are content to receive it like children.

The story would certainly be a challenge to Mark's readers to face up to the demands of discipleship. But since few of his community were likely to have been wealthy, they probably found more comfort in the promise of reward for those who gave up **brothers or sisters or mother or father** rather than for those who left **home. . .or land**; the ominous addition 'with persecutions' may reflect the situation of the community.

17 Jesus **was setting out on his journey**. Mark refers simply to 'a journey' and, if the story were told on its own, we should have to translate it in this way. But in its present context Mark presumably thinks of Jesus continuing on the journey which is bringing him ever

---

1 A C D Θ fams. 1 and 13 and other MSS add: *for those who trust in riches.*
2 A few MSS read κάμιλος, *rope*, for κάμηλος, *camel.*
3 Some MSS, (including אB C Δ Ψ) read: *and said to him.*

closer to Jerusalem. Moreover, the word for 'journey' is once again ὁδός, which can also mean 'road' or 'way', and which is used later in the chapter for the road leading to Jerusalem (vv.46, 52); perhaps it conveys something of this meaning of Christian pilgrimage here. The only information which Mark gives us about the **man** who **ran up** to Jesus is that he **was a man of great wealth** (v.22). Matthew describes him as young, and Luke tells us that he was a ruler – hence the usual designation, 'the rich young ruler'. His gesture in **kneeling before** Jesus seems as extravagant for a Jew as his form of address, but Jesus' reaction in v.21 suggests that the man is sincere, rather than indulging in flattery. He asks how he may **inherit eternal life** – that is, life in the coming age, about which Jesus has spoken in 8.34ff. and 9.42ff. 'Inheriting eternal life' is equivalent to 'entering the Kingdom of God', and in this section the phrases alternate (cf. vv.23–5, 30); in the Fourth Gospel, 'eternal life' is used regularly in place of 'the Kingdom of God'.

**Why do you call me good? No one is good except God alone.** 18 Jesus' response is an enigma, and many different explanations have been given. Montefiore suggested that in rejecting the description 'good' he betrayed a consciousness of sin, but we can be sure that Mark, at least, did not understand the rejoinder in that way. Popular among the Fathers was the suggestion that Jesus was explaining why the word was, in fact, an appropriate one: the questioner is meant to realize that Jesus, being good, is in fact divine. This explanation reflects the doctrinal suppositions of a later age. The problem itself, however, was already obvious to Matthew, who dealt with it by altering the wording. Precisely because of its difficulty, the saying has a considerable claim to authenticity, and indeed it fits in well with the emphasis in the rest of Jesus' teaching on the Kingdom of God: Jesus makes no claims to independent authority – he calls on men and women to respond to the claims of God. It is appropriate, then, that he should point away from himself to the character and demands of God. Yet it is typical of Mark's presentation of the gospel that the crucial test of this man's obedience should be whether or not he is prepared to become a follower of Jesus.

**You know the commandments**: Jesus quotes the last six com- 19 mandments (numbers 5–10, with number 5 last) – i.e. those which are concerned with human relationships – but **do not defraud** has somewhat surprisingly replaced 'do not covet'. No satisfactory explanation of this has ever been given. 'Defrauding' – or perhaps 'depriving' someone of property – might be regarded as a specific example of covetousness, and a temptation to which the wealthy were especially prone. Nevertheless, we expect Jesus to substitute the inner cause for the consequential action, not vice versa . Perhaps the verb ἀποστερέω, which can mean also 'to rob', suggested a neat contrast with the demand that the man give everything he had to the poor. It occcurs rarely in the LXX, but it is interesting to find it used in Mal. 3.5, in a list of evil-doers which contains echoes of the Decalogue, and which includes 'adulterers' and 'those who swear falsely'. Matthew and Luke omit the phrase altogether. The claim to **have kept all these** sounds

20 arrogant but is apparently made without pride; the man is dissatisfied and thinks something more is necessary. The challenge of Jesus demands total commitment: to the man's enquiry – **what must**

21 **I do?** – he replies 'everything'. In spite of the man's awareness that obedience to the Torah alone was inadequate, he is nevertheless approaching religion from the same viewpoint as the Pharisees in vv.1–9, asking 'How much need I do?' His obedience is based on calculations of self-interest rather than on a single-hearted love of God which is prepared to fling everything away. Jesus' command, **Come! Follow me**, takes on a new significance within the context of the believing community; what was probably originally a summons to join him in his way of obedience to God, in response to the demands of God's eschatological Kingdom, has become a call to commitment to Jesus himself as Lord. In the context of Mark's story, the summons to follow Jesus echoes his earlier challenge to would-be disciples to deny themselves and to take up a cross (8.34). It is a call to follow him on the journey he is about to resume (10.17), but for this man, the

22 challenge is too great: **his face fell and he went away sad at heart, for he was a man of great wealth.**

23 As so often in Mark, Jesus spells out the significance of this incident for the benefit of **his disciples.** If his exclamation that it is difficult **for those who have riches to enter the Kingdom of God** astonished them, this was presumably because they, like many of their contemporaries, saw wealth as an indication of God's pleasure. There is an alternative tradition, however, reflected in many of the psalms and in the teaching of Jesus, which identifies the poor with the pious, and the rich with the ungodly; this interpretation comes to the fore in Luke's gospel.

24–5 A few manuscripts reverse the order of vv.24 and 25, and some commentators have argued that this is more logical, a view that was presumably shared by an early copyist. The present order is, however, perfectly natural: **to enter the Kingdom of God is difficult** enough; the reason why the **rich** in particular find it difficult is that they are not prepared to exchange all they have for the sake of the one pearl of great price (Matt. 13.45f.). The attitude required is once again that set out in 8.36. The additional phrase in v.24, though found in many manuscripts, is probably another attempt to 'improve' the logic.

The saying in v.25 is probably proverbial; there is a parallel saying about an elephant in the Talmud. It is only the extraordinary inability of commentators to appreciate the hyperbole and humour in the illustration that has led them to suggest that the **camel** (κάμηλος) should be reduced in size to a rope (κάμιλος – a reading adopted in a few late MSS), or that **the eye of a needle** should be enlarged to an imaginary gate in the wall of Jerusalem. Jesus wished to make his hearers think by presenting them with an absurd picture of the largest animal attempting to go through the tiniest aperture. The disciples, 26 however, **were more astonished than ever**; once again they demonstrate their total misunderstanding of Jesus' teaching. Their question, '**Then who can be saved?**' (whether it is addressed **to one another** or **to him**), and Jesus' reply in v.27, set out two opposing 27 approaches: on the one hand, belief in merit, which deserves reward, on the other, trust in God's grace.

The exchange between **Peter** and Jesus makes an appropriate 28 contrast to the story in vv.17–22, since Peter and his companions have in fact **left everything and followed** Jesus, responding to the call which the rich man rejects. The members of Mark's own church have also answered Jesus' call, and no doubt these words would have seemed pertinent to them. We are again reminded of the cost of discipleship – but also of its rewards. Joyous abandonment of earthly possessions leads to fulness of life. The reference to **brothers, or sisters, or mother**, reminds us that Jesus himself rejected his own relatives in 3.31–5, claiming that those who did the will of God (presumably a much larger number) were his brother, sister and mother. It may seem anomalous that Jesus promises rewards which 29–30 sound so remarkably down to earth – but the motive for their action is **for my sake and for the sake of the gospel** rather than personal gain. Because εὐαγγέλιον (elsewhere 'good news') is clearly used here as a technical term, we have translated it as **gospel**. If lost human relationships are **repaid a hundred times**, this is presumably in the fellowship found in the Christian community (cf. Mark 3.34f.). The phrase **with persecutions** sounds like an artificial addition. It is possible that both this and the next phrase – **and in the age to come, eternal life** – were added at a time when it was felt that the promise of a hundredfold reward was slow in its fulfilment!

**Many who are first will be last, and the last first.** This final saying 31 is found in other contexts also (cf. Matt. 20.16 and Luke 13.30), and does not fit particularly well here. We might have expected it to follow the sayings about wealth and the Kingdom in vv.23–7. In its present context, Mark perhaps regards it as summing up both the promise to the disciples and the warning to the rich.

## 14 JESUS PREDICTS HIS DEATH FOR THE THIRD TIME 10.32-4

*(Matt. 20.17–19; Luke 18.31–4)*

(32) Now they were on the road, travelling up to Jerusalem, and Jesus was going ahead of them, and they were amazed; and those who followed were afraid. And taking the Twelve aside again, he began to tell them what was going to happen to him. (33) 'Look, we are going up to Jerusalem, and the Son of man will be delivered up to the chief priests and the scribes, and they will condemn him to death and deliver him up to the Gentiles. (34) And they will mock him and spit at him and flog him and kill him; and after three days he will rise up.'

This third prediction of Jesus' death and resurrection is much fuller than the previous two, and contains precise details which seem to derive from a knowledge of the passion story. Either Mark is drawing here on a different tradition, or he has deliberately spelt out the details of the passion as it draws closer. Mark's three passion predictions serve to remind his readers not only that Jesus' death and resurrection were part of God's purpose, but that Jesus himself was totally obedient to God's will.

These verses mark another important stage in the story; the course of Jesus' journey through Judaea is no longer vague but takes on a definite aim: Jesus is openly heading for **Jerusalem**. In one sense this can be described as the beginning of the passion narrative, for at this point the events which lead inevitably to his death are put in motion. Is this perhaps the reason for the amazement or awe which fall upon the company? Mark's meaning is far from clear. He tells us that **Jesus was going ahead of them, and they were amazed**. Does he mean to distinguish between this group and **those who followed** who **were afraid**? Most commentators assume that the **they** refers to the disciples (i.e. the Twelve) and that two groups are being referred to here. But the disciples are commonly described as 'those who follow' (cf. v.28); and why should one group be **amazed**, and the other **afraid**? Some suppose that the **they** refers to the wider group, and that **those who followed** are therefore the disciples, who are most aware of what may happen and are therefore afraid. One attractive suggestion is that the first of these verbs should be read in the singular, and that it was Jesus who was amazed or distressed. The verb used here is θαμβέω, and the compound, ἐκθαμβέω, is used of Jesus in Gethsemane. But there is no textual support for this emendation, and it is perhaps best to assume that Mark means that the whole company

32

244

(both Jesus and his disciples) were distressed, but that **those who followed** (the disciples, in contrast to Jesus himself) **were afraid.** The fear experienced by those wondering whether they were heading for persecution and martyrdom may have been all too familiar to Mark's readers. He has probably used the phrase **those who followed** deliberately, because he wants to stress that discipleship means doing precisely this – following Jesus. **The road** (ὁδός, cf. v.17) on which Jesus' followers travel with him is also 'the Way', an early term for discipleship (cf. Acts 9.2, and see below, v.52). It is significant that each of the passion predictions is apparently made while Jesus and his disciples are 'on the road' (see 8.27; 9.33f.).

This introductory verse is clearly editorial, leading into a separate introduction, **and taking the Twelve. . . .**As before, the teaching 33–4 about the passion is given privately to the Twelve, but this time in far greater detail.

# 15  THE COST OF DISCIPLESHIP                10.35–45

*(Matt. 20.20–8)*

(35) **And James and John, the sons of Zebedee, approached him and said, 'Teacher, we want you to do something for us.'** (36) **'What do you want me to do for you?' he asked.** (37) **They replied, 'Allow us to sit, one at your right hand and one at your left, in your glory.'** (38) **And Jesus said to them, 'You do not know what you are asking. Can you drink the cup that I drink, or be baptized with the baptism with which I am baptized?'** (39) **They replied, 'We can.' But Jesus said to them, 'The cup that I drink you shall drink, and with the baptism I am baptized with, you shall be baptized.** (40) **But to sit at my right or my left is not mine to give; that belongs to those for whom they have been prepared.'**

(41) **And when the ten heard this, they were indignant with James and John.** (42) **And Jesus summoned them and said to them, 'You know that those who are supposed to be rulers among the Gentiles lord it over them, and those in high positions make them feel the weight of their authority.** (43) **It is not to be that way with you. But whoever wants to be great among you must be your servant,** (44) **and whoever wants to be first among you must be slave of all.** (45) **For the Son of man himself did not come to be served, but to serve, and to give his life as a ransom for many.'**

The third prediction of the passion, like the previous one, is followed by an incident which demonstrates the failure of the disciples to grasp Jesus' meaning and see the implications of his teaching for their own lives. Vv.42–5 may be a separate saying which Mark has used here because it is on a similar theme; Luke has placed his version of the saying (once again arising out of a dispute about greatness) in his account of the Last Supper – an appropriate context for a saying about serving at table (Luke 22.24–7). In both the saying addressed to James and John and that addressed to the ten, the attitudes which Jesus demands of his disciples are based on and imitative of his own life of service and his acceptance of death.

It is significant, moreover, that this incident is recorded immediately after the statement that Jesus was now going up to Jerusalem (v.32). No sooner is the end in sight, than the disciples begin to ask for a share in Jesus' future kingly power. Mark once again skilfully reminds his readers that Jesus is indeed going to be proclaimed king in Jerusalem, but that it will be through shame and crucifixion. The final saying in v.45 makes a similar point but refers also to the redemptive nature of Christ's death.

The application of this teaching to the life of Mark's own community would have been clear: there may well have been church leaders there whose attitude was similar to that of James and John, seeing leadership in terms of status and privilege. For them, the teaching that true greatness is seen in service was certainly necessary. At the same time, the threat of persecution was a very real one; the warning that being Jesus' disciple was likely to mean sharing his suffering may have been all too relevant to their situation.

35 Matthew places the request made here by **James and John, the sons of Zebedee**, in the mouth of their mother – perhaps in an attempt to show the two disciples in a less discreditable light; Mark's frank account of the disciples' behaviour suggests that the story may be authentic. They address Jesus as **Teacher** (see on 9.38). **We want you to do something for us**: their request shows how far they are from comprehending Jesus' teaching, since they appear to think they have a right to demand a reward, and what they have in mind is nothing less than the best positions in the messianic kingdom which they believe Jesus is about to set up. They perhaps imagine that Jesus is entering Jerusalem in order to claim the Davidic throne and rule

37 the nation. The seats at his **right hand and. . .left** could be either adjacent thrones (cf. Luke 22.30) or the seats of honour at the messianic banquet; in either case, James and John are thinking of the future only in terms of **glory**.

38 Jesus' reply reminds us once again of the necessity for suffering. The metaphor of **the cup** is used in the Old Testament of what God has in store for an individual, whether this is good (Ps. 23.5) or bad (Ps. 75.8); James and John may **not know what** they **are asking**, but the reader of Mark's gospel is well aware that the cup which Jesus

drinks is one of suffering and death (cf. 14.36). Water was another
metaphor used of calamity in the Old Testament (e.g. Ps. 42.7; Isa.
43.2) and the verb to **be baptized** (βαπτίζομαι) was used in contemporary Greek of being flooded with calamities (cf. also Luke 12.50).
**They replied, 'We can'**; the disciples' ready answer shows that they 39
do not understand what Jesus is asking them, any more than they understand the implications of their own request.

The promise that James and John will share the **cup** and **baptism**
of Jesus is sometimes seen as a prophecy after the event, reflecting
knowledge of the later martyrdom of the brothers. James was put to
death by Herod at an early date (Acts 12.2), but the fate of John is
uncertain; according to one tradition (backed only by late manuscript
evidence), he too was martyred, but according to another, he lived to
a ripe old age in Ephesus. It may be that it was the saying in Mark
10.38f. which created the story of his martyrdom, rather than vice
versa. In fact, the references to cup and baptism are not sufficiently
precise to be regarded as *vaticinia ex eventu*: they indicate suffering
rather than death, though knowledge of the fate of Jesus naturally
makes the reader interpret the words in a narrower sense.

The contrast between glory and the way of suffering is typical of
this section in Mark. But Jesus' words to the brothers, **'You do not
know what you are asking'**, seem almost to identify the two – a
paradox which reappears explicitly in the Fourth Gospel, where
Jesus' death is spoken of as his glorification. The request to sit at 40
Jesus' **right** and **left** reminds us inevitably of the account of the death
of Jesus, when two robbers are crucified on his right and left. This is
probably deliberate irony, though the promise that the seats of glory
belong **to those for whom they have been prepared** refers to places
of honour in the Kingdom of God.

If **the ten...were indignant with James and John**, it was perhaps 41
not because their own attitudes were any different, but because the
two brothers had stolen a march on them. So, at least, Mark suggests 42
in telling us that **Jesus summoned them** and addressed the whole
group. The saying about the **rulers among the Gentiles** indicates
that the brothers' request is understood as a demand to hold positions
of authority. The phrase **those who are supposed to be** is ambiguous, but is probably intended to indicate that their rule is only apparent and is unreal in the eyes of God.

**Whoever wants to be great among you must be your servant, and** 43-4
**whoever wants to be first among you must be slave of all**: these
words are reminiscent of the paradoxical teaching given in 8.35, 9.35
and 10.31. In v.45, however, we have a new idea, since for the first 45
time Jesus explains the significance of his death instead of speaking
simply of its necessity. The introductory **for** (καὶ γάρ) is casual: the
disciples must behave in the way set out in vv.43-4, not simply be-

cause **the Son of man** is their model, whom they imitate (v.45a), but because his death is for their benefit and provides them with the means to follow his example. The authenticity of this saying has been the subject of constant debate. Many scholars reject the possibility that it goes back to Jesus himself, on the grounds that it is without parallel in the rest of Mark and out of harmony with its context. The parallel in Luke 22.27 speaks only of Jesus as 'one who serves' and is thought by many to be an earlier version of a saying of which Mark 10.45 is a dogmatic reformulation; some earlier commentators (e.g. Branscomb) argued that the Markan form of the saying betrays the influence of Paul.

Much depends on the interpretation that is given to the saying itself. Almost all commentators assume that it is based on Isaiah 53, and the debate then centres on the question of the use of this chapter in the early stages of the tradition: did Jesus see himself as the fulfilment of Isaiah 53, or was the link made after his death? Those who have assumed that Jesus saw himself in the role of the Suffering Servant have accepted Mark 10.45 as authentic; those who attribute the identification to the community tend to reject it.

The influence of Isaiah 53 is, however, by no means as clear as has been believed. The word **serve**, which seems to form an obvious link, represents a Greek verb (διακονέω) which is never used in the LXX. Moreover, the lowly service of others described in Mark 10.45 is a very different idea from the honour implied in the appellation 'God's servant', used in Deutero-Isaiah. It is true that the LXX speaks of someone who serves many in Isa. 53.11 (δουλεύοντα πολλοῖς), though this is a variation from the Hebrew, but the only word common to the Greek versions of Isaiah 53 and Mark 10.45 is the word **many**. The Hebrew word for 'servant', *'ebed*, is normally translated by παῖς in the LXX, occasionally by δοῦλος: neither word is applied to Jesus in the gospels. The willingness of Jesus to give his life has often been linked with the statement in Isa. 53.12 that the servant 'poured out his soul to death', but these words mean little more than the English phrase 'he gave up the ghost'; the comparison in Isa. 53.7 with an animal brought to slaughter suggests submission to what is inevitable rather than a willing acceptance of death. Finally, the word **ransom** bears no relation, in spite of many statements to the contrary, to the Hebrew word *'āšām* used in Isa. 53.10, which means 'an offering for sin'. The noun **ransom** (λύτρον) and the cognate verb 'to redeem' (λυτρόω) are both used in the LXX to describe a variety of transactions – e.g. the payment of money given to free a slave (Lev. 25.47–55, where the Hebrew root is *g-'-l*), or the sacrifice offered in place of the first-born (Exod. 13.13–16, where the root is *p-d-h*). It is hardly a coincidence that both these passages link the notion of redemption with God's saving action in bringing his people up from slavery in Egypt, since this is a common theme in passages where the verb λυτρόω is used.[1] The influence of Isaiah 53 on this saying has therefore been grossly exaggerated, though the theology of Isaiah 40–55 as a whole is certainly an important part of its background. (It is interesting to note that W. Grimm, *Weil Ich dich liebe*, argues that Isaiah 43 is more important for our understanding of Mark 10.45 than Isaiah 53.)

The preposition **for** (ἀντί) can have a variety of meanings, according to the context. If **ransom** were here understood to be a substitutionary sacrifice, then it would mean 'instead of', but it is important not to read back into this saying ideas which belong to later centuries, and if the noun has the more general sense of 'redemption' suggested above, then the preposition will mean 'for the sake of' or 'on behalf of'. In some mysterious way, which is not spelt out, the sufferings of one man are used by God to bring benefit to others. His death is said to benefit **many**. To us, this word suggests exclusion: 'many but not all'. In Semitic thought, the emphasis is more likely to be inclusive: the contrast is not between the many who are saved and others who are not, but between the many and the one who acts on their behalf. It is this contrast that we find in Isa. 53.11f. Interesting parallels have also been discovered in the Qumran material, where one of the terms used for the congregation is 'the many' (e.g. 1QS 6.1, 7–25; CD 13.7; 14.7). The organization of the Qumran community demonstrates that they regarded themselves as the embodiment of 'true Israel', and 'the many' were therefore the people of God. If Jesus' life is given for many, therefore, this may well be understood to mean that he dies on behalf of all God's people. But the interpretation of this concept of God's people varies according to the context. Within the ministry of Jesus himself, one might well think in terms of Israel – the people to whom Jesus proclaimed the coming of the Kingdom – or at least, to those Jews who responded to his preaching: cf. with this the comment in John 11.51 to the effect that Jesus' death benefits the nation. Cf. also 4 Macc. 17.21f., where the martyrs are described as having become a ransom for the nation's sin. For Mark, however, the constituency of God's people had changed; they were no longer 'Israel according to the flesh' (as Paul puts it), but a much smaller community, consisting of those – whether Jew or Gentile – who followed Jesus. (See below, on Mark 14.28.)

If these are the ideas that lie behind this verse, then the two parts of the saying are not as far apart from each other as is frequently

---

1 The Hebrew roots *g-'-l* and *p-d-h*, the two terms most commonly rendered by λυτρόω, are both used to describe God's deliverance of Israel. The former, a word used elsewhere of the practical support provided by one's nearest kinsman, whose duty it was to take up one's cause, is used in particular in Deutero-Isaiah to describe God's new act of redemption in bringing Israel back from exile in Babylon (see Isa. 41.14; 43.1,14; 44.22–4; 52.3).

supposed. The statement in v.45a that **the Son of man himself did not come to be served, but to serve**, is clearly presented as a paradox: this is obvious from the construction – 'not this. . .but that' (οὐκ . . . ἀλλά). Whatever the origin of the Son-of-man sayings, it seems that behind this particular one there lies an expectation that the Son of man should be served. This is in keeping with the picture in Daniel 7 (see especially vv.14 and 27). The paradox presented in this first part of the verse is parallel to that presented in vv.43b–4; for here, as elsewhere in Mark, there is a clear link between the saying about discipleship and the saying about the Son of man – indeed, v.45a provides the basis for vv. 43b–4. But the second part of v.45 also speaks of a form of service: the Son of man is to give his life in order to bring redemption to others. An interesting parallel to these words is found in 4 Maccabees, which was composed in Greek in the first century AD, probably a little earlier than Mark's Gospel. In 17.21 the sufferings of the martyrs are described as 'like a ransom (ἀντίψυχον) for the nation's sin'; earlier, in 6.29, the dying prayer of one of them is for God's people, that his life (ψυχή) may be taken, 'a ransom (ἀντίψυχον) for theirs'. These passages interpret the martyrs' deaths specifically as an atonement for sin – an idea which, as we have seen, is not explicitly used in Mark 10.45; there is a closer verbal link here, however, than there was with Isaiah 53. Moreover, these passages are of particular interest because their theme is the same as that of Daniel 7, where the righteous in Israel are trampled under foot by the last of the beasts, and where it is only when the obedience of the faithful has been tested by suffering that the one like a son of man (the representative of the saints of the Most High) is vindicated and rewarded. In both Daniel 7 and 4 Maccabees, the martyrs suffer on behalf of others: they die, not as substitutes, but as *representatives* of their nation; and because of their faith and fortitude their countrymen are delivered. The Maccabaean martyrs, whose tortures are described in 4 Maccabees, might well have been said to have given their lives **for many**.

What is striking about Mark 10.45 is that it is **the Son of man** who **gives his life...for many**. In Daniel 7, it is others who die, the one like a son of man who is pronounced the victor. The saying of Jesus turns this upside down, as the introductory **not. . .but** might lead us to expect. Moreover, this reversal is precisely what we expect after the repeated emphasis in earlier sayings about the paradoxical road to greatness. But since those who die and those who triumph are members of the one community, each of them can be the representative of that community; the martyrs represent faithful Israel, steadfast even under persecution, while the one like a son of man represents the victorious saints. What Mark 10.45 does is to remind us that suffering and victory belong to each other, and that it is only through the former that the latter is achieved.

A modern parallel to the idea of one man as the representative of his people, dying on behalf of his nation, can be seen in the description given to the French resistance leader, Jean Moulin. Tortured and killed by the Nazis, he has been called 'the face of France' – a term more commonly given to those who represent their country in happier circumstances. In dying for his fellow countrymen, Moulin represented both them and the honour of his nation, as well as contributing toward their final liberation.

It seems clear that the final words of 10.45 are not as alien to the context (or to the rest of Mark's gospel) as is often argued, and that there is an inner logic which holds together the ideas of the Son of man, service, the giving of one's life, and a ransom. It is also of interest to note that the Lukan parallel to this saying, though it lacks these final words, is set in the context of the Last Supper, where the theme of Jesus' death is dominant; moreover, it is followed by a saying in which Jesus 'covenants' to his disciples the kingdom which God has covenanted to him (Luke 22.28f.) – the kingdom whose coming is closely associated with his death (22.16,18). Luke, also, has linked this saying about service with Jesus' sacrifice, and by his ordering of the material has suggested that Jesus dies on behalf of others. Our decision as to whether or not the saying in Mark 10.45 goes back to Jesus himself will depend very much on whether we think that he spoke of his own death in these terms. (See, further, C.K. Barrett, 'The background of Mark 10.45'; M.D. Hooker, *Jesus and the Servant*, pp. 74–9; *The Son of Man in Mark*, pp. 140–7.)

# 16 A BLIND MAN SEES THE WAY 10.46–52

*(Matt. 20.29–34; Luke 18.35–43)*

**(46) They reached Jericho; and as he left Jericho with his disciples and a large crowd, the son of Timaeus – Bartimaeus – a blind beggar, was seated at the side of the road. (47) And hearing that it was Jesus of Nazareth, he began to cry out, 'Son of David, Jesus, have pity on me.' (48) And many of them told him to keep quiet, but he cried out all the more, 'Son of David, have pity on me.' (49) Jesus stopped and said, 'Call him.' So they called the blind man; 'Courage,' they said to him, 'Get up! He is calling you.' (50) And throwing aside his cloak, he jumped up and came to Jesus. (51) And Jesus asked him, 'What do you want me to do for you?' 'Master,' the blind man replied, 'let me see again.' (52) And**

**Jesus said to him, 'Go: your faith has saved you.' And straight away he recovered his sight and followed him on the road.**

This is the final healing miracle in the gospel, and Mark has clearly included it because of its double meaning. Like the recovery of the blind man in chapter 8, the story of Bartimaeus stands in contrast to the preceding failure of the disciples and symbolizes the ability of those who have faith in Jesus to see the truth. The story is an appropriate climax to a section which has spelt out the meaning of discipleship, but it also points forward to the incidents that follow. Just as the story in chapter 8 of the blind man who gains his sight introduces an incident in which Jesus challenges the disciples to see his true identity, so the healing of Bartimaeus, who hails Jesus as Son of David, introduces a series of incidents which, in Mark's eyes, clearly demonstrate Jesus' messianic status: Jesus rides into Jerusalem to the acclamation of the crowd (11.1–11) and pronounces judgement on Jewish worship (11.12–25); then follow various disputes which centre on the unique authority of Jesus (11.27–12.44), in the course of which the 'claims' of Jesus come to the fore. So the true identity of Jesus becomes clearer the closer we move to the Cross.

Mark's story is a final challenge to his readers to join Bartimaeus in following Jesus on the road (or 'way') of discipleship, even though that road leads to Jerusalem and all that happens there.

46     Mark provides us with both the name of the place and the name of the beggar. These precise details are rare in his narrative and have been variously interpreted by earlier commentators, either as eyewitness details preserved in the tradition (so Branscomb and Taylor) or as artificial additions (so Bultmann). As far as Mark is concerned, he may well have thought it important to include these particular details at this point for the following reasons: (a) **Jericho** is only fifteen miles from Jerusalem and the goal of Jesus' journey is therefore almost within sight; **the road** on which Jesus is travelling is now inevitably the path of suffering. (b) **Bartimaeus** is not simply the recipient of a healing miracle, but becomes a disciple of Jesus: at the beginning of the story he is **seated at the side of the road**, but at its conclusion we are told that he **followed him on the road**. It is true that **a large crowd** also accompanies Jesus (v.46), but the **blind beggar's** faith sets him apart from the crowd.

47     Apart from Peter at Caesarea Philippi, and those possessed by unclean spirits, Bartimaeus is alone in addressing Jesus by any kind of messianic title. **Son of David** became a fairly common title for the messianic king in later Jewish literature and would have been understood in that sense by Mark (its first known use is in Pss. Sol. 17.21). It is sometimes suggested that, because Bartimaeus is blind, Mark understands the confession to be wrong (e.g. D.O. Via, *The*

*Ethics of Mark's Gospel*, p. 162). It is true that in Mark's eyes 'Son of David' is not an adequate title for Jesus (12.35–7), but it is typical of Mark's irony that the blind should see more than those with sight, and the title points forward to the story of the triumphal entry into Jerusalem which immediately follows. **And many of them told him 48 to keep quiet:** it is notable that it is now the crowd, not Jesus, that attempts to silence him (the verb, ἐπιτιμάω, was used in 1.25 and 8.30); there is no question here of an artificially kept secret. The blind man sees something at least of the truth which the crowd is unable to see. His persistence is rewarded by Jesus' response to his need. 49 (See additional note on miracles, pp. 71–5.)

A beggar's **cloak** was commonly spread out on the ground to 50 receive alms, so that we are perhaps to think of Bartimaeus pushing it aside in his eagerness rather than taking it off. Like others who are called by Jesus, he abandons everything he has (cf. 1.18, 20; 2.14; 10.21, 28; see C.D. Marshall, *Faith as a Theme in Mark's Narrative*, pp. 141f.). He addresses Jesus as **Master** – ῥαββουνί, lit., 'my rabbi', a more reverential form of address than the more common word 'rabbi' used by Peter in 9.5 and 11.21. Jesus commends the man's **faith,** 52 which has **saved** him. The reference to salvation suggests more than physical healing, since we are told that Bartimaeus not only **recovered his sight,** but **followed him on the road** (ὁδός), an echo of v.32. His faith in Jesus' power, his confession of his authority, and his willingness to follow him all mark him out as a disciple; his response forms an interesting contrast to the poor showing of the Twelve in the previous story.

# F  The King comes to Jerusalem                    11.1–13.37

Superficially, these chapters seem to be a success story. Jesus rides into Jerusalem and is hailed as king by the crowds; he teaches in the temple, stands up to the authorities, and is applauded by the people. For Mark, however, they are a story of failure – the failure of Israel and of her leaders to worship and serve God, and her failure to receive his Messiah. The mounting antagonism of the authorities points forward to their inevitable rejection of Jesus and so seals their own rejection by God. Nevertheless, there are signs of hope: a scribe is not far from the Kingdom; a widow gives everything she has to God; and there are hints, in dramatic incident and parable, that Gentiles will come to worship God and will inherit what Israel throws away.

Throughout these chapters, Mark's presentation of the material points clearly to the messianic status of Jesus, even though none of the characters in the story makes any statement about who he is.

Jesus rides into Jerusalem, while the crowds greet 'the one who comes in the name of the Lord', and 'the coming kingdom of our father David'. Jesus enters into the temple and purges it, an incident which Mark sets in parallel with Jesus' condemnation of a fruitless fig tree symbolizing Israel: asked about his authority to do these things, Jesus points back to the mission of John the Baptist, thereby identifying himself as the one whose coming John foretold. As hints about the true status of Jesus grow stronger, so also do indications of what his coming will mean for Israel. In 12.1–12, we have a story which shows how the two themes are related: because the religious authorities reject Jesus (who is clearly to be identified as the 'beloved son' in the story), they too will be rejected. This is followed by four short accounts of his teaching which demonstrate Mark's earlier statement, in 1.22, that Jesus taught with authority. The first three stories also imply judgement on certain groups: those who fail to give to God what belongs to him (12.17); those who doubt the power of God to raise the dead and are therefore totally wrong (12.24, 27); those who substitute burnt offerings and sacrifices for the whole-hearted love of God (12.33). The fourth contrasts an inadequate belief that the Messiah is the son of David with the acknowledgement of him as Lord: Mark's readers are well aware that the question, while it is posed here as though it were an academic one, is in fact for them an existential one about their own commitment to Jesus. The element of judgement is found again in the last two incidents in this chapter – clearly pronounced in vv.38–40, implied in vv.43f. This theme comes to a climax in chapter 13, but here again it is linked with the question of Jesus' own authority, since we are well aware that judgement is now pronounced on Jerusalem because the city's religious leaders have failed to accept Jesus and are about to succeed in their plans to put him to death. And throughout the chapter there are references to the authority of Jesus – 'my name' (v.6), 'for my sake' (v.9), 'the son of man coming in the clouds' (v.26), 'the Son' (v.32).

By his juxtaposition of statements hinting at the authority of Jesus with Jesus' pronouncements of judgement on Israel's religious leaders, Mark suggests to his readers that the climax of the nation's sin was in the failure of her leaders (and the great bulk of the people) to accept Jesus: the catastrophe which overcomes Jerusalem is thus seen as God's judgement on Israel for rejecting her Messiah. At the same time, the ever increasing reminders regarding the nature of Jesus' authority prepare us for the final act in the drama, in which Jesus will be revealed to the world as Messiah and Son of God, above all in the accusation brought against him (14.61) and at the moment of his death (15.39).

# 1 JESUS RIDES INTO JERUSALEM                    11.1-11

*(Matt. 21.1-11; Luke 19.28-40; John 12.12-16)*

(1) And when they were approaching Jerusalem, and had reached Bethphage[1] and Bethany, near the Mount of Olives, he sent two of his disciples, (2) telling them, 'Go into the village opposite you, and straight away, as you enter, you will find tethered there a foal which no one has ever ridden; loose it and bring it here, (3) and if anyone should ask you, "Why are you doing that?" say "The Master needs it and will send it back[2] straight away."' (4) And they set off and found the foal, tethered by a door, outside in the street, and they untied it. (5) And some of the bystanders said to them, 'What are you doing, untying the foal?' (6) But they replied as Jesus had instructed them, and they allowed them [to take it]. (7) And they brought the foal to Jesus and spread their outer garments on it, and he sat on it. (8) Many spread their outer garments on the road – others, greenery cut from the fields; (9) and those who went before and those who followed shouted

'Hosanna!
Blessed is the one who comes in the name of the Lord.
(10) Blessed is the coming kingdom of our father David.
Hosanna in the highest!'

(11) And he came into Jerusalem, into the temple, and looked round at everything; then, because it was already evening, he went out to Bethany with the Twelve.

Mark has told us nothing of previous visits by Jesus to Jerusalem, and this account of Jesus' entry is therefore the more dramatic. It seems very likely that Jesus had been in Jerusalem before and perhaps taught there. Apart from the evidence of the Fourth Gospel, there are hints in the Synoptics that Jesus had visited the city at an earlier stage (e.g. Luke 13.34). One possibility is that Mark has telescoped two visits, and that the triumphal entry (and perhaps some of the teaching) belongs to the earlier of the two. In any case, the period between Jesus' arrival in Jerusalem and the crucifixion was probably much greater than the five days assigned to it in the Church's calendar; Mark's account does not have to be compressed within those five days, for although – unusually – he links together the incidents in the temple as occurring on three successive days (11.12, 20), the teaching in the temple was not necessarily all given on the third day (cf. 14.49), while his dating in 14.1 gives no indication as to how long

1 *Bethphage* is omitted in D and some Latin MSS.
2 The word order is confused; some MSS omit πάλιν, *back*.

had elapsed since Jesus arrived in Jerusalem.

The question of chronology arises also in connection with a problem concerning the crowd which accompanied Jesus into the city. This has customarily been explained as made up of festival pilgrims arriving for Passover. Even if we impose a strict time-scheme on Mark, however, and accept the traditional dating, these pilgrims were arriving in Jerusalem remarkably early for a festival the following Friday. Moreover, the details of the story are reminiscent of the celebration of the Feast of Tabernacles, when the people carried branches of greenery (presumably cut in the countryside near Jerusalem), which were waved during the recital of the Egyptian Hallel (Psalms 113–18, the psalms of praise recalling the Exodus); according to the Talmud (B. Sukkah 37a–b), these branches were waved at the word 'Hosanna' (Ps. 118.25).[1] It has therefore been suggested that the incident took place in the autumn, at Tabernacles, rather than at Passover (so T.W. Manson, *B.J.R.L.*, 33, 1951, pp. 271–82). But a similar ceremony took place at the winter Feast of *Hanukkah* (Dedication), which celebrated the cleansing of the temple by Judas Maccabaeus in 165 BC – a festival with strong nationalistic significance – and this would provide an even more appropriate setting for Jesus' action in the temple (see F.C. Burkitt, *J.T.S.*, 17, 1916, pp. 139ff). It must be noted, however, that John, who knows of earlier visits by Jesus to Jerusalem, agrees with Mark in placing not only the triumphal entry but the cleansing of the temple at Passover (John 12.12; 2.13).

The suggestion that in crying **'Hosanna'** the pilgrims were in fact celebrating the festival, rather than acclaiming Jesus as king, and that they were calling down blessings on all those who were travelling to Jerusalem, accords well with some of the problematic features of Mark's story. One of these is the apparent fickleness of the crowd which later demands Jesus' death (15.6–15) – though perhaps Mark thinks of those travelling with Jesus as acclaiming him, rather than of the crowd, since in v.9 he refers to **those who went before and those who followed**; this is how Luke interpreted the scene, though in Matthew and John it is clearly the crowd which welcomes Jesus to Jerusalem. More important is the lack of any reference to the triumphal entry at the trial of Jesus: had the incident been interpreted as a messianic demonstration at the time, it would have provided useful evidence for the prosecution. As Mark tells the story, the incident is certainly not the unambiguous assertion of messiahship which later interpretation has made it, even though Mark himself regards it as

---

1 At a much later period, these branches apparently came to be known as 'Hosannas' (Targum II to Esther 3.8), but by this stage the true meaning of the word (see below) had been so long forgotten that it was being treated as a noun.

clear enough to those with eyes of faith. Nor is this simply Mark's understanding of the incident; John also sees significance in the story which he says was not obvious at the time, even to the disciples. With hindsight, and read in the light of scripture, the incident took on a meaning which had not been clear when it took place (John 12.16).

Unless the whole story is a legend based on the prophecy in Zech. 9.9, however – and had that been the case, we might have expected much clearer reference to that passage in Mark's account (cf. Matt. 21.4f.; John 12.14f.) – or is a projection back by Mark of a celebration of Jesus' kingship into his lifetime (see D.R. Catchpole, 'The "triumphal" entry'), we still have to account for the action of Jesus in riding into the city. Since pilgrims normally entered the holy city on foot, Jesus' decision to ride this last stage of the journey looks like some kind of claim to authority; the action is the more extraordinary, since throughout his ministry he has walked everywhere. The choice of an ass has generally been interpreted as an act of humility, but to ride any animal in these circumstances rather than walk was scarcely humble. In fact, the ass was an appropriate mount for a king in the ancient world, and the fundamental contrast between ass and horse was that the latter was used in battle. The notion of humility has come through the influence of Zech. 9.9, for though the Hebrew word used of the king could mean 'afflicted', it was interpreted by both the LXX and the Targum as 'humble'. But Mark makes no reference to Zechariah 9, and there is no evidence that the verse was of any importance for messianic belief at the time of Jesus. It is true that in the middle of the third century AD, Rabbi Joshua ben Levi is reported as saying that if Israel was worthy, the Messiah would come with the clouds of heaven, and if not, lowly and riding on an ass (B. Sanh. 98a), but his words suggest that the lowly Messiah of Zech. 9.9 would not be recognized and confirm the lack of contemporary interest in this verse. Although the later evangelists made the link with Zechariah 9, therefore, we cannot be sure that Mark had already done so, though he may well have had it in mind. We certainly cannot assume that this passage appeared relevant to Jesus himself, though this in no way diminishes the implicit claim in Jesus' action.

In Mark's account, Jesus enters the city of David as king, heralded as 'Son of David' by a blind beggar on the road, and welcomed by the plaudits of other pilgrims who, whether they are his own disciples or simply members of the crowd, do not grasp the full significance of their own greeting, any more than Peter, at Caesarea Philippi (following the healing of another blind man), grasped the significance of his acclamation of Jesus as the Christ. Readers of the gospel, on the other hand, understand the true significance of Jesus' entry into Jerusalem and the welcome given to him by the crowd.

**Bethany** was about two miles from **Jerusalem**, and **Bethphage** 1 somewhat closer, only a sabbath-day's journey (about half a mile) away. Both villages were on the slopes of **the Mount of Olives**, and from Jericho Jesus would have reached Bethany first. The omission of the refererence to Bethphage by some MSS is probably due to an early attempt to sort out Mark's geography. According to Zech. 14.4, God would stand on the Mount of Olives on the final day of judge-

2  ment. Jesus' detailed instructions to **two of his disciples** appear to rest on supernatural knowledge, yet the disciples express no surprise, even when events happen exactly as he foretold. The instructions could, of course, have been the result of a private agreement between Jesus and the owner of the animal; but if so, why should the story be told in this detail? Anthony Harvey suggests that its purpose is not to impress us with Jesus' supernatural knowledge but to underline the real significance of the story (*Jesus and the Constraints of History*, pp. 122f.). For this, we need to turn to a suggestion by Duncan Derrett that what Jesus does here is to 'impress' the ass, thereby exercising the authority of a king who had the right to commandeer an animal in this way (*Studies in the New Testament*, II, pp. 165–83); the acquisition of the ass was as much a signal of Jesus' kingship as the riding of it into the city. The fact that the **foal** was one **which no one** had **ever ridden** made it suitable for a sacred purpose; it would also make it appropriate for use by a king, since according to the Mishnah (M. Sanh. 2.5), no one else may ride a king's horse.

3  The reference to **the Master** has been interpreted in various ways. The title used here – ὁ κύριος – is used in the LXX in the sense of 'the Lord' to refer to God, but this meaning hardly fits the context. One possibility is that it means 'the owner'; any worried neighbours are to be reassured by a message that it was the animal's owner (perhaps now one of Jesus' company of followers) who had sent them – a logical reply in the circumstances, as the use of similar statements by countless conmen shows! It is also possible that the phrase is used here in the sense which it came to have in the Christian community as a title for Jesus himself. Nowhere else (except perhaps in 5.19) does Mark allow the title to slip into his narrative in this anachronistic way, but it is possible that Mark felt that at this point in his narrative the identity of Jesus is being made sufficiently plain by events for him to use the title: it is 'the Lord' who is entering Jerusalem and coming to the temple (cf. Mal. 3.1). There is no basis for the *N.E.B.*'s 'our Master', which seems to be an attempt to guess at what might have beeen present in an earlier stage of the tradition. Derrett's suggestion at this point is that ὁ κύριος αὐτοῦ does indeed mean 'its owner', but that this refers to Jesus himself: as king, he is entitled, when he **needs it**, to claim it as his. If this is Mark's meaning, then these words underline the claim to kingship which he understands Jesus to be making by his actions.

The disciples are to assure those who question their right to take the animal that it will be sent **back straight away**. This seems a natural enough comment in the circumstances, though Derrett notes that it implies that Jesus takes full responsibility for the animal and so scrupulously observes the laws of borrowing in the Mishnah. Those MSS which omit the word πάλιν (= again) must be interpreted as meaning that whoever is given Jesus' message will send it here immediately – i.e., to him; however, this omission is probably secondary.

The exact fulfilment of Jesus' words suggests not simply his **4–6** foreknowledge of events, but his deliberate carrying-out of his destiny and the importance of what is taking place.

**They brought the foal to Jesus and spread their outer garments** **7** **on it**, so making an impromptu throne. Since Jesus is not on foot, the carpeting of **the road** with **garments** seems a somewhat strange **8** feature; it is, however, reminiscent of the proclamation of Jehu as king in 2 Kgs. 9.13, and though Jehu was certainly not an ideal monarch, so that we would hardly expect this story to be modelled on that incident, it may be that that passage reflects a recognized custom. Moreover, those who **spread** their clothes **on the road** (ὁδός once again) are 'preparing the way of the Lord' (1.3) as he reaches his goal and enters Jerusalem. The word στιβάς, translated **greenery**, really means a layer of something forming a bed, and the emphasis is therefore on the soft leaves. At the Feasts of Tabernacles and of the Dedication of the Temple the crowds would have carried branches (see 2 Macc. 10.7), rather than throwing them on the ground, but it is only in the Fourth Gospel that we are told that the crowd carried branches (there specified as palm), a detail which has become a feature of the traditional picture of Palm Sunday.

**Hosanna!** is the transliteration of a Hebrew phrase meaning 'save **9** now'; in the first century AD it would presumably have been understood by Jews as an appeal to God to save his people from foreign domination. Mark, however, seems to understand it as a shout of praise. The word is found in Ps. 118.25, and the following verse is quoted here from the LXX version (117.26), where the meaning (following the Hebrew) is: 'Blessed in the name of the Lord is he who comes' (i.e. to the feast); Mark probably means us to link the phrase **in the name of the Lord** with **the one who comes**, however, as in our translation, so turning a general welcome of the festival pilgrims into a specific proclamation of the arrival of the one who comes in God's name – a phrase which could well have messianic significance. **Blessed is . . .**: both v.9b and v.10a should be understood as affirming **10** what is true rather than as conveying blessing to the recipient. In Greek, the two greetings are clearly parallel (εὐλογημένος ὁ ἐρχόμενος . . . εὐλογημένη ἡ ἐρχόμενη . . .), confirming that the one who is wel comed also brings the kingdom. The second greeting is odd, since the phrase **our father David** is unknown in Judaism, where the term 'father' is normally used of the patriarchs; the reference to his **coming kingdom** is also an unusual expression, although there was widespread hope of a future Davidic king: the language probably reflects Christian beliefs, or else has been used deliberately to make the parallel with v.9b. In Mark, the words serve to confirm the earlier proclamation of Jesus as Son of David as he approached Jerusalem (10.47f.). **Hosanna in the highest!** makes no sense if taken literally; this phrase shows that the word **Hosanna** had become simply a cry of jubilation.

Jesus' arrival in **the temple** seems something of an anticlimax, confirming the suggestion that the triumphal entry was not a messianic demonstration. Jesus simply **looked round at everything; then...went out to Bethany with the Twelve**: contrast the accounts in Matthew and Luke. It is possible, of course, that Mark has deliberately made Jesus' arrival a 'non-event', because he wished to place the cleansing of the temple in the context of the story of the withered fig tree. Though apparently tame, however, this inspection of the temple by Jesus is of great importance for Mark, since it leads to its subsequent condemnation.

# 2 ISRAEL'S FAILURE 11.12–26–

*(Matt. 21.12–22; Luke 19.45–8; John 2.13–17; Thomas 106)*

**(12) And on the following day, as they were leaving Bethany, he felt hungry, (13) and seeing in the distance a fig tree in leaf, he went to see if he could find anything on it; but when he came up to it he found nothing but leaves, for it was not the season for figs. (14) And he said to the tree, 'May no one ever eat fruit from you again!' And his disciples were listening.**

**(15) And they came into Jerusalem, and entering the temple, he began to drive out those who bought and sold in the temple; and he overturned the tables of the money-changers and the seats of those who sold doves, (16) and he would not allow anyone to carry goods through the temple. (17) And he began to teach them, and said, 'Is it not written, "My house shall be called a house of prayer for all the nations"? But you have made it "a robbers' den".'**

**(18) The chief priests and the scribes were listening, and they looked for a way to destroy him; for they were afraid of him, since the whole crowd was astonished at his teaching. (19) And when evening came, they[1] left the city.**

1 Some MSS (including **ℵ** C D Θ fams. 1 and 13) read *he left the city.*

(20) Early next morning, as they passed by, they saw the fig tree,
him, 'Look, Rabbi; the tree which you cursed has withered!'
(22) Jesus answered them, 'Have faith in God.[1] (23) Truly I tell
you, that if someone should say to this mountain, "Be taken up and
that if someone should say to this mountain, "Be taken up and
hurled into the sea," and does not doubt in his heart but believes
that what he says will happen, it will be done. (24) Therefore I tell
you, whatever you ask for in prayer, believe that you have received it, and it will be yours. (25) And whenever you stand praying, forgive, if you have anything against anyone, so that your
Father in heaven may also forgive you your wrongdoings.[2]

In this next section we once again find one event sandwiched within
another – a device used elsewhere in Mark, and almost certainly due
to his editing. We are clearly meant to see a link between the fate of
the barren fig tree and Jesus' action in the temple. But this triple
grouping of material has been placed within two paragraphs dealing
with Jesus' identity and authority (vv.1–10, 27–33), so building up
another, more complex 'sandwich'. The judgement pronounced on
Israel in vv.12–26 is thus firmly linked with her failure to recognize
her Messiah.

The incident of the fig tree is a difficult one. It is the only 'negative'
miracle in the gospels, for instead of pronouncing a word of salvation,
which brings life, Jesus here utters a curse – apparently out of pique –
which kills the tree. The story is dismissed by some commentators as
out of character for Jesus (though akin to some miracles found in the
apocryphal gospels); it has been explained as an aetiological legend
about a withered tree, or the result of the disciples misunderstanding
some words of Jesus; as an 'acted parable' ('oracle' might be a better
word) similar to those performed by Old Testament prophets, or as a
story which has developed out of a parable (cf. Luke 13.6–9). Whatever its origins, however, the story is certainly used symbolically by
Mark and probably had this symbolic significance from the beginning. The fig tree represents Israel, which has failed to produce
the appropriate fruits when her Messiah looked for them. The
background of this imagery is found in passages in the Old Testament
which speak of the Lord looking in vain for grapes or figs on his vine
or fig tree, and of the judgement which necessarily follows: especially relevant are Hos. 9.10, 16f., Mic. 7.1 and Jer. 8.13:

'When I would gather them, says the Lord,
    there are no grapes on the vine,

---

1 Some MSS (including א D Θ fam. 13) read *If you have faith in God.* . . .
2 A C D Θ fams. 1 and 13, and some versions add v.26: *But if you do not forgive,
neither will your Father in heaven forgive your wrongdoings.*

nor figs on the fig tree;
even the leaves are withered,
and what I gave them has passed away from them.'

This, then, is why Jesus curses the tree: not out of pique, but because it represents Israel, and Israel has fallen under the judgement of God.

Equally important is the expectation that in the messianic age the fig tree will bear fruit. The fig tree is an emblem of peace and prosperity: hope for the future is expressed in terms of sitting in security under one's vine and one's fig tree (e.g. Mic. 4.4; Zech. 3.10) and gathering fruit from them (Hag. 2.19). William Telford (*The Barren Temple and the Withered Tree*) argues that the fig tree would have been understood as a symbol for Israel, which should have borne fruit in the messianic era: yet when Jesus comes to the city, the tree is without fruit, and judgement inevitably follows.

Further difficulties arise from the inconsistencies in the story: Jesus looks for fruit because he is hungry – logical enough, except that we are then told that it was not the season for figs! One possible solution is that this story, like the preceding one, concerns events which took place, not in spring, but in autumn, when some fruit might still be left on the tree; the comment about the season was then added when the setting was changed. Another is that Jesus was not looking for fruit to eat but simply inspecting it to see what kind of harvest could be expected; in this case the remark that Jesus was hungry is a misunderstanding, and the fact that it was not the season for ripe figs is irrelevant. Both comments will have been added to the story at some stage. But why should Mark have included the comment that it was not the season for figs? It may be that this is a deliberate hint to us to take the story symbolically. The tree could not provide Jesus with figs to eat because it was not the season for figs, but though it was the wrong time of year for normal fruit the tree should in fact have been covered with fruit to greet the Messiah. Because Israel does not recognize her Messiah she does not welcome him, and because she does not receive him, the messianic age – the season of figs – cannot arrive.

The story thus forms a fitting context for Jesus' violent action in the temple. There has been a great deal of discussion regarding the correct dating of this so-called cleansing of the temple. Mark and John agree in linking the incident with a Passover visit (see also on v.15), but while Mark places the incident at the very end of Jesus' ministry, John puts it at the beginning. The Markan dating has often been defended in the past on the basis that the Fourth Gospel is governed by theological motives, but the recognition that Mark, also, is a theological writer means that he, too, may have placed the story where he does in accordance with theological purposes. Moreover, since Mark records only one visit of Jesus to Jerusalem, there was no other setting which he could have given the story in the framework which he chose to use. If – as seems most likely – the tradition reached the evangelists without any indication of when the incident took place, it is not necessary to suppose that either Mark or John has deliberately altered the dating, but rather that each of them placed it where he thought appropriate; this means that perhaps neither of these dates is the correct one, since the incident could have happened at any stage in the ministry, on another visit of Jesus to Jerusalem.

In placing the story at the end of Jesus' life, Mark presents it as the climax of Jesus' challenge to the Jewish religious authorities and of his claim to authority: the incident sets the seal on Jesus' own fate (and so on that of the nation). John, too, though he places the story at the beginning of his narrative, links it with the death of Jesus; the saying about the temple in John 2.19 is not just a play on words but arises from the belief that the Jewish attempt to destroy Jesus led to God's rejection of Jerusalem and its temple, and the whole incident (like that of the marriage feast in Cana) symbolizes the replacement of Judaism by Christianity. Mark, also, throughout these final chapters, binds together the themes of Israel's rejection of her Messiah and her own inevitable rejection by God.

What was the motive behind Jesus' action? Some have seen it as an attack on the sacrificial system. But since the demand to offer sacrifice was included in the commands of God, set out in the Torah, Jesus would hardly have challenged the whole system. It must also be remembered that the prophets, who were at one time commonly interpreted as attacking sacrifices, were concerned rather with the attitude which made sacrifice a sufficient expression of religion without regard to social justice. Was it then the misuse of the sacrificial system which Jesus was attacking? The complaint that the authorities have prevented the temple from being a **house of prayer for all the nations** supports this suggestion. So does the Johannine version of Jesus' protests, which attacks the merchants for making the temple a house of trade. The sale of animals in the court of the Gentiles meant that it was impossible to worship there, and Jesus was not alone in complaining about the way in which the priestly authorities extracted money from worshippers. Obviously they charged for their services in providing appropriate sacrifices and offerings, though opinions vary as to whether or not their charges were extortionate (I. Abrahams, *Studies in Pharisaism and the Gospels*, pp. 82–9, maintains that they were not). It has been argued recently by E.P. Sanders (*Jesus and Judaism*, pp. 61–76) that it was not the commercial enterprises themselves that were polluting the temple, since these were essential to the system: it was necessary to provide animals without blemish and money of a certain quality to the worshippers.

Nevertheless, from at least the time of Malachi there had been protests about the priests, whose corruption meant that the sacrifices offered in the temple were neither pure nor pleasing to the Lord (Mal. 3.3f.). Similar complaints are found in the Psalms of Solomon (2.3–5; 8.11–13), at Qumran (1Qp Hab. 8.8–13; 12.1–10; CD 5.6–8; 6.12–17) and in the Talmud (B.Pes.57a), while Josephus describes the way in which the servants of the priestly aristocracy stole tithes from the ordinary priests (*Antiquities*, XX. 8.8; 9.2). There is thus good reason to think that Jesus may have been aiming his protests at the priests, and though Sanders objects that there is no indication that Jesus attacked the priesthood, this story is perhaps sufficient evidence that he did so. His action may have been a protest against the way in which a concern with the outward niceties of religion (the insistence that a sacrificial animal must be without blemish, guaranteed pure, and that temple taxes were paid in the appropriate currency) led to realities being ignored (cf. Matt. 5.23f.); in other words, his protest about the priests' activities is exactly on a parallel with his protests about the teaching of the scribes and Pharisees – hardly surprising, then, if the outcome was a collusion between priests and scribes.

But Jesus' protest may well have been wider than this. In Malachi 3 the corruption of the priests is only half the story: it is symbolic of the sin of the whole people. God will execute judgement against those who break his commandments and oppress the poor (v.5); the people have been robbing God and withholding tithes and offerings (vv.6–10). When the priests 'present right offerings to the Lord, then the offering of Judah and Jerusalem will be pleasing to the Lord' (vv.3f.). It would be in the prophetic tradition for Jesus to protest about worship in the temple which was hollow because it was offered by those whose behaviour was unjust: true love of God always goes hand in hand with love of neighbour (Mark 12.28–34). The quotation from Jer. 7.11 attributed to Jesus in v.17 does not refer in its original context to commercial transactions in the temple. The people are there described as 'robbers' or 'brigands' because their behaviour outside the temple means that when they enter the temple they cannot worship God sincerely: they rob God in the temple as surely as they have robbed the poor outside. Since by driving out the buyers and sellers and by overturning the table of the money-changers Jesus prevents would-be worshippers buying sacrifices or offering the half-shekel tax, this suggests that he is protesting that their worship is a sham, not simply attacking the malpractices of the authorities.

It is possible, then, that the traditional interpretation of Jesus' action as a 'cleansing' of the temple is correct. The temple had been cleansed in the past – by Josiah, who removed the altars of other deities and deposed their priests (2 Kgs. 23), and by Judas Maccabaeus, after its desecration by Antiochus Epiphanes (1 Macc. 4.36–59): the latter restoration was celebrated annually in the Feast of Dedication. If, as has been suggested (see above, p. 256), the incident took place during this festival, the link with cleansing would be obvious.

Since the temple symbolized the relationship between God and his people, it was natural that hopes of renewal should be linked with it. The Jewish hope of the End included the expectation of a new temple, which would be built either by God himself or by his Messiah (e.g. 1 Enoch 90.28f.). Mal. 3.1–4, as we have seen, promises that the Lord will come to his temple and purge the priests and their offerings. Was Jesus, by his actions, therefore, demanding a thorough purging of both priests and people? Was this a symbolic action, equivalent to his proclamation: 'The Kingdom of God is at hand: repent'?

Clearly, as an act of reforming zeal, the incident would have to be judged a failure: the money changers no doubt soon recovered their coins, and the place was restored to order. The evangelists, however, see Jesus' actions as much more than a mere gesture of protest: they are to be understood as prophetic actions, symbolizing a divine judgement which will be worked out in future events. John interprets the incident as both a sign of the coming cessation of Jewish worship, and a symbol of the way in which Jesus himself fulfilled the functions once served by the temple. Mark, by embedding the incident in the story of the fig tree, shows clearly that he interprets it as a sign of God's condemnation of Israel because of her failure to bear fruit. This suggests that he sees it as a symbol of the future destruction of the temple and the final cessation of worship. On their own, Jesus' words are not the equivalent of the curse in v.14, nor (*pace* the commentators) are his actions an obvious symbol of the future destruction of the temple, but both words and actions are a condemnation of the nation for her failure to produce fruit, and in the context of the story of the barren fig tree they imply judgement and destruction. Moreover, it is possible that something more is implied in the story as Mark gives it. He alone, of the four evangelists, includes the words **for all the nations** in the quotation from Isa. 56.7 – reminding us that the words were originally a promise about the future; by omitting them, Matthew and Luke make Jesus' words a straightforward contrast between what the temple should have been and what it had become. Was Mark aware of the eschatological dimension of the words? If so, did he include them because he saw in Jesus' action a symbol of the fact that through his coming death, Gentiles were to be brought to worship God? Certainly this would agree with passages such as 12.9 and 15.39; this interpretation is also close to that of John, who interprets the event positively, of the future worship of the Christian community, as well as negatively, and who links the death of Jesus with the drawing in of the Gentiles (John 12.32). Perhaps, then, Mark understands Jesus' actions as a 'messianic' act – not merely a condemnation of Israel for her failure, but a claim that the time has come for the purpose of God to be fulfilled – though this will be via the paradoxical path of rejection.

It has, indeed, been suggested (C. Roth, *N.T.*, 4, 1960, pp. 174–81) that Jesus himself saw his action as a 'messianic act' fulfilling the prophecy of Zech. 14.21 about the temple (the Hebrew reads 'Canaanite', but both the Targum and Aquila understand it to mean 'trader'). Certainly the setting of the story within that of the barren fig tree suggests that *Mark* may have seen it in terms of the fulfilment of eschatological hopes: when Jesus comes to Jerusalem, he expects the promises to be fulfilled – the fig tree should provide fruit, and the temple of the Lord should be holy, 'and there shall no longer be a trader in the house of the Lord of hosts on that day'.

But eschatological hopes involve judgement as well as renewal. Our interpretation of the story thus disagrees with that of E.P. Sanders (*loc. cit.*), who sees Jesus' action in the temple as a symbol not of its condemnation, but of its forthcoming destruction, and who believes that he intended to indicate simply that the End was at hand and that a new temple was about to appear. To see it simply as an announcement of destruction and restoration, however, is to ignore the prior question: '*Why* should the temple be destroyed and rebuilt?' For Sanders, the answer is simple: because the time has come. But Jesus' call to repentance suggests that the outcome was not yet inevitable: there was still time to respond. No doubt Jesus' protest in the temple (like that of the prophets before him) implied that if the people did not repent, judgement would follow: his words and actions were thus a warning of possible judgement to come. But it was Mark, looking back on events, who saw the incident as a final judgement rather than as a warning, interpreting it as a symbol of forthcoming destruction. It is hardly surprising if Mark, writing at a time when the Jewish people appeared to have rejected the gospel, gave an interpretation to events which was somewhat different from Jesus' own. If, as we believe, he was writing after AD 70, it is not surprising if he saw the story as pointing inevitably to the temple's destruction. (See further, M.D. Hooker, *B.J.R.L.*, 70, 1988, pp. 7–19.)

Mark's community, probably largely Gentile, would have found in these incidents the explanation of Israel's apparent rejection as the people of God. At the same time, the stories serve as a warning against repeating the mistakes of those whose failure, both to worship God with sincerity and to embrace the gospel, had led to their downfall.

12    The story begins with the words **on the following day** – an unusual temporal link in Mark. With the similar note in v.20, it serves to join

the story of the fig tree with the entry of Jesus into the temple. The statement that Jesus **felt hungry** might have been added as an obvious explanation; but it may perhaps reflect an Old Testament passage such as Mic. 7.1.

**Jesus inspects the fig tree, going to see if he could find anything** 13 **on it,** just as on the previous day he had inspected the temple. Fig trees come into leaf in late March in the Jerusalem area; the first crop of fruit begins to form before the leaves appear, even though it takes several months to ripen, but Mark understands Jesus to have been looking for edible fruit. **But when he came up to it he found nothing but leaves,** a symbol of Israel's outward show of religion and failure to produce anything of worth. The statement that **it was not the season for figs** makes nonsense of the narrative at the ordinary level (see the discussion above). Once the story is understood symbolically, however, it is entirely appropriate that the Lord should look for fruit at the most unexpected time of year (cf. 13.35).

**'May no one ever eat fruit from you again!'** It has been suggested 14 that Jesus' words were not a curse, but a declaration that the fruit of the tree would never be eaten – either by Jesus himself, or perhaps by anybody at all (T.W. Manson, *B.J.R.L.*, 33, 1951, pp. 271–82). In the former case, the saying would have been a declaration about the imminence of his death (cf. a similar statement in 14.25); in the latter case, it would have been a prophecy of the inevitable and early judgement of Jerusalem (cf. 13.26–31). These suggestions arise from the ambiguity of the possible underlying Aramaic sentence and offer a fascinating example of the way in which a saying or story can take on a completely different meaning in a different context. Whatever the original meaning however (and here we can only speculate), Mark has understood the words as an emphatic curse: the tree is condemned because of its failure to produce fruit. In pronouncing judgement and carrying it out, Jesus exercises the authority of God himself to condemn and destroy, but since the fig tree is a symbol for the nation, it is possible that Mark sees this action as a symbol for future divine action, and supposes that God himself – rather than Jesus – will carry out the final, eschatological judgement of Israel. The comment that **his disciples were listening** warns us that this is not the end of the story; it will be picked up in v.21.

The scene shifts back to **Jerusalem** again. **The temple** was a large 15 building made up of various areas, the outermost being the court of the Gentiles, which is the scene of this incident. Here worshippers could buy what they needed from traders who seem to have had a virtual monopoly in sacrificial animals, since theirs alone were guaranteed to be without blemish. If Jesus **began to drive out those who bought and sold in the temple,** he would be interrupting the offering of sacrifices. Each year, for a few days immediately before

1st Nisan (which fell two weeks before Passover), **money-changers** set up their **tables** for the exchange of Greek or Roman money into the special Tyrian currency in which the temple-tax had to be paid; this tax was payable each year by every adult male Jew by the 1st Nisan (M. Shek. 1.3; cf. Ex. 30.11–16). Provision for the exchange was also made earlier the same month (i.e. between the 15th and 25th Adar) in other towns (see I. Abrahams, *Studies in Pharisaism*, pp. 82–9). If, as seems likely, this was the only occasion in the year when these tables were set up in the temple, and if this detail in the narrative is correct, then the incident must have taken place two to three weeks before Passover. In relation to both sacrifice and temple-tax therefore, attempts to preserve the purity of Jewish worship may well have prevented any Gentiles who wished to do so from using the temple for prayer – though in the case of the tax, the disturbance would have lasted for only one week.

16    The temple precincts were apparently being used as a short-cut by the inhabitants of Jerusalem – a practice which is forbidden in the Mishnah (M. Berakoth 9.5). In this instance, by refusing to **allow anyone to carry goods through the temple**, Jesus is seen as demanding the fulfilment of a regulation where the authorities had grown lax. Yet his attitude is consistent: he condemns whatever indicates that men are insincere in their worship of God – whether it is the too

17    scrupulous observance of a regulation or the flouting of it. **And he began to teach them, and said**: this somewhat ponderous phrase introduces what Mark believes to be the basis of Jesus' attack. It is not clear who is being addressed, but it is natural to think of everyone in the temple precinct: they have failed to offer God true worship and have polluted the temple by their wickedness. The quotation in v.17 is from Isa. 56.7. '**My house shall be called a house of prayer for all the nations**': the final phrase, 'for all the nations' (missing from both Matthew and Luke), hints at the ultimate outcome: though this temple will be destroyed, another temple, made without hands, will enable Gentiles to worship God (14.58; 15.38f.). The phrase '**a robber's den**' is found in Jer. 7.11, in a denunciation of those whose moral behaviour was repugnant to God, but who nevertheless came to the temple to worship.

18    Jesus' action is a clear condemnation of the priestly authorities, who have permitted these practices: the result is that **the chief**

19    **priests** join **the scribes** in plotting his death (cf. 3.6). The **crowd**, on the other hand, was as usual **astonished at his teaching** (cf. 1.22; 6.2). **And when evening came, they left the city**: the variation between 'they' and 'he' in v.19 is understandable, since Mark has the singular in v.18, the plural in v.20, and a slip could easily be made.

20    The story continues on the following morning: **the fig tree** was not

21    simply wilting, but completely destroyed, **withered from the roots**.

Peter's awestruck exclamation – 'Look, Rabbi; the tree which you cursed has withered!' – underlines the fulfilment of Jesus' word of condemnation, and the word remembering makes doubly certain that we think back to vv.12–14. The conclusion to the story is quickly told, but various sayings have been added to it – chiefly by word association, for the story itself has little to do with faith, prayer or forgiveness. In the context of v.23, Jesus' injunction to the disciples **22–3** to have faith in God naturally suggests that the withering of the tree is the result of his own faith in God and is offered to them as an example of what faith can do. But if we detach these added sayings, the words become far more appropriate to the symbolic meaning of the miracle: even though God's judgement is inevitable and Israel's fate is sealed, the disciples must continue to trust in God (cf. the similar theme in chapter 13). If this is the original significance of the saying, then it may have formed the original climax to the story and, if so, this suggests that the story was already interpreted in a symbolic way in the pre-Markan tradition. (This is the only place in the New Testament where the notion of 'faith in God' is expressed by the phrase πίστις θεοῦ. A similar phrase is used in Rom. 3.3, but there the genitive is clearly subjective, not objective, and ἡ πίστις τοῦ θεοῦ refers to the faithfulness of God. The use of the unusual expression in Mark 11.22 serves to remind us that the exhortation to have faith in God is in fact based on God's own faithfulness.) The variant reading in v.22, which makes the saying conditional, 'If you have faith in God, truly I tell you . . .' is probably the result of assimilation to Matt. 21.21.

The sayings in vv.22–6 appear to have been collected together at some stage: the word faith (πίστις) in v.22 is picked up in the saying about believing (πιστεύω) in v.23. It seems likely that this saying was soon linked with the one that follows, in v.24, since this also refers to belief, and that this in turn, being about prayer, led to the addition of the saying about prayer and forgiveness in v.25. Commentators often assume that the sayings have been used here simply because of the verbal links (e.g. Taylor, Nineham). However, the reference to **this mountain** in v.23 may well have been understood by Mark as a reference to the temple mount, in which case he may well be responsible for adding the collection at this point. If this is the correct explanation, then Mark has here reminded us that the withered fig tree and the action in the temple have the same significance.

**Truly I tell you that if someone should say to this mountain, 'Be taken up and hurled into the sea,' and does not doubt in his heart but believes that what he says will happen, it will be done.** Moving a mountain appears to have been a proverbial saying for doing difficult tasks. It seems more likely that this is the explanation for the origin of this saying, rather than that it was a reference to one particular mountain. Matthew has a parallel saying in a different context in

17.20, Thomas has a similar promise in 106, and Luke records a similar saying about a sycamine tree in 17.6 – either a mulberry or a sycomore (a tree quite unlike the English sycamore), both of which belong to the same family as the fig. Since it refers to a tree, Luke's version of the saying might have appeared a more appropriate one to include here. Whatever its origin, the inclusion of the saying at this point suggests that Mark is now interpreting it of the temple mount. In contrast to Jewish expectation that at the Last Day 'the mountain of the house of the Lord' would be exalted and 'established as the highest of the mountains' (Mic. 4.1), Jesus now pronounces judgement on it and declares that it will be submerged in the sea. **The sea** was the place of destruction (cf. 5.13; 9.42).

24 The introductory words, in vv.23 and 24 – **truly I tell you** and **therefore I tell you** – indicate originally independent sayings. **Whatever you ask for in prayer, believe that you have received it:** the aorist (you have received) has probably been used to represent the Semitic prophetic present, which expressed the certainty of future

25 action. The wording of the saying in v.25, **forgive...so that your Father in heaven may also forgive you your wrongdoings**, echoes that of the Lord's Prayer (Matt. 6.12; Luke 11.4; cf. also Matt. 6.14f.).

26 The saying found in some MSS, and noted in the footnote, is probably an addition from Matt. 6.15.

# 3 THE AUTHORITY OF JESUS 11.27–33

*(Matt. 21.23–7; Luke 20.1–8)*

**(27) And they came into Jerusalem once more, and as he was walking in the temple, the chief priests and scribes and elders came to him (28) and asked, 'By what authority are you doing these things? Who has given you authority to act in this way?' (29) Jesus replied, 'I have a question to put to you; if you answer me, I will tell you by what authority I do these things. (30) Was the baptism of John from heaven or from men? Answer me!' (31) And they discussed it among themselves: 'If we say "from heaven",' they said, 'he will say, "Then why did you not believe him?" (32) But should we say "from men"?' – they feared the people, for all held John to have been a true prophet. (33) So they answered Jesus, 'We do not know'. And Jesus replied, 'Neither will I tell you by what authority I do these things.'**

This is the first of another group of conflict stories, in which Jesus meets opposition from various sources. In this one, he is confronted by representatives of all the religious authorities in Jerusalem, who raise the ultimate question regarding the source of his authority. In doing so, they return to the issue which was raised in 3.22–30 by the scribes who came from Jerusalem. But the story also links up with 11.1–10, where Jesus first entered Jerusalem and the temple. By placing events in this order, Mark implies that, had the religious authorities understood the significance of Jesus' entry into Jerusalem, they would have had no need to ask about his authority in acting as he does in the temple.

Mark's readers, of course, understand very well the source both of Jesus' authority and of John's, and the reason why they are related (see below).

**As he was walking in the temple**: the scene is probably once again   27 the court of the Gentiles. **The chief priests and scribes and elders** are the three groups which made up the Sanhedrin or supreme Jewish court. They question Jesus about the **authority** by which he is   28 **doing these things**, and ask **who has given** him **authority to act in this way**. In the context in which Mark has placed the encounter, the questions clearly refer to Jesus' actions in the temple on the previous day; the author of the Fourth Gospel also links the cleansing of the temple with a question about Jesus' authority (John 2.18). It is possible that the questions posed here originally had a wider reference and were asked of Jesus' activity of preaching and healing in general. D. Daube has suggested that the point at issue was the authority to teach, and the fact that Jesus had not been formally trained as a rabbi and given rabbinic authority (*J.T.S.*, 39, 1938, pp. 56f.).

Although his questioners may be thinking of authority at a human level and complaining that he is acting without their authorization, Jesus raises a more important issue in his reply: '**I have a question to**   29 **put to you; if you answer me, I will tell you by what authority I do these things**. The device of countering one question with another was fairly common in rabbinic debates. If the Jewish leaders answer his question correctly, they will have answered their own, since the two are bound together. **Was the baptism of John from heaven or**   30 **from men?** Jesus here links his own mission with that of John the Baptist. It is not that their two cases are simply analogous: for Mark, at least, John is the forerunner of Jesus, and the source of their authority must be the same. Looking back at the opening verses of the gospel, we remember that John's message was concerned entirely with the one who followed him and who was mightier than he; even his baptism was said to point forward to the baptism with Holy Spirit to be brought by his successor. For Mark, an incident in which Jesus answered a question about his own authority by pointing back to the activity of John must have seemed a clear claim to be the mightier one whom John foretold. But there may well be particular significance in the fact that Jesus is at this point being challenged in the

271

temple about his activities there. In 1.2, Mark quoted Mal. 3.1 of John. It is possible that Mark would have understood the link between Jesus and the Baptist, who is the messenger of Mal. 3.1, to indicate that Jesus must be the Lord who comes suddenly to his temple (Mal. 3.1–4): those who accept the messenger will accept the Lord who follows. Since in chapter 1 he attributes the Malachi quotation to Isaiah, however, and since there is no direct link with Malachi here or in vv.15–19, we cannot be certain that this passage was in Mark's mind. Nevertheless, the fact that at this particular point in the story Jesus is said to have referred back to John the Baptist suggests that Mal. 3.1 has been influential at some stage.

**31–2** His opponents debate what they shall say. The verb translated **discussed** (διαλογίζομαι) was used in 2.6, 8 of scribes who (as here) questioned the authority of Jesus (cf. also 8.16f.); the use of the same verb suggests to us that their discussion stems from unbelief. **Heaven** is a typical Jewish circumlocution for God; the contrast is not with Satan, as in 3.22–30, but with **men**, suggesting that the questioners had thought only in terms of human authorization. Their perplexity in deciding what answer to give is due, not to a desire to give the correct reply, but to a concern to preserve their own position. Bultmann (*Synoptic Tradition*, p. 20), has pointed out the unexpectedness of the words **'Then why did you not believe him?'** and suggested that the most natural response from Jesus, if the Jewish leaders replied **'from heaven'**, would have been to claim that his authority also was from the same source. If John is regarded as an authentic prophet, why should Jesus be denied the same title? The emphasis on disbelief looks like a later Christian comment, possibly due to Mark himself. We have noted earlier (1.14; 6.14–29; 9.9–13) that Mark understands the fate of John and the fate of Jesus to be woven together. The implication here is not only that the authority of both was from heaven, but also that the divine authority of both was denied by the Jewish leaders. Had they believed the witness of John, they would have accepted the one who followed him. It is because of their hardness of heart that the question posed by Jesus has become, for them, unanswerable.

**33** The admission from the religious leaders that they **do not know** is extraordinary: Mark's account of their discussions indicates that he believed them to be deliberately refusing to acknowledge the truth. Jesus' refusal to answer is typical of the way in which he claims authority throughout Mark's gospel. In reality, of course, the answer has been given – but men refuse to accept it as the truth.

# 4  A PARABLE ABOUT REJECTION                          12.1–12

*(Matt. 21.33–46; Luke 20.9–19; Thomas 65f.)*

(1) And he began to speak to them in parables: 'A man planted a vineyard, and he built a wall round it and dug out a winepress and built a tower; then he let it out to tenants and went abroad. (2) And at the proper season, he sent a servant to the tenants to collect from them some of the produce, (3) and they seized him, beat him and sent him away empty-handed. (4) Again, he sent another servant to them, but they struck him on the head and treated him shamefully. (5) He sent another – him they killed – and many others: some they beat and some they killed. (6) He still had one left – a beloved son; in the end he sent him to them, saying, "They will respect my son." (7) But these tenants said to one another, "This is the heir; come! – let us kill him, and the inheritance will be ours." (8) So they seized him and killed him and threw him out of the vineyard. (9) What will the owner of the vineyard do? He will come and put the tenants to death, and he will give the vineyard to others. (10) Have you not read this scripture:

"The stone which the builders rejected –
This has become the chief cornerstone.
(11) This was the Lord's doing,
And it is marvellous in our eyes"?'

(12) And they tried to arrest him, for they realized that he had told the parable against them, but they feared the crowd; so they left him and went away.

The parable of the vineyard tenants introduces another section of teaching, all of it set in the temple, which thus forms a bridge between Jesus' action in 11.15–19, and his clear pronouncement of doom in 13.1–2. Throughout the whole of this teaching there runs a note of hostility and tension: the underlying theme is the authority of Jesus, already challenged in 11.27–33. This series of conflict stories is in many ways similar to the earlier collection, in 2.1–3.6, but it is now the teaching of Jesus, rather than his activity, that comes under scrutiny. The parable itself is the most clearly allegorical of all Jesus' parables. Those scholars who are convinced that Jesus never used allegory are obliged to conclude, either that this particular story originated in the Church and is to be understood as an allegory about Jesus' rejection and death, or that an original parable has been radically changed through being overlaid with allegorical details. Certainly in its present context it demands to be read as an allegory of the failure of Israel's rulers to accept God's messengers. However, it is well nigh impossible to remove traces of allegory from the story altogether, even when all details are removed, and Jeremias' attempts do do so (*The Parables of Jesus,* pp. 70–7) are a failure. Since the image of Israel as God's vineyard goes back to Isaiah 5, there is no reason why Jesus himself should not have taken this over, and this means that the original parable contains a certain basic allegorical character. A comparison between Mark's version and the parallel passages in Matthew, Luke and the Gospel of Thomas demonstrates the different ways in which details in the narrative have been either added or allegorized. Whether or not the original story referred to a son who was killed, such details certainly held for the early Church a significance which they could not have had for those who first heard the parable. Mark has understood the purpose of the parable to be an attack on the religious leaders, as v.12 makes clear: these men have consistently refused to hear God's word and do so still in their refusal to listen to Jesus (cf. 11.27–33). The parable might have had this significance from the beginning or perhaps, like the original image in Isaiah and Mark's own account of the withered fig tree, was intended as an indictment of Israel in general for her failure to produce fruit.

The theme of the story is not unusual; similar parables are found in rabbinic sources. Its background lies in the fact that much of the land in Galilee was owned by absentee landlords who must have entrusted the task of rent-collection to agents. The behaviour of the tenants seems absurdly foolish, but that, of course, is the point of the story! Moreover, it is not impossible to imagine that Galilean Jews, resentful at the demands of foreign landowners, might have felt themselves justified in their behaviour and have imagined that they could escape retribution. It has been argued recently, moreover, that their action is explicable in view of Jewish law, which allowed a presumption of ownership to those who had possession of property and enabled those whose rights to possess it had not been disputed for a certain period to claim to be the true owners (J. Duncan Derrett, *Law in the New Testament,* pp. 286ff.).

The parable ends with the punishment of the tenants. The meaning is clear: those who have rejected God's messengers will themselves be rejected; others will inherit the promises. An appropriate setting can be found, either in Jesus' own challenge to the religious authorities, or in the situation of the early Church. It is worth noting, however, that the story speaks only of the rejection and death of the various messengers, and there is no hint of Jesus' resurrection: this suggests that the original parable belonged to Jesus' ministry and was delivered as another warning to his hearers not to reject the final messenger, lest judgement overtake them. When the story was retold after the resurrection, however, then the death of the final messenger was interpreted allegorically of the crucifixion, and it seemed to Christians that something vitally important was missing from the story – something which could not, however, be forced into the story itself and could only be added as a scriptural comment. So the story was 'rounded off' with a 'proof-text' of the resurrection, the Old Testament citation in v.10. The addition reminds us of the shift in perspective between the occasion when Jesus first used the parable and the time when Mark's community heard it. The parable is still an indictment of Israel and her leaders, but it is also a reassurance to Christians that they are the ones to whom the vineyard has been given, and so the legitimate tenants; this has come about because (changing the metaphor) the stone has been made the 'cornerstone' of the new community.

**Jesus began to speak to them in parables,** no longer 'plainly', as 1 he has been doing to his disciples (8.32). Nevertheless, those to whom this parable is addressed understand its meaning, and there is no need for explanation (v.12). Mark does not specify who this group are, but it is clear that he is thinking of the religious authorities in Jerusalem – **the chief priests and scribes and elders** mentioned in 11.27 who have refused to accept that Jesus' authority is from heaven. The description of the **vineyard,** with its references to the protective **wall,** the trough dug under the **winepress** for collecting juice and the **tower** which provided a look-out, echoes that given in Isa. 5.1f.; Mark's Greek is very close to that of the LXX, so that even though the details are what we would expect in a Palestinian vineyard, the present form of the story must be the work of a Greek-speaking Christian (possibly Mark himself). It is interesting at this point to compare the version of the parable found in the Gospel of Thomas (Logion 65), which is much simpler, and perhaps closer to the original out of which Mark's version has grown: 'A good man had a vineyard. He gave it to husbandmen. . . .' Luke, also, has a much simpler version than Mark's, and his only echo of Isaiah 5 is the phrase 'planted a vineyard' (Luke 20.9). This is a useful reminder that, even if Mark is our earliest gospel, its version of a particular pericope is not necessarily the earliest which we have. Even without the additional details, however, it is difficult to think that a story beginning in this way would not have reminded Jewish hearers of the story in Isaiah 5 (and cf. also Ps. 80.8–13 and Jer. 2.21) where the vineyard represents Israel, whose owner is God. But whereas in Isaiah the point of the 2 story is the failure of the vineyard to produce fruit (cf. Mark 11.12–14), the point of this story is the failure of the **tenants** to recognize the claims of the legitimate owner by handing over **some of the produce,** which was apparently the agreed rent.

The first **servant** having failed in his mission, the owner sent a 3–5 second and a third; the tension in the story mounts as the treatment dealt out to the servants grows progressively worse: the first is merely beaten, the second is **struck. . .on the head and treated. . . shamefully,** while the third is **killed.** The reference to **many others,** though it is intended to underline the villainy of the tenants, in fact detracts from the climax. Both Luke and Thomas omit this detail; in the Gospel of Thomas there are only two servants, and the third messenger is the son. Three is a common number in popular stories, so that once again Thomas' version, with its total of three messengers, may be closer to the original: when the servants were interpreted allegorically of the prophets, and the son of Jesus, then it was natural to speak of a long succession of servants.

6      Finally, we have the last messenger. The landowner's action in sending his **beloved son** seems rash, but this is explained by his

7–8    comment that '**They will respect my son.**' But his fate is the worst of all: hoping to gain the vineyard for themselves, the tenants **seized him and killed him and threw him out of the vineyard** – i.e., left his body to rot without burial. Matthew and Luke, influenced by their knowledge of the crucifixion, reverse the phrases and have the son cast out before he is killed. Although Christians cannot read the story without giving christological significance to the term **son,** the word might have been used originally as much to emphasize the finality of the landowner's demand, as to differentiate the last messenger himself from the others. The point of the story is the obduracy and criminal irresponsibility of the tenants, and there is no need to assume that Jesus intended his hearers to identify him with the son in the story. For Mark's readers, however, this is an obvious echo of the phrase used in 1.11 and 9.7; for those with eyes to see and ears to hear, the parable is a clear reminder of Jesus' identity.

It is possible that Jesus himself told a story about three servants, and that the figure of the beloved son is an allegorical detail which has been added at a later stage. However, the killing of the heir forms the natural climax to the story; it may also be a necessary part of it if Derrett (*loc. cit.*) is right in suggesting that the point is that a son could act as his father's legal representative in a way that the slaves could not, and that this was the owner's last opportunity of establishing his

9      claim to ownership. **What will the owner of the vineyard do?** Jesus often poses questions in his teaching but does not normally provide answers. The answer provided here may be a later addition; in Matthew, it is attributed to those who heard the parable. The **others** to whom the vineyard is to be given ought logically – at least in the setting Mark gives the parable – to be new leaders, since it is said to be directed against the Jewish authorities. But by Mark's day the new tenants who are taking over the vineyard are Gentiles.

10–11   The proof-text from Ps. 118.22f. (here following the LXX (117)) is quoted elsewhere in the New Testament (cf. Acts 4.11; 1 Pet. 2.7) but seems out of place in its present context, since the point of the parable is not the vindication and restoration of the wounded messengers, but the punishment of the tenants. **The stone which was rejected** and is now honoured might, of course, refer to those who are now given the vineyard, but the text is used elsewhere of the resurrection, and the image of the stone is used of Jesus (cf. Rom. 9.32f.; Eph. 2.20). In the present context, the quotation serves to complete the story of the son, who has been killed by the tenants: once this figure was understood to represent Jesus, it seemed necessary to refer to the resurrection. The addition must have been made at an early stage, since a reference to the same passage occurs immediately after the parable in the Gospel of Thomas (though without being linked to it). Matthew Black, however, has argued that there is a word-play on the Hebrew *ben* (son) and *'eben* (stone) underlying the parable and the saying, and that they therefore belonged together from the very beginning: he claims, indeed, that the parable 'may be regarded as itself a *pesher* of the testimonia' (*N.T.S.*, 18, 1971–2, pp. 1–14). It is equally possible, of course, to see in this word-play an explanation for the addition of the proof-text.

It is not clear whether **the chief cornerstone** (κεφαλὴ γωνίας, lit. 'the head of the corner') is to be understood as a large cornerstone in the foundation or as the keystone of an arch. The idea is used elsewhere in the New Testament in descriptions of the Christian community as a temple. Here it represents an abrupt change of imagery. Since Jesus is teaching in the temple, however, Mark may well expect us to see a link with the incident in 11.15–19: just as Jesus' action is a symbol of God's judgement on the temple, so the vineyard which is handed over to new tenants signifies the fact that true worship of God is now centred on the risen Christ, not in the Jerusalem temple. If so, then Mark presents us with an idea expressed more explicitly and succinctly in the Fourth Gospel (2.18–22).

**They tried to arrest him.** Jesus' teaching in the temple produces 12 the same result as his actions. Mark's account of the events leading to the passion is full of dramatic irony: Jesus' parable is directed against the religious leaders and foretells their future destruction, but it is of course their rejection of Jesus (and his teaching) which leads to their own rejection by God. The parable is acted out in the passion narrative which follows: in seeking to destroy Jesus, the authorities succeed only in destroying themselves.

Mark tells us that the religious authorities **realized that he had told the parable against them.** As Mark retells it, they could hardly fail to do so. But how much of the parable does he believe that they understood? For Mark, the reference to the beloved son must have seemed a clear messianic claim on Jesus' part, however indirectly made: did he believe that the Jewish leaders also understood it in this way? If so, then this story, with the previous one, is for Mark the real turning-point of the gospel, the moment at which the Jewish authorities reject their Messiah, and when his fate – and theirs – is sealed.

# 5   A TRICK QUESTION ABOUT TAX          12.13–17

*(Matt. 22.15–22; Luke 20.20–6; Thomas 100)*

**(13) And some of the Pharisees and Herodians were sent to him to trap him in speaking; (14) they came to him and said, 'Teacher, we know that you are sincere and court no one's favour, for you do not show partiality, but teach the way of God with sincerity. Is it lawful to give tribute to Caesar or not? Should we pay or should we not?' (15) Realizing their hypocrisy, he said to them, 'Why are you testing me? Bring me a denarius, so that I may see it.' (16) So they brought one, and he asked them, 'Whose image is this? Whose inscription?' They replied, 'Caesar's.' (17) Then Jesus said to them, 'Give to Caesar what belongs to Caesar, and to God what belongs to God.' And they were totally amazed.**

This is the first of a series of incidents in which Jesus deals in turn with four different questions. The first of these questions is put to him, we are told, by **some of the Pharisees and Herodians**, specifically in hope of catching him out. The second, from the Sadducees (a group not mentioned elsewhere by name in Mark) is equally hostile. The third is put by a scribe who is impressed by Jesus' answers, and the fourth is raised by Jesus himself. David Daube (*The New Testament and Rabbinic Judaism*, pp. 158–69) has pointed to an interesting parallel between these four questions and similar groupings found in Jewish literature. There is a passage in the Babylonian Talmud (B. Nid. 69b–71a) where twelve questions are put to R. Joshua b. Hananiah: of these, three were concerned with *Halakah* (matters of Law), three with *Haggadah* (a term used of non-legal material: in this context, consisting of questions about apparent contradictions within scripture), three were mocking questions (ridiculing belief in the resurrection) and three concerned matters of conduct. These four types of question correspond, Daube suggests, with the four questions in Mark 12, though there the question concerning exegesis comes last. R. Joshua taught at the beginning of the second century AD, and the Talmud itself was compiled much later, but there is another example of four questions grouped together in the Passover Haggadah (the liturgy used at the Passover meal), though it is impossible to be certain whether the earliest form of this known to us corresponds with what was done in Jesus' time. At the meal, passages from scripture are read, and four questions about the Passover found there (in Deut. 6.20; Ex. 12.26; 13.14 and 8) are attributed to four sons: the wise son is said to put a question about Law, the wicked son a contemptuous question, the pious son a simple question; the fourth son does not know how to ask, and his father takes the initiative and instructs him. These four questions also form an interesting parallel to the four questions in Mark 12, and this time they occur in the same order. Professor Daube suggests that the collection of narratives that we have in Mark 12.13–37 was deliberately based on the Passover Haggadah and might well have been brought together during the celebration of Passover in a Jewish-Christian community.

Even if Professor Daube is not correct in all his suggestions, it may be that the idea that there are basically four types of question provides the explanation for Mark's ordering of the material at this point. Taken together, the four incidents show Jesus as one who teaches with authority – the authority he claims in 11.27–33; by dealing with every possible kind of question, Jesus demonstrates his superiority to everyone who opposes or questions him, for his authority, unlike theirs, is from heaven. They come to a fitting climax with a story which raises, implicitly, the question of Jesus' own status. For Mark and his readers, these incidents unfold at the historical level the story depicted in allegorical form in 12.1–12 – the story of the hostility which met one whose claims were (as it seemed to the believing community, looking back) clearly presented before his people.

The first incident provides us with a good example of a pronouncement story: its purpose is to lead up to the punch-line at the end which consists of Jesus' reply to the question put to him. In its present context the story leads on naturally from 12.12: having failed to arrest Jesus, the Jewish leaders try to ensnare him by sending a group of men to trap him with their question. The incident itself sounds likely enough: the question reflects the situation during Jesus' ministry, and the saying could well be authentic. Nevertheless, it seems more likely that the saying was the result of long reflection on the problem, rather than an instantaneous response thought up on the spur of the moment.

The story centres on the payment of the κῆνσος, or poll-tax, a tax imposed on the population of Judaea, Samaria and Idumaea in AD 6, when these districts became a Roman province under the rule of a procurator. The imposition of the tax, like the arbitrary parcelling out of Jewish territory to suit the convenience of Rome, was regarded by the Jews as an outrageous act of interference on the part of their foreign rulers. It caused the simmering hatred of Rome to boil over in the revolt under Judas referred to in Acts 5.37, and according to Josephus (*Antiquities* XVIII.1.1,6) it gave rise to the Zealot movement, and so led to the revolt of AD 70. The issue of whether or not the poll-tax should be paid was therefore a burning one, and the question put to Jesus was a direct challenge to him to declare on which side of the fence he stood. The trap is obvious: if Jesus sides with the nationalists, he can be denounced to the Roman authorities and arrested as a political agitator; if he sides with the government, he will lose popular support. If there was at this stage any speculation that Jesus might be a messianic leader, his acceptance of Rome's authority would certainly discredit him in the eyes of the crowd. Jesus' answer accepts the legitimate demands of the Roman government, but immediately switches our attention to the far more important demands of God.

From early times, commentators have used these words to support the doctrine of two kingdoms. This holds that there are two separate and distinct realms – that of the state and that of the Kingdom of God – which are not in rivalry, and each of which has its separate sphere of influence. Unfortunately, however, experience has shown that the demands of the state and obedience to God do very often clash. By shifting our attention immediately from the command to give Caesar his due to that to give God what is due to him, Jesus' answer in fact suggests that obedience to God's demands is the primary requirement.

13    The trap is set by **Pharisees and Herodians** – the same unholy alliance that we encountered in 3.6. It is probable that both groups would have voted – however reluctantly – for the payment of the tax: the Pharisees because the *status quo* suited them better than open rebellion; the Herodians because they were supporters of Herod, who was a lackey of Rome. Jesus was a threat to them both because he challenged the established order: he must either be destroyed or be rendered harmless.

14    Readers of the gospel may well see irony in the acknowledgement that Jesus teaches **the way of God**, for though his questioners do not realize it, this is 'the way of the Lord', the way trodden by Jesus and by those who follow him as disciples (see 1.3; 10.32, etc.) Since Jesus does not care for men's opinion, the attempt to flatter him by praising his **sincerity** seems ill conceived! These words are presumably intended to sharpen the challenge to Jesus to speak out fearlessly and so land himself in trouble. Jesus, however, is well aware that their question – **Is it lawful to give tribute to Caesar or not?** – is not an honest one but is intended to catch him out: these men have been

15    **sent to him to trap him in speaking.** So **realizing their hypocrisy**, he asks for a Roman **denarius** – the silver coin with which the poll-tax had to be paid; in contrast to the smaller copper coins in everyday use in Palestine, it bore the head of the emperor. The engraving of any human likeness was, of course, contrary to the Jewish Law, and so made the coins themselves an offence to Jews.

16    Nevertheless, when Jesus asked for a denarius, his opponents **brought**

one. The fact that they were able to do so demonstrated that they had at least one in their possession. The logic of Jesus' reply is that those who use the money clearly owe some kind of allegiance to Caesar, since the **image** and **inscription** are **Caesar's**, and the coin therefore belongs to him.

The verb translated **give** (ἀποδίδωμι) implies the payment of a 17 debt. Jesus' answer is often interpreted as a clever evasion of the trap, but his reply is in fact unequivocal. However much the inhabitants of Judaea dislike it, they cannot escape the authority of **Caesar** and the obligations that entails. This reply is immediately balanced, however, by the command to render **to God what belongs to God**. It has been suggested that there is here an allusion to Gen. 1.26f., and that the meaning is that those who bear the image of God belong to him and owe him all that they are. Although the saying is probably less subtle than this, it certainly suggests that man's duty to God is something much more important than his duty to Caesar. The Zealots believed that they could serve God by denying the authority of Caesar; by placing his two commands side by side, Jesus denies that men will come to God's Kingdom by destroying Caesar's. As for the opponents of Jesus, they have as usual concentrated on a minor issue – the payment of taxes – and so ignored the fundamental question, which was whether or not they were paying to God what they owed to him. Jesus' own answer to this question, *vis-à-vis* the religious leaders, has just been set out for us by Mark in the preceding parable: they have consistently refused to give God what they should.

The final comment, that the people **were totally amazed**, is typical of Mark. Probably he thinks of them being astonished at the authority of Jesus' reply, rather than at its cleverness.

# 6   ANOTHER TRICK QUESTION: ABOUT THE RESURRECTION                     12.18–27

*(Matt. 22.23–33; Luke 20.27–40)*

(18) Then Sadducees came to him (it is they who say that there is no resurrection) and asked him, (19) 'Teacher, Moses laid this down for us: if a man's brother dies and leaves a wife but does not leave children, his brother should take the wife and raise up children for his brother. (20) Now there were seven brothers; the first took a wife, and when he died he left no children; (21) the second took her and died, leaving no children, and so did the third. (22) None of the seven had any children; finally, the woman

died as well. (23) In the resurrection, whose wife will she be, since all seven married her?' (24) Jesus said to them, 'Is this not why you are wrong? You are ignorant both of the scriptures and of the power of God. (25) When they rise from the dead, they will neither marry nor be given in marriage, but will be like the angels in heaven. (26) As for the resurrection of the dead, have you not read in the book of Moses, in the passage about the bush, how God spoke to him, saying, "I am the God of Abraham, and the God of Isaac and the God of Jacob"? (27) He is not the God of the dead, but of the living: you are totally wrong.'

Another pronouncement story continues the theme of controversy between Jesus and the religious authorities. This time the attack is made by a group of **Sadducees**, members of the Jewish priestly aristocracy. Their name apparently derives from Zadok, high priest in the time of David, but it is not clear why or how it came to be used; they do not seem to have formed any kind of organized party. What is clear is that the Sadducees belonged to privileged, priestly families, and that they were conservative in outlook, distrusting anything new or progressive. This is illustrated by the fact that they rejected such comparatively recent beliefs as the resurrection and the existence of angels. They regarded only the written Law as binding, and in this they were at odds with the Pharisees, who accepted not only the written Law, but the oral tradition as well. It is often said that the Sadducees rejected the authority of the Prophets and Writings and accepted the Pentateuch alone, but there is nothing in Josephus' account of their teaching to support this; nevertheless, it is likely that they regarded the Pentateuch as having far greater authority than the other books. Clearly there was a great gulf, not only between Sadducees and Pharisees, but between Sadducees and the ordinary people. (See Josephus, *Wars*, II.8.14; *Antiquities*, XIII.10.6; XVIII.1.4; Schürer, *History*, II, pp. 404–14).

The topic raised by the Sadducees' question was therefore one on which they were in fundamental disagreement with the Pharisees. If the incident goes back to Jesus' own lifetime, then it is interesting to note that Jesus sided with the Pharisees. Moreover, since it seems unlikely that the Sadducees regarded Jesus as an authority on doctrine or genuinely respected his opinion, they presumably set their question in order to ridicule his beliefs: in other words, they assumed that his views on this matter would agree with those of the Pharisees. This is a useful reminder that Jesus was probably a great deal closer to the Pharisaic party than the reader of the New Testament, influenced by its anti-Pharisaic propaganda, often realizes.

Jesus' answer falls into two parts. The first (v.25) deals with the question by explaining that the manner of resurrection life is quite different from that which is presupposed in the problem: in other words, the Sadducees' ridicule of the fashionable belief in the resurrection is met by Jesus' scornful dismissal of their crude understanding of what the resurrection will be like. The second (v.26) leaves the question which has been put to Jesus on one side and deals with the real issue which lies behind it – whether or not the dead will be raised. This second answer 'proves' the resurrection (in typical rabbinic manner) by means of a citation from **the book of Moses** – the one authority accepted by the Sadducees. It is possible that one or other of these two responses is a later addition to the story. The first interrupts the logic which links v.24 with vv.26f., and it is as much an answer to the Pharisees (whose debates the Sadducees are mocking) as to the Sadducees themselves. The second begins awkwardly with the new introduction in v.26. Both answers are relevant to the debate, and both would have been useful in the controversies on this topic between Jews and Christians which must certainly have taken place. It is impossible now to sort out the history of the pericope: if two traditions have been combined this may have taken place before the story came into Mark's hands. The topic is obviously a suitable one for **Sadducees** to raise, even though their question would certainly have been posed in a scoffing or contemptuous manner (see above on Daube's interpretation, p. 278f.). There is Markan irony in the picture of Sadducees scoffing at the notion of resurrection in the context of the passion narrative: those who know the end of the story know very well that God **is not the God of the dead, but of the living.**

**It is they who say that there is no resurrection.** This seems to 18 have been one of the most important features of the Sadducees' position; it is remarked on by Josephus (*Antiquities*, XVIII.1.4 and *Wars*, II.18.14). They address Jesus as **Teacher**, the form of address 19 used by the previous group of questioners in v.14: it is the natural term to use when Jesus is being asked to pronounce on matters of conduct and doctrine. The question that is put to him is based on the law about levirate marriage set out in Deut. 25.5–10: **Moses laid this down for us: if a man's brother dies and leaves a wife but does not leave children, his brother should take the wife and raise up children for his brother.** The law was intended to provide a man with heirs, who would preserve his name and inherit his property. The point of the Sadducees' argument is that it is clear from his legislation that Moses did not believe in the resurrection.

**Now there were seven brothers**; the number is typical of such 20 stories. **Whose wife will she be?** Similar questions about the relevance 23 of Mosaic legislation in the world to come were apparently seriously debated by the rabbis.

**Is this not why you are wrong?** The Greek is obscure. Probably it 24 means 'The reason why you make the mistake you do – in failing to accept the resurrection – is that you do not really know either the scriptures or the power of God'. The Sadducees, who based every-thing on **the scriptures**, are accused of failing to understand their true significance. **The power of God** presumably refers to his power to raise the dead (cf. 1 Cor. 6.14); the Sadducees, by denying the re-surrection, are denying the power of God to create life. Power is so much a characteristic of God that the word is used instead of the divine name in Mark 14.62. The twin appeal to the witness of the scriptures and the power (or Spirit) of God, experienced in the resur-rection, became characteristic of Christian preaching (e.g. Gal. 3; 1 Cor. 1.18–31; Acts 2.14–36).

It has been suggested that the word 'power' in this verse has in fact replaced 'powers', and that this was a reference to the 'Geburoth' or 'Powers', the term by which the second of the Eighteen Benedictions in the synagogue service is known. The first benediction, 'Aboth', praises the God of the patriarchs, the second praises him for his mighty acts, which include raising the dead. If, as is probable, these two benedictions date from pre-Christian times, then perhaps the Sadducees are being attacked for ignoring the witness of both the scriptures and the liturgy (see H. Loewe in *A Rabbinic Anthology*, ed. C.G. Montefiore and H. Loewe, p. 369). This ingenious theory does not really explain the argument here, however, for though the Sad-ducees certainly claimed to believe the scriptures (or at least the Torah), and maintained that they alone took them seriously, they did not accept the tradition which included the prayers. Indeed, the re-ference to resurrection in this particular benediction may well have been introduced precisely in order to refute the Sadducees' denial of the doctrine: they were scarcely likely, then, to 'know' the prayer!

25     **When they rise from the dead, they will neither marry nor be given in marriage, but will be like the angels in heaven.** This say-ing raises problems, since it suggests that the life of heaven is a blood-less existence where the warmth of human relationships has ceased to matter. In speaking of marriage, however, Jesus would have been concerned – as was normal at that time – with questions of property and legitimacy, and what he is rejecting is therefore the notion that this social contract continues in the resurrection life. The implication is perhaps that the limitations of this bond will be removed in the age to come, allowing a wider and deeper experience of human relation-ships in an existence which will be very different from that of this present age. Jesus rejects materialistic notions of the resurrection life: its nature will be quite different from life in the present age. Compare Paul's comments in 1 Cor. 15.35–50 on the differences between the earthly and the resurrection bodies. Since angels were thought to be immortal, marriage was, for them, clearly unnecessary. By bringing angels into the argument, Jesus affirms another of the contemporary beliefs denied by the Sadducees.

The non-materialistic view of the future world is echoed by a saying in the Talmud attributed to Rab, a teacher of the third century AD: 'The world to come is not like this world. In the world to come there is no eating or drinking or begetting or bargaining or envy or hate or strife; but the righteous sit with crowns on their heads and are satisfied with the glory of God's presence' (B. Berakoth 17a). Other descriptions of the world to come are far less spiritual, but it is by no means clear that accounts of sumptuous feasting and drinking were intended to be taken literally. Such descriptions were more appropriately applied to the messianic age, which was a this-worldly concept, though popular opinion probably confused the two.

**As for the resurrection of the dead. . . .** The resumptive phrase 26 suggests an independent saying, but the argument follows on from the complaint in v.24 that the Sadducees **are ignorant . . . of the scriptures.** Jesus quotes from **the book of Moses, in the passage about the bush.** This method of referring to a particular passage by a key phrase (here lit. 'at the bush') was the normal one at the time, since chapter and verse divisions were unknown.

The belief that the patriarchs were still alive is found elsewhere – cf. 4 Macc. 7.19; 16.25. The way in which the text is used here to 'prove' that they must be living seems entirely artificial to modern readers, but it was a normal method of exegesis at the time. The argument is that since God describes himself as **the God of Abraham, and the God of Isaac and the God of Jacob,** these patriarchs must still exist. This does not depend on the use of the present tense, **I am,** since there is no verb, either in the Greek here or in the Hebrew of Ex. 3.6; rather it depends on the belief that God would not have described himself as the God of dead heroes, since **He is not the God of the** 27 **dead, but of the living.** Strictly speaking, this argument says nothing about resurrection: it could point equally well to immortality of the soul. But in Jewish thought, the future life was identified with the resurrection of the body, without which it was impossible to experience anything except some kind of shadowy existence that was worse than extinction. Although the method of argument may seem strange, the conviction that underlies it is perhaps more familiar: if God is the God of the patriarchs (and of those who came after them), he does not cease to be their God at their death; experience of fellowship with God demands belief in some kind of continuing relationship with him.

**You are totally wrong.** Instead of the usual comment about the crowd's astonishment, Mark repeats Jesus' emphatic declaration that the Sadducees were in error. Matthew prefers to note the reaction of the crowd (Matt. 22.33) and Luke tells us that Jesus' answer impressed the scribes and silenced his opponents (Luke 20.39f.). But Mark's ending also, in its own way, serves to underline the authority of Jesus, who can dismiss the arguments of the Sadducees in this way.

# 7   A QUESTION ABOUT THE LAW   12.28–34

*(Matt. 22.34–40; Luke 10.25–8)*

(28) One of the teachers of the Law came up and heard them disputing, and observing how well he answered them, he asked him, 'Which commandment is first of them all?' (29) Jesus answered, 'The first is, "Hear, O Israel! The Lord our God is the one [Lord], (30) and you shall love the Lord your God with all your heart and with all your soul and with all your mind and with all your strength." (31) The second is this: "You shall love your neighbour as yourself." There is no other commandment greater than these.' (32) And the scribe said to him, 'Well said, Teacher. You are right in saying that he is one, and that there is none but he. (33) And to love him with all one's heart and with all one's understanding and with all one's strength, and to love one's neighbour as oneself is far more than all burnt offerings and sacrifices.' (34) Then Jesus, seeing how thoughtfully he had answered, said to him, 'You are not far from the Kingdom of God.' And after that, no one dared to ask him anything.

Mark portrays the scribe as an honest questioner in search of truth. This is surprising in view of the hostile attitude of the previous questioners; it is even more surprising when we remember the antagonism shown to Jesus by the scribes elsewhere in Mark. In contrast, both Matthew and Luke (who has the story in a different context) say specifically that the question was put to Jesus in order to test him (Matt. 22.35; Luke 10.25). In Luke there is a further difference: Jesus throws the ball back to his questioner and asks him what is written in the Law, so that it is the lawyer who makes the reply which Mark attributes to Jesus. Commentators are unable to agree as to whether the Markan or Lukan version of the story is more likely to be the earlier. In favour of Mark, it is argued that the presence of a friendly scribe is unusual (and therefore authentic) and that Luke's account shows signs of adaptation to fit the context (introducing the parable which follows) and has been conformed to the typical pattern of a conflict story used in early Church controversies. In favour of Luke, it can be argued that it is more likely that a story which attributed a notable saying to one of Jesus' opponents would have been altered by the Church to a story where Jesus pronounces the words than vice versa, and that Mark's repetition of the saying by the scribe in vv.32f. reflects the earlier version. This is a good example of the difficulties involved in tracing the development of the tradition, and a further reminder that the earliest gospel does not necessarily contain the earliest account of a particular incident. Perhaps the right conclusion in this case is that both accounts show development: Luke in emphasizing the hostility between Jesus and the Jewish leaders, Mark in attributing the saying to Jesus. Matthew appears to have amalgamated the two versions, presumably taking them from Mark and 'Q'. Either Mark inherited the story with its approbation of the scribe, or for some reason he changed a conflict story into the form it has in his gospel. The former is possible, the latter requires explanation. One possible solution is provided by Daube's suggestion about the grouping of these stories (see above, p. 278f.): if the third questioner represents the 'pious son' who is ready to accept good teaching, this could explain the scribe's readiness to hear Jesus. Another is that Mark thought it appropriate that the central demands of God to his people should be found in Jesus' mouth.

It is significant that Jesus appeals to the Torah in his answer: he endorses what the scriptures say. There is no conflict between the commands of God which are set out there and the demands of the gospel. The challenge to love God and to love one's neighbour, once addressed to Israel, is addressed now to Mark's readers and is as appropriate for them as it was for the scribe in the story.

**One of the teachers of the Law**: Mark uses the term γραμματεύς 28 which has been translated elsewhere as 'scribe' for brevity's sake (as in v.32); we have varied the translation here as a reminder that the man was in fact engaged in expounding the Torah. **Which commandment is first of them all?** The question put to Jesus was one that was commonly discussed by the rabbis. There were said to be 365 prohibitions and 248 positive commands in the Torah, and attempts were made to summarize its demands. The issue was not which of the commandments was the most important (since all were important and must be kept), but whether there was some basic principle from which the whole Law could be derived. In reply, Jesus 29 quotes the opening words of the *Shema* (Deut. 6.4), which is recited daily by pious Jews: **Hear, O Israel! The Lord our God is the one [Lord].** Matthew and Luke do not include these words, and they could perhaps have been included here simply because in Deuteronomy they introduce the commandment which Jesus declares to be the 'first'. Nevertheless, they are certainly relevant to what follows, since the whole Law is understood as the nation's response to God's call of Israel to be his people. **You shall love the Lord 30 your God with all your heart and with all your soul and with all your mind and with all your strength.** The Hebrew of Deut. 6.5 reads 'heart ... soul ... and might' (translated in the LXX by καρδία ... ψυχή ... δύναμις). The Markan διάνοια (mind) is used as an alternative translation in the LXX for 'heart', and ἰσχύς (strength) is used here instead of 'might'.

**The second is this**: asked for one commandment, Jesus gives two. 31

Luke runs the two together into one. Certainly they belong together and are therefore held together in the concluding comment: **There is no other commandment greater than these.** Faith and ethics are so closely bound together in the Old Testament as to be virtually indistinguishable. The command to **love** one's **neighbour** arises from the command to love God, and the love of God is empty unless it issues in love of neighbour. This second quotation is from Lev. 19.18, and between them these two Old Testament citations sum up the demands of the Decalogue. In Leviticus, it is clear from the parallelism that the neighbour referred to is a fellow Israelite, but by the time of Jesus the term seems to have been extended to include non-Jews resident in Israel.

Others beside Jesus quoted these passages in reply to similar questions; e.g. R. Akiba (second century AD) quoted Lev. 19.18 (Sifra 89b), while R. Hillel (first century AD) is said to have taught: 'what is hateful to yourself, do not do to your neighbour; this is the whole Law, the rest is commentary' (B. Sab. 31a; cf. Matt. 7.12 = Luke 6.31). The Law is summarized as love of God and love of neighbour in Test. Issachar 5.2 (cf. 7.6) and Test. Dan 5.3, but the Testaments of the Twelve Patriarchs have been subjected to Christian editing and so cannot be relied on as witnesses to Jewish beliefs. Nevertheless, there is enough evidence to suggest that the answer attributed here to Jesus might well have been given by the scribe, as Luke indicates. His reply can be interpreted in two ways, however. One is to take these two commands as the basis from which all others can be deduced: ultimately, all the regulations in the Torah can be understood as ways of spelling out how one should love God and love one's neighbour. The other is to say that, since what matters is loving God and one's neighbour, the other laws are fulfilled in these and therefore need no longer be assiduously kept. The former view seems to be held by Matthew who adds to Jesus' words the comment 'On these two commandments depend all the Law and the prophets' (22.40), and who attributes to him also the saying 'till heaven and earth pass away, not an iota, not a dot, will pass from the Law' (5.18). This is presumably the way in which Jewish rabbis who quoted similar summaries would have understood the saying here: it underlined the purpose of all the Law's commandments without in any way undermining their necessity. It is easy, on the other hand, to see how some Christians were able to interpret the saying in the second way, as meaning that love was the essential feature of the Law, and particular regulations unimportant. While the first way of understanding the saying could be used to support a rigorist view of the Law, we need to remember that the second could lead to to the opposite extreme, since it was open to the danger of being interpreted as justification for antinomianism.

The view that love is the one essential element of the Law is expressed by Paul in Rom. 13.8, when he says that the person 'who loves his neighbour has fulfilled the Law'. The comparative evaluation 33 offered by the scribe in Mark 12.33, when he says that the principle of love **is far more than all burnt offerings and sacrifices,** reflects a similar approach, though, of course, the words do not necessarily imply that the burnt offerings and sacrifices are unimportant: since the conversation is said to have taken place in the temple, where burnt offerings and sacrifices were offered up, the scribe himself has presumably come to worship there. The insistence that attitudes and behaviour are more important than religious observance echoes similar statements in the Old Testament, e.g. Jer. 7.22f.; Hos. 6.6. But the fact that Mark has placed this incident in the temple, following after Jesus' dramatic action there (11.12–17) and almost immediately before his prophecy of its destruction in 13.1f., suggests that for him the scribe's words would have been understood as an endorsement of Jesus' condemnation of the worship offered in the temple as inadequate. For the members of Mark's church, who probably did not offer the sacrifices set out in the Jewish Law, the story would have been of great value, encouraging them in the belief that the real demands of God lay elsewhere.

In Matthew and Luke, the pericope ends with the words of Jesus – the normal form for a pronouncement story. Mark's version includes the scribe's approval and elaboration of Jesus' saying. Christians are inclined to assume that any teaching in the gospels which challenged current Jewish orthodoxy must derive directly from him, but it is worth noting that on this issue – and no other – Mark believes Jesus and his interlocutor to have been in agreement: the scribe fully endorses Jesus' reply. Jesus himself may have been more concerned with stressing the purpose of the Law than with drawing the corollary that some of its regulations were unimportant. Certainly this story reminds us again that Jesus may have been closer to some of his Jewish contemporaries than the gospels often suggest: others shared his concern for what was essential.

Jesus, in turn, endorses the scribe's answer; his commendation is 34 somewhat strange, in view of the fact that the scribe has done little more than repeat Jesus' own reply. This is perhaps an indication that, in an earlier version of the story, it was the scribe who provided the answer to his own question (cf. Luke 10.25–8). But Mark's account makes an interesting theological point: the teacher of the Law assumes that he is entitled to approve Jesus' teaching, but in fact the roles are reversed, and it is Jesus who approves his. The statement that the scribe is **not far from the Kingdom of God** is understood by some to mean that he does not have far to go to qualify, by others to be a promise that he will enter when the Kingdom arrives. Whether the

Kingdom is understood to be present or future – or half and half – the point of the saying is that by his response the scribe has shown that his attitude is the right one. He is honest in his desire to love God **with all one's heart and with all one's understanding and with all one's strength.** Contrast Luke 10.29, where the same scribe is said to have attempted to justify himself and is portrayed as a legalist. **Then Jesus. . .said to him, 'You are not far from the Kingdom of God.'** Mark has already told us that it is those who accept the teaching of Jesus who are given the secret of the Kingdom of God (4.11), so that it is not surprising to find him presenting someone who readily accepts Jesus' teaching as being near the Kingdom. By describing the scribe's enthusiastic response, Mark once again underlines the authority of Jesus' teaching – something he normally does by saying that Jesus silenced his opponents (cf. 11.33; 12.12, 17, 27). The final effect, however, is the same: after that **no one dared to ask him** any question (but see below, on v.35).

# 8   JESUS ASKS A QUESTION                   12.35–7

*(Matt. 22.41–6; Luke 20.41–4)*

**(35) And as Jesus was teaching in the temple, he said. 'How is it that the teachers of the Law say that the Christ is the son of David? (36) David himself, [inspired] by the Holy Spirit, said,**

> **"The Lord said to my Lord,**
> **Sit at my right hand.**
> **Until I have put your enemies**
> **Under your feet."**

**(37) David himself calls him "Lord", so how can he be his son?" And a great crowd listened to him eagerly.**

Having silenced all who questioned him, Jesus now poses a question himself. In Matthew, this is addressed to the Pharisees and concerns their own teaching, and the incident has thereby become a conflict story, but in Mark it is presented as part of Jesus' teaching to the crowd. The theme is totally unexpected, since Jesus here initiates a discussion about the nature of his messiahship and does so in public. This in itself raises obvious questions for the modern reader. Even stranger is the fact that Jesus apparently attacks what the Church believed, namely that he was of Davidic descent: if the Messiah is David's lord, he asks, **how can he be his son?** One explanation of the pericope is that it originated in disputes between Jews and Christians regarding the latter's claim that Jesus was the Messiah: it provides a defence of this claim, against Jewish objections that he could not be the Messiah because he was not of Davidic descent. An alternative explanation is that it reflects internal Christian debates and represents an attack on the assumption of some Christians that, because Jesus was the Messiah, he must be of Davidic descent. Strangely enough, there is very little reference to Jesus' Davidic descent elsewhere in the New Testament. We have only Rom. 1.3 (which is echoed in 2 Tim. 2.8), Rom. 15.12 and Acts 2.30 (by implication); the genealogies of Matthew and Luke and the reference to the house of David in Luke 1.69; and three passages in Revelation (3.7; 5.5; 22.16). We may accept Rom. 1.3 as early evidence (especially if it is a pre-Pauline formula), and the genealogies, which are hardly consistent with the belief in the virgin birth, since they trace Jesus' ancestry through Joseph, may represent early attempts to establish Jesus' Davidic ancestry. But apart from John 7.42 there is no evidence that Jesus' Davidic descent was ever questioned. There is, then, little indication that this was an issue, either in Jewish-Christian debates, or within the Christian community.

The quotation from Ps. 110.1, on the other hand, is not only used elsewhere (Acts 2.34f.; Heb. 1.13), but is widely echoed in passages where Jesus is said to be seated at God's right hand (e.g. Mark 14.62; Col. 3.1; Heb. 1.3; cf. also 1 Cor. 15.25). If this psalm was widely used in Christian apologetic, it would have been natural to discuss how it was to be related to the traditional Jewish belief in a Davidic Messiah. This would provide an understandable *Sitz im Leben* for the argument developed in Mark 12.35–7; the pericope is likely to have been used, therefore, in christological debates in the Church concerning the best way of understanding Jesus' role and status.

It is much more difficult to suggest a possible setting in the life of Jesus himself. In his mouth, it could be understood only as a clear messianic claim, and this is totally out of character with the rest of our evidence. The argument that the Messiah is greater than David belongs to the theology of the Church, not the teaching of Jesus. It is true that some commentators (e.g. Taylor) have argued for its authenticity on the grounds that it is at once allusive (concealing and revealing Jesus' identity) and challenging. But it is allusive precisely because it is put into the mouth of Jesus (without a Johannine 'I am' to make the identification clear), and it is challenging because the unsolved riddle is left for us to work out. Challenging the teaching of Jesus certainly is, but it is a characteristic of Mark's style to challenge his readers by posing questions about the true identity of Jesus (cf. 4.41; 8.29; 11.28).

For Mark, the saying must have been understood as a statement about Jesus' messiahship: although Jesus' claim to be himself

David's lord is only implicit, it is nevertheless plain. Certainly Mark did not imagine that Jesus happened to discuss the significance of this particular passage by chance! The challenge to the Jewish authorities to accept Jesus as their Messiah is here made clear. It is significant that both here and in 8.27–30 the initiative is taken by Jesus himself. There is in Mark's view no excuse for those who fail to recognize Jesus as Lord. In chapter 8, Jesus' questioning led us to see that he is greater than the prophets; in chapter 12, it points us to the fact that he is greater than David.

What is less clear is the logic of the pericope itself. Is it a denial of Jesus' Davidic descent? If so, Mark does not seem to have thought so, since he apparently sees no contradiction with the title 'Son of David' used in 10.47. Matthew and Luke, also, were happy to take the story over, even though they were at pains in their opening chapters to trace the descent of Jesus from David. The evangelists apparently saw no problem, and this suggests that they understood this passage, not as a denial of Jesus' Davidic descent, but as an affirmation of something more important – his lordship, which made him superior to the political Messiah of Jewish patriotic hopes, superior even to David himself. If it is objected that the straightforward logic of the passage must mean that David's lord cannot be his descendant, then we need to remember not only the Semitic idiom whereby a comparison could be expressed by using a negative (cf. Hos. 6.6 with Mark 12.33), but also that the saying is put in the form of a question, almost a conundrum. It challenges its hearers to think about the position of the one who is now being proclaimed as Christ and to recognize that he is not simply 'Son of David' but much more. An interesting parallel is to be found in Rom. 1.3f., our earliest testimony to Jesus' descent. Here we are told that Jesus 'was descended from David according to the flesh', but that he was 'designated Son of God in power according to the Spirit'. 'Son of David' and 'Son of God' are held together as complementary truths; Jesus' Davidic descent is not denied, but it is clear that for Paul, at least, the fact that Jesus is Son of God is of far greater significance. The inadequacy of the term 'Son of David' explains why it is so little used in the New Testament. But it was inadequate not simply because it accorded too low a status to the exalted Jesus, but because its background made it misleading in a Jewish context and meaningless in a Gentile one. Our pericope seems to reflect an important stage in the formulation of christological ideas, as the Church sought for ways of expressing its beliefs about Jesus. Certainly it would have assured Mark's community that Jesus' lordship was universal.

Why has Mark placed the pericope here? The message it conveys is that Jesus is to be acknowledged as 'Lord'. Once again, we are reminded of Mal. 3.1, which speaks of the Lord coming to his temple. It is perhaps significant that it is in the temple that Jesus comes closer to revealing his identity than anywhere else. Is this perhaps why Mark describes the incident as taking place **as Jesus was teaching in** 35 **the temple?** This is usually said to be a somewhat unnecessary phrase, resulting from Mark's use of traditional material, since according to his own narrative Jesus has been engaged in continuous dialogue in the temple since 11.27. But perhaps it is a deliberate reminder that Jesus is in the temple, put there to help us to see the significance of the disclosure which he is about to make.

Whatever the reason for the repetition, Mark's emphasis on Jesus' activity in teaching is typical. Daube suggests that the last sentence of v.34 belongs to this pericope, and that it explains why Jesus now takes the initiative: he puts the question on behalf of those who cannot ask for themselves (see above, p. 278f.). **How is it that the teachers of the Law say that the Christ is the son of David?** Daube's suggestion would perhaps give some point to Mark's redundant ἀποκριθεὶς (lit. 'answering', but here left untranslated) at the beginning of v.35. Once again, we have translated γραμματεύς by 'teacher of the Law', rather than 'scribe', because the discussion concerns the teaching of scripture.

The whole argument depends on the belief that Psalm 110 was 36 written by **David himself.** Like many of the psalms, this one is attributed to David, and this would naturally have been assumed to be correct by any Jew living in the first century AD. Old Testament scholars now believe the psalm to be later than the time of David, possibly much later, though the view that it contains a hidden reference to Simon Maccabaeus seems fanciful. David is said to have spoken the words when **[inspired] by** (lit. 'in') **the Holy Spirit;** that is, they are understood as a prophecy with divine authority. **The Lord** refers, of course, to God, while **my Lord** was, for the author of the psalm, the king: in other words, the psalm was about the king rather than by him. The psalm is assumed here to be about the Messiah, and this was probably the interpretation given to it in first-century Judaism, though of this we have no evidence. For Christians, **Lord** was a term used of Jesus himself. The use of the Aramaic phrase *māranā thā* in 1 Cor. 16.22 indicates that he was addressed as 'our Lord' from the early days of the Church. The invitation to **sit at my right hand** will be echoed in Jesus' claim before the high priest in 14.62.

**Under your feet:** this is the one phrase in the quotation which varies from the LXX version of Psalm 110. In Greek, in fact, only one word has been changed, giving us 'under' (ὑποκάτω) for 'footstool' (ὑποπόδιον). The exact phrase is, however, used in Ps. 8.6, and its presence in Mark may reflect the influence of another psalm which became popular in Christian circles. **David himself calls him 'Lord',** 37

293

so how can he be his son? For the significance of this comment, see the discussion above.

And a great crowd listened to him eagerly. Mark often rounds off a pericope with an account of the crowd's reaction, so it is natural that he should do so here, though many editors prefer to understand this sentence as the introduction to the next paragraph. The Greek could perhaps mean 'the mass of the people' – i.e. the ordinary people as distinct from the religious authorities.

## 9  JESUS ATTACKS THE TEACHERS OF THE LAW
12.38–40

*(Matt. 23.1–36; Luke 20.45–7)*

**(38) And in his teaching he said, 'Beware of the scribes, who like to walk about in long robes, and to be acknowledged in the market places, (39) to occupy the front seats in the synagogues, and places of honour at feasts. (40) They eat up the property of widows and say long prayers for show: they will receive the greater condemnation.'**

The previous paragraph could be understood as an attack on the teaching of the scribes – of whom the one scribe in vv.28–34 was not typical; certainly this paragraph is an attack on their behaviour. Perhaps it is this link which explains its present position. Not all **scribes** were guilty of the hypocrisy which is attacked here, as the story in vv.28–34 demonstrates, but warnings about the behaviour of particular scribes tended to become sharpened into blanket condemnation of the whole party in the bitter conflict between the Church and the Jewish authorities. Those who are condemned here care nothing for true religion but are concerned only with their own position.

Once again, what is under attack here is false piety, acting as a cloak to injustice. Jesus' words in v.40 echo those of several of the prophets, but it is perhaps worth noting that in Mal. 3.5, judgement is pronounced on those who oppress the widow: Mark may have chosen to include these verses here because they were appropriate to the picture of the Lord, come in judgement to the temple.

38 **And in his teaching he said**: Mark's new introduction gives the impression that he has picked this passage out of a longer section of teaching. This impression may be accidental, but it is of course possible that he has done precisely that. It is interesting to note that vv.38f.

form part of a much longer condemnation of the scribes and Pharisees found in Matt. 23, and this suggests that Mark may have made a selection from the tradition about Jesus' teaching on this particular theme. The use made of this material illustrates the complexity of the relationship between the Synoptics. Matthew has placed his long section attacking the scribes and Pharisees in the equivalent position to this one, immediately after the question concerning the Messiah. Luke has taken over Mark 12.38–40 at the corresponding point in his gospel, but instead of expanding it he has placed his attack on the Pharisees and scribes, containing material parallel to that used in Matthew 23, in a totally different context in chapter 11.

**Beware of the scribes, who like to walk about in long robes.** The scribes apparently wore a particularly long version of the *tallith*, or outer garment, when they were at prayer or engaged in other religious activities. They are condemned here for parading their religion and wearing these clothes in order to be seen and so admired for their piety. As men of superior learning, they expected to receive salutations **in the market places. The front seats in the synagogues were** 39 regarded as the best; to sit there, facing the rest of the congregation, gave one eminence over the ordinary worshippers. **They eat up the** 40 **property of widows**: this is a separate saying which is not found after the 'Q' version of vv.38f. (Matt. 23.6 = Luke 11.43). It is not at all clear that it is the same group of men who are being condemned, and it is possible to translate: 'As for those who. . . .' Exploitation of the poor was not a sin to which the scribes were particularly prone, and this accusation might have been made more appropriately against the rich priestly party; condemnation of those who exploit the helpless is familiar enough (e.g. Isa. 10.2). Duncan Derrett makes the interesting suggestion that the accusation here was directed against trustees or guardians who had been appointed to look after estates, but who took more than their proper share as expenses; similar complaints about such men are found in later Jewish sources (*Studies in the New Testament*, I, pp. 118–27). But why should such men be accused here not simply of exploitation, but of false piety? Derrett suggests that their long prayers were an attempt to encourage possible clients to entrust them with their property, and that the word προφάσει (translated **for show**) implies an ulterior motive, rather than a false pretext. Whichever way we interpret it, the accusation brought against these men is similar to that made in vv.38f., though their guilt is greater than those who are attacked there. We are left to work out for ourselves why this group deserves **the greater condemnation**. The answer can be suitably summed up by reference back to vv.28–34: those who parade their piety are merely guilty of silly ostentation, but those who oppress the defenceless are certainly failing not only to love God, but also to love their neighbour.

# 10   A WIDOW'S GIFT                          12.41–4

*(Luke 21.1–4)*

(41) While he was sitting opposite the treasury, he saw the crowd throw money into the treasury; and many who were rich threw in large sums. (42) And a poor widow came up and threw in two tiny coins (the equivalent of a penny). (43) And calling his disciples, he said to them. 'I tell you truly that this poor widow has thrown in more than all who have contributed to the treasury, (44) for they all contributed out of their surplus, but she, out of her need, has put in everything she possessed – all that she had to live on.'

In contrast to the men who exploit poor widows, we have the **poor widow** who sacrifices all she has. It is often assumed that this pericope has been linked to the preceding one in the oral tradition because they each contained the word 'widow', and this is certainly one possibility. But it is also possible that they have been deliberately brought together (perhaps by Mark) because of their content. Certainly the illustration of true worship and generosity provided by the widow stands in sharp contrast not only to the rich who gave large sums, but to the scribes condemned for their ostentatious piety in the preceding verses. Jesus praises the woman for giving all that she has – though an infinitesimal amount; it is interesting to compare 14.3ff., where another woman is praised by him for making a gift – this time of a vastly expensive jar of perfume. Each woman makes an extravagant gesture by her gift, though in a very different way. The story is a reminder to Mark's readers that the humblest and poorest of them can make a worthy offering to God.

41    **He saw the crowd throw money into the treasury**; this is sometimes taken as a reference to a special room in the temple to which offerings could be brought, but it is more likely that it means one of the thirteen chests, shaped like a trumpet, which stood round the court of women. In contrast to the **many who were rich** who **threw**
42    **in large sums**, the woman threw in **two tiny coins**. The coin referred to here (τὸ λεπτόν – a *lepton* – 'mite' in the A.V.) was the smallest in circulation in Palestine. It is possible that it was not in use in the West, and that this is why Mark explains that two of them are **the equivalent of a penny**. But perhaps he merely wishes to emphasize that the widow might, had she chosen, have made a gift to the temple without parting with her last coin: she was down to her last penny, but she could at least have divided it. The value of the coins was infinitesimal. There were two *lepta* in a *quadrans*, and four *quadrans* in an *assarion* or *as*, which was worth one-sixteenth of a *denarius*: the two *lepta* together were therefore worth one-sixty-fourth of the amount that a

labourer might expect to earn in a day. **I tell you truly that this poor** 43–4 **widow has thrown in more than all who have contributed to the treasury, for they all contributed out of their surplus, but she, out of her need, has put in everything she possessed – all that she had to live on.** The story's climax comes in the saying of Jesus, which brings out the contrast between the widow and the other visitors to the temple, whose piety cost them little. Her offering is acceptable because it arises out of the love for God and neighbour commended in vv.30–3.

## *INTRODUCTORY NOTE TO MARK 13*

Mark 13 is unlike any other section of Mark's gospel. First of all, it is unusual in form, in that it is a connected discourse with a unifying theme. It is true that, like the collections of sayings earlier in the gospel, it shows clear signs of having been pieced together, but here the material has been so arranged that the theme of the speech is developed stage by stage. The closest similarity is with chapter 4, but that is a collection of parables on the same theme, rather than a discourse. There are, however, literary precedents elsewhere for a speech of this kind being placed on a great man's lips at the very end of his life. In Gen. 49.2–27, for example, Jacob predicts what will happen to his descendants; in Deuteronomy 32, Moses addresses the people shortly before his death; and in 1 Chronicles 28, David hands over the kingdom to Solomon. Whole books were written in the form of farewell discourses (The Testaments of the Twelve Patriarchs and the Assumption (or Testament) of Moses) and in the classical world we may compare Socrates' farewell in *Phaedo* (though that is written in the typical form of a Platonic dialogue). There are parallels elsewhere in the New Testament (John 14–17 and Acts 20.17–38).

Secondly, Mark 13 is unusual in theme, since it is concerned with setting out future events right up to the parousia; once again, we can find partial parallels in the earlier Markan material, in so far as some of the sayings which make up the discourse are similar to sayings used in earlier chapters, but we have to turn elsewhere to find real parallels to the overall theme. Here, the background is to be found in Jewish apocalyptic writing, the clearest examples of which are perhaps 4 Ezra 13 and 1 Enoch 37–71, and, in the Old Testament, Daniel 7–12.

Apocalyptic is a notoriously complex area of study, and there are many problems involved in attempting to define it or trace its origins. The word 'apocalypse' means 'revelation', and the adjective 'apocalyptic' is used strictly of a particular form of writing in which the secrets of the universe are revealed – usually in the form of a vision, and often with the aid of certain accepted images, each of which has a particular meaning. The vision is usually attributed to some great figure in the past, so that 'future' events foretold in the vision but lying in the reader's past serve to authenticate the writer's message. It seems probable that apocalyptic writing grew out of prophecy, and it is not always easy – or indeed helpful – to say which is which: Isaiah 24–7, for example, is differently categorized by different commentators. It is in general terms true to say that apocalyptic writing is more stylized than prophetic, and that it is concerned to a large extent with the last things. It is often said that apocalyptic is more pessimistic than prophecy, but this is misleading; what is meant by this statement is that Israel's situation became so desperate that the apocalyptic writers abandoned the hope that God would set things right through the ordinary processes of history and looked instead for a more direct form of divine intervention which would involve the break-up of the present order.

One theory about the origin of Mark 13, which has been popular among commentators since it was put forward by T. Colani in the middle of the nineteenth century, is that the chapter is built on an earlier Jewish-Christian document – the so-called 'Little Apocalypse'. The tensions and apparent contradictions within the chapter, the basic structure of the chapter and its artificial setting, the expectation of an interval before the parousia and the descriptions of the events that would precede it, together with the phrases which echo apocalyptic mood and tone, are all explained, if it is recognized that the discourse goes back, not to Jesus himself, but to a document that Mark has taken over and edited. This document, it is suggested, was a 'fly-sheet', written during the Jewish War of AD 66–70 to encourage Christians (or possibly Jews, since the apocalypse was not necessarily Christian in origin) living in Judaea. Those who have accepted this idea have not always agreed about which verses to assign to the document, but it has generally been held to have included at least vv.7–8, 14–20 and 24–7. These three sections give us an outline of future events similar to those we find in Jewish apocalyptic writings:

(i) vv.7-8 *the birth-pangs* (αἱ ὠδῖνες, v.8),
(ii) vv.14–20 *the tribulation* (ἡ θλίψις, vv.19, 24),
(iii) vv.24–7 *the End* (τὸ τέλος, vv.7.13).

The existence of the 'Little Apocalypse' cannot be either proved or disproved, but this is not of great importance, since the hypothesis in fact helps us little in understanding Mark 13 as it now is. What we can say with certainty is that, whether Mark took over an already existing outline or is himself responsible for its plan, the discourse in its present form is clearly composite and shows signs of Markan editing.

It contains a number of sayings from different sources, some possibly Jewish, some of them going back to Jesus himself, and others reflecting the concerns of the Christian community in the middle of the first century. At the same time, however, the chapter is marked by an 'apocalyptic style' which sets it apart from the rest of the gospel.

Mark 13 is often referred to as 'the Markan Apocalypse', but the description is perhaps not entirely appropriate, since the discourse lacks many of the features of apocalyptic writing: there is no heavenly vision, no use of bizarre imagery, no description of what happens after the parousia – no resurrection, no judgement, no punishment or reward – and the idea that one can pinpoint the time of the End is specifically denied. The writer is more concerned to warn his readers about the dangers in store and to urge them to be prepared for a long struggle than to encourage them by suggesting that the End is near: indeed, he seems concerned to dampen down over-enthusiastic expectation of the End which can lead only to disappointment. On the other hand there is plenty of variety among the apocalyptic writings, none of which has all the features listed above, and Mark's discourse certainly has some of the characteristics of apocalyptic, since we have a programme of the events that lead up to the End, authenticated (as is the manner of apocalyptic writing) by being attributed to Jesus, and set out in the familiar language and style of apocalyptic. In fact, the label we put on this chapter matters little; what matters is that we should realize that Mark is using and adapting the ideas and imagery of his day.

One thing is certainly clear: the message of Mark 13, though ostensibly to Peter and James, John and Andrew, is in fact directed to the readers of the gospel. This emerges not only in the aside in v.14 – 'let the reader understand!' – but also in the frequent use of the pronoun 'you' throughout the chapter. Jesus specifically warns those who hear his words to be on their guard, and his warnings punctuate the discourse: vv.5, 9, 23, 33; many of the verbs are in the second person plural. Those who first heard the gospel read could hardly hear these words without realizing that the warnings were addressed to them.

This chapter is sometimes appealed to by those who wish to date Mark's gospel before AD 70 – e.g. M. Hengel, *Studies in the Gospel of Mark*, pp. 14–28. It is argued that Mark's description of the Church's troubles reflects the situation during the Jewish War, but that the reference to the desolating sacrilege in v.14 is vague and reminiscent of earlier predictions because he is writing about something that still lies in the future, whereas Luke, writing after the event, refers to the Roman armies surrounding Jerusalem (Luke 22.10). Yet it is by no means certain that Mark might not have chosen to use this mysterious phrase in order to make clear the deeper significance of the historical happenings; his parenthesis in v.14 suggests that his original readers would understand well enough to what particular event he referred and were being urged to see its real meaning (see below, on v.14).

An even more precise setting has been suggested by W. Marxsen (*Mark the Evangelist*, pp. 151ff.), who also places it in the years AD 66–70, and who argues that the purpose of Mark's gospel reaches its climax in this chapter, which was intended to urge the Christians in Jerusalem to flee to Galilee, there to wait for the parousia: his arguments are unconvincing, not least because it is difficult to understand why Mark should have written at such length and have taken so long to get to the point, if his purpose was to urge his readers to flee from Jerusalem without delay.

The purpose of Mark 13 seems, indeed, to be to urge inaction rather than action, for its overall theme is that the time is not yet. It is true that three of its sections refer to signs that some great event is about to occur (vv.14–20, 24–7, 28–31); but interwoven with these are sections which describe events which might be taken as signs but in fact are not to be understood as such (vv.5–8, 9–13, 21–3). The warning to take heed is attached to these three sections (vv.5, 9, 23), and is a warning against misunderstanding what is happening and not, as we might perhaps expect, against being caught off guard by the parousia. The final command to be on guard belongs to the last section in the chapter (vv.32–7), a passage which apparently contradicts everything preceding it by urging the need to watch constantly, since the time of the parousia is unknown to anyone. Here is the real tension in this chapter. Whatever the origin of the rest of the material (and Mark may well have adapted it to suit his purpose), it has been arranged into a coherent pattern which runs 'Do not be misled by these events; the End is not yet. . . . But when *this* happens, then watch out.' This basic message is repeated twice, in vv.5–20 and 21–7.

5–8    Take heed: the End is not yet.
9–13    Take heed: you must endure.
14–20    But when this happens, then act.
21–3    Take heed: do not be misled.
24–7    But when this happens, it is the End.
28–31    And when this happens, he is near.

The final section, by contrast, suggests the need for constant vigilance and offers no signs of the End, either true or false.

Paradoxically, it may well be this last section, which seems out of place in the discourse, that comes closest to representing Jesus' own attitude. It is understandable if an original message which ran 'Be prepared, watch: the Kingdom of God may come at any time' encouraged the early Christian community to expect an imminent end to the world; in time a new warning was needed in a situation of over-enthusiasm: 'Do not get too excited: the End is near – but not as near as all that.' This, in fact, is precisely the development which – if the epistles addressed to the Thessalonian church are both genuinely Pauline – apparently took place in the Christian community at Thessalonica. At the same time, events that had been interpreted as signs that God was working his purpose out, and therefore as warnings to Christians to be alert, became distorted into signs by which one could plot the time of the Lord's return, and so as indications that the period of the Church's suffering was over. Mark's chapter seems to reflect this second situation, and it looks very much as though he has adapted the material to fit it. The overall message is a warning that there may be more suffering yet in store – a familiar enough theme in a gospel which has emphasized that following Jesus means taking up the cross. Nevertheless, Mark encourages his readers by his confidence in the final parousia of the Son of man in glory, which brings victory not only for the Son of man, but also for the elect.

Mark 13 repeats, therefore, Mark's persistent message that the path of discipleship involves suffering, and that it is those who follow this way faithfully who will be vindicated. It is hardly surprising, then, that some of the language used in vv.9–13 and 26 about the tribulations and rewards facing the disciples 'echoes' the language that will be used about Jesus himself in the next two chapters. But linked with this theme is that of another kind of suffering – the suffering which leads not to vindication but to destruction, and in this Mark 13 is the climax of what precedes it. The previous two chapters have described Jesus' teaching ministry in the Jerusalem temple and have been concerned with Israel's failure to respond to her Messiah and with the judgement which will inevitably follow. Mark 13 thus holds together two themes which for Mark are inseparably linked: the suffering and vindication of Jesus and his followers, and the failure and punishment of his people.

We have suggested that there is a tension in this chapter between the final section in vv.32–7, which urges constant vigilance, and the carefully structured order of events in vv.5–31. In the earlier part of the discourse Mark's readers are three times told to be on guard lest they are misled by false signs (vv.5–8, 9–13, 21–3), and three times given true signs that great events are about to occur (vv.14, 24, 28). The final section suggests that the End may come at any time: the rest of the chapter expresses confidence that it will not arrive until certain things have taken place. But was Mark himself unaware of this tension? Now it is notable that the three 'true signs' that Mark gives are all of them followed so swiftly by the events they herald that they provide scarcely any warning at all; moreover, in each case the sign is of such a nature that it cannot be misunderstood, being part of the event itself. They are analogous to the four-minute warning promised to the modern world in the event of a nuclear attack – a warning given only when the missile is launched, and when real preparations are too late. So: when you see the abomination that makes desolate standing in the temple (v.14), then there is time for nothing, except to flee; when you see the heavens disintegrate (vv.24f.), then there can be no possible mistake that the End has come; when you see the fig-tree burst into leaf (v.28), then summer is upon you. What Mark has set out, then, are three false signs of the End which might mislead the faithful, and three signs that provide no real warning at all. Mark's purpose may perhaps be to discourage apocalyptic speculation – though by a strange irony his own 'timetable' of events has been used as the basis for innumerable such speculations ever since. But he is perhaps also concerned to encourage Christians who have endured persecution such as is described in vv.9–13, and who are wondering why they are still waiting for the promised day of vindication. Mark assures them that Jesus did not promise the disciples that such things would be the immediate prelude to the End. But whether to discourage those who are concerned to calculate the End, or whether to encourage those who wonder why the End has not yet come, Mark uses the traditional material he has inherited to build up a picture in which he demonstrates that the events which seemed to some to have been signs that the Lord was near were never intended to be seen in that way.

If we have correctly understood Mark's purpose, then it seems that the parable in vv.32–7 of the man on a journey may be more appropriate to his theme than at first appeared. This final paragraph of the discourse urges the need for constant watchfulness. But if the overall message of the earlier verses is that the only signs that will be given will leave no time for further preparation, then there is no inconsistency. If there is no timetable of events to lull us into the belief that there are still several events that must take place before the End, then there is need for constant vigilance. But equally, since there will be no mistaking the End when it arrives, this vigilance means patient waiting at one's post, not speculation about how much longer the delay will be.

This suggests that Mark believes himself to be living in the period after the clear sign described in v.14 – a period described vaguely by the phrase **in those days** (v.19). There has already been trouble and distress; there has already been persecution directed against Christians; clearly some had expected these to lead to the End and were disappointed. The distress described in vv.14–18 is, however, of a different kind: this refers to one particular event in one particular place, and it is interpreted by Mark as a sign of the desolation of the temple and the punishment of God's people. The fact that Mark puts two questions into the mouths of the disciples in v.4 and separates the events in Judaea from the cosmic events in vv.24–7, suggests that he regards the two as linked together, yet not identical. Perhaps the destruction of Jerusalem – prophesied so clearly by Jesus in word and sign in chapters 11 and 12 – had seemed to some like the End itself. Certainly Mark seems to regard it as the beginning of the tribulation which will continue till the End arrives. But the fact that he describes further false signs in vv.21–3 suggests that Mark and his readers are living after the fall of Jerusalem in AD 70. The temple's desolation was the sign of disaster and destruction for Israel, inaugurating the final period of tribulation, but it was not the End of all things. Of that End there will be no more signs until the heavens themselves presage the arrival of the Son of man.

See, on Mark 13, the special studies by G.R. Beasley-Murray, *Jesus and the Future* and *A Commentary on Mark 13*. Also S.G.F. Brandon, *N.T.S.*, 7, 1961, pp. 126–41; K. Grayston, *B.J.R.L.*, 56, 1974, pp. 371–87; L. Hartman, *Prophecy Interpreted*; M.D. Hooker, *B.J.R.L.*, 65, 1982, pp. 78–99.

# 11 THE TEMPLE'S DESTRUCTION                    13.1–4

*(Matt. 24.1–3; Luke 21.5–7)*

**(1) And as he left the temple, one of his disciples said to him, 'Look, teacher! What huge stones! What wonderful buildings!' (2) And Jesus said to him, 'Do you see these great buildings? There will not be one stone left here on another – not one that will not be thrown down.'**

**(3) And as he was sitting on the Mount of Olives opposite the temple, Peter and James and John and Andrew asked him privately, (4) 'Tell us, when will these things happen? What will be the sign that all these things are about to be fulfilled?'**

These opening verses serve as an introduction to Jesus' discourse. 1 First we have a link with the previous section – **as he left the temple**. The disciples' exclamation at the magnificence of the temple might have come more naturally as they were approaching, rather than leaving, the building. But their words are needed here as the cue for Jesus' prophecy of the temple's destruction. As for their reaction, that in itself is natural enough; the incident may be historical, even though Jesus' reply has been greatly extended. The magnificence of Herod's temple was famous. Begun about 20 BC, it is often said that it was still unfinished in the time of Jesus, but Josephus tells us that the sanctuary was completed in eighteen months and the outer buildings in eight years (*Antiquities*, XV.11.5–6). Certainly he speaks elsewhere of work being done on the building as late as AD 62, and John 2.20 refers to a period of 46 years, which suggests that minor work continued long after the official completion. However, this does not seem to have detracted in any way from its splendour which was, according to Josephus' description, awe-inspiring, sufficient to impress seasoned travellers, let alone men who rarely travelled anywhere. Josephus provides us with detailed descriptions of the building, its enormous size, its ornamentation, its white marble and the gold which covered the front face and reflected the sun's rays (*Antiquities*, XV.11; *Wars*, V.5). As for its **huge stones**, Josephus gives different measurements for the largest of these in different accounts – both 45 × 5 × 6 cubits and 25 × 8 × 12 cubits. (A cubit measured approximately 18 ins., or half a metre.) Even allowing for exaggeration, it seems that some of the stones were enormous, and it was no doubt their size which impressed visitors such as the disciples. But the exclamation here also sums up the sense of security felt by the Jews, confident that God would protect his own people, and encouraged by the sight of these **wonderful buildings** – the symbol of his presence with them (cf. Jer. 7.4).

2    Jesus' answer is a prophecy of the temple's destruction. This saying has a good claim to be an authentic utterance of Jesus, since it is found (in different forms) in several contexts. In John 2.19, the saying takes the form of a challenge to the Jews, 'Destroy this temple', which is interpreted by the evangelist as Jesus' body. In the Markan and Matthaean accounts of Jesus' trial, he is accused of saying that he himself will destroy the temple, but this accusation is said to be false; nevertheless it is repeated at the crucifixion (Mark 14.57f.; 15.29; Matt. 26.59–61; 27.40). Luke omits these accusations, though he relates instead how a similar charge is brought against Stephen to the effect that he has prophesied the destruction of the temple by Jesus (Acts 6.14). These various traditions look like developments from the saying we find here. There is nothing particularly surprising in Jesus' words. According to a tradition in the Talmud, Rabbi Johanan ben Zakkai, a contemporary of Jesus, also foretold the destruction of the temple forty years before it occurred (B. Yoma 39b). Perhaps the political intrigues of the time and the threats of revolt by extreme patriots made Roman retaliation seem inevitable. Perhaps Jesus thought only of the divine judgement which must fall on Israel because of her refusal to hear his message. Certainly prophecy of the temple's destruction was in keeping with prophetic tradition: cf. Jer. 7.14; 26.6; Mic. 3.12. Such statements were never popular. They sounded like disloyalty – even blasphemy, since the temple symbolized the presence of God with his people (cf. the accusation against Stephen, Acts 6.13f.). There is no reason to suppose that Jesus' quarrel was

with the temple itself: indeed, in Matthew this passage follows Jesus' lament over Jerusalem and the temple (Matt. 23.37–9; cf. Luke 13.34f.). His complaint was against the nation, and the destruction of the temple is part of their punishment.

The temple was destroyed by fire in AD 70 and subsequently razed to the ground (cf. Josephus, *Wars*, VI. 4.5–7 and VII. 1.1). It has been argued that, if Mark were writing after this event, he would have made the saying fit the facts more precisely, but the statement that **there will not be one stone left here on another** is accurate enough, and its wording gives no clue as to whether the disaster had taken place when it was written. The mode of destruction is not important: what matters is that Israel's punishment is complete.

Jesus **was sitting** – the usual posture for a teacher, cf. 4.1, Matt. 5.1. 3 **The Mount of Olives** lies to the east of Jerusalem, on what may have been the road to Bethany. Higher than Jerusalem itself, it provided a panoramic view of the city and the temple, with the valley of Kidron between. It is the natural setting for the discourse which follows. But it is appropriate for other reasons also. In Zech. 14.1ff. we read of the 'day of the Lord' when Jerusalem will be overrun by her enemies, until the Lord defeats them in turn; then he will stand on the Mount of Olives and inaugurate his reign over the whole earth. The mountain is a fitting spot, then, for Jesus to unfold teaching about the End.

The four disciples to whom the teaching is given are those whose call Mark described in 1.16–20. If **Andrew** appears last, separated from his brother, it is perhaps because the names of the other three, **Peter and James and John**, have by Mark's time become firmly linked together; cf. 5.37; 9.2; 14.33. They **asked him privately** for further explanation of his words – a familiar theme in Mark – cf. 4.10; 7.17; 9.28; 10.10.

The question **when will these things happen?** is a natural one: 4 these things (ταῦτα) refer back to the temple's destruction. The next question, however, asking about **the sign that all these things** (ταῦτα πάντα) **are about to be fulfilled**, suggests much more, and seems to look forward to the discourse that follows. It is perhaps an attempt by Mark to make the discourse relevant to the disciples' question. Commentators often echo the complaint of Victor of Antioch who, writing in the fifth century, remarked that the disciples asked one question, and Jesus answered another. In so far as this is true, it is perhaps an indication that the opening verses of this chapter may be Mark's attempt to provide a setting for this material. The criticism is not entirely fair, however, for though the temple is not referred to in the discourse (except for an oblique reference in v.14), its fate was inevitably linked with that of Jerusalem. Moreover, for Mark himself, as we have seen in chapter 11, the temple was a symbol of the nation, its destruction the result of Israel's wickedness, and part of the nation's punishment. For Mark it would have been entirely natural to move from one theme to another. It is true that the discourse moves beyond the destruction of Jerusalem to the parousia and the End of all things, but it is clear that these events are understood to belong together, so that one heralds the other. The disciples' request for a sign is not met until vv.14f. Before that, we have prophecies of disasters and sufferings that have to be endured before the final disaster can come.

## 12 THE BEGINNING OF SUFFERINGS 13.5–8

*(Matt. 24.4–8; Luke 21.8–11)*

**(5) Then Jesus began to tell them: 'Be on guard, lest someone misleads you. (6) Many will come in my name, saying, "I am [he]!", and they will mislead many. (7) When you hear of wars and rumours of wars, do not be alarmed; this must happen – but it is not yet the End. (8) For nation will rise against nation, and kingdom against kingdom; there will be earthquakes everywhere, there will be famines: these things are the beginning of birthpangs.'**

5 The first section of the discourse provides a warning about things that might be misunderstood as the sign which the disciples have requested: they must not be led astray by false signs into thinking that the final judgement and disaster are imminent. The opening warn-
6 ing, **Be on guard** (βλέπετε), is characteristic of the discourse (cf. vv.9, 23, 33). These constant warnings balance the injunctions to hear (ἀκούετε) which punctuate the parable chapter (4.3, 9, 23, 24, 33; cf. also v.12).

Three events are mentioned here. The first is the arrival of men who **will mislead many** by saying 'I am [he]'. There is Markan irony here, for the claim 'echoes' that of Jesus himself in 14.62: but whereas his claim will be rejected, that of the 'false Christs and false prophets' (cf. vv.21f.) will be believed. It is extraordinarily difficult to know who these imposters are, or what it is that they are claiming. The most obvious interpretation is perhaps that they are pseudo-Messiahs, claiming to be God's promised leader. That would make sense in a Jewish setting, and there seem to have been a number of messianic pretenders, the last being Bar Cochba, who led the revolt of AD 132. But why should they also mislead Jesus' own followers, and how could they claim to speak in Jesus' name when they declared 'I am he'? An imposter could hardly claim to be the Messiah if he also claimed to speak in Jesus' name. One possible solution to the dilemma is that the situation here is similar to that reflected in 2 Thessalonians, where we find evidence of undue excitement being caused in the Church by people who declared that the day of the Lord had arrived – and so, presumably, that the Lord himself had come: cf. 2 Thess. 2.1f., where Paul, in a passage very similar to this, goes on to explain that other things must happen first. Could the saying in Mark be a reference to false teachers who made this kind of announcement? (So W. Manson, *J.T.S.*, 48, 1947, pp. 137f.) Luke's addition of the words 'The time is at hand!' (21.8) perhaps supports this. The difficulty with this suggestion is that it is still difficult to make sense of the words attributed to those who claim to be speaking in Jesus' name; we expect them to cry 'he is here', not 'I am he' – or rather, since the Greek is simply ἐγώ εἰμι, 'I am'. Whoever these men are, they seem to be making claims for themselves, not claims about Jesus.

The alternative seems to be to understand the phrase **in my name** as meaning 'claiming to be me' or 'usurping my name'. But if these men were actually claiming to be Jesus, we are dealing with a problem for which there is no evidence elsewhere, and it is difficult to imagine how such a claim could be made, unless perhaps by some deluded prophet: were there many such?

This impasse leads us back to the first possibility – that the speakers might be Jewish claimants to messiahship – but understanding the phrase **in my name** to have this alternative sense of usurpation. The 'name' that they are claiming will be the name 'Christ', not 'Jesus'. This suggestions seems to have the support of Matthew, who interprets Mark's ἐγώ εἰμι as meaning 'I am the Christ' (Matt. 24.5). But what relevance does this have to the situation that Mark is describing? At this point it is well to notice that the **many** who are misled by these men are not necessarily members of the Church. We tend to assume that they are Christians, because the warning to the disciples in v.5 not to be misled (βλέπετε μή τις ὑμᾶς πλανήσῃ) is echoed by the statement in v.6 that **many. . .will mislead many** (πλανήσουσιν). In fact there is nothing to indicate that the members of either of the two groups referred to as 'many' in v.6 are disciples: it is men and women in general who will be led astray by these false messianic claimants. (It is true that in Luke 21.8 it is the hearers of Jesus who are warned not to be misled by the 'many' who make false claims; but in Luke the setting is different, and this whole section of teaching is delivered openly, not to the disciples in private.) Moreover, if we read on, we will discover that the other disasters described in this first section are wars and 'natural disasters' (earthquakes and famines). These are certainly not in any sense troubles that come only to Christians; logically, then, we might expect this first trouble to be of the same character. If in fact the men whom Mark describes are Jewish claimants to messiahship, the link is even closer, for it is obvious that messianic uprisings would lead, almost inevitably, to wars, and they in turn to famine.

This suggests that the danger against which the disciples are warned is quite different from that which confronts the **many** in v.6. The disciples must not be misled into thinking that all the things described in vv.6–8 are the sign for which they have asked, since these things are only **the beginning**. Since there is nothing specifically Christian in these verses (apart from the phrase **in my name**), it is possible that they have been taken over from a Jewish source, but, if so, they have been re-interpreted by the introductory warning to the disciples that these disasters are not to be seen as the immediate prelude to the End.

7    **Wars and rumours of wars** are a common enough feature in Old Testament prophecy, and were understood as a mode of divine punishment (e.g. Jer. 4.16f.; Zech. 14.2). From being part of the divine 'setting right' of the world, they came to be seen as part of the turmoil which preceded the end in apocalyptic expectation, and which necessitated divine intervention (e.g. 4 Ezra 8.63–9.3). **This must happen**, because it is part of God's plan, but the disciples are **not** to **be alarmed** or agitated. The same verb (θροέω) is used in 2 Thess. 2.2, when Paul warns the Thessalonians not to be alarmed by false rumours that the day of the Lord has arrived. In Mark, also, we are
8    assured that **it is not yet the End**: life in this world continues. **For nation will rise against nation, and kingdom against kingdom**; cf. Isa.19.2; 4 Ezra 13.31. Both **earthquakes** (Isa. 13.13; Jer. 4.24; 1 Enoch 1.6f.) and **famines** (Isa. 14.30; Joel 1; 2 Bar. 27.6) are included in prophetic pronouncements and apocalyptic expectations. All these things, however, are but **the beginning of birthpangs**: the Greek word ὠδίν means a 'pang', and the plural form used here often has this specific meaning. Later, the rabbis spoke of the suffering which would precede the End as 'the birthpangs of the Messiah', and it is possible that the phrase was already a semi-technical one in the first century. But the image of a woman in labour is often used in the Old Testament of Israel's sufferings; it symbolized the agony which can lead to a new beginning (cf. Isa. 26.17f.; 66.8f.; Hos. 13.13; Mic. 4.9f. The disasters that Jesus foretells here are a necessary prelude to the last days: but they are only the beginning of the sufferings which must take place before the End arrives.

Mark's readers will have been familiar with wars and rumours of wars, with famines (cf. Acts 11.28) and with accounts of earthquakes, such as that which partly destroyed Pompeii in AD 62, and there may well have been both Jews and Christians who reacted to such events in an alarmist manner, imagining that this was the End of all things. To them the message is clear: these things were all expected, and they are the preliminary stages in the count-down to the last days, but they are not themselves the sign of the End, for it is not yet the time of the End.

# 13  PERSECUTION                                          13.9–13

*(Matt. 24.9–14; Luke 21.12–19)*

(9) 'As for yourselves – be on guard! They will hand you over to the courts; you will be beaten in synagogues, and brought before governors and kings for my sake, to bear testimony to them. (10) (And first the good news must be preached to all nations.) (11) When they hand you over and take you to court, do not worry beforehand about what you will say, but say whatever is given to you when the time comes; for it is not you who speak, but the Holy Spirit. (12) Brother will betray brother to death, the father his child; children will rise up against their parents and put them to death. (13) And you will be hated by everyone for my sake. But whoever holds out to the End will be saved.'

The next section opens with a repetition of the warning to the disciples 9 in v.5: **be on guard!** This time, the warning concerns sufferings that may befall them as Christians, but it is a warning to expect these things, not to try to escape them. Even here, in reply to the disciples' questions about the destruction of the temple, they are reminded once more that their discipleship means suffering. Matthew omits vv.9, 11 and 12, having used them already in the instruction to the Twelve in 10.17–21, but both he and Luke include similar sections at this point, though their wording differs from Mark and from each other. Once again, the experiences foretold here are ones with which Mark's first readers were probably all too familiar. The **courts** to which the disciples could expect to be handed over were the συνέδρια, the local Jewish courts, which had the powers of discipline; each town had its sanhedrin (Sanh.1.6), and what we know as the Sanhedrin was the Great Sanhedrin, the most important court of all, in Jerusalem. The sentence of 'forty lashes less one' (as laid down in Deut. 25.1–3), which Paul says he received five times (2 Cor. 11.24), was imposed by these courts, and was apparently carried out **in synagogues.** In addition to punishment from the Jewish authorities, the disciples would have to face trial at the hands of Gentile rulers – **governors and kings:** we find in Acts accounts of the apostles being brought before Roman officials (23.33; 25.6) and kings (Acts 12.1–3; 25.23). These warnings remind us of something else besides the persecution suffered by the early Church, however, for the vocabulary 'echoes' the story of Jesus' own sufferings (see R.H. Lightfoot, *Gospel Message*, pp. 51f.): the verb **hand...over** (παραδίδωμι) has been used already in predictions of the passion (9.31; 10.33) and occurs repeatedly in the passion narrative itself (14.10–15.15). Jesus himself is handed over to the Sanhedrin, the supreme Jewish court, and brought before Pontius Pilate, the governor of Judaea. John the Baptist, the forerunner of Jesus has already been handed over (1.14) and brought before King Herod (6.17–29). The warning that the disciples must expect to endure these things **for my sake** reminds us of Jesus' warning that those who wish to follow him must do so by carrying a cross. The demand that his followers share his sufferings will not be abrogated by their failure in Gethsemane. They will be required **to bear testimony to them**: the word 'testimony' is a legal one, but it is not clear here whether this testimony is given *to* them or *against* them. The same Greek phrase is used in Mark 1.44 with the former sense, in 6.11 with the latter. It is possible to understand the phrase to mean that the punishment that is inflicted on Jesus' disciples will be used in evidence against their judges: those who condemn his followers will themselves be arraigned in a heavenly court. In the present context, however, it seems more natural to understand the phrase in the sense of 'testifying to them concerning the gospel' (cf. Acts 26.22, where Paul stands before both a governor and a king, testifying to them the truth of the gospel). Interpreted in this way, the phrase provides an introduction to the following verse: **first the good news must be preached to all nations**.

10    This saying is an enigma. It interrupts the argument abruptly, and without it the argument progresses smoothly from v.9 to v.11. Matthew and Luke seem to agree with this judgement, since the former moves it to the end of the section, and the latter omits it altogether. It is also missing from the parallel passage in Matt. 10.17–21. It looks very much as though Mark has inserted the saying into the tradition. But why? First, we need to note that it is possible to punctuate vv.9–10 differently, following the interpretation of some early Latin and Syriac versions which read: 'to bear testimony to them and to all the Gentiles. The good news must first be preached.' This punctuation is given some support by Matt. 10.18, which reads '. . .to bear testimony before them and the Gentiles', and has been strongly argued for by G.D. Kilpatrick (in *Studies in the Gospels*, ed. D.E. Nineham, pp. 145ff.; he argues also for a different punctuation in v.9, but this does not alter the sense materially). The saying then becomes a reminder to the disciples that their primary task is that of evangelizing: it is in pursuing this that they will be brought before the courts. The significance of this interpretation is that it removes the clear reference to a Gentile mission which the normal punctuation provides. Since the reluctance of the disciples to evangelize the

Gentiles makes it difficult to believe that Jesus gave such clear instructions on this subject, this interpretation appeals to those who wish to maintain that Jesus spoke these words. However, the intrusion of the verse into the context suggests that it is more likely to be a Markan editorial comment than a saying of Jesus, and in view of the hints in the rest of the gospel, it would be no surprise to find him pointing forward to the Gentile mission here.

The word **first** could mean 'before you are arrested', but in the context of Mark 13 it is more likely to refer to the events which signify the arrival of the End. Matthew has clearly understood the saying in this way, since in his version he adds the words 'and then the End will come' (24.14). Moreover, we find that a similar idea occurs in Matt.. 10.17–23, following Jesus' warning to the disciples. After the passage that is almost identical with Mark 13.9,11–13, Matthew adds v.23: if the disciples are prevented from preaching in one city they are to flee to another, since they will not have completed their task before the Son of man comes. Matt. 10.23 concerns an unfinished mission to Israel, Mark 13.10 and Matt. 24.14 a mission to the Gentiles which must be completed before the End comes. Matt. 10.23 suggests a sense of urgency, Mark 13.10 and Matt. 24.14 emphasize that the End is not yet here. But all three passages stress the need to preach before the parousia, and link this with warnings about the persecution which those who follow Jesus must expect. The fact that Matthew makes this link in two different passages (using non-Markan material as well as Markan) suggests that the ideas of preaching, persecution and the parousia were related, and that Mark 13.10 may not be such an arbitrary insertion as at first appears.

A comparison between Matthew 10 and Mark 13 demonstrates the way in which tradition can be differently used in different contexts. In Matthew 10, the sayings about persecution form part of the warnings to the disciples about the treatment they can expect in the course of their mission; the saying about the parousia stresses the urgency of this mission. In Mark 13, on the other hand, the same sayings are a warning of what the disciples must expect to endure before the End. Although the persecution results from preaching, the reference to preaching in v.10 serves the same function as the comment in v.7 that the End is not yet here. For Mark, the sufferings of the disciples are not signs that the End is at hand, but signs that the proclamation of the good news (or 'gospel' – τὸ εὐαγγέλιον) is taking place: he is concerned lest these sufferings be misunderstood. The emphasis is on endurance (v.13); instead of Matthew's urgency, we have the belief that the End cannot come until the Gentile mission is completed. This idea echoes what Paul says in Rom. 11.25, and suggests that Mark was writing in a similar situation.

The function of the saying perhaps explains its position. Mark could not begin the section with it, since it does not belong with his warning to be on guard. He might have ended with it, as Matthew does in chapter 24: this is neater, but in Matthew the comment has no real relevance to the warning about persecution and is simply treated as something else that must happen before the End. In Mark, however awkward the order may be, and however intrusive v.10 may seem, the saying nevertheless belongs within Mark's overall structure. The disciples must expect to suffer as followers of Christ; but those sufferings are not signs that the End is at hand. Rather they result from the preaching of the gospel; the End will arrive only when the proclamation of the good news is complete.

11    **When they hand you over (παραδίδωμι) and take you to court, do not worry beforehand about what you will say.** The promise that those on trial would be provided with words to say...**when the time comes** seems to have circulated as a separate saying, since it is found in a totally different context in Luke 12.11f. It also occurs in Matthew 10 (but not 24). Luke has a different version of the saying in 21.15 which ascribes the guidance to Jesus himself instead of **the Holy Spirit.** In Luke 21 the promise is apparently of victory in the courts (vv.15, 18), but for Mark the saying is a part of the warning about what lies ahead, and an encouragement to endure: even this experience is not one about which they need to be anxious! The verb προμεριμνάω, unknown before Mark, refers to anxiety about what is going to happen, and the warning is parallel to the injunction not to

12    be alarmed in v.7. **Brother will betray brother to death:** the verb 'betray' represents yet another use of παραδίδωμι. The prophecy of dissension and betrayal within the family echoes the description in Mic. 7.6 more closely than any of the passages in apocalyptic literature which have been suggested as parallels. No doubt it will have corresponded all too closely to the experience of many first-century Christians.

13    The idea that Christians **will be hated** and persecuted for the **sake** of Jesus (lit. 'for my name') is found in 1 Pet. 4.14. Jesus may well have warned his followers to expect hatred, but the form of the saying suggests a time when they were being persecuted as 'Christians'. **Whoever holds out to the End will be saved.** The phrase εἰς τέλος, translated **to the End,** can be used as an adverbial phrase meaning 'completely'. Since the persecution described in vv.9–13 is not one of the signs that indicate that the End is imminent, we ought perhaps to understand the word τέλος in a non-technical sense; if so, then the promise concerns those who remain faithful right to the end – even when that end is death; cf. Rev. 2.10, where those who are faithful to death are promised the crown of life. Salvation is then the reward promised to those who are prepared to die because of their loyalty to Christ (cf. Mark 8.35): if the saying circulated separately, that must

almost certainly have been its meaning. In the present context, however, Mark's readers could hardly avoid linking the word τέλος with the 'End' already referred to in v.7; it may even have been the catchword which caught Mark's attention and led him to put the saying at this point. In this case the meaning would be that those who remain faithful under persecution until the End comes will be saved: a similar idea is found in 4 Ezra 6.25 and 7.27. It is also worth noting that in the Greek version (Theodotion) of Dan. 12.12, the verb to hold out (ὑπομένω) is used to translate the Hebrew word meaning 'waits' in describing the faithful who survive until the End arrives. Such a promise might seem a little odd, following after the statement that the disciples can expect to be put to death, since it suggests that they will be excluded from salvation! But the two statements are not incompatible: some of Jesus' followers will be called on to be faithful to death, and others will endure to the End; but Mark would no doubt have agreed with Paul that those 'who are alive, who are left until the coming of the Lord, shall not precede those who have fallen asleep' (1 Thess. 4.15).

# 14 THE SIGN OF DESTRUCTION 13.14–20

*(Matt. 24.15–22; Luke 21.20–4)*

**(14) 'But when you see the abomination of desolation standing where it should not be (let the reader understand!), then those who are in Judaea should flee to the hills. (15) Anyone who is on the roof should not go down into the house to fetch anything out of it, (16) and anyone who is in the field should not turn back for his cloak. (17) Alas for those women who are pregnant or who have children at the breast at that time! (18) Pray that it does not happen in winter. (19) For in those days the distress will be such as has never been before, from the beginning of the world which God created until now, and never will be again. (20) And if the Lord had not shortened the time, no one would be saved. But for the sake of the elect, whom he has chosen, he has shortened the time.'**

From general predictions about wars and catastrophes (vv.5–8) and 14 prophecies of persecution (vv.9–13) we turn to a particular, local disaster. The pace of the discourse changes abruptly at this point, and we are at last given a **then** (τότε) in response to the disciples' initial **when?** (πότε). Until now, the message has been 'Wait! Do not be overwhelmed. Endure!' But now the time for action has arrived.

The sign that this moment has arrived will be the appearance of **the abomination of desolation,** or desolating sacrilege (τὸ βδέλυγμα

313

της ἐρημωσεως). This phrase comes from the LXX of Dan. 12.11, where it refers to the altar to Zeus which was set up on the altar of burnt offering by Antiochus Epiphanes in 168 BC (cf. 1 Mac.1.54, 59). Anything connected with idolatry was an 'abomination' to God, and this particular abomination put an end to temple worship and so caused its 'desolation'. Now, however, the phrase is being used of a future desecration, presumably of a similar kind. Many commentators believe that this event lay in the future for Mark, as well as for Jesus, in which case the evangelist may have had in mind the threat by Caligula in AD 40 to erect his own statue in the temple – an act of impiety which he did not in fact carry out – and perhaps expected that something similar might eventually take place. If, as we have argued, Mark is writing *after* the destruction of Jerusalem, then he is presumably thinking of the desecration of the temple in AD 70 when, according to Josephus, the soldiers of Titus set up their standards in the temple and sacrificed to them, acclaiming Titus himself as Emperor (*Wars*, VI.6.1). The fact that Mark uses a masculine participle, **standing** (ἐστηκότα), with a neuter noun, suggests that he was thinking of the person behind the symbol (perhaps Titus) rather than a statue or standard: the figure will stand **where it should not be**. Similar imagery to Mark's is used in 2 Thess. 2.3f., where we read of 'the man of lawlessness...who...takes his seat in the temple of God', an event which heralds the arrival of the day of the Lord. Mark seems to be thinking of an event which will occur in the temple, and which will be the sign of its imminent destruction.

**Let the reader understand!** This has sometimes been understood as meaning 'the reader of Daniel', but this seems very unlikely, and the suggestion was probably made in an attempt to explain how Jesus came to be addressing 'the reader'. An alternative explanation is that Mark has simply copied a written source, without realizing the absurdity of attributing these words to Jesus. But there is no need for these explanations: the words are Mark's own parenthesis, a typical apocalyptic aside, alerting his readers to the fact that his somewhat enigmatic language needs to be decoded. But why the enigma? Why does he use obscure language? One suggestion is that Mark has deliberately obscured a straightforward historical prediction (preserved in Luke 21.20) because of the dangerous political situation when he wrote (so Taylor); but it seems more probable that Luke has given an explanation of Mark's conundrum in the light of his knowledge of past historical events. It is possible that Mark himself did not have any precise idea as to what these words describe. In the previous verses, Jesus' 'prophecy' has described the Christian community's past and present experience; if this is the point at which Mark himself moves into the unknown, this may explain his mysterious language. Nevertheless, when the event occurs, his readers will recognize it and be ready to act. The most likely explanation, however, is that Mark intends us to understand that what Jesus says is to take place in the temple is both the fulfilment of Daniel's prophecy, and also the sign of the arrival of the last things. The person who desecrates the temple is at one level a human being, but he is also the embodiment of evil, who came later to be known as Antichrist. This figure appears in different forms in Jewish and early Christian literature (e.g. the beast in Revelation 13.11ff. and the man of lawlessness in 2 Thess. 2.3) and symbolizes the forces of evil that are to be let loose in the world before the End, in a re-enactment of the myth of creation in which chaos is finally defeated by God and all things set in order. Behind the historical event in the temple, then, Mark intends us to see its real significance, and to understand why this should be the sign that unparalleled disasters are to be let loose in the world.

Then those who are in Judaea should flee to the hills. They are to flee because Jerusalem's destruction is imminent. The instruction reads somewhat strangely, since Jerusalem itself was in the hills, and a lot of Judaea was hilly country. But the injunction to flee to the hills is reminiscent of the flight of the Maccabees to the hills following the earlier desecration of the city (1 Macc. 2.28). They, however, had already left Jerusalem and moved to Modin, which was situated in the lower countryside to the north-west of Jerusalem, and it was from this city that they fled to the hills. The present command is perhaps an echo of this passage. The urgency of the instructions suggests a sudden invasion or uprising. If anyone. . .is on the roof, he must not 15 stop to go down into the house: he must escape down the outside staircase, and must not pause to enter the house, for there is no time to fetch anything out of it. Nor is there time for someone who is 16 stripped for work in the field to turn back for his cloak – a phrase reminiscent of the action which proved fatal to Lot's wife when she was fleeing from Sodom to the mountains and turned back (Gen. 19.26: the parallel is underlined by Luke in his version of the saying, which is included in a different context in 17.31f.). Women who are weighed 17 down by unborn or tiny children will have little hope of escape. If the flight takes place in winter, the fugitives will be in great distress, 18 since there will be little shelter from the weather and little food. Moreover, the swollen *wadis* will be impassable and make escape difficult.

So far, this section has described a disaster which, though it brings 19 terrible suffering for those involved in it, is like many other disasters which have taken place in the course of history. Now, however, we learn that the flight from Jerusalem will herald the beginning of unprecedented suffering. The distress will be such as has never been before, from the beginning. . .until now. These words are a quotation from Dan. 12.1 and suggest that Mark is interpreting this period

20 of suffering as the great tribulation which precedes the end of this age. Once again, a quotation from Daniel serves to give historical events an eschatological significance. The distress is such that **the Lord** has **shortened the time. . .for the sake of the elect.** In Daniel and in later apocalyptic writing, we find the idea that the timetable of the last days is already fixed: so many years must elapse before the end finally comes (e.g. Dan. 12.7). The statement that God has **shortened the time** seems to suggest that God has, in his mercy, brought the completion date forward, in order to save those **whom he has chosen** from further torment. The alleged parallels to this idea in Jewish literature are unconvincing, since what we find there is either the threat that the length of the years will be changed and the seasons upset – part of a general corruption of nature resulting from man's wickedness, 1 Enoch 80.2 – or the statement that, since the last day is fixed, the world is hurtling on towards final judgement (4 Ezra 4.26; 2 Bar. 20.1; 83.1; cf. 1 Cor. 7.29). It seems more likely that what is meant here is not any alteration in the divine plan, but simply that God has from the beginning set a limit to the sufferings of the elect by decreeing that they should last for a certain fixed period of time.

**No one would be saved:** the sense (of ἐσώθη) is probably 'be left alive', cf. 4 Ezra 6.25 and 7.27. A remnant will survive the horrors of the tribulation and live to see the wonders of the End. But those who survive to the End share in the eschatological salvation, and the verb σῴζω would inevitably suggest this idea also. Once again, as in v. 13, this does not mean that those who fall victim to the distress are excluded from salvation. **The elect:** used in the Old Testament of Israel in general (e.g. Ps. 105.6, 43; Isa. 65.9), this term or its equivalent came to be used of the righteous few in later literature (e.g. 1 Enoch 1.1; 62.8; 1QS 8.6; 1QH 2.13). Mark's readers would naturally see themselves as members of this chosen group.

# 15 MORE FALSE ALARMS                    13.21–3

*(Matt. 24.23–5)*

**(21) 'And if anyone says to you then, "Look – here is the Christ!" or "Look, there he is!", do not believe it. (22) For false Christs and false prophets will appear and will perform signs and wonders in order to mislead, if possible, the elect. (23) Be on guard! I have told you everything beforehand.'**

21 The four disciples have been given an answer to their original question: now we are dealing with the period following the destruc-

tion of Jerusalem. **And if anyone says to you then, 'Look – here is the Christ!' or 'Look, there he is!', do not believe it.** There is a 'Q' saying parallel to this one in Luke 17.23, which Matthew seems to have incorporated into his version of the discourse (cf. Matt. 24.26f.). The idea that the Messiah will be discovered **here** or **there** suggests a human figure, not a heavenly one descending to earth, and once again the saying may have referred originally to Jewish expectation of a Messiah. V.21 is also similar to the warning in v.6 and may be another version of that saying. This time, however, Mark understands 22 the warning as specifically addressed to the disciples; the danger is such that even **the elect** may be led astray – if such a thing is **possible**. Since Mark's story records continual failures on the part of the twelve men whom Jesus has chosen, it is clear that he believes that such a thing *is* possible. The situation depicted by Mark is now quite different from that in v.6: the time to expect the Son of man is near. In this context, the saying certainly reminds us of the false rumours mentioned in 2 Thess. 2.2 to the effect that the Day of the Lord has come. The faithful must beware false rumours – **false prophets** who announce the end, and even **false Christs**. Warnings against false prophets are familiar (e.g. Jer. 14.14; 23.32), but once again it is impossible to be sure how Mark understood the second group. Jewish messianic pretenders were hardly likely to mislead Christians; yet it is difficult to believe that there were many in the Church who were so deluded as to believe themselves to be the returning Christ. Perhaps Mark thinks of those who oppose Christ and who try to mislead the elect with false teaching – those whom 1 John 2.18 describes as the 'many antichrists' who accompany Antichrist. The term ψευδόχριστοι is probably a more general one than the translation 'false Christs' suggests. It is worth noting also that the antichrist figure in 2 Thess. 2, who is termed 'the lawless one', is accompanied by the same false **signs and wonders** that are attributed here to the false Christs and false prophets. The recognition that false prophets are capable of performing signs and wonders, and so of deceiving the people, is found in Deut. 13.1f. Mark seems to be using common tradition about the troubles associated with the coming of the Antichrist (cf. v.14), which perhaps explains why he has placed the warning at this point.

**Be on guard!** The warning given in v.5 is repeated and underlined. 23 For Mark's readers, the thought that the sufferings and difficulties they faced had been foreseen by Jesus would give them comfort. Just as the sufferings and death of Jesus had been part of God's plan and had been foretold by Jesus himself, so too were the persecution and disasters which they were enduring.

## 16  THE COMING OF THE SON OF MAN  13.24–7

*(Matt. 24.29–31; Luke 21.25–8)*

(24) 'But in those days, after that distress,

"The sun will be darkened
(25) And the moon will not give her light.
The stars will fall from heaven,
And the celestial powers will be shaken."

(26) And then they will see the Son of man coming in the clouds with great power and glory. (27) And then he will send out the angels and gather the elect from the four winds, from the end of earth to the end of heaven.'

24–25  The drama moves on another step, beyond the horrors of **that distress**, described in vv.14ff., to the final act. Cosmic disasters herald the arrival of **the Son of man**. The imagery is familiar from passages in the Old Testament, where the failure of **sun** and **moon** is used to describe the horror of disasters such as wars and earthquakes which overwhelm their victims: cf. Ezek. 32.7f.; Joel 2.10; 3.15; Amos 8.9. The four parallel lines in vv.24f. seem, indeed, to be a composite quotation from Isa. 13.10 and 34.4, two passages which describe the wrath which will overtake the world on the day of the Lord. It is often said by commentators that apocalyptic writers took over this imagery and understood it literally, but there is little evidence for this. The clearest examples are Rev. 6.12f.; 8.10 (though even these are part of a vision and perhaps to be understood symbolically) and Test. Moses 10.5. Where we do find references to strange phenomena in the heavens (e.g. the sun and moon shining at the wrong time, 4 Ezra 5.4; 1 Enoch 80.4–7; Sib. Or. 3.801–3), these are understood as cosmic portents of the approaching end. A rather different idea occurs in Sib. Or. 5.512–31, where the stars make war on one another and are finally all destroyed.

Are these verses in Mark to be understood simply as poetic imagery, describing the terrors of war, earthquake and famine? This seems unlikely, since these disasters have been described already in vv.6–8; we appear to have moved on beyond the course of historical events to the winding-up of history. Are they to be understood literally, as signs of the approaching End? If so, then unlike earlier false alarms, there can be no mistaking these particular portents. It is not simply that the heavens have gone awry, but that they have broken up: to us these words suggest total cosmic disintegration, but we must be careful not to impose our Copernican understanding of the universe on Mark. Perhaps he means only what Luke describes as 'signs in sun and moon and stars' (Luke 21.25). The language is the traditional language used by the prophets for the day of the Lord, and it is used because it evokes all the ideas associated with that day of judgement. It is more than metaphorical, less than literal: the closest parallels are in the passages he uses – Isaiah 13 and 34 – which are equally ambiguous. In this context, commonsense questions about what will actually happen are out of place, for the language is the language of myth.

**And then....** A second 'then' provides an answer to the disciples' 26 question in v.4: the coming of **the Son of man** means that all things are to be accomplished. **They will see**: the words are no longer addressed to the disciples, perhaps because this saying or section was originally independent. It is by no means clear who the people referred to as 'they' are: perhaps the word refers simply to all those who have survived the great tribulation, but in its present context it could mean specifically the elect of v.22. The picture of **the Son of man coming in the clouds** is based on Dan. 7.13, though the figure who comes on clouds there is described as '*like* a son of man'. Clouds are frequently associated with God in the Old Testament, at one and the same time concealing and revealing his glory (cf. Exod. 34.5). In Dan. 7.13 the 'one like a son of man' comes 'with clouds' in contrast to the four evil beasts who emerge from the great sea: the symbolism provides the reader with information about who is on which side. The Son of man here is thus seen to come with the power and authority given to him by God. Mark does not tell us in what direction he moves: in Daniel, the one like a son of man comes to God, and in isolation the saying here could have the same meaning; in the context Mark gives it, however, it is natural to think that **they will see the Son of man coming** *towards* them. **With great power and glory**: in Mark 8.38–9.1, the glory is linked with the coming of the Son of man, the power with the Kingdom of God: here, they are both interpreted as attributes of the Son of man. **And then he will send out the angels** 27 **and gather the elect.** The idea that God would gather the remnant of his people from other countries and bring them back to Judaea is found in the Old Testament, e.g. Isa. 11.11; 43.6. Now, however, the elect who will be gathered must be the members of the 'new' Israel. **From the four winds**: from all directions; cf. Zech. 2.6. **From the end of earth to the end of heaven**: this somewhat mixed combination of two metaphors (cf. Deut. 13.7; 30.4) seems to be an attempt to be all-embracing.

For Mark's readers, this passage is an assurance that, whatever sufferings they may have to endure, their faithfulness to Jesus will be rewarded on the Last Day, when they are acknowledged by the Son of man. This is the other half of the picture painted in 8.38.

## 17 A PARABLE ABOUT THE FIG TREE 13.28–31

*(Matt. 24.32–5; Luke 21.29–33)*

(28) 'Learn a lesson from the fig tree: when its branch becomes tender and it puts out leaves, you know that summer is near. (29) In the same way, when you see these things happening, you will know that he is near – at the very door. (30) I tell you truly that this generation will not pass away until all these things take place. (31) Heaven and earth will pass away, but my words will not pass away.'

At the end of the discourse we have two parables and a number of sayings which seem to have been linked together because of certain words and phrases that they have in common. The first is a parable about a sign – a natural enough pericope to have added here. Yet it fits badly into its context: **these things** in v.29 cannot refer to the events in vv.26f., since they were themselves the climax to the period of waiting. The parable has been added here because it was thought to be on the same theme as the rest of the discourse, but in the setting of Jesus' own life-time it may well have had a different emphasis. Even in its present setting, Luke takes it to be a parable about the Kingdom of God, and he may well be right. If so, then perhaps the signs which showed that the Kingdom was near were originally the activities of Jesus himself (cf. Luke 11.20; 12.54–6). Mark may perhaps have had another reason for adding the parable at this point. The parable is about a fig tree, and it was a fig tree that was cursed in chapter 11, when Jesus first pronounced judgement on the temple and on Israel. It is significant that now, when Jesus has spelt out the nature of Israel's punishment and the final gathering of the elect, we have a story about another fig tree. The dormant tree, apparently dead, bursts into new life, and its young leaves are a promise of coming summer: hope, and not destruction, is the final word.

28 **Learn a lesson from the fig tree:** the fig tree is one of the commonest trees in Palestine. It is the most obvious harbinger of **summer**, since so many of the other trees are evergreen. Moreover, the fig tree was commonly used in Jewish literature to symbolize the joys of the messianic age (see W.R. Telford, *The Barren Temple and the Withered*
29 *Tree*, pp.128–204). **When you see these things happening:** the awkwardness of the reference to 'these things' (ταῦτα) here betrays the fact that the parable is an addition. It is by no means clear what Mark has in mind. Perhaps he sees the parable as a parallel way of expressing the theme of vv.24–7, in which case 'these things' must refer to the signs in vv.24f. Perhaps he is thinking back to the ταῦτα in v.4, and is therefore referring to the events in Judaea described in vv.14ff.

In this case it is the destruction of the temple and the punishment of Israel which warn the Christian community that they must be constantly on the lookout. **He is near:** there is no subject in the Greek, and the verb (ἐστίν) can be translated equally well by 'it is'. Mark might mean 'the Son of man' or 'the End'. Luke supplies a subject – the Kingdom of God (Luke 21.31). **At the very door:** this phrase (which might have come more naturally in the next parable) suggests that Mark has a person, rather than a thing in mind. Cf. James 5.9.

**I tell you truly that this generation will not pass away until all** 30 **these things take place.** This is a separate saying, perhaps added here becaues the words 'these things take place' echo the previous verse. It supplies an answer to the 'When?' in v.4f, but since it refers to 'all these things' it is presumably applied here to everything described in vv.5–27. Many attempts have been made to understand the Greek for **this generation** (ἡ γενεὰ αὕτη) in some other way, but they are all unconvincing. The reason for these attempts was the embarassment caused by an apparently unfulfilled prediction in the mouth of Jesus. An alternative solution was to limit the application of the phrase 'all these things'. Once it is recognized that the saying did not originally belong in its present context, the difficulties become rather different. If it is an authentic saying, to what did it originally refer? The similarity with Mark 9.1 suggests that it could have referred to the Kingdom of God. A comparison of that saying with the Matthaean parallel shows how easily a saying about the coming of the Kingdom could be reapplied to the coming of the Son of man. But perhaps it is a warning of unknown origin, couched in traditional apocalyptic language and used here by Mark because it seemed appropriate – at once ominous and vague. Used here, the saying provides an important clue to Mark's purpose in this chapter. If all these things are to take place within this generation, then we understand why he ends the discourse with the warnings in vv.33–7. The fact that some Christians have been misled by false signs of the parousia does not mean that there is no need for continual vigilance: sooner or later the End will come, and Mark's readers must therefore keep watch.

**Heaven and earth will pass away, but my words will not pass** 31 **away.** This is another independent saying, presumably added at some stage because of the verb 'pass away', which links it with the previous saying. A similar saying is found in Matt. 5.18 (cf. Luke 16.17), but what is said there about the Law is said here about the words of Jesus: indeed, the claim made here is greater, since it is said that his words will endure even when heaven and earth have ceased to exist. If the saying is authentic, it is a remarkable claim to authority, similar to the 'But I say to you' in Matt. 5.22 etc.: it is the word of God (not of man) that remains 'for ever' (Isa. 40.8). On its own, the saying may have referred to the teaching of Jesus in general. In its present context, it underlines the importance of the teaching which has just been given.

# 18 ANOTHER PARABLE 13.32–7

## (Matt. 24.36,42; 25.13–15; Luke 12.38, 40)

**(32) 'But no one knows about that day or about that hour – neither the angels in heaven nor the Son, only the Father. (33) Be on guard; be alert;[1] for you do not know when the time will come. (34) It is like a man who is away from home; when he leaves his house he puts his servants in charge, giving each his task, and he commands the doorkeeper to keep watch. (35) Keep watch, then, for you do not know when the master of the house is coming – whether in the evening, or at midnight, or at cock-crow or in the early morning – (36) lest he should come suddenly and find you asleep. (37) And what I say to you I say to all: keep watch!'**

The second parable is introduced by another independent saying which strikes a new note: no one knows when these things will happen, and the disciples must therefore be always on the alert. The parable contains the same message: since the master of the house will arrive home without warning, there is need for constant vigilance. There is no suggestion here of any 'sign' which might herald his approach, and the parable belongs to a period where men were being urged to be ready for the future crisis, rather than one in which they were being warned that the crisis might not be as near as they had expected. On its own, the parable may well have had a setting within the ministry of Jesus (see above, pp. 300f.). If Mark uses it here, in apparent tension with the rest of his material, it is probably because it has a firm place in the tradition. There are signs, however, that he has adapted it to suit his own purposes. Luke's parallel speaks of a man at a marriage feast (Luke 12.36–8), but Mark thinks of a longer absence (a man on a journey), and of servants going about their work while their master is away – a detail which may have come from the parable of the talents (Matt. 25.14–30//Luke 19.12–27), or possibly from the parable of the faithful and wicked servants (Matt. 24.45–51//Luke 12.42–8). According to Luke, the parable of the talents was told because Jesus' followers were expecting the imminent arrival of the Kingdom. As for the parable of the faithful and wicked servants (which in Matthew replaces Mark's parable of the absent house-

1 Following B D and a few other MSS. Many MSS add *and pray.*

holder), this emphasizes the unexpected delay of the master. In both cases, the emphasis is on the reward and punishment of the servants. Mark's version of the parable neatly holds together the twin emphases of the eschatological tension: the End will come suddenly (when one least expects it), so one must be ready now; nevertheless, the time of its coming is unknown, so one must be prepared for a long wait. But, sooner or later, the End will come. Mark's readers must not be misled by premature announcements of Jesus' glorious return, but neither must they cease to expect him.

**But no one knows about that day or about that hour – neither** 32 **the angels in heaven nor the Son, only the Father.** Many commentators assert that v.32 contradicts v.30, but the two sayings are not necessarily incompatible: it is possible to be confident that an event will occur within a certain span of time without being certain of the precise day or hour. This saying's authenticity has been endlessly debated. On the one hand, it is argued that it must go back to Jesus, since no one would have attributed ignorance to him; indeed, the saying caused problems for the early Church – problems which are reflected in the omission of the words 'nor the Son' from some MSS in the Matthaean parallel (Matt. 24.36). On the other hand, it seems unlikely that Jesus spoke of himself openly as the Son, since evidence that he did so is rare outside the Fourth Gospel: the only comparable passage in the Synoptics is Matt. 11.27//Luke 10.22. One possible explanation is that an original saying by Jesus has been modified by the addition of the title. Whatever its origin, the verse serves here to warn Mark's readers about the folly of thinking that one could predict the exact time of the End. If Jesus himself confessed ignorance, how can his followers claim greater knowledge? The reference to **that day** echoes the warnings in the Old Testament about 'the Day of the Lord' (e.g. Isa. 2.12; Amos 5.18; cf. 2 Thess. 1.10). Since it was a day of judgement, it is not surprising to find the warning **Be on guard** 33 repeated once more. There is plenty of MS evidence for the words *and pray*, following the command to **be alert**, but they are probably an addition which has crept in from 14.38. The need for constant vigilance is due to the fact that **you do not know when the time will come.** This suggests that there are no signs to warn the disciples of impending judgement, and it is this which makes it difficult to reconcile this paragraph with the previous one, where there are said to be clear signs of the End.

The parable in v.34 illustrates the theme of v.33. It presents a 34 somewhat odd picture, since a man going on a journey in Palestine in the first century AD would not travel at night, and his servants could hardly be blamed for not waiting up for him. Luke's version of the parable is about a man who has gone out to a banquet, and this makes much better sense (Luke 12.36). Mark seems to have combined a parable about a man expected home at night with one about a man . . . away from home who entrusts his servants with various responsibililties (cf. Matt. 25.14–30 and Luke 19.11–27). The point of Mark's parable about the man who returns at night is not that his arrival is unexpected, but that his servants are given no warning about the precise time that he will come and must therefore be constantly vigilant. The detail about putting **his servants in charge, giving each his task**, which has probably come from the parable of the talents, seems designed to remind Mark's readers that keeping watch for the master's return does not excuse the servants from faithfully carrying out their duties. This detail may have been added by Mark himself in order to emphasize that the command to keep watch for the master's return does not in fact conflict with the belief that a certain period of time must elapse first. Mark's allegorical interpretation of the parable is plain, and the moral is spelt out with only a thin

35   disguise in v.35: the disciples must **keep watch**, since they **do not know when the master of the house is coming**. This command suggests that he is already at hand, and the urgency here contrasts with the earlier part of the discourse which emphasized that the End could not be expected yet. The four points of time – **in the evening, or at midnight, or at cock-crow or in the early morning** – are the four watches of the night according to Roman reckoning. R.H. Lightfoot (*The Gospel Message of St Mark*, p. 53) has suggested that it may not be accidental that three out of the four phrases are echoed in the account of the passion which follows (14.17; 14.72; 15.1): the events leading up to Jesus' crucifixion take place **in the evening** (the Last Supper), in the middle of the night (Gethsemane, arrest and trial), **at cock-crow** (Peter's denial) and **in the morning** (trial before Pilate). Certainly in the course of that fateful night three of the four disciples are again commanded to watch, but when Jesus returns to them he

36   finds them **asleep** (14.34, 37f., 40, 41); one of them is caught off guard
37   at cock-crow (14.72). The warning to **keep watch**, however, is not meant for the disciples alone: the final words of the discourse – **And what I say to you I say to all** – remind Mark's readers that the warning is addressed to them also.

# G   The story of the Passion            14.1–15.47

It has often been argued that the Passion narrative is different in character from the rest of Mark's material, being based on a pre-Markan connected narrative, with incidents arranged in a specific order (see, e.g., Schweizer, pp. 284–6; Jeremias, *Eucharistic Words*, pp. 89–96). However, the impression of continuity given by this section may well result from the fact that there is (on the whole) an inevitable logic about the order of events, which follow on naturally one from another when the story is being recounted *in toto*. But many of the incidents can stand alone: a notable example is 14.17–25, since we know that this story *was* told on its own (see 1 Cor. 11.23–6; cf. also the use of the Gethsemane tradition (Mark 14.32–42) in Heb. 5.7f.). Other passages could certainly have circulated independently and been used alone (as, indeed, they still are, when read as part of a lectionary): e.g. 14.3–9 (cf. Luke 7.36–8); 14.26–31, 53f. and 66–72; 14.55–65; 15.1–15, 15.16–20 and 15.21–39.

Whatever the origin of this section, it shows as much evidence of Markan editing as does the rest of Mark's material. A summary of the arguments is given by J. Donahue in W.H. Kelber, *The Passion in Mark*, pp 8–16.

# 1  THE PLOT                                                    14.1–2

*(Matt. 26.1–5; Luke 22.1–2; John 11.47–53)*

**(1) It was now two days before the Festival of Passover and Unleavened Bread, and the chief priests and the scribes were looking for a way to seize him by stealth and kill him: (2) 'Not during the festival,' they said, 'lest the people riot'.**

This short paragraph picks up a theme which is by now familiar: the authorities' determination to destroy Jesus (cf. 3.6; 11.18; 12.12). It serves to set the scene for the narrative that follows.

The seemingly straightforward statement that **it was now two days before the Festival of Passover** causes complex problems of dating. The Passover was eaten on the 15th Nisan, the lambs having been killed on what we should reckon to be the afternoon of the same day but which was by Jewish reckoning the 14th Nisan, since the Jewish day began at sunset. The feast of **Unleavened Bread**, originally a separate festival, was celebrated at the same time, from 15th to 21st Nisan, so that the two festivals had become in effect one (cf. 2 Chron. 35.17; Josephus, *Antiquities*, XIV.2.1; XVII.9.3). If Mark is counting in the Jewish way – i.e. inclusively – as seems probable (cf. 8.31), then he means 'the day before'. Since Mark dates the crucifixion on the day before the sabbath (i.e. Friday; cf. 15.42), and the passover meal the previous evening (i.e. Thursday), he is probably thinking of some time on the day before that (i.e. Wednesday). Some commentators suggest that Mark is counting in a Roman manner, and that if on this reckoning we count two days on from what we call Wednesday, we come to the day on which Jesus died; they then argue that this supports the dating we find in the Fourth Gospel, according to which the Last Supper was not a passover meal and Jesus died on the 14th Nisan, at the time the passover lambs were killed. But this conclusion does not follow, since **two days before the Festival of Passover** could just as easily refer to our *Tuesday*, two days before *Thursday*.

2 The real puzzle of the paragraph, however, is the fact that in the narrative that follows, the Jewish leaders are described as doing the very thing that they here reject as impossible. Why do they apparently abandon their decision **not** to take Jesus **during the festival**? And did that decision mean that they planned to take Jesus *before* the feast began, or after it was all over? Luke has seen the problem and avoided it. One suggestion is that they intended to wait until the end of the feast, but that the treachery of Judas altered the situation and led them to seize the opportunity to take Jesus: this may well have been Mark's understanding of events, even though this is not necessarily what happened. An alternative suggestion is that the phrase **not during the festival** should in fact be translated 'not in the presence of the festival crowd' (so J. Jeremias, *Eucharistic Words*, pp. 71–3), and that the real emphasis should be placed on the phrase **by stealth**; the arrest in the garden avoided the danger of a public riot (cf. 14.49). But perhaps the implication is that **the chief priests and the scribes** decided that they must act swiftly, before the feast, and that this is what they proceeded to do with the aid of Judas' act of treachery – in which case this paragraph seems to provide support for the Johannine view that Jesus was dead and buried before the feast began; since it conflicts with Mark's own view, it may well represent pre-Markan tradition.

# 2  JESUS IS ANOINTED 14.3–9

*(Matt. 26.6–13; John 12.1–8)*

**(3) And he was in Bethany, in the house of Simon the leper, and as he sat at table, a woman entered, holding an alabaster jar of very costly perfume – genuine nard – and she broke the jar and poured the ointment over his head. (4) Some of those present said indignantly to one another, 'Why this waste of perfume? (5) For this perfume could have been sold for more than three hundred denarii, and given to the poor.' And they scolded her. (6) But Jesus said, 'Leave her alone; why do you bother her? She has done a fine thing for me. (7) For you have the poor among you always, and you can do good to them whenever you wish, but you do not always have me. (8) She has done what she could: she has anointed**

**my body for burial beforehand. (9) Truly I tell you, wherever the good news is preached, throughout the whole world, what she has done will be told as her memorial.'**

This section provides an interesting example of the way in which a story could be adapted and given different interpretations by different evangelists. Matthew's version is similar to Mark's; the only significant difference is that he says that it was the disciples who objected to the woman's action. In Luke, however, the story is not only found in a totally different context (7.36–50) but is itself very different – so much so that some commentators have assumed it to be the record of another incident: the Simon with whom Jesus dines is a Pharisee, not a leper, and the woman, who is described as 'a sinner', anoints the feet of Jesus, not his head, an unusual action, and possibly a confusion with her previous act in wiping his feet; the objection which is made does not concern the woman's extravagance but her immorality, and the incident is used to demonstrate the loving response of the forgiven sinner. The concern with forgiveness is typically Lukan; cf. Luke 15; 18.9–14; 19.1–10. In John, the incident takes place in Bethany, as in Mark, but in the home of Lazarus, not Simon, and six days before the Passover instead of two; the woman is identified as Mary, the sister of Lazarus, and she anoints Jesus' feet, not his head, and then, surprisingly, wipes them with her hair – confused details which seem to derive from Luke's version of the story; the protest is made by Judas (who has become, as it were, the scapegoat for the other disciples), and the woman's action is linked (though much more obscurely than in Mark) with Jesus' burial. The tradition identifying the woman as Mary Magdalene is not found in any of the gospels and is first recorded in the fourth century.

It was customary to pour oil on the hair of guests at dinner parties given by the well-to-do, and the incident can be understood, at one level, as an act of devotion to Jesus by the woman. She breaks the jar and pours out everything she has in gratitude to Jesus. Her action contrasts with the niggardly complaints of the onlookers. The story forms an interesting pair with that of the poor widow in the temple who throws everything she has into the treasury – in contrast to the rich who contribute out of their wealth (12.41–4), and the men who devour widows' houses (vv.39f.). Perhaps Mark has deliberately used these two stories to enclose Jesus' judgement on Jerusalem in chapter 13 – a passage which spells out the condemnation of those who have refused to respond to God in love and devotion.

For Mark, however, this story has another significance, and that is the way in which the woman's action points forward to Jesus' imminent death. Indeed, since in 16.1 the attempt to anoint his corpse is frustrated by his resurrection, this premature action symbolizes the fact that in his case the normal ceremony will not take place: Jesus is anointed for burial before death because he will not be anointed after death – and he will not be anointed for burial then because God will raise him from the dead. The woman's action is thus a summary of the gospel, and this is why it will be recalled **wherever the good news is preached.** Typically, Mark intercalates the story between the two sections describing the authorities' plot to arrest Jesus – a reminder that the events that are now taking place are the result of more than merely human plans. Within this setting, the story is then placed as close as possible to the actual burial of Jesus (contrast the earlier dating in John 12).

But Mark may well have seen yet another significance in this story. Jesus has entered Jerusalem as king (11.1–10), he is about to be challenged as the Messiah by the high priest (14.61), crucified as 'King of the Jews' (15.26), mocked by his opponents as 'Christ, the King of Israel' (15.32), and acknowledged by his executioner as 'Son of God' (15.39). Since Mark's story shows us that it is through death that Jesus is revealed as 'Messiah' or 'anointed', it seems likely that he interpreted this anointing for burial as the symbol of Jesus' messianic anointing also. The fact that the ritual was performed by a woman rather than a priest was one more anomaly in a story that was already anomalous from beginning to end.

For those who know the end of the story then, the woman's action epitomizes Jesus' death and resurrection, proclaims his status as king, and challenges others to share her devotion to him.

3 **And he was in Bethany.** Mark clearly thinks of Jesus as lodging at Bethany – cf. 11.11, 20. Nothing else is known about **Simon the leper.** Since lepers were automatically excluded from ordinary society, Simon must either have been cured of his leprosy (perhaps by Jesus) or have become a leper subsequently. The words probably shocked Mark's original hearers, reminding them once more that Jesus deliberately associated with outsiders. **As he sat at table, a woman,** who is unnamed, **entered**; she flouts convention by coming in while the men are at their meal, presumably in her anxiety to do Jesus this service. The **jar** was an **'alabaster'** (ἀλάβαστρος), or globular vase without handles, used for perfume and not necessarily made of alabaster. The **perfume** was an aromatic oil made from **nard,** a highly valued Indian plant. The meaning of the word translated **genuine** (πιστίκος) is uncertain: the most widely accepted view is that it is derived from πίστις, meaning 'faith' or 'reliability', and hence 'genuine'; an alternative interpretation links it with an Aramaic word for a nut used in making ointments. This section is full of awkward Greek phrases that look very much like clumsy translations from Aramaic. Whatever the exact meaning, the substance is said to have been **very costly,** an apt description in view of the valuation given in

v.5: if a denarius was an appropriate rate of pay for one day's labour (Matt. 20.4, 10), then **three hundred denarii,** was the best part of a year's wages. **She broke the jar:** this woman's gift (like that of the widow in 12.41–4) is total, and the destruction of the jar symbolizes its totality. But Mark's first readers might well have seen another symbolism in the action, since the ointment jars used in anointing the dead were often broken and left in the tomb.

**Some of those present said indignantly to one another, 'Why**  4–5
**this waste of perfume? For this perfume could have been sold for more than three hundred denarii, and given to the poor.' And they scolded her.** The indignation of the onlookers contrasts with the woman's generosity – a point that Luke elaborates in his version of the story (Luke 7.44–6). It was an act of courtesy to refresh a guest with oil, but to break open the whole jar was an act of absurd extravagance.

**But Jesus said, 'Leave her alone; why do you bother her? She**  6
**has done a fine thing for me.'** In spite of his concern for the poor and the oppressed, Jesus sides with the woman. His response to criticism reminds us of the occasion earlier in the gospel when he was questioned about the failure of his disciples to fast (2.18–20): on both occasions, demands for the more rigorous performance of religious duties (fasting and almsgiving) on the part of his associates are met by a justification of their behaviour in view of the short time that Jesus himself is with them. Here he supports the woman's action by declaring: **'You have the poor among you always, and you can do**  7
**good to them whenever you wish, but you do not always have me.'** Matthew attributes the criticism to the disciples, but Mark's account suggests that (as in 2.18–20) it comes from outsiders. The contrast in both Mark 2 and 14 is between those who rejoice in the presence of Jesus and those who are concerned – however sincerely – to do what the Law requires. John makes a similar point in the story of the changing of water into wine, which contrasts the duties of Judaism and the joy experienced in the presence of Jesus. Mark's story is not intended to minimize the needs of the poor, but to emphasize that religious observance is less important than one's response to Jesus: cf. 10.21, where response to Jesus involves the giving of all that a man has – to the poor. The woman's action is described as **a fine thing**, a good or praiseworthy work (χαλὸν ἔργον). Daube suggests that the phrase is a technical term for a work of charity (*The New Testament and Rabbinic Judaism*, pp. 315f.): the woman's service to Jesus is as much a 'good work' as the almsgiving her critics advocate. This saying in vv.6–7 is probably the earliest comment on the woman's action and may go back to Jesus himself, though it is possible that here, as in 2.20, the reference to Jesus' departure may have been sharpened later. It forms a natural climax to the story, and there is need for nothing more.

8    **She has done what she could.** This sentence reads very oddly in Greek, meaning literally 'what she had she has done'. It is possible that this is a deliberate echo of 12.44, where the widow puts in everything she had. It is not suggested that this woman spent everything she had on her gift, but her action represents a similar generous response. This comment introduces a new interpretation of the woman's action: **she has anointed Jesus' body for burial beforehand.** Commentators have sometimes suggested that the fact that Jesus' body was not anointed caused his friends and disciples distress, and that they therefore came to interpret this incident as rectifying the omission (so, e.g., Branscomb and Nineham). But though the circumstances of the burial might have caused distress at the time, the suggestion that it was this distress that gave rise to the interpretation given here hardly accords with the community's resurrection faith: this particular omission proved to need no rectification. It is more likely that this comment was added to the story by someone (possibly by Mark himself, since this is for him the key significance of the incident) who saw the woman's action as a symbolic one, foreshadowing Jesus' coming death.

9    **Truly I tell you.** These words introduce what seems to be yet another addition – a saying about the world-wide mission of the Church already referred to in 13.10. If it seems strange that the story should **be told as a memorial** to a woman whose name Mark does not record, this is because it is **what she has done** that is all important. In pouring out her gift over his head, she has in one action anointed him Messiah, proclaimed his death and resurrection and made an act of total commitment to him as Lord: the story is itself a proclamation of **the good news** which is to be **preached throughout the whole world.**

## 3  THE TRAITOR                                    14.10–11

*(Matt. 26.14–16; Luke 22.3–6)*

**(10) And Judas Iscariot, one of the Twelve, went to the chief priests in order to betray him to them. (11) When they heard, they were glad and promised to give him money, and he looked for an opportunity to betray him.**

This paragraph takes up the theme of vv.1–2, and may have followed on from them in Mark's source. Whatever their origin, Mark has used these two short paragraphs as a framework for the story of the anointing: those who plot Jesus' death are only subsidiary actors in the real drama.

The historicity of this incident is unquestioned: the presence of a traitor among Jesus' closest disciples was too much of an embarrassment to have been invented. There has been a great deal of discussion about why Judas betrayed Jesus, and what information he supplied to the authorities. Regarding the former question, Mark is silent. The only hint he provides is the reference to money in v.11, which is taken up by Matthew in his account (26.15; cf. John 12.6), but Mark shows no interest in the traitor's motives: they are unimportant, since Judas is – unwittingly – part of the divine plan. Speculations that Judas was a fervent patriot, disillusioned by Jesus' failure to lead an armed uprising, receive no support from Mark's account.

As to what Judas betrayed, there is no suggestion in Mark that he provided the priests with information about Jesus' teaching which might have given them a basis on which to bring charges: Judas does not appear at the trial as a witness. According to Mark's account, Judas led the temple officials to the Garden of Gethsemane at night, and it seems to have been the whereabouts of his master that he betrayed; this is made explicit by John (18.2). It seems odd that the authorities should need an informer to provide this information, but the account of the arrest suggests that Jesus was not as well-known a figure in Jerusalem as Christian tradition assumes (14.44–6; cf. John 18.4f.).

**Judas** is described as **one of the Twelve**. The Greek is strange, lit. 10 'the one of the Twelve' (ὁ εἷς τῶν δώδεκα), but there are parallels to the construction in the everyday letters preserved in the papyri found in Egypt. There is no reason to think that the phrase is used to distinguish this Judas from someone else of the same name, for the name **Iscariot** already does that: rather it serves to emphasize the fact that even the traitor was one of the twelve disciples whom Jesus had chosen (cf. 3.19); there is already a hint here of the idea that he was chosen deliberately, because he was necessary to the divine plan (cf. John 13.27). The word **betray**, from the verb παραδίδωμι, echoes the word used in two of the passion predictions, where it suggests a 'handing-over' by God (9.31; 10.33; cf. 1.14; 14.41): even this supreme act of treachery by Judas can be used by God in working out his purpose. **He looked for an opportunity to betray him.** According to 11 Mark's account, this opportunity occurred on the following night, but it is possible that Mark has telescoped events.

# 4  PREPARATIONS FOR THE PASSOVER    14.12–16

*(Matt. 26.17–19; Luke 22.7–13)*

**(12) And on the first day of Unleavened Bread, when the passover**

lambs were slaughtered, his disciples said to him, 'Where do you wish us to go, to make preparations for you to eat the Passover?' (13) And he sent two of his disciples and told them, 'Go into the city, and a man carrying a jar of water will meet you: follow him. (14) And wherever he enters, say to the householder, "The Teacher says, 'Where is my room, where I may eat the Passover with my disciples?'" (15) And he will show you a large upstairs room, furnished and ready: prepare for us there.' (16) And the disciples set off and went into the city and found [everything] as he had told them, and they prepared the Passover.

It is quite clear from this passage that Mark believed the Last Supper to have been a passover meal. However, this is the only place in Mark where the identification is clearly made, and this section may be a late addition to the tradition about the passion. One indication of this, it is often suggested, is the use of the word **disciples** in vv.12, 13, 14 and 16, whereas we find references to **the Twelve** in the rest of the chapter. But this is not as significant as it seems, since the other references, apart from v.17, are all to Judas, who is described throughout the passion narrative as **one of the Twelve**.

One interesting feature of this section is its similarity to the story in 11.1–6, where Jesus sends two disciples into the village, telling them what they will find and what they are to say and do. The similarity extends even to the vocabulary (eleven consecutive words in 14.13 are identical with those in 11.1f.), and it looks very much, therefore, as though Mark is responsible for the present form of both stories.

This raises the question whether, if this is a Markan addition to an earlier narrative, Mark is in fact right in depicting the Last Supper as a passover meal, or whether this belief is itself a late development in the tradition. The main reason for doubting Mark's identification is the fact that John is equally clear in stating that Jesus died *before* the passover meal was eaten (John 18.28; 19.14); Matthew and Luke follow Mark's version, but Luke 22.15, which is probably intended to convey an unfulfilled wish, may support John's dating.

Since John has traditionally been regarded as the theologian among the evangelists, there has been a tendency to accept the synoptic tradition at this point, and to assume that the Johannine dating, which places the crucifixion one day earlier, is the result of theological interpretation. According to the Johannine chronology, Jesus died in the afternoon of the 14th Nisan, the day when the passover meal was being prepared, at the every hour when the lambs were being killed in the temple. This dating might well have arisen as a result of interpreting Jesus' death in terms of a paschal lamb, an interpretation that we find as early as Paul (1 Cor. 5.7). But it is equally possible that the Johannine dating is the correct one, and that it is the synoptic tradition that has been influenced by theological motives: if Jesus died at passover time, it was natural enough that the Last Supper of Jesus with his disciples should in time be assumed to have been a passover meal, especially since Jesus' actions at that meal were interpreted as symbolizing his death – an interpretation that is at least as early as Paul (cf. 1 Cor. 11.23–6). The question of whether or not the meal was a passover one must therefore be decided in other ways.

There are certain features in the evangelists' accounts of the supper and the events afterwards which seem particularly appropriate if it were in fact a passover meal. Among these are the late hour at which it is eaten (v.17), the wine that replaced the water drunk at ordinary meals (vv.23–5), the fact that the participants are said to recline at table (v.18), the hymn sung at the end of the meal (v.26), the way in which Jesus interprets what is taking place (vv.22–5), and the fact that Jesus and his disciples spend the night within the city limits (v.26). On the other hand, central features of the passover meal – the passover lamb, the bitter herbs, the explanation of the ritual as a re-enactment of the Exodus – are missing. If this was a passover meal, then we must assume that Mark's account omits these details because he is emphasizing what was distinctive and different on this particular occasion. Much more difficult are those elements in the story that seem inconsistent with the synoptic dating: chiefly, the extraordinary events which are said to take place on a feast day. If this was a passover meal, it means that the arrest, trial and crucifixion of Jesus all took place on 15th Nisan, which was a holy day. Although Jeremias, in his book *The Eucharistic Words of Jesus*, has argued that all the difficulties can be explained as permissible exceptions to the Jewish Law, there are really too many anomalies to make this convincing. It is much easier to understand, however, why Mark should have added details consistent with the meal being a Passover, if he in fact believed that this was what it was.

Some scholars have tried to maintain that both the Johannine and the synoptic traditions are in fact correct. The suggestion that Jesus might have celebrated the Passover 24 hours in advance – without a lamb – cannot be supported, but there is more to be said for the explanation given by A. Jaubert (*The Date of the Last Supper*). She argued that Jesus and his disciples celebrated the Passover on the 14th Nisan but calculated the date according to an ancient calendar set out in the book of Jubilees which was apparently followed by the community living at Qumran. This theory enabled her to maintain that Mark was right in describing the meal as a Passover (though she argued that it was held on the Tuesday, not the Thursday evening), and that John was correct in speaking of the day of the crucifixion as the day of preparation for the (official) Passover. This is an ingenious theory and has other advantages, for example, in allowing much more time between Jesus' arrest and crucifixion for the judicial procedures to take place. But it does not explain how Jesus and his disciples were able to eat the passover meal in Jerusalem three days before the official celebration – or, indeed, why they should wish to do so; what happened in Qumran (which had dissociated itself from what happened in Jerusalem) was a somewhat different matter. Nor does it explain why John should keep firmly to the official calendar and say nothing about the true character of the meal.

The weight of the evidence therefore seems to be in favour of the Johannine dating: in other words, it is likely that the Last Supper took place 'before the feast of the Passover' (John 13.1), and that the identification with the passover meal was made after the event. But though the chronology may be inaccurate, it can be argued that the change is not a serious distortion of the tradition, since men who had travelled to Jerusalem to celebrate the Passover and who gathered together for what was clearly a somewhat solemn meal on the eve of the festival must certainly have had that festival very much in their minds. More important still, Mark's account reflects the significance given to the tradition by the Christian community in the light of Jesus' subsequent death. (A useful summary of the arguments about the date for the Last Supper can be found in G. Ogg's essay, 'The chronology of the Last Supper'.)

12    Mark frequently places two temporal clauses together, presumably to make things clearer, but on this occasion he has only caused further confusion, since **the first day of Unleavened Bread** was the 15th Nisan, the day when the Passover was eaten, whereas the day **when the passover lambs were slaughtered** was the 14th Nisan. However, since the Jewish day began at sunset, it is true that the lambs were killed in the afternoon and eaten in the evening of what we should regard as the same day, and that the Feast of Unleavened Bread began on that evening. This probably explains Mark's dating, which suggests that this, at least, represents a non-Jewish viewpoint rather than early tradition. Alternative explanations are that the opening phrase is a mistranslation from the Aramaic, or that the 14th Nisan (when leaven was removed from the house) had come to be known in popular usage as the first day of the festival.

Although the **disciples** take the initiative in the story by asking what they are to do, everything centres on Jesus. It is natural that they should recognize his authority by asking him where he wishes them to prepare the meal, but remarkable that they should describe this as making **preparations for you to eat the Passover** rather than 'for

13    us'. **He sent two of his disciples,** as he had done in 11.1, to make the necessary preparations. **A man carrying a jar of water** was a fairly unusual sight, since water-carriers normally used leather bottles. It is useless to speculate as to whether or not this story owes its origin to

some pre-arrangement between Jesus and the householder; for Mark, that is beside the point. The significance of the story for him is quite different: he sees Jesus as totally in control of the situation and demonstrates how everything needed by Jesus is provided. There is no suggestion that Jesus is in hiding, or that the preparations are being carried out in secret; anyone could have followed the disciples, just as they followed their guide.

In 11.1–7 the statement that 'the Master needs it' (with the possible **14** hint that Jesus is the real owner) was a sufficient reason for Jesus to be sent a colt; so now, the message from **the Teacher**, asking **'Where is my room?'** (with the strangely proprietary 'my') will evoke a willing response from the householder. **The Passover** had to be eaten in Jerusalem, and it was therefore normal – and necessary – to make a request to use a room for the evening. Jesus is offered **a large 15 upstairs room**, which suggests unusually spacious accommodation, and this room is found **furnished and ready.** It is pointless to discuss to what extent the room was in fact furnished: for Mark, the significant fact is that the room is ready, and that Jesus is therefore provided with all he needs. **The disciples found [everything] as he had told 16 them.** As in 11.1–7, when the disciples do what Jesus commands, they find his word fulfilled. Mark reminds us again that, though Jesus' enemies are plotting to kill him, he not only knows beforehand what will happen, but is deliberately carrying out something which is in God's control, not theirs. **And they prepared the Passover:** the preparations included the provision of unleavened bread, wine and bitter herbs, and the roasting of the lamb, which was killed in the temple in the afternoon.

# 5  PROPHECY OF BETRAYAL                                    14.17–21

*(Matt. 26.20–5; Luke 22.14, 21–3)*

**(17) And when it was evening, he came with the Twelve; (18) and as they sat at table eating, Jesus said, 'Truly I tell you, one of you will betray me – one who is eating with me.' (19) They began to be distressed, and to ask him one after another, 'Surely you do not mean me?' (20) 'It is one of the Twelve,' he told them, 'who is dipping with me into the dish. (21) For the Son of man goes as it is written of him, but woe to that man by whom the Son of man is betrayed! It would have been better for that man if he had never been born.'**

The significance of this passage lies in the fact that Jesus is shown as fully aware of what is about to take place. He is not taken by surprise

335

by Judas' treachery but accepts it as part of his destiny. The story therefore underlines the obedience of Jesus to God's will, and the belief that the divine purpose is set out in scripture.

17    The incident is set in the context of the Last Supper. Since it is **evening**, it must now be 15th Nisan according to Mark's reckoning. Neither in this section nor the next (vv.22–5) is the meal specifically identified as a passover celebration, though the previous paragraph makes Mark's own understanding clear. Some of the features of the narrative support Mark's interpretation, but these may in fact represent adaptations that have been made to the story in the belief that the meal was a Passover; they are not necessarily accurate reports of what took place.

18    The statement that they were **eating** will be echoed in v.22, an indication that Mark has here combined two originally independent pericopae. The Greek verb translated **sat at table** (ἀνακειμένων) means literally 'were reclining'. This posture was adopted by the Jews for eating the Passover as a symbol of their liberation from slavery in Egypt; at other meals it would have been unusual for first-century Jews to recline. The verb **betray** (παραδίδωμι) has been used repeatedly in Mark, both to describe the action of Judas (3.19; 14.10f.), and to prophesy the fate of Jesus (9.31; 10.33) – a fate shared already by his forerunner (1.14) and prophesied for his followers (13.9, 11f.): Judas' act of treachery is seen by Mark as part of the divine plan. The reference to Judas as **one who is eating with me** is reminiscent of Ps. 41.9, a passage that is quoted in John 13.18 and was used in attempting to explain the defection of one of Jesus' close friends. The disciples' response is strange. We might expect them to

19    ask 'Who is it?' and to take action; instead, **one after another**, they ask **'Surely you do not mean me?'** It is true that the form of the question (μήτι ἐγώ;) means that it looks for the answer 'no', but we hardly expect them to raise the question, even in this negative form. Peter's indignant reaction a few verses later (v.29) is much more

20    natural. Their question serves, however, to introduce Jesus' next words: **it is one of the Twelve. . .who is dipping with me into the dish.** Since eating together was a sign of fellowship, these words underline Judas' treachery. The common dish is an essential part of the passover ceremony, though it was used at other meals also; in Mark's setting, we naturally think of the passover ritual. In Matthew, the story is expanded in order to make it clear that Jesus knew which of the Twelve it was (Matt. 26.25; cf. also John 13.21–30). The saying

21    about **the Son of man** which rounds off this section stresses the same themes – the divine plan, set out in scripture, and Jesus' obedience to it. Jesus **goes** on the way ordained by God, a way that leads to death. The verb to go (ὑπάγω) is taken up by the fourth evangelist and used of Jesus going to the Father (e.g. John 7.33; 8.14; 16.5) but is not nor-

mally used in the sense of 'to die': here, it strengthens the sense of necessity that governs Jesus' destiny. Nevertheless, the belief that what happens to Jesus **is written of him** in no way exonerates Judas, **by whom the Son of man is betrayed.** The verb 'betray' (παραδίδωμι once again) might well be translated here by 'handed over' and demonstrates the way in which Mark holds together divine predestination and human freedom: Judas is the one by whom Jesus is betrayed, an act of treachery so vile that **it would have been better for that man if he had never been born;** but he is also the one through whom God achieves his purpose to hand Jesus over to his executioners.

# 6  THE LAST SUPPER                                14.22-5

*(Matt. 26.26-9; Luke 22.15-20)*

**(22) And as they were eating, he took bread and praised [God]; and he broke [it] and gave [it] to them and said, 'Take, this is my body.' (23) Then he took a cup and gave thanks [to God]; and he gave it to them, and they all drank from it. (24) And he said to them, 'This is my blood of the covenant,[1] poured out for many. (25) Truly I tell you: I will never drink again from the fruit of the vine, until that day when I drink it new in the Kingdom of God.'**

Mark's account of the Last Supper is brief and almost certainly reflects the form of wording used at the celebration of the eucharist in his own church. The setting he gives it establishes his understanding of its character: the meal is a Passover (vv.12–16), the celebration of Israel's redemption from Egypt; and Jesus' conversation at the meal concerns his imminent betrayal and death (vv.17–21). St Paul, similarly, links this Last Supper closely with the theme of Jesus' death when he introduces his account of the meal in 1 Cor. 11.23 with the words 'the Lord Jesus on the night when he was betrayed....' Mark's account (which is followed closely by Matthew) is independent of Paul's, but Luke's version seems to reflect both traditions and is further complicated by the different textual readings at Luke 22.19f. The question of what happened in the upper room, and which account is closest to Jesus' original words, is an extremely complex one. The answer depends in part on the nature of the meal, and whether Mark is right in depicting it as a Passover: it needs to be remembered that this information is given only in Mark 14.12–16,

1 Following א B C D^c L Θ Ψ. A fams. 1 and 13 and many other MSS and versions read *of the new covenant.*

and that none of the accounts of the Last Supper states that it was in fact a passover meal. It depends also on Jesus' own understanding of his role, and in particular of his death, and the extent to which his words and actions were given a sacrificial interpretation subsequently by the Church. Did not the fact that this meal took place just before Jesus' death inevitably change the significance of his words in retrospect? Was the original importance of the meal perhaps primarily that it was the last of a number of 'fellowship meals' eaten by Jesus and his disciples, and do Luke's references to the breaking of bread in Acts indicate that the early Church continued to gather for such meals in the presence of their risen Lord? If so, has the celebration of the eucharist developed out of one particular interpretation of these meals, which emphasized the significance of Jesus' death for the community, or did the Church celebrate a memorial of the Lord's death – as distinct from fellowship meals – from the very beginning? Perhaps we should not try to distinguish too sharply between these explanations. Clearly the Last Supper was remembered, not simply because it was the last meal of Jesus with the Twelve, but because he did and said something memorable. Nevertheless the occasion, special though it may have been, was presumably one of many meals which Jesus ate with his disciples, and we need to remember that eating together was seen as an important means of establishing fellowship. The suggestion that the meals eaten together by early Christians fell into two distinct categories – eucharists (celebrations of the Last Supper) and agapes (fellowship meals) is probably too rigid. It seems more likely that such gatherings would have reflected a spectrum of ideas and associations.

A comparison of the various accounts of the meal reveals different emphases. Matthew adds to Mark the commands to eat and drink, and thereby shifts attention from the act of sharing to the elements themselves. His further addition of the phrase 'for the forgiveness of sins' may be derived from Jeremiah's words about the new covenant (31.34) but could simply spell out his understanding of the nature of the sacrifice implied by Mark's **poured out**. The shorter Lukan text stresses only the sharing of the *cup*, while the longer text describes the bread as 'given', and the wine as 'poured out', so stressing the sacrificial interpretation of Jesus' death.[1] A similar adaptation can be seen taking place in 1 Cor. 11.24, where the most likely explanation of the textual variant is that an original statement that Christ's body is 'for you' has been filled out by the words 'broken' or 'given'. Paul's version in 1 Corinthians 11 lacks the Markan formula **gave it to them** and so links the explanatory words more closely with the bread and the cup: the emphasis is on the eating and drinking, which are a

1 There is a major textual problem in Luke 22: some MSS omit vv.19b–20.

means of fellowship with Jesus (1 Cor. 11.26; cf. 10.16). Paul stresses that the symbolic actions with bread and cup are a 'memorial' of Jesus, but this 'memorial' is an act which proclaims not only his death but his coming again. All the accounts link the cup with the theme of the covenant, with the exception of the shorter Lukan version; but even here the cup is linked with the coming Kingdom, and in Luke 22.28–30 Jesus speaks of this Kingdom as something which has been 'covenanted' to him and which he now 'covenants' to his disciples. All the evangelists link the wine with the wine which will be drunk in this coming Kingdom, and Paul sees both eating and drinking as pointing to the future (1 Cor. 11.26).

It is clearly impossible for us now to reconstruct the original scene underlying this variety of interpretation. Some scholars maintain that Mark's account represents reasonably faithfully what Jesus did and said (e.g. J. Jeremias, *Eucharistic Words*); others suggest that the significance of what Jesus did and said has been drastically changed in the light of his death and resurrection. It is interesting to note that the directions for holding the eucharist given in the Didache, a Christian writing of the second century, include a totally different tradition from the biblical one about the words that are to be said over the cup (there mentioned first, as in Luke 22.17) and the bread. One possibility is that the symbol of the bread goes back to the Last Supper, but that the interpretation of the wine was added later. Certainly we have references to meals where bread was broken but no wine was drunk (Acts 2.42; Acts of Peter 5, Acts of John 109f. and Acts of Thomas 27 all refer to this breaking of bread as a eucharist), and 1 Cor. 11.25 also suggests that wine was not always drunk. Of course, this may have been due to the fact that wine was not a normal constituent of everyday meals, rather than because it was not given a symbolic interpretation by Jesus at the Last Supper. But it may be that the symbolic actions with bread and wine belong to separate traditions and have been brought together: there is some support for this in John, where the eucharistic teaching is attached to the feeding narrative and the discourse about bread in chapter 6. It is possible that the symbolic sharing of wine had its origin in the theme of the messianic banquet. In this connection, it is worthy of note that the Qumran community not only looked forward to the meal which would be eaten in the last days in company with the anointed priest and the Messiah of Israel (1QSa. 2) but modelled their present community meals on this pattern: these meals were therefore pointers to this future fellowship (1QS 6). (For a recent discussion of the issues, see X. Léon-Dufour, *Sharing the Eucharistic Bread*.)

Mark's own community would presumably have gathered together regularly to celebrate the Lord's Supper and would therefore have been very much aware that in doing so they were sharing in and appropriating what took place in the upper room.

22     **And as they were eating.** This new introduction echoes that in
v.18 and would follow more appropriately immediately after v.17.
Mark has apparently combined two separate traditions about what
happened at the meal, and this one was probably already in use at
Christian gatherings (cf. 1 Cor. 11.23–5). The statement that they
were already eating when Jesus distributed the **bread** indicates that
this was a special meal, at which a preliminary course was served –
another indication of the belief that this was a passover celebration.

**He took bread and praised [God]; and he broke [it] and gave [it]
to them.** The four verbs echo those used in 6.41 and 8.6f.: they were
familiar actions at any meal, for it was normal for the head of the
family to offer thanksgiving in this way. It is not the bread that is
blessed but God, probably in the words of the Jewish prayer of
thanksgiving: 'Blessed art Thou, Lord our God, King of the universe,
who bringest forth bread from the earth'. The ritual establishes the
fellowship of those who share in the meal, a factor that is underlined
by Jesus' first word, **take**; by sharing the bread, they share in fellowship together.

The interpretation of some of the elements in the meal was another
feature of the passover ritual, and the words **this is my body...this is
my blood** are reminiscent of those used at the passover meal to
describe unleavened bread: 'this (is) the bread of affliction'. Whatever the origin of the sayings over the bread and the cup, by the time
of Mark the Christian community is looking back on the death of
Jesus in a way similar to that in which the Jews looked back to the
Exodus, and the eucharist has become a celebration of God's saving
activity, centred on the death of Jesus. His self-sacrifice is seen as the
new act of redemption, establishing a covenant between God and his
people which supersedes the old covenant between God and Israel.
The words of institution inevitably reflect the Church's understanding of that event, as well as its celebration in the eucharist.

The two sayings are parallel and stand side by side. Wine was drunk
only on special occasions, not at ordinary meals, but it was an essential part of the celebration of Passover. If the Last Supper was a
passover meal, then the most natural **cup** to be interpreted was the
last one, or cup of blessing, at the conclusion of the meal. Paul reflects
this tradition, when he says that Jesus took the cup 'after supper'
(1 Cor. 11.25; so too Luke 22.20) and when he refers to 'the cup of
blessing' (1 Cor. 10.16). If this is the original setting, and if the words
go back to Jesus himself, then these two sentences were not spoken
together but at the beginning and the end of the meal. However, we
have already seen that the Johannine dating is more likely to be
correct than the Markan, in which case the meal was not a Passover;
and though we might nevertheless expect the approaching festival to
dominate the thoughts of all who were present, we would not expect

the participants to enact the ritual of the feast itself. If the sayings do go back to Jesus, therefore, we should not necessarily link his words and actions with particular parts of the passover celebration.

What do the words **this is my body** signify? Although the Greek has ἐστιν, there would have been no copula in Aramaic, which means that interpretations which have stressed the material identity of Jesus' body with the bread are certainly mistaken. Yet the translation 'represents' is inadequate. Jesus' actions in breaking and distributing the bread are not just a dramatic illustration of his teaching; they are a symbolic representation of what is actually taking place, and the words explain the actions. Because the term **body** stands in parallel with **blood**, there is a tendency to understand it as meaning 'flesh'. This interpretation had already been made by the time John 6.52–8 was written. But the Greek word σῶμα, translated body, is ambiguous in meaning and can denote not only the physical body, but also the 'person' or 'self'. It may be that the word σῶμα translates a similar term in Aramaic, *gūp*, but since the Markan words are a liturgical formula, they may well be a summary rather than a full account of Jesus' words. Taking words and actions together, it seems likely that in sharing the bread among his disciples, Jesus was sharing something of his own personality with them. How should we understand this? Is it a promise to be with them? This is certainly one way in which the Christian community understood the celebration of the Lord's Supper (so, e.g., 1 Cor. 10.21). Is it perhaps a handing-over of authority and mission? This idea is found in Luke's account of the conversation at the meal (Luke 22.28–30). In this case, Jesus' distribution of bread would be to some extent analogous to Elijah's action in 1 Kings 19.19, where he throws his cloak over Elisha and so marks him out as his successor. Taken on their own, the distribution of the bread and the saying linked with this action suggest ideas of fellowship and joint enterprise. It is the close association with the saying over the cup that throws emphasis on the bread itself and suggests sacrificial ideas. Although Mark does not include the command to the disciples to repeat the rite which is found in 1 Corinthians 11 and Luke 22, the account of the Last Supper that he gives must have been familiar to the members of the Christian community for whom he is writing, for they would have been aware of the link between what happened in the upper room and what happens when Christians meet to eat and drink together. Just as Jews, celebrating the Passover, identify themselves with their forefathers fleeing from slavery in Egypt, so that the unleavened bread becomes for them the bread of affliction, so the Christian community, in taking the bread, shares in the body of Jesus, given to his disciples. In this sense, the words and actions of Jesus become a new passover rite, whether or not the original setting was a passover meal.

23    The **cup** is a communal one, since **they all drank from it**. Information about whether or not this was normal at celebrations of the
Passover at this date is uncertain. Customary or not, the passing
round of one cup, like the action of breaking and sharing bread,
stresses the disciples' participation in what Jesus gives them. A
similar emphasis is found in the independent Lukan tradition about
the cup in Luke 22.17, where Jesus tells the disciples to 'divide' the
cup among themselves. To share someone's cup is to have close
fellowship with them.

24    **This is my blood.** These words are extremely difficult. No Jew
could have regarded the drinking of blood with anything but horror,
for the blood represented the life of an animal and belonged to the
Lord. The blood of any sacrifice was poured out as an offering, and
animals killed for human consumption must be drained of all blood
before being eaten. Once again, therefore, the word **is** should not be
understood to mean material identity. Even the notion of drinking
wine which 'represents' blood is difficult. Nevertheless, red wine is
an obvious image for blood, and this link was certainly made at an
early stage (see 1 Cor. 10.16). It is worth noting (1) that according to
Mark the interpretation is given after the disciples drink from the cup,
not before – i.e., it seems to be an interpretation of the act of sharing the
wine, rather than of the wine itself; (2) that in the parallel Pauline
account, the words are 'This cup is the new covenant in my blood'
(1 Cor. 11.25): the emphasis there falls on the cup, and on the fact that
it signifies a new covenant, ratified in Jesus' blood; (3) that Mark does
not find the statement **this is my blood** sufficient explanation but
continues with the words **of the covenant, poured out for many**.

Although it has been argued by some that the words **'this (is) my
blood'** represent the earliest form of the tradition (so Jeremias,
*Eucharistic Words*, pp. 168–203, who dates it to the decade following
Jesus' death), it seems impossible that Jesus himself could have used
these words about the wine, even as a comparison. It is more likely
that they are a liturgical development which brings the saying over
the wine into line with that over the bread. Certainly it looks as
though Mark has brought together different traditions, for Aramaic
scholars maintain that it is impossible to translate the phrase **my
blood of the covenant** into Aramaic. If so, then the interpretation in
terms of a covenant may be earlier than that which referred to 'my
blood': certainly the covenant interpretation was known already to
Paul (1 Cor. 11.25), whose version of the saying avoids some of the
problems found in Mark. The **covenant** was seen in the Old Testament as the means by which God established a relation between himself and men, and the covenant on Sinai was ratified by blood,
sprinkled on the people (Exod. 24.8). The word 'new' which is found
in some MSS is probably the result of assimilation to Paul's account in

1 Corinthians 11. The final clause is couched in sacrificial language: the blood of Jesus is **poured out**, i.e. his life is offered up to God, for the sake of **many**. As in 10.45, the 'many' stand in contrast to the 'one' who gives up his life. How his death benefits them is not explained: Matthew adds the phrase 'for the forgiveness of sins', but in view of the passover setting of the story, Mark may well have the passover lamb in mind and so be thinking of the death of Jesus as the redemptive act which brings the new community of God's people into existence.

The final saying of Jesus over the cup echoes words used in the 25 passover liturgy, where God is blessed as the one who 'creates **the fruit of the vine**'. It also points forward to the time when Jesus will **drink** wine **new in the Kingdom of God**. The image is that of the messianic banquet, which symbolized the joy that was expected to accompany the new age (see e.g. Isa. 25.6; 2 Baruch 29.5–8; Matt. 8.11; Luke 14.15; Rev. 19.9). Here is yet another tradition about the significance of the cup, and one that may well be the earliest of all. In the Lukan tradition, which appears to be independent of Mark, Jesus tells the disciples to take and share the cup, since he himself will not drink 'from now on...of the fruit of the vine until the Kingdom of God comes'. In their Lukan version, these words are sometimes interpreted as a vow of abstention, but linked as they are with Jesus' action in giving the cup to the disciples, they seem to indicate that Jesus is understood to be handing over authority to his disciples, who will now have to carry on his work – an idea which, we have already suggested, may be conveyed by his action in distributing the bread. In Mark, however, the words lack both the phrase 'from now on' and the implication that the disciples will carry on what Jesus cannot do: the emphasis here is on what Jesus himself does and achieves. Placed where it is, the saying suggests that Mark perhaps sees the death of Jesus as being in some way instrumental in bringing about the arrival of God's Kingdom.

# 7   PROPHECY OF DENIAL                         14.26–31

*(Matt. 26.30–5; Luke 22.39, 31–4)*

**(26) And when they had sung a hymn, they went out to the Mount of Olives. (27) And Jesus said to them, 'You will all fall away, for it is written,**

> **"I will strike the shepherd,**
> **and the sheep will be scattered."**

(28) But after I am raised, I shall go before you into Galilee.'[1] (29) Then Peter said to him, 'Even if they all fall away, yet I will not.' (30) And Jesus said to him, 'Truly I tell you, today, this very night, before the cock crows twice, you will deny me three times.' (31) But he declared emphatically, 'Even if I have to die with you, I will never deny you'; and so said they all.

The account of the Last Supper is flanked by two pericopes in which Jesus foretells the disloyalty of his disciples. This paragraph shows signs of Markan redaction. V.28 seems an intrusion between Jesus' words in v.27 and Peter's reply in v.29, but it is a key saying for Mark, since it points forward to 16.7. Without it, the pericope speaks only of failure – the disciples will fall away (σκανδαλισθήσεσθε – 'you will be tripped up') and deny (ἀπαρνήσῃ) Jesus: their failure puts them among those who are ashamed of Jesus and his words (8.38). Throughout the gospel, Mark has stressed the failure of the disciples to comprehend, but they have at least followed him. Now they will fail to do even that. But v.28 introduces a different note: since the risen Jesus will still summon them to follow him as his disciples, his resurrection will mean restoration for them, also.

26    And when they had sung a hymn. Mark is no doubt thinking of the second part of the so-called Egyptian Hallel (Pss. 114/5–118, which are psalms of praise inspired by the Exodus; there was disagreement between the schools of Hillel and Shammai about whether Psalm 114 was included in the first or the second part) which was sung at the end of the passover meal. The Mount of Olives fell within the boundary of greater Jerusalem, in which passover night had to be spent. Once again, these details are compatible with Mark's belief that the meal was a Passover, but are by no means proof that he was right.

27    Jesus' prophecy of the disciples' failure is backed up by a quotation from Zech. 13.7, which introduces a new image – that of the sheep who are scattered. This quotation has probably been added at some stage to the prediction that the disciples will fall away. The saying from Zechariah may originally have been used by the Christian community as a proof-text for the death of Jesus, but in this context it serves to show that the flight of the disciples (v.50) was also part of God's plan. The change from the imperative (Strike!) in Zech. 13.7 to the first person singular, I will strike, underlines the point which is by now familiar in Mark's story: even human weakness and hard-heartedness are part of the divine purpose. What takes place is both foretold in scripture and accepted in obedience by Jesus.

28    It is interesting to discover that v.28 is missing from a third-century papyrus fragment found in Egypt known as the Fayyum gospel-fragment, which consists of part of this pericope. This might be evidence

1 V.28 is missing from the Fayyum fragment.

for a pre-Markan form of the story, but the fragment could equally well be an abridgement of the Markan story. The verb to **go before** (προάγω) is as ambiguous in Greek as in English: Jesus' words can mean either that he is going on ahead of the disciples to **Galilee** (where they will see him – cf. 6.45) or that he will lead them there (cf. 10.32). In 16.7 the promise is perhaps interpreted in the former sense, but here the image of the **shepherd** in the previous verse compels us to think of a shepherd leading his flock. Not only will Jesus himself be **raised**; the scattered flock will be brought together again, under their shepherd's leadership. In spite of their failure, the shepherd will still acknowledge his sheep; this is perhaps the significance of the reference to Galilee, which has been the centre of Jesus' ministry and their discipleship, in contrast to Jerusalem, the place of suffering. This prophecy remains unfulfilled in Mark's story. But since Jesus' other predictions – including those immediately before and after, in vv.27 and 30 – are fulfilled, we may have every confidence that this one will be also. It is confirmed in 16.7.

Peter's protest picks up Jesus' prophecy in v.27 that **all** the disciples  29
will **fall away**: he at least, he claims, **even if they all fall away…will
not.** But his boast serves to introduce a worse prediction. Peter will
not only fall away, but will **deny** Jesus **three times.** Once again, Jesus  30
foresees all that will take place, and this time his knowledge is emphasized by the accuracy with which he forecasts the moment of
Peter's apostasy – **this very night, before the cock crows twice.**

Peter protests his readiness to share Jesus' sufferings: **even if I**  31
**have to die with you, I will never deny you.** To fail at this point will
be to disown Jesus in deed as well as in name, since in calling men to
discipleship, Jesus called them to share his fate (8.34; cf. 13.9–13). But
the disciples have not grasped what it means to save one's life by
losing it (8.35), and they are not yet ready to share Jesus' cup and
baptism (10.38f.), though they all join Peter in protesting their
willingness to die with their master.


# 8   GETHSEMANE                                    14.32–42

*(Matt. 26.36–46; Luke 22.40–6; John 18.1)*

**(32) They reached a place called Gethsemane, and he said to his
disciples, 'Sit here while I pray.' (33) And he took with him Peter
and James and John and began to be troubled and distressed.
(34) And he said to them, 'My heart is overwhelmed with grief and
is ready to break. Stay here and keep watch.' (35) And going forward a little, he threw himself on the ground and prayed that if it
were possible, the hour might pass from him. (36) And he said,**

'Abba, Father, all things are possible to you. Take this cup away from me: yet not my will, but yours.' (37) And he came and found them sleeping and said to Peter, 'Simon, are you asleep? Did you not have the strength to keep watch for one hour? (38) Keep watch, and pray that you do not fall into temptation. The spirit is willing, but the flesh is weak.' (39) And going away again, he prayed, saying the same words.[1] (40) And returning again, he found them sleeping, for their eyes were very heavy; and they did not know how to answer him. (41) And he cane the third time and said to them: 'Are you still sleeping and taking your rest? Enough![2] The hour has come. Look, the Son of man is handed over into the hands of sinners. (42) Get up! Let us go. Look, my betrayer is here.'

Although this story betrays some signs of artificiality (e.g. the three-fold return of Jesus, the words of a prayer which no one is awake to hear), there is no reason to deny its historical basis. The incident is unusually well attested, being referred to in Heb. 5.7, in addition to the echoes of Jesus' words in John 12.27, 14.31 and 18.11. Moreover, Luke's version may be an independent one, and Mark's account looks very much like the amalgamation of two sources. We notice, for example, that Jesus first leaves all the disciples (v.32), then three of them (v.34); that we are given the substance of the prayer in v.35f, followed by precise words in v.36; Jesus is said to leave the three disciples twice (vv.34, 39) but returns to them three times (vv.37, 40, 41), though the larger group is not mentioned again. Either Mark has combined two versions of the story, or he has expanded the tradition he inherited in order to emphasize the role of Peter, James and John, who figure prominently elsewhere in his gospel. Another reason for affirming the historical basis of the tradition underlying this story is the fact that the picture of Jesus given here is in tension with Mark's usual presentation. We have seen how Mark elsewhere demonstrates his belief that the death of Jesus is part of God's purpose, set out in scripture and accepted by Jesus, who speaks of it as necessary and inescapable. Here, however, we find Jesus praying that the cup may be removed, and he is pictured as **troubled and distressed**. It is difficult to believe that this scene would have been invented by Jesus' followers, for the tendency would have been to present him facing death calmly and serenely. It is interesting to compare John 12.27, where Jesus describes himself as 'disturbed', but where he is nevertheless presented as free from stress and totally in control of the situation. Mark's picture of Jesus in Gethsemane rings true, for it

---

1 The phrase *saying the same words* is omitted by D and old Latin MSS.
2 Reading ἀπέχει. D W Θ Ψ fam. 13 and some Latin and Syriac MSS read ἀπέχει τὸ τέλος.

shows us the struggle of someone who faces up to the likelihood of imminent suffering, not knowing what the outcome of events will be. Jesus grapples with the horror of violent death, recognizing it, as did every Jew, as an outrage. Within Mark's framework, this struggle is bound to look artificial: can Jesus really suppose that the cup he has long accepted as inevitable can be taken away? But in the context of Jesus' life, it is believable. There is no reason to doubt that Jesus had reckoned with the possibility of death and was aware of the danger involved in going to Jerusalem. He must have been aware that faithfulness to the commands of God would probably lead to a collision with the authorities, and so to disaster and death. But if we recognize that the theme of inevitability in the gospel narrative is the result of hindsight then there is every reason to believe that in preaching the Kingdom of God, Jesus hoped that Israel would respond to his call to repent and accept God's rule, and that, in challenging the authorities in Jerusalem, he hoped that even they would respond. If this was Jesus' hope, then to the end there must have been two possibilities before him: on the one hand, the success of his mission, on the other, apparent failure and inevitable suffering for himself. It was perhaps the realization that his mission had 'failed', and that Israel was deaf and blind to his message, that is reflected in the Gethsemane tradition. For Mark, of course, and for the whole Christian community, the death of Jesus was now seen to be the fulfilment of his mission, since apparent failure had been turned into victory by the resurrection: it is hardly surprising if such a momentous belief has affected the way in which much of the story is told.

The name **Gethsemane** means 'oil press', which suggests that the 32 **place** (or plot of ground) was probably an olive orchard; John refers to a 'garden' (18.1). The traditional site of Gethsemane is situated on the lower slopes of the Mount of Olives, on the eastern side of the Kidron valley. It is dominated on the west by the temple mount which lowers over it, and is still an impressive and evocative site. Jesus leaves **his disciples** in order to **pray** alone (cf. 6.46). V.35 would follow on naturally here, but instead we have what may be either an 33 independent version of the story in vv.33f., or an addition of Mark's own. Jesus takes **with him Peter and James and John**, but then leaves them with instructions to keep watch while he prays. These three disciples have been mentioned together at various points in the narrative (with Andrew in 1.16–20, 29ff.; in 5.37ff.; in 9.2–8; with Andrew in 13.3ff.), as well as appearing on their own from time to time (John, in 9.38; James and John, 10.35–45; Peter, 1.36; 8.29, 32f.; 9.5; 10.28; 11.21; 14.29ff.). Possibly this simply means that Mark found their names in the tradition. But it may be significant that these three disciples have throughout Mark's story been Jesus' closest companions. Those who have seen Jesus raise the dead (5.37ff.), witnessed his transfiguration and seen the glory that can be spoken of only after his own resurrection (9.2ff.), and who have heard his teaching about the suffering and final vindication that await his followers (13.3ff.), ought to be able to strengthen him as he approaches death. Moreover, all three have boasted of their ability to share his suffering (10.35–40; 14.29ff.); now they are given the opportunity to prove their boast. But since they have consistently failed to understand that glory comes only through suffering, the outcome is inevitable.

The anguish of Jesus is described in two forceful words which both express strong emotion: he was **troubled and distressed**. A similar

34 picture is given in Heb. 5.7. His first words – **My heart is overwhelmed with grief** – echo the lament which forms the refrain of Psalms 42–3. The command to the three disciples to **keep watch** picks up a theme which dominates the final parable in Mark 13. There the disciples are commanded to keep watch, because they do not know when the End will come. The injunction here means more than simply 'keep awake': the time of testing has already begun, and if the disciples are not to succumb they must be ready to meet it.

35 **He threw himself on the ground.** The action conveys the urgency of Jesus' supplication. His prayer that **the hour might pass from him** picks up a term (ὥρα) that Mark has used already in 13.11 and 32 of the crucial hour of testing. For Jesus, this hour comes with his arrest and death. The fourth evangelist takes over the term and uses it in a distinctive way of the death of Jesus, but he sees this, not as an hour of testing, but as an hour of triumph and glory (John 2.4; 7.30; 12.23, 27).

36 The Aramaic word **Abba** – a form of address meaning **Father** – is retained not only here but in Rom. 8.15 and Gal. 4.6, where the sign of Christian freedom is the fact that Christians are able to address God with these words because the Spirit of his Son lives in them. Its retention suggests that it was remembered as Jesus' distinctive way of addressing God, though somewhat surprisingly this is the only place in the gospels where it is found. **Abba** was used not only by a child addressing a parent but also, according to the Babylonian Talmud, as a courtesy by a disciple addressing his rabbi. It has been argued (notably by J. Jeremias, *The Prayers of Jesus*, pp. 11–65, 108–12; *Theology* I, pp. 62–8) that this particular form of the Aramaic word is an especially intimate one, and that it is used nowhere else in Judaism as an address to God, so that Jesus' prayer is unique. In fact, the evidence is not quite so unambiguous, nor can we be certain that we have access to it all (see G. Vermes, *Jesus and the World of Judaism*, pp. 39–43, and J. Barr, *J.T.S.*, n.s. 39, 1988, pp. 28–47 for criticism of Jeremias' view). Nevertheless, the use of the Aramaic word here and in Romans and Galatians does suggest that this mode of address was regarded as unusual and was therefore remembered. The word 'Father' is the first of several 'echoes' of the Lord's Prayer in Jesus'

words: 'Father...not my will, but yours...pray that you do not fall into temptation.' It would not be surprising if Jesus used on this occasion petitions that he had taught his disciples, but it would be equally natural if others later attributed to him language which echoes the prayer used by the Christian community. Jesus prays that God will remove the **cup** which he has to drink. This image has been used already for Jesus' sufferings and death in 10.38. The prayer is set in the context of an affirmation of God's power – **all things are possible to you** – and the acknowledgement that God's will must be done – **not my will, but yours.** Once again we are reminded by Mark that Jesus is obedient to God's will.

Then, in contrast, we return to the familiar theme of the disciples' 37 failure. Jesus finds the three whom he has commanded to keep watch **sleeping:** they have failed him. **Peter** – who has been so vigorous in declaring his ability to stand by Jesus – is singled out for rebuke. The use of his own name, **Simon**, indicates the seriousness of this failure to support Jesus: he is no true disciple. If they fail **to keep watch** even **for one hour** they will fail in the coming test, and that means that Jesus' words in 14.27 will be fulfilled: they will fall away and deny Jesus by deserting him. But Jesus charges them a second time to **keep** 38 **watch.** They are to **pray that** they **do not fall into temptation.** This prayer is less a prayer to escape testing, than to be able to withstand it. Since they have declared their willingness to share Jesus' suffering, their prayer ought to echo his – 'Save us from this hour; take this cup away from us; yet not our will, but yours'. In the event, they refuse to drink the cup. By running away, they save their lives, but succumb to temptation. The saying that **the spirit is willing, but the flesh is weak** sums up the disciples' dilemma: 'spirit' represents human response to God, while 'flesh' represents human weakness (cf. Isa 31.3).

**And going away again, he prayed, saying the same words.** The 39 last phrase may be a later gloss, since it is missing from some MSS; whether it is original or not, its purpose is to emphasize the intensity of Jesus' struggle. The statement that **they did not know how to** 40 answer him echoes 9.6. **And he came the third time.** The three-fold 41 pattern is a familiar one and serves to emphasize the disciples' failure. Three times they fail to watch and fall asleep. We are not surprised, however, since Jesus warned them three times what was to happen to him, and they failed to understand. Mark probably intends us to see a link also with Peter's three-fold denial in the next chapter: if he fails to watch three times, it is hardly surprising if he fails to withstand temptation three times also.

The word **Enough!** represents an attempt to translate a Greek word (ἀπέχει) which is totally obscure. It has to be admitted that there is very little evidence for this particular interpretation, but the Vulgate, which reads *sufficit*, seems to have understood it in this way. But what is enough? Perhaps we should understand it to mean 'Enough of sleeping'. Some MSS add the words 'the end' (το τέλος) which would enable us to give the verb a more usual sense and translate the whole sentence as another question: 'Is the end far off?' (i.e. are you assuming that there is no imminent danger?). However, this reading was probably an attempt to make sense of a word which was already proving difficult to understand. But this is certainly a feasible meaning of the verb, and possibly Mark was thinking of either the hour or the betrayer (both of which have now arrived) as its subject, in which case the sense would be 'Far off? No! Already here!' The suggestion that the verb is used in its technical sense to mean 'the account is paid', and therefore means that Judas has already received his money, seems a desperate expedient. It would be nice if this technical sense could be stretched to mean 'The time is up!', but once again, evidence for this is lacking.

**The hour** from which Jesus has prayed to be delivered **has come.** What he has foretold is fulfilled – **the Son of man is handed over** (or betrayed) **into the hands of sinners.** Once again, the verb παραδίδωμι has a double sense and conveys both the idea that Jesus is betrayed by the treachery of men, and that what is taking place is part of the divine purpose. Equally important for Mark is the theme of Jesus' obedience, which is demonstrated in his words '**Get up! Let us go.**' Jesus is ready to meet the suffering which he knows awaits him. His final comment, **Look, my betrayer is here,** shows that Mark believes him to have been fully expecting what was taking place.

# 9  THE ARREST                                14.43–52

*(Matt. 26.47–56; Luke 22.47–53; John 18.2–11)*

**(43) And suddenly, while he was still speaking, Judas, one of the Twelve, arrived, and with him a crowd armed with swords and cudgels, sent by the chief priests and scribes and elders. (44) Now his betrayer had given them a signal, saying, 'The man I kiss – he is the one: seize him, and take him away under guard.' (45) And when he arrived, straight away he went up to him and said 'Rabbi' and kissed him. (46) Then they laid hands on him and held him fast. (47) But one of the bystanders drew his sword and struck the high priest's servant, cutting off his ear.**

**(48) Then Jesus said to them, 'You have come out with swords and cudgels, as though against a robber, to seize me! (49) Day after day I have been with you in the temple, teaching, and you did not seize me. But let the scriptures be fulfilled.' (50) And [the**

disciples] all left him and fled.

(51) And a certain young man, who was wearing nothing but a linen cloth, was following him; and they seized him. (52) But he slipped out of the linen cloth, and ran away naked.

The kernel of this story is found in vv.43–6, ending with the words **held him fast**. The rest of the material may consist of separate pieces of tradition (v.47, vv.48–50 and 51–2) which Mark has pieced together and added to this core. However, the theme of the fulfilment of scripture and the incident of an ear being cut off are found also in John's account, so that the piecing together may have been done already before Mark.

Mark links this story to the preceding one with his characteristic 43 phrase, καὶ εὐθὺς, here translated **and suddenly**, and also with his next words, **while he was still speaking**, which underline the idea that Jesus knows precisely what is going to happen and is in control of the situation. **Judas** is introduced as **one of the Twelve**, as though we were hearing about him for the first time. Many commentators regard this as a sign that the story circulated as an independent unit before Mark incorporated it into the gospel, but his use of the phrase may have been deliberate, rather than unthinking, for it serves to emphasize Judas' treachery. The **crowd armed with swords and cudgels** sounds like a rabble rather than a posse of officials. They are **sent by the chief priests and scribes and elders**, the three groups making up the Sanhedrin. The same three groups have already challenged Jesus in 11.27ff.

Mark once again emphasizes Judas' villainy by describing him as 44 **his betrayer**. The pre-arranged **signal** identifies Jesus, which suggests that his captors did not recognize him. In John's account no signal is given and Jesus identifies himself. It is interesting that the evangelists are agreed that Jesus' captors did not know who he was, since it suggests that he was not in fact as well known in Jerusalem as we might imagine from the gospels. A kiss was a common way for a disciple to greet a rabbi. Judas does not hesitate. He greets Jesus 45 **straight away**, addressing him as **Rabbi** and kissing him; the compound verb used for 'kiss' (καταφιλέω rather than φιλέω) underlines his action and so serves to emphasize his act of treachery.

**Then they laid hands on him and held him fast.** Mark does not 46 identify the **bystander** who **drew his sword and struck the high** 47 **priest's servant**. In John 18.10f. it is said to be Peter, but since Mark so often names Peter, he is unlikely to have omitted this tradition had he known it. It is not even clear that Mark is thinking of a disciple. In the other three gospels Jesus rebukes the man who tries to defend him, but in Mark the incident is something of an intrusion into the narrative, and Jesus' next words are addressed to his captors. He protests 48

against the manner of his arrest: they **have come out with swords**
49 **and cudgels, as though against a robber.** He has taught openly **in
the temple**, and they have come by stealth, at night. The phrase
translated **day after day** (καθ' ἡμέραν) may perhaps have the meaning 'in the daytime' in this context (cf. the summary in Luke 21.37). If
we are correct in taking it in its more usual meaning, however, this is
evidence that Jesus perhaps spent a much longer period **teaching** in
the temple than Mark describes. The reference to Jesus in the temple
reminds us of the scene in chapter 11, where Jesus condemned those
who had made the temple into a den of robbers and was challenged
concerning his authority by the chief priests and the scribes and the
elders; on that occasion they failed to arrest him. Possibly Mark sees
irony in the fact that those whom Jesus accused of behaving like
robbers now treat him as though he were a robber: if so, we have a
parallel to a theme which is most clearly set out in 7.1–13, where the
Pharisees, who accuse Jesus of breaking the Law, were shown to be
the real lawbreakers.

Jesus' final words – **But let the scriptures be fulfilled** – emphasize
once more Mark's conviction that everything that takes place is part
of God's plan. The term 'the scriptures' is a general one, and Mark
does not pick out any particular passage: rather they are all fulfilled.
50 But it is not only scripture that is fulfilled: Jesus' own predictions
about the disciples are now fulfilled also, since they **all left him and
fled,** just as he foretold.

51–2 The next two verses are a total enigma. Mark gives no hint as to the
identity of the **young man** – or if he does, we do not recognize it.
Because Mark has included a story which has no obvious theological
significance, it is often suggested that the young man may have been
the author himself, but this suggestion can, of course, only be speculation. Since the young man is said to have been **following** Jesus
(meaning, presumably, that he followed behind Jesus as he was led
away), Mark clearly does not number him among the disciples, who
have all deserted Jesus. In describing him as **wearing...a linen cloth**
(σινδών), Mark was perhaps thinking of a garment rather than a piece
of cloth. The picture of the young man fleeing **naked** is reminiscent
of Amos 2.16, but the suggestion that the incident has been created
out of this text has little to commend it. Nevertheless, the fact that
Mark includes a story with so little obvious theological point suggests
that an historical reminiscence concerning the arrest may have been
interpreted as the fulfilment of scripture, and that it is to this that the
story owes its preservation. Matthew and Luke both omit the story.
One possible explanation of the inclusion of the story in Mark is that
the young man's faithfulness in following Jesus (however short-
lived) emphasizes yet again the failure of the disciples to do even that.
Another links the story with the young man (here too a νεανίσκος)

dressed in a white garment who announces Jesus' resurrection in 16.5, interpreting both references in the light of later baptismal practice, where a convert took off his/her garment before immersion and put on a white one afterwards (R. Scroggs and K.I. Groff, *J.B.L.*, 92, 1973, pp. 531–48). It has been suggested that Mark's readers would inevitably have been reminded of their own baptism. But the young man sheds his garment at the moment of failure, not at the confession of faith, and so fails to 'die with Christ'. Jesus dies alone, and it is *he* who is wrapped in a 'linen cloth' (σινδών) in 15.46! It seems unlikely that Mark intended his readers to see this as a symbol of Jesus' vicarious death.[1]

# 10 JESUS BEFORE THE SANHEDRIN     14.53–65

*(Matt. 26.57–68; Luke 22.54–5,63–71; John 18.12–16,18–23)*

(53) Then they led Jesus away to the high priest, and all the chief priests and elders and scribes gathered together. (54) And Peter followed him at a distance, right into the high priest's courtyard; and he sat there, with the attendants, warming himself by the fire.

(55) The chief priests and the whole Sanhedrin tried to find evidence against Jesus, in order to put him to death, and they could not. (56) Many gave false evidence against him, but their statements were not consistent. (57) And some stood up and gave false evidence against him, saying, (58) 'We heard him say, "I will destroy this sanctuary, made with [human] hands, and in three days I will build another, made without hands."' (59) Yet even so their evidence was not consistent. (60) The high priest rose [and came] forward and questioned Jesus: 'Have you nothing to reply? What is it that these men witness against you?' (61) But he was silent and made no reply. The high priest questioned him again: 'Are you the Christ, the Son of the Blessed?' he asked. (62) Jesus said, 'I am,[2] and you will see the Son of man, seated at the right

---

1 In 1973 Morton Smith published an eighteenth-century MS containing a copy of what purports to be a letter written by Clement of Alexandria, which refers to an expanded version of Mark (*Clement of Alexandria and a Secret Gospel of Mark*). This expanded 'secret' version includes a story in which Jesus raises a 'young man' (νεανίσκος) from the dead; the young man then comes to see Jesus at night, wearing a linen cloth over his naked body, and Jesus teaches him the mystery of the Kingdom of God. Controversy has raged over the authenticity of the fragment: if it is genuine it suggests that in the late second century AD the story of the young man was being elaborated in terms of an initiation ceremony.

2 Θ fam. 13 and a few other MSS read: *You say that I am.*

hand of power and coming with the clouds of heaven.' (63) Then the high priest tore his clothes and said, 'What need do we have now of witnesses? (64) You have heard the blasphemy. What is your decision?' They all condemned him as being worthy of death.

And some of them began to spit on him; and they blindfolded him[1] and hit him. 'Prophesy!' they said. And the attendants slapped him in the face.

Mark's account of Jesus' appearance before the Sanhedrin raises considerable historical problems. If the proceedings he describes are meant to be a formal trial, then they contravene the regulations set out in the Mishnah for the conduct of trials by the Sanhedrin (M. Sanh. 4.1). Since the Mishnaic regulations were drawn up almost a century after AD 70, however, when the Sanhedrin ceased to exist in its previous form, they cannot be relied on to give us an accurate picture of first-century customs. Yet even their somewhat idealized picture is probably based on earlier tradition. It seems unlikely that the Sanhedrin would have blatantly broken its own rules of procedure in order to condemn Jesus, though it would certainly be consistent with Mark's portrait of the Jewish authorities to depict them as doing so. The problems are eased if we suppose that what is described in 14.55–65 is not an official trial but a preliminary hearing, intended to formulate a charge which could be brought against Jesus later. The question of the nature of the proceedings is tied up with another problem: did the Jews have the authority at this time to carry out the death penalty? According to John 18.31 they did not, and this is supported by statements in the Jerusalem Talmud (J. Sanh. 1.18a, 34; 7.24b, 41) that they lost this power forty years before the destruction of the temple – a period which is generally assumed to be an underestimate for the time of the procuratorship, which lasted from AD 6 to 70. These statements are contradicted, however, by the provision of regulations in the Mishnah about capital charges and their punishment, as well as by references to various executions in the New Testament (e.g. that of Stephen in Acts 6–7) and in Jewish sources. Scholars have argued with equal vehemence on either side of this issue (e.g. P. Winter, *On the Trial of Jesus*, that the Sanhedrin could try capital cases, A.N. Sherwin-White, *Roman Society and Roman Law*, that it could not). Whatever the truth of this matter, the evangelists are all clear that Jesus was put to death by the Romans, on what was to Rome a political charge. Whatever the nature of the examination by the Sanhedrin, therefore, it was in effect no more than a prelimi-

---

1 The words *and they blindfolded him* are omitted by D and few MSS of the old Latin, Syriac and Bohairic.

nary hearing: whether or not this body had the power to carry out the death sentence, for some reason it did not do so.

This raises another question, regarding the role played by the Jewish leaders in these proceedings. Was it in fact the Roman authorities who instigated the charge against Jesus? It seems highly probable that the evangelists have exaggerated the part played by the Jews in the proceedings, and that this may have been due to apologetic motives. It was natural for the Christian community to stress the guilt of the Jewish leaders in rejecting their Messiah, and politic to play down the part played by Rome, in the hope that this would minimize Roman opposition to the Church. Nevertheless, there is no reason to doubt that the Jewish leaders had some hand in Jesus' death. If they did not carry out the execution themselves, then this was either because they lacked the necessary authority, or because they found no opportunity, or because it suited their purpose to have Jesus executed by the civil power.

The Great Sanhedrin (i.e. the Jerusalem Sanhedrin, as distinct from local gatherings) consisted of 71 members. There is some debate as to the exact role of the Sanhedrin at the time of Jesus, since, as we have already pointed out, information in the Mishnah reflects the situation after the Fall of Jerusalem and does not necessarily provide accurate information about the earlier period. The Hebrew term *Sanhedrin* was a loan-word from the Greek συνέδριον, and though tradition traces the origin of the Sanhedrin to the seventy elders who assisted Moses (Num. 11.16–25), its true origin is much later. After AD 70, the Sanhedrin was replaced by the *Beth Din*, whose powers were solely religious and moral. It has recently been argued by Ellis Rivkin (*What Crucified Jesus?*) that the Sanhedrin was in fact a political body with no jurisdiction over religious matters, which were always dealt with by a *beth din*, and that the charge brought against Jesus was a political one, not religious. It seems unlikely, however, that such a body, exercising political powers only, would have existed under Roman rule; the charges brought against Jesus are thus likely to have been religious ones. On the Sanhedrin, see also Schürer, *History*, II, pp. 199–226.

The rules of procedure set out in the Mishnah for the judgement of capital cases gave the accused the benefit of the doubt. A verdict of guilty could not be passed immediately but had to be left over until the following day, and since none of the proceedings could take place at night, on a sabbath or on a festival day, this means that (if these rules applied at that time) a trial could not have been held at the time or in the manner that Mark describes. Mark 15.1 suggests that a second gathering of **the whole Sanhedrin** took place the following morning, and though this is described as **a consultation** (and may not even be a separate gathering), it is possible that Mark's account reflects the rule that the verdict must be postponed until the following day. But according to Jewish reckoning the day began at sunset, so that if a nocturnal meeting was held in order that two sessions could take place before the festival began, this would have been contrary to the regulations, both because it was held at night, and because it was held on the same day. The matter is made worse by the fact that, according to Mark's dating, the festival had already begun, so that we need to adopt the Johannine dating in order to make sense of Mark's account! Another possibility is that the impression that there were two meetings of the Sanhedrin may be due to Mark's intercalation of the story about Peter in vv.66–71, with the resulting contrast between Jesus under interrogation and Peter's failure when questioned; in this case 15.1 simply resumes the account of the proceedings before the high priest and records its conclusion. Luke records only one assembly of the Sanhedrin, in the morning, which seems historically more plausible; nevertheless, Mark's account of an examination of Jesus by the high priest at night is supported by John (18.19–24). Perhaps the most likely explanation of the anomalies is that the proceedings were entirely informal and therefore not bound by the normal rules of procedure, though the evangelists have assumed that it was an official trial. To this we must add the possibility that details may have been altered in the course of retelling the story.

In addition to these legal anomalies, there are other historical problems in relation to the narrative of the trial. While Mark is followed fairly closely by Matthew, there are significant differences in the accounts given by Luke and John. Luke includes a trial before Herod, while John provides a very different version of the trial before Pilate. These differences suggest that the Christian community lacked detailed information about the course of events after Jesus' arrest. Since the disciples had fled, the only 'eyewitness' (apart perhaps from a disciple who was 'known to the high priest', referred to in John 18.15) was Peter, and even he was not in a position to follow the proceedings. We may be sure that there was some kind of preliminary hearing before the Jewish authorities, and that the sentence of death was pronounced and executed by the Romans. The accounts of what was said at the various proceedings vary considerably and may well represent later reflection on the meaning of these events. One of the factors which influenced the way in which the story was told was the increasing tendency to blame the Jews for Jesus' death and to exonerate the Romans. We have already seen how the former of these themes is important for Mark, and in later gospels we find that the role of the Roman authorities is played down at the expense of emphasizing Jewish guilt (cf. Matt. 27.19, 24–6; Luke 23.4,13–16; John 18.28–38; 19.4–6,12–16). The picture of Pilate vacillating and giving in to pressure seems unlikely, since according to other sources he was a particularly obstinate man (see references below, p. 366). In particular, the accounts of the actual charges brought against Jesus and his responses to those charges have probably been moulded by later interpretation.

Whatever historical problems this scene may raise, however, its impact at the theological level is profound. Confronted by his accusers, Jesus finally acknowledges that he is **the Christ, the Son of the Blessed**. But the words are in fact spoken by the high priest, and it is fitting that it is he who (unknowingly!) proclaims God's chosen one to Israel. No sooner is the Messiah revealed, however, than he is rejected: **the high priest tore his clothes and. . .they all condemned him as being worthy of death**. The two themes of Israel's rejection of her Messiah and Israel's own rejection by God are woven skilfully together. The accusation brought against Jesus is that he has threatened to destroy the temple; in fact, his words have been words of warning and judgement, not threats, and it is the religious leaders themselves who are responsible for the destruction of the temple, since in rejecting Jesus they bring down divine judgement on the nation. There is, then, irony in the accusation: Jesus has not threatened to destroy the temple, but because of him it will indeed be destroyed. Perhaps the tearing of the high priest's garment points forward to the tearing of the sanctuary curtain in 15.38; certainly at this moment the fate both of Jesus and of the temple is sealed.

Mark's picture is full of anomalies: the witnesses cannot agree; the high priest improperly asks Jesus to respond to charges which have not been substantiated and then accuses him of blasphemy, even though his words apparently do not constitute blasphemy; the nocturnal gathering of the court and the immediate passing of sentence are illegal. The proceedings are a farce – and Mark has perhaps deliberately presented them as such. It is not Jesus who is guilty of breaking the Law, but his opponents, who claim to uphold it! Although Jesus is now on trial before the high priest, his accusers will soon be on trial before the Son of man, and Jesus' announcement of his vindication involves their own condemnation: '**You will see the Son of man, seated at the right hand of power and coming with the clouds of heaven.**'

Mark does not name **the high priest**, but Matthew (26.3, 57) adds 53 the information that it was Caiaphas. A gathering of **all the chief priests and elders and scribes** sounds like a meeting of the Sanhedrin, but the normal meeting-place for that body was a special hall on the temple mount (M. Sanh. 11.2). Mark, however, is clearly thinking of the high priest's house, since he refers to **the high priest's** 54 **courtyard**. It is also clear from 15.1 that Mark thinks of the meeting as taking place at night, in breach of the regulations (M. Sanh. 4.1).

**And Peter followed him.** The account of Jesus' examination before the high priest is interwoven with another story, in typically Markan fashion, and this reference to Peter prepares the way for the second story, which is taken up in vv.66–72. Whether or not the phrase **at a distance** is meant to emphasize the gap between master and disciple, Mark's aim is certainly to demonstrate the difference between them when they are confronted by testing. The reference to **the fire** supports Mark's picture of a night session of the council. The house would have been built round the centre courtyard, so that Peter took a risk in venturing inside.

55 **The chief priests and the whole Sanhedrin tried to find evidence against Jesus.** Mark presents the whole scene as a travesty of justice. According to the Mishnah (M. Sanh. 4.1), a trial on a capital charge should begin with a statement of the reasons for acquittal, not with reasons for conviction: here, however, the judges' minds are made. up from the outset, since they are determined **to put him to death.**

56 The statement that **many gave false evidence against him** is reminiscent of Ps. 27.12 (cf. 35.11), which would probably have been familiar to Mark's first readers; the incident is not necessarily based on that passage, however. The inability of the false witnesses to make their testimony agree seems extraordinarily incompetent, but Mark

57 is insistent on this point: twice he speaks of men giving **false evidence,**
59 and twice he says that **their statements were not consistent.** This failure to agree serves to emphasize Mark's belief that their testimony was false and Jesus innocent. A man could be condemned only on the evidence of two or more witnesses (Num. 35.30; Deut. 17.6): if two witnesses could not be found in agreement out of the **many** who

58 came forward, then clearly their testimony was false. The specific charge brought against Jesus is that he threatened to destroy the **sanctuary** and **build another.** The accusation is repeated in Mark 15.29. The term for 'sanctuary' used in both places and in 15.38 is ναός, instead of Mark's more usual word for the temple, ἱερόν. It is possible that the choice of term is deliberate and refers more specifically to the inner sanctuary containing the Holy Place and the Holy of Holies, so emphasizing the gravity of the charge brought against Jesus. A similar interesting change from ἱερόν to ναός takes place in John 2.14–22. Since Mark regards it as false, he perhaps sees it as a misrepresentation of Jesus' saying in 13.2, which refers only to the temple's destruction and certainly does not suggest that Jesus threatened to destroy it himself. According to Matthew, two men (who are not described as bearing false witness) agreed in their accusation but claimed only that Jesus had said that he was able to destroy the temple, not that he had threatened to do so. The incident is missing altogether in Luke, but in Acts 6.14 Stephen is accused of saying that Jesus will destroy the temple. In John 2.19, Jesus chal-

lenges the Jews to destroy the temple and promises that he will then raise it up in three days – a saying which the evangelist immediately interprets of Jesus' death and resurrection. This evidence (together with the incident in Mark 11) suggests a widespread tradition that Jesus did make some statement about the destruction of the temple (see 13.2). The claim that he will build a new one is a natural corollary, since Jewish expectation about the eschaton included the hope that God (or his Messiah) would rebuild the temple (see, e.g., 1 Enoch 90.28f.; Jub. 1.17, 27–9). Whether Jesus himself spoke of the rebuilding, or whether this is a Christian expansion (as in 12.10f.), Mark perhaps regarded it as equivalent to a messianic claim, since, when the testimony of the witnesses fails, the high priest challenges Jesus directly (v.61). The contrast between what is **made with [human] hands** (χειροποίητον) and that which is **made without hands** (ἀχειροποίητον) is primarily between what belongs to this age and that which belongs to the age to come, when God himself would rebuild the temple. The words are missing from 15.29, and may be a later addition to the tradition. It is often suggested that they reflect the views of the Hellenistic Church and of those Christians who questioned the value of temple worship, but the idea of a heavenly Jerusalem which will finally be established on earth is a feature of apocalyptic: see 2 Bar. 4.2–6 and 4 Ezra 10, and cf. Gal. 4.26. Since the Christian community thought of itself as already living in the age to come in some degree, we naturally find it adapting this idea of the new temple: for the author to the Hebrews, the sanctuary not made with hands was the heavenly counterpart of the earthly building, a spiritual sanctuary into which Christ entered at his death (Heb. 9.11, 24), while Paul speaks of the Christian community itself as God's temple (1 Cor. 3.16f.; 2 Cor. 6.16). For Mark's readers, therefore, the new temple was probably understood in a spiritual sense, of God's presence in their own community. The phrase **in three days** could mean simply 'in a short time' but inevitably would have been linked, sooner or later, with the period between Jesus' crucifixion and resurrection: this link is made explicit in John 2.18–22.

'**Have you nothing to reply? What is it that these men witness** 60 **against you?**' The high priest's questions to Jesus are manifestly absurd, since the charge brought against him has collapsed: they make sense, however, in the Matthaean context, where two witnesses are found who agree, and for this reason the passage lends some support to the belief that Matthew was written before Mark. If we accept Markan priority, then the discrepancy can be explained by supposing that v.59 has been added to the story at some stage – an addition which is either subsequent to Matthew's editing of the material, or which he chose to ignore. Certainly there is in Mark no reason for Jesus to be anything but **silent** when he is asked to reply to false accusations, and his silence emphasizes his innocence. But perhaps it is for this very reason that Mark has included the high priest's questions – to underline Jesus' silence before his accusers, just as he included v.59 to emphasize that the accusations were false. It is possible that the evangelist had in mind the silence of the innocent sufferer in Pss. 38.13 (37.14); 39.9 (38.10) and Isa. 53.7, but the language is quite different, and there is no obvious influence from these passages.

61    The high priest's next question – 'Are you the Christ, the Son of the Blessed?' – is a direct challenge to Jesus, and this too contravenes the proper procedure. Unless the notion of rebuilding the temple is meant to be understood as a messianic claim, there seems to be no logic linking this verse with those that precede it. The form of the question suggests that it has been formulated by the Church and represents Christian confession rather than Jewish accusation. Nevertheless, the belief that Jesus was put to death as a messianic claimant is firmly established in the tradition, and if there was collusion between the religious and the secular authorities, as the evangelists suggest, then the high priest's question may represent the substance of the accusation. It is typical of Jewish piety to avoid using the name of God, but **the Blessed** is not a normal periphrasis. There is no clear evidence in the literature that has come down to us that 'Son of God' was used by Jews as a synonym for **Christ** in the first century, though the idea that Israel, the king (and so the future king) and righteous individuals could be described in this way was certainly known. But to use the phrase as a description that could be applied appropriately to various individuals is not the same as using it as a recognizable title for a particular individual. In the present passage, the phrase hovers between these two functions: it is not used on its own, as an independent title (as it is in Luke 22.70), but in order to fill out the meaning of the term 'Christ'. For Mark, however, the phrase 'the Son of God' was itself a title – indeed, the title which best expressed Jesus' identity – and he uses it here as though it were equivalent to 'Christ'. In this way he is able to link his belief that Jesus was the Jewish Messiah with the confession that he was the Son of God – a title that would have made more sense to his Gentile readers than the term 'Christ'. The fact that he substitutes 'the Blessed' for 'God', and so depicts the high priest as avoiding the divine name, adds irony to a scene in which the religious authorities manipulate the evidence in an attempt to convict Jesus, while carefully avoiding the possibility of any technical infringement of the commandment not to dishonour God's name.

62    This time, **Jesus'** reply is unequivocal: **I am** (ἐγώ εἰμι). His affirmative answer is perhaps surprising in view of the secrecy about his identity up to this point, and especially after the silence with which he greeted

Peter's confession at Caesarea Philippi. It is even more surprising to compare the other Synoptics at this point, and to find less positive answers there: in Matthew, 'You have said so' (σὺ εἶπας), and in Luke, 'You (pl.) say that I am' (ὑμεῖς λέγετε ὅτι ἐγώ εἰμι). Some MSS of Mark do in fact read 'You say that I am' (σὺ εἶπας ὅτι ἐγώ εἰμι) which might, if original, explain the other evangelists' versions of the saying, but it is much more likely that this represents an assimilation to Matthew. If it seems odd that Matthew and Luke should make Jesus' reply less direct, it is nevertheless easy enough to find explanations. In Matthew, Jesus not only refuses the demand that he should answer on oath (as we might expect – cf. Matt. 5.33–7), but throws the onus back on to the high priest: 'You have said so' – it is the high priest (whom we would expect to proclaim God's Messiah to his people) who has unwittingly declared Jesus' true identity. In Luke, the scene develops into a discussion about belief in Jesus: his enemies will not believe him to be the Messiah, even if he makes messianic claims (Luke 22.67f.); faith in him as the Son of God is something that men must declare for themselves (v.70). There is no need then to assume, as many commentators do, that I am is not the original reading in Mark. Moreover, it is entirely appropriate that at this point in Mark's story Jesus should acknowledge his messianic status. It is not something that he claims for himself, though he acknowledges the truth when the high priest unwittingly declares his true identity as Messiah and Son of God. It is because Jesus acknowledges that he is Messiah and Son of God that he is put to death, it is as Messiah that he is crucified, and it is through death that he is proclaimed as Messiah and Son of God (cf. 15.18, 26, 32, 39). In contrast to the claims of false messiahs proclaiming 'I am' (13.6), Jesus' words will be substantiated. But the only 'evidence' that he has to back his claim refers to his future vindication. In 8.38 and 13.26 we have references to a glorious future manifestation of the Son of man, and a judgement scene in which those who suffer persecution for the sake of Jesus will be vindicated, while those who reject him will be ashamed. Now it is Jesus himself who suffers, and he who will be vindicated.

As at Caesarea Philippi, the question of Jesus' messianic status is no sooner raised than Jesus begins to talk of his mission as the Son of man; but this time it is to affirm the triumph which lies beyond the suffering. **You will see the Son of man, seated at the right hand of power**: these words are addressed to Jesus' enemies who will find themselves judged hereafter because of their refusal to acknowledge him: in this context, therefore, they are a challenge, not a reassurance. Matthew and Luke both add a temporal clause, 'from now on' (Matthew: ἀπ' ἄρτι, Luke: ἀπὸ του νυν) and apparently think of Jesus' immediate exaltation to God's right hand (cf. Acts 2.33; 5.31), rather than of a future judgement. But it is difficult to understand how

Matthew can think of Jesus' enemies 'seeing' the Son of man 'from now on'; certainly Mark's version implies a future judgement scene, in which the Son of man's true position is recognized by everyone. Now his judges see only the accused prisoner, but hereafter they will see the glorified Son of man. As in the earlier saying in 8.38, therefore, the declaration that Jesus is to be vindicated proves to be a threat rather than a promise. The phrase **seated at the right hand** echoes Ps. 110 (109).1, which has been quoted already in 12.36, and this has been combined with a reference to **the Son of man...coming with the clouds of heaven**, taken from Dan. 7. 13. Whether or not Mark thinks of the sitting and the coming as two distinct events is not clear. It is possible that both words are ways of expressing the triumph and vindication of the Son of man, rather than indicating two separate activities: if so, then perhaps the much debated question as to whether Mark is thinking of the coming of the Son of man as an approach to earth (as is traditional) or to the throne of God (as has been maintained by T.F. Glasson, *The Second Advent*) is misplaced. In Daniel 7, the figure like a Son of man comes to God to receive authority, glory and the kingdom, and it matters little where the throne of God is set, whether in heaven or on earth. The essential point in Mark 14 is not a future parousia, but the contrast between the present situation and the future vindication – a contrast which was summed up in the earlier saying at 8.38. Since Mark mentions being **seated** before **coming**, however, it is natural that his words have been interpreted in terms of a scheme of future exaltation for Jesus, to be followed by the parousia.

63     **Then the high priest tore his clothes.** From being a sign of grief (Job 1.20), this became the gesture used at the end of a trial, when the accused was convicted of blasphemy. According to the Mishnah (M. Sanh. 7.5), the chief witness was ordered to utter the exact words spoken by the accused, whereupon the judges tore their garments. Yet according to the same passage, no one could be convicted of blasphemy 'unless he pronounces the divine Name itself', and this, according to Mark, Jesus has avoided, by using the circumlocution: the **power.** Possibly Mark assumes that the claim that he will sit at God's right hand would have been seen as tantamount to blasphemy; perhaps he deliberately depicts the high priest as ignoring the rules, and so condemning Jesus falsely, or perhaps the Mishnaic regulation is too late to apply. Another possibility is that Mark understands the words **I am** (ἐγώ εἰμι) as a use of the divine name, and so not merely as a claim by Jesus to be the Messiah (which certainly was not blasphemy), but as a claim to divine status (cf. John 8.28; 18.5ff.). Certainly it is

64     clear from the high priest's next words that Mark assumed that something in Jesus' reply could be interpreted as blasphemous. The penalty for **blasphemy** was death by stoning (Lev. 24.10–16), though it seems doubtful whether this was in fact still enforced.

362

Since **they all condemned him,** they were themselves all guilty of his death. They pronounce him **worthy of death.** The word translated 'worthy' (ἔνοχος) was used in 3.29 of those who are guilty of blaspheming against the Holy Spirit: the context there forms an interesting parallel to the present scene. On that occasion scribes from Jerusalem accused Jesus of working by the power of Satan, and by their own condemnation of Jesus they were themselves condemned. Whether or not this final condemnation by the Sanhedrin was a formal death sentence, or merely the opinion of the court, makes little difference to Mark's story.

**And some of them.** . . . In the Markan context, this seems to mean 65 'some of the Sanhedrin'; this is improbable, though Mark may well have intended to suggest that they were capable even of this. The idea that it was the attendants who treated Jesus with physical abuse seems more likely, and in Luke 22.63 the whole incident is attributed to 'the men who were holding Jesus' (cf. John 18.22). It is not clear who **the attendants** were: perhaps servants of the high priest or officers of the court. The words **spit, face** and **slapped** all echo words used in Isa. 50.6, and it is possible that the description of the righteous sufferer in that passage has influenced Mark's vocabulary, but the similarity stops with the use of individual words. **Prophesy!** Jesus is mocked as a false prophet; according to Deut. 18.20, false prophets were to be put to death. The fact that he is blindfolded suggests that he is asked to identify his assailant, as in Matt. 26.68 and Luke 22.64. But the taunt could be less specific, and a few MSS omit the words **and they blindfolded him.** Perhaps for Mark there is irony in this demand that Jesus should prophesy, since immediately afterwards we have the account of the fulfilment of Jesus' prophecy that Peter would deny him three times before cockcrow (D. Juel, *Messiah and Temple,* pp. 71–2). The final statement – they **slapped him in the face** – is colloquial and untranslatable: literally, it means 'they received him with blows'.

# 11 PETER DISOWNS JESUS 14.66–72

*(Matt. 26.69–75; Luke 22.56–62; John 18.17, 25–7)*

**(66) While Peter was below in the courtyard, one of the high priest's servant-girls came by, (67) and seeing Peter warming himself, looked hard at him. 'You, too,' she said, 'were with this man from Nazareth, this Jesus.' (68) But he denied it. 'I don't know**

---

1 Following A C D Θ Ψ<sup>c</sup> fams. 1 and 13 and many other MSS and versions. The words *and a cock crew* are omitted by ℵ B L W Ψ* and a few other MSS and versions.

– I don't understand – what you are saying.' And he went outside, into the porch; and a cock crew.[1]
(69) And the maid saw him and began to say again to the bystanders, 'He is one of them.' (70) But again he denied it. And again, a little later, the bystanders said to Peter: 'You are certainly one of them, for you are a Galilean.' (71) Then he began to curse and to swear: 'I do not know this man you are talking about.' (72) And straight away a cock crew for the second time. And Peter remembered how Jesus had said to him: 'Before the cock crows twice, you will disown me three times.' And he threw himself down and wept.

The story of Peter's failure under testing stands in sharp contrast to that of Jesus before the Sanhedrin, and Mark draws our attention to this by interleaving the two stories: the scenes for both were set in vv.53 and 54. The three-fold denial of Jesus by Peter follows his three-fold failure to watch with him in Gethsemane and fulfils Jesus' words in vv.29–31. Each denial marks a worse failure on Peter's part, since he begins by denying that he knows Jesus to one girl, then does so again in the presence of all the bystanders, and finally reiterates his denial with curses and oaths. Though told with dramatic skill there is no reason to doubt the historical basis of a narrative which shows Peter in such a bad light. The story may well have been a timely reminder to Mark's readers that following Jesus was by no means an easy thing: when persecution threatened, it was all too easy to be ashamed of Jesus and his words (Mark 8.38).

66  **Peter** is challenged by **one of the high priest's servant-girls**, who
67  recognizes him as a companion of **this man from Nazareth, this**
68  **Jesus** (cf. 1.24). **But he denied it.** The verb 'deny' (ἀρνέομαι) echoes the compound verb (ἀπαρνέομαι) used in v.30; the two are used interchangeably in the New Testament. **'I don't know – I don't understand – what you are saying.'** The punctuation and translation of this reply are uncertain, but the general meaning is clear enough. **The porch** (τὸ προαύλιον) is the vestibule or passage leading into the court. The words **and a cock crew**, found in some MSS, might have been omitted from others accidentally (they are not found in Matthew or Luke) but may well have been added by someone anxious to explain the statement in v.72 that **a cock crew for the second time.**

69  **And the maid saw him and began to say again to the bystanders,**
'He is one of them.' The charge is now more specific: not simply to have been with Jesus (v.67) but to belong to his company of disciples;
70  **but again he denied it.** Finally, **the bystanders** pick out Peter as **a Galilean**; according to Matt. 26.73, it is Peter's accent that gives him away. There must have been plenty of Galileans in Jerusalem at festi-

val time but not, presumably, inside the high priest's house. **Then he began to curse and to swear.** The object of the curse is not stated in 71 Greek, but we should probably understand it as meaning that he invoked a curse on himself if he is lying. This time Peter's denial is spelt out for us: **I do not know this man you are talking about.**

**And straight away.** Mark's characteristic phrase this time has 72 real point: it underlines the inevitability with which Jesus' words are fulfilled: **a cock crew for the second time. And Peter remembered how Jesus had said to him: 'Before the cock crows twice, you will disown me three times.'** Luke makes the link clear by adding the unlikely detail that 'the Lord turned and looked at Peter' (22.61), but Mark's stark account is more dramatic. **And he threw himself down:** the meaning of the Greek (ἐπιβαλὼν) is an enigma. The verb ἐπιβάλλω means 'to throw...over' or 'to lay...on' (hence suggestions such as 'he covered his face' or 'he pulled on his cloak'), but here it is used intransitively. Whatever its meaning, Peter's remorse is clearly seen in the final words **and wept.**

## 12　JESUS BEFORE PILATE　　　　　　　　15.1–15

*(Matt. 27.1–2,11–26; Luke 23.1–5, 18–25;*

*John 18.28–40; 19.1, 4, 12–16)*

**(1) And straight away, when it was morning, the chief priests held a consultation[1] with the elders and the scribes and the whole Sanhedrin; and having bound Jesus, they led him away and handed him over to Pilate. (2) Pilate questioned him: 'Are you the King of the Jews?' 'You say so,' he replied. (3) And the chief priests brought many accusations against him. (4) Pilate questioned him again. 'Have you nothing to reply?' he said. 'See how many accusations they bring against you!' (5) But Jesus made no further reply, and Pilate marvelled.**

**(6) At the festival he used to release one prisoner for them – one whom they requested. (7) Now there was a man called Barabbas in prison, among those rebels who had committed murder in the uprising. (8) And when the crowd appeared and began to ask that he should do what was customary, (9) Pilate replied, 'Do you want me to release for you the King of the Jews?' (10) – for he knew that it was out of envy that the chief priests had handed him over. (11) But the chief priests stirred up the crowd to ask rather for the release of Barabbas. (12) And Pilate asked them again, 'What then**

1 ℵ C L and a few other MSS read συμβούλιον ἑτοιμάσαντες (*reached a decision*) for συμβούλιον ποιήσαντες.

do you want me to do with the man whom you call "King of the Jews"?' (13) And they cried out again, 'Crucify him!' (14) And Pilate said to them: 'Why, what evil has he done?' But they cried out all the louder, 'Crucify him.' (15) So Pilate, wishing to satisfy the crowd, released Barabbas for them; and he had Jesus flogged and handed him over to be crucified.

The so-called trial before Pilate is hardly properly so described. Although the members of the Sanhedrin bring accusations against Jesus (which he refuses to answer), sentence is never passed. Instead, Pilate offers to release Jesus under the passover amnesty – this implies that he has been convicted already – and finally hands him over to be crucified. Probably Mark had no tradition regarding Pilate's verdict and sentence, though it is possible that he had traditions which he chose not to use. Certainly the effect of his narrative is to suggest that the sentence was pronounced by the Sanhedrin, in 14.64, and that Pilate was simply the instrument through whom they were able to carry it out.

The responsibility of the Jews for the whole affair is stressed: it is the Jewish leaders who hand Jesus over to Pilate (v.1), bring accusations against him (v.3) and stir up the crowd to prevent his release (v.11). It is the Jewish crowd who demand the death penalty for Jesus (vv.13, 14). In contrast, Pilate is astonished by Jesus (v.5), attempts to release him (vv.5ff.), and declares him innocent (v.14).

Pilate was prefect of Judaea from AD 26–36. Although he is normally referred to as 'procurator', a Latin inscription found at Caesarea bearing the name 'Pontius Pilate' refers to him as 'prefect', and this seems to have been the correct term at the time (Josphus describes Pilate as ἐπίτροπος, procurator, but Matthew refers to him as ἡγεμών, governor). Normally resident in Caesarea, the prefects, when visiting Jerusalem, would have stayed either in the palace of Herod the Great or in the Fortress of Antonia adjacent to the temple. The idea that Pilate made vain attempts to release Jesus is scarcely credible, though it is one that is developed by the other evangelists in various ways. According to information elsewhere, Pilate was an 'inflexible, merciless and obstinate' man and hardly likely to have been browbeaten in this way (Philo, *De Legatione ad Gaium*, XXXVIII; cf. Josephus' description of Pilate's cruelty, *Antiquities*, XVIII.3.2 (= *Wars*, II.9.4) and 4.1f.). It is true that Josephus records that Pilate gave way to pressure on one occasion, but only because he was confronted by determined opposition from the Jews (*Antiquities*, XVIII.3.1 = *Wars*, II.9.2f.). Nor, as a Roman official, is he likely to have indulged the crowd in this way. Moreover, there is no evidence anywhere else for the custom of releasing a prisoner at Passover. Possibly the tradition that Barabbas had been released led Mark to assume that it was an annual custom. In any case, this part of the story looks very much like an attempt to stress the guilt of the Jewish leaders and the reluctance of the Roman authorities to put Jesus to death – themes which would have served the apologetic purposes of the early Christian community.

According to the question put by Pilate in v.2, the charge against Jesus is that he claims to be **the King of the Jews**, and it is as such that he is handed over for execution (vv.12,15). Mark emphasizes that it is as King of the Jews that Jesus dies. Paradoxical as it may seem, the crucifixion does not destroy the Christian claim that Jesus is the Messiah but rather proclaims him as such. He died, not because of any wrongdoing (even Pilate recognized his innocence, vv.5,14), but because he was the Messiah. It is no longer necessary to conceal the truth about Jesus, but now that Pilate declares it openly, no one accepts it, least of all Pilate himself!

**When it was morning.** According to Jewish reckoning, this is still 1 the same day, so that Mark can hardly be thinking of the rule that a second meeting of the court, on the following day, was necessary before sentence was passed; moreover, this has already been done. Possibly Mark does not understand the purpose of the second meeting, or perhaps this verse is a (very short) doublet of 14.53–64, though this seems unlikely since the verse bears the signs of being a Markan construction – the typical beginning, **and straight away** (καὶ εὐθὺς), and the repetitious **the whole Sanhedrin.** It is possible that Mark has created the impression that a second meeting was held by his insertion of the story of Peter, and if we adopt the variant reading, the reference to a separate meeting is in fact eliminated. Whether or not Mark is thinking of a new gathering of the council, this verse serves to link the examination of Jesus by the Jewish authorities with that by Pilate: Mark probably assumed that the Sanhedrin decided on their strategy in dealing with Pilate. **Having bound Jesus, they led him away and handed him over to Pilate.** The verb for 'hand over' is the familiar παραδίδωμι, used frequently in the passion predictions and passion narrative.

**'Are you the King of the Jews?'** Mark omits any preliminary 2 negotiations between Pilate and the Jews and goes straight to what becomes the central theme of the crucifixion narrative (vv.9, 12, 18, 26, 32). Pilate's question is the Graeco-Roman equivalent of the high priest's question in 14.61 and amounts to a political charge. The 'you' is emphatic (perhaps implying astonishment or contempt), and so is the 'you' in Jesus' reply – **'You say so'.** Jesus here uses the same ambiguous response which Matthew and Luke attribute to him in answering the high priest. Mark can hardly have understood it as equivalent to a straightforward 'Yes', or Pilate would have had no choice but to convict Jesus straight away of insurrection. But neither can it be a straightforward denial; the response is non-committal. Jesus makes no claims for himself, and the onus of deciding who he is is thrown back on others – both those who take part in the story and those who read it. The question Pilate puts is not 'Do you claim to be the King of the Jews?' but **'Are you?'**, and to Mark's readers the meaning of Jesus' words ought to be clear. As in the case of the high priest in 14.61, it is Pilate himself who has, unwittingly, announced the truth about Jesus. The irony is that he will proclaim it to the world by nail-

3 ing Jesus to the cross (v.26). The reference to the **many accusations** which are brought against Jesus is vague, and something of an anticlimax after the question in v.2. Mark seems to be trying to stress the part played by **the chief priests**. Their accusations are the equivalent of the testimony of the false witnesses in 14.56–9, and

4 Pilate's next question – **'Have you nothing to reply?'** – echoes that put by the high priest in 14.60. Here, as there, Jesus is silent, refusing

5 to take part in the proceedings. **Pilate marvelled**: the verb θαυμάζειν expresses astonishment; it was used in 5.20 of the amazement caused by reports of Jesus' miracles, and in 6.6 of Jesus' own amazement at the lack of faith shown by his own countrymen. Pilate is shown as one who recognizes that something quite remarkable is taking place. The verb may be a deliberate echo of the LXX rendering of Isa. 52.15 – 'so shall many nations be amazed at him'.

6 **At the festival he used to release one prisoner for them.** There is no reference anywhere to such a custom, nor is there any real parallel

8 from any other part of the Roman Empire, and the idea that it **was customary** may be a misunderstanding of the tradition. While it is feasible that some such concession could have been made in order to placate the Jews, the notion that a Roman official would release any

7 particular prisoner **whom they requested** is incredible. **The uprising** is mentioned as though it were a recent well-known event. There were plenty of uprisings, and plenty of rebels who were ruthlessly destroyed by the Romans. Again, Pilate is hardly likely to have pardoned someone **who had committed murder**. The prisoner who is now identified is **a man called Barabbas**: the Greek phrase (ὁ λεγόμενος Βαραββᾶς) suggests a surname rather than a first name, and Barabbas is found elsewhere as a second name. Some MSS read 'Jesus Barabbas' in the equivalent verse of Matthew (27.16), and it has been argued that it may be the original reading there, since the subsequent omission of the word 'Jesus' is much easier to understand than its addition. This has led, in turn, to the suggestion that the origin of the story of the choice beween Jesus and Barabbas was a confusion of two separate incidents, one of which concerned Jesus, and the other a man called Jesus Barabbas. But this idea can only be speculative, and Mark certainly provides no evidence to support it. In spite of the implausibilities in the story as he relates it, which may

well be the result of theological motifs, the story of Barabbas is probably grounded in some historical incident, though it is now impossible
to discover what that was.

Pilate offers **to release. . .the King of the Jews**, though this is 9
hardly a favour, since Jesus has not yet been found guilty. Indeed
Mark's next comment implies that Pilate regarded him as innocent, 10
since **he knew that it was out of envy that the chief priests had
handed him over** (παραδίδωμι). The wickedness of **the chief priests** 11
is compounded by the fact that they **stirred up the crowd** to demand
**the release** of the wrong man. This crowd is not the one the authorities feared in 14.2. If Mark is correct in depicting a crowd coming to
Pilate, it may well have consisted of supporters of Barabbas, demanding his release. For Mark, the significance of the crowd is that it 12–13
represents the Jews, who reject the one whom Pilate calls **the King of
the Jews** and demand his crucifixion. Once again, the story is implausible. Pilate is hardly likely to have asked the crowd how to deal
with his prisoner; nor was there any reason why the fate of Jesus
(whom Pilate has not found guilty) should depend on the decision to
release Barabbas. But the story provides an interesting 'parable' of
the wider truth that is being enacted: Jesus, acknowledged as innocent, is put to death, while Barabbas, justly condemned to death for
his crimes, goes free.

Pilate's final question, '**Why, what evil has he done?**', depicts him 14
once again as one who believes in Jesus' innocence (cf. Herod's
assessment of John in 6.20). In contrast, the Jews shout out '**Crucify
him**' once more and are thereby shown as responsible for his death.
**So Pilate. . .had Jesus flogged**: flogging was the normal prelude to 15
crucifixion. It was a savage affair, carried out with leather whips, to
whose thongs pieces of metal and bone had been attached. Pilate
then **handed** Jesus **over** to be crucified: the familiar verb παραδίδωμι,
'to hand over' or 'to deliver', which has already been used in this
chapter at vv.1 and 10, is used once more, this time of the final handing over of Jesus to death.

# 13    THE KING IS MOCKED                    15.16–20a

*(Matt. 27.27–31a; Luke 23.11; John 19.2–3)*

**(16) The soldiers took him away inside the palace (that is, the
Praetorium) and called the whole company together. (17) Then
they dressed him in purple, and plaiting a thorny crown, set it on
his head. (18) And they began to salute him: 'Hail, King of the
Jews!' (19) And they beat him about the head with a cane and spat
on him, and falling on their knees, did obeisance to him. (20) And**

**when they had finished mocking him, they stripped the purple off him and dressed him in his own clothes.**

Some commentators argue that this section has been added to the passion narrative at some stage, since the story reads just as well without it. If so, the addition was made by Mark or someone before him, since no MS is without it. The incident is found in all four gospels, though in Luke it is Herod's soldiers who are said to mock Jesus (23.11). Various parallels have been found to the story: Philo records an incident in which Agrippa I was mocked by the inhabitants of Alexandria after being made King of Judaea – though it was not Agrippa himself but a half-wit, Carabas, who was dressed up and addressed and saluted as king (*In Flaccum* V–VI). There is also evidence of various ceremonies in different places involving the dressing up of a mock king, and sometimes his sacrificial death. The existence of these parallels does not undermine the historicity of this particular incident; rather they suggest that it was entirely natural. For Mark, however, its significance lies in its dramatic irony: Jesus has been proclaimed king, and men salute him as such.

16  **The soldiers took him away inside.** This suggests that the scene so far has been enacted outside, and this is certainly what John depicts (18.28f.). A similar scene is described by Josephus (*Wars*, II. 14.8–9), where Florus, a later procurator, sat in judgement on a tribunal which had been set up in front of the palace. **The palace:** the word αὐλή, normally used of a courtyard, is here used of the procurator's headquarters, **the Praetorium.**

**The whole company:** the σπεῖρα was a cohort, the proper strength of which was 600 men. Mark seems to be using the phrase loosely.

17  **They dressed him in purple,** the colour worn by emperors. The **thorny crown** is usually assumed to be an instrument of torture, but it is possible that it was made from the long spines of a date palm, worn with the point of the thorns facing away from the head, and that it was a deliberate caricature of the radiate crown (imitating the rays of the sun-god) with which 'divine' rulers were portrayed on coins of

18  the period (see H.St.J. Hart, *J.T.S.*, n.s. 3, 1952, pp. 66–75). **'Hail, King of the Jews!'** These mocking words echo the salutation given to the Emperor – *Ave Caesar!* – but they also emphasize once again that it is as King of the Jews that Jesus dies: throughout Mark's passion narra-

19  tive, Jesus' enemies unwittingly proclaim the truth about him. **And they beat him about the head with a cane:** in Matthew, the cane is given to Jesus as a sceptre (27.29). **And spat:** spitting is mentioned in Isa. 50.6, but there is no real indication that the account here has been influenced by that passage. The ill-treatment here is parallel to that given to Jesus in the high-priest's house in 14.65. **Falling on their knees,** they **did obeisance to him,** as though to a king; the irony of

the scene is once again clear to those who recognize that Jesus is
indeed a king.

# 14　THE CRUCIFIXION　　　　　　　15.20b–32

*(Matt. 27.31b–44; Luke 23.26,32–9; John 19.17–24)*

**(20) And they led him out to crucify him. (21) And they compelled
a certain passer-by, Simon from Cyrene (the father of Alexander
and Rufus), who was on his way from the country, to carry his
cross. (22) And they brought him to a place called Golgotha
(which means 'Place of a skull'). (23) And they offered him wine,
drugged with myrrh, but he would not take it. (24) Then they
crucified him and shared out his clothes, casting lots to decide
what each should take. (25) It was the third hour when they
crucified him; (26) and the inscription giving the charge against
him read, 'The King of the Jews'. (27) And they crucified two bandits with him, one on his right and the other on his left.[1]**

**(29) And the passers-by hurled insults at him, shaking their
heads and saying, 'Aha! The man who destroys the sanctuary and
builds it in three days! (30) Save yourself, and come down from
the cross!' (31) In the same way, too, the chief priests ridiculed
him, together with the scribes: 'He saved others,' they said to one
another, 'but he cannot save himself. (32) Let the Messiah, the
King of Israel, come down now from the cross, so that we may see
and believe.' Even those who were crucified with him reviled him.**

Mark's account is brief but nevertheless shows signs of expansion:
the crucifixion itself is mentioned twice (vv.24, 25, as is Jesus' loud
cry, vv.34, 37); vv.21–24a (with their stark historic presents) probably
belong to the nucleus of the story. The three-fold mockery (vv.29–32)
suggests elaboration, as do the solemn references to the hours (vv.25,
33). Crucifixion was a barbaric mode of execution. Widely practised
in the ancient world, it was adopted by the Romans for slaves and for
the worst kind of criminal; they also came to employ it in dealing with
rebels against Roman rule. Since the victim was stripped naked and
fixed immobile to suffer the torments of pain, thirst, insects and
taunts, sometimes for days, it was a particularly humiliating, as well
as a prolonged and agonizing form of death.

Mark presents the crucifixion of Jesus almost as though it were an
enthronement: Jesus has been hailed by the crowds as he entered

---

1 Some MSS add: (28) *And the scripture was fulfilled which says, 'He was numbered with the lawless'.*

Jerusalem (11.1–10), anointed (by a woman! – 14.3–9), 'identified' by the high priest (14.61), proclaimed to the people by Pilate (15.9, 12) and saluted as king by the soldiers (15.17–19). Now he is 'enthroned' on the cross, with an inscription telling the world who he is, and with two thieves occupying the places of honour at his right and his left (10.37). Although Mark (typically) hints at the scene's significance rather than spelling it out clearly, his presentation reminds us of the fourth evangelist's insistence that Jesus' crucifixion is the moment of his glorification. Yet Mark could never have put it in those terms, since to do so is to run the risk of minimizing the anguish: in his story the shame, the humiliation, the suffering and the agony remain to the fore. It is left to the reader to see a deeper significance in all these events.

21    **And they compelled a certain passer-by, Simon from Cyrene... to carry his cross.** Criminals were normally compelled to carry their own cross (i.e. the cross-beam, which would be fixed to the upright post at the place of execution); Mark does not explain why Jesus did not carry his own; the suggestion that he was too weak is later inference. Mark's account differs from that of John, who insists that Jesus carried the cross himself (19.17). But John may have been reacting against Gnostic assertions that Simon had been crucified instead of Jesus, so Mark's version could be based on an historical incident. **Alexander and Rufus** were presumably known to Mark's readers (by name if not in person). Mark may well see irony in the fact that it is Simon of Cyrene (who has not been heard of before) who is compelled to carry the cross, since these words – ἵνα ἄρῃ τὸν σταυρὸν – echo the challenge of Jesus to the would-be disciple in 8.34: 'let him...take up his cross'. Luke emphasizes the link by adding the words 'behind Jesus' (23.26). Simon is said to have been **on his way from the country,** but whether this means from his work in the fields or from his house outside Jerusalem is not clear, and the remark therefore throws no light on the question as to whether or not the day was a festival.

22    **They brought him to a place called Golgotha.** The Aramaic word, meaning **skull,** suggests that the place of crucifixion may have been a hill, deriving its name from its shape, though legend later associated it with the spot where Adam's skull was buried. The exact location is uncertain, since what came to be known as the traditional site was not identified until the fourth century AD. Crucifixions were generally held in public places, in order to provide the maximum possible

23    deterrent, and v.29 suggests a site near a road. The drink of **wine, drugged with myrrh,** would have been offered to Jesus by Jewish sympathizers (perhaps women from Jerusalem) rather than by his Roman executioners. The custom of offering a pain-killing drink to those condemned to death is mentioned in the Talmud (B. Sanh. 43a),

where it is said to be based on Prov. 31.6. The statement that Jesus refused to drink it supports Mark's picture of him as willingly accepting the path of suffering.

**They crucified him.** The victim's arms and feet were fixed to the 24 cross with rope or nails; John 20.25 refers to nailprints in Jesus' hands. **And shared out his clothes:** the clothes of those who were crucified were regarded as the perquisites of their executioners. Mark's account clearly echoes the wording of Ps. 22.18: 'they divide my garments among them, and for my raiment they cast lots'. This does not necessarily mean that the incident has been created out of the quotation, though the reference to **casting lots** may be an elaboration based on the psalm. Nevertheless, Mark would probably not have mentioned this particular incident at all if he had not seen in it the fulfilment of scripture.

**It was the third hour when they crucified him.** Mark divides 25 Good Friday into three-hour periods (see vv.1, 33f., 42). The scheme seems somewhat artificial and is at variance with the tradition used by the fourth evangelist (19.14). The solemn marking of the hours is perhaps intended to remind us that what is taking place is in accordance with God's plan and is the fulfilment of his purpose. **The inscription** (or *titulus*) **giving the charge** on which a criminal had 26 been condemned was normally displayed on the cross. If the wording given here is authentic, it must have been intended as sarcasm. For Mark, however, the title is profoundly true: it is through crucifixion that Jesus is proclaimed as Messiah, and as **the King of the Jews.**

There is further irony in the crucifixion of **two bandits with him,** 27 **one on his right and the other on his left.** Two criminals occupy the places of honour which were requested by James and John in 10.37. 28 The quotation from Isa. 53.12 is missing from the earliest and best MSS and has apparently been added at some stage, probably from Luke 22.37, where it is used in a somewhat different context. In both passages the quotation has been used to explain the scandal of the circumstances of Jesus' death: even the fact that he was executed in the company of other criminals was explained as part of the divine plan.

**And the passers-by hurled insults at him.** The verb (βλασφημέω) 29 echoes the accusations brought against Jesus by his opponents (14.64; cf. 2.7): the irony is that it is his enemies who 'blaspheme' him (cf. also 3.28f.)! The derision of **passers-by** is probable enough, even though Mark's description of them **shaking their heads** (a gesture of contempt) echoes Lam. 2.15 and Ps. 22.7(21.8). Mark uses the threefold account of mockery in vv.29–32 skilfully to make theological comment on Jesus' death. **Aha! The man who destroys the sanctuary and builds it in three days!** This first taunt echoes the accusation brought against Jesus at his 'trial' (14.58): Jesus is invited 30 to use the supernatural powers which he is accused of claiming to save himself by coming **down from the cross.**

31    It is unlikely that **the chief priests** and **the scribes** would have attended the execution. Possibly vv.31f. are an expansion of the story, since the words of mockery are similar to the previous taunt: Jesus is again invited to save himself. There is supreme irony in the words Mark attributes to the Jewish leaders, for if he is to save **others**, then

32   **he cannot save himself.** This time, the taunt picks up the second charge brought against Jesus, that of claiming to be God's **Messiah.** The demand that he should **come down...from the cross, so that we may see and believe,** shows a false understanding of the nature of faith, which is not dependent on miracles, but is a necessary condition for them. These words remind us of the demand for a sign made by the Pharisees in 8.11f. In both cases, the demand for a special sign is itself a demonstration of unbelief. In chapter 8, Mark underlines this by placing the Pharisees' words immediately after the second feeding of the crowd: they demand special signs while failing to see the evidence in front of their eyes. Now Jesus' enemies demand that he 'proves' himself to be **the King of Israel** by coming down from the cross. But for Mark it is on his cross that Jesus is proclaimed to be the King of Israel, and by his death that he is affirmed as Messiah: to save himself would in fact be to deny that he is Messiah, not to establish it. It would also be to deny the principle set out by Jesus in 8.35 that it is by losing one's life that one gains it.

**Even those who were crucified with him reviled him.** With this reference to a third group's mocking Jesus, Mark completes the picture of desolation. Even those who shared Jesus' torments joined in jeering at him: he is now totally isolated.

# 15   THE DEATH OF JESUS                                    15.33–41

*(Matt. 27.45–56; Luke 23.44–9; John 19.28–30)*

**(33) At the sixth hour, darkness fell over the whole land, [and remained] until the ninth hour; (34) and at the ninth hour Jesus cried with a loud voice, 'Eloi, Eloi, lema sabachthani?' which means, 'My God, my God, why have you abandoned me?' (35) When some of the bystanders heard, they said, 'Listen! He is calling Elijah.' (36) Someone ran and soaked a sponge with sour wine, put it on a cane and offered it to him to drink, saying, 'Let us see if Elijah will come to take him down.' (37) Then Jesus gave a loud cry and died. (38) And the curtain in the sanctuary was torn in two, from top to bottom. (39) When the centurion, who was**

standing there opposite him, saw how[1] he died, he said, 'Truly, this man was [the] son of God.'
(40) Some women were also there, watching from a distance; among them were Mary Magdalene, Mary – mother of James the younger and of Joses[2] – and Salome, (41) who had followed him when he was in Galilee and had looked after him, and many others, who had come up to Jerusalem with him.

Central to Mark's understanding of the death of Jesus is the cry of dereliction in v.34. Deserted and betrayed by his disciples, rejected and condemned by the nation's leaders, taunted by passers-by and fellow-victims, Jesus now experiences utter desolation: even God has forsaken him! Whether or not the words were spoken by Jesus himself we cannot, of course, know. They are a quotation from Psalm 22 which has influenced the telling of the passion story, but though these precise words may have been introduced into the story at some stage, the cry of dereliction has a more authentic ring than the very different final sayings attributed to Jesus by Luke (23.46) and John (19.30). Moreover, these words provide a profound theological comment on the oneness of Jesus with humanity, and on the meaning of his death, in which he shares human despair to the full. Commentators who insist that Jesus (or Mark) must have had the rest of the psalm (with its message of hope) in mind fail to grasp the significance of Mark's picture of Jesus as utterly desolate. Jesus now experiences the most bitter blow which can befall the religious man: the sense of having been abandoned by God. Mark reminds his readers of the horror of Jesus' sufferings; not for a moment does he sentimentalize the cross. This is true obedience to God's will (14.36) – what Paul describes as being 'obedient to death, even death on a cross (Phil. 2.8). At this moment Jesus experiences what Paul elsewhere describes as 'becoming a curse' (Gal. 3.13) or 'being made sin' (2 Cor. 5.21). His willingness to 'deny himself and. . .lose his life' has been tested to the full. Only because he is willing to drain the cup of suffering to the full (10.38; 14.36) will he be vindicated, and his proclamation as king be turned from a mockery into a reality. And at the moment of his death comes the first sincere (if uncomprehending) acknowledgement of Jesus since his arrest: not simply as the King of the Jews, for they have rejected him, but as Son of God!

The **darkness** which **fell over the whole land from the sixth hour** 33 **...until the ninth hour** is a sign of the terrible nature of what is taking place. Attempts to explain it by some natural phenomenon miss the point. It matters not at all, therefore, that an eclipse of the sun was

1 Some MSS add: *crying out.*
2 Some MSS add *the* before *mother*, assuming that there are two women: lit. *Mary of James the younger and the mother of Joses..*

impossible at the time of the full moon. And though Luke explains the darkness by saying that 'the sun's light failed' (23.45), he is not necessarily using the verb (ἐκλείπω) in a technical sense. The evangelists are more likely to have been thinking of a fulfilment of Amos 8.9: 'On that day. . .I will make the sun go down at noon and darken the earth in broad daylight.' The darkness at midday symbolizes the judgement that comes upon the land of Israel with the rejection of Israel's king.

34    'Eloi, Eloi, lema sabachthani?' This is the only saying from the cross that Mark records. The words are a quotation from the beginning of Psalm 22. It has often been argued that Mark (or Jesus himself) intended to refer not to these words alone, but to the rest of the psalm, in which the psalmist goes on to speak of his hope of deliverance. But the suggestion seems to be an attempt to disguise the horror of the scene as it is portrayed by Mark, and the narrative supplies no evidence to support the contention that Mark had the rest of the psalm in mind. Earlier commentators (e.g. Rawlinson, Branscomb) often found it impossible to believe that Jesus could have died with words of despair on his lips, and since Luke and John both omit the cry of dereliction they may have experienced the same

35    difficulty. The quotation is given in Aramaic, though the confusion with the name Elijah is possible only in Hebrew. Matthew appears to have seen this difficulty (or to have made use of an earlier tradition), since he quotes the opening words in Hebrew – 'Eli, Eli'. The suggestion that Jesus is calling Elijah is presumably based on the tradition that Elijah, who had been translated to heaven at the end of his life (2 Kgs. 2.11f.), would come to the aid of the righteous in time of trouble. (In Jewish rabbinic material we find a number of bizarre episodes in which Elijah is said to have made a sudden appearance and come to someone's assistance; e.g. B.Ber. 58a; B. Ab. Zara 17b, 18b; Midrash Esther 10.9.) If so, Mark must think of the bystan-

36    ders as Jews, not Romans. The person who ran and soaked a sponge with sour wine, put it on a cane and offered it to him to drink, on the other hand, is more likely to have been a Roman soldier than a member of the crowd: the sour wine (ὄξος) could well be wine which the soldiers had with them (cf. Luke 23.36, where wine is offered to Jesus in mockery). According to Mark, however, it is the man who offers Jesus the drink who also suggests that Elijah may come to his rescue: Let us see (taking the verb ἄφετε with the following one, ἴδωμεν, which seems the most natural translation) if Elijah will come to take him down, an unlikely comment from a Roman soldier. This difficulty, together with the fact that there is no real relationship between the action and the words, may indicate that we have here a weaving together of two traditions, one about Elijah (vv.34f., 36b), and the other about a soldier offering Jesus a drink (v.36a), and this is supported by the fact that both Luke and John have independent

accounts of how Jesus was offered wine to drink (Luke 23.36; John 19.29). The significance of this second tradition for all the evangelists, though they use it in different ways, would certainly derive from the fact that the incident was seen as a fulfilment of Ps. 69.21 (68.22): 'they gave me vinegar to drink'. The LXX uses here the same word ὄξος, employed by all the evangelists, but it is clear from the context that in the psalm it has the meaning 'vinegar': the psalmist's enemies have given him 'poison for food', and vinegar to assuage his thirst. In the gospels, however, if we are to make sense of the incident (especially in John) we must understand the word in its other sense of cheap everyday wine such as the soldiers might drink. The offering of wine to drink would have been a humane gesture, but in the light of Psalm 69 it came to be interpreted (most clearly in Luke) as an act of mockery. This perhaps explains why the incident has been inserted into the tradition about Elijah: in the moment of extremity, when even God appears to have deserted him, Jesus receives no aid but is mocked by his enemies' offer of sham comfort. The suggestion that Elijah might come to his aid may be a deliberate irony on Mark's part. For earlier in the gospel Jesus himself has spoken of Elijah and identified him with John the Baptist (9.11–13): Elijah has come, his message has been spurned, and he himself has been put to death. How, then, can Elijah now come to aid Jesus?

**Then Jesus gave** another **loud cry.** This time Mark offers no inter- 37 pretation, whether true or false. There is nothing in his account to support the suggestion of some commentators (e.g. Anderson) that he understands it as a word of judgement on the world. It seems rather to be another cry of anguish, as in v.34: in Ps. 22.2 the psalmist declares that he cries to God by day and night but receives no response. Earlier references in Mark to loud cries have been to the cries of unclean spirits in the moment of defeat (1.26; 5.7). This final inarticulate cry accords with Mark's stark account in v.34. As we have seen, Luke and John give a different picture. In Luke, there is only one loud cry in which Jesus commits himself obediently into God's hands (23.46): in John, Jesus dies with the triumphant words 'It is finished' (19.30).

**And the curtain in the sanctuary was torn in two, from top to** 38 **bottom.** Mark could be thinking either of the inner curtain which separated the Holy of Holies from the Holy Place, or of the outer curtain at the doorway of the Holy Place itself. The same word (τὸ καταπέτασμα) was used of both (Josephus, *Antiquities*, VIII.3.3; LXX Exod. 26.33, 37). The latter was unimportant, however (there was a door as well), while the former was of great significance: there was no other barrier to the Holy of Holies, and through it the high priest alone was permitted to pass, and that only once a year. In view of 13.2, 14.58 and 15.29, it seems clear that Mark understands the symbolic rending to be a sign of the temple's future destruction. A similar idea was used later in the Gospel of the Nazarenes, according to which the lintel of the temple fell down in pieces (Fragments 21 and 36). We find a similar story also in Josephus (*Wars*, VI.5.3) who tells how the gate of the inner court one night opened of its own accord. This was, he says, a sign of the temple's future destruction, though the uninitiated interpreted it as a good omen. For Mark, the rending of the curtain may well have a positive as well as a negative interpretation. With Jesus' death, the fate of Israel is sealed: she has rejected her Messiah, and her judgement is inevitable, since her condemnation has already been pronounced. But at the same time others are brought into the community of God's people. In the Epistle to the Hebrews, Jesus is seen as a new high priest, entering the Holy of Holies through his death, and so dealing with sin once and for all (Heb. 9.11f., 24–8); moreover he opens the way for others to enter through the curtain, which is interpreted as his flesh (10.19f.; cf. 6.19f.). Mark does not spell out the symbolism in terms of the ritual of the Day of Atonement, but he may well have in mind the idea of the removal of a barrier which kept men out of God's presence (so R.H. Lightfoot, *The Gospel Message of St Mark*, pp. 55f.). This is supported by the next verse where, astonishingly, the confession of faith is made by a Gentile. If barriers are broken down through the death of Jesus, even Gentiles can now enter; cf. a similar possible use of symbolism in the breaking down of the 'dividing wall' in Eph. 2.14, which may well refer to the barrier in the temple beyond which Gentiles were not permitted to pass.

39    **The centurion** was in charge of the company of soldiers and was Jesus' executioner. When he **saw how he died, he said, 'Truly, this man was [the] son of God.'** The centurion's words are understood by Mark to be a response to the death of Jesus. The verb 'crying out' occurs in many MSS of different types and may be original but makes no real difference to the sense. Matthew interprets the incident differently, since he makes the confession a response to the signs and wonders which accompany Jesus' death in his gospel. For Mark, however, it is the death of Jesus that is the significant event and which leads men to confess him as **the son of God**. This phrase is anarthrous (υἱὸς Θεοῦ) and the translation 'a son of God' adopted in some versions is thus technically correct, yet probably misleading, for while it is true that the centurion, if he uttered these words, could only have meant by them a divine man or demi-god, yet for Mark they are a proclamation of the truth about Jesus. In 1.1, the same phrase is translated as 'the son of God', and it therefore seems best to adopt the same translation here (see E. Schweizer, *T.D.N.T.*, VIII, p. 379; Colwell, *J.B.L.*, 52, 1933, pp. 12–21; Bratcher, *Exp. Tim.*, 68, 1956, pp. 27f.). For Mark, it is this Gentile soldier who gives to Jesus the title which hitherto has been spoken only by the heavenly voice or by unclean

spirits acknowledging their master (1.11; 9.7; 3.11; 5.7). Whether Mark thinks that the centurion is aware of the true significance of his words is not clear. Perhaps Mark regards them as an unconscious acknowledgement of Jesus' identity, like the taunts of those who mocked the dying Jesus, unaware of the true meaning of their words (15.18, 26, 29f., 31f.), and the incredulous questions of the high priest and Pilate (14.61; 15.2). The truth is thus spoken by Jesus' judges and by his executioner. Nevertheless, the centurion stands at this point as the representative of those who acknowledge Jesus as God's son. His words form the climax of Mark's gospel, for they are the words used in the confession of Christian faith, and they are found in the mouth of a Gentile at the moment of Jesus' death.

The **women** who witness Jesus' death are mentioned here in order 40 to prepare for their role in the next two sections. They play no part in the story at this point, but in contrast to the disciples they are at least present at the crucifixion, even if they observe events only **from a distance**. Mark's picture is certainly more probable than John's (19.25). **Mary Magdalene** is identified in Luke 8.2 as a woman from whom Jesus had expelled seven demons. There is no scriptural evidence for the traditional picture of Mary as a prostitute. She came from Magdala, on the west coast of Galilee. The second **Mary** is described literally as 'of James. . .and of Joses, mother'; she could be either the **mother of James the younger** or the daughter; the variant reading understands the mother **of Joses** to be another woman. Nothing is known about **James the younger** or **Joses**, but presumably they were well known to Mark's readers (cf. v.21); James is described literally as 'small', which could be a reference to his age or his height. **Salome** is not mentioned by name in Matthew, who does, however, refer to the mother of the sons of Zebedee (27.56); most commentators assume that the two evangelists are referring to the same person, though we cannot be certain that this is so. It may be that each evangelist has picked out those women whose names would be known in his community. Mark mentions here for the first 41 time that women had been among those **who had followed** Jesus **when he was in Galilee** (cf. Luke 8.2f.), and that they had **looked after him** and **had come up to Jerusalem with him**.

# 16   THE BURIAL                                    15.42–7

*(Matt. 27.57–61; Luke 23.50–6; John 19.38–42)*

**(42) It was now evening, and because it was Preparation – that is the day before the sabbath – (43) Joseph of Arimathea, an influential member of the Council, who was himself waiting for the King-**

dom of God, summoned up his courage and went to Pilate to ask for Jesus' body. (44) Pilate was astonished that he should have died so soon, and sending for the centurion, he asked him whether he was already dead.[1] (45) After learning [the facts] from the centurion, he granted the corpse to Joseph. (46) And he bought a linen sheet, took him down from the cross, and wrapped him in the sheet. Then he laid him in a tomb cut out of the rock, and rolled a stone across the entrance to the tomb. (47) Mary Magdalene and Mary [the mother] of Joses saw where he was laid.

The story of Jesus' burial was important, since it confirmed the reality of his death. It is notable that it is included in the brief summary of the kerygma quoted by Paul in 1 Cor. 15.3ff. The suggestion that the incident was created in order to show that Isa. 53.9 was 'fulfilled' by Jesus has nothing to commend it. Indeed, the circumstances of Jesus' death and burial are the reverse of those set out there! The basic story is described by Bultmann as 'an historical account which creates no impression of being a legend' (*The History of the Synoptic Tradition*, p. 274).

42    **It was now evening.** Strictly speaking, this would mean that the sabbath had already begun, but the point of the hasty burial was to dispose of Jesus' body before dusk, **because it was Preparation – that is the day before the sabbath.** Burials took place on the day of death whenever possible, and on the following day at the latest, so that a death late on Friday required instant action. Mark carefully explains the meaning of the term 'Preparation' for Gentile readers, but appears to be less careful in his reference to the time: presumably he means that Joseph acted during the brief interval between Jesus' death at the ninth hour and dusk. Many commentators point out that Mark's account here conflicts with the chronology he adopts in 14.12–16 which makes Friday the Feast of Passover: it makes little sense for Joseph to avoid desecration of the sabbath by burying Jesus on another holy day. Strangely the Mishnah does not tell us what was to be done with a corpse when two holy days fell on subsequent days, but a festival day differed from the sabbath only in that preparation of needful food was permitted (M. Betz. 5.2; Meg. 1.5), and on the sabbath it was permitted to wash a corpse, but not to move it (M. Shab. 23.5). Once again, it seems that Mark's narrative supports the Johannine dating of the crucifixion (according to which Passover coincided with the sabbath) rather than his own. It is true that he refers here to the following day as the sabbath, not as the Passover, but obviously he could not make the latter identification in view of his interpretation of the Last Supper.

1 Some MSS read: *had been some time dead.*

Arimathea is usually identified with Ramathaim, a village 20 miles **43**
from Jerusalem. Joseph is described as **influential**, a man of some
position, and a **member of the Council** (perhaps the Sanhedrin). The
fact that he was **waiting for the Kingdom of God** does not necessarily mean that he was sympathetic to Jesus' cause, though Matthew
and John describe him as a disciple (Matt. 27.57; John 19.38) and
Luke exonerates him from blame in Jesus' death (Luke 23.51). It
could have been simple piety which led him to give Jesus burial.
Jewish custom demanded the speedy disposal of a corpse, and if a
dead man had no friends or relatives to bury him, someone else must
act instead. Moreover, Deut. 21.23 demanded that a malefactor's
body should be removed from the tree on which it was hung before
sundown. Although the Roman authorities often left the bodies of
criminals on crosses until they decayed, as a warning to others
(Mark's comment that it needed **courage** on Joseph's part to approach
**Pilate** indicates that his request might well have been refused), it
seems that Jews were sometimes allowed to remove the bodies in accordance with Deuteronomy 21. Certainly Josephus (*Wars*, IV. 5.2)
describes them doing so. This would provide another motive for
Joseph to bury Jesus before sundown: it was not simply because the
next day was the sabbath, but because the Law decreed that a criminal's corpse must be taken down and disposed of before nightfall. Far
from being a secret follower of Jesus acting out of devotion to him,
therefore, Joseph may have regarded Jesus' body as a curse to the
land which needed to be disposed of as soon as possible.

The next two verses may be an addition to the story, which reads **44–5**
more smoothly without them; Matthew and Luke both omit them.
Whatever their origin, their effect is to stress the fact that Jesus really
was dead: Pilate's surprise at the speed of Jesus' death serves to introduce the confirmatory evidence of **the centurion** who had witnessed
the scene. Mark perhaps wished to deny rumours that there had been
a mistake and that Jesus had been taken down prematurely from the
cross. The variant reading in v.44 seems less appropriate, though it
could for that reason have been 'corrected' to that followed in the
text. The word **corpse** (το πτῶμα) underlines the brute reality of
Jesus' death.

The purchase of **a linen sheet** on a festal day would have been, **46**
strictly speaking, contrary to the Law, but there were ways of bending
the regulations if the matter was urgent. It was possible to make
purchases, provided that financial arrangements were discussed
subsequently (M. Shab. 23.1; Tos. Shab. 17.13; B. Shab. 151a). Mark's
description of the burial shows that it was a hasty affair, and he makes
no reference to the use of any ointment (cf. 16.1 and 14.8). Rock-hewn
tombs were common in the vicinity, and the use of **a stone** to seal **the
entrance to the tomb** was normal. The women – or rather two of **47**

them, Mary Magdalene and Mary [the mother] of Joses – appear again, this time as witnesses of the spot where he was laid. The second Mary is described this time simply as 'of Joses', which might well be taken to mean 'daughter of Joses', but which in view of v.40 has been understood here to mean 'mother of Joses'.

## H The Epilogue: the Resurrection 16.1–8

## 1 THE EMPTY TOMB 16.1–8

*(Matt. 28.1–8; Luke 24.1–11; John 20.1, 11f.)*

(1) When the Sabbath was over Mary Magdalene, and Mary [the mother] of James and Salome bought spices,[1] so that they might go and anoint him. (2) And very early in the morning on the first day of the week they came to the tomb, just after sunrise. (3) They were saying to one another, 'Who will roll the stone away for us from the entrance to the tomb?' (4) when they looked up and saw that the stone had been rolled away (for it was extremely large). (5) Then they entered the tomb and saw a young man sitting on the right-hand side, wearing a white robe, and they were astounded. (6) But he said to them, 'Do not be alarmed. You are looking for Jesus of Nazareth, who was crucified. He has been raised – he is not here! Look – there is the place where they laid him. (7) But go and say to his disciples – and Peter! – "He is going before you into Galilee; you will see him there, just as he told you."'

(8) Then they went out and fled from the tomb, overcome by trembling and terror, and they said nothing to anyone, for they were afraid.

These eight verses make up the last section of the gospel to have been written by Mark himself. Everything after v.8 is written in a different style and has quite clearly been added later. Since neither Matthew nor Luke show signs of having used this additional material (indeed, vv.9–20 look like a summary of the tradition used in the other gospels), it is probable that this was added to Mark some considerable time after the gospel was written, probably in the second century. The great problem, to which we must return, is whether Mark intended to end at v.8, or whether his gospel is incomplete – either because he was unable to finish it, or because the original ending was

---

1 The first part of the verse is omitted by D, which reads: *and they bought spices.*

lost. The suggestion that Mark intended to end at v.8 is best considered after we have examined his treatment of this section. If in fact he broke off here but intended to write more, then perhaps he himself suffered – just too soon! – the martyrdom which throughout his narrative he had so clearly foreseen as the likely fate of those who became disciples of Jesus. If, on the other hand, he wrote more and the ending was lost, then this loss was presumably due to the fact that the original copy of the gospel was read and reread until the final page of the codex or end of the scroll wore away. In this case, however, it is puzzling that the missing portion was not copied out and replaced. Though the problem is the abrupt ending, it is remarkable, nevertheless, that an accidental break should have occurred at a point where a case can at least be made for arguing that Mark intended to stop.

In common with the other evangelists, Mark does not describe the resurrection itself. He describes only the scene at the empty tomb, and the message of the risen Jesus to his disciples, which is entrusted to the women who had come to anoint his corpse.

The story begins as soon as **the Sabbath was over**, that is on 1 Saturday evening. It is strange that the women are named again, so soon after v.47, unless this is the beginning of another independent tradition which Mark has incorporated as it stands (though the rest of the story looks like Markan composition, using many of his favourite words); this part of the verse is indeed omitted in one MS, which makes the whole thing read more smoothly, but this is unlikely to be the original reading. Even stranger, the names do not tally exactly with 15.47 (or even with 15.40), though Mark's purposes seems to be to establish this small group of women as witnesses of Jesus' death, burial and resurrection. Only **Mary Magdalene** is constant. **Salome**, mentioned in 15.40, reappears. The other **Mary** is this time described as being **of James**, and once again this phrase might most naturally be understood to mean 'daughter' rather than **mother**. However we understand the relationship, the three different descriptions of this Mary cause problems: either there are two different women, one related to James, the other to Joses (and according to 15.40, his mother), or there is one woman, who is mother of Joses and either mother or daughter of James. The discrepancies suggest that Mark has taken over different traditions and reproduced them faithfully, at least in these details; they also warn us against assuming that there must be theological significance in the minor details of Mark's narrative! The three women **bought spices** – that is perfumed ointments – at the earliest opportunity, in order to **anoint** Jesus' body. It was customary to prepare bodies for burial by anointing them; to do so 36 hours after burial was at best pointless, at worst extremely unpleasant. Only Luke (23.56–24.1) agrees with Mark at this point. Matthew

(28.1) says simply that the women went to see the tomb, John (19.39f.) that Joseph and Nicodemus anointed the body before burial. However, it may well be that there was no opportunity to anoint the body, and that the Johannine tradition merely reflects the assumption that the rite was performed by those who buried Jesus. The women may have wished to do belatedly what ought to have been done, even though it was too late to be anything but an expression of their devotion. Even if Mark and Luke have misinterpreted their motive, we would expect the women to come to the grave at the first opportunity, since such visits were customary. For Mark, of course, the reference to their desire to anoint the body has particular significance and underlines their inability to comprehend what is taking place. The women plan to anoint Jesus belatedly, after his burial; they are too late, not (as we might assume) because the body has begun to decay, but because it is no longer there. For Mark, the story recorded in 14.3–9 thus took on a new significance – the women fail to do belatedly what was in fact done by another woman prematurely. Her action was a prophetic sign of his death; theirs is made impossible because of his resurrection.

2    **Very early in the morning on the first day of the week.** According to Jewish reckoning this means in the early hours before dawn. The other evangelists seem to agree (cf. in particular John 20.1: 'while it was still dark'). But Mark's next temporal reference is inconsistent: the women, he says, **came to the tomb, just after sunrise.** Attempts were made at an early stage to tidy up this anomaly by altering one phrase or the other. The explanation is probably that Mark was not

3    being as precise as his critics. **They were saying to one another, 'Who will roll the stone away for us from the entrance to the tomb?'** The women's conversation on the journey is clearly illogical: it is little use their going to the tomb for their stated purpose if they cannot enter it when they arrive. But Mark's purpose is to underline the fact that the tomb had been firmly closed, and that the women had no expectation of finding it open, so he enables us to share their sur-

4    prise at finding **that the stone had been rolled away.** At this point Mark adds the comment: **for it was extremely large.** Many commentators and translators have been offended by Mark's abrupt style at this point and have shifted this comment to the end of v.3. But Mark's purpose is not to stress the inability of the women to move the rock (which is obvious), but the significance of what has now taken place: the huge rock has been rolled away. By whom, Mark does not say. Matthew attributes the deed to an angel (28.2), but this is simply another way of speaking of God's activity.

5    The **young man sitting on the right-hand side, wearing a white robe** is recognizably an angel. (Cf. the 'young men' in 2 Macc. 3.26, 33, and the description of Jesus' garments in Mark 9.3.) His appearance

strikes the women with terror. The verb translated **astounded** in v.5 and **alarmed** in v.6 (ἐκθαμβέομαι) is used by Mark alone among New Testament writers. He used it in 9.15 of the crowd's astonishment at seeing Jesus on his descent from the mountain, and in 14.33 of Jesus' own emotion in Gethsemane. Clearly Mark means that the women were terrified, rather than simply amazed. They have no expectation 6 of the announcement which they are to be given, for they are **looking for the body of Jesus of Nazareth, who was crucified.** The somewhat formal language suggests that of an early summary of the scandal of the gospel (cf. 1 Cor. 1.23; 2.2; Gal. 3.1). So, too, does the divine message delivered by the angel: **He has been raised.** The verb (ἠγέρθη) is an Aorist Passive and, though it might be understood (as in the *R.S.V.*) in an active sense ('He has risen'), it is better to translate it as we have done here. It is God who has raised Jesus to life, and it is his mighty act that is announced to the women. Jesus is not to be found among the dead; **the place where they laid him** is empty, for **he is not here.**

Where, then, is he to be found? The rest of the angel's words are a 7 commission to the women to deliver a message to the disciples. It has sometimes been argued that v.7 is an addition to the narrative, since the women's silence in v.8 is incomprehensible after such a commission. But if so, the addition must have been made by Mark (Matthew includes the verse) who therefore presumably did not consider this a difficulty. The message is addressed to Jesus' **disciples – and Peter!** – who is mentioned specifically because he has denied that he is a disciple. The message sums up the forgiveness which Jesus offers his followers. Strictly, none of them has any right to be summoned to follow the risen Lord, for all of them by their actions, and Peter by his words, have been ashamed of Jesus. But the warning of Mark 8.38 is not yet put into operation: instead of being ashamed of those who have failed him, Jesus calls them to begin again. **He is going before you into Galilee.** These words echo those attributed to Jesus himself in 14.28 – words which introduced Peter's protestations and Jesus' prediction of Peter's failure. In that context, the verb (προάξω – I will go before) had to be understood in the sense of 'lead': after his resurrection, Jesus would lead the disciples into Galilee (as a shepherd leads his sheep). Here, the same verb (προάγει) has been translated in the same way, as 'go before', but this is generally understood in the sense of 'go ahead' or 'precede', since it is only when they arrive in Galilee that they **will see** Jesus. Yet the final words, **just as he told you,** show clearly that Mark has the earlier passage in mind, and he is certainly saying something far more significant than that Jesus will arrive in Galilee before the disciples. This is no mere rendezvous, but a call to the disciples to follow Jesus once again. On the way to Jerusalem, Jesus had gone ahead (10.32 – ἦν προάγων), and the disciples had seen him and followed. Now they are called to follow him, even though they cannot see him. What looks like an inconsistency in Mark may be a deliberate attempt on his part to underline that this is what discipleship means, now that Jesus has been raised from the dead.

The promise that the disciples will see Jesus in Galilee suggests a resurrection appearance there, and this is how Matthew understood it (cf. Matt. 28.16ff.). But why should the disciples be sent to Galilee? Some commentators have followed Lohmeyer (*Markus*, p. 355f.) in thinking that Galilee is mentioned because it is the place of eschatological fulfilment: the promise that they will see Jesus is thus a reference to the parousia. (So also W. Marxsen, *Mark the Evangelist*, pp. 75–95). Lohmeyer argued that the verb 'to see' was normally used of the parousia rather than the resurrection (e.g. 14.62). But his arguments are flimsy: the verb 'to see' is used of the risen Lord elsewhere (e.g. 1 Cor. 9.1; John 20.18) and could have that sense here, and there is no reason why Galilee (rather than Jerusalem) should be the place of the parousia. If the saying *is* understood of the parousia, then it becomes more of a threat than a promise! (Cf. 8.38 and 14.62.)

The question therefore remains – why are the disciples sent back to Galilee? The message might perhaps reflect traditions that Galilee was the place where Jesus was seen after the resurrection, but there are in fact very few such traditions in the gospels: Matthew has only 28.16ff. (whose introduction suggests that it depends on Mark 16.7), Luke has no appearances in Galilee, and John has one story in chapter 21, which is clearly a supplement to the gospel. Perhaps, then, Mark has the angel direct the disciples to Galilee because that is where his own community is situated. This is possible, though the composition of the gospel is not normally located in Galilee. An alternative explanation could be that Mark has used traditions from Galilaean communities which naturally associated their experience of the risen Lord with their own area. But if Mark himself is not writing for a Galilaean community, it may be that we have to look for another explanation for the message. Perhaps in picturing the disciples as returning to Galilee – the place where they were originally called – Mark thinks of them as beginning again: they have failed Jesus, failed to take up their crosses and follow him to crucifixion, but now they are being summoned once again to follow him, and to learn once again what discipleship means. Mark may perhaps interpret the message as one of forgiveness and renewal.

There is, however, a much simpler explanation of the reference to Galilee. Presumably Mark believes that the disciples obeyed the message and returned to Galilee – and in spite of Luke's account of events in Acts, it is most likely that they did in fact return there. Perhaps, then, the message reflects, not traditions about appearances of the risen Lord to the disciples, but a tradition that the disciples did indeed return to Galilee. If so, then the command to go to Galilee may originally have been an explanation for the disciples' return; they went back, not because they ran away, but because they were sent back by the risen Lord.

The reaction of the women is entirely natural: **they went out and** 8 **fled from the tomb.** The **trembling and terror** which overcame them are familiar Markan themes: this is precisely how many other characters in the story have reacted up to this point when confronted with the power of God. Now that they are confronted with the mightiest act of all, how else could they react? Equally understandable is their silence. Some commentators have suggested that this is an apologetic note, meant to explain why the story of the empty tomb was unknown in the earliest tradition. But the women's silence when they are told of the resurrection is of a piece with their terror. So, too, is their disobedience. Up to this point, the women in Mark's story have done well: individual women have been commended for their faith and their actions (5.34; 7.29; 12.41–4; 14.3–9), and the women who followed Jesus from Galilee have alone stood by him at the end: they alone witnessed his death (15.40f.) and burial (15.47). But at this point, even they fail. Their disobedience and fear demonstrate their inability to believe the good news. Throughout Mark's gospel, men and women have been blind and deaf to the truth about Jesus, and now at the end, when the divine message is delivered to the women, they are struck dumb, and fail to deliver it: **they said nothing to anyone, for they were afraid.** Here is Mark's final irony. In the rest of the story, Jesus has commanded men and women to say nothing about the truth they have glimpsed, and they have frequently disobeyed. Now that the time has at last come to report what has happened, the women are silent!

# 2   A SHORT ENDING

**They reported all these instructions briefly to Peter's companions. Afterwards, Jesus himself sent out through them, from east to west, the sacred and imperishable proclamation of eternal salvation. Amen.**

This brief ending was clearly written by a subsequent writer in an attempt to round off Mark's gospel. It is found in a few late Greek MSS and a few of the versions. With the exception of one Latin MS (k), they all continue with vv.9–20.

**They reported all these instructions briefly to Peter's compan-**

ions. The author of this brief paragraph attempts to deal with the problem of the women's silence but can only do so by contradicting Mark's concluding statement. Perhaps the use of the word 'briefly' is an attempt to soften this. As in 16.7, Peter is singled out for special mention. No resurrection appearance is described, though it is implied in the statement that **Jesus himself sent out** the gospel by means of the disciples. The universal scope of the mission is emphasized in the phrase **from east to west**. The description of the gospel as **the sacred and imperishable proclamation of eternal salvation** suggests that the ending was written by someone familiar with Hellenistic thought.

# 3  A LONGER ENDING                    16.9–20

*(Matt. 28.18–20; Luke 24.13–43, 48, 51; John 20.14–23)*

**(9) After he had risen, early on the first day of the week, he appeared first to Mary Magdalene, from whom he had driven out seven demons; (10) she went and told his companions, who were mourning and weeping. (11) But when they heard that he was alive, and that she had seen him, they did not believe.**

**(12) After that, he appeared in another form to two of them as they were walking into the country. (13) They went back and told the others; but they did not believe them either.**

**(14) Finally, he appeared to the eleven as they sat at table, and he reproached them for their lack of faith and hardness of heart, because they had not believed those who had seen him after he had been raised. (15) Then he said to them, 'Go into the whole world and proclaim the good news to the whole creation. (16) Whoever believes and is baptized will be saved, but whoever does not believe will be condemned. (17) These are the signs that will accompany believers: in my name they will cast out demons; they will speak in strange tongues; (18) they will pick up snakes in their hands, and if they drink any deadly poison, it will not harm them; they will lay hands on the sick who will recover.'**

**(19) After the Lord Jesus had spoken with them, he was taken up into heaven and sat down at the right hand of God. (20) They went out and preached everywhere, the Lord working with them, and confirming their message through the signs that accompanied them.**

These verses were certainly not written by Mark: in style and vocabulary they are quite different from the rest of the gospel. It has, indeed, been argued (W.R. Farmer, *The Last Twelve Verses of Mark*) that the differences can be explained by Mark's use of traditional material, but this solution fails to explain why Mark should have handled the tradition so differently in this last section of the gospel. This passage is in fact missing from some of the earliest MSS (including ℵ and B); in others, it occurs after the alternative, shorter ending. Eusebius, writing in the fourth century, said that the best MSS ended at v.8. These verses were, however, apparently known to Tatian in about AD 140, and Irenaeus, writing in about AD 180, quotes from them and assumes them to be written by Mark. Since the author seems to have known Luke-Acts (and possibly the other gospels), the verses were probably written at the beginning of the second century. A tenth-century MS attributes them to the elder Aristion (c. AD 100), but no reliance can be placed on this tradition.

Although this section was obviously added to Mark in an attempt to 'complete' the gospel, it could hardly have been written for that purpose. It does not attempt to deal with the problems caused by Mark's abrupt ending – the women's silence and the unfulfilled promise to the disciples that they would see Jesus in Galilee – and it shows no reliance on vv.1–8. It consists of three brief accounts of appearances of the risen Lord.

**After he had risen, early on the first day of the week.** The intro- 9 duction suggests an independent composition. Jesus is not named, but **Mary Magdalene** is reintroduced. The statement that Jesus saved her from **seven demons** echoes Luke 8.2. There is an account of the appearance to Mary in John 20.11–18, but the reference to it here is so brief that one cannot tell whether it is dependent on John. The failure of the disciples to believe her report is recorded in Luke 10–11 24.11, though there she brings them news of the empty tomb. The statement that the disciples **did not believe** is repeated in v.13, after the account of a second resurrection appearance. This second story 12–13 is a summary of that given in Luke 24.13–35. The statement that Jesus **appeared in another form to two of them as they were walking into the country,** is reminiscent of Luke's story of the two disciples walking to Emmaus who fail to recognize Jesus.

The third appearance is to **the eleven.** The statement that they 14 were **at table** is reminiscent of Luke 24.41f. The author again stresses the disciples' slowness to believe: Jesus **reproached them for their lack of faith and hardness of heart.** To this extent at least these verses are in agreement with the rest of Mark: by their failure to believe the reports of those who have announced the resurrection, the disciples have once again demonstrated their lack of faith and hardness of heart. Even now, there is no compelling evidence to make men believe. Perhaps it is this theme that made some early editor regard the section as an appropriate conclusion to the gospel. At this point one MS includes a conversation between the disciples and the risen Lord. The passage is known as the Freer Logion (the MS, W, is now in the Freer Museum in Washington), and part of it is quoted by Jerome in Latin. The Greek is not clear but may be translated roughly as follows:

And they excused themselves, saying, 'This age of lawlessness and unbelief is under Satan, who by means of the unclean spirits does not allow the true power of God to be comprehended. Therefore,' they said to Christ, 'reveal your righteousness now.' And Christ replied to them, 'The limit of the years of Satan's power has been completed. But other terrible things draw near, even for the sinners for whom I was delivered to death that they might turn back to the truth and sin no more, in order that they might inherit the spiritual and imperishable glory of righteousness which is in heaven.'

The passage appears to be an attempt by one copyist of the gospel to explain both the failure of the disciples to believe the accounts of the resurrection, and the unbelief of men and women of his own time. He longs for the end (the revelation of Christ's righteousness) but is confident that Satan's power is limited, even though Christians may have to endure a period during which fearful things occur.

15 Jesus' command to **Go into the whole world and proclaim the good news** is reminiscent of Acts 1.8 and Matt. 28.19. The disciples'
16 mission is to be universal: it is **to the whole creation. Whoever believes and is baptized will be saved, but whoever does not believe will be condemned.** Once again, the importance of believing is emphasized; and, as in Matt. 28.19, baptism is now seen as an important
17 element in the response to the gospel. **The signs that will accompany believers** include the casting out of **demons** and the healing of **the sick**, both of which have been attributed by Mark to the disciples
18 already (cf. 3.15; 6.13). Speaking **in strange tongues** and picking up **snakes** are described in Acts (cf. 2.4; 28.3–6). The idea that Christians will be immune from **poison** is not found elsewhere in the New Testament,though stories of miraculous escapes are recorded later. In describing these various feats as 'signs' which 'accompany' the disciples, the approach of this author has changed somewhat from that of Mark himself. The emphasis now is on the mighty works for their own sake, as demonstrations of the power of Christ's name – **the Lord. . .confirming their message through the signs that accompanied them** (v.20) – rather than as an integral part of the gospel. Like Jesus, the disciples are to cast out demons and heal the sick; but, unlike him, they are to speak in tongues and be preserved from physical danger.
19 **After the Lord Jesus had spoken with them, he was taken up into heaven.** This brief summary of the ascension, following im-

mediately on the mission charge, echoes the language of Acts 1.11. The author speaks now of the Lord Jesus, a title which Mark himself has not used, but which expresses the Church's faith and becomes appropriate at this point, since at his exaltation Jesus **sat down at the right hand of God**. The language (echoing Ps. 110.1) is used frequently in the New Testament to express Christ's lordship and was used by Mark in 14.62; the proof-text itself is found in the mouth of Jesus in 12.36.

Unlike Mark, the author rounds the passage off with an account of 20 the obedient response of the disciples. **They went out** – presumably from Jerusalem. No location has been mentioned, but in the other gospels the three appearances referred to here are associated with Jerusalem, and it is the most natural setting. There is no suggestion here that the eleven were in Galilee, so that the problem of v.7 remains unsolved. The picture of the disciples preaching **everywhere, the Lord working with them**, is reminiscent of Acts.

## Additional note: Mark's ending

At least two of Mark's readers in antiquity shared the feeling of many modern readers that his gospel was unfinished. To some extent, this feeling results from our knowledge of the other gospels: we expect more because they include more. Yet clearly the other evangelists considered that more was necessary and by their own endings demonstrated that for them, too, Mark stopped short.

This sense that Mark is incomplete may be misleading however. If, as seems probable, Mark was the first evangelist, he was not conditioned by preconceptions about the proper shape of a gospel. Even if all his readers and successors found his model unsatisfactory, that would not mean that Mark himself intended to write anything other than what we now have. It may be that Mark's original idea of the shape of a gospel seemed to others to be stunted because they did not understand what he was trying to do.

The suggestion that Mark intended to end his gospel at 16.8, first made by Wellhausen in 1903, has often been rejected: three reasons have been given. First it has been regarded as an impossible ending for syntactical reasons: it was long argued that it was impossible to end a paragraph, let alone a book, with the conjunction γάρ (for). In fact, however, examples of paragraphs ending in this way have been found elsewhere. (For examples, see R.H. Lightfoot, *Locality and Doctrine in the Gospels*, pp. 1–48, and *The Gospel Message of St Mark*, pp. 80–97. To those he cites we may add Menander's *Dyscolos*, lines 437–8.) Moreover, Mark's style is notoriously rough, and his final sentence is complete, however inelegant it may seem.

Second, it seems impossible to many that Mark should end with the statement that the women disobeyed the divine command because **they were afraid**. But we have seen that these reactions to the stupendous event of the resurrection were entirely in keeping with those of men and women throughout Mark's gospel. It would be surprising if the women had reacted in any other way! Moreover, their silence almost compels us to stop here. Certainly the attempt to solve the problem in the 'shorter ending' is a failure, for it contradicts Mark's clear statement that **they said nothing to anyone**. If Mark himself wrote more, it must have been an account of an appearance of the risen Jesus, either to the women, or to the disciples in Galilee.

This introduces us to the third objection to Mark's ending. The story seems to us to demand an appearance of the risen Lord. The 'passion' predictions have referred to the resurrection as well as to the crucifixion. Moreoever, the announcement that Jesus has been raised in vv.6f. promises that the disciples will see him. In the other gospels, as in Paul (1 Cor. 15.3–8), the appearances of the risen Jesus are all important. Mark seems to break off just before the climax of his story and leaves us waiting to meet the risen Lord. But again, we must ask whether it would have seemed necessary to Mark to record an appearance of the risen Lord, or whether it is not entirely in keeping with the method he uses throughout the gospel to leave his readers to make the crucial step of faith for themselves, without presenting them with less ambiguous evidence for the resurrection. Throughout his story, the truth of Jesus has been clear to those with eyes to see and ears to hear but has been at least partially concealed from all the characters in the story, apart from Jesus himself. Only those who read (or hear) the gospel with eyes and ears of faith – members of the Christian community – see its true significance. At this point in the story, the vital question is not whether Peter and his fellow-disciples finally grasped the truth (we may assume that they did, or the story would not have been told), but whether we, reading Mark's words, are prepared to hear the angel's message and follow Jesus into Galilee on the path of discipleship. If we remember the rest of the story, it is not, after all, surprising if the women told no one. Their silence corresponds with the secret in the rest of the gospel: the truth can be heard only by those who are prepared to believe. Nevertheless, their silence is culpable – it represents a failure to comprehend: like the other references to silence it reflects the inability of men and women to respond to the good news. Throughout the gospel, the disciples have been blind and deaf to the truth: now that the time has come to proclaim it, we should not be surprised if the women are dumb.

It is part of the scandal of the gospel that the only 'evidence' for the resurrection is a message entrusted to a group of women. Even if they had delivered it, their words would have had no value, since Jewish law demanded the evidence of two male witnesses to establish anything! Yet in Mark's gospel the women are faithful to Jesus even when his disciples have fled: they are the only witnesses to his death (15.40f.), burial (15.47) and resurrection (16.1–8). Moreover, individual women have been singled out in earlier chapters for their faith (5.25–34; 7.24–30) and devotion (12.41–4; 14.3–9). It is ironic that on Easter morning those who had faithfully followed Jesus to his crucifixion should flee from the tomb – just as the disciples fled from arrest (14.50, 52): this stupendous act is too great even for their loyalty.

Mark ends his gospel, therefore, with two pieces of non-evidence: a message delivered to women, who failed to pass it on (and whose evidence was in any case useless); and a promise to the disciples that they will see Jesus in Galilee, which is left hanging in mid-air. But was this promise never fulfilled? Since the angel's words refer back to a prophecy of Jesus, set out in 14.28, and since all Jesus' other prophecies have proved to be true, we may be confident that this one was also fulfilled. But, of course, it depends on the disciples' obedience and response – they must go to Galilee if they wish to see him. It is typical of Mark's gospel that the message should be in the form 'Go and you will see him', for it demands response. Earlier in the gospel, Jesus commanded a paralysed man to stand up and walk. It was impossible for a paralysed man to stand up and walk: nevertheless he obeyed. Again, he told a man with a shrivelled hand to stretch out his hand. It was impossible for him to stretch out a shrivelled hand: nevertheless he obeyed. Restoration came through obedience. And now Jesus commands men paralysed with fear to go to Galilee: since Mark's story is only 'the *beginning* of the good news' we know that in fact they obeyed, went to Galilee and saw the risen Lord.

If we are unhappy with the ending of Mark's gospel as he has left it, it is perhaps because we expect him to 'round it off' with an appearance of the risen Lord; we want assurance that Jesus met the disciples, pronounced forgiveness and recommissioned them. Instead, we have the 'evidence' of the women, who are invited to inspect the empty tomb and told 'He is not here; he has been raised', and we have the message to the disciples to return to Galilee, where they had seen Jesus before, and where they will see him again. Though they have denied Jesus and been ashamed of him, they are nevertheless offered a second chance of learning, once again, what it means to be disciples – disciples, this time, of the crucified and risen Lord. We are offered nothing more. But is this, perhaps, because Mark is inviting us to make our own response? Is it because this was the starting-point for Mark's own readers? They could not go and inspect the tomb for themselves: they had to rely on the evidence of others that it was indeed empty. As for 'seeing' the risen Lord, that was a possibility for them all – not, indeed, in the special way reported by the other evangelists and by Paul, in the so-called 'resurrection appearances', but by accepting the invitation of the risen Lord to 'go to Galilee', the place of discipleship. The promise is intended for them – for us – as well as for the eleven frightened disciples: if you want to see Jesus, then follow where he leads. This is the end of Mark's story, because it is the beginning of discipleship.

Some have objected that this kind of interpretation is too 'modern' and sophisticated for it to correspond to Mark's own intention: like those who added the 'shorter' and 'longer' endings, these critics insist that Mark's gospel is incomplete as it stands. It is impossible for us to know, now, whether the insights into the nature of the gospel which we have been discussing are Mark's own. We believe that they are: but if they are not, then at least the gospel's ending offers us a fine example of the value of 'reader response' criticism, since it provides us with an interpretation of the text to which author and reader together can contribute – an interpretation which corresponds with the experience of many readers of the gospel, whether or not it was in the mind of the evangelist.

# SELECT BIBLIOGRAPHY

## Biblical and other texts

*NOTE BY THE GENERAL EDITOR*
Because the New Testament writings belong to their times as well as to ours, and come from a society with a mentality often distant from that of this age, their correct understanding is often advanced by referring to other ancient writings of the same general period. To readers without a 'classical background', or who are relative newcomers to the subject, allusions to these writings can appear obscure and technical.

Most important of all are the books of the Old Testament, including the books of the so-called Apocrypha consisting of the writings included in the Greek Old Testament but not regarded as canonical in the Hebrew synagogues.

In addition there are numerous Jewish documents which circulated and were probably published under the names of eminent Old Testament figures; they are therefore called Pseudepigrapha, or works with false titles. Examples are the book of Enoch, part of which is called the Similitudes, the Assumption or Testament of Moses, the book of Jubilees, the Testaments of the Twelve Patriarchs, the Psalms of Solomon, 2 Baruch. There are good translations of these in H.F.D. Sparks (ed.), *The Apocryphal Old Testament*, Clarendon Press, 1984, or in J.H. Charlesworth, *The Old Testament Pseudepigrapha*, London and New York, 1983–5.

Texts found in the community library at Qumran by the Dead Sea, in process of publication in the series *Discoveries in the Judaean Desert* (Oxford University Press), are referred to by special abbreviations. Qumran has six caves in which manuscripts were found; so those in Cave I are abbreviated as 1Q. This 'code' is followed by the first Hebrew letter of the text in question. 1QS is the Community Rule, 1QSa the Rule of Congregation. Pesher means commentary; so 1QpHab means the Qumran commentary on Habakkuk. 1QH is a collection of Thanksgiving Hymns. One document found in the sixth cave at Qumran was already known in two medieval manuscripts, first published by S. Schechter, *Fragments of a Zadokite*

*Work,* Cambridge, 1910. This document was written at Damascus for a community akin to that at Qumran. It is abbreviated CD.

A convenient translation of the principal Dead Sea texts is that by Geza Vermes (Penguin).

Contemporary with the New Testament writers are two major Jewish authors who wrote in Greek: Philo of Alexandria, much of whose work is a commentary on the Pentateuch, and Josephus, historian of the Jews and especially of the war of AD 66–70 which ended with the sack of Jerusalem. Both Philo and Josephus were edited and translated in the Loeb Classical Library. Widely available is the English version of Josephus made by William Whiston (1667–1752), first published in 1737.

Jewish writings later than the New Testament, but often preserving old rabbinic traditions, are found in the tracts of the Mishnah (M) of the late second century, the commentaries on these tracts in the Babylonian Talmud (B) and the Jerusalem Talmud (J) of the fifth and sixth centuries, and in the Tosefta ('supplement') roughly contemporary with the Mishnah. H. Danby made an English translation of the Mishnah (Oxford University Press). The Babylonian Talmud can be read in the Soncino translation, the Tosefta in that edited by Jacob Neusner. For the Jerusalem Talmud it is necessary to go to the French version by Schwab. The different tracts are customarily cited by abbreviations of their Hebrew titles.

Other rabbinic texts are the Midrash ('investigation' or study) with exegesis of scripture, translated by M. Freedman; Mekilta or exegesis of Exodus; Megilloth ('rolls') on the Song of Songs, Ruth, Ecclesiastes and Esther; Sifra or an exegesis of Leviticus; and the Targum ('interpretation') consisting of Aramaic paraphrases of the Hebrew biblical text.

Texts from the Gentile world can illustrate the world of ancient society. In this volume reference is made to Xenophon's memoirs of Socrates, *Memorabilia*; Menander (342–291 BC), witty author of comedies, whose play *The Bad Tempered man (Dyskolos)* was recovered in 1958 in a papyrus now in the Bodmer library at Geneva (translated by Philip Vellacott, 1960); Cicero, greatest of Latin orators in the first century BC; Plutarch, author of biographies and moral essays, writing in Greece about 100 AD; Tacitus, sombre historian of the early Roman emperors, writing about the same time as Plutarch – contemptuous of Jews and Christians but not much more so than of everyone else.

Christian writings can also provide important material for understanding the world from which the New Testament came. Some of these are 'apocryphal' texts produced in rivalry to the canonical gospels, acts, epistles, and apocalypse. The *Gospel of Thomas,* complete only in a Coptic version, often cited as simply Thomas, contains 114 sayings of Jesus in a tradition clearly independent of the synoptic tradition. The *Gospel of the Nazarenes,* current among communities of Christian Jews, is closely related to the canonical St Matthew. The Acts of Peter, John, and Thomas were composed for popular reading and fostered a missionary dedication which asked believers to forgo marriage. These and other apocryphal texts can be read in translation in R.McL. Wilson, *New Testament Apocrypha,* 2 volumes, and in M.R. James, *The Apocryphal New Testament.*

The Christian writings of the generation following the end of the apostolic age, commonly called the Apostolic Fathers, include the Didache or Teaching of the Twelve Apostles which could be as early as parts of the New Testament itself. Later second-century authors were concerned with the vindication of Christianity against pagan critics or against heretical deviation, e.g. Justin, writing in Rome about 150–60, his pupil Tatian who made a Gospel harmony, his admirer Irenaeus, bishop of Lyons, about 180, Clement of Alexandria, and Origen (184–254) whose reply to the anti-Christian Celsus (*contra Celsum*) was composed in 248 at Caesarea in Palestine.

Lastly the Bible itself: the Hebrew Bible received more than one Greek translation. The most widely used, and that quoted by New Testament writers, is that ascribed to the Seventy, Septuaginta, produced at Alexandria in the third century before Christ. A very literal translation, highly valued by early Christian commentators like Jerome, was produced by Aquila in the second century AD.

The transmission of the New Testament text is more intricate than that of other ancient texts because of the huge number of manuscripts and numerous ancient translations into Latin, Syriac, Coptic, Armenian, and other tongues. In medieval or Byzantine times, the Greek churches had a standard form of text commonly called the received Text or Textus Receptus, which is that underlying the King James version of 1611. This form of text developed rather late. Before it there were wide regional variations, reflected in different families of manuscripts; and study suggest that these may often bring us closer to the original than the Received Text. Two books by Bruce M. Metzger provide reliable guides in this area: *The Text of the New Testament* and *The Early Versions of the New Testament* (Oxford University Press).

The Greek text underlying the translation in this commentary is that of Nestle-Aland published by the German Bible society (*Novum Testamentum Graece,* Deutsche Bibelstiftung, Stuttgart).

Many manuscripts of the revision of the Latin Bible made by Jerome at the end of the fourth century, now commonly called the Vulgate, contain prologues to the gospels of Mark, Luke, and John. Probably there was one for Matthew too, but if so it does not survive. These prologues have been thought by some to be as early as the second century AD, directed against the heresy of Marcion who denied that the Old and New Testaments come from the same God. It is now usual to date the prologues later.

H.C.

TEXTS

*Biblia Hebraica*, ed. R. Kittel, Stuttgart, 1950.
*The Old Testament Pseudepigrapha*, ed. J.H. Charlesworth, 2 vols., London, 1983, 1985.
*The Dead Sea Scrolls in English*, trans. G. Vermes, Sheffield, 3rd edn, 1987.
*Septuaginta*, ed. A. Rahlfs, 2 vols., Stuttgart, 1935.
*The Targum of Isaiah*, trans. and ed. J.F. Stenning, Oxford, 1949.
*Josephus*, ed. H.St.J. Thackeray *et al.*, Loeb Classical Library, 9 vols., London, 1926–65.
*Philo*, ed. F.H. Colson *et al.*, Loeb Classical Library, 12 vols., London, 1929–53.
*Novum Testamentun Graece*, ed. E. Nestle, rev. K. Aland *et al.*, Stuttgart, 26th edn, 1979.
*New Testament Apocrypha*, ed. E. Hennecke and W. Schneemelcher, E.tr. R.McL. Wilson, 2 vols., London, 1963, 1965. (A translation of the revised German edn is in preparation.)
*Midrash Rabbah*, ed. H. Freedman and M. Simon, 10 vols., London, 1939.
*The Mishnah*, trans. H. Danby, Oxford, 1933.
*The Babylonian Talmud*, ed. I. Epstein, 18 vols., London, 1935–52.
*Le Talmud de Jérusalem*, trans. M. Schwab, new edn, Paris, 1932–3.
*The Tosefta*, trans. J. Neusner, 6 vols., New York, 1977–86.

## *Literature on St Mark and related topics*

The literature published on Mark is immense: H.M. Humphrey's *A Bibliography for the Gospel of Mark 1954–1980* (New York, 1981) lists 1,599 items for those few years alone! Since 1980, scholarly work on Mark has multiplied. Clearly it is impossible to include here more than a tiny fraction of what is available. Moreover, there are many books on related topics, such as Synoptic studies, problems of history and christology, and methods of criticism and analysis, all of them apposite. The books and articles included in this bibliography have been chosen because they are likely to be particularly helpful to readers of this commentary, or because they represent a particular point of view, or because they are specifically referred to in the course of the discussion. The great majority of those selected for inclusion are therefore in English.

M.D.H.

COMMENTARIES

Achtemeier, P.J., *Mark*, Proclamation Commentary, Philadelphia, 1975.

Anderson, H., *The Gospel of Mark*, New Century Bible, London, 1976.

Beasley-Murray, G.R., *A Commentary on Mark 13*, London, 1957.

Branscomb, B.H., *The Gospel of Mark*, Moffatt New Testament Commentary, London, 1937.

Cranfield, C.E.B., *The Gospel according to St Mark*, Cambridge Greek Testament Commentary, Cambridge, 4th edn, 1972.

Grundmann, W., *Das Evangelium nach Markus* (Kritisch-exegetischer Kommentar über das Neue Testament), Göttingen, 17th edn, 1967, with supplement by G. Sass.

Haenchen, E., *Der Weg Jesu*, Berlin, 2nd edn, 1968.

Johnson, S.E., *A Commentary on the Gospel according to St Mark*, Black's New Testament Commentaries, London, 1960.

Klostermann, E., *Das Markusevangelium: Handbuch zum Neuen Testament*, Tübingen, 2nd edn, 1926.

Lohmeyer, E., *Das Evangelium des Markus: Kritisch-exegetischer Kommentar*, Göttingen, 17th edn, 1967.

Loisy, A., *L'Évangile selon Marc*, Paris, 1912.

Montefiore, C.G., *The Synoptic Gospels*, 2 vols., London, 2nd edn, 1927.

Nineham, D.E., *The Gospel of St Mark*, Pelican Gospel Commentary, Harmondsworth, 1963.

Rawlinson, A.E.J., *St Mark*, Westminster Commentaries, London, 7th edn, 1949.

Schniewind, J., *Das Evangelium nach Markus*, Göttingen, 4th edn, 1947.

Schweizer, E., *The Good News according to Mark*, E.tr. London, 1971.

Swete, H.B., *The Gospel according to St Mark*, London, 1898.

Taylor, V., *The Gospel according to St Mark*, London, 1952.

Wellhausen, J., *Das Evangelium Marci*, Berlin, 2nd edn, 1909.


OTHER LITERATURE

Abrahams, I., *Studies in Pharisaism and the Gospels*, First Series, Cambridge, 1917.

Achtemeier, P.J., 'Toward the isolation of pre-Markan miracle catenae', *J.B.L.*, 89, 1970, pp. 265–91.

Achtemeier, P.J., et al., 'Essays on Mark' in *Interpretation*, 32, 1978, pp. 339–99.

Bammel, E. and Moule C.F.D., eds., *Jesus and the Politics of His Day*, Cambridge, 1984.

Barr, J., "Abba isn't Daddy', *J.T.S.*, n.s., 39, 1988, pp. 28–47.

Barrett, C.K., 'The background of Mark 10.45' in *New Testament Essays: Studies in Memory of Thomas Walter Manson*, ed. A.J.B.

Higgins, Manchester, 1959, pp. 1–18.

Barrett, C.K., *The Holy Spirit and the Gospel Tradition*, London, 1947.

Barrett, C.K., *Jesus and the Gospel Tradition*, London, 1967.

Bauckham, R., 'Jesus' demonstration in the temple', in *Law and Religion*, ed. B. Lindars, Manchester, 1988, pp. 72–89.

Beasley-Murray, G.R., *Baptism in the New Testament*, London, 1962.

Beasley-Murray, G.R., *Jesus and the Future*, London, 1956.

Beavis, M.A., *Mark's Audience: The Literary and Social Setting of Mark 4.11–12*, Sheffield, 1989.

Belo, F., *A Materialist Reading of the Gospel of Mark*, Maryknoll, New York, 1981.

Best, E., *Following Jesus: Discipleship in the Gospel of Mark*, Sheffield, 1981.

Best, E., *Mark: The Gospel as Story*, Edinburgh, 1984.

Best, E., 'Mark's use of the Twelve', *Z.N.W.*, 69, 1978, pp. 11–35, reprinted in *Disciples and Discipleship: Studies in the Gospel according to St Mark*, Edinburgh, 1968, pp. 131–61.

Best, E., *The Temptation and the Passion: The Markan Soteriology*, Cambridge, 1965.

Black, C. Clifton, *The Disciples according to Mark*, Sheffield, 1989.

Black, Matthew, *An Aramaic Approach to the Gospels and Acts*, Oxford, 3rd edn, 1967.

Black, Matthew, 'The christological use of the Old Testament in the New Testament', *N.T.S.*, 18, 1971–2, pp. 1–14.

Boobyer, G.H., *St Mark and the Transfiguration Story*, Edinburgh, 1942.

Boobyer, G.H., 'The secrecy motif in St Mark's Gospel', *N.T.S.*, 6, 1960, pp. 225–35.

Booth, Roger P., *Jesus and the Laws of Purity*, Sheffield, 1986.

Boucher, Madeleine, *The Mysterious Parable*, C.B.Q. Monograph 6, Washington D.C., 1977.

Bowman, J., *The Gospel of Mark: the New Christian Jewish Passover Haggadah*, Leiden, 1965.

Brandon, S.G.F., 'The date of the Markan gospel', *N.T.S.*, 7, 1961, pp. 126–41.

Brandon, S.G.F., *Jesus and the Zealots*, Manchester, 1967.

Bratcher, R.G., 'A note on υἱός θεοῦ (Mark xv. 39)', *Exp. Tim.*, 68, 1956, pp. 27f.

Bultmann, R., *The History of the Synoptic Tradition*, E.tr., Oxford, 1963.

Bultmann, R., *Theology of the New Testament*, 2 vols., E.tr., London, 1952 and 1955.

Burkill, T.A., *Mysterious Revelation*, Ithaca, N.Y., 1963.

Burkill, T.A., *New Light on the Earliest Gospel*, New York, 1972.

Burkitt, F.C., *The Gospel History and its Transmission*, Edinburgh,

1906.

Burkitt, F.C., 'Hosanna', *J.T.S.*, 17, 1916, pp. 139–52.

Butler, B.C., *The Originality of St Matthew*, Cambridge, 1951.

Campbell, J.Y., 'The kingdom of God has come', *Exp. Tim.*, 48, 1936–7, pp. 91–4.

Carrington, P., *The Primitive Christian Calendar*, Cambridge, 1952.

Casey, Maurice, *Son of Man: The Interpretation and Influence of Daniel 7*, London, 1979.

Catchpole, D.R., 'The "triumphal" entry' in *Jesus and the Politics of His Day*, ed. E. Bammel and C.F.D. Moule, Cambridge, 1984, pp. 319–34.

Chilton, B., ed., *The Kingdom of God*, London, 1984.

Colwell, E.C., 'A definite rule for the use of the article in the Greek New Testament', *J.B.L.*, 52, 1933, pp. 12–21.

Conzelmann, H., *An Outline of Theology of the New Testament*, E.tr., London, 1969.

Daube, David, *The New Testament and Rabbinic Judaism*, London, 1956.

Daube, David, 'ἐξουσία in Mark 1.22 and 27', *J.T.S.*, 39, 1938, pp. 45–59.

Derrett, J. Duncan M., *Law in the New Testament*, London, 1970.

Derrett, J. Duncan M., *Studies in the New Testament*, I, II, III, Leiden, 1977, 1978, 1982.

Dewey, Joanna, *Markan Public Debate*, Chico, 1980.

Dodd, C. H., *The Founder of Christianity*, London, 1970.

Dodd, C.H., 'The framework of the gospel narrative', *Exp. Tim.* 43, 1932, pp. 396–400, reprinted in C.H. Dodd, *New Testament Studies*, Manchester, 1953, pp. 1–11.

Dodd, C.H., *The Parables of the Kingdom*, London, 1935.

Drury, J., *The Parables in the Gospels*, London, 1985.

Drury, J., 'The sower, the vineyard and the place of allegory in the interpretation of Mark's parables', *J.T.S.*, n.s., 24, 1973, pp. 367–79.

Evans, C.F., 'I will go before you into Galilee', *J.T.S.*, n.s., 5, 1954, pp. 3–18.

Farmer, W.R., *The Last Twelve Verses of Mark*, Cambridge, 1974.

Farmer, W.R., *The Synoptic Problem*, New York and London, 1964.

Farrer, A.M., *A Study in St Mark*, London, 1951.

Fitzmyer, J.A., *Essays on the Semitic Background of the New Testament*, London, 1971.

Flemington, W.F., *The New Testament Doctrine of Baptism*, London, 1948.

Fowler, Robert M., *Loaves and Fishes*, Chico, 1981.

Fuller, R.H., *The Foundations of New Testament Christology*, London, 1965.

Fuller, R.H., *Interpreting the Miracles*, London, 1963.

Fuller, R.H., *The Mission and Achievement of Jesus*, London, 1954.

Gerhardsson, B., 'The parable of the sower and its interpretation', *N.T.S.*, 14, 1968, pp. 165–93.

Gerhardsson, B., *The Testing of God's Son*, Lund, 1966.

Glasson, T.F., *The Second Advent*, London, 3rd edn, 1963.

Glasswell, M.E., 'The use of miracles in the Markan gospel' in *Miracles*, ed. C.F.D. Moule, London, 1965, pp. 51–62.

Goulder, M.D., *The Evangelists' Calendar*, London, 1978.

Grayston, K., 'The study of Mark XIII', *B.J.R.L.*, 56, 1974, pp. 371–87.

Grimm, W., *Weil Ich dich liebe*, Frankfurt am Main, 1976.

Hahn, F., *The Titles of Jesus in Christology*, E.tr. London, 1969.

Hart, H.St.J., 'The crown of thorns in John 19, 2–5', *J.T.S.*, n.s., 3, 1952, pp. 66–75.

Hartman, L., *Prophecy Interpreted*, Lund, 1966.

Harvey, Anthony, *Jesus and the Constraints of History*, London, 1982.

Hengel, M., *Studies in the Gospel of Mark*, London, 1985.

Hooker, M.D., 'Is the Son of Man problem really insoluble?' in *Text and Interpretation: Studies in the New Testament presented to Matthew Black*, Cambridge 1979, pp. 155–68.

Hooker, M.D., *Jesus and the Servant*, London, 1959.

Hooker, M.D., 'The Johannine Prologue and the messianic secret', *N.T.S.*, 21, 1974, pp. 40–58.

Hooker, M.D., 'The Kingdom of God', in *A Dictionary of Biblical Interpretation*, eds. R. Coggins and L. Houlden, London, 1990, pp. 374–7.

Hooker, M.D., 'Mark', in *It is Written: Scripture Citing Scripture: Essays in Honour of Barnabas Lindars, SSF*, Cambridge, 1988, pp. 220–30.

Hooker, M.D., *The Message of Mark*, London, 1983.

Hooker, M.D., *The Son of Man in Mark*, London, 1967.

Hooker, M.D., 'Traditions about the Temple in the Sayings of Jesus', *B.J.R.L.*, 70, 1988, pp. 7–19.

Hooker, M.D., 'Trial and tribulation in Mark XIII', *B.J.R.L.*, 65, 1982, pp. 78–99.

Hooker, M.D., 'What doest thou here, Elijah?', in *The Glory of Christ in the New Testament: Studies in Christology in Memory of George Bradford Caird*, eds. L.D. Hurst and N.T. Wright, Oxford, 1987, pp. 59–70.

Hull, J.M., *Hellenistic Magic and the Synoptic Tradition*, London, 1974.

Jaubert, A., *The Date of the Last Supper*, E.tr., New York, 1965.

Jeremias, J., *The Eucharistic Words of Jesus*, E.tr., London, 2nd edn, 1966 (based on 3rd German edn, revised and enlarged).

Jeremias, J., *Jesus' Promise to the Nations*, E.tr., London, 1958.

Jeremias, J., *The Parables of Jesus*, E.tr., London, rev. edn, 1963 (from 6th German edn).

Jeremias, J., *The Prayers of Jesus*, E.tr., London, 1967.

Jeremias, J., *Theology of the New Testament*, I, E.tr., London, 1971.

Juel, D., *Messiah and Temple*, Missoula, 1977.

Kallas, J., *The Significance of the Synoptic Miracles*, London, 1961.

Kealey, S., *Mark's Gospel: A History of Its Interpretation*, New York, 1982.

Keck, L.E., 'The introduction to Mark's gospel', *N.T.S.*, 12, 1966, pp. 352–70.

Keck, L.E., 'The spirit and the dove', *N.T.S.*, 17, 1970, pp. 41–67.

Kee, H.C., 'Christology in Mark's gospel', in *Judaisms and Their Messiahs at the Turn of the Christian Era*, eds. J. Neusner, W.S. Green and E.S. Frerichs, Cambridge, 1987, pp. 187–208.

Kee, H.C., *Community of the New Age*, London, 1977.

Kelber, W.H., ed., *The Passion in Mark*, Philadelphia, 1976.

Kermode, F., *The Genesis of Secrecy: On the Interpretation of Narrative*, Cambridge, Mass., 1979.

Kilpatrick, G.D., 'The Gentile mission in Mark and Mark 13⁹⁻¹¹', in *Studies in the Gospels*, ed. D.E. Nineham, Oxford, 1955, pp. 145–58.

Kilpatrick, G.D., 'Some problems in New Testament text and language', in *Neotestamentica et Semitica: Studies in Honour of Principal Matthew Black*, eds. E.E. Ellis and M. Wilcox, Edinburgh, 1969, pp. 198–202.

Koch, D.A., *Die Bedeutung der Wundererzählungen für die Christologie des Markusevangeliums*, Berlin, 1975.

Kümmel, W.G., *Promise and Fulfilment*, E.tr. London, 1957 (from 3rd German edn, 1956).

Lambrecht, J., *Die Redaktion der Markus-Apokalypse*, Rome, 1967.

Lambrecht, J., 'Jesus and the Law: an Investigation of Mark 7.1–23', *Eph. Th. L.*, 53, 1977, pp. 24–79.

Léon-Dufour, X., *Sharing the Eucharistic Bread*, E.tr., New York, 1987.

Lightfoot, R.H., *The Gospel Message of St Mark*, Oxford, 1950.

Lightfoot, R.H., *History and Interpretation of the Gospels*, London, 1934.

Lightfoot, R.H., *Locality and Doctrine in the Gospels*, London, 1938.

Lindars, B., *Jesus Son of Man*, London, 1983.

Manson, T.W., 'The Cleansing of the Temple', in *B.J.R.L.*, 33, 1951, pp. 271–82.

Manson, T.W., *The Sayings of Jesus*, London, 1949.

Manson, T.W., *The Teaching of Jesus*, Cambridge, 2nd edn, 1935.

Manson, W., 'The ΕΓΩ ΕΙΜΙ of the messianic presence in the New Testament', *J.T.S.*, 48, 1947, pp. 137–45.

Marcus, Joel, *The Mystery of the Kingdom of God*, S.B.L. dissertation, Atlanta, 1986.

Marshall, C. D., *Faith as a Theme in Mark's Narrative*, Cambridge, 1989.

Martin, R.P., *Mark: Evangelist and Theologian*, Exeter, 1972.

Marxsen, W., *Mark the Evangelist*, E.tr. Nashville, 1969.

Mauser, U.W., *Christ in the Wilderness*, London, 1963.

Meagher, J.C., *Clumsy Construction in Mark's Gospel*, New York and Toronto, 1979.

Montefiore, C.G. and Loewe, H., ed., *A Rabbinic Anthology*, London, 1938.

Moule, C.F.D., *An Idiom Book of New Testament Greek*, Cambridge, 1953.

Moule, C.F.D., 'Mark 4: 1–20 yet once more' in *Neotestamentica et Semitica: Studies in Honour of Matthew Black*, ed. E. Earle Ellis and M. Wilcox, Edinburgh, 1969, pp. 95–113.

Moule, C.F.D., *The Origin of Christology*, Cambridge, 1977.

Neirynck, F., *Duality in Mark: Contributions to the Study of the Markan Redaction*, Leuven, rev. edn, 1988.

Nineham, D.E., 'The order of events in St Mark's Gospel', in *Studies in the Gospels: Essays in Memory of R.H. Lightfoot* (ed. Nineham), Oxford, 1955, pp. 223–39.

Ogg, G., 'The chronology of the Last Supper', in *Historicity and Chronology in the New Testament*, D.E. Nineham *et al.*, London, 1965, pp. 75–96.

Perrin, Norman, 'The christology of Mark: a study in methodology', *J.R.*, 51, 1971, pp. 173–87, reprinted in *A Modern Pilgrimage in New Testament Christology*, Philadelphia, 1974.

Perrin, Norman, *Jesus and the Language of the Kingdom*, London, 1976.

Perrin, Norman, *The Kingdom of God in the Teaching of Jesus*, London, 1963.

Perrin, Norman, 'Towards an interpretation of the gospel of Mark', in *Christology and a Modern Pilgrimage: A Discussion with Norman Perrin*, ed. H.D. Betz, Missoula, rev. edn, 1974, pp. 1–52.

Petersen, N.R., ed., 'Perspectives on Mark's Gospel', *Semeia* 16, Missoula, 1980.

Pryke, E.J., *Redactional Style in the Marcan Gospel*, Cambridge, 1978.

Quesnell, Q., *The Mind of Mark: Interpretation and Method through the Exegesis of Mark 6.52*, Rome, 1969.

Räisänen, H., *Das 'Messiasgeheimnis' im Markusevangelium*, Helsinki, 1976.

Räisänen, H., 'Jesus and the food laws', *J.S.N.T.*, 16, 1982, pp. 79–100.

Rhoads, D. and Michie, D., *Mark as Story*, Philadelphia, 1982.

Richardson, A., *The Miracle Stories of the Gospels*, London, 1941.

Riesenfeld, H., *Jésus transfiguré*, Copenhagen, 1947.

Rivkin, Ellis, *What Crucified Jesus?*, London, 1984.

Robbins, Vernon K., *Jesus the Teacher: A Socio-rhetorical Interpretation of Mark*, Philadelphia, 1984.

Robinson, James, *The Problem of History in Mark*, London, 1957.

Robinson, J.A.T., *Redating the New Testament*, London, 1976.

Roth, C., 'The cleansing of the Temple and Zechariah', *N.T.*, 4, 1960, pp. 174–81.

Rowley, H.H., 'The baptism of John and the Qumran sect' in *New Testament Essays: Studies in Memory of Thomas Walter Manson*, ed. A.J.B. Higgins, Manchester, 1959, pp. 218–29.

Sabbe, M., ed., *L'Évangile selon Mark: tradition et rédaction*, Leuven, rev. edn, 1988.

Sanders, E.P., *Jesus and Judaism*, London, 1985.

Schnackenburg, R., *God's Rule and Kingdom*, London, 1963.

Schürer, Emil, *The History of the Jewish People in the Age of Jesus Christ*, rev. by Geza Vermes, Fergus Millar and Matthew Black, 3 parts (in 4 vols.), Edinburgh, 1973, 1979, 1986, 1987.

Schweitzer, A., *The Mystery of the Kingdom of God*, E.tr. London, 1925.

Scobie, C.H.H., *John the Baptist*, London, 1964.

Scobie, C.H.H., in *The Scrolls and Christianity*, ed. M. Black, London, 1969, pp. 58–69.

Scroggs, R. and Groff, K.I., 'Baptism in Mark: dying and rising with Christ', *J.B.L.* 92, 1973, pp. 531–48.

Sherwin-White, A.N., *Roman Society and Roman Law in the New Testament*, Oxford, 1963.

Smith, C.W.F., 'Fishers of men', *H.T.R.*, 52, 1959, pp. 187–203.

Smith, Morton, *Clement of Alexandria and a Secret Gospel of Mark*, Cambridge, MA., 1973.

Standaert, B., *L'Évangile selon Mark: composition et genre littéraire*, Bruges, 2nd edn, 1984.

Stoldt, H.-H., *History and Criticism of the Marcan Hypothesis*, E.tr., Edinburgh, 1980.

Strack, H.L. and Billerbeck, P., *Kommentar zum Neuen Testament aus Talmud und Midrasch*, 4 vols., Munich, 1922–8.

Talbert, C., *What is a Gospel? The Genre of the Canonical Gospels*, Philadelphia, 1970.

Telford, W., *The Barren Temple and the Withered Tree*, Sheffield, 1980.

Telford, W., ed., *The Interpretation of Mark*, London, 1985.

Thrall, M.E., 'Elijah and Moses in Mark's account of the Transfiguration', *N.T.S.*, 16, 1970, pp. 305–17.

Trocmé, E., *The Formation of the Gospel according to Mark*, E.tr. London, 1975.

Tuckett, C., ed., *The Messianic Secret*, London, 1983.

Tuckett, C., *The Revival of the Griesbach Hypothesis*, Cambridge, 1983.

Turner, C.H., 'Marcan usage: notes, critical and exegetical, on the Second Gospel', in *J.T.S.* 25–9, 1924–8.

Vermes, G., *Jesus the Jew*, London, 1973.

Vermes, G., *Jesus and the World of Judaism*, London, 1983.

Via, Dan O., *The Ethics of Mark's Gospel*, Philadelphia, 1985.
Vielhauer, P., 'Jesus und der Menschensohn', *Z.Th.K.*, 60, 1963, pp. 133–77.
Weeden, T., *Mark – Traditions in Conflict*, Philadelphia, 1971.
Wenham, D. and Blomberg, C., eds., *Gospel Perspectives 6: The Miracles of Jesus*, Sheffield, 1986.
White, K.D., 'The parable of the sower', *J.T.S.*, n.s., 15, 1962, pp. 300–7.
Winter, P., *On the Trial of Jesus*, Berlin, 1961.
Wrede, W., *The Messianic Secret*, E.tr. by J.C.G. Greig, Cambridge and London, 1981.

# INDEX OF AUTHORS

# SUBJECT INDEX

# INDEX OF ANCIENT SOURCES

12.2, 133
12.8f., 210
12.9, 208, 210
12.10, 117
12.11f., 312
12.36, 323
12.36–8, 322
12.38, 322
12.40, 322
12.42–8, 322
12.50, 247
12.54–6, 320
13.6–9, 261
13.16, 80, 186
13.18f., 135
13.19, 136
13.20f., 194
13.30, 243
13.34, 255
13.34f., 305
14.15, 343
14.27, 208
14.34, 230
15, 327
16.16, 136
16.17, 321
16.18, 237
17.1f., 230
17.6, 136, 270
17.14, 80
17.23, 317
17.31f., 315
17.33, 208
18.9–14, 327
18.12, 98
18.15–17, 238
18.18–30, 239
18.31–4, 244
18.35–43, 251
19.1–10, 327
19.11–27, 324
19.12–27, 322
19.26, 133
19.28–40, 255
19.45–8, 260
20.1–8, 270
20.9, 275
20.9–19, 273
20.20–6, 278
20.27–40, 281
20.39f., 285
20.41–4, 290
20.45–7, 294
21.1–4, 296
21.5–7, 303
21.12–19, 309
21.15, 312
21.18, 312
21.20, 314
21.20–4, 313
21.25, 319
21.25–8, 318
21.29–33, 320
21.31, 321
21.37, 352
21.8, 307
21.8–11, 306
22, 341

22.1–2, 325
22.3–6, 330
22.7–13, 331
22.10, 299
22.14, 335
22.15, 332
22.15–20, 337
22.16, 251
22.17, 339, 342
22.18, 251
22.19f., 337
22.19b–20, 338
22.20, 340
22.21–3, 335
22.24–7, 246
22.26, 227
22.27, 248
22.28f., 251
22.28–30, 339, 341
22.30, 111, 246
22.31–4, 343
22.37, 373
22.39, 343
22.40–6, 345
22.47–53, 350
22.54–5, 353
22.56–62, 363
22.61, 365
22.63, 363
22.63–71, 353
22.64, 363
22.67f., 361
22.70, 360, 361
23.1–5, 365
23.4, 356
23.11, 369, 371
23.13–16, 356
23.18–25, 365
23.26, 371, 372
23.32–9, 371
23.36, 376, 377
23.44–9, 374
23.45, 376
23.46, 375, 377
23.50–6, 379
23.51, 381
23.56–24.1, 383
24.1–11, 382
24.11, 389
24.13–35, 389
24.13–43, 388
24.41f., 389
24.48, 388
24.51, 388

John
1.1–18, 18, 31
1.11, 152
1.19, 18
1.21, 221
1.29ff., 39
1.33, 39, 42
1.40, 59
2.1–10, 100
2.4, 348
2.13, 256
2.13–17, 260
2.14–22, 358

2.18, 191, 271
2.18–22, 359
2.19, 263, 304, 358
2.20, 304
3.22–30, 53
3.25, 43
6, 164, 167
6.1–17, 163
6.15, 167
6.15–21, 168
6.24, 171
6.30, 73
6.30f., 191
6.30–5, 167
6.52–8, 341
6.52–9, 165
7.30, 348
7.33, 336
7.42, 291
8.14, 336
8.28, 362
9, 197
9.1–3, 85
10.37, 373
11, 225
11.4, 150
11.11–14, 150
11.33, 80
11.38, 80
11.47–53, 325
11.51, 249
12, 328
12.1–8, 326
12.6, 331
12.12, 256
12.12–16, 255
12.14f., 257
12.16, 257
12.23, 348
12.23–6, 207
12.25, 208
12.27, 346, 348
12.32, 266
12.34, 89
13.1, 334
13.18, 336
13.21–30, 336
13.27, 331
14–17, 297
14.31, 346
16.5, 336
18.1, 345, 347
18.2, 331
18.2–11, 350
18.4f., 331
18.5f., 170
18.5ff., 362
18.10f., 351
18.11, 346
18.12–16, 353
18.15, 356
18.17, 363
18.18–23, 353
18.19–24, 356
18.22, 363
18.25–7, 363
18.28, 332
18.28f., 370

18.28–38, 356
18.28–40, 365
18.31, 354
19.1, 365
19.2–3, 369
19.4, 365
19.4–6, 356
19.12–16, 356, 365
19.14, 332, 373
19.17, 372
19.17–24, 371
19.25, 379
19.28–30, 374
19.29, 377
19.30, 375, 377
19.38, 381
19.38–42, 379
19.39f., 384
20.1, 382, 384
20.11f., 382
20.11–18, 389
20.14–23, 588
20.18, 386
20.23, 84
20.25, 373
21, 386

Acts
1.8, 390
1.11, 391
1.13, 112
1.21f., 111–12
1.22, 33
2, 38
2.4, 390
2.14–36, 284
2.27, 65
2.30, 291
2.33, 361
2.34f., 291
2.38, 53
2.42, 339
3.14, 64
3.19, 53
4.11, 276
5.31, 361
5.37, 279
5.38f., 191
6–7, 354
6.4, 131
6.13f., 304
6.14, 304, 358
7.56, 89
8.4, 85
8.14, 156
8.36, 239
9.2, 202, 245
10.36f., 131
10.37, 33
11.28, 308
12.1–3, 309
12.2, 247
12.12, 6
12.25, 6
13.1f., 156
13.24f., 33
13.35, 65
15.7, 53